OPERATIONS AND SUPPLY CHAIN MANAGEMENT FOR MBAs

OPERATIONS AND SUPPLY CHAIN MANAGEMENT FOR MBAS

EIGHTH EDITION

Jack R. Meredith
Professor of Management and Broyhill Chair, Emeritus
Wake Forest University

and

Scott M. Shafer
Associate Dean of MS in Business Analytics Programs and Professor of Management
Wake Forest University

WILEY

VP AND DIRECTOR, PORTFOLIO MANAGEMENT	Nancy Gerome
DIRECTOR, PORTFOLIO MANAGEMENT	Lise Johnson
EDITOR	Jennifer Manias
EDITORIAL ASSISTANT	Campbell McDonald
SENIOR MANAGING EDITOR	Judy Howarth
PRODUCTION EDITOR	Umamaheswari Gnanamani
MARKETING COORDINATOR	Jessica Spettoli
COVER PHOTO CREDIT	©VectorMine/Shutterstock

This book was set in 10/12 TimesLTStd by Straive™.

Founded in 1807, John Wiley & Sons, Inc. has been a valued source of knowledge and understanding for more than 200 years, helping people around the world meet their needs and fulfill their aspirations. Our company is built on a foundation of principles that include responsibility to the communities we serve and where we live and work. In 2008, we launched a Corporate Citizenship Initiative, a global effort to address the environmental, social, economic, and ethical challenges we face in our business. Among the issues we are addressing are carbon impact, paper specifications and procurement, ethical conduct within our business and among our vendors, and community and charitable support. For more information, please visit our website: www.wiley.com/go/citizenship.

Evaluation copies are provided to qualified academics and professionals for review purposes only, for use in their courses during the next academic year. These copies are licensed and may not be sold or transferred to a third party. Upon completion of the review period, please return the evaluation copy to Wiley. Return instructions and a free of charge return shipping label are available at: www.wiley.com/go/returnlabel. If you have chosen to adopt this textbook for use in your course, please accept this book as your complimentary desk copy. Outside of the United States, please contact your local sales representative.

ISBN: 978-1-119-89869-6 (PBK)
ISBN: 978-1-119-89868-9 (EVALC)

Library of Congress Cataloging-in-Publication Data

LCCN number: 2022056816

Printing identification and country of origin will either be included on this page and/or the end of the book. In addition, if the ISBN on this page and the back cover do not match, the ISBN on the back cover should be considered the correct ISBN.

SKY10088813_102324

Brief Contents

CONTENTS

PART 2   OUTPUT AND PROCESS PLANNING

3   DESIGNING THE OUTPUT AND ITS DELIVERY PROCESS   90

4   CAPACITY AND SCHEDULING   138

PREFACE

The enthusiasm of the users of this MBA-oriented book has been greatly rewarding for us, and we thank them for their comments, suggestions, criticism, and support. Although the book is not the massive seller that an undergraduate textbook can become, it is clear that there is, as we felt, a need for a solely MBA-level text. The book was originally written because of the express need we felt in our many MBA programs at Wake Forest University for an operations management textbook directed specifically to MBA students and especially to those who had some real-world experience. We tried all of the current texts but found them either tomes that left no time for the cases and other materials we wanted to include or shorter but simplistic quantitative books. Moreover, all the books were so expensive; they did not allow us to order all the cases, readings, and other supplements and class activities (such as the "Beer Game"; see Appendix A in Chapter 5) that we wanted to include in our course.

What we were looking for was a short, inexpensive book that would cover just the introductory, basic, and primarily conceptual material and terminology. This would allow us, as the professors, to tailor the course through supplementary cases and other materials for the unique class we would be teaching: executive, evening, full time, short course, and so on. Although we wanted a brief, supplementary-type book so that we could add other material, we have colleagues who need a short book because they only have a half-semester module for the topic. Or, they may have to include another course (e.g. statistics) in the rest of the semester.

Changes in This Eighth Edition

In the previous edition, we felt compelled to reorganize the book to reflect the many significant changes that had occurred. Our focus in the current revision was building on the new structure, mainly by updating the content to reflect important changes and trends that have occurred since the last revision. Two major additions were the incorporation of "sustainability" throughout the book, especially in Chapter 5, and the addition of considerable material on "innovation" and "design thinking" in Chapter 3. We also updated the chapter introduction examples to reflect these major changes.

Other key changes made include:

- As a part of sustainability, discussions about the environment and waste were inserted in the appropriate chapters.

- The new concept of "the project economy," in contrast to the mass production economy, is introduced in Chapter 1.

- More material was added about the importance and use of the "business case" for projects in Chapter 2.

- Finally, many new end-of-chapter discussion questions have been added, especially regarding innovation and sustainability.

The material continues to be organized into three parts. In Part I: Strategy and Execution, we discuss operations and supply chain strategy in Chapter 1 and then follow this up with executing strategy through project management in Chapter 2. Part II: Output and Process Planning then covers four chapters. Output and process planning is described first in Chapter 3 and then the planning of capacity and schedules in Chapter 4. Chapter 5 covers the more strategic topics associated with managing the supply chain followed by Chapter 6 that addresses issues related to supply chain planning. Part III: Managing and Improving the Process then begins with Chapter 7 on monitoring and controlling processes, followed by Chapter 8 on process improvement through the use of Six Sigma. The last chapter, also on process improvement, covers the concepts of lean management. The book then concludes with six cases, followed by a Glossary of key terms to help students quickly refresh their memories on the terminology used in the chapters.

In revising the book, we have kept the elements of our earlier philosophy. For example, we kept the other majors such as marketing and finance in mind – what did these students need to know about operations to help them in their careers? And we still minimize the heavier quantitative material, keeping only discussions and examples that illustrate a particular concept, since finance and marketing majors would not be solving operations problems. Moreover, even operations managers probably wouldn't themselves be solving those problems; more likely, they would be assigned to an analyst. For those chapters in which exercises are included, they are intended only to help illustrate the concept we are trying to convey rather than make experts of the students.

We continued to add service examples throughout the text, since the great majority (over 80% these days!) of our students would be, or are already, employed in a service organization. And since these students will be working and competing in a highly global economy, we employ many international examples. We also kept the textual flow of material in the chapters away from the current undergraduate trend of fracturing the material flow with sidebars, examples, applications, solved problems, and so forth, in an attempt to keep the students' interest and attention. Given the maturity of MBA students, we instead worked these directly into the discussions to attain a smoother, clearer flow. As noted below, the Instructor's Manual includes suggestions for readings, cases, videos, and other course supplements that we have found to be particularly helpful for MBA classes since this book is intended to be only a part of the MBA class.

Supplements

Our approach to supplementary MBA-level material here is to reference and annotate in the Instructor's Manual additional useful cases, books, video clips, and readings for each of the nine textbook chapters. The annotation is intended to help the instructors select the most appropriate materials for their unique course. Although we have added some of our own and our colleagues' cases to the rear of this edition, we also rely on our favorite Harvard, Darden, Western Ontario, and European cases, plus *Harvard Business Review* readings to fully communicate the nature of the chapter topic we are covering. PowerPoint slides and Case Data and Solutions are available on the instructor website at www.wiley.com/go/meredith/operationsmanagementmbas8e. The publisher can also custom bind selected content from this text or any other Web text, along with cases and articles, should this approach be of interest to the professor. Please visit https://custom select.wiley.com/ or contact your local Wiley representative for more details.

Your Inputs Appreciated

We would once again like to encourage users of this book to send us their comments and suggestions. Tell us if there is something we missed that you would like to see in the next edition (or the Instructor's Manual or website) or if there is perhaps material that is unneeded for this audience. Also, please tell us about any errors you uncover or if there are other elements of the book you like or don't like. We hope to continue keeping this a living, dynamic project that evolves to meet the needs of the MBA audience, an audience whose needs are also evolving as our economy and society evolve and change.

We want to thank the many reviewers of this book and its previous editions: Joseph Akpovi, California State University, Stanislaus; Alexander Ansari, Seattle University; Dennis Battistella, Florida Atlantic University; Linda Brennan, Mercer University; David Cadden, Quinnipiac University; Satya Chakravorty, Kennesaw State University; Yaneth Correa, Colorado State University, Pueblo; Giovani da Silveira, University of Calgary; Douglas J. Dinon, Rensselaer Polytechnic Institute; Okechi Geoffrey Egekwu; Michael H. Ensby, Clarkson University; James A. Fitzsimmons, University of Texas; Ronald Frank, RPI Lally School of Management; Lawrence D. Fredendall, Clemson University; William C. Giauque, Brigham Young University; Mike Godfrey, University of Wisconsin–Oshkosh; Damodar Golhar, Western Michigan University; Suresh Kumar Goyal, Concordia University, Canada; Hector Guerrero, The College of William & Mary; Adel Guitouni, University of Victoria; Robert Handfield, North Carolina State University; Mark Gerard Haug, University of Kansas; Janelle Heineke, Boston University; Zhimin Huang, Hofstra University; David Hollingworth, Rensselaer Polytechnic Institute; James L. Hoyt, Troy State University; Kendra Ingram, Texas A&M University–Commerce; Patrick Jaska, University of Mary Hardin–Baylor; Jonatan Jelen, NYU–Poly; Mehdi Kaighobadi, Florida Atlantic University; Deborah Kellogg, University of Colorado, Denver; Casey Kleindienst, California State University–Fullerton; Archie Lockamy III, Samford University; Manoj Malhotra, University of South Carolina; Gus Manoochehri, California State University–Fullerton; JD McKenna, Colorado Technical University; Robert F. Marsh, Sacred Heart; Ron McLachlin, University of Manitoba; Ivor P. Morgan, Babson College; Rob Owen, Thunderbird School of Global Management; Seungwook Park, California State University–Fullerton; Madeleine Pullman, Portland State University; Ranga V. Ramasesh, Texas Christian University; Jaime S. Ribera, IESE–Universidad de Navarra, Spain; Gary D. Scudder, Vanderbilt University; Sue Perrott Siferd, Arizona State University; Samia Siha, Kennesaw State University; Donald E. Simmons, Ithaca College; Anthony Steigelman, California Lutheran University; Scott Swenseth, University of Nebraska, Lincoln; William J. Tallon, Northern Illinois University; Forrest Thornton, River College; Richard Vail, Colorado Mesa University; Asoo J. Vakharia, University of Florida; Jerry C. Wei, University of Notre Dame; and Jack Zhang, Hofstra University.

JACK MEREDITH

Professor of Management and Broyhill Chair, Emeritus
School of Business
Wake Forest University, P.O. Box 7897
Winston-Salem, NC 27109
meredijr@wfu.edu
www.business.wfu.edu/emeritus/jack-meredith/

SCOTT SHAFER

Associate Dean of MS in Business Analytics Programs and Professor of Management
School of Business
Wake Forest University, P.O. Box 7897
Winston-Salem, NC 27109
shafersm@wfu.edu
www.mba.wfu.edu/faculty/shafer
336.758.3687

STRATEGY AND EXECUTION

In this first part of the book, we describe the importance of operations and the supply chain to the global competitiveness of all organizations. We then move into a discussion of their role in designing and executing a competitive strategy for the organization. Chapter 1 first describes the functions of operations and the supply chain in an organization and then lists the aspects of value that customers and clients desire for the products and services they buy. Next, a range of strategic frameworks are described that organizations can employ to develop and evaluate their business strategy. However, selecting and carefully designing a strategy for the organization is only half the battle for survival in a very competitive global economy – the organization must be able to successfully execute the strategy. As discussed in Chapter 2, a major tool for achieving this is project management, which has developed into a field in itself, with a full range of tools and techniques for executing projects of all kinds, including strategy.

Operations and Supply Chain Strategy for Competitiveness

It is widely recognized that the environment confronting organizations today is increasingly competitive due to the globalization of markets, shorter product life cycles, and rapidly changing technology. As a result, organizations in all industries are searching for ways to improve their competitive position and attain world-class standards. From an Operations Management perspective, firms can enhance their competitiveness by developing new products and services, developing new processes, and/or improving their existing business processes. Thus, a central theme of this book is the critical role Operations Management plays in contributing strategically to an organization's overall competitiveness.

In this first chapter, we begin by describing the nature of the operations function within the global competitive environment utilizing the holistic systems perspective. Included in this discussion are key trends in operations and supply chain management. Then we analyze the aspects of products and services that customers value such as innovativeness, functionality, quality, customization, responsiveness, and low cost. Next, several strategic frameworks that can be used to align the operations function with the benefits valued by customers and the overall business strategy are discussed. We conclude the chapter with a discussion of productivity, which is not only an important overall measure of the efficiency of an organization's operations, but also is important to the prosperity of an entire society as well.

1.1 Introduction

- No discussion of the critical role operations and supply chain management can play in an organization's global competitiveness would be complete without a discussion of Amazon. Founded on July 5, 1994, Amazon received its first book order in 1995. And perhaps somewhat surprising, the first book ordered was not on the bestseller list. Rather, *Fluid Concepts and Creative Analogies: Computer Models of the Fundamental Mechanisms of Thought* earned the distinction of being the first book ordered on Amazon. Apart from its unusual start, Amazon's trajectory has been nothing short of breathtaking. By 2004 Amazon's sales rose to almost $7 billion. By 2014 its sales were just shy of $89 billion, and by 2017 its sales reached $178 billion. Indeed, no other company reached the $100 billion in sales milestone faster than Amazon. And as a further reflection of its success, by the end of 2018, Amazon had the third highest market capitalization trailing only Microsoft and Apple.

From its modest beginnings as an online book retailer, Amazon has transformed the entire retail industry. Undoubtedly, a key driver of Amazon's success is the value proposition it provides to its customers including low prices, fast delivery, and an enormous selection of merchandise. But what makes it possible for Amazon to deliver on this value proposition? As it turns out, the foundation of Amazon's ability to deliver on its value proposition is its ground-breaking supply chain strategy facilitated by its brilliant use of technology.

While entire articles and even books could be written about Amazon's supply chain practices, our present purpose is well served by briefly highlighting a few aspects of its supply chain strategy. For example, one key aspect of its supply chain strategy is the way it manages its warehouse operations. Strategically, Amazon locates its warehouses in proximity to major metropolitan areas. More tactically, it tailors its warehouses to the types of products that will be stored in them and organizes the merchandise within the warehouses based on criteria such as the level of demand. In a related vein, another key aspect of Amazon's supply chain strategy is its inventory management practices. Interestingly, Amazon outsources much of its inventory management and focuses on managing the inventory levels of frequently purchased items or what are referred to as its standard inventory. Another category of inventory is its just-in-time inventory, which includes products that are purchased less frequently. In the case of books, Amazon creates partnerships with publishers to ship books to Amazon or in some cases directly to the customer as orders come in. Because of its ability to efficiently manage its inventory, Amazon achieved a −33.5 day cash conversion cycle in 2017 compared to cash conversion cycles of 4.4 and 9.3 at Costco and Walmart, respectively. Amazon's negative 33.5 cash conversion cycle means that it gets paid from its customers 33.5 days before it pays its suppliers. Effectively then, Amazon is using its suppliers' cash to fund and expand its own operations! Amazon has continued its outstanding performance regarding its cash conversion cycle. While fluctuating quarter to quarter, in the third quarter of 2021 Amazon achieved a record negative 48 days cash conversion cycle according to Marketplace Pulse, an e-commerce intelligence firm.[1]

Beyond its rapidly increasing sales, high market capitalization, and negative cash conversion cycle, another key performance metric is market share. This is yet another area where Amazon excels. Analytics provider One-Click Retail estimated that Amazon accounted for 44% of all online retail sales in 2017 and 4% of all retail sales. Such a large volume of sales translates into economies of scale that help keep unit costs down by spreading fixed costs over a larger volume of sales. The large sales volume leads to other opportunities as well. For example, having a large base of customers allowed Amazon to move into manufacturing, and it currently produces a variety of products including backpacks, Bluetooth speakers, and cell phone chargers. Additionally, its large sales volume makes it possible to invest in new technologies and continue to innovate. For example, by 2017 Amazon had 45,000 warehouse robots that it hoped would eventually be able to pick and pack customer orders without human assistance. By January of 2020 it was reported that the number of robots utilized in its warehouses had increased to 200,000.[2] In 2013 Amazon began developing drone-based delivery systems. By December of 2016 Amazon completed its first drone delivery without human intervention in a remarkable 13 minutes from order to delivery.[3] More recently, Amazon has been exploring the feasibility of offering one-hour delivery through its Amazon Prime Now Service. With its diversification into manufacturing, its acquisition of Whole Foods, and its investment in a drone delivery service, it is exciting to speculate on how Amazon will continue to evolve.

- As in sports, numerous intense rivalries exist in the world of business, such as the rivalries between Visa and MasterCard, Microsoft and Apple, Ford and General Motors, Energizer

---

[1] Marketplace Pulse, Amazon Cash Conversion Cycle, https://www.marketplacepulse.com/stats/amazon/amazon-cash-conversion-cycle-96, 5/18/2022.

[2] Edward, D., Amazon now has 200,000 robots working in its warehouses, https://roboticsandautomationnews.com, January 21, 2020.

[3] Amazon, First Prime Air Delivery, amazon.com, May 18, 2022.

and Duracell, and Nike and Reebok. Certainly, any list of top business rivalries would be incomplete without Coke and Pepsi. Interestingly, while these two firms compete in the same industry, one has had considerable success on the important dimension of share price performance, while the other's performance has been rather dismal. More specifically, over the 10-year period ending in February 2015, Pepsi's stock price increased by 85.6%, while Coke's increased by 100.6%. The result was that Coke's market capitalization increased to $182.4 billion compared to Pepsi's market capitalization of $145.8 billion. This difference in market capitalization was even more dramatic when one considers the fact that Pepsi's sales were significantly higher than Coke's – $66.4 billion versus $46.9 billion in 2013.

A question that naturally arises is: What accounted for these very different outcomes? One explanation offered by analysts and critics was that Pepsi simply took its eye off the ball. In particular, while Coke focused its attention on beverages, Pepsi had been distracted by attempting to develop nutritious snacks. One result was that Pepsi Cola went from being the number-two soda to the number-three soda behind Coke and Diet Coke. To address its weakened performance, Pepsi's board of directors initiated a strategic review of the company (Esterl 2012).

- Brad Smith, President and Vice Chair, refers to Microsoft's ambitious 10-year commitment to sustainability as its "moonshot." The program launched in January of 2020 established the goals for Microsoft to be carbon negative (i.e. removing more carbon each year than it emits) by 2030 and removing from the environment by 2050 all the carbon the company has emitted since its founding in 1975. Microsoft has also committed to becoming water positive or replenishing more water than it consumes and zero waste by 2030. In pursuing its sustainability goals, Microsoft seeks to help advance the United Nations Sustainability Goals adopted by all member nations in 2015. Based on its belief that there is an urgent need for all organizations to become carbon zero, Microsoft's focus extends beyond improving its own environmental impact to helping all organizations minimize their environmental impact. A key aspect of Microsoft's approach to sustainability is to both reduce its carbon emissions and to remove existing carbon. In its first year, Microsoft reduced its carbon emissions by 6% or 730,000 metric tons and supported projects that removed an additional 1.3 million metric tons of carbon. In its second year, Microsoft decreased emissions stemming from its operations by an additional 17% mainly by purchasing energy from renewable sources. However, when Microsoft calculated the emissions created by its entire supply chain, it determined that emissions actually increased by 23% highlighting both the importance and challenges associated with addressing sustainability across the entire supply chain. One way Microsoft is addressing the sustainability challenges across its supply chain is that it changed its supplier code of conduct to require suppliers to disclose their greenhouse gas emissions. Looking to the future, Mr. Smith notes that further progress toward Microsoft's sustainability goals will require having accurate standards, appropriate economic incentives, and utilizing technology to provide effective measurement data. Regarding the development of economic incentives, Microsoft imposes an internal tax of $15/metric ton of emissions generated via internal operations and a $5/ton tax (that will increase over time) on emissions generated by supply chain partners. Other important steps Microsoft has taken to advance its sustainability agenda include factoring in progress on sustainability goals in executive compensation and the creation a $1 billion climate innovation fund that invests in new technologies that address key aspects of climate including emissions, water, and waste. Microsoft is also developing tools such as its cloud for sustainability by monitoring emissions and partnering with a wide range of other companies to help organizations reduce their environmental impact. At Microsoft, the commitment to sustainability has gone beyond the development of lofty goals to becoming an important part of its culture (Smith 2021).

These brief examples highlight the critical role operations and supply chain management can play in an organization's competitiveness. While having a clearly articulated strategy and value proposition is critically important, even more important is the ability to execute the strategy and deliver the desired value proposition. For example, Amazon has clearly defined its value proposition, namely, to offer its customers low prices, fast delivery, and an enormous selection of merchandise. However, it is Amazon's innovative and effective supply chain management practices that made it possible to actually deliver on its value proposition. The Pepsi example illustrates a fundamental principle in strategy and competitiveness – namely, the organizations that focus on doing a few things well usually outperform organizations that lack this focus. The Microsoft vignette discusses the topic of sustainability that is becoming increasingly important. As will be discussed later in this chapter and throughout this book, the operations function of organizations plays a critically important role in helping organizations achieve their sustainability goals.

Amazon's success further demonstrates how quickly technology can upend an industry and change the major players and their competitiveness. And despite its current success, Amazon's continued innovation in technologies such as drones and robotics and its continued innovation in its service offering through its acquisition of Whole Foods and exploring a one-hour delivery option make it clear how competitive the marketplace is and that competitive success is a moving target. As General Eric Shinseki so aptly put it, "If you don't like change, you're going to like irrelevance even less." With a focus on change via the design, management, and improvement of the processes that create value for the customers, it is a fair characterization to say that operations is fundamentally concerned with helping organizations stay relevant. So, with this lofty mission in mind, we now turn our attention to introducing you to the world of operations and supply chain management.

Today, in our international marketplace, consumers purchase their products from the provider that offers them the most "value" for their money. To illustrate, you may be doing your course assignments on a notebook computer made in China, driving a German automobile, or watching a movie on a TV made in Taiwan while cooking your food in a Korean microwave. There is a reason why products may be produced in part, or wholly, by foreign firms, and it concerns an area of business known as operations.

A great many societal changes are also occurring today that intimately involve activities associated with operations. For example, there is great pressure among competing nations to ensure they have fair access to foreign markets as they seek to increase their exports. And businesses are intent on building efficient and effective supply chains, improving their processes through "Six Sigma," and successfully applying the precepts of "lean management" and other operations-based programs.

Another characteristic of our modern society is the explosion of new technology, an important aspect of operations. Technologies such as smartphones, social media, tablet computers, and cloud computing, to name a few, are profoundly affecting business and are fundamentally changing the nature of work. For example, some banks are shifting their focus from building new branch locations to using the Web as a way to establish and develop new customer relationships. Banks rely on technology to carry out more routine activities as well, such as transferring funds instantly across cities, states, and oceans. Our industries also rely increasingly on technology: robots carry and weld parts together, and workerless, dark "factories of the future" turn out a continuing stream of products. And soft operations technologies, such as "supply chain management" and "lean production" (Feld 2000; Womack and Jones 2003), have transformed world markets and the global economy.

This exciting, competitive world of operations is at the heart of every organization and, more than anything else, determines whether the organization survives in the international marketplace or disappears into bankruptcy or a takeover. It is this world that we will be covering in the following chapters.

1.2 Operations

Why do we argue that operations be considered the heart of every organization? Fundamentally, organizations exist to create value, and operations is the part of the organization that creates value for the customer. Bestselling author Michael Hammer (2004) maintains that operational innovation can provide organizations with long-term strategic advantages over their competitors. Regardless of whether the organization is for profit or not for profit, primarily service or manufacturer, or public or private, it exists to create value. Thus, even nonprofit organizations like the Red Cross strive to create value for the recipients of their services in excess of their costs. Moreover, this has always been true, from the earliest days of bartering to modern-day corporations.

Consider McDonald's as an example. This firm uses a number of inputs, including ingredients, labor, equipment, and facilities; transforms them in a way that adds value to them (e.g., by frying); and obtains an output, such as a hamburger, that can be sold at a profit. This conversion process, termed as *production system,* is illustrated in Figure 1.1. The elements of the figure represent what is known as a *system*[4]: *a purposeful collection of people, objects, and procedures for operating within an environment.*

Note the word *purposeful*; systems are not merely arbitrary groupings but goal-directed or purposeful collections. Managing and running a production system efficiently and effectively are

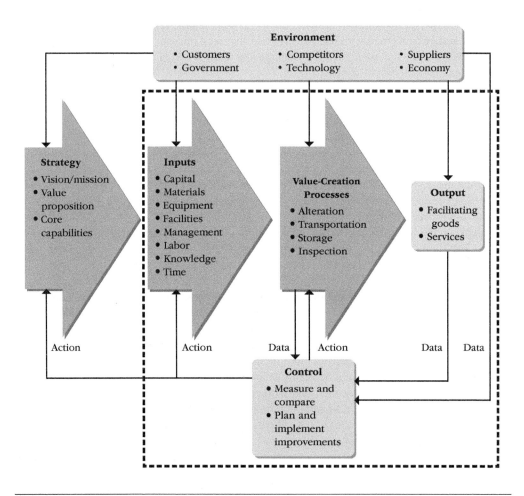

FIGURE 1.1 The Production System

---

[4]Note the word *system* is being used here in a broad sense and should not be confused with more narrow usages such as information systems, planning and control systems, or performance evaluation systems.

at the heart of the operations activities that will be discussed in this text. Since we will be using this term throughout the text, let us formally define it. ***Operations*** **is concerned with creating value by transforming inputs into useful outputs in support of an agreed-upon strategy**; this constitutes the primary activity of virtually every organization.

Not only is operations central to organizations, it is also central to people's personal and professional activities, regardless of their position or role. People, too, must operate productively, adding value to inputs and producing quality outputs. For example, a marketing professional creates value by developing effective promotional campaigns and conducting market research that leads to a better understanding of customer needs. Finance professionals create value by cost-effectively raising capital to run the business, by managing the organization's cash flows, and by evaluating the benefits of purchasing other organizations. Human resource professionals create value by recruiting talent, partnering with other areas of the organization to train and develop employees, and developing procedures and policies for evaluating employee contributions. Furthermore, in our personal lives we create value by transforming inputs into outputs such as when we host a Super Bowl party, plant a garden in our backyard, and paint our bedroom. As these examples illustrate, the work across all professions and in our personal lives can be viewed fundamentally as transforming inputs into outputs. Combining this insight with a central operations management principle that all work processes can be improved makes it clear that operations management should be of major interest to all readers not just professionally but also personally.

1.2.1 Systems Perspective

As Figure 1.1 illustrates, a production system is defined in terms of the environment, the organization's overarching strategy, a set of inputs, the value-creation process, the outputs, and some mechanism for controlling the overall system. The strategy includes determining elements such as the vision and mission of the organization, what customers value (often referred to as the value proposition), and the core capabilities of the organization. We discuss the strategy in detail a bit later. The environment includes those things that are outside the actual production system but that influence it in some way. Because of its influence, we need to consider the environment, even though it is beyond the control of decision makers within the system.

For example, a large portion of the inputs to a production system are acquired from the environment. Also, government regulations related to pollution control and workplace safety affect the production system. Think about how changes in customers' needs, a competitor's new product, or a new advance in technology can influence the level of satisfaction with a production system's current outputs. As these examples show, the environment exerts a great deal of influence on the production system.

Because the world around us is constantly changing, it is necessary to monitor the production system and take action when the system is not meeting its strategic goals. Of course, it may be that the current strategy is no longer appropriate, indicating a need to revise the strategy. On the other hand, it may be found that the strategy is fine but that the inputs or value-creation processes, or both, should be modified in some way. In either case, it is important to continuously collect data from the environment, the transformation processes, and the outputs; compare that data to the strategic plan; and, if substantial deviations exist, design and implement improvements to the system, or perhaps the strategy, so that results are aligned with the strategic goals.

Thinking holistically in terms of systems provides decision makers with numerous advantages. To begin with, the systems perspective focuses on how the individual components that make up a system interact. Thus, the systems perspective provides decision makers with a broad and complete picture of an entire situation. Furthermore, the systems perspective emphasizes the relationships between the various system components. Without considering these relationships, decision makers are prone to a problem called *suboptimization*. Suboptimization occurs when one part of the system is improved to the detriment of other parts of the system and, perhaps, the organization as a whole. For example, if a promotion created by the marketing department leads to an increase in demand beyond what operations has the capacity to supply, the result may be increased customer dissatisfaction. Thus, decisions need to be evaluated in terms of their effect on the *entire* system, not simply in terms of how they will affect one component of the system.

In the remainder of this section, we elaborate on inputs, the value-creation processes (also referred to as the transformation processes), and outputs. In later sections and chapters, we further discuss both strategy and elements of the control system in more detail.

1.2.2 Inputs

The set of inputs used in a production system is more complex than might be supposed and typically involves many other areas such as marketing, finance, engineering, and human resource management. Obvious inputs include facilities, labor, capital, equipment, raw materials, and supplies. Supplies are distinguished from raw materials by the fact that they are not usually a part of the final output. Oil, paper clips, pens, tape, and other such items are commonly classified as supplies because they only aid in producing the output.

Another very important but perhaps less obvious input is knowledge of how to transform the inputs into outputs. The employees of the organization hold this knowledge. Finally, having sufficient time to accomplish the operations is always critical. Indeed, the operations function quite frequently fails in its task because it cannot complete the *value-creation (transformation activities)* within the required time limit.

1.2.3 Value-Creation Processes

The value-creation processes are the part of the system that add value to the inputs. Value can be added to an entity in a number of ways. Four major ways are described here:

1. *Alter:* Something can be changed physically. This approach is basic to manufacturing industries, where raw material inputs are cut, stamped, formed, assembled, and so on. But it need not be a separate object or entity that is physically changed; for example, what is altered may be *us.* We might get our hair cut, or we might have our teeth straightened.

    Other, more subtle, alterations may also have value. *Sensual* alterations, such as heat when we are cold, or music, or beauty, may be highly valued on certain occasions. Beyond this, even *psychological* alterations can have value, such as the knowledge from obtaining a college degree or the feeling of friendship from a phone call or text message.

2. *Transport:* An entity, again including ourselves, may have more value if it is located somewhere other than where it currently is. We may appreciate having things brought to us, such as merchandise from an online retailer, or removed from us, such as garbage.

3. *Store:* The value of an entity may be enhanced for us if it is kept in a protected environment for some period. Some examples are wills kept in a safe-deposit box, our pet boarded at a kennel while we go on vacation, or ourselves staying in a hotel.

4. *Inspect:* Last, an entity may be more valued if we better understand its properties. This may apply to something we own, plan to use, or are considering purchasing, or, again, even to ourselves. Medical exams, elevator certifications, home inspections, and jewelry appraisals fall into this category.

Thus, we see that value may be added to an entity in several different ways. The entity may be changed directly, in space, in time, or even just in our mind. Additionally, value may be added using a combination of these methods. To illustrate, an appliance retailer may create value by both storing merchandise and transporting (delivering) it. Of course, there are other ways of adding value as well beyond the operations function, such as by "guaranteeing" something. However, the majority of value is created through the operations function, and the management of this function is the focus of this book. These many varieties of transformations, and how they are managed, constitute some of the major issues to be discussed in this text.

1.2.4 Outputs

Two types of outputs commonly result from a production process: services and products. Generally, products are physical goods, such as a tablet computer, and services are abstract or nonphysical. More specifically, we can consider the characteristics in Table 1.1 to help us distinguish between the two.

However, this classification may be more confusing than helpful. For example, consider a pizza delivery chain. Does this organization produce a product or provide a service? If you answered "a service," suppose that instead of delivering its pizzas to the actual consumer, it made the pizzas in a factory and sold them in the frozen food section of grocery stores. Clearly, the actual process of making pizzas for immediate consumption or to be frozen involves basically the same tasks, although one may be done on a larger scale and use more automated equipment. The point is, however, that both organizations produce a pizza, and defining one organization as a service and the other as a manufacturer may seem to be a little arbitrary.

We avoid this ambiguity by adopting the point of view that *any physical entity accompanying a transformation that adds value is a facilitating good* (e.g. the pizza). In many cases, of course, there may be no facilitating good; we refer to these cases as *pure services*.

The advantage of this view is that every transformation that adds value is simply a service, either with or without facilitating goods! If you buy a notebook computer, you have not purchased a product. Rather, you have purchased a bundle of services, many of them embodied in a facilitating good: services that assembled and tested the computer, that provided advice on the features needed, and that installed the key software on the computer. We refer to these services as a bundle of "benefits," of which some are tangible (the computer's memory, processor speed, weight, display resolution) and others are intangible (knowledgeable salesclerks, a convenient location, and convenient payment options). Some services may of course even be negative, such as an audit of your tax return. In summary, *services* are bundles of benefits, some of which may be tangible and others intangible, and they may be accompanied by a facilitating good or goods.

Firms often run into major difficulties when they ignore the service aspect of their operations. They may think of, and even market themselves as a "computer manufacturer" and not as

Table 1.1 Characteristics of Products and Services

Products	Services
Tangible	Intangible
Minimal contact with customer	Extensive contact with customer
Minimal participation by customer in the delivery	Extensive participation by customer in the delivery
Delayed consumption	Immediate consumption
Equipment-intense production	Labor-intense production
Quality easily measured	Quality difficult to measure

providing a bundle of services. They may recognize that they have to include certain tangible services (such as installing software) but ignore the intangible services, which might even be more important (helping customers decide on key features). Another reason for not making a distinction between manufacturing and services is that when a company views itself as a manufacturer, it tends to focus on measures of internal performance such as efficiency and utilization. But when companies view themselves as providing services, they tend to focus externally and ask questions such as "How can we serve our customers better?" This is not to imply that improving on internal performance measures is not important or desirable. Rather, it suggests that improved customer satisfaction should be the primary impetus for all improvement efforts. It is generally not advisable to seek internal improvements if these improvements do not ultimately lead to corresponding improvements in customer service and customer satisfaction.

In this text, we will adopt the point of view that all value-adding transformations (i.e., operations) are services, and there may or may not be a set of accompanying facilitating goods. Figure 1.2 illustrates how the tangible product (or facilitating good) portion and the intangible service portion for a variety of outputs contribute to the total value provided by each output. The outputs shown range from virtually pure services to what would be known as products. For example, the upscale restaurant appears to be about 75% service and 25% product. Although we work with "products" as extensively as with services throughout the chapters in this book, bear in mind that in these cases we are working with only a *portion* of the total service, the facilitating good. In general, we will use the generic term *outputs* to mean either products or services.

One particular type of output that is substantially different from products and many other types of services is that of knowledge or information. These outputs often have the characteristic that the more they are used, the more valuable they become. For example, in a network, the more entities that belong to the network, the more useful it may be. If you are on Linked-In®, Facebook®, or an online dating site, the more other people that are also there, the more valuable it is to you. Some other characteristics of information or knowledge that differ from normal goods and services are as follows:

- Giving or selling the information/knowledge to someone doesn't mean you can't give or sell it to someone else.

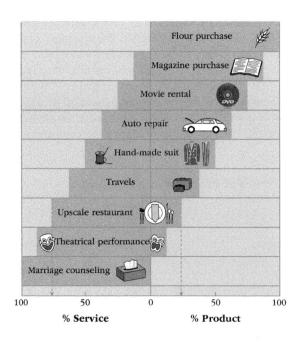

FIGURE 1.2 The Range from Services to Products

- The information/knowledge doesn't wear out the more it is used.

- The information/knowledge isn't subject to the law of diminishing returns.

- The information/knowledge can be replicated at minimal cost and trouble.

- The more the knowledge is used, the more valuable it becomes.

1.2.5 Control

Suppose that in our production system, we make a mistake. We must be able to observe this through, for example, accounting records (measurement data), compare it to a standard to see how serious the error is, and then, if needed, plan and implement (perhaps via a project as discussed in Chapter 2) some improvements. If the changes are not significantly affecting the outputs, then no control actions are needed. But if they are, management must intercede and apply corrective control to alter the inputs or the value-creation processes and, thereby, the outputs. The control activities illustrated in Figure 1.1 are used extensively in systems, including management systems, and will be encountered throughout this text.

One example of the components of the production system for a school would be as follows: A strategy of providing a safe, trustworthy, friendly environment for passing knowledge on to the students. The inputs would be, among others, the teachers, facility, books, and students that are exposed to a value creation-processes of learning, counseling, motivating, and so on to produce outputs of educated, skilled students. Control is exercised through examinations, budgets, and taking attendance. This all occurs in a physical and structural environment that includes state and county school boards to provide oversight policies and tax systems to provide the resources.

1.2.6 Operations Activities

Operations includes the activities associated specifically with the production system and a variety of other activities that support the production system. For example, purchasing or procurement activities are concerned with obtaining many of the inputs needed in the production system. Similarly, shipping and distribution are sometimes considered marketing activities and sometimes considered operations activities. Because of the important interdependencies of these activities, many organizations are attempting to manage these activities as one process commonly referred to as *supply chain management.*

As organizations begin to adopt new organizational structures based on business processes and abandon the traditional functional organization, it is becoming less important to classify activities as operations or non-operations. However, to facilitate an understanding of the role operations plays, we commonly divide the field into a series of subject areas such as scheduling, process design, inventory management, maintenance, and quality control. These areas are quite interdependent, but to make their workings more understandable, we discuss them as though they were easily separable from each other. In some areas, a full-fledged department may be responsible for the activities, such as quality control or scheduling, but in other areas, the activities (such as facility location) may be infrequent and simply assigned to a particular group or project team. Moreover, some of the areas such as supply chain management are critically important because they are part of a larger business process or because other areas depend on them. Finally, since we consider all operations to be services, these subject areas are equally applicable to organizations that have traditionally been classified as manufacturers and services.

1.2.7 Trends in Operations and Supply Chain Management

As has been previously discussed in this chapter and will be a central theme throughout the remainder of this book, an organization's operations play a critical role in its overall competitiveness and long-term success. This is yet another reason why people in all business disciplines need to have an appreciation and understanding of the operations function. Furthermore, given the critical role played by operations, it is important to stay abreast of the significant trends in the operations area as well as general business trends that may impact the operations function.

1.2.7.1 Technology

As in other disciplines, technology is having a significant impact on the practice of operations. For example, communication technologies such as the Web and cloud computing are greatly facilitating the ability of organizations to share real-time information with their suppliers and customers. Having more timely information enhances the opportunities for supply chain partners to coordinate and integrate their operations, which ultimately leads to a more effective and efficient supply chain that benefits both the end customer and the trading partners in the supply chain.

One exciting technology that promises to greatly enhance the ability of organizations to have real-time information on their inventory and other assets is radio-frequency identification (RFID); RFID tags are attached to individual inventory items, and these tags transmit identification and location information. For example, by attaching an RFID tag to a part, its progress through the production process can be monitored and, when finished, its location in the warehouse tracked.

As an example of the use of RFID tags, in 2016 Delta Airlines invested $50 million in RFID technology to track passenger bags. The use of RFID tags on baggage helped Delta increase both the efficiency with which it handles baggage and its customer satisfaction. To illustrate this, in May 2018 Delta had only 1.54 mishandled baggage claim reports per 1000 passengers compared to an industry average that is greater than 5. Delta is deploying RFID technology in a number of other areas to improve its supply chain performance including adding RFID to monitor the expiration dates and inventory levels of emergency equipment on its planes and using RFID tags on key spare parts such as airplane wheels in order to track when a replenishment order is needed.

RFID tags are classified as passive or active. Passive RFID tags contain no power source and therefore rely on the power source of an RFID reader to transmit their information. Active RFID tags contain a power source such as a battery and use this power source to periodically transmit a signal that provides identification information. Perhaps the greatest challenge to greater adoption of RFID tags is the cost of the tags themselves. As with other technologies, the cost of RFID has decreased dramatically and is expected to continue on this trajectory. The cost of basic passive RFID tags range from a few cents to a dollar or more depending on the volume of tags purchased and the environmental factors they are designed to withstand. The tags that Delta uses to track baggage are similar to the tags used in retail and cost 3 to 5 cents each. The cost of active RFID tags starts from $15 to $20 and again increases depending on the features desired.

More recently, another technology generating a great deal of enthusiasm is blockchain. While the blockchain technology was originally deployed in 2009 to track transactions for the cryptocurrency Bitcoin, the technology is applicable to a wide variety of situations that require the ability to securely record and share transactional information. As one example, in 2018 Walmart experimented with blockchain to manage the supply chain data for 30 products. Using mobile apps supplied by Walmart to its supply chain partners, Walmart was able to track a mango from the time it was picked in Mexico through the packing house and other processing points along the supply chain to its store shelves. The blockchain included a wealth of data including the harvest date, location of the fruit at any given time, and even digital images of the fruit. Based on early results of the experiments, managers at Walmart have found the blockchain technology to be both simpler and more secure than the use of the more traditional approach that employs bar codes, paper records, and conventional databases. Furthermore, in a test of the technology's ability to trace the source of an item needing to be recalled, the blockchain technology was able to identify the source of a bag of sliced mangoes in less than three seconds with the blockchain technology. Using its traditional technology and systems, it took over six days to track the same bag of mangoes. We will have more to say about blockchain in Chapter 5 when we discuss supply chain management in more detail.

1.2.7.2 Supply Chain Considerations

As a result of the advances in technology as well as an intensifying competitive environment, another important trend in business is the increasing emphasis organizations are placing on effectively managing their supply chains. Indeed, to remain competitive, organizations are discovering the importance of leveraging the volumes of customer data that are a natural by-product of our computerized society, developing stronger relationships with their supply chain partners, and proactively managing the risks associated with disruptions to their supply chain. Regarding the increasing volumes of data, as will be discussed in greater detail in Chapter 5, many organizations are finding ways to combine the volumes of data they accumulate with advanced analytical techniques to manage and improve their supply chains in ways that were unthinkable in the past.

Another area gaining increasing attention in supply chain management is the development of strong relationships with supply chain partners through increased collaboration. It is now widely accepted that all supply chain partners can benefit through greater collaboration. For example, including all supply chain partners in the development of the demand forecast not only increases the amount of information available from different perspectives but also helps ensure that the detailed plans of suppliers and customers are aligned and working toward achieving the same goals. We return to the issue of building relationships with supply chain partners and the benefits of greater collaboration in Chapter 5.

Related to the area of developing stronger relationships with supply chain partners is the emphasis organizations are placing on the sourcing of their products. In the past, sourcing decisions were frequently viewed as primarily tactical in nature with the overarching goal of obtaining the lowest possible unit cost. Often, the strategy used to obtain the lowest cost was to play one supplier against another. Now, we see organizations increasingly discussing *strategic sourcing* and thinking more holistically in terms of the total cost of ownership, not just the unit cost. Likewise, the potential benefits of outsourcing overseas are being increasingly questioned, and new terms such as reshoring and next-shoring have entered the lexicon. The topic of strategic sourcing is discussed in greater detail in Chapter 6.

Managing the risk of disruptions to the supply chain is yet another area gaining increasing attention. For example, consider the impact of the earthquake and the tsunami that hit Japan in 2011 on the availability of product components and finished goods. More recently the COVID-19 pandemic has disrupted numerous supply chains resulting in shortages for a wide variety of products including baby formula, semiconductors, and automobiles. Disruptions to the supply chain are generally either the result of nature (natural disasters such as earthquakes, blizzards, floods, and hurricanes) or human behavior (terrorist strikes, glitches in technology, and workers going on strike). Managing such disruptions is especially challenging because they are often difficult to predict. The best approach for dealing with these types of disruptions to the supply chain is to brainstorm potential disruptions, assess the impact of the identified disruptions, and develop contingency plans to mitigate the risk of the disruption. Because of the increasingly important role supply chain management plays to an organization's competitiveness, we address the topic in greater detail in Chapters 5 and 6.

1.2.7.3 Sustainability

A final important trend impacting the practice of operations management is the increasing levels of concern for the environment, which in turn has led many organizations to place greater emphasis on issues related to sustainability. Regardless of your personal point of view regarding whether climate change should be of concern or not, many leading and high-profile businesses are making significant commitments to sustainability as the Microsoft vignette at the beginning of the chapter illustrates. As other examples, Apple has committed that its entire supply chain will be carbon neutral by 2030. Unilever has committed to being carbon neutral by 2039, Amazon by 2040, and the world's largest ship container company Maersk by 2050. Google is already carbon neutral and has further committed to sourcing all its energy needs from carbon free sources by 2030. More broadly, in a survey conducted by Deloitte of over 2,000 C-suite executives in late 2021, 97% of the respondents indicated they have already experienced negative impacts from climate change and 89% agreed that climate change is a global emergency. On a more optimistic note, 88% agreed that the worst impacts of climate change can be limited with immediate action.

Beyond genuine interest, perhaps another key driver of business' interest in climate change is increasing regulations, many of which directly impact the operations area. Perhaps the best-known regulation related to climate change is the COP 21 or Parris Agreement that was signed by almost 200 countries and is a legal agreement to limit the increase in global temperatures to less than 2°C. Regardless of the rationale, it is clear that sustainability is both a current and important focus of business.

Addressing environmental concerns impacts virtually all aspects of operations management from the design of the organization's output, to the sourcing of parts, to the distribution of the product, and even to the disposal or recycling of the product or its components once it reaches the end of its useful life. Green sourcing, for example, seeks to identify suppliers in such a way that the organization's carbon footprint and overall impact on the environment are minimized.

Because of both its timeliness and importance, the topic of sustainability has been integrated throughout this book. Broadly speaking, sustainability refers to taking responsibility for the impact an organization's operations have on all stakeholders including employees, customers, suppliers, shareholders, the communities they operate in, and the environment.

As a result of the increasing importance organizations are placing on sustainability, some organizations are adopting the triple bottom line approach for assessing their performance. In addition to assessing profits, organizations that employ the triple bottom line approach also assess themselves on social responsibility (people) and their environmental responsibility (planet). Committing to people relates to employing business practices that treat people fairly such as eliminating discrimination, employing appropriate labor practices such as ensuring safe and appropriate working conditions. Committing the planet relates to employing business practices that do not negatively impact the environment such as using renewable energy, eliminating pollution, and not depleting natural resources. Reducing waste associated with products is another top sustainability priority of organizations that seek to minimize the negative impact they have on the planet. Along these lines, organizations can deploy a strategy referred to as the three Rs: reduce, reuse, and recycle. As its name suggests, the reduce strategy seeks to decrease the amount of waste associated with a product. One way to accomplish this is to minimize the amount of product packaging used. For example, Apple committed to eliminating all plastic used in its packaging by 2025. In services, switching to electronic copies of documents helps reduce waste, such as when a bank switches to electronic statements. Reuse is a second strategy for minimizing waste. The idea underlying reuse is to identify alternative uses for an item after its initial use. For example, there are kits available for converting old computer monitors into fish aquariums. Finally, recycling involves using the materials from old products to create new products. For example, many greeting cards are made from recycled paper.

Returning to the first P of the triple bottom line, namely profits, it is also worth mentioning that many organizations have discovered that they can simultaneously increase their competitiveness while at the same time pursue sustainability objectives. Indeed, rather that view sustainability and profitability as tradeoffs, progressive companies seek to identify approaches that accomplish both simultaneously. Even a high-level assessment suggests this is possible. For example, it is not hard to imagine how becoming more energy efficient and producing less waste can translate into lower costs. Indeed, numerous companies including Microsoft, Apple, Google, Patagonia, and Walmart have discovered that they can continue to grow their businesses while at the same time reduce their emissions. The appendix to this chapter provides an overview of some key concepts associated with sustainability.

1.2.7.4 The Project Economy

Another important trend affecting operations today is the one that we are just beginning to see – the change in our economic environment from one of *mass production* of both products and services to one of *projects* (Nieto-Rodriguez 2021). During the last century, mass production created tremendous value for society through increases in productivity and efficiency. This was due to advances in knowledge about how to manage factories and services, how to create better machinery and processes, and how to improve quality, accessibility, speed, and variety.

However, ever-increasing efficiency seems to have run its course and productivity has stagnated, in spite of amazing recent advances in technology (robotics, artificial intelligence, and data analytics) and communication (cell phones, the Web, and 5G). Our efficient operations of the past cannot satisfy the constantly increasing expectations of our society, and every organization today also faces continual and constant disruptive changes due to competition and expectations.

Making more of the same is not the solution; change is required in our organizations themselves. It is commonly said that organizations need to both *exploit* their existing capabilities but also *explore* new capabilities, typically through innovation and technological change. This means that *projects* are needed to successfully bring about these innovative capabilities. Mass production capabilities require investing in assets that will keep costs low and accessibility high for what customers want now, but that is a short-term investment. The production process is focused on productivity through a hierarchical, command and control structure. Projects focus on medium- to long-term capabilities such as quick response to changing needs and more attention to the human assets of the organization rather than the machinery, resulting in a flatter, more egalitarian, diverse, and motivating structure.

Projects are about change and new benefits – innovative new outputs, transformed processes, strategic initiatives, new ways of managing, and greater satisfaction from work. Nieto-Rodriguez (2021) notes that workers are most proud of the work they performed on projects, whether a success or a failure, not production lines. Projects are highly motivating for workers, and teams too. Perhaps this is why projects are slowly displacing mass production as the economic thrust of organizations these days.

Unfortunately, most people and too many managers feel that their regular job is what is important, and projects only get in the way of their job. This is understandable since their pay and the promotion system is typically tied to their regular job, not the innovations and breakthroughs that come from their efforts on projects. But if managers ignore the effort that people put into projects, strategic initiatives will fail, re-orgs will not deliver, and innovations will flop. In the past, mass production was the norm and projects were temporary distractions, but in the future, projects will become the norm and production the temporary jobs.

To make this transformation, managers will have to change dramatically, instituting flat organizations that value their workers' capabilities and diversity, and supporting projects as the main job of their organization. This "support" however is not just a matter of *approving projects*. The management of projects will become their primary job, including governance, business case development, benefits realization, and many other competencies. This means that budgets, resources, attention, decisions, and all else will have to move toward projects and their teams instead of functional departments. The organizational culture will also have to evolve toward a project-based structure with managers helping their workers develop the required project management competencies, such as training in collaboration and innovation. The transformation will not be easy, but it will much better for the organization, its managers, its workers, and for society.

1.3 Customer Value

As was noted earlier, organizations exist to create value for their customers. It is also worth repeating that the operations function is the part of the organization that has the primary responsibility for creating this value. In this section, we discuss the aspects of products and services that customers value including innovativeness, functionality, quality, customization, responsiveness, and low cost.

1.3.1 Costs

In the "Introduction" to this chapter, we mentioned that customers support the providers of goods and services who offer them the most "value." In this section, we elaborate on this concept. The equation for value is conceptually simple:

$$Value = perceived\ benefits/costs$$

While the perceived benefits can take a wide variety of forms, the costs are usually more straightforward:

- The upfront cost of the product/service

- Other monetary life-cycle costs of using the service or product, such as maintenance

- The hassles involved in obtaining the product or service, such as travel required, obtaining financing, the friendliness of service, and so on.

The cost to the customer is, of course, the price paid, but this is usually highly correlated with the cost of producing the service or product, which is itself largely based on the "efficiency" of the production process. *Efficiency* or productivity is always measured as output/input; for example, a standard automobile engine that uses gasoline is usually about 15–20% efficient (i.e. the energy put into the engine in terms of gasoline vs. the energy put out in terms of automobile motion). In comparison, electric and jet engines are more efficient, and rocket engines can reach almost 70% efficiency. We will return to the topic of productivity at the end of this chapter.

In addition to costs, the benefits provided by the output are another key factor in determining how the customer values the output. We next consider five ways these benefits are created: innovativeness, functionality, quality, customization, and responsiveness.

1.3.2 Innovativeness

With competition intensifying and product life cycles becoming shorter, one key to competitive success is the ability to continuously create new products and services. It is the field of research and development (known as R&D) that is primarily responsible for developing innovative new product and service ideas. R&D activities focus on creating and developing (but not producing) the organization's outputs. On occasion, R&D also creates new production methods by which outputs, either new or old, may be produced.

Research itself is typically divided into two types: pure and applied. Pure research is simply working with basic science to develop new knowledge. Applied research is attempting to develop new knowledge along particular lines. For example, pure research might focus on developing a material that conducts electricity with zero resistance, whereas applied research could focus on further developing this material to be used in products for customers. *Development* is an attempt to utilize the findings of research and expand the possible applications, often consisting of modifications or extensions to existing outputs to meet customers' interests. The focus of Chapter 3 is on designing the output, including innovation, and its delivery process so we will postpone our discussion of this topic until Chapter 3.

1.3.3 Functionality

Many people confuse *functionality* with quality (discussed next). But functionality involves the activities the product or service is intended to perform, thereby providing the benefits to the customer. A contemporary example is the ubiquitous smartphone. These days, it is rare to find a cell phone that is only a phone; smartphones include many additional features such as cameras, the ability to check e-mail and the weather, browsers to surf the Web, and a myriad of apps that greatly expand the functionality of the phone.

1.3.4 Quality

Quality is a relative term, meaning different things to different people at different times. Moreover, quality is not an absolute but, rather, is based on customers' perceptions. Customers' impressions can be influenced by a number of factors, including brand loyalty and an organization's reputation. Richard J. Schonberger has compiled a list of multiple quality dimensions that customers often associate with products and services:

1. *Conformance to specifications.* Conformance to specifications is the extent to which the actual product matches the design specifications, such as a pizza delivery shop that consistently meets its advertised delivery time of 30 minutes.

2. *Performance.* Customers frequently equate the quality of products and services with their performance. Examples of performance include how quickly a sports car accelerates or the battery life of a cell phone.

3. *Features.* Features are the options that a product or service offers, such as heated seats on a car and using facial recognition to unlock a smartphone.

4. *Quick response.* Quick response is associated with the amount of time required to react to customers' demands. However, we consider this to be a separate benefit, discussed further in the section on responsiveness.

5. *Reliability.* Reliability is the probability that a product or service will perform as intended on any given trial or for some period of time, such as the probability that a car will start on any given morning.

6. *Durability.* Durability refers to how tough a product is, such as a cell phone that still functions after being dropped in a swimming pool or a knife that can cut through steel and does not need sharpening.

7. *Serviceability.* Serviceability refers to the ease with which maintenance or a repair can be performed.

8. *Aesthetics.* Aesthetics are factors that appeal to human senses, such as the taste of a steak or the sound of a sports car's engine.

9. *Humanity.* Humanity has to do with how the customer is treated, such as a private university that maintains small classes so students are not treated like numbers by its professors.

It is worth noting that not all the dimensions of quality are relevant to all products and services. Thus, organizations need to identify the dimensions of quality that are relevant to the products and services they offer. Market research about customers' needs is the primary input for determining which dimensions are important. Of course, measuring the quality of a service can often be more difficult than measuring the quality of a product or facilitating good. However, the dimensions of quality described previously apply to both.

1.3.5 Customization

Customization refers to offering a product or service precisely tailored to a customer's desires or needs. However, there is a range of accommodation to the customer's needs, as illustrated in Figure 1.3. At the left, there is the completely standard, world-class (excellence suitable for all markets) product or service. Moving to the right is the standard with options, continuing on to variants and alternative models and ending at the right with made-to-order customization. In general, the more customization, the better – if it can be provided quickly, with acceptable quality and cost.

1.3.5.1 Flexibility

However, to offer customization demands flexibility on the part of the firm. Professor Upton (1994), formerly of the Harvard Business School, defines flexibility as "the ability to change or react with little penalty in time, effort, cost, or performance" (p. 73). There are more than a dozen different types of flexibility that we will not pursue here – design, volume, routing through the production system, product mix, and many others. But having the right types of flexibility can offer the following major competitive advantages:

- Faster matches to customers' needs because change over time from one product or service to another is quicker

- Closer matches to customers' needs

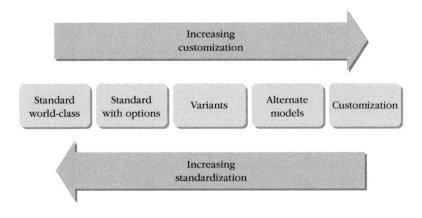

FIGURE 1.3
Continuum of
Customization

- Ability to supply the needed items in the volumes required for the markets as they develop

- Faster design-to-market time to meet new customer needs

- Lower cost of changing production to meet needs

- Ability to offer a full line of products or services without the attendant cost of stocking large inventories

- Ability to meet market demands even if delays develop in the production or distribution process.

1.3.5.2 Mass Customization

Until recently, it was widely believed that producing low-cost standard products (at the far left in Figure 1.3) required one type of transformation process and producing higher-cost customized products (far right) required another type of process. However, in addition to vast improvements in operating efficiency, an unexpected by-product of the continuous improvement programs of the 1980s was substantial improvement in flexibility. Indeed, prior to this, efficiency and flexibility were thought to be trade-offs. Increasing efficiency meant that flexibility had to be sacrificed and vice versa.

Thus, with the emphasis on continuous improvement came the realization that increasing operating efficiency could also enhance flexibility. For example, many manufacturers initiated efforts to reduce the amount of time required to set up (or change over) equipment when switching from the production of one product to another. Obviously, all time spent setting up equipment is wasteful, since the equipment is not being used during this time to produce outputs that ultimately create revenues for the organization. Consequently, improving the amount of time a resource is used productively directly translates into improved efficiency. Interestingly, these same reductions in equipment times also resulted in improved flexibility. Specifically, with shorter equipment setup times, manufacturers could produce economically in smaller-size batches, making it easier to switch from the production of one product to another.

In response to the discovery that efficiency and flexibility can be improved simultaneously and may not have to be traded off, the strategy of mass customization emerged (see Pine 1993; Gilmore and Pine 1997). Organizations pursuing *mass customization* seek to produce low-cost, high-quality outputs in great variety. Of course, not all products and services lend themselves to being customized. This is particularly true of commodities, such as sugar, gas, electricity, and flour. On the other hand, mass customization is often quite applicable to products characterized by short life cycles, rapidly advancing technology, or changing customer requirements. However, research suggests that successfully employing mass customization requires an organization to first develop a transformation process that can consistently deliver high-quality outputs at a low cost. With this foundation in place, the organization can then seek ways to increase the variety of its offerings at the same time ensuring that quality and cost are not compromised.

In an article published in the *Harvard Business Review,* Gilmore and Pine (1997) identified four mass customization strategies:

1. *Collaborative customizers.* These organizations establish a dialogue to help customers articulate their needs and then develop customized outputs to meet these needs. For example, one Japanese eyewear retailer developed a computerized system to help customers select eyewear. The system combines a digital image of the customer's face and then various styles of eyewear are displayed on the digital image. Once the customer is satisfied, the customized glasses are produced at the retail store within an hour.

2. *Adaptive customizers.* These organizations offer a standard product that customers can modify themselves, such as fast-food hamburgers (ketchup, etc.) and closet organizers. Each closet-organizer package is the same but includes instructions and tools to cut the shelving and clothes rods so that the unit can fit a wide variety of closet sizes.

3. *Cosmetic customizers.* These organizations produce a standard product but present it differently to different customers. For example, Planters packages its peanuts and mixed nuts in a variety of containers based on specific needs of its retailing customers, such as Walmart, 7-Eleven, and Safeway.

4. *Transparent customizers.* These organizations provide custom products without the customers knowing that a product has been customized for them. For example, Amazon.com provides book recommendations based on information about past purchases.

1.3.5.3 Example: Hewlett-Packard

Faced with increasing pressure from its customers for quicker order fulfillment and for more highly customized products, Hewlett-Packard (HP) wondered whether it was really possible to deliver mass-customized products rapidly at the same time continuing to reduce costs (Feitzinger and Lee 1997). HP's approach to mass customization can be summarized as effectively delaying tasks that customize a product as long as possible in the product supply process. It is based on the following three principles:

- Products should be designed around a number of independent modules that can be easily combined in a variety of ways.

- Manufacturing tasks should also be designed and performed as independent modules that can be relocated or rearranged to support new production requirements.

- The product supply process must perform two functions. First, it must cost-effectively supply the basic product to the locations that complete the customization activities. Second, it must have the requisite flexibility to process individual customers' orders.

HP has discovered that modular design provides three primary benefits. First, components that differentiate the product can be added during the later stages of production. This method of mass customization, generally called *postponement,* is one form of the assemble-to-order production process, discussed in more detail in Chapter 3. For example, the company designed its printers so that country-specific power supplies are combined with the printers at local distribution centers and actually plugged in by the customer when the printer is set up. Second, production time can be significantly reduced by simultaneously producing the required modules. Third, producing in modules facilitates the identification of production and quality problems.

1.3.6 Responsiveness

Organizations that can respond faster to shifts in customer needs and meet these needs more dependably are able to obtain significant competitive advantages. Indeed, the competitive advantages of faster, dependable response to new markets or to the individual customer's needs have been frequently noted in the business media (Eisenhardt and Brown 1998; Stalk 1988; Vessey 1991). For example, in a study of the U.S. and Japanese robotics industry, the National Science Foundation found that the Japanese tend to be about 25% faster than Americans, and to spend 10% less, in developing and marketing new robots. The major difference is that the Americans spend more time and money on marketing, whereas the Japanese spend five times more than the Americans on developing more efficient production methods.

Table 1.2 identifies a number of prerequisites for and advantages of fast, dependable response. These include higher quality, faster revenue generation, and lower costs through elimination of overhead, reduction of inventories, greater efficiency, and fewer errors and scrap. One of the most important but least recognized advantages for managers is that by responding faster, they can

Table 1.2 Prerequisites for and Advantages of Rapid Response

1 *Sharper focus on the customer.* Faster response for both standard- and custom-designed items places the customer at the center of attention

2 *Better management.* Attention shifts to management's real job, improving the firm's infrastructure and systems

3 *Efficient processing.* Efficient processing reduces inventories, eliminates nonvalue-added processing steps, smoothes flows, and eliminates bottlenecks

4 *Higher quality.* Since there is no time for rework, the production system must be sufficiently improved to make parts accurately, reliably, consistently, and correctly

5 *Elimination of overhead.* More efficient, faster flows through fewer steps eliminate the overhead needed to support the remaining steps, processes, and systems

6 *Improved focus.* A customer-based focus is provided for strategy, investment, and general attention (instead of an internal focus on surrogate measures such as utilization)

7 *Reduced changes.* With less time to delivery, there is less time for changes in product mix, engineering changes, and especially changes to the order by the customer who just wanted to get in the queue in the first place

8 *Faster revenue generation.* With faster deliveries, orders can be billed faster, thereby improving cash flows and reducing the need for working capital

9 *Better communication.* More direct communication lines result in fewer mistakes, oversights, and lost orders

10 *Improved morale.* The reduced processing steps and overhead allow workers to see the results of their efforts, giving a feeling of working for a smaller firm, with its greater visibility and responsibility

allow a customer to delay an order until the exact need is known. Thus, the customer does not have to change the order – a perennial headache for most operations managers.

Faster response to a customer also can, up to a point, reduce the unit costs of the product or service, sometimes significantly. On the basis of empirical studies reported by Meredith et al. (1994) and illustrated in Figure 1.4, it seems that there is about a 2:1 (i.e. 0.50) relationship between response time and unit cost. That is, starting from typical values, an 80% reduction in response time results in a corresponding 40% reduction in unit cost. The actual empirical data indicated a range between about 0.60 and 0.20, so for an 80% reduction in response time, there could be a cost reduction from a high of 0.60 × 80% = 48% to a low of 16%.

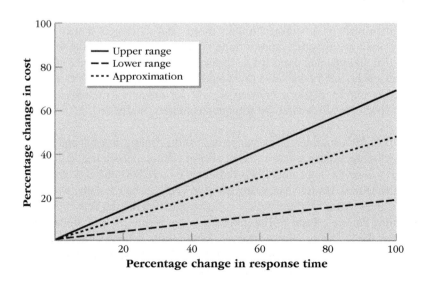

FIGURE 1.4 Cost Reductions with Decreases in Response Time

This is an overwhelming benefit because if corresponding price reductions are made, it improves the value delivered to the customer through both higher responsiveness and lower price. The result for the producer is a much higher market share.

If the producer chooses not to reduce the price, then the result is significantly increased profitability.

1.4 Strategy and Competitiveness

As the part of the organization that creates value for the customers, operations plays a key role in the competitiveness of the organization. *Competitiveness* can be defined in a number of ways. We may think of it as the long-term viability of a firm or organization, or we may define it in a short-term context such as the current success of a firm in the marketplace as measured by its market share or its profitability. We can also talk about the competitiveness of a nation, in the sense of its aggregate competitive success in all markets. The U.S. President's Council on Industrial Competitiveness gave this definition in 1985:

> *Competitiveness for a nation is the degree to which it can, under free and fair market conditions, produce goods and services that meet the test of international markets while simultaneously maintaining and expanding the real incomes of its citizens.*

1.4.1 Global Trends

The United States provides a graphic example of global trade trends. Indeed, some find the trend in the trade of goods and services for the United States alarming. Although U.S. *exports* have grown considerably over the last 50 years, *imports* have increased at a faster rate over this period. More specifically, beginning in 1971 the United States has experienced a trade deficit where the total value of what it imported exceeded the value of its exports. Perhaps of greater concern to the United States is its trade deficit. The trade deficit in the United States peaked in 2006 at approximately $771 billion or approximately 5.6% of GDP while during the period of 2013–2019 it remained below 3% of GDP. In 2021 the U.S. exports were $2.5 trillion and its imports were $2.4 trillion, making the United States the second largest exporter (behind China) and the largest importer.

A key factor influencing trade is the exchange rate between the currencies of countries. Let's consider in more detail what it means when a country's currency declines in value relative to foreign currencies. A weaker currency means that citizens in that country will have to pay more for products imported from foreign countries. Meanwhile, the prices for products produced in that country and exported to foreign countries will decline, making them more desirable. Thus, a decline in the value of a country's currency is a double-edged sword. Such a decline makes imported goods more expensive for citizens to purchase but at the same time makes exports less expensive for foreign consumers, increasing the demand for domestic products.

As an example, let's consider the exchange rates of the American dollar and the Chinese Yuan. In the early 1980s, the exchange rate or the number of Chinese Yuan a U.S. dollar could purchase was below 2.0. However, in the mid-1990s through the mid-2000s the U.S. dollar became much stronger relative to the Chinese Yuan, rising above 8. Thus, each U.S. dollar was able to purchase more than 8 Chinese Yuan. Throughout the period from 2008 on, the Yuan weakened a bit, generally fluctuating between 6 and 7. The implications for a stronger U.S. dollar depend on your perspective. For the U.S. consumer, a stronger dollar results in cheaper goods that are imported from China. However, for manufacturers, exports to China become more expensive, which in turn makes them less competitive from a cost standpoint.

According to economic theory, a stronger dollar should make American products less desirable (or competitive) in foreign markets and imports more desirable in American markets. However, some market actions that governments and businesses often take to keep from losing customers can alter this perfect economic relationship. For instance, in the 1990s, when the price of Japanese products in the United States started increasing in terms of dollars, Japanese firms initiated huge cost-cutting drives to reduce the cost (and thereby the dollar price) of their products, to keep from losing American customers, which was largely successful. Similarly, China controls the exchange rate of its currency to stay at about 7 to the dollar so it always sells its goods at a competitive price.

In the last decade, particularly with the economic rise of China and India, global markets, manufacturers, and service producers have evolved in a dramatic manner. With the changes occurring in the World Trade Organization (WTO), international competition has grown very complex in the last two decades. Previously, firms were domestic, exporters, or international. A domestic firm produced and sold in the same country. An exporter sold goods, often someone else's, abroad. An international firm sold domestically produced as well as foreign-produced goods both domestically and in foreign countries. However, domestic sales were usually produced domestically, and foreign sales were made either in the home country or in a plant in the foreign country, typically altered to suit national regulations, needs, and tastes.

Now, however, there are global firms, joint ventures, partial ownerships, foreign subsidiaries, and other types of international producers. For example, Canon is a global producer that sells a standard "world-class" camera with options and add-ons available through local dealers. And automobile producers frequently own stock in foreign automobile companies. Mazak, a machine tool company, is the U.S. subsidiary of Yamazaki Machinery Company of Japan. Part of the reason for cross-ownerships and cross-endeavors is the spiraling cost of bringing out new products. New drugs and memory chips run in the hundreds of millions to billions of dollars to bring to market. By using joint ventures and other such approaches to share costs (and thereby lower risks), firms can remain competitive.

Whether to build offshore, assemble offshore, use foreign parts, employ a joint venture, and so on is a complex decision for any firm and depends on a multitude of factors. For example, the Japanese have many of their automobile manufacturing plants in foreign countries. The reasons are many and include to circumvent foreign governmental regulation of importers, to avoid the effects of currency fluctuations, to avoid import fees and quotas, and to placate foreign consumers. Of course, other considerations are involved in producing in foreign countries: culture (e.g. whether women are part of the labor force), political stability, laws, taxes, regulations, reducing an organization's carbon footprint, and image.

Other complex arrangements of suppliers can result in hidden international competition. For example, many products that bear an American nameplate have been totally produced and assembled in a foreign country and are simply imported under a U.S. manufacturer's or retailer's nameplate, such as Nike shoes. Even more confusing, many products contain a significant proportion of foreign parts or may be composed entirely of foreign parts and only assembled in the United States (e.g. automobiles, aircraft). This recent strategic approach of finding the best mix of producers and assemblers to deliver a product or service to a customer has come to be known as "supply chain management," a topic we discuss in detail in Chapters 5 and 6.

1.4.2 Strategy

The organization's business strategy is a set of objectives, plans, and policies for the organization to compete successfully in its markets. In effect, the business strategy specifies what an organization's competitive advantage will be and how this advantage will be achieved and sustained through the decisions the organization's business units make in the future. A key element of the business strategy is determining the window of opportunity for executing this strategy before competitors do the same. The strategic plan that details this business strategy is typically formulated at the executive committee level (CEO, president, vice presidents) and is usually long range, at least three to five years.

In fact, however, the actual decisions that are made over time *become* the long-range strategy. In too many firms, these decisions show no pattern at all, reflecting the truth that they have no active business strategy, even if they have gone through a process of strategic planning. In other cases, these decisions bear little or no relationship to the organization's stated or official business strategy. The point is that an organization's actions tell more about its true business strategy, or lack thereof, than its public statements.

But devising a winning strategy is only the first step in being competitive. The organization and its various business units still need to successfully *implement* this strategy, and that is where so many fail. It is now clear that more organizational strategies fail not so much for being a poor strategy but instead for poor execution. As Morgan, Levitt, and Malek note in their widely heralded book, *"Executing Your Strategy; How to Break It Down and Get It Done"* (Morgan et al. 2007, p. 1), "Corporations spend about $100 billion a year on management consulting and training, most of it aimed at creating brilliant strategy. Yet studies have found that . . . something like 90% of companies consistently fail to execute strategies effectively." They confirm that thousands of such strategies fail every year because of poor execution.

Executing a winning strategy is a major project or set of projects that must be implemented within a limited time, taking substantial resources and experienced talent, the province of *project management* (Meredith and Shafer 2022). Unfortunately, as Morgan et al. point out, top managers consider the tedious work of project management as "too 'tactical' to take up their precious time . . . leaving the grunt work of execution to the lower echelons. Nothing could be further from the truth . . . that is precisely where strategy goes awry" (pp. 2, 4). Morgan et al. suggest that a simple test of this failure in perspective of top executives is to examine the set of projects – the *project portfolio* – to see whether it is aligned with the organization's stated strategy or not. The execution of strategic initiatives through project management will be dealt with in the next chapter of this first part of the book concerning strategy *and* execution.

1.4.3 Strategic Frameworks

We now turn our attention to several frameworks that can facilitate the development of discipline-specific strategies, where each in turn support the overall strategy of the organization. These discipline-specific strategies are also executed via projects or sets of projects. There will be a marketing strategy, a financial strategy, an R&D strategy, and so on. Here, of course, we are interested in the operations and supply chain strategy. One factor that needs to be considered in the development of a strategy is the stage an output is in during its life cycle, which is where we will begin our discussion.

1.4.3.1 The Life Cycle

A number of functional strategies are tied to the stages in the standard *life cycle* of products and services, as shown in Figure 1.5. Studies of the introduction of new products indicate that the life cycle (or *stretched S growth curve,* as it is also known) provides a good pattern for the growth of demand for a new output. The curve can be divided into three major segments: (1) introduction and early adoption, (2) acceptance and growth of the market, and (3) maturity with market saturation. After market saturation, demand may remain high or decline, or the output may be improved and possibly start on a new growth curve.

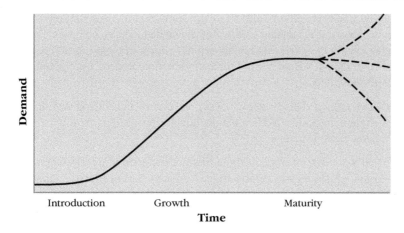

Introduction   Growth   Maturity

Time

FIGURE 1.5 The Life-cycle Curve

The length of product and service life cycles has been shrinking significantly in the last decade or so. In the past, a life cycle might have been five years, but it is now six months. This places a tremendous burden on the firm to constantly monitor its strategy and quickly change a strategy that becomes inappropriate to the market.

The life cycle begins with an *innovation* – a new output or process for the market, which we discuss in greater detail in Chapter 3. The innovation may be a patented product or process, a new combination of existing elements that has created a unique product or process, or some service that was previously unavailable. Initial versions of the product or service may change relatively frequently; production volumes are small, since the output has not caught on yet; and margins are high. As volume increases, the design of the output stabilizes and more competitors enter the market, frequently with more capital-intensive equipment. In the mature phase, the high-volume output is a virtual commodity, and the firm that can produce an acceptable version at the lowest cost usually controls the market.

Clearly, a firm's business strategy should match the life-cycle stages of its products and services. If a firm such as Apple is good at innovation, it may choose to focus on the introduction and growth phases of the product's life cycle and then introduce new products before the product reaches the mature phase. On the other hand, if an organization's strength is in high-volume, low-cost production, it may wait until a product proves itself and reaches the maturity stage before entering the market with its offering.

One approach to categorizing an organization's business strategy is based on its timing of introductions of new outputs. Two researchers, Maidique and Patch (1979), suggest the following four product development strategies:

1. *First-to-market.* Organizations that use this strategy attempt to have their products available before the competition. To achieve this, strong applied research is needed. If a company is first-to-market, it has to decide if it wants to price its products high and thus skim the market to achieve large short-term profits or set a lower initial price to obtain a higher market share and perhaps larger long-term profits.

2. *Second-to-market.* Organizations that use this strategy try to quickly imitate successful outputs offered by first-to-market organizations. This strategy requires less emphasis on applied research and more emphasis on fast development. Often, firms that use the second-to-market strategy attempt to learn from the mistakes of the first-to-market firm and offer improved or enhanced versions of the original products.

3. *Cost minimization or late-to-market.* Organizations that use this strategy wait until a product becomes fairly standardized and is demanded in large volumes. They then attempt to compete on the basis of costs as opposed to features of the product. These organizations focus most of their R&D on improving the production process, as opposed to focusing on product development.

4. *Market segmentation.* This strategy focuses on serving niche markets with specific needs. Applied engineering skills and flexible manufacturing systems are often needed for the market-segmentation strategy.

Be aware that a number of implicit trade-offs are involved in developing a strategy. Let us use the first-to-market strategy to demonstrate. A first-to-market strategy requires large investments in product development in an effort to stay ahead of the competition. Typically, organizations that pursue this strategy expect to achieve relatively higher profit margins, larger market shares, or both as a result of initially having the market to themselves. The strategy is somewhat risky because a competitor may end up beating them to the market. Also, even if a company succeeds in getting to the market first, it may end up simply creating an opportunity for the competition to learn from its mistakes and overtake it in the market. To illustrate, although Sony introduced its Betamax format for VCRs in 1975, JVC's VHS format – introduced the following year – was the standard that ultimately gained widespread market acceptance. As a more recent example, Research in Motion introduced its smartphone in 1999 and Handspring introduced its smartphone the Treo 180 in 2002. Both of these phones had small physical keys and were ultimately replaced by smartphones with virtual keyboards such as Apple's iPhone that was introduced in 2007.

Such trade-offs are basic to the concept of selecting a business strategy. Although specific tasks must be done well to execute the selected strategy, not everything needs to be particularly outstanding – only a few things. And, of course, strategies based on anything else – acquisitions, mergers, tax loss carry-forwards, even streams of high-technology products – will not be successful if the customer is ignored in the process.

1.4.3.2 Performance Frontiers

As we know from the earlier "Customer Value" section, there are a wide range of benefits and costs that organizations can compete on and various groups of customers value. If, say, n of these factors are important for an organization to consider, we might then conceive of a graph or space with n dimensions on it showing the organization's measures on each of the n factors as well as their competitors' measures. The curve connecting all these measures would then be called the organization's *performance frontier* (Clark 1996). For simplicity, let us use just two factors, say, cost and variety, as shown in Figure 1.6, with the performance frontier curve labeled 1.

As illustrated by the points A, B, and C, improvement on one dimension can usually only be attained by sacrificing performance on another dimension. For example, as shown in Figure 1.6, increasing output variety may result in higher unit costs. In effect, this curve represents the level of performance that organizations in an industry can achieve across two dimensions given the technology available at a given point in time. According to the figure, company A is apparently pursuing more of a customization strategy than the two other competitors shown, offering a wider variety of outputs but incurring greater cost. We might think of a high-end furniture store as perhaps fitting point A. Company C, perhaps Costco, seems to be pursuing a standardization strategy, offering a smaller range of furniture but incurring lower unit costs.

An interesting use of this framework is to investigate and evaluate the impact of a change in technology or operational innovation. For example, in Figure 1.7, assume a new innovation such as "cross-docking" has been developed by company B, perhaps represented by Walmart, shifting

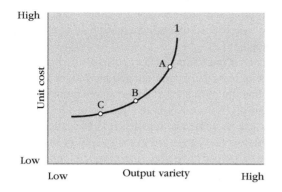

FIGURE 1.6
Example Performance
Frontier

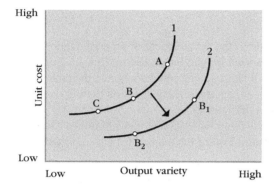

FIGURE 1.7
Development of New
Technology Results
in Shift in the Perfor-
mance Frontier

its performance frontier to curve 2. In this case, company B could hold its unit price constant and offer higher output variety than company A and at lower unit costs (position B_1). Alternatively, company B could maintain its current level of output variety and lower its unit cost to levels below company C's (position B_2) or perhaps choose a position somewhere between points B_1 and B_2.

Suppose you were employed at company A and company B chose to operate at point B_1. In effect, company B can now offer a wider variety of outputs and at lower unit costs. What are your options? As it turns out, there are two generic options or *improvement trajectories* company A could try to follow. One improvement trajectory would be for company A to streamline its operations and make cost–variety trade-offs, moving down curve 1 toward company C. Upon streamlining its operations, company A could then attempt to adopt the new technology and choose a position on the new frontier. A second improvement trajectory would be for company A to attempt to directly adopt the new technology and move to the new frontier without streamlining its current operations.

There are advantages and disadvantages associated with both trajectories. An advantage of streamlining operations first is that this might provide a better understanding of current processes. In turn, this better understanding might increase company A's options in choosing a location on the new frontier and might even better position it to adopt the new technology. One drawback of streamlining its current operations first is that the knowledge gained might be irrelevant when the new technology is eventually adopted and delaying the adoption of the new technology might mean reduced market share and profits. Another important factor is the amount of time required to execute the improvement trajectory and get to the new position on the new performance frontier. However, although it might appear that streamlining the current operation first before adopting the new technology should take more time than immediately adopting the technology, when ease of implementation is considered, the former approach might in fact be more expedient.

On a more practical note, Kmart some years ago tried to challenge Walmart on low prices but was unsuccessful. Then, Sears and Kmart merged instead, but that didn't seem to work well either as there are only a handful of Sears and Kmart stores remaining.

One final point. In Figure 1.7, it was assumed that the result of the new technology/innovation was simply a shift in the performance frontier. It is also important to be aware of the possibility that a new technology can change the shape as well as the location of the performance frontier. Such a change in shape can have important implications regarding choosing a location on the new frontier as well as the nature of the trade-off facing the industry. In either case, the way to beat your competition is through developing or using new technology to move to a new frontier.

1.4.3.3 Focus

Another key consideration in the development of an organization's strategy is its focus. In the past, firms primarily competed on one factor, such as low cost or innovation, because that was what they were good at. Obviously, they could not ignore the other factors of competition, which they had to do acceptably on, but their heavy attention to their one strength was based on a strategic concept called *focus* (Skinner 1974).

McKinsey & Company, a top management consulting firm, studied 27 outstanding firms to find their common attributes. Two of the major attributes reported in *Business Week* are directly related to focus:

1. *Stressing one key business value.* At Apple, the key value is developing innovative new products that are easy to use; at Dana Corporation, it is improving productivity.

2. *Sticking to what they know best.* All the outstanding firms define their core capabilities (or strengths) and then build on them. They resist the temptation to move into new areas or diversify.

When an organization chooses to stress one or two key areas of strength, it is referred to as a *focused organization*. For example, Apple is known for its user-friendly designs, Walmart for its low cost, and Nordstrom for its customer service. In general, most but not all areas of focus relate to operations. Some firms, such as those in the insurance industry, focus on financial strength and others focus on marketing strengths. For example, Harley-Davidson considers its strength to be in building relationships with its dealers and motorcycle owners. And many health-care organizations are achieving significant operational efficiencies by focusing on a narrow range of ailments. For example, by treating only long-term acute cases, Intensiva HealthCare has been able to reduce its costs to 50% of those of a traditional intensive-care ward. Clearly, adopting a focus strategy means knowing not only what customers to concentrate on but also what customers you do *not* want.

Table 1.3 identifies several areas of focus that organizations commonly choose when forming their competitive strategy; all are various forms of differentiation. Recent competitive behavior among firms seems to be dividing most of the factors in Table 1.3 into two sets that Hill (2000), an operations strategist and researcher in England, calls *order qualifiers* and *order winners*.

An *order qualifier* is a characteristic of the product or service that is required if the product is even to be considered or in the running. In other words, it is a prerequisite for entering the market. An *order winner* is a characteristic that will win the bid or the purchase. These qualifiers and winners vary with the market, of course, but some general commonalties exist across markets. For

Table 1.3 Common Areas of Organizational Focus

Innovation. Bringing a range of new products and services to market quickly

Customization. Being able to quickly redesign and produce a product or service to meet customers' unique needs

Flexibility of products and services. Switching between different models or variants quickly to satisfy a customer or market

Flexibility of volume. Changing quickly and economically from low-volume production to high volumes and vice versa

Performance. Offering products and services with unique, valuable features

Quality. Having better craftsmanship or consistency

Reliability of the product or service. Always working acceptably, enabling customers to count on the performance

Reliability of delivery. Always fulfilling promises with a product or service that is never late

Response. Offering very short lead times to obtain products and services

After-sale service. Making available extensive, continuing help

Price. Having the lowest price

example, response time, performance, customization, innovation, and price seem to be frequent order winners, and the other factors (e.g. quality, reliability, and flexibility) tend to be order qualifiers. Working with marketing and sales to properly identify which factors are which is clearly of major strategic importance.

In addition to the advantages of being focused, there are some dangers. A narrowly focused firm can easily become uncompetitive in the market if the customers' requirements change. In addition to being focused, a firm must be flexible enough to alter its focus when the need changes and to spot the change in time. Frequently, a focus in one area can be used to an advantage in another way if there is enough time to adapt, for example, to move into a new product line or alter the application of the focus. Moreover, as products go through their life cycle, the task of operations often changes, as shown in Figure 1.8, from being flexible enough to accept changes in design, to meeting the growing demand in the marketplace, and to cutting costs. Throughout this life cycle, the focus of the organization has to change if it stays with the same output. Another option is to choose to compete at only one stage of the life cycle and abandon other stages so that they can keep the strength of their original focus.

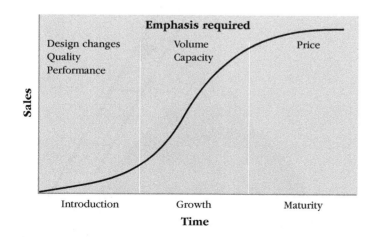

FIGURE 1.8 Product Life Cycle: Stages and Emphasis

An organization can also easily lose its focus. For example, in the traditional functional organization, purchasing may buy the cheapest materials it can. This requires buying large quantities with advance notice. Scheduling, however, is trying to reduce inventories, so it orders materials on short notice and in small quantities. Quality control is trying to improve the output, so it carefully inspects every item, creating delays and extensive rework. In this example, each functional department is pursuing its own objectives but is not focusing on how it can support the organization's overall business strategy.

However, the most common reason a firm loses its focus is simply that the focus was never clearly identified in the first place. Never having been well defined, it could not be communicated to the employees, could therefore not gain their support, and thus was lost. Sometimes, a focus is identified but not communicated throughout the organization because management thinks that lower-level employees don't need to know the strategic focus of the firm in order to do their jobs.

1.4.3.4 The Sand Cone

For many organizations that relied on the focus framework of strategy, the traditional view was that competing on one competitive dimension required trading off performance on one or more other dimensions (e.g. higher quality results in higher costs). However, research suggests that, at least in some cases, building strengths along alternative competitive dimensions may in fact be cumulative and that building a strength on one dimension may facilitate building strengths on other dimensions (Ferdows and De Meyer 1990).

Furthermore, according to this research, there is a preferred order in developing strengths on various competitive dimensions. According to the sand cone model (as it is called), shown in Figure 1.9, organizations should first develop the capability to produce quality outputs. Once an organization has developed this proficiency, it is next appropriate to address the issue of delivery dependability. Next, according to the model, the competitive dimensions of speed and cost should be addressed, respectively.

In addition to providing guidance to organizations regarding the order in which to focus their attention and initiatives, the model has intuitive appeal. For example, it makes little sense to focus on improving delivery dependability before an organization can provide a consistent level of quality. In today's competitive marketplace, providing defective outputs in a timely fashion is not a recipe for long-term success.

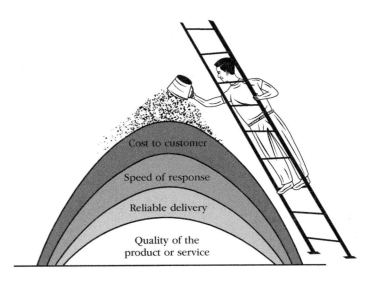

FIGURE 1.9 The Sand Cone Model. Adapted from Ferdows and De Meyer (1990, p. 175)

Likewise, organizations should achieve consistent quality levels and delivery dependability before attempting to reduce lead times. Of course, the model is not set in stone (remember that it is called the sand cone), and organizations facing different circumstances may choose to address the competitive dimensions in a different order.

1.4.4 Core Capabilities

One important result of developing a business strategy is identifying the organization's core competencies and capabilities that provide those product/service dimensions important to customers and hence are the source of customer value. *Core competencies* (Prahalad and Hamel 1990) are the collective knowledge and skills an organization has that distinguish it from the competition. In effect, these core competencies become the building blocks for organizational practices and business processes, referred to as *core capabilities* (Stalk et al. 1992). (Hereafter, we will refer to both of these simply as "core capabilities.") The importance of these core capabilities derives from their strong relationship to an organization's ability to integrate a variety of technologies and skills in the development of new products and services. Clearly, then, one of the top management's most important activities is the identification and development of the core capabilities the organization will need to successfully execute the business strategy.

In effect, core capabilities provide the basis for developing new products and services and are a primary factor in determining an organization's long-term competitiveness. Hammer (2004) points out the importance of "operational innovation" in the organization as one basis for sustained competitive advantage, the clear result of a core capability. Therefore, two important parts of strategic planning are identifying and predicting the core capabilities that will be critical to sustaining and enhancing the organization's competitive position. On this basis, an organization can also assess its suppliers' and competitors' capabilities. If the organization finds that it is not the leader, it must determine the cost and risks of catching up with the best versus the cost and risks of losing that core capability.

Hayes and Pisano (1994) stress the importance of a firm not looking for "the" solution to a current competitive problem but rather the "paths" to building one or two core capabilities to provide the source of customer value for the indefinite future. Moreover, the firm should not think in terms of "trade-offs" between core capabilities (e.g. moving from flexibility as a strength to low cost), but rather of "building" one capability on top of others and determining which *set* will provide the most customer value.

Often, it is more useful to think of an organization in terms of its portfolio of core capabilities, rather than its portfolio of businesses or products. For instance, Sony was known for its expertise in miniaturization; 3M for its knowledge of substrates, coatings, and adhesives; Black and Decker for small electrical motors and industrial design; Boeing for its ability to integrate large-scale complex systems; and Honda for engines and power trains. Had Sony initially viewed itself as primarily a manufacturer of Walkmans, rather than as a company with expertise in miniaturization, it might have overlooked several profitable opportunities, such as entering the camcorder business. As another example, Boeing has successfully leveraged its core capability related to integrating large-scale systems in its production of commercial jetliners, space stations, fighter-bombers, and missiles.

As these examples illustrate, core capabilities are often used to gain access to a wide variety of markets. Canon used its core capabilities in optics, imaging, and electronic controls to enter the markets for copiers, laser printers, cameras, and image scanners. In a similar fashion, Honda's core capabilities in engines and power trains comprise the basis for its entry into other businesses: automobiles, motorcycles, lawn mowers, and generators.

In addition to providing access to a variety of markets, a core capability should be strongly related to the benefits provided by the product or service that customers value. In Sony's case, its expertise in miniaturization translates directly into important product features such as portability and aesthetic designs. Alternatively, suppose Sony developed a core competence in writing understandable user manuals. Since people who purchase an HD TV or a camcorder rarely base their purchase decision on the quality of the user manual (when was the last time you read a user manual?), this core capability would provide little of any competitive advantage.

Another characteristic of core capabilities is that they should be difficult to imitate. Clearly, no sustainable competitive advantage is provided by a core capability that is easily imitated. For example, Sony's expertise in miniaturization would mean little if other electronics manufacturers could match it simply by purchasing and taking apart Sony's products (this is called *reverse engineering*). Bartmess and Cerny (1996) identify three elements of a core capability that hinder imitation:

- It is complex and requires organizational learning over a long period of time.

- It is based on multiple functional areas, both internal and external to the organization.

- It is a result of *how the functions interact* rather than the skills/knowledge within the functions themselves.

The topic of core capabilities is also strongly related to the recent surge in outsourcing and offshoring. *Outsourcing* involves subcontracting out certain activities or services. For example, a manufacturer might outsource the production of certain components, the management and maintenance of its computer resources, employee recruitment, or the processing of its payroll.

When we consider the concept of core capability, it is important to recognize that not all parts, services, and activities are equal. Rather, these activities and parts can be thought of as falling on a continuum ranging from strategically important to unimportant. Parts and activities are considered strategically important in the following cases:

- They are strongly related to what customers perceive to be the key characteristics of the product or service.

- They require highly specialized knowledge and skill, a core capability.

- They require highly specialized physical assets, and few other suppliers possess these assets.

- The organization has a technological lead or is likely to obtain one.

Activities that are not strategic or core are candidates for outsourcing. These parts or activities are not strongly linked to key product characteristics, do not require highly specialized knowledge, and do not need special physical assets, and the organization does not have the technological lead in this area. Thus, if it is beneficial to outsource these parts or activities – perhaps because of lower cost or higher quality – no loss in competitiveness should result. On the other hand, when a firm's strategic parts and activities have been outsourced, particularly to a foreign supplier, called *offshoring,* the firm has become *hollow* (Jonas 1986). As we have stated, the wise firm will outsource only nonstrategic, simple, relatively standard parts and processes such as screws or types of processes that are not worth the time for the firm to produce itself; the complex, proprietary parts and processes that give their products an edge in the marketplace are produced internally. If the firm outsources these parts and processes as well, it soon finds that the engineering design talent follows the production of the part outside the firm, too, and its core capabilities have been lost. Then, the firm has been *hollowed out,* becoming merely a distributor of its supplier's products.

Given the huge potential effects of outsourcing, both positive and negative, a firm should consider such a move *very* carefully. Management needs to think about both the long- and short-term effects. They also need to consider the impact of this decision on their core capabilities and everything else they do within the company. Such a major decision as outsourcing will affect other decisions as well, such as sourcing materials, hiring/releasing labor and management, marketing, finance, and a wide range of other areas.

So what is the problem? If a supplier can deliver the parts at lower cost and better quality when they are needed, why not use the supplier? The problem is that the supplier gains the expertise (and core capabilities) to produce the critical parts you need, and as Hayes and Pisano (1994), among others, note, organizations quickly forget how they produced those critical parts. After a while, when the supplier has improved on the process and you have forgotten how to make the parts, it is likely to start competing with you, producing the products you have been selling and dropping you as a customer. This is even more dangerous if, as already noted, the product and transformation system has also been hollowed out, following the production activities to the supplier. This happened extensively in the television industry, where the Japanese learned first how to produce and then how to engineer black-and-white and, later, color television sets. They then started tentatively introducing their own brands, to see if U.S. customers would buy them. Their products were inexpensive, of high quality, and caught on quickly in the free-enterprise American markets. The Japanese and Koreans now virtually control this industry.

1.5 Productivity

As has been discussed in this chapter, operations is that part of the organization that creates value for the customer by transforming inputs into outputs. Operations management, in turn, is concerned with overseeing the systems and processes that transform inputs into customer-valued outputs. With a focus on managing the value-creating processes, it is helpful to have measures that assess how well the value-creating processes are performing in terms of transforming inputs into outputs. One such measure is *productivity*.

More precisely, productivity is the ratio of outputs to inputs. In managerial terms, productivity is the output that is generated for a given level of input. In effect then, productivity assesses how efficiently value-creating processes transform inputs into outputs. Productivity increases as more output is produced for a given level of input or when less input is needed to produce a given level of output. Thus, productivity is a measure of efficiency and the terms efficiency and productivity are often used interchangeably.

Productivity is normally defined as output per worker hour. This definition of productivity is known as a *single measure* of productivity since it only considers one factor of production (or one input), namely, labor hours. The productivity of other inputs could also be determined such as the material productivity by taking the ratio of output to the materials used or the energy productivity by taking the ratio of the output to the energy used to produce the outputs.

Labor productivity is the most common measure of productivity because in the past, labor often constituted the vast majority of the cost of a product, however presently it is frequently as little as 5%. Thus, labor productivity is no longer a representative measure of the overall efficiency of a value-creating process.

Yet another problem with labor productivity, or any single measure of productivity for that matter, is that the single measure of productivity can be easily increased by substituting another input for it. For example, labor productivity could easily be increased by substituting machinery for labor, but that doesn't mean that this is a wise or even cost-saving decision. To address this problem associated with single measures of productivity, *multifactor* productivity measures that use several inputs, such as both labor and capital, can be used. And if we take this idea to the extreme, the gold standard for calculating productivity is what is called *total factor productivity* where all the inputs used – labor, capital, materials, and energy – are included in the denominator. Of course, the different inputs must be measured in the same units, such as dollars, so they can be added up to calculate the total input used. Because total factor productivity provides the most comprehensive view of the inputs needed to produce the outputs, it is the preferred approach for assessing an organization's productivity.

While productivity can be used to make comparisons such as comparing different factories in the same organization or comparing one organization to another, perhaps the best use of a productivity measure is tracking how it changes over time. Ideally, productivity should exhibit a general upward trend over time. A drop in productivity indicates that efficiency is deteriorating and should be investigated to determine if corrective action is warranted. Of course, an organization may choose to place less emphasis on efficiency to enhance its competitive position. For example, an organization may choose to increase its staffing level or inventory levels to provide higher levels of customer service.

This brings us to another important topic, namely, the distinction between efficiency and effectiveness. While these terms are often used interchangeably, in actuality they are concerned with markedly different aspects of organizational performance. In particular, "effectiveness" relates to the achievement of goals and is frequently defined as "doing the right thing." Efficiency, on the other hand, can be defined as "doing the thing right." Thus, effectiveness relates to being focused on the proper task or goal, while efficiency relates to how well the task or goal is done.

1.5.1 Improving Productivity Rates

Productivity is not only important to organizations but also important to countries. Indeed, in order for a country, or more generally a society, to increase its standard of living, it must first increase its productivity. Most often the productivity of countries is assessed by dividing its gross domestic product (GDP) by its population to get what is referred to as its GDP per capita. Since GDP represents the total value of the goods and services created by the country, dividing a country's GDP by its population represents the amount of goods and services the country created per person. The more goods and services created per person, the higher the country's productivity and its standard of living.

According to the International Monetary Fund (IMF), Luxembourg was estimated to be the most productive country in the world in 2022 (the most recent data available at the writing of this book) producing over $135,000 of goods and services for each person in its population. By comparison, the United States' GDP per capita in 2022 was a little more than half of this at just over $76,000 placing it as the eighth most productive country. To help put this in context, here are the GDP per capita of some other countries in 2022 and their ranking in parentheses: Ireland $101,509 (2), Norway $99,481 (3), Switzerland $96,390 (4), Germany $51,104 (19), Japan $39,243 (28), South Korea $34,994 (32), Italy $34,777 (33), and China $14,905 (64). What if anything do you find surprising about these results?

While GDP per capita provides insight into a country's current standard of living, also of importance is how the country's productivity is changing over time, which in turn reflects how the standard of living of the country's residents is changing over time. Figure 1.10 shows the multifactor productivity for six select countries over the period from 1985 to 2020. To make the comparisons possible across countries, the multifactor productivity for each country was indexed to 100 for the year 2010. Thus, the line for each country shows the relative multifactor productivity of that country relative to its multifactor productivity in 2010. Index values less than 100 indicate multifactor productivity levels below the multifactor productivity for that country in 2010, while index values greater than 100 indicate multifactor productivity levels above the 2010 level for that country.

As can be seen in Figure 1.10, Korea and Ireland have increased their respective multifactor productivity levels the fastest over this 30 plus year period. The results for Korea may not be

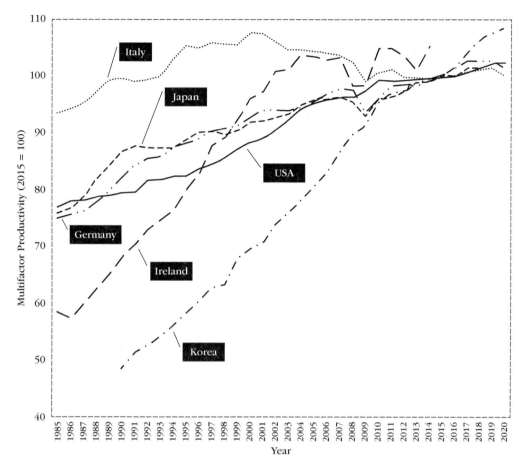

FIGURE 1.10
Comparison of GDP
per Capita for Select
Countries
Source: Organization for
Economic Co-Operation
and Development.

particularly surprising to you given the substantial imports in the United States from Korean companies that have become household names including Samsung, LG, Kia, and Hyundai. Ireland is also particularly noteworthy as it was the second most productive country in 2022. Thus, Ireland is not only one of the most productive countries, it is also among the countries with the highest rate of improvement in multifactor productivity.

The United States also experienced an upward trend in multifactor productivity; however, its rate of improvement lagged Korea's and Ireland's. Italy's multifactor productivity, on the other hand, remained relatively flat, exhibiting only a very slight increase over this 30 plus year period.

We observe that while a country's productivity level provides a measure of country's current standard of living (e.g. the value of all goods and services produced by the country per resident), the growth rate of productivity assesses the rate at which the standard of living is improving. Increasing GDP per capita means that on average each person in the country produced more goods and services. For this reason, economists often refer to productivity as the engine of the economy.

Given its direct link to standard of living, a logical question is how can a country improve its productivity growth? Fundamentally, there are four drivers of a country's productivity: physical capital, human capital, natural resources, and technology. Here we focus on technology as it is often considered to hold the most promise for continued increases in productivity.

In the past, technology typically equated to the substitution of mechanical power for human physical labor or what is referred to as *mechanization*. This trend continues today where we now see electronic equipment replacing human sensing skills or what is referred to as *automation*. Indeed, mechanization, automation, and computerization are so common that they have become an everyday aspect of the workplace and are considered business as usual. The use of robots to pick and pack orders at Amazon, as discussed at the beginning of the chapter, provides a contemporary example of automation.

But by the same token, we must be careful not to focus solely on productivity as the problem. Rather whether our focus is at the individual worker level, organization level, or the country level, our focus should be on overall competitiveness and recognize that productivity is but one dimension of competitiveness. One framework for more broadly considering the major factors that shape an organization's competitiveness is the Balanced Scorecard, as described next.

1.6 The Balanced Scorecard and Strategy Map

The balanced scorecard approach (Kaplan and Norton 1996) is becoming increasingly recognized as a way to help organizations translate their strategy into appropriate performance measures in order to monitor their success. In the past, it was not uncommon for managers to rely primarily on financial performance measures. However, when the inadequacies of these measures were discovered, managers often responded either by trying to improve them or by abandoning them in favor of operational performance measures such as cycle time and defect rates. Many organizations now realize that no single type of measure can provide insight into all the critical areas of the business. Thus, the purpose of the balanced scorecard is to develop a set of measures that provide a comprehensive view of the organization.

Organizations that have developed a balanced scorecard report numerous benefits, including the following:

- An effective way to clarify and gain consensus on the strategy

- A mechanism for communicating the strategy throughout the entire organization

- A mechanism for aligning departmental and personal goals to the strategy

- A way to ensure that strategic objectives are linked to annual budgets

- Timely feedback related to improving the strategy.

One problem with traditional performance measurement systems based primarily on financial measures is that they often encourage shortsighted decisions, such as reducing investments in product development, employee training, and information technology. The balanced scorecard approach corrects this problem by measuring performance in four major areas: (1) financial performance, (2) customer performance, (3) internal business process performance (e.g., operations, marketing), and (4) organizational learning and growth.

The financial performance measures included in the balanced scorecard are typically related to profitability, such as return on equity, return on capital, and economic value added. Customer performance measures focus on customer satisfaction, customer retention, customer profitability, market share, and customer acquisition. The internal business process dimension addresses the issue of what the organization must excel at to achieve its financial and customer objectives. Examples of performance measures for internal business processes include quality, response time, cost, new product launch time, and the ratio of processing time to total throughput time. Finally, the learning and growth dimension focuses on the infrastructure the organization must build to sustain its competitive advantage. Learning and growth performance measures include employee satisfaction, employee retention, worker productivity, and the availability of timely and accurate information.

The process of developing a balanced scorecard begins with top management translating the mission and strategy into specific customer and financial objectives. Based on the customer and financial objectives, related measures for the internal business processes are identified. Finally, investments in employee training and information technology are linked to the customer, financial, and internal business process objectives. Note that a properly constructed balanced scorecard contains an appropriate mix of outcome measures related to the actual results achieved and measures that drive future performance.

The balanced scorecard is based on the premise that a strategy is a set of hypotheses about cause-and-effect relationships that can be stated as if–then statements. For example, management of a department store might hypothesize that increasing the training that sales associates receive will lead to improved selling skills. These managers might further hypothesize that better selling skills will translate into higher commissions for the sales associates and will therefore result in less turnover. Happier and more experienced sales associates would likely lead to increased sales per store, which ultimately translates into an increase in return on investment (ROI). Since a properly developed balanced scorecard tells a story about the cause-and-effect relationships underlying the strategy, all measures included in the scorecard should be elements in the chain of cause-and-effect relationships.

In extending their earlier work on the balanced scorecard, Kaplan and Norton (2000) proposed the development of strategy maps (see also Scholey 2005) as a way to illustrate and monitor the cause-and-effect relationships identified through the development of a balanced scorecard. In particular, strategy maps provide organizations with a tool that helps them better monitor important details about their strategic business processes, thereby enhancing their employees' understanding of the strategy interactions, which in turn facilitates implementing the business strategy.

Like the balanced scorecard, strategy maps address four perspectives: the financial perspective, the customer perspective, the internal business process perspective, and the learning and growing perspective. A sample strategy map for a department store that wants to improve its performance is shown in Figure 1.11.

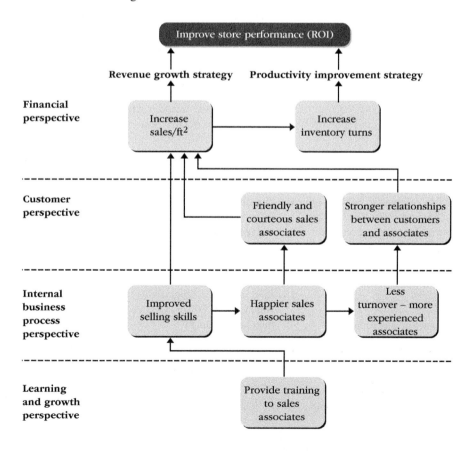

FIGURE 1.11 Sample Strategy Map for a Department Store

At the top of the strategy map, the goal is specified, which in our example is to improve the store's ROI. Management has determined that the goal of improving the store's ROI can be accomplished by increasing revenue and/or improving the store's productivity. The remainder of the strategy map explicitly shows the chain of cause-and-effect relationships management has hypothesized about how the store's ROI can be improved. For example, it is believed that providing the sales associates with additional training will lead to improved selling skills, which should then result in increased sales per square foot of retail space and happier associates. Happier associates in turn should result in both friendly and courteous sales associates and less turnover among the associates. Ultimately, the strategy map hypothesizes that increased sales per square foot will help the store increase its revenue and its inventory turns, which will then lead to revenue growth and productivity improvements. In the end, management should develop measures for each element in the strategy map and then track these measures to validate the hypothesized relationships proposed in the strategy map. In cases where the hypothesized relationships are not supported, new relationships should be hypothesized.

EXPAND YOUR UNDERSTANDING

1. Why is it so hard to increase productivity in the service sector?

2. Many foreign firms have been successful in the following areas: steel, autos, cameras, and televisions. Are services more protected from foreign competition? How?

3. It is commonly said that Japanese firms employ 10 times as many engineers per operations worker as U.S. firms and 10 times fewer accountants. What effect would you expect this to have on their competitiveness? Why?

4. How might the concept of a "facilitating good" alter the way we perceive a product? A service?

5. Is it wise for a firm to stick to what it knows best, or should it expand its market by moving into adjoining products or services? How can it avoid losing its focus?

6. Can you think of any other areas of possible focus for a firm besides those identified in Table 1.3?

7. What core capabilities do you think China possesses? India? Japan? The United States?

8. According to K. Blanchard and N. V. Peale (*The Power of Ethical Management*, New York: Morrow, 1988), the following three ethical tests may be useful: (1) Is it legal or within company policy? (2) Is it balanced and fair in the short and long term? (3) Would you be proud if the public or your family knew about it?

Apply these tests to the following situations:

    a. A foreign firm subsidizes its sales in another country.

    b. A foreign firm dumps its products (sells them for less than cost) in another country.

    c. A country imports products that, had they been made domestically, would have violated domestic laws (e.g. laws against pollution).

9. In responding faster to customers' needs, where might the cost savings come from? What benefits would result?

10. Can you think of companies that have moved the performance frontier of their industries?

11. Why do Americans invest more in marketing new products while the Japanese invest more in engineering? What advantages accrue to each investment?

12. Using new technologies, it is not uncommon for firms to cut their response times by a factor of 10. What effect would you expect this to have on their unit costs?

13. What are the order winners and order qualifiers for Walmart? Toyota? BMW? Sony?

14. Given the recent trends in products and services, does the focus strategy or sand cone strategy seem most applicable these days?

15. How does the way a system's boundary is defined affect the results of a systems analysis?

16. How might the addition of equipment to a production system lower efficiency? What does this say about replacing labor with equipment?

17. What hard decisions might have to be made to increase a firm's productivity? Are firms generally willing to make them?

18. How could the productivity of resources such as a pump, warehouse, $1000 of capital, a market survey, and a kilowatt-hour be measured?

19. What is more important, efficiency or effectiveness?

20. Does the balanced scorecard monitor all the elements of the production system of Figure 1.1? If not, what does it miss? Does it include anything not in Figure 1.1? If so, why, and why isn't it in Figure 1.1?

21. For many years, the balanced scorecard was seen as more appropriate for implementing strategy than for planning it. Now that the strategy map has been conceived, does this replace the balanced scorecard or does each do something different and, if so, which one is concerned with implementing strategy?

22. In some advanced economies, projects now constitute over 40% of their GDP. By what year do you think they will constitute the majority of GDP?

23. Do you think the project transformation can occur in organizations with their current managers, or will the managers have to be replaced? What would have to be the characteristics of those managers who could successfully institute this dramatic change?

24. Review the chapter titles in the table of contents. Which areas do you imagine have the greatest opportunity to support an organization's sustainability objectives?

Apply Your Understanding

Izmir National University

Izmir National University (INU) was chartered in 2010 to facilitate Turkey's expected eventual entry into the economy of Europe, via the EU. To foster growth and development in the European economy, engineering, science, and business were deemed to be the institution's primary areas of intellectual endeavor. The university grew rapidly during its first three years. By 2015, the enrollment had reached just over 9300 students. However, with this rapid growth came a number of problems. For example, because the faculty had to be hired so quickly, there was little real organization, and curriculum seemed to be decided on the basis of which adviser a student happened to consult. The administrative offices were often reshuffled, with vague responsibilities and short tenures.

The faculty of the new Business School was typical of the confusion that gripped the entire university. The 26 faculty members were mostly recent graduates of doctoral programs at major European and Turkish universities. There were 21 Assistant Docents and Lecturers, 3 Docents, and 2 full Professors, spread fairly evenly over the four departments, each overseen by a Kursu professor (department head). In addition, funds were available to hire three additional faculty members, either assistant or regular Docents. The background of the newly recruited Dekan (administrative head, dean) of the Business School included five years of teaching at a primarily Muslim university in Turkey and two years of departmental administration at a large southern European university.

Upon arriving at the Business School, the Dekan asked the faculty to e-mail their concerns to her so that she could begin to get a handle on the major issues confronting the school. Her office assistant selected the following comments as representative of the sentiments expressed:

- "Our student–teacher ratio is much higher than what it was at my former university. We need to fill those open slots as quickly as possible and ask the university to fund at least two more faculty positions."

- "If we don't get the quality of enrollments up in the MBA program, the graduate school will never approve our application for a doctoral program. We need the doctoral program to attract the best faculty, and we need the doctoral students to help cover our courses."

- "Given that research is our primary mission, we need to fund more graduate research assistants."

- "The travel budget isn't sufficient to allow me to attend the meetings I'm interested in. How can we improve and maintain our visibility if we get funding for only one meeting per year?"

- "We need better staff support. Faculty members are required to submit their exams for copying five days before they are needed. However, doing this makes it difficult to test the students on the material covered in class right before the exam, since it's difficult to know ahead of time exactly how much material we will cover."

- "I think far too much emphasis is placed on research. We are here to teach."

- "Being limited in our consulting is far too restrictive. In Europe, we were allowed one day a week. How are we supposed to stay current without consulting?"

- "We need to update our computers more often."

Questions

1. What do the comments by the faculty tell you about INU's strategy?

2. What would you recommend the Dekan do regarding the Business School's strategic planning process? What role would you recommend the Dekan play in this process?

3. Productivity is defined as the ratio of output (including both goods and services) to the input used to produce it. How could the productivity of the Business School be measured? What would the effect be on productivity if the faculty all received a 10% raise but continued to teach the same number of classes and students?

Taracare, Inc.

Taracare, Inc., operates a single factory in Ensenada, Mexico, where it fabricates and assembles a wide range of outdoor furniture for the U.S. market, including chairs, tables, and matching accessories. Taracare's primary production activities include extruding the aluminum furniture parts, bending and shaping the extruded parts, finishing and painting the parts, and then assembling the parts into completed furniture. Upholstery, glass tabletops, and all hardware are purchased from outside suppliers.

Jorge Gonzalez purchased Taracare in 2014. Before that, Jorge had distinguished himself as a top sales rep of outdoor furniture for the western region of one of the leading national manufacturers. However, after spending 10 years on the road, he wanted to settle down and spend more time with his family back in Mexico. After searching for a couple of months, he came across what he believed to be an ideal opportunity. Not only was it in an industry that he had a great deal of knowledge about, but he would be his own boss. Unfortunately, the asking price was well beyond Jorge's means. However, after a month of negotiation, Jorge convinced Jesus Garza, Taracare's founder, to maintain a 25% stake in the business. Although Jesus had originally intended to sell out completely, he was impressed with Jorge's knowledge of the business, his extensive contacts, and his enthusiasm. He therefore agreed to sell Jorge 75% of Taracare and retain 25% as an investment.

Jorge's ambition for Taracare was to expand it from a small regional manufacturer to one that sold to major national retailers. To accomplish this objective, Jorge's first initiative was to triple Taracare's sales force in 2015. As sales began to increase, Jorge increased the support staff by hiring an accountant, a comptroller, two new designers, and a purchasing agent.

By mid-2018, Taracare's line was carried by several national retailers on a trial basis. However, Taracare was having difficulty both in meeting the deliveries its sales reps were promising and in satisfying the national retailers' standards for quality. To respond to this problem, Jorge hired Alfredo Diaz as the new manufacturing manager. Before accepting Jorge's offer, Alfredo was the plant manager of a factory that manufactured replacement windows sold by large regional and national retailers.

After several months on the job – and after making little progress toward improving on-time delivery and quality – Alfredo scheduled a meeting with Jorge to discuss his major concerns. Alfredo began:

> I requested this meeting with you, Jorge, because I am not satisfied with the progress we are making toward improving our delivery performance and quality. The bottom line is that I feel I'm getting very little cooperation from the other department heads. For example, last month purchasing switched to a new supplier for paint; and although it is true that the new paint costs less per gallon, we have to apply a thicker coat to give the furniture the same protection. I haven't actually run the numbers, but I know it is actually costing us more, in both materials and labor.

> Another problem is that we typically run a special promotion to coincide with launching new product lines. I understand that the sales guys want to get the product into the stores as quickly as possible, but they are making promises about delivery that we can't meet. It takes time to work out the bugs and get things running smoothly. Then, there is the problem with the designers. They are constantly adding features to the product that make it almost impossible for us to produce. At the very least, they make it much more expensive for us to produce. For example, on the new "Destiny" line, they designed table legs that required a new die at a cost of 250,000 pesos. Why couldn't they have left the legs alone so that we could have used one of our existing dies? On top of this, we have the accounting department telling us that our equipment utilization is too low. Then, when we increase our equipment utilization and make more products, the finance guys tell us we have too much capital tied up in inventory. To be honest, I really don't feel that I'm getting very much support.

Rising from his chair, Jorge commented:

> You have raised some important issues, Alfredo. Unfortunately, I have to run to another meeting right now. Why don't you send me a memo outlining these issues and your recommendations? Then, perhaps, I will call a meeting and we can discuss these issues with the other department heads. At least our production problems are really no worse than those of our competitors, and we don't expect you to solve all of our problems overnight. Keep up the good work and send me that memo at your earliest convenience.

Questions

1. Does Alfredo's previous experience running a plant that made replacement windows qualify him to run a plant that makes outdoor furniture?

2. What recommendations would you make if you were Alfredo?

3. Given Jorge's background and apparent priorities, how is he likely to respond to Alfredo's recommendations? On the basis of this likely response, is it possible to rephrase Alfredo's recommendations so they are more appealing to Jorge?

EXERCISES

1.1 Compare the productivity of the organizations below. Which organization is the most productive?

Organization	Output (Units/Year)	Annual Labor Hours
Estec	432,000	217,328
Teckore	756,000	428,926
Stekpro	584,000	331,817

1.2 Able Electronics produces 1700 units with $3.5 million of equipment. Micro Devices produces 2500 units using $4.5 million worth of equipment.

a. Compare the capital productivity of Able and Micron.

b. If the equipment in both firms is new but is depreciated linearly over 10 years at Able and 8 years at Micron, recalculate the capital productivity on an annual basis. What does this tell you about the pitfalls in calculating capital productivity?

1.3 Reynard Shoes employs 10 workers and $500,000 of equipment to produce 10,000 pairs of shoes annually. Assume that workers are paid $25 per hour and work a 50-hour work week, 50 weeks a year.

a. Calculate the multifactor productivity for Reynard.

b. Recalculate the multifactor productivity by including materials of $700,000 per year.

c. How would you compare Reynard's productivity to Cincinnati Shoes, which produces 20,000 pairs of shoes per year with 15 workers, $200,000 of equipment, and $300,000 of materials a year? Assume a 40-hour work week, 50 weeks a year, and a wage rate of 27.50 per hour. What accounts for the difference?

1.4 The printed circuit board (PCB) industry in one state produced $1,783,457,850 worth of product last year and paid $372,876,515 for labor, $490,313,297 for materials, and $511,387,216 for equipment. Compare the multifactor productivities of the PCB industry with the state's integrated circuit industry, which produced $2,318,746,019 worth of silicon microprocessors and paid $518,255,899 for labor, $711,341,866 for materials, and $686,377,103 for equipment.

1.5 HiTeck International's workers earn $15 per hour and work fifty 40-hour weeks per year. Capital expenses run $1 million per year, $10 million of materials are purchased annually, and its annual energy costs are $300,000 per year. It runs a full double shift half the year for its seasonal product and a single shift of 90 workers the other half of the year. Its annual output is 15,000 appliances.

a. Calculate HiTeck's total factor productivity.

b. Compare the total factor productivity of HiTeck with Fastec, which outsources its production and spends $10 million to purchase 9500 appliances. What is the potential danger to Fastec?

c. Suppose that HiTeck's 15,000 appliances consisted of 5000 microwaves, 6000 ovens, and 4000 dishwashers. If you now wanted to calculate HiTeck's productivity, what additional information would you like to have?

1.6 A company has collected the data shown in the spreadsheet below for the two plants it operates. The plants are of similar size and capacity. All data are in thousands of dollars.

a. Calculate the labor, capital, and multifactor (including labor, capital, and materials) productivity for each plant for all years.

	A	B	C	D	E	F	G	H	I
1				Plant A				Plant B	
2	Year	Sales	Labor	Capital	Materials	Sales	Labor	Capital	Materials
3	20X0	35100	1800	8780	20800	34800	1780	8705	17800
4	20X1	38200	1950	10230	20600	37900	1910	9670	20300
5	20X2	39600	2000	10800	21050	40300	2005	10500	22100
6	20X3	41000	2150	11170	23300	40600	1990	10800	21800
7	20X4	42900	2175	12570	24300	42700	2060	11600	21900
8	20X5	46500	2325	12000	26600	45800	2180	12600	24100
9	20X6	47500	2400	12100	24400	48300	2260	13600	28500
10	20X7	47900	2495	12900	27600	48900	2255	14050	27500
11	20X8	50400	2520	13800	29200	50200	2280	14700	29700
12	20X9	53400	2700	14500	31200	50500	2260	15100	29900
13	20Y0	56300	2900	15300	29600	55100	2430	16800	31000

b. Plot Plants A's and B's labor productivity on the same graph.

c. Plot Plants A's and B's capital productivity on the same graph.

d. Plot Plants A's and B's multifactor productivity on the same graph.

e. Evaluate each plant's performance over time both independent of the other plant and relative to the other plant. (Refer to parts b–d above.)

1.7 Referring to Exercise 6, calculate the percent change in labor, capital, and multifactor productivity for each plant for all years. Plot the percentage change in multifactor productivity for both plants on the same graph. Compare the performance of the two plants.

1.8 Referring to Reynard Shoes from Exercise 3, the plant manager was asked to estimate the multifactor productivity for next year. The plant manager expects that the employment level will remain at 10 workers. She further estimates that equipment expenses will be $500,000 next year, but it is possible they will be as low as $425,000 or as high as $600,000. In consulting with the marketing department, the forecast is that demand will be 10,000 pairs of shoes next year but may be as low as 9000 or as high as 10,700. The wage rate will remain flat at $25 per hour, and the plant will operate a 50-hour work week, 50 weeks a year. Finally, the plant manager estimates that material costs will be $70 per pair of shoes but could be as low as $60 or as high as $85 per pair. Use this additional information to build a model to predict the multifactor productivity for next year.

BIBLIOGRAPHY

Akram, S., World's Top Exporters and Importers, uk.worldoptions.com, February 4, 2022.

Bartmess, A., and K. Cerny. "Building Competitive Advantage Through a Global Network of Capabilities." Chapter 7 in R. A. Hayes, G. P. Pisano, and D. M. Upton, *Strategic Operations: Competing Through Capabilities*. New York: Free Press, 1996.

Cheng, J., and B. Intindola. "Apple's Size Clouds Market." *Wall Street Journal* (February 15, 2012).

Clark, K. "Competing Through Manufacturing and the New Manufacturing Paradigm: Is Manufacturing Strategy Passé?" *Production and Operations Management*, 5 (1996): 42–58.

Deloitte, Deloitte 2022 CxO Sustainability Report, www2.deloitte.com, May 20, 2022.

Doerr, J., *Speed and Scale: An Action Plan for Solving our Climate Crisis Now*. Portfolio/Penguin, 2021.

Eisenhardt, K., and S. Brown. "Time Pacing: Competing in Markets That Won't Stand Still." *Harvard Business Review* (March–April 1998): 59–69.

Esterl, M., "PepsiCo Board Stands by Nooyi–Shareholders Grouse but Company Unlikely to Break Up; Marketing Dollars Will Shift Back to Soda," *Wall Street Journal* (January 13, 2012), p. B1.

Feitzinger, E., and H. L. Lee. "Mass Customization at Hewlett Packard: The Power of Postponement." *Harvard Business Review* (January–February 1997): 116–121.

Feld, W. M. Lean. *Manufacturing: Tools, Techniques, and How to Use Them*. Boca Raton, FL: CRC Press, 2000.

Ferdows, K., and A. DeMeyer. "Lasting Improvements in Manufacturing Performance: In Search of a New Theory." *Journal of Operations Management*, 9 (1990): 168–184.

Gilmore, J. H., and B. J. Pine II. "The Four Faces of Mass Customization." *Harvard Business Review* (January–February 1997): 91–101.

Grant, D. B., Trautrims, A., and Wong, C. Y. *Sustainable Logistics and Supply Chain Management, 2nd Edition*. Kogan Page, 2017.

Hammer, M. "Deep Change: How Operational Innovation Can Transform Your Company." *Harvard Business Review* (April 2004): 85–93.

Hayes, R. H., and G. P. Pisano. "Beyond World Class: The New Manufacturing Strategy." *Harvard Business Review* (January–February 1994): 77–86.

Hill, T. *Manufacturing Strategy: Text and Cases*, 3rd ed. Homewood, IL: Irwin, 2000.

Jonas, N. "The Hollow Corporation." *Business Week* (March 3, 1986): 57–85.

Kaplan, Deborah Abrams. "Wheels Up: How Delta Uses RFID to Ensure a Smooth Supply Chain." Supply Chain Dive, www.supplychaindive.com, July 31, 2018.

Kaplan, R. S., and D. P. Norton. "Having Trouble with Your Strategy? Then Map It." *Harvard Business Review* (September–October 2000): 167–176.

Kaplan, R. S., and D. P. Norton. *The Balanced Score–Card*. Boston, MA: Harvard Business School Press, 1996.

Leblanc, R. "How Amazon Is Changing Supply Chain Management." The Balance Small Business, www.thebalancesmb.com/how-amazon-is-changing-supply-chain-management-4155324, November 4, 2018.

Macrotrends, U.S. Trade Balance 1970–2022, https://www.macrotrends.net/countries/USA/united-states/trade-balance-deficit, May 19, 2022.

Maidique, M. A., and P. Patch. *Corporate Strategy and Technological Policy*. Case 9-679-033. Boston, MA: Harvard Business School, 1979.

Meredith, J. R., D. M. McCutcheon, and J. Hartley. "Enhancing Competitiveness Through the New Market Value Equation." *International Journal of Operations and Production Management*, 14 (November 11, 1994): 7–21.

Meredith, J. R., and S. M. Shafer. *Project Management: A Strategic Managerial Approach*, 11th ed. New York: Wiley, 2022.

Morgan, M., R. E. Levitt, and W. Malek. *Executing Your Strategy: How to Break It Down and Get It Done*. Boston, MA: Harvard Business School Press, 2007.

Nash, Kim S. "Firms Try Out Blockchain." *Wall Street Journal* (February 7, 2018), p. B5.

Nieto-Rodriguez, A. "The Project Economy Has Arrived." *Harvard Business Review*, November–December, 2021.

OECD., "Multifactor Productivity." data.oecd.org/lprdty/multifactor-productivity.htm#indicator-chart, May 19, 2022.

Pine, B. J., II. *Mass Customization: The New Frontier in Business Competition*. Boston, MA: Harvard Business School Press, 1993.

Prahalad, C. K., and G. Hamel. "The Core Competence of the Corporation." *Harvard Business Review* (May–June 1990): 79–91.

Scholey, C. "A Step-by-Step Guide to Measuring, Managing, and Communicating the Plan." *Journal of Business Strategy*, 26(3) (2005): 12–19.

Skinner, W. "The Focused Factory." *Harvard Business Review* (May–June 1974): 113–122.

Smith, B., "One year later: The path to carbon negative – a progress report on our climate 'moonshot,'" blogs.mircosoft.com, January 28, 2021.

Stalk, G. "Time—The Next Source of Competitive Advantage." *Harvard Business Review* (July–August 1988): 41–51.

Stalk, G., P. Evans, and L. E. Shulman. "Competing on Capabilities: The New Rules of Corporate Strategy." *Harvard Business Review* (March–April 1992): 57–69.

Upton, D. M. "The Management of Manufacturing Flexibility." *California Management Review* (Winter 1994): 72–89.

US Census Bureau, Foreign Trade, www.census.gov/foreign-trade/statistics/historical/index.html, November 30, 2018.

Vessey, J. T. "The New Competitors: They Think in Terms of 'Speed to Market.'" *Academy of Management Review*, 5 (April 1991): 23–33.

Wikipedia, List of Countries by GDP (nominal) per capita, en.wikipedia.org/wiki/List_of_countries_by_GDP_(nominal)_per_capita, May 19, 2022.

Womack, J. P., and D. T. Jones. *Lean Thinking: Banish Waste and Create Wealth in Your Corporation*, rev. ed. New York: Free Press, 2003.

Appendix A

Some Sustainability Concepts

 With sustainability gaining increasing interest in business and society, it is becoming increasingly important for all business professionals to have a working knowledge of the key concepts associated with sustainability. This is especially true for operations and supply chain professionals as the decisions made in these areas are often directly connected to sustainability.

Broadly speaking, sustainability can be defined as the ability of an entity such as a person, organization, society, or even the entire planet to maintain itself and thereby endure over time. Businesses and governments address sustainability by enacting policies that seek to minimize the negative impacts current practices have on the environment. Increasingly, many business leaders are coming to the realization that the way we currently live and interact with our environment is leading to irreparable damage to planet Earth and therefore that major changes are urgently required. The Brundtland Commission report (also called Our Common Future) released in 1987 by the World Commission on Environment and Development expresses well what is meant by sustainability as "meeting the needs of the present without compromising the ability of future generations to meet their needs."

Implicit in this view is the need to balance long- and short-term benefits. One way to operationalize this view is through the use of the triple bottom line as was discussed in the chapter. Along these lines, sustainability can be thought to be comprised of three overarching and interrelated concepts: economic (profit), environmental (planet), and social (people). As was discussed in the chapter, businesses and governments are increasingly making commitments to sustainability, although they are often met with skepticism. For example, the term "greenwashing" has entered the business lexicon to refer to the business practice of organizations providing false or misleading evidence to create the impression that they are more environmentally friendly than they actually are. And even with the proper intentions, significant challenges must be addressed in the pursuit of implementing sustainable practices such as simply quantifying the impact the business has on the environment. By the same token, organizations that have adopted sustainable practices have realized numerous benefits including enhanced competitiveness. In fact, research is emerging that shows a link between high Environmental, Social, and Governance (ESG) ratings and improved financial performance such as having lower debt and equity costs. There is also evidence that suggests that investors are increasingly considering ESG criteria, which in turn could have an impact on a firm's valuation.

Much of the focus related to sustainability relates to greenhouse gases (GHGs). Some gases in our atmosphere, including nitrogen and oxygen, allow thermal energy (heat) to pass through from the Earth's surface to space. GHGs, on the other hand, are gases in our atmosphere that absorb thermal energy and reflect a portion of it back to the Earth's surface. The six major GHGs are:

- Carbon dioxide (CO_2): The main source of CO_2 is the burning of fossil fuels such as from cars with internal combustion engines. There are also natural sources of CO_2 including forest fires, volcanic activity, and decomposing vegetation.

- Methane CH_4: Some major sources of methane gas are landfills and agriculture activities (raising of beef and dairy cows). While methane diffuses from the atmosphere in approximately 10 years, versus 100 years or more for CO_2, it is more potent in radiating heat back to the Earth's surface.

- Nitrous oxide (N_2O): The major source of nitrous oxide is from the use of fertilizers and animal waste. Nitrous oxide remains in the atmosphere for 100 years longer than CO_2 and traps heat at 300 times the rate of CO_2.

- Hydrofluorocarbons (HFC): The main source of HFC are leakages from refrigeration and air conditioning equipment.

- Perfluorocarbons (PFC): The major source of PFC is from the production of aluminum. PFC are also used as solvents in the electronics industry.

- Sulfur hexafluoride (SF_6): SF_6 is used primarily in the electric power industry in products such as high-voltage circuit breakers. According to the U.S. Environmental Protection Agency, SF_6 is 22,800 times more effective in trapping infrared radiation than CO_2 and has an estimated lifetime of 3,200 years.

In examining the sources and uses of GHGs, it is clear that some amount of GHGs is necessary. However, mounting evidence suggests that too much of these gases creates a problem in the form of extra warming of the planet. Because the GHGs have varying impacts on the environment, it is helpful to express the emissions of organizations, industries, countries, and the planet in terms of CO_2 equivalents (CO_2e). As such, CO_2e is a measure for assessing the combined impact of alternative GHGs. For example, one ton of CH_4 is equivalent to 25 tons CO_2 while one ton of N_2O is equivalent to 295 tons of CO_2.

BIBLIOGRAPHY

Doerr, J., *Speed and Scale: An Action Plan for Solving our Climate Crisis Now*. Portfolio/Penguin, 2021.

Mollenkamp, D. T. Sustainability, Investopedia.com, November 15, 2021

Spiliakos, A. What Does Sustainable Mean in Business, online, hbs.edu, Oct 10, 2018.

U.S. EPA, Sulfur Hexafluoride (SF6) Basics, epa.gov, May 20, 2022.

2

Executing Strategy: Project Management

CHAPTER IN PERSPECTIVE

In the previous chapter, we discussed the importance of successfully implementing the organization's strategic plans. Such efforts are executed through major projects involving changes in the organization's systems and procedures. In this chapter, we address the management of such projects. We use a process improvement project as an example, but projects are used in all kinds of organizations for every conceivable purpose. They range from simple combinations of tactical tasks to strategic organizational change and from setting up a party to putting a person on the moon.

The chapter begins with a discussion of the project planning, which includes the topics of the project portfolio, how projects fit within the organizational structure, and organizing the project team. We then move on to an explanation of some project scheduling techniques including the contemporary topics of sustainable project management, the critical chain and Agile project management.

The chapter continues with an examination of cost–time trade-offs for speeding up the completion of the project. The chapter concludes with a discussion of controlling project cost and performance, primarily through the use of "earned value."

As suggested by the title of this chapter, the topics discussed in the chapter are critically important toward the attainment of the organization's strategy. For example, in our discussion of project planning, it is noted that an organization's success is typically not dependent on the success or failure of any single project, but rather the development and execution of an appropriate portfolio of projects. Likewise, while the topic and mechanics of project scheduling may tend to be more tactical in nature, it is important to keep in mind the strategic implications associated with project scheduling. For example, in many projects such as transitioning to a new software platform, updating a product or service with new features, or constructing a new distribution center, nothing is more visible to senior management and customers than a project that misses its public deadline. In addition to increasing the cost of the project, missed deadlines can seriously damage an organization's brand and reputation. And with much shorter product life cycles, missed deadlines can have serious consequences in terms of the ability of the organization to gain market share and may significantly limit the amount of time the organization has to recoup its investment in the project. With the vast amount of work that is organized as projects and the strategic implications associated with executing this work well, it is critical that people in all business disciplines have a solid foundation in project management.

2.1 Introduction

- In 2012, a leak was discovered in a 40-year-old, 750,000-gallon underground nuclear waste storage tank at the U.S. Department of Energy's Hanford, Washington state site. The danger was that the waste could reach the nearby Columbia River, which provided drinking water for hundreds of thousands of people in Washington and Oregon. A project team was set up to figure out how to transfer all the radioactive waste from the leaking tank into a new underground safe storage container. Initial estimates, however, were that even with the most aggressive schedule, it would take five years to retrieve all the waste, two years beyond a court order to complete the effort within three years.

  The project team didn't panic however and initiated their planning by first trying to identify all the potential risks, both known and unknown, regarding the project. They also immediately started filling gaps in the resources that would be needed for the project and engaged the nervous public to assure them that the region would remain safe, safety always being a top priority in nuclear waste cleanup projects. However, a preliminary simulation analysis of the project forecast that the team had only a 12% chance of success.

  Since the schedule was so tight, a major focus was put on the schedule, which used two full-time schedulers to oversee the project's 9000 activities. The result was that the critical path software package became their most important rescheduling tool as the project's schedule status and progress were constantly revised. Since there was no built-in time for contingencies, the goal of the team was to look for innovative ways to cut down the time on the activities in order to build up slack in the schedule for later possible setbacks. The team also met weekly to constantly revisit the risk register to update and reprioritize potential risks that might impact the schedule and budget. The team thus became proficient at using opportunities that emerged during the project and smart risk management to build up slack, resulting in a final total of 71 days.

  The team also set up a plan for managing community leaders and other stakeholders to earn and maintain their trust in the project. This included frequent press releases, meetings with reporters to update them on project progress, and creating a Hanford Advisory Board consisting of community leaders and state representatives of both Washington and Oregon. As one of the project's managers noted, people normally won't trust a company or agency, but if they get to know the project manager personally and see your integrity and commitment to the project and their own interests, you can earn their trust.

  As a result of the project team's efforts, the project closed 17 days ahead of schedule. Efforts are now ongoing to identify what caused the leak and to share lessons learned from this project so that if another leak occurs in one of the other 177 buried storage tanks, they will now know how to save time, money, and resources addressing the problem (Schur 2017).

- The U.S. Veterans Health Administration (VHA) is the largest health-care system in the United States and serves almost nine million veterans annually. Prior to 2008, each of its 153 medical centers was responsible for processing its own claims for medical services provided to U.S. veterans. After benchmarking other health-care providers to identify best practices, administrators at the VHA believed they could improve the efficiency of claims processing by centralizing the insurance billing from the 153 medical centers to seven Consolidated Patient Account Centers (CPACs).

  A five-year project was planned to transition from the decentralized claims process approach to the more centralized approach. The project plan entailed incrementally phasing in one CPAC at a time over a five-year horizon. Asheville, NC, was selected as the location for the first CPAC as it was already processing the claims for eight medical centers and was therefore already functioning as a sort of CPAC. It took about two years to fully convert the Asheville unit into a completely functioning CPAC. After converting the Asheville site, the number of medical centers it served more than doubled to 18 and its staff was increased by 400% to 530 employees.

Once the Asheville CPAC was completed, the project team turned its attention to identifying the sites for the other six CPACs. Ultimately, the project team selected six sites across the United States for the CPACs: Wisconsin, Tennessee, Florida, Nevada, Kansas, and Pennsylvania. With the sites selected, the next step was to develop a project plan that detailed timelines for the build-outs and outfitting of each site. Another project plan was created for employee training and implementation.

Within three years of the program, four of the seven CPACs had been successfully implemented. For the final three CPACs, the project team decided to implement them simultaneously, rather than sequentially to reduce the project duration by an entire year. Of course, doing this increased the risk of the project, so the team developed a structured risk management plan and assessed project risk continuously.

By all accounts, the project was an overwhelming success. The project was finished an entire year early and came in slightly under budget. With the new centralized approach to claims processing, collections increased to 18.4%, and the number of days to collect payments decreased from 56 to 41 days. It is also worth noting that implementing each successive CPAC went smoother than the ones before it as the project team leveraged the lessons learned at each stage of the project (Schupak and Stains 2014).

- Sinebrychoff, a subsidiary of the Carlsberg Group, is one of Finland's largest beverage companies (beer, soft drinks, energy drinks). Sinebrychoff set the goal that its production facilities would be carbon neutral by 2030 and the entire organization by 2035. In pursuit of these goals, the company initiated a project to install a battery storage system in its Helsinki production facilities. One key benefit of the project was improving the company's energy efficiency, which in turn would help reduce energy costs and carbon emissions. Additionally, the battery storage system would help decouple the company's use of energy from the procurement of its energy thereby allowing the company to avoid purchasing its energy at peak times. While the project was expected to provide these and other benefits, there were also a number of challenges facing the project. For example, despite significant cost reductions over the last decade for battery storage systems, the project still required a large upfront investment. Additionally, Sinebrychoff had no inhouse expertise in managing or maintaining battery storage systems. To address these challenges, Sinebrychoff partnered with a number of other companies. For example, the project was financed by MW Storage International AG which also specialized in integrating and managing energy storage facilities. The battery storage equipment, a 20-megawatt gridstack system, was provided by Fluence, a joint venture of Siemens and AES. The Finish firm Vibeco supplied the needed expertise on operating virtual power plants and also developed a trading platform that allowed the venture to participate in energy markets. Finally, Siemens constructed the medium voltage switchgear and the connection to the high voltage grid (Siemens 2021).

- Although it was 2013, almost 6000 Mecklenburg County, NC, employees were still using e-mail software from 2003. This resulted in a problem that the database was 98% full, which required the employees to frequently clean out their inboxes in order to be able to send out new messages. Having fallen so far behind, the county decided the best course of action was to leap forward from using on-site e-mail servers to migrating to the cloud.

  The migration project was divided into two major phases. In the first phase, the physical infrastructure for communicating with the cloud storage was to be set up. With the infrastructure in place, the second phase would then migrate the employees to the current version of the software. The county brought in a consultant to execute the first phase of the project that focused on setting up the technology infrastructure. In three months, the consultant successfully set up the infrastructure that linked the on-site servers to the cloud.

Unfortunately, while the contractor had successfully completed the first phase of the project, it was considerably less successful in completing the second phase. For example, over a three-month period, it had succeeded in only converting 15 of the 5800 employees to the newer version of the software. With the project falling behind schedule, the county decided to move the second phase of the project, that of migrating employees to the new software, inhouse. Furthermore, to get the project back on schedule, the internal project manager (PM) decided to move away from the traditional waterfall approach where the stages of a project are completed sequentially to an Agile approach where the project is completed in short sprints, and then, project priorities are reevaluated after each sprint. With the Agile approach, the project team was able to migrate all 5800 employees in only eight weeks. In the end, this helped make up some of the schedule delays created by the consultant and allowed the project to finish only two months after its original deadline (Schupak 2014).

Although projects are often used to address more tactical aspects of organizational performance (e.g. the e-mail migration project in Mecklenburg County), they are the most common way organizations structure and implement more strategic and even mission critical organizational changes (e.g. moving to 7 CPACs at the VHA, and achieving organizational sustainability goals at Sinebrychoff).

From the previous examples, we see the ubiquitous role of project management for implementing these more strategic projects in a variety of organizations. Indeed, the selection and execution of projects is one of the primary tools used by organizations to accomplish their strategic objectives. Although there are all types of strategic projects, they typically all involve some form of major change in the organization. In the VHA example, the focus of the project was improving its business processes, while the Mecklenburg County project addressed the need to implement new technology. Sinebrychoff's battery storage project illustrates the increasing importance of partnering with other organizations in planning and executing projects. While the scope of each of these projects differed, the last three projects broadly addressed issues related to helping the organizations better accomplish their missions and goals. Dealing with this type of strategic change is sometimes referred to as "change management," and there are even positions called "Change Managers" whose job is to help employees adjust to role and organizational changes in the organization.

As we stated in Chapter 1, deciding on or creating a strategy is only the first step in making a major change in an organization – it still must be implemented! As Morgan et al. note (2007, pp. 4, 7): "Effective strategy consists of choosing to do the right things. Effective execution means doing those things right. Whatever the cause, competent and well-meaning executives routinely fail to integrate and align the work of the organization with the strategic vision of the organization." Morgan et al. point out that since most organizations have many more potential projects than they can successfully execute, making the hard choices to select the *right* projects for their scarce resources and energy also means, even more importantly, actively deciding where they *won't*. A company's de facto strategy is defined by what projects it is actually pursuing, not what it says. But this is not a one-time effort; the organization must continuously review their project portfolio against the evolving environment and carefully reallocate their resources among potential projects.

When projects are selected for implementation, it is important for top management to realize that the assigned project manager (PM) is an expert in delivering a specific project output – a machine, a tunnel, a new organizational structure – made difficult due to typically tight constraints on project cost and time. In the past, it was assumed that having the output would automatically deliver the benefits expected. However, no one was assigned the responsibility of making sure the output was used to actually deliver the benefits desired. We now know that someone needs to be responsible for this task as well and hence organizations now name a senior manager as the "project owner" (other terms include the project sponsor, project champion, and program manager) whose responsibility is to obtain the benefits described in the project's business case (Zwikael and Meredith 2018; Nieto-Rodriguez 2021).

The project owner oversees the project and alters its direction if changes or updates are made to the business case. This person acts as an "agent" for the CEO or group that authorized the project since neither the CEO nor a group, or even the project manager has the time to attend to these tasks. The project owner also works continuously with all the stakeholders in the project, especially the project manager, and helps prepare the intended users of the project's outputs for the changes that are coming. Inevitably, problems arise in projects and the project owner helps the project manager in solving these problems, which may require obtaining additional resources. More serious issues may require that the business case be altered, and this usually impacts all stakeholders in the project.

Project management is fundamentally concerned with managing organizational activities that result in some particular, desired output to achieve some specific benefit(s). Although we have titled this chapter, "Executing Strategy: Project Management," it should be clear that this is only one use among many for project management. For example, in the traditional functional organization, a product development team with representatives from production, finance, marketing, and engineering can be assembled to ensure that new product designs simultaneously meet the requirements of each area. Ensuring that each area's requirements are being met as the new design is developed reduces the likelihood that costly changes will have to be made later in the process. The result is that new products can be developed faster and less expensively, thereby enhancing the firm's overall responsiveness. Perhaps, a better product is developed as well, owing to the synergy of including a variety of different perspectives earlier in the design process.

In this chapter, we describe the many activities required in the successful management of projects. We start with the definition of a project and why project management is different from managing functional activities. We then move into the project life-cycle activities, starting with planning the project, which includes an understanding of the role of the project in the organization's strategy. We next describe the two major types of project life cycles and why it is important to be able to tell which is applicable for the project at hand. This is then followed by a discussion about organizing the project team, the various techniques available to the PM for planning the project activities, and sustainable project management. Following this, we discuss the major topics of scheduling the project and determining the probability of completing it by its due date. In the process, we describe the capabilities and outputs of some project management software packages. Moving along the project life cycle, we then address the topics of controlling the project's cost and performance. The chapter includes discussions of the "critical chain" and Agile concepts of project management.

2.2 Defining a Project

Up to this point, you might not have realized that projects are actually a special type of process. The term *process* refers to a set of activities that, taken together, create something of value to customers. Typically, the term *process* is used to refer to a set of activities that are routinely repeated, such as processing insurance forms, handling customers' complaints, and assembling a smartphone. The term *project* also refers to a set of activities that, taken together, produce a valued output. However, unlike a typical process, each project is unique and has a clear beginning and end. Therefore, projects are processes that are performed infrequently and ad hoc, with a clear specification of the desired objective.

One important characteristic of all projects is that they have some unique aspect(s) about them that prohibits them from being performed in a routine manner. It may concern the tasks involved in meeting the performance requirements of the project (called "scope"), or the time window, or the resource limits, or something else, but it cannot be performed by the organization's regular business processes.

The choice of the project form often indicates the importance of the project's objective to the organization and to the many other *stakeholders,* such as the client, the project owner and manager, subcontractors, consultants, the project team, the project management office, the government (sometimes), the community, and possibly others. Thus, top-grade resources, including staff, are often made available for project operations. As a result, project organizations become professionalized and are often managed on that basis. That is, minimal supervision is exercised, administrative routine is minimized, and the project team professionals are charged with solving the problem and obtaining the required results (cost, performance, and deadline). The project team is then given the privacy and freedom to decide *how* to solve the problem.

Projects frequently require different emphases during their life cycle. For example, technical performance may be crucial at the beginning, cost overruns in the middle, and ontime completion and benefit realization at the end. The flexibility of making spur-of-the-moment changes in emphasis by trading off one criterion for another is fundamental to project management. This ability results from the close contact of the PM with the technical staff – there are few, if any, "middle managers."

The following are some examples of projects:

- Organizing conferences, banquets, conventions, and weddings

- Managing R&D projects such as the Manhattan Project (which developed the atomic bomb)

- Running political campaigns, war operations, advertising campaigns, or forest firefighting operations

- Chairing ad hoc task forces, overseeing planning for government agencies, or conducting corporate audits

- Converting from one computer system to another

- Locating and laying out amusement parks, camping grounds, and refuges

- Constructing highways, bridges, tunnels, and dams

- Building ships, planes, and rockets, or a doghouse

- Erecting skyscrapers, steel mills, homes, and processing plants

In physical project operations, such as bridge construction, most of the *production* per se is completed elsewhere and brought to the project area at the proper time. As a result, great many project activities are *assembly* operations. With projects, resources are concentrated on the achievement of specific objectives, primarily through proper *scheduling* and *control* of activities, many of which are simultaneous. Some of the scheduling considerations in project management are knowing what activities must be completed and in what order, how long they will take, when to increase and decrease the labor force, and when to order materials so that they will not arrive too early (thus requiring storage and being in the way) or too late (thus delaying the project).

The control activities include anticipating risks concerning what can and might go wrong, knowing what resources can be shifted among activities to keep the project on schedule, and so forth.

2.3 Planning the Project

In this section, we focus in detail on the planning of projects. In the area of project management, planning is probably the single most important element in the success of a project, and considerable research has been done on the topic. We start with the role of the organization's many projects in achieving its strategy, known as the organization's *project portfolio*. This portfolio evolves over time, since projects have a finite life cycle, as mentioned earlier and discussed in the next subsection. Following this, we discuss the project team and its tie to the parent organization. Last, we describe the actual project planning tools.

2.3.1 The Project Portfolio

The long-term purpose of projects in the organization is to ultimately achieve the organization's goals. This is accomplished through the project portfolio, also known as the organization's *aggregate project plan*. In making project selection decisions, it is vital to consider the interactions among various projects and to manage the projects as a set. This is in stark contrast to the common practice of simply setting a project budget and specified return on investment (ROI) hurdle rate and then funding projects until either the budget or supply of acceptable projects is exhausted.

Organizations that fund all projects that meet their ROI criterion typically end up with significantly more ongoing projects than they can competently manage, and thus, their contribution to the organization's long-term goals can be lost. Because ROI is an insufficient selection criterion, the set of projects chosen may not constitute close to an optimal portfolio for achieving their purpose.

In an attempt to better tie one firm's product development projects to its strategic objectives, Professors Wheelwright and Clark (1992) of the Harvard Business School developed a framework for categorizing the firm's product development projects that they call the "aggregate project plan." The purpose of their framework was to convey the *distribution* of all the organization's product/service design projects across the measures of importance to the firm such as resource demands, innovativeness, product lines, time, and project type. Thus, the portfolio for an organization's strategic projects should illustrate how the projects map out over the measures of importance to the organization. Having a visual map of the projects in the organization's portfolio is an important tool for helping senior management make crucial project selection decisions.

It is also important to point out, however, that it is typically not a single project that determines the organization's long-run success, but rather the *set* of research projects pursued by the organization in its project portfolio. Therefore, in making project selection decisions, it is vital to consider the interactions among various projects and to manage the projects as a set in order to achieve the organization's strategic objectives. The visual map of the portfolio is extremely useful in facilitating the analysis of these factors.

Using Wheelwright and Clark's framework, output development projects are categorized along two dimensions: (1) the extent of changes made to the output and (2) the degree of process change. Based on these two dimensions, projects can then be categorized into the following four categories, as we illustrate in Figure 2.1:

1. *Derivative projects.* Derivative projects seek to make incremental improvements in the output and/or process. Projects that seek to reduce the output's cost or make minor product line extensions exemplify these types of projects. Developing a stripped-down version of a notebook computer or adding a new menu item at a fast-food restaurant would qualify as a derivative project. This category accounts for a large majority of all innovations.

2. *Breakthrough projects.* These projects are at the opposite end of the continuum from derivative projects and involve extensive changes in both the products and processes, typically seeking the development of a new generation of outputs. A self-driving car and an entirely online grocery store are examples of breakthrough projects.

3. *Platform projects.* Platform projects fall between derivative and breakthrough projects, involving substantial changes either in the product, the process or both. In general, the

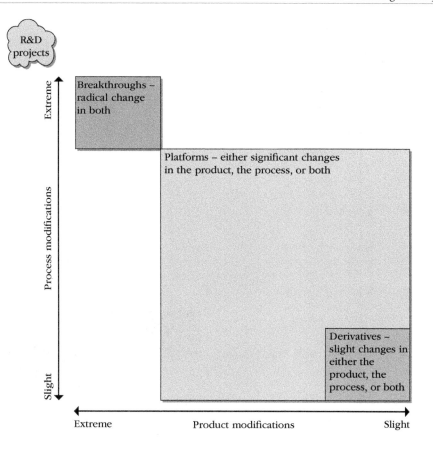

FIGURE 2.1 The Aggregate Project Plan

result of these projects is an output that can serve as the *platform* for an entire line of new outputs. A key difference between platform projects and breakthrough projects is that platform projects stick with existing technology. As an example, the development of an ultrathin netbook computer would qualify as a platform project. If this computer succeeds, it could serve as the basis for a number of derivative projects focusing on cost improvement and the development of other computer models with different features.

4. *R&D projects.* R&D projects entail working with basic technology to develop new knowledge. Depending on its focus, an R&D project might lead to breakthrough, platform, or derivative innovations. The R&D project category is a cloud because it is unclear how much product or process change may be involved in these projects.

The use of the aggregate project plan requires that all projects be identified and plotted. The size of the points plotted for each project should be proportional to the amount of resources the project will require. In Figure 2.2, we have used different shapes to indicate different types of projects. Internal projects are plotted using circles, while projects pursued as part of a strategic alliance with other firms are plotted using squares.

There are a number of ways the aggregate project plan can be used. The identification of gaps in the types of projects being undertaken is probably most important. For example, are the types of projects undertaken too heavily skewed toward derivative-type projects? This might indicate an inadequate consideration of the firm's long-run competitive position. Also, the aggregate project plan facilitates evaluation of the resource commitments of the ongoing as well as proposed projects. Finally, this framework can serve as a model for employee development. New employees can

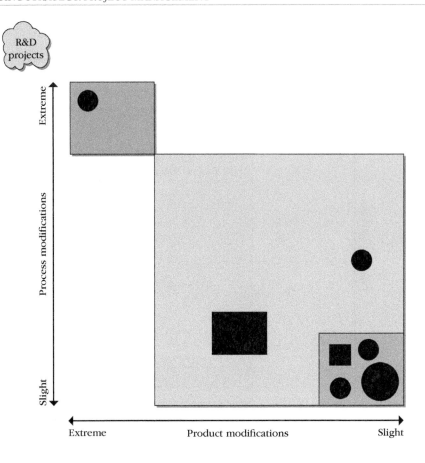

FIGURE 2.2 An Example Aggregate Project Plan

be initially assigned to a team working on a derivative project. After gaining experience, employees can be assigned to a platform project and then assigned to *manage* a derivative project. As managerial skill accumulates, the employee will qualify for larger and more valuable projects. Of course, we must remember that the fundamental purpose of this entire process is to ensure that the set of projects accurately reflects the organization's strategic goals and objectives.

As one example, Hewlett-Packard (HP) found itself in the common position of having more ongoing projects than it could effectively control, so it turned to the use of an aggregate project plan. By intensely scrutinizing all their projects and taking into consideration the gaps and excesses on their aggregate project plan, HP was able to prioritize the projects and concentrate on those that made the greatest contribution to their strategic goals for the least resource use. The initiative helped one HP organization systematically reduce 120 projects down to 30, and another organization from 50 to 17, thereby increasing the chances of success for the most important projects (Englund and Graham 1999).

One final aspect of the project portfolio is the risk profile of various projects, an especially important consideration when choosing among competing projects to fund. Risks arise mainly in two major phases of every project – the project execution phase where project outputs are delivered and the benefits realization phase where the benefits desired by the organization and detailed in the business case come to pass. The primary risks in the execution phase involve what's known as the "iron triangle" of requirements: missing the *deadline*, exceeding the *budget*, and failing to meet the *specifications* for the output, all three of which will undoubtedly change as the project progresses. The risks in this phase of the project can often be anticipated and handled with standard process control procedures and tools (described in Chapter 7) such as control charts and failure mode and effect analysis. The risks in the benefits realization phase are subtle and more nuanced, involving human behavior, motivation, user resistance, fear of change, and other more difficult aspects of implementing the project's outputs. The role of the project owner is specifically directed to identifying and addressing these types of risks, which can arise from within the organization, from entities outside the organization such as subcontractors, or from any of the many stakeholders in the project such as the local community.

2.3.2 The Business Case

The business case is a document that outlines not only the project that is being proposed but more importantly, how the results of that project will benefit the organization. That is, it clearly articulates how the project's goals and benefits fit into the strategic vision of the organization. It also includes the other project options that were considered and the reasons why this particular option is being recommended. In addition, it gives a first estimate of the scope of work required for the project, the costs that will be involved, the time frame anticipated, and all the risks that may impede the project. Thus, it lays out the rationale for investing in the project and justifies it, hopefully gaining the commitment of top management and authorization to proceed with the project.

Some important additional elements of the business case have recently been recommended (Einhorn 2019, 2020, 2022).One major addition is the specification of the governance of the project, including not just the project manager but also the project owner/sponsor, any oversight committee, and the other key stakeholders in the project. Another important element of the business case is the specification of how "success" will be measured. Zwikael and Meredith (2019) recommend three distinct generic measures: (1) project management success, (2) project ownership success, and (3) project investment success. The first measure is solely based on the successful completion of the desired output of the project, which is the responsibility of the project manager. The second measure is based on the successful attainment of the anticipated benefits, the responsibility of the project owner. And the third measure is based on how worthwhile the client or organization that funded the project was satisfied with the outcome, regardless of whether it was a success or failure. That is, knowing ahead of time what the outcome would turn out to be, would they have still invested in the project?

Of course, things change as a project that has never been done before progresses: the environment changes, project activities do not turn out as planned, assumptions may turn out to be wrong, top management may change, or the strategic plan may change. And these changes may impact the internal or external stakeholders in the project in undesirable ways, which then has to be taken into account and rectified. Hence, current thinking about the business case (Einhorn 2020, 2022) is that it needs to be constantly updated, and the plans will likely need to be changed or at least adjusted, and the benefits may need to be altered. If these alterations make the project less attractive, top management will have to reconsider the project and perhaps change its direction, or possibly even terminate it.

2.3.3 The Project Life Cycle

It has been found, for example, that progress in a project is rarely uniform, but instead often follows one of two common forms, as shown in Figure 2.3. In the stretched-S life-cycle form, illustrated in Figure 2.3*a*, when the project is initiated, progress is slow as responsibilities are assigned and organization takes place. But the project gathers speed during the implementation stage, and much progress is made. As the end of the project draws near, the more difficult tasks that were postponed earlier must now be completed, yet people are being drawn off the project, and activity is "winding down," so the end keeps slipping out of reach.

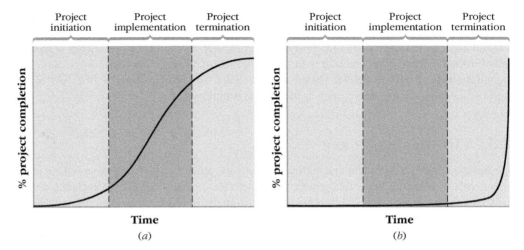

FIGURE 2.3 Two Project Life Cycles: (*a*) Stretched-S, (*b*) Exponential

In the exponential form, illustrated in Figure 2.3*b*, after the project is initiated, there is continuous activity on numerous aspects of the project, but until all the elemental parts come together at the end, there is no final output. This is typical of projects that require final assembly of components to produce the whole (like a car) or goods (like a cake, which is only glop until it is baked in the oven). It is especially typical of office and other such service work where the final output is a life insurance policy, or ad piece, or perhaps even an MBA degree. Without that last signature, or piece of paper, or earned credit, there is virtually no product. (However, if a student is auditing courses with the goal of understanding rather than getting a degree, the progress toward their goal may indeed be linear with every day spent in class.)

The reason it is important to contrast these two forms, besides pointing out their differences in managerial needs, is that during the budgeting stage, if there is a flat across-the-board budget cut of, say, 10% and the project is of the stretched-S form, then not being able to spend that last 10% of the budget is of no urgency, since probably 97% of the benefits will be achieved anyway. However, if the project is of the exponential form, then missing the last 10% is catastrophic because this is where all the value is attained. Another perspective on the same issue is the effect of early termination of the project. Terminating the stretched-S form early will have negligible impact, but terminating the exponential form will be a complete disaster. It is imperative that the PM and top management know which type of project they are working with before taking such actions.

2.3.4 Projects in the Organizational Structure

One of the factors in the success of a project is making sure that it is reporting to the proper level of management in the organization. In a functionally structured organization with the typical departments of marketing, finance, operations, human resources (HR), engineering, and so on, projects are frequently housed in the department or division that has a major interest in the project's success or has the special skills to ensure that it will be executed properly. More generic projects, such as a divisionwide effort to speed up product development, might report to the division head or a vice president, and the project team is composed of members drawn from many of the individual departments.

Some organizations are structured by projects, called "projectized" organizations. Construction, engineering, legal, consulting, and auditing firms are frequently structured this way; the line units are the particular contracts the firm is working on, while the administrative support groups, such as HR and finance, are staff units that report higher up in the organization but render support to all the projects. If some of the contracts are very large and long running, the project may have its own dedicated staff.

In some ways, the projectized organization is at the opposite end of the spectrum from the functional organization, and, as might be suspected, each has its own advantages and disadvantages. For example, functionally organized projects have the advantage of tremendous depth of knowledge in the department relating to the goals of the project. But projectized projects have the advantage of having the entire project team all directed to the same goal and reporting to a single PM.

In an attempt to obtain the benefits of each of these ways of organizing projects, some firms have adopted what is known as a "matrixed" structure, where projects draw their workers from each appropriate functional department (the columns of the matrix), but the workers are grouped together into independent projects (the rows). Thus, each worker has two bosses, a functional boss and a project boss. This arrangement often does gain some of the advantages of each of the two major organizational arrangements, but it also has some additional disadvantages, such as conflicts between the two bosses. Combinations of these forms are also common, such as the "weak" or functional matrix and the "strong" or project matrix. Each way of organizing the project has its own advantages and disadvantages, and what works best depends largely on the circumstances of the organization and the reason it started a project.

2.3.5 Organizing the Project Team

Next we will talk about the important role of the PM and their team, and then discuss the project owner. Regardless of the form of the project, a team will be required to run it. Some members of the team may be directly assigned to the PM for the duration, while others may have only partial responsibilities for the project and still report to their functional superior. There are three types of team members who should report directly to the PM, however:

- Those who will be having a long-term relationship with the project

- Those with whom the PM will need to communicate closely or continuously

- Those with rare skills necessary to project success

Yet even if these people report to the PM, it is still not common for the PM to have the authority to reward these people with pay bonuses, extra vacation, or other such personnel matters – that authority normally still resides with the functional manager. Thus, there are not a lot of incentives the PM can give people for working hard on the project. The main ones are the fun and excitement of the challenge and doing something that will be important to the organization.

With the pressures that tend to gravitate toward such important and high-profile projects, it may be assumed that there is also a lot of opportunity for conflict to arise. This is true, and not only between the PM and other organizational units but even among members of the project team. According to Thamhain and Wilemon (1975), at project formation, the main sources of conflict are priorities and procedures. As the project gets under way, priorities and schedules become the main points of conflict. During the main implementation stage, conflict shifts to technical issues and schedules. But toward the end of the project, when timing is becoming crucial, only schedules are a source of conflict. Knowing when to expect trouble, and what kinds, throughout the project can help the PM keep peace within the project team and facilitate smooth project progress.

Another major factor in the success of a project is selecting the proper PM. The responsibilities of and special demands on a PM are extensive (e.g. acquiring resources, motivating the team, dealing with obstacles, making goal trade-offs, and communicating across a range of stakeholders), but four major attributes stand out (Meredith and Shafer 2022):

1. *Credibility.* The PM needs both technical and administrative credibility, technical to handle the project's details and administrative to handle the range of important stakeholders.

2. *Sensitivity.* The PM must be sensitive to both politics and personalities. Projects are pressure cookers and interpersonal conflicts can erupt without warning, not only between team members but also with higher administration and outsiders. The sensitive PM will detect a potential conflict and then confront and defuse it before it turns into a crisis.

3. *Leadership, ethics, and managerial style.* Clearly, the PM needs many competencies to run complex projects, but different types of projects need more emphasis on certain competencies than others. For example, the PM will require vastly different competencies in an HR versus a construction project.

4. *Ability to handle stress.* Projects are created because the normal functioning of the organization isn't able to handle the special requirements of the project. Hence, stress is expected in every project, but tight schedules, insufficient resources, and difficult (or constantly changing) goals add substantially to a PM's stress level.

Some people enjoy the job of a PM and others don't, so selecting a PM who has a good record on past projects is one indicator of the proper PM for a project. Another is whether the person shows interest in the profession of project management, such as by joining the Project Management Institute (PMI), knowing the project management body of knowledge (PMBOK), or becoming certified as a Project Management Professional or holding one of the other certifications offered by PMI and other organizations. (For more on PMI, PMBOK, and certification, refer to Table 1.1 in Meredith and Shafer 2022.)

The demands on the project owner are just as difficult as those on the PM but broader, involving communication with everyone from the CEO or other project authorizing entity to individual users of the project output, such as front-line employees or local citizens. Most of the interactions for the project owner will usually be with the PM, however, since project execution is typically the major cost and time element of each project. Clearly, the attributes required for the job of the project owner will be different from that of the PM. It has been found (Zwikael et al. 2018) that the best project owner candidates come from two categories of employees, former highly experienced PMs who are known for being good managers of people and senior managers who are also good at managing others, especially if they have some project management experience.

2.3.6 Project Plans

The initiation of a project should in most cases include the development of some level of *project charter* (the basis for the final *project plan*), unless the project is highly routine. The elements that constitute the project charter and form the basis for more detailed planning of the budgets, schedules, work plan, and general management of the project are described in the following text. It should be noted that the process of developing the project charter varies from organization to organization, but any project charter should contain some level of information regarding the following elements:

- *Purpose and justification.* This is a short summary directed to top management and those unfamiliar with the project. It contains a statement of the general goals of the project and a brief explanation of their relationship to the firm's objectives. Often this section is referred to as the Business Case. A properly crafted Business Case should succinctly provide the financial and strategic justification for the project.

- *Objectives.* This contains a more detailed statement of the general goals of the project and their priorities, what constitutes success, and how the project will be terminated. The statement should include measurable objectives such as profit and competitive aims from the Business Case as well as technical goals.

- *Overview.* This section provides a high-level description of the project, its requirements and its boundaries (i.e. what is in and not in the project's scope). Both the managerial and the technical approaches to the work may also described. Also included here is a description of the assumptions the project is based on and contingency plans if the assumptions don't prove to be correct and the procedures for changes in the project, including scope, budget, and schedule.

- *Schedule and milestones.* This outlines the schedule and lists milestone events and/or phase gates. Each major/summary task is listed, and the estimated time for each task should be obtained from those who will do the work. The project master schedule is constructed from these inputs.

- *Resources.* There are two primary aspects to be considered here. The first is the *project budget.* Both capital and expense requirements, as well as any contractual requirements, are detailed here. Second, cost monitoring and control procedures should be described.

- *Stakeholders.* Besides the client, community, and other external stakeholders, this section also lists who must be involved in the review and approval process, such as the sponsor, the project owner, as well as the time-phased personnel requirements of the project, that is, the *team* and other involved departments. The name and authority level of the PM should also be included here. Special skills, types of training needed, possible recruiting problems, legal or policy restrictions on workforce composition, and any other special requirements, such as security clearances, should be noted. Time phasing the personnel needs makes clear to management and other departments when the various types of contributors are needed and in what numbers.

- *Risk management plan.* This covers potential problems that could affect the project at a high level. One or more issues, such as subcontractor default, unexpected technical breakthroughs, strikes, hurricanes, new markets for the firm's technology, tight deadlines and budgets, and sudden moves by a competitor, are certain to occur – the only uncertainties are which, when, and their impact. Plans to deal with unfavorable (or favorable) contingencies should be developed early in the project's life.

- *Evaluation method.* Every project should be evaluated against standards and by methods established at the project's inception. This includes a brief description of the procedures to be followed in monitoring, collecting, storing, and evaluating the history of the project.

Almost by definition, a project is an attempt to meet specified performance or "scope" requirements by a specific deadline within a limited budget. These objectives are generally illustrated in Figure 2.4 and are known as the "iron triangle" or "triple constraint." The project plan described previously lays out these three objectives in detail, but the task for the PM is to "make it happen."

To achieve these three project objectives, one of the PM's first responsibilities is to define all the tasks in as much detail as possible so that they can be scheduled, their costs determined, and responsibility assigned. This set of task descriptions are captured in the *work breakdown structure* (WBS), which provides the inputs for the *project schedule* (usually put into a format known as the *project Gantt chart*) and the RACI matrix that shows who is responsible for performing the tasks. More specifically, the RACI matrix uses the letters R, A, C, and I for each task to document project responsibilities: responsible (for a task), accountable, consult (or coordinate for support), and inform (notify), respectively.

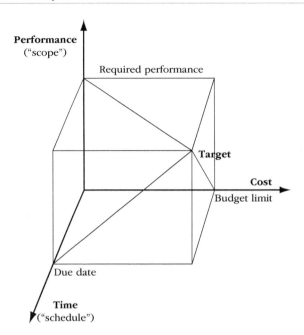

FIGURE 2.4 Three Project Objectives. Reprinted with permission from J. R. Meredith and S. M. Shafer (2022)

A typical WBS is illustrated in Figure 2.5 for a project to develop "Quick Response Teams" for the government.

Figure 2.6 illustrates RACI matrix for the project.

The scheduling of project activities is highly complex because of (1) the number of activities required, (2) the precedence relationships among the activities, and (3) the limited time of the project. The primary method of project scheduling is based on two historical network approaches – *program evaluation and review technique* (PERT) and *critical path method* (CPM).

A network approach is useful because a project schedule has to handle an enormous number of different activities, which must be coordinated in such a way that the subsequent activities can take place and the entire project (job) can be completed by the due date.

The scheduling procedure for project operations must be able not only to identify and handle a variety of tasks that must be done but also to handle their time sequencing. In addition, it must be able to integrate the performance and timing of all the tasks with the project as a whole so that

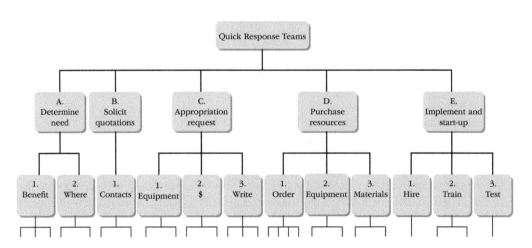

FIGURE 2.5 Work Breakdown Structure

| WBS | | Project Office | | | | Field Oper. | |
Subproject	Task	Project Manager	Contract Admin.	Program Mgr.	Portfolio Mgr.	Field Manager	
Determine need	A1	A		C	R		
	A2	I	A	R	C		
Solicit quotations	B1	A	I	R		C	
Write approp. request.	C1	I	R	A	C		
	C2		C	A	R		
	C3	C	I	R		I	
"	"						
"	"						
"	"						

Legend:
R Responsible
A Accountable
C Consult
I Inform

FIGURE 2.6 RACI Matrix. Reprinted with permission from J. R. Meredith and S. M. Shafer (2022)

control can be exercised, for example, by shifting resources from operations with slack (permissible slippage) to other operations whose delay might threaten the project's timely completion. The tasks involved in planning and scheduling project operations are as follows:

- *Planning.* Determining what must be done and which tasks must *precede* others.

- *Scheduling.* Determining *when* the tasks must be completed; when they *can* and when they *must* be started; which tasks are *critical* to the timely completion of the project; and which tasks have *slack* in their timing and how much.

2.3.7 Change Management

As noted earlier, there is sometimes another player involved in a project known as a *change manager*. For smaller and/or more tactical projects, the role of change manager may be taken on informally. For larger and more strategic projects, it is essential that this role be formally assigned. Regardless of whether the role is assigned formally or informally, the change manager's responsibility is to help people and teams successfully transition to new roles or responsibilities in an organization, but there is no intended responsibility for successfully executing the project or accomplishing its objectives and benefits. Wikipedia defines change management as all approaches to prepare and support individuals, teams, and organizations in making organizational changes. Such changes may be due to technology, crises, new competitors to the organization, efficiency or effectiveness improvements, or organizational acquisitions, mergers, or restructurings.

Change managers have a variety of tools at their disposal to help others such as information technology, behavioral science techniques, education, social science approaches, training workshops, and many others. These managers stress the importance of thinking through the organizational change before initiating it and then monitoring the change through various metrics as the change is implemented. For example, upper management should try to identify the assumptions they are making with the change, any risks that could occur, what the change may be dependent upon, what it will cost, how it will alter the culture of the organization, what the return on the investment (ROI) will be, what other changes may also be required, and finally what disbenefits may occur as well. In term of metrics to monitor during the change, some good indicators are the financial results, the efficiencies of the workers, the managerial commitment to the change, how effective communication is becoming, and what the stakeholders are thinking.

John Kotter at Harvard Business School has developed a well-known change model (Mind Tools: "Kotter's 8-Step Change Model": www.mindtools.com/pages/article/newPPM_82.htm) that many organizations use consisting of the following steps:

1. Create a sense of urgency about the change.

2. Form a powerful coalition for the change.

3. Create a strategic vision for the change.

4. Communicate this vision across the organization.

5. Remove any obstacles and barriers to the change.

6. Create short-term wins and publicize them.

7. As change occurs, build on it to accelerate the change.

8. Anchor the change in the organizational culture.

2.3.8 Sustainable Project Management

Sustainable project management (SPM) refers to the combination of traditional project management concepts with sustainability concepts, including both social and environmental concerns. More formally, SPM has been defined as

> *the planning, monitoring, and controlling of project delivery and support processes, with consideration of the environmental, economical, and social aspects of the life-cycle of the project's resources, processes, deliverables, and effects, aimed at realizing benefits for stakeholders, and performed in a transparent, fair and ethical way that includes proactive stakeholder participation.* (Silvius and Schipper, 2014, p. 79)

Per this definition, it is worth emphasizing that SPM refers to projects that deliver sustainable outcomes (such as the Sinebrychoff example at the beginning of the chapter) as well as to projects that employ sustainable practices in completing the project.

It has been argued that incorporating sustainability concepts into the project management field has fundamentally changed the practice of project management (Sánchez 2015). Accordingly, the topic of SPM is an area of increasing interest in the academic community. For example, one research stream has investigated the factors that influence PMs to incorporate sustainability practices into the projects they lead. In some cases, the main driver for incorporating sustainability considerations into projects stem from the PM's intrinsic motivation based on their personal values and principles. In other cases, PMs may incorporate sustainability into their projects to comply with regulations, directives from senior management, or to conform to the expectations of other stakeholders. In yet other cases, the PM may not be strongly concerned with sustainability but will happily take advantage of opportunities to incorporate sustainability objectives when they are available. From an organizational and practitioner point of view, the use of SPM can be justified based on moral arguments, enhanced resilience, improved organizational or technological performance, and firm profitability and competitiveness.

Earlier in the chapter we discussed the three objectives of a project (see Figure 2.4), namely, time, cost, and performance. Considering issues related to sustainability effectively adds a fourth constraint that further complicates the PM's job of managing the tradeoffs associated with completing the project. Furthermore, beyond creating conflicts with the three traditional project objectives, there can be tradeoffs associated with the sustainability objectives themselves. For example, a temperature control system added to an office building to reduce the energy consumed in heating and cooling the building also consumes energy. Given the increasingly difficult task of addressing all of these tradeoffs, it has been argued that PMs must concede that it is not possible to solve all of them, and therefore the PM should focus on managing the tradeoffs as opposed to attempting find solutions that resolve the tradeoffs (Sabini and Aldernman 2021).

As has been discussed throughout this chapter, projects play a critical role in helping organizations achieve long-term objectives. And while sustainability is a high priority objective in many organizations, even considering projects more narrowly, it is clear that projects impact key aspects of sustainability (e.g. the environmental impact of the project and the labor practices employed in executing the project). Along these lines PMBOK recognizes this and discusses the importance of conducting an environmental analysis in the Introduction and first stewardship "principle" of PMI's new *Standard for Project Management* (PMI 2022) to ensure PMs are accountable for the impacts of the projects they lead. A clear implication for PMs, project team members, and stakeholders is that the definition of project success should include the impact the project has on aspects related to sustainability.

2.4 Scheduling the Project

The project scheduling process is based on the activities that must be conducted to achieve the project's goals, the length of time each requires, and the order in which they must be completed. If a number of similar projects must be conducted, sometimes these activities can be structured generically to apply equally well to all the projects.

Two primary techniques have been developed to plan projects consisting of ordered activities: PERT and CPM. Although PERT and CPM originally had some differences in the way activities were determined and laid out, many current approaches to project scheduling minimize these differences and present an integrated view, as we will see here. It will be helpful to define some terms first.

- *Activity.* One of the project operations, or tasks; an activity requires resources and takes some amount of time to complete.

- *Event.* Completion of an activity, or series of activities, at a particular point in time.

- *Network.* The set of all project activities graphically interrelated through precedence relationships. In this text, boxes (called *nodes*) represent activities and arrows between the boxes represent precedence. (This is typical of the CPM approach; in PERT, the arrows represent activities.)

- *Path.* A series of connected activities from the start to the finish of the project.

- *Critical path.* Any path that, if delayed, will delay the completion of the entire project.

- *Critical activities.* The activities on the critical path or paths.

We next illustrate the process of scheduling with a Six Sigma process improvement project example. We use the DMAIC approach (see Chapter 8) to improve a bank's process for handling mortgage refinancing applications.

2.4.1 Project Scheduling with Certain Activity Times: A Process Improvement Example

The primary inputs to project planning are a list of the activities that must be completed, the *activity completion times* (also called activity *durations*), and precedence relationships among the activities (i.e. what activities must be completed before another activity can be started). In this section, we assume that activity completion times are known with certainty. Later, we relax this assumption and consider situations in which activity completion times are uncertain.

Important outputs of project scheduling include the following:

- Graphical representation of the entire project, showing all precedence relationships among the activities

- Time it will take to complete the project

- Identification of critical path or paths

- Identification of critical activities

- Slack times for all activities and paths

- Earliest and latest time each activity can be started

- Earliest and latest time each activity can be completed.

2.4.1.1 Project Completion and Critical Paths

Table 2.1 shows the activity times and precedence for the 10 activities that must all be finished to complete a bank's strategic process improvement project for their most profitable activity, mortgage refinancing. According to Table 2.1, activities A, B, and C can be started at any time. Activity D can be started once activity A is completed. Activities E, F, and G cannot be started until both activities B and C are finished, and so on. The network diagram for this project is shown in Figure 2.7, in which ellipses show the start and end of the project, arrows represent the required precedence, and rectangular nodes represent activities A–J in Table 2.1. The rectangular nodes list the activity by letter, followed by its expected time (in days). This way of depicting a project is known as activity-on-node (AON) and is typical of CPM; the PERT alternative, activity-on-arrow (AOA), is also common, however (see, e.g., Meredith and Shafer 2022).

To determine the window of completion times of each of the nodes on the network and thus the entire project, *early start times* T_{ES} and *early finish times* T_{EF} are calculated for each activity,

Table 2.1   Data for a Bank's Mortgage Refinancing Project

Activity	Expected time, t_e	Preceding activities
A: Identify all stakeholders	10	–
B: Develop the project charter	10	–
C: Uncover all relevant regulations	5	–
D: Set up project procedures	7	A
E: Determine total refinancing time	5	B, C
F: Use accounting data for total cost	7	B, C
G: Interview to determine unknown risks	2	B, C
H: Redesign so as to reduce task times	5	C
I: Determine cost reductions of new design	8	G, H
J: Uncover any new constraints on design	4	D, E

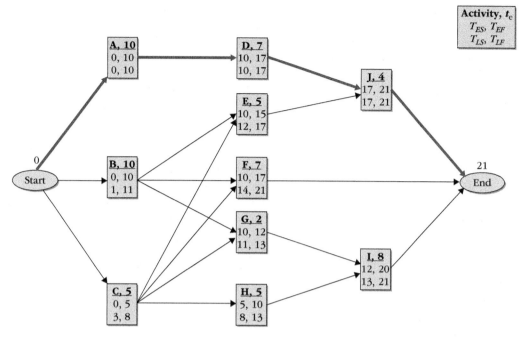

FIGURE 2.7
Network Diagram for
Mortgage Process
Improvement Project

as shown in Figure 2.7. The values of T_{ES} and T_{EF} are calculated moving left to right through the network. Thus, we begin with the Start node and work our way to the End node. To illustrate, the project starts at time zero (sometimes this is not the case), and then, activities A, B, and C can also be started as early as time zero, since none of them are preceded by another activity. Since activity A requires 10 days, if it is started at time zero (T_{ES}), it can be completed (T_{EF}) as early as day 10. Likewise, if activity B is started at time zero, it can be completed as early as day 10, and activity C can be completed by day 5. Continuing on, since activity A can be finished as early as day 10, activity D can start as early as day 10 and, since it takes seven days, can finish as early as day 17. The same logic applies to activities E–H.

Now consider activity J. Activity J cannot be started until activities D and E are *both* completed. Since activity D can be finished as early as day 17 and E can be finished as early as day 15, activity J can be started only as early as day 17, the *latest* of its preceding activities (remember, J cannot start until both activities D and E are completed). Since J takes four days, then it can be finished as early as 21 days. The same logic applies to activity I. It cannot start until the latest of its predecessors is completed, 12 for G and 10 for H, and hence 12. Since it takes eight days, it can be completed by day 20. Now that T_{ES} and T_{EF} have been calculated for all the activities, we can determine the earliest time that the project can be completed. Since the project "End" cannot be completed until all its predecessors are completed, the earliest it could be completed is day 21, based on activity J.

We can now find the critical path and critical activities for the project. Since the End of the project depended on activity J, we bold the arrow from J to End. Similarly, J's start time depended on activity D, rather than E, so we bold the arrow from D to J. And D depended on the completion of A, so we bold that arrow and then the arrow from the Start node to A, resulting in the critical path A–D–J and the critical activities A, D, and J.

Once T_{ES} and T_{EF} have been calculated for each activity, the *latest* times each activity can be started and finished without delaying the completion of the project can be determined. In contrast to T_{ES} and T_{EF}, the *latest start time* (T_{LS}) and *latest finish time* (T_{LF}) are calculated by moving *backward* through the network, from right to left. These T_{LS} and T_{LF} times are also shown in Figure 2.7.

In calculating T_{ES} and T_{EF}, we determined that the project could be completed by day 21. If the project is to be completed by day 21, then activities J, F, and I can be completed as late as day 21 without delaying completion of the project. Thus, the latest finish time for activities J, F, and I is 21. Since activity J requires four days, it can start as late as $21 - 4$, or 17, and still finish by day 21. Likewise, activity I can start as late as $21 - 8$, or 13, and still finish by day 21, and activity F can start as late as $21 - 7 = 14$. Continuing on, since activity J can start as late as day 17, activity D can finish as late as day 17. Since activity D requires seven days, it can start as late as day 17 $- 7 = 10$ without delaying the entire project. Activities G and H are handled similarly, resulting in the late start and finish times for activities G and H.

Now let's look at activity B, which precedes activities E, F, and G. The latest it can finish is the *earliest* late start date of activities E, F, and G since if it doesn't start by then, that activity will be late and will delay the entire project. Since the late start dates of these three activities are 12 (for E), 14, and 11, activity B's latest finish date must be 11, because if it doesn't finish by 11, activity G can't start and will delay activity I, which will delay the project. The latest finish date for activity C is found in the same manner.

Note in Figure 2.7 that the latest dates for the critical activities (A, D, and J) are identical to the earliest dates. That is, the latest dates cannot be delayed from the earliest dates at all, or else the entire project will be delayed! This will always be the case since this represents the critical path of the project.

2.4.1.2 Slack Time

The times T_{ES}, T_{EF}, T_{LS}, and T_{LF} can be used by the PM to help plan and develop schedules for the project. For example, if an activity requires a key resource or an individual, its earliest and latest start times provide a window during which that resource can be acquired or assigned to the project. Alternatively, if an activity falls behind schedule, the latest completion time provides an indication of whether the slippage will delay the entire project or can simply be absorbed.

Notice in Figure 2.7 that for some activities, T_{ES} is less than its T_{LS} and its T_{EF} is less than its T_{LF}. In these cases, the PM can exercise some discretion in terms of when the activity is started and when it is completed. The amount of flexibility the PM has in terms of starting and completing an activity is referred to as its *slack* (or *float*) and is calculated as

$$\text{Activity slack} = T_{LS} - T_{ES} = T_{LF} - T_{EF}$$

All activities on the critical path have zero slack, that is, there is no room for delay in any activity on the critical path without delaying the entire project. But activities off the critical path may delay up to a point where further delay would delay the entire project. For example, activity H has a late start time of 8 and an early start time of 5, leaving three days of possible slack. If resources for activity H are sitting idle and could be used to expedite activity A, for example, the PM may choose to do this, perhaps reducing the duration of activity A by one day and bringing the project in at day 20 instead of 21, for an early completion!

In addition to calculating slack times for individual activities, slack times can be calculated for entire paths. Since all paths must be finished to complete the project, the time to complete the project is the time to complete the path with the longest duration. Thus, the path with the longest duration is critical in the sense that any delay in completing it will delay the completion of the entire project. Path slacks are calculated as

$$\text{Path slack} = \text{duration of critical path} - \text{path duration}$$

If we consider path C–H–I, it has a duration of 18, so its path slack is $21 - 18 = 3$ days, but path B–G–I has a path slack of only one day. Since activity I is on both paths, its slack is always the lesser of the two paths, one day in this case.

Before leaving the topic of slack, it is important to point out that the slack times computed for individual activities are not additive over a path. To illustrate, both activities C and H have slacks of three days, but if we use those three days for activity C, starting it at day 3 instead of 0, there is then no slack for activities H or I. The point is that slack times for individual activities are computed on the assumption that only one particular activity is delayed.

2.4.2 Project Scheduling with Uncertain Activity Times

The previous section discussed project planning in situations where the activity completion times were known with certainty before the project was actually started. In reality, however, project activity times are frequently not known with certainty beforehand. In these cases, PM often develops three estimates for each activity: an optimistic time t_o, a pessimistic time t_p, and a most likely time t_m. The *optimistic time* is the amount of time the PM estimates it will take to complete the activity under ideal conditions; that is, only one time in a hundred would it take less time than this. The *pessimistic time* refers to how long the activity will take to complete under the worst-case scenario; again, there is only a 1% chance it would ever take longer than this. The *most likely time* is the PM's best estimate of how long the activity will actually take to complete. In addition to these three time estimates, the precedence relationships among the activities are needed as inputs to the project planning process.

The primary outputs of project planning when activity times are not known with certainty include the following:

- Graphical representation of the entire project, showing all precedence relationships among the activities

- Expected activity and path completion times

- Variance of activity and path completion times

- Probability that the project will be completed by a specified time

- The time corresponding to a specified probability of the project being complete

In Table 2.2, we present the three activity times that gave rise to the expected times in Table 2.1. Table 2.2 also includes the variance of the expected time, whose calculation, as well as the calculation of the expected time, we describe next.

2.4.2.1 Calculating Activity Durations

The estimates of the three activity times in Table 2.2 are based on the assumption that the activities are independent of one another. Therefore, an activity whose duration is changed will not necessarily affect the duration of the other activities. Additionally, it is assumed that the difference between t_o and t_m need *not* be the same as the difference between t_p and t_m. For example, a critical piece of equipment may be wearing out. If it is working particularly well, this equipment can do a task in two hours that normally takes three hours; but if the equipment is performing poorly, the task may require 10 hours. Thus, we may see nonsymmetrical optimistic and pessimistic task times for project activities, as for activities E and H in Table 2.2. Note also that for some activities, such as B, the durations are known with certainty.

The general form of nonsymmetrical or skewed distribution used in approximating PERT activity times is called the beta distribution and has a mean (expected completion time t_e) and a variance, or uncertainty in this time, σ^2, as given in the following text. The beta distribution is used because it is flexible enough to allow one tail of the distribution to be longer than the other (more things will typically go worse-than-expected than will go better-than-expected in

Table 2.2   Six Sigma Activity Times (Days)

Project activity	Optimistic time t_o	Most likely time t_m	Pessimistic time t_p	Expected time t_e, and variance σ^2
A	5	11	11	10, 1
B	10	10	10	10, 0
C	2	5	8	5, 1
D	1	7	13	7, 4
E	4	4	10	5, 1
F	4	7	10	7, 1
G	2	2	2	2, 0
H	0	6	6	5, 1
I	2	8	14	8, 4
J	1	4	7	4, 1

a project) and is thus a more appropriate distribution for activity completion times. The following formulas are used to calculate the expected activity time and the variance of the activity time, respectively:

$$t_e = \frac{t_o + 4t_m + t_p}{6}$$

$$\sigma^2 = \left(\frac{t_p - t_o}{6}\right)^2$$

The previous equation for the expected completion time is simply a weighted average of the three time estimates, with weights of 1, 4, and 1, and the denominator of 6 is, of course, the sum of the weights. The value of 6 in the estimate of the variance, however, comes from a different source, the assumption that the optimistic and pessimistic times are each 3 standard deviations from the mean. This only applies, however, to estimates made at the 99% certainty level. If a manager is reluctant to make estimates at that level and feels that a 95%, or 90%, level is easier to estimate, then the equations for the standard deviation change (the approximation for the mean is still acceptable, however) to

$$95\% \text{ level}: \quad \sigma = \left(t_p - t_o\right)/3.3$$

$$90\% \text{ level}: \quad \sigma = \left(t_p - t_o\right)/2.6$$

The results of these calculations (at the 99% level) are listed in Table 2.2.

The discussion of project management with known activity times included critical paths, critical activities, and slack. These concepts are not quite as useful in situations where activity times are not known with certainty. Without knowing the activity times with certainty, any of the paths may have the potential to be the longest path. Furthermore, we will not know which of the paths will take longest to complete until the project is actually completed. And since we cannot determine with certainty before the start of the project which path will be critical, we cannot determine how much slack the other paths have. We can, however, use probability estimates and simulation to help us gain more confidence, as described in the next two subsections.

2.4.2.2 Probabilities of Completion

When activity times are not known with certainty, we cannot determine how long it will actually take to complete the project. However, using the variance of each activity (the variances in Table 2.2), we can compute the likelihood or probability of completing the project in a given time period, assuming that the activity durations and paths are independent of each other. The distribution of a path's completion time will be approximately normally distributed if the path has a large number of activities on it. (Recall from the central limit theorem in statistics that this is true regardless of the distribution of the activities themselves, beta in our case.) For example, the mean time along path A–D–J was found to be 21 days. The variance is found by summing the variances of each of the activities on the path. In our example, this would be

$$V_{\text{path A–D–J}} = \sigma_A^2 + \sigma_D^2 + \sigma_J^2 = 1 + 4 + 1 = 6$$

The probability of completing this path in, say, 23 days is then found by calculating the standard normal deviate of the desired completion time less the expected completion time, and using the table of the standard normal probability distribution (inside rear cover) to find the corresponding probability:

$$Z = \frac{\text{desired completion time} - \text{expected completion time}}{\sqrt{V}} = \frac{23 - 21}{\sqrt{6}} = 0.818$$

which results in a probability of 79% (see Figure 2.8). This can also be found in Excel® using the NORM.DIST function with the syntax = NORM.DIST(D, t_e, σ, TRUE), where D is the desired project completion time, 23 days in our case. Similarly, we can calculate that completion time by which we would be, say, 90% sure the project would be completed. From Appendix A, we find the standard normal deviate corresponding to 90% as about 1.28, so $21 + (1.28\sqrt{V}) = 24.14$ days. Again, this could also be found in Excel® from the NORM.INV function with syntax = NORM.INV (probability, t_e, σ), which in our case would be = NORM.INV (0.90, 21, 2.449) = 24.14 days.

So far, we have determined only that there is a 79% chance that path A–D–J will be completed in 23 days or less. If we were interested in calculating the probability that the entire project will be completed in 23 days, we would need to calculate the probability that all paths will be finished within 23 days. To calculate the probability that all paths will be finished in 23 days or less, we first calculate the probability that each path will be finished in 23 days or less, as we just did for path A–D–J. Then, we multiply these probabilities together to determine the probability that all paths will be completed by the specified time. The reason we multiply these probabilities together is that we are assuming that path completion times are independent of one another. Of course, if the paths have activities in common, they are not

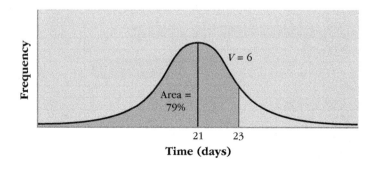

FIGURE 2.8
Probability Distribution of Path Completion Time

truly independent of one another, and a more complex analysis such as simulation, illustrated next, is necessary.

To simplify the number of calculations required to compute the probability that a project will be completed by some specified time, for practical purposes it is reasonable to include only those paths whose expected time plus 2.33 standard deviations is more than the specified time. The reason for doing this is that if the sum of a path's expected time and 2.33 of its standard deviations is less than the specified time, then the probability that this path will take longer than the specified time is very small (i.e. less than 1%), and, therefore, we assume that the probability that it will be completed by the specified time is 100%. Finally, note that to calculate the probability that a project will take longer than some specified time, we first calculate the probability that it will take less than the specified time and then subtract this value from 1.

2.4.2.3 Simulating Project Completion Times

When activity times are uncertain, it is usually not possible to know which path will be the critical path before the project is actually completed. In these situations, simulation analysis can provide some insights into the range and distribution of project completion times. To illustrate this, we use the network diagram in Figure 2.9 consisting of six activities labeled A–F.

Based on historical data, it has been determined that all the activity times are approximately triangularly distributed, with the optimistic, most likely, and pessimistic times given in the nodes of Figure 2.9 following the letter of the activity. Inspection of the network diagram reveals three paths: A–C–F, B–D–F, and B–E.

To simulate the completion of this project using Crystal Ball® (see www.oracle.com/crystalball/index.html for details on Crystal Ball®), the spreadsheet in Figure 2.10 was developed.

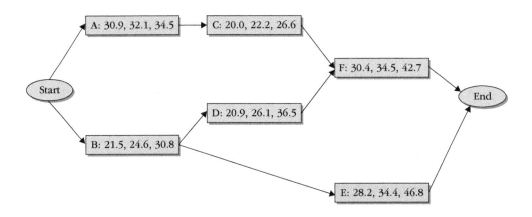

FIGURE 2.9
Example Network for Simulating

	A	B	C	D	E	F	G	H	I	J
1	Activity	Activity	Activity	Activity	Activity	Activity	Path	Path	Path	Completion
2	A	B	C	D	E	F	ACF	BDF	BE	Time
3	32.1	24.6	22.2	26.1	34.4	34.5	88.8	85.2	59	88.8
4										
5										
6							Assumption Cells		Forecast Cell	
7										
8										
9	Formulae:									
10	Cell G3	= A3 + C3 + F3								
11	Cell H3	= B3 + D3 + F3								
12	Cell I3	= B3 + E3								
13	Cell J3	= MAX (G3:I3)								

FIGURE 2.10
Spreadsheet for Simulating the Project

FIGURE 2.11
Simulation Results

In the spreadsheet, completing the project is simulated by generating random numbers for the six activities and then adding up the activity times that make up each path to determine how long the paths take to complete. The longest path determines the project completion time.

In the spreadsheet, randomly generated activity times from a triangular distribution for each activity are generated in cells A3:F3 by defining these cells as assumption cells. For example, cell A3 was defined as an assumption cell with a triangular distribution with minimum, likeliest, and maximum values of 30.9, 32.1, and 34.5, respectively. In column G, the time to complete path A–C–F is calculated based on the activity times generated in cells A3:F3. For example, in cell G3,the formula =A3+C3+F3 was entered. In a similar manner, cells H3 and I3 are used to calculate the time to complete paths B–D–F and B–E, respectively. Cell J3 keeps track of when the project is actually completed on a given replication. Since the longest path determines the time when the project is completed, =MAX(G3:I3) was entered in cell J3.

The results of simulating the project 10,000 times are summarized in Figure 2.11. The results indicate that, on average, the project required 92.18 days to complete. Furthermore, across the 10,000 replications of the project, the fastest project completion time was 83.64 days and the longest was 106.64 days. The simulation package can also show the probabilities of completing the project before any given date, or after any given date, or even between any two dates.

2.4.3 Project Management Software Capabilities

A wide range of project management software packages and capabilities are available, depending on the project needs and the funds available. The main aspects to consider when selecting a package are the capabilities required and the time and money available to invest in a package. If the project is very large and complex, or if it interacts with a number of other projects that must also be managed with the software, then some of the more sophisticated packages are appropriate. However, not only do these cost more, but they also take longer to learn. On the other hand, if the project is simpler, a less elaborate package that is easier to learn and use may be the best choice.

A yearly survey and analysis of such packages are conducted by the PMI. These surveys give details on the friendliness of each package, their capabilities (schedules, calendars, budgets, resource diagrams and tables, graphics, migration capabilities, report generation, tracking capability, etc.), their computer requirements, and their cost.

Probably, the most commonly used package these days is Microsoft's Project. This package is fairly sophisticated for the cost and is extremely easy to learn and use. Examples of some of its report capabilities are given in Figures 2.12 and 2.13.

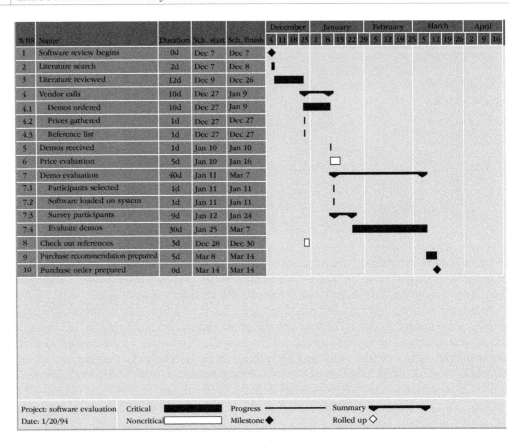

FIGURE 2.12
Microsoft Project's
Gantt Chart for a
Software Information
System Upgrade

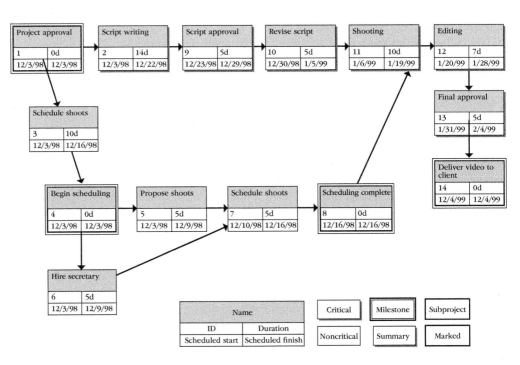

FIGURE 2.13 PERT
Chart Generated by
Microsoft Project for a
Video Sales Tool

2.4.4 Goldratt's Critical Chain[1]

In *Critical Chain*, Eliyahu Goldratt (1997) applies his theory of constraints (described in Chapter 9) to the field of project management. In this theory, he primarily focuses on three phenomena that tend to bias the expected completion time of projects, based on the network techniques we described previously, toward shorter times than occur in reality. These three phenomena are inflated activity time estimates, activity time variability with path interdependencies, and resource dependence.

2.4.4.1 Inflated Activity Time Estimates

Assuming that project workers have a general desire to be recognized for good performance, what do you imagine they do when they are asked to provide time estimates for tasks they will be responsible for completing? Do you imagine they provide their most likely estimate which may have only a 50% chance of being met? Or, more likely, do you imagine they inflate, or *pad,* their estimate to increase the likelihood of successfully completing the task on time? What would you do?

We suspect that if you are like most people, you would tend to somewhat inflate your time estimate. Unfortunately, inflated time estimates tend to create even more problems. First, inflating the time estimate has no impact on the actual probability distribution of completing the activity. Second, what happens in cases where a project team member finishes early? More than likely, the team member believes that it is in his or her best interest to remain silent about completing activities in less than the allotted time so that future time estimates are not automatically discounted by management based on a track record of early task completions. Moreover, there are sometimes penalties for completing early, such as storage of materials.

Third, just as things tend to fill the available closet and storage space in your home, work tends to fill the available time. Thus, the scope of the task may be expanded to fill the available time. Perhaps even more dangerous than the inflated estimate becoming a self-fulfilling prophecy is that, after receiving approval for a task based on an inflated time estimate, workers may perceive that they now have plenty of time to complete the task and therefore *delay starting the task.* Goldratt refers to this as the *student syndrome,* likening it to the way students often delay starting assignments until the last minute. The problem of delaying the start of a task is that obstacles are frequently not discovered until the task has been under way for some time. If the start of the task is delayed, the opportunity to effectively deal with these obstacles and complete the task on time is greatly diminished.

2.4.4.2 Activity Time Variability with Path Interdependencies

Another factor that tends to favorably bias the expected project completion time is the effect of variability in the activity times when there are multiple and interconnecting paths in a network. First, consider a project with, say, 10 activities all in a line (i.e. in series), each of the same expected duration and variability. It seems clear that if random events affect the activities, some will finish early and others late, but the general overall effect will be that the early completions will largely offset the late completions and the project will finish about when expected. However, suppose now that another project also has 10 activities, but they are all in parallel, and all must be completed to complete the project. Since the project will not be done until every activity is completed, the slowest activity of the 10 – that is, the one whose random events delay the activity the most – will be the one that determines when the project is actually completed.

---

[1] Adapted from J. R. Meredith, and S. M. Shafer. *Project Management in Practice*, 7th ed. Hoboken, NJ: Wiley, 2021.

Most projects are not like either of the previous two examples but instead have many activities in series and many in parallel. As we saw previously, the activities in series tend to cancel out their random effects, but this is not true of the parallel activities, which tend to delay the project. Eventually, all the interacting paths of activities throughout the network act like our parallel activities and have a delaying effect on the project due to their random variations. In particular, if there is another path(s) through the network that is close to the length of the path with the longest expected duration and has substantial variability, it is quite likely that this path, rather than the supposedly "critical path," will determine when the project is completed.

2.4.4.3 Resource Dependence

Last, it frequently happens that some activities need the same (scarce) resource (perhaps a machine, or a particularly skilled person) at the same time. If this happens, then there is no alternative but for one activity to wait until the other activity has finished with the resource, unless, of course, the organization is willing to spend extra funds to acquire or rent another resource – but this will then negatively affect the budget. As a result, resource dependence within a project can also seriously delay a project beyond its expected completion time based on the critical path.

Goldratt's approach for addressing these three issues is based on elementary statistics. It is easily shown that the amount of safety time needed to protect a particular path in a project is less than the sum of the safety times required to protect the individual activities making up the path. The same approach is commonly used in inventory management, where it can be shown that less safety stock is needed at a central warehouse to provide a certain service level to customers than the amount of safety stock that would be required to provide this same service level if carried at multiple distributed (e.g. retail) locations.

Based on this intuition, Goldratt suggests reducing the amount of safety time added to individual tasks and using some fraction of that reduction as a safety buffer for the entire project, called the *project buffer*. The amount of time each task is reduced depends on how much of a reduction is needed to get project team members to change their behavior. For example, the allotted time for tasks should be reduced to the point that the student syndrome is eliminated. To motivate the project team members, Goldratt suggests using activity durations where in fact there is a high probability that the task will *not* be finished on time.

To address the need to consider both precedence relationships and resource dependencies, Goldratt proposes thinking in terms of the longest chain of consecutively dependent tasks where such dependencies can arise from a variety of sources, including precedence relationships among the tasks and resource dependencies. Goldratt coined the term *critical chain* to refer to the longest chain of consecutively dependent activities.

Based on this definition of the critical chain, there are two potential sources that can delay the completion of a project. Similar to the critical path concept, one source of delay is the tasks that make up the critical chain. The project buffer discussed earlier is used to protect against these delays (see Figure 2.14). But, as noted previously, tasks external to the critical chain can also delay the completion of the project if these delays end up delaying one or more of the tasks on the critical chain. As shown in Figure 2.14, safety time can be added to these paths as well to ensure that they do not delay tasks on the critical chain. The safety time added to chains other than the critical chain is called a *feeding buffer*, since these paths often feed into the critical chain. Thus, the objective of feeding buffers is to ensure that noncritical chains are completed so that they do not delay tasks on the critical chain.

Clearly, activities on the critical chain should be given the highest priority. Likewise, to ensure that resources are available when needed, they should be contacted at the start of the project. It is also wise to keep these resources updated on the status of the project and to remind them periodically of when their input will be needed. Goldratt suggests reminding these resources two weeks before the start of their work, then three days prior to their start, and finally the day before they

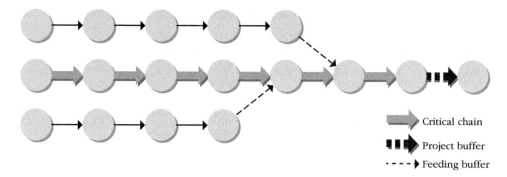

Critical chain

Project buffer

Feeding buffer

FIGURE 2.14
Project and Feeding
Buffers

start. Since any delay of an activity on the critical chain can cause a delay of the entire project, it is important that a resource immediately switch to the task on the critical chain when needed.

2.4.5 Agile Project Management[2]

With Agile project management (APM), a project is completed in stages that last from one to four weeks. These stages are commonly referred to as iterations, sprints, or milestones. During each stage, project team members are given detailed instructions on the work that is to be completed during the stage. Furthermore, a key element of APM is that the quality of the work for a given stage must be approved before the next stage can be started. Verifying that the quality standards are met at the end of each stage well positions the project team to identify the causes of problems and make rapid adjustments. In the old, traditional approach to project management before business case updating, long gaps between the creation and identification of problems could impede correcting the problems.

In contrast to the traditional waterfall approach to project management where progress flows from one stage to another, APM utilizes fixed length stages or iterations. Also, based on lean principles (discussed in Chapter 9), APM emphasizes maximizing the value of the project *as defined by the customer*. Another key characteristic of APM is that it incorporates adaptive planning such that the project plan and business case are updated as circumstances change. Table 2.3 further contrasts APM from the previous traditional waterfall approach.

While APM was originally developed for software development, it has been applied to other areas including product development and engineering. A number of benefits are commonly attributed to APM including:

- Better project outcomes as a result of issues being identified earlier.

- Increased customer satisfaction as a result of receiving customer input and feedback throughout the project.

- Improved morale of project team members resulting from the use of self-managed teams and having greater autonomy. Furthermore, the short iterations help mitigate employee burnout.

- Increased collaboration and project visibility resulting from daily sprint reviews.

With all the attention that APM is receiving, it is important to point out that many of its tenants can be easily incorporated in more traditional project management approaches. For example, there is nothing that prevents increasing customer involvement in the traditional waterfall

---

[2] Adapted from Meredith and Shafer (2021).

Table 2.3   Comparison of Agile Project Management with Traditional Waterfall Approach

Dimension	Agile project management	Traditional waterfall approach
Planning	Short-term plans that are adjusted as project progresses	Attempts to stick to long-term plans made in advance
Client involvement	Throughout the project	Beginning and end of project
Project execution	Broken down into incremental stages called iterations	Work completed based on comprehensive and highly structured plan
Communication	Open, frequent (daily) communication among stakeholders encouraged	Mainly for project control
Feedback on results	At the end of each iteration	At the end of the project
Work structure	Integrated cross-functional team	Team members tend to work independently and rely on project manager to coordinate tasks
Project leadership	Self-managed teams	Project manager allocates work to team members
Team member feedback	Open communication encouraged by all team members	Feedback typically provided confidentially by project manager
Process ownership	Team	Project manager
Experimentation	Encouraged to identify ways to best meet customer requirements	Discouraged in order to meet project deadline and stay on budget
Scope	Flexible	Rigid
Change	Welcome and expected part of project	Resisted and often requires formal change order request

approach. Likewise, there is nothing inherent to traditional project management that prohibits greater experimentation. The point being, that rather than viewing APM as an all or nothing approach to project management, there is nothing that precludes a project manager from adopting a subset of APM best practices. That is, there is a continuum between traditional project management and Agile. Some projects will do better with something close to Agile and some better with the blend closer to traditional. Finally, it is worth noting that related to the popularity of APM, the Project Management Institute offers a certification in APM-the Agile Certified Practitioner (PMI-ACP).

2.5 Expediting the Project: Trade-Offs Between Cost and Time

In the previous section, we examined how statistical analysis and computer simulation can be used to estimate the probability of completing a project by a specified time. But what if this analysis indicates that the probability of completing the project within the desired timeframe is too low? This is precisely the issue we address in this section. More specifically, we examine cost–time trade-offs for speeding up the completion of the project.

So what do we mean by time–cost trade-offs? In the case of completing a project, it is often possible to add additional resources to or use better resources for one or more project activities to complete these activities in less time. Doing so is useful in cases where completing the project at a normal pace would result in completing the project after the desired completion time. Adding additional resources may also be desirable in cases where the project falls behind schedule.

Of course, adding additional resources or better resources will almost certainly result in additional costs.

Managing these types of trade-offs is indeed one of the primary roles of the PM. In fact, it is almost always possible for the PM to trade-off one of the three generic project objectives of performance, budget, and time that comprise the triple constraint to perform better on one or two of the other objectives. In this section, our focus is to evaluate the desirability of incurring additional costs relative to the impact this will have on reducing the project completion time.

Adding additional resources or using better resources to reduce the time it takes to complete one or more project activities is referred to as *crashing*. More specifically, project crashing or "crashing", for short, refers to reducing the project completion time by using additional resources or perhaps utilizing better resources. The crash time refers to the shortest amount of time an activity can be completed and the crash cost refers to the cost of reducing the activity to the crash time.

As alluded to a moment ago, our goal then is to find the most cost-effective way for reducing the project duration. This is perhaps best understood by looking at it visually.

The graph shown in Figure 2.15 corresponds to one of the activities in a project. More specifically, the graph provides information related to how long the activity will take to complete and what it will cost to complete it working at both a normal pace and an expedited pace. From the graph, we observe that completing the activity at a normal pace will take seven days and cost $250. Furthermore, we observe that by using additional resources, the duration of the activity can be shortened or crashed to four days but at a cost of $340. Thus, we observe that by spending an extra $90 this activity's duration can be shortened or crashed by three days.

Typically, an activity can be shortened in increments. In other words, it is not an all or nothing decision. For the activity shown in the graph, this means that while the activity will take seven days to complete at a normal pace and that it can be completed in as little as four days by spending an extra $90, there may be other possibilities between these two extremes. For example, it may be possible to spend half of the $90 to shorten the duration of the activity by 1.5 days instead of shortening it by a full three days. This logic is also reflected in the graph. More specifically, the slope of the line segment between the normal activity point and the crashed activity point represents the crash cost per day. Unless stated otherwise, we generally assume that an activity can be partially crashed. In our example, this means the PM could consider crashing the activity 1 day, 2 days, 3 days, or even a fraction of a day such as 1.5 days or 2.75 days.

With this background on crashing, let's now turn our attention to applying these concepts to an entire project. For this example, we will refer to the project shown in Figure 2.16. Table 2.4 provides additional information for the project activities including the activity normal times and costs and the activity crash times and costs. From the information given, we can easily determine

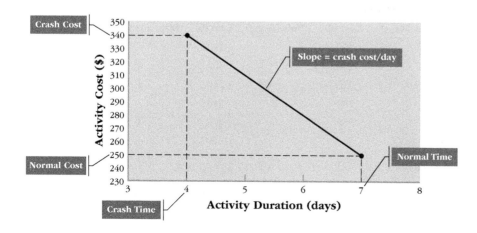

FIGURE 2.15
Time–Cost Trade-off
for an Activity

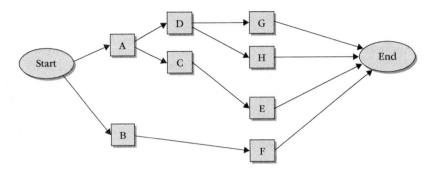

FIGURE 2.16
Example Project

that there are four paths through this project including: A–D–G with a duration of 20 days, A–D–H with a duration of 22 days, A–C–E with a duration of 17 days, and B–F with a duration of 20 days. Thus, path A–D–H is the critical path and activities A, D, and H are the critical activities. It is important to recognize this because if the goal is to shorten the duration of the project, then it is the critical path that must be shortened. Of course, as we shorten the critical path, one or more other paths will eventually become the critical path.

Referring to Table 2.4, the normal times or the amount of time it will take to complete the activities working at a normal pace is provided in the second column. The third column provides the normal costs or the cost of completing the activities working at a normal pace. The fourth column provides the crash times or the shortest amount of time the activities can be completed in, while the fifth column provides the crash costs or the cost to complete the activities in the shortest amount of time. In the sixth column, the total allowable crash times are calculated as the difference between the normal times and crash times. Finally, the last column provides the cost slopes or in this case the crash costs per day. The formula for calculating the cost slope is

$$\text{Cost Slope} = \frac{\text{Crash Cost} - \text{Normal Cost}}{\text{Normal Time} - \text{Crash Time}}$$

For example, activity B has a normal cost of $200 and a crash cost of $300. Subtracting $200 from $300 indicates that crashing this activity as much as possible would result in spending an extra $100. Furthermore, crashing this activity as much as possible would reduce its duration by

Table 2.4 Time and Cost Information for the Example Project

Activity	Normal Time (days)	Normal Cost ($)	Crash Time (days)	Crash Cost ($)	Max crash days	Cost slope ($/day)
A	5	100	4	140	1	40
B	9	200	7	300	2	50
C	7	250	4	340	3	30
D	9	280	7	340	2	30
E	5	250	2	460	3	70
F	11	400	7	720	4	80
G	6	300	4	420	2	60
H	8	80	6	140	2	30
Total		$1860		$2860		

two days from nine days to seven days. In other words, an extra $100 can be spent to shorten activity B by two days which works out to spending $50 per day the activity is crashed:

$$\text{Cost Slope}_{\text{Activity B}} = \frac{300 - 200}{9 - 7} = \$50/\text{day}$$

Let's now examine the cost of gradually shortening the duration of the project one day at a time. To perform this analysis, we will rely on the last two columns of Table 2.4, namely, the total allowable crash time and the crash cost per week for each activity. A summary of the steps taken to shorten the project one day at a time is provided in Table 2.5. In particular, Table 2.5 shows the sequence in which the activities are crashed and the incremental costs incurred in crashing the activities.

As noted earlier, path A–D–H is the longest path with a duration of 22 days. However, because some of the activities are on more than one path, we need to keep track of the durations of all paths as we crash the activities so we know at each step which path or paths are critical.

Referring to the first row in Table 2.5 we observe that completing the project without crashing any of the activities will result in a project duration of 22 days (first column) at a total project cost of $1860 (last column). To shorten the project by one day would require crashing either activity A, D, or H by one day. Referring to Table 2.4, we observe that the costs of crashing activities A, D, and H by one day are $40, $30, and $30, respectively. While activities D and H are tied as having the lowest crash cost per day, we will start by crashing activity D since it appears on more paths and therefore will shorten more paths simultaneously.

Thus, referring to the second row in Table 2.5, activity D was selected as the first activity to crash. Crashing activity D shortens path A–D–G to 19 days and path A–D–H to 21 days. The other two paths are not impacted since activity D is not on these paths. Finally, crashing activity D by one day increases the project costs by $30 bringing the total project costs to $1890.

After crashing activity D by one day, path A–D–H remains as the sole critical path. Thus, to shorten the project duration by another day requires that this path be shortened another day. In the previous step, we determined that crashing activity D was the best strategy, and since activity D can be crashed by a total of two days (see Table 2.4), we will crash activity D another day. The result of doing this is shown in the third row of Table 2.5 where the project's duration has been reduced to 20 days and activity D has been crashed as much as possible.

With path A–D–H being reduced to 20 days, it now has the same duration as path B–F. Thus, there are now two critical paths, and shortening the project's duration requires that both paths be crashed. Since there are no activities in common on these two paths, shortening the project by another day will require crashing separate activities on each path. Activity D has already been

Table 2.5 Summary of Analysis to Shorten Project One Day at a Time

Project duration	Activity to crash	Path Durations				Added crash cost	Project cost
		A–D–G	A–D–H	A–C–E	B–F		
22		20	22	17	20	$0	$1,860
21	D	19	21	17	20	$30	$1,890
20	D	18	20	17	20	$30	$1,920
19	B, H	18	19	17	19	$80	$2,000
18	B, H	18	18	17	18	$80	$2,080
17	A, F	17	17	16	17	$120	$2,200

crashed the maximum amount so either activity A or H will have to be crashed on path A–D–H. Likewise, on path B–F either activity B or F will have to be crashed. Referring to Table 2.4, we observe that it is cheaper to crash activity H than activity A and that it is cheaper to crash activity B than F. This is reflected in the fourth row in Table 2.5.

After crashing B and H one day, paths A–D–H and B–F remain as the only critical paths. Furthermore, since both of these activities can be crashed two days, we choose to crash them another day to shorten the project by yet another day. The result of doing this is shown in the fifth row in Table 2.5. Also observe that we now have three critical paths: A–D–G, A–D–-H, and B–F.

Referring to path A–D–H, activities D and H have both been crashed their maximum two days. Therefore, the only option available to further reduce the duration of path A–D–H is to crash activity A. This has the benefit that also shortens path A–D–G. However, path B–F also has to be reduced by a day and activity B has been crashed its maximum of two days. Thus, activity F will also have to be crashed. The results of crashing activities A and F are shown in the last row of Table 2.5. At this point, all the activities on path A–D–H have been crashed their maximum amount, and it is therefore not possible to shorten this path any further. And while we could crash the other activities more, the project cannot be completed in any less time than 17 days since the duration of the longest path determines the duration of the project. Thus, 17 days is the fastest this project can be completed and would result in a total project cost of $2200.

As this example illustrates, there is a lot to keep track of when doing time–cost analysis including the activity crash costs, how much each activity can be crashed, which path(s) is currently the critical path, and so on. Creating a table similar to Table 2.5 is very helpful for keeping track of this information. While beyond our present scope, it is also worth pointing out that optimal crashing solutions can be found using mathematical programming.

So now that we have completed this time–cost trade-off analysis, what do we do with it? To make use of this analysis, it is helpful to create a graph that visually shows the time–cost trade-off that exists in the project. The graph for this example is shown in Figure 2.17. As you can see, the graph plots the project's duration taken from the first column of Table 2.5 on the horizontal axis and the total project costs from the last column of Table 2.5 on the vertical axis. This allows the PM to visually see the relationship between the project duration and the project cost. In the graph created for the example project, we observe that the project cost increases very slightly as the project duration is reduced from 22 days to 20 days. However, beyond this point, the cost of reducing the project's duration further increases more rapidly given the steeper slope of the line. Thus, in this case, it would likely be justified to crash the project to 20 days, but probably not justified to crash it further unless there were other strategic reasons or incentives for further reducing its duration.

FIGURE 2.17
Visualizing the Project
Cost–Duration
Trade-off

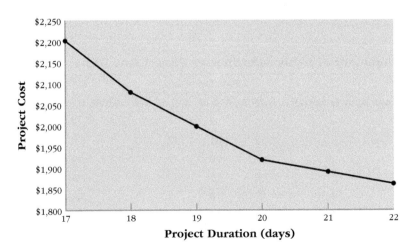

2.6 Controlling the Project: Cost and Performance

One of the control systems most widely used in projects is the cost variance report. Cost standards are determined through engineering estimates or through analysis of past performance. They become the target costs for the project. The actual costs are then monitored by the organization's cost-accounting system and are compared with the cost standard. Feedback is provided to the PM, who can exert any necessary control if the difference between standard and actual (called a variance) is considered significant.

As an example, consider the cost–schedule charts in Figure 2.18. In Figure 2.18a, actual progress is plotted alongside planned progress, and the "effective" progress time (TE) is noted. Because progress is less than planned, TE is less than the actual time (TA). On the cost chart (Figure 2.18b), we see that the apparent variance between the planned value and the actual cost at this time (PV – AC) is quite small, despite the lack of progress (earned value, EV). But this is misleading; the variance should be much more given the lack of progress.

These two graphs are combined for PM into an *earned value* chart – Figure 2.19 – where the planned value (PV), actual cost (AC), and earned value completed (actual earned dollars of progress, EV) are plotted. Here, we see that the actual cost variance is now substantial, given the poor progress and large schedule variance. Plotted in this manner, one chart will serve to monitor both progress and cost. We can then define three variances: (1) a *cost variance* equal to the value completed less the actual cost (EV – AC), where a cost overrun is negative; (2) a *schedule variance* equal to the value completed less the planned value (EV – PV), where "behind" is negative; and (3) a *time variance* equal to the effective time less the actual time (TE – TA), where a delay is negative.

When these variances are significant, the PM must identify (or at least attempt to identify) an *assignable cause* for the variance. That is, he or she must study the project to determine why the variance occurred. This is so that the proper remedy can be used to keep the variance from recurring. A corrective action is called for if some inefficiency or change in the prescribed process caused the variance.

Variances can be both favorable and unfavorable. A significant *favorable variance* (e.g. a variance resulting from a large quantity discount on material) will usually not require corrective action, though investigation is still worthwhile so that this better-than-expected performance can be repeated.

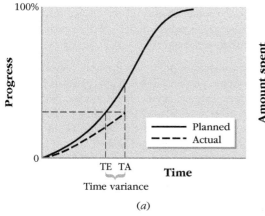

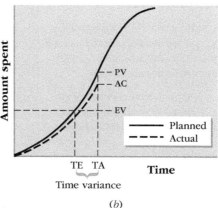

FIGURE 2.18
Cost–schedule
Reconciliation Charts

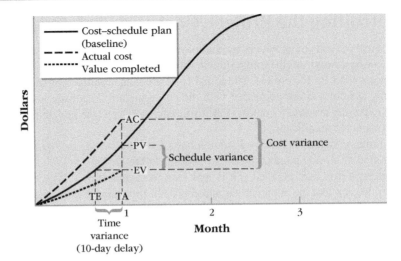

FIGURE 2.19
Earned Value Chart

EXPAND YOUR UNDERSTANDING

1. Frequently, the project's tasks are not well defined, and there is an urge to "get on with the work," since time is critical. How serious is it to minimize the planning effort and get on with the project?

2. Contrast the cost–schedule reconciliation charts with the earned value chart. Which one would a PM prefer?

3. How would a manager calculate the value completed for an earned value chart?

4. Do you think people's estimates are more accurate for optimistic or pessimistic activity times?

5. What do you think are the reasons for the tremendous growth in project management in our society?

6. Why doesn't it make sense to think in terms of a critical path when activity times are not known with certainty?

7. In calculating the probability that a project will be finished by some specified time, the probabilities of each path are multiplied together, on the assumption that the paths are independent of one another. How reasonable is this assumption?

8. Is the stretched-S life-cycle project form more common or the exponential form? What other aspects of managing a project are affected by the nature of the project form besides budgeting and early termination?

9. What do you think are the reasons for the topics of conflict among the project team in each stage of the project?

10. Given the powerful nature of project management software packages today, why should a PM have to know how to construct a PERT chart or WBS?

11. Given the ease of use of simulation software such as Crystal Ball®, what other data used in project management should probably be simulated?

12. Describe how to actually calculate earned value.

13. What does the project portfolio illustrate? How might it be useful to management?

14. Why do you think the need for a "project owner" is only now coming to be realized?

15. Do you think the risks to the project team's results are more or less difficult to overcome than the risks to the benefits of the project? Why?

16. Given the responsibilities of the PM vs. the project owner, which one do you think you would be better at?

17. How do the responsibilities of the change manager differ from those of the project owner? What responsibilities are different between them?

18. When calculating the probability that a project will finish by a specified time, the probabilities of each path being completed by the specified time are multiplied together. Why can't we multiply the probabilities of each path not finishing by the specified time together to get the probability of the project taking longer than the specified time?

19. Consider the differences between Agile Project Management and the traditional waterfall approach summarized in Table 2.3. Which practices associated with Agile do you see as having the greatest potential to complement the traditional waterfall approach?

20. Do you see any similarities between the Morgan et al. quote at the beginning of the chapter and the discussion of efficiency and effectiveness in Chapter 1?

21. How should a project manager go about determining which goal should be traded off for another?

22. Does the introduction of the extensive use of the business case throughout the execution of the project and the realization of its benefits bring it closer to the Agile approach? What is still different?

23. How might changes in the project to adjust to environmental changes initiate problems with external stakeholders?

24. Previously, the project "sponsor" was a senior manager with regular duties but now also responsible for obtaining the resources needed for a project. How responsive do you think a project's sponsor would have been to a resource problem in a project? Does the addition of a separate project "owner" help resolve those issues, and if so, how might it?

25. The chapter discusses sustainability as a fourth trade-off. Is it necessarily the case that pursuing sustainability objectives will require tradeoffs in cost, schedule, and performance?

Apply Your Understanding

E-Razor, Inc., A Strategic Budgeting Decision

After four years as a new start-up, e-Razor has expanded its line of programmable razors to include both linear and rotary models, as well as women's and teenagers' versions. Programming is simply done by the user through icons that adjust the speed of the cutting head, adjust the distance from the skin (to avoid ingrown hairs or give the sexy look of a day's growth), activate the trimmer, and so on. All the razors use the same electronics module to keep costs down.

e-Razor is now planning their budget for next year, including their investment in razor research, development, and product improvement, as well as investments in their production process to improve quality and lower costs. Eight projects have been proposed for top management's consideration, as follows:

A. Marketing would like to see the programmable functions extended to stay ahead of the competition, which might involve a new electronics module, the brain of the razor. Projected cost: $25,000.

B. Manufacturing believes a mixed model flow line would reduce costs and improve quality at the same time. To a large extent, the same production equipment as currently used in their job shop process could be reconfigured for the line and only a few new items would be needed. Projected cost: $11,000.

C. Marketing would also like to see the programmable feature extended to other health/beauty products, such as hair dryers, facial saunas. Projected cost to investigate and report: $16,000.

D. Sales has received feedback from customers that an engineering modification to the razor head allowing the razor to be used in the shower would make it much more useful. The production process would need to be modified somewhat. Projected cost: $9000.

E. Engineering has been evaluating a new user interface that would allow many new functions to be easily added. Moreover, it is faster and easier for the user to program. The current production process can be used. Projected cost: $17,000.

F. A consultant in chemistry who has been investigating the properties of tiny strands of cut hair for the firm believes there may be a way to keep the shaving head clean without opening the head enclosure and emptying or rinsing the head – a distasteful task for most people. Such a change would substantially change the production process. Projected cost: $22,000.

G. Sales has had inquiries from customers about whether a cheap, limited use version of the razor is available for business trips and vacations. A new production line would be required. Projected cost: $28,000.

H. Along the same line, customers have asked if a purely battery-driven (nonrechargeable) razor is available. This would primarily involve a change in the type of battery being used; the production process would be only slightly affected. Projected cost: $8000.

Questions

1. Construct an aggregate project plan for this portfolio of projects and place the projects on the diagram with the diameters of the circles representing their projected costs.

2. Analyze the diagram for balance across the categories. Are there any gaps or excesses? What should the distribution of projects look like for a firm of this age?

3. The total budget for these projects is limited to $100,000. Which projects would you suggest implementing?

Nutri-Sam: The Latin American Expansion Decision

Nutri-Sam produces a line of vitamins and nutritional supplements. It recently introduced its Nutri-Sports Energy Bar, which is based on new scientific findings about the proper balance of macronutrients. The energy bar has become extremely popular among elite athletes and others. One distinguishing feature of the Nutri-Sports Energy Bar is that each bar contains 50 mg of eicosapentaenoic acid (EPA), a substance strongly linked to reducing the risk of cancer but found in only a few foods, such as salmon. Nutri-Sam was able to include EPA in its sports bars because it had previously developed and patented a process to refine EPA for its line of fish-oil capsules.

Because of the success of the Nutri-Sports Energy Bar in the United States, Nutri-Sam is considering offering it in Latin America. With its domestic facility currently operating at capacity, the president of Nutri-Sam has decided to investigate the option of adding approximately 10,000 square feet of production space to its facility in Latin America at a cost of $5 million.

The project to expand the Latin American facility involves four major phases: (1) concept development, (2) definition of the plan, (3) design and construction, and (4) start-up and turnover. During the concept development phase, a project owner is chosen to oversee all four phases of the project and is given a budget to develop a plan. The outcome of the concept development phase is a rough plan, feasibility estimates for the project, and a rough schedule. Also, a justification for the project and a budget for the next phase are developed.

In the plan definition phase, the project owner selects a PM to oversee the activities associated with this phase. Plan definition consists of four major activities that are completed more or less concurrently: defining the project scope, developing a broad schedule of activities, developing detailed cost estimates, and developing a plan for staffing.

The output of this phase is a detailed plan and proposal for management specifying how much the project will cost, how long it will take, and what the deliverables are.

If the project gets management's approval and management provides the appropriations, the project progresses to the third phase, design and construction. This phase consists of four major activities: detailed engineering, mobilization of the construction employees, procurement of production equipment, and construction of the facility. Typically, the detailed engineering and the mobilization of the construction employees are done concurrently. Once these activities are completed, construction of the facility and procurement of the production equipment are done concurrently. The outcome of this phase is the physical construction of the facility.

The final phase, start-up and turnover, consists of four major activities: prestart-up inspection of the facility, recruiting and training the workforce, solving start-up problems, and determining optimal operating parameters (called centerlining). Once the prestart-up inspection is completed, the workforce is recruited and trained at the same time that start-up problems are solved. Centerlining is initiated upon the completion of these activities. The desired outcome of this phase is a facility operating at design requirements.

The following table provides optimistic, most likely, and pessimistic time estimates for the major activities.

Activity	Optimistic time (months)	Most likely time (months)	Pessimistic time (months)
A: Concept development	3	12	24
Plan definition			
B: Define project scope	1	2	12
C: Develop broad schedule	0.25	0.5	1
D: Detailed cost estimates	0.2	0.3	0.5
E: Develop staffing plan	0.2	0.3	0.6
Design and construction			
F: Detailed engineering	2	3	6
G: Facility construction	8	12	24
H: Mobilization of employees	0.5	2	4
I: Procurement of equipment	1	3	12
Start-up and turnover			
J: Prestart-up inspection	0.25	0.5	1
K: Recruiting and training	0.25	0.5	1
L: Solving start-up problems	0	1	2
M: Centerlining	0	1	4

Questions

1. Draw a network diagram for this project. Identify the four "near-critical" paths through the network diagram.

2. Find the probability that the project can be completed within 30 months. What is the probability that the project will take longer than 40 months? What is the probability that the project will take between 30 and 40 months?

3. [3]Use Crystal Ball® (or another simulation package) to simulate the completion of this project 10,000 times, assuming that activity times follow a triangular distribution. Estimate the mean and standard deviation of the project completion time. Compare your results to your answer to Question 2.

4. What types of information does Nutri-Sam's top management need that relate to the schedule to decide if they should approve this project at the end of the plan definition phase?

5. Will the project owner be helpful for this project? If so, with what aspects?

EXERCISES

2.1 The following AON chart was prepared at the beginning of an important software upgrade project. The duration, in days, follows the letter of each activity. What is the critical path? Which activities should be monitored most closely?

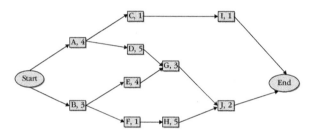

At the end of the first week, it was noted that activity A was completed in 2.5 days, but activity B required 4.5 days. What impact does this have on the project? Are the same activities critical?

2.2 Refer to Exercise 1. Compute the earliest start and finish times, the latest start and finish times, and the slack times for each activity. Also, calculate the slack for each path.

2.3 Given the following German Autobahn repair project, find the probability of completion by 17 weeks and by 24 weeks using the traditional statistical approach.

Activity	Times (weeks)			Required precedence
	Optimistic	Most likely	Pessimistic	
A	5	11	11	—
B	10	10	10	—
C	2	5	8	—
D	1	7	13	A

Activity	Times (weeks)			Required precedence
	Optimistic	Most likely	Pessimistic	
E	4	4	10	B
F	4	7	10	B
G	2	2	2	B
H	0	6	6	C
I	2	8	14	G,H
J	1	4	7	D, E

If the firm can complete the project within 18 weeks, it will receive a bonus of €10,000. But if the project is delayed beyond 22 weeks, it must pay a penalty of €5000. If the firm can choose whether or not to bid on this project, what should its decision be if this is normally only a breakeven project?

2.4 Construct a network for the project below and find its expected completion time.

Activity	t_e (Weeks)	Preceding activities
a	3	None
b	5	a
c	3	a
d	1	c
e	3	b
f	4	b, d
g	2	c
h	3	g, f
i	1	e, h

---

[3]Optional instructor-assigned question.

2.5 Estimated activity times and precedences are given below:

| | Times (days) | | | Required |
Activity	Optimistic	Most likely	Pessimistic	precedence
A	6	7	14	—
B	8	10	12	—
C	2	3	4	—
D	6	7	8	A
E	5	5.5	9	B, C
F	5	7	9	B, C
G	4	6	8	D, E
H	2.7	3	3.5	F

Using the traditional statistical approach, what is the probability that the project will be completed within:

(a) 21 days
(b) 22 days
(c) 25 days

2.6 Pusan Iron and Steel, located on the eastern coast of South Korea, is a major supplier of both girder and rolled steel to the emerging construction, appliance, and automobile companies of China. Due to growing sales volumes and the need for faster delivery, Pusan is converting its current single weigh station into a larger, multiple drive-through station. The new drive-through weigh station will consist of a heated, air-conditioned building with a large floor and a small office. The large room will have the scales, a 15-foot counter, and several display cases for its equipment.

Before erection of the building, the PM evaluated the project using CPM analysis. The following activities with their corresponding times in weeks were recorded.

| | | | Times | | |
#	Activity	Optimistic	Most likely	Pessimistic	Preceding tasks
1	Lay foundation	8	10	13	—
2	Dig hole for scale	5	6	8	—
3	Insert scale bases	13	15	21	2
4	Erect frame	10	12	14	1, 3
5	Complete building	11	20	30	4
6	Insert scales	4	5	8	5
7	Insert display cases	2	3	4	5
8	Put in office equipment	4	6	10	7
9	Give finishing touches	2	3	4	8, 6

Using CPM analysis, find the expected completion time.

2.7 As in the situation illustrated in Figure 2.19, an Irish Web-design project at day 70 exhibits only 35% progress when 40% was planned, for an effective date of 55. Planned value was €17,000 at day 55 and €24,000 at day 70, and actual cost was €20,000 at day 55 and €30,000 at day 70. Find the time variance, cost variance, and schedule variance at day 70.

2.8 As in the situation shown in Figure 2.19, a project at month 2 exhibited an actual cost of $78,000, a planned value of $84,000, and a value completed of $81,000. Find the cost and schedule variances. Estimate the time variance.

2.9 A project at month 5 had an actual cost of $34,000, a planned value of $42,000, and an earned value of $39,000. Find the cost and schedule variances.

2.10 Given a network:

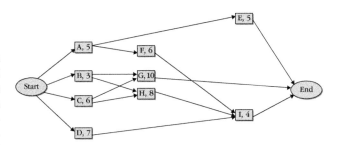

Note that four activities can start immediately. Find the following:

(a) Critical path
(b) Earliest time to complete the project
(c) Slack on activities E, F, and H

2.11 Given the activities data in the table below:

Activity	Times (weeks)	Preceding activities
A	3	—
B	6	—
C	8	—
D	7	A
E	5	B
F	10	C
G	4	C
H	5	D, E, F
I	6	G

(a) Draw the network.
(b) Find the critical path.
(c) Find the slacks on all activities.

2.12

Activity	Duration	Preceding activities
1	1	–
2	2	–
3	3	–
4	4	3
5	3	2, 4
6	8	3
7	2	2, 4
8	4	1, 5
9	2	17
10	6	2, 4
11	5	6, 10
12	10	7, 8, 11
13	11	7, 8, 11
14	1	6, 10
15	9	12
16	3	6, 10
17	8	12
18	6	13, 14, 15

(a) Draw the network diagram
(b) Find the critical path
(c) Find the completion time

2.13 In the project network shown in the following figure, the number alongside each activity designates its known duration in weeks. Determine the following:

(a) Earliest and latest start and finish times for each activity
(b) Earliest time that the project can be completed
(c) Slack for activities
(d) Critical activities
(e) Critical path

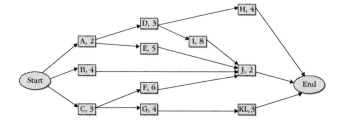

2.14 Referring to Exercise 2.3, find the probability of completing the project by 17 and 24 weeks using simulation and assuming the activity times are triangularly distributed. How do your answers compare using simulation and the traditional statistical approach? Which approach do you have the most confidence in?

2.15 Referring to Exercise 2.5, find the probability of completing the project by 21, 22, and 25 days using simulation and assuming the activity times are triangularly distributed. How do your answers compare using simulation and the traditional statistical approach? Which approach do you have the most confidence in?

2.16 Referring to Exercise 2.15, what is the probability that the path with the longest expected duration is actually the critical path? What does this suggest about the applicability of attempting to identify the critical path at the beginning of the project when activity times are uncertain?

2.17 Referring to Exercise 2.6, find the distribution of the project completion time using simulation and assuming the activity times are triangularly distributed. How is having the distribution of project completions times useful to a project manager? What is the probability the project can be completed between 65 and 70 weeks?

2.18 Given the following project (all times are in days):

Activity	Predecessor	Normal time	Normal cost	Crash time	Crash cost
A	—	3	$40	2	$80
B	A	2	20	1	80
C	A	2	20	2	20
D	A	4	30	1	120
E	B	3	10	1	80

(a) How much will it cost to complete the project at a normal pace?
(b) What is the shortest amount of time the project can be completed in? What is the cost of completing the project in the shortest amount of time?
(c) Create a graph showing the time–cost trade-off. Based on the graph, how much would you recommend the project be crashed?

2.19 Given the following project (all times are in days):

Activity	Predecessor	Normal time	Normal cost	Crash time	Crash cost
A	—	5	$50	3	$150
B	—	4	40	2	200
C	B	7	70	6	160
D	A, C	2	20	1	50
E	A, C	3	30	—	—
F	B	8	80	5	290
G	D	5	50	4	100
H	E, F	6	60	3	180

(a) How much will it cost to complete the project at a normal pace?

(b) What is the shortest amount of time the project can be completed in? What is the cost of completing the project in the shortest amount of time?

(c) Create a graph showing the time–cost trade-off. Based on the graph, how much would you recommend the project be crashed?

BIBLIOGRAPHY

Einhorn, F., J. Meredith, and C. Marnewick. "A Model to Guide the Effective Use of a Business Case for IT Projects," *International Journal of Managing Projects in Business*, 15(1) (2022):36–57.

Einhorn, F., J. Meredith, and C. Marnewick. "Business Case Effectiveness: The Critical Role of the Organization," *International Journal of Managing Projects in Business*, 13(5) (2020)):1051–1075.

Einhorn, F., C. Marnewick, and J. Meredith. "Achieving Strategic Benefits from Projects: The Critical Importance of Using the Business Case Over the Entire Project Lifetime," (with F.), *International Journal of Project Management*, 37(8) (2019):989–1002.

Englund, R. L., and R. J. Graham. "From Experience: Linking Projects to Strategy." *Journal of Product Innovation Management*, 16(1) (1999): 52–64.

Goldratt, E. M. *Critical Chain*. Great Barrington, MA: North River Press, 1997.

Keen, J. M. (2011). *Making Technology Investments Profitable: ROI Road Map from Business Case to Value Realization*. Hoboken, N.J.: Wiley.

Kopmann, J., Kock, A., Killen, C. P., and Gemunden, H. G. "Business Case Control in Project Portfolios – An Empirical Investigation of Performance Consequences and Moderating Effects." *IEEE Transactions on Engineering Management*, 62(4, 2015): 529–543.

Meredith, J. R., and S. M. Shafer. *Project Management in Practice*, 7th ed. New York: Wiley, 2021.

Meredith, J. R., and S. M. Shafer. *Project Management: A Strategic Managerial Approach*, 11th ed. New York: Wiley, 2022.

Meredith, J. R., and O. Zwikael. "Achieving Strategic Benefits from Project Investments." *Business Horizons*, 63 (September, 2020): 61–71.

Morgan, M., R. E. Levitt, and W. Malek. *Executing Your Strategy: How to Break It Down and Get It Done*. Boston, MA: Harvard Business School Press, 2007.

Project Management Institute. *The Standard for Project Management* and *A Guide to the Project Management Body of Knowledge*, 7th ed. Newtown Square, PA: Project Management Institute, 2022.

Sabini, L., and M. Alderman. "The Paradoxical Profession: Project Management and the Contradictory Nature of Sustainable Project Objectives." *Project Management Journal*, 52(4) (2021): 379–393

Sánchez, M.A. "Integrating Sustainability Issues into Project Management." *Journal of Cleaner Production*, 96 (2015): 319–330.

Silvius, G., and R.P.J. Schipper. "Sustainability in Project Management: A Literature Review and Impact Analysis." *Social Business*, 4(1) (2014): 63–96.

Schupak, A. "Migratory Patterns." *PM Network* (February 2014): 54–59.

Schupak, A., and T. Stains. "Consolidated Effort." *PM Network* (May 2014): 60–67.

Schur, M. "Waste Makes Haste." *PM Network*, 31 (November 2017): 30–35.

Siemens, "Battery storage: Efficient, sustainable and lucrative," new.siemens.com, May 12, 2021.

Thamhain, H. J., and D. L. Wilemon. "Conflict Management in Project Life Cycles." *Sloan Management Review* (Summer 1975): 31–50.

Wheelwright, S. C., and K. B. Clark. "Creating Project Plans to Focus Product Development." *Harvard Business Review* (March–April 1992): 2–14.

Zwikael, O., J. R. Meredith, and J. Smyrk. "The Responsibilities of the Project Owner in Benefits Realization." *International Journal of Operations and Production Management*, 39 (4, 2019): 503–524.

Zwikael, O., and J. R. Meredith. "Who's Who in the Project Zoo? The Ten Core Project Roles." *International Journal of Operations and Production Management*, 38 (2, 2018):474–492.

Zwikael, O., and J. R. Meredith. "Evaluating the Success of a Project and the Performance of its Leaders," *IEEE Transactions on Engineering Management*, 68 (6, 2019):1745–1757.

OUTPUT AND PROCESS PLANNING

In this second part of the book, "Output and Process Planning," we first describe in Chapter 3 output design and how to plan and design the organization's value-creating transformation and supply processes to produce and deliver the outputs. In Chapter 4, we expand our discussion of output and process planning and elaborate on the importance of planning for the amount to be offered as well as its timing through proper scheduling of the processes. In Chapters 5 and 6, we describe how to plan and manage the supply chain. Chapter 5 focuses on the supply chain strategy and the design of the supply chain. Chapter 6 then gets into the planning and analysis of the supply chain and its critical ties to the sales function.

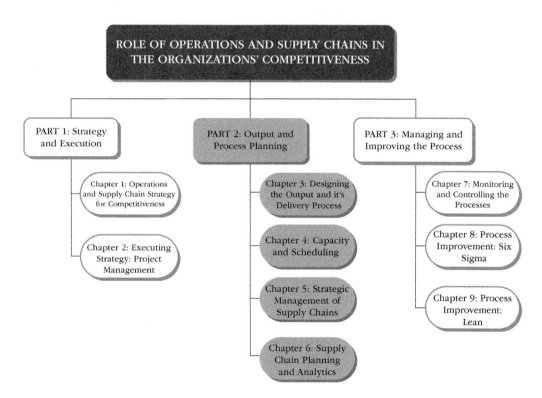

Designing the Output and its Delivery Process

CHAPTER IN PERSPECTIVE

Chapters 1 and 2 in Part 1 focused on determining a competitive strategy for the organization and planning its implementation. As we start Part 2, our first task is the design of the organization's outputs and the selection and design of the value-creating transformation process that will produce and deliver these outputs. Naturally, the organization's strategy should guide the choices and decisions made in these areas.

However, it is also important to emphasize that while output and process design should be guided by the organization's strategy, they also play a critical role toward achieving that strategy. With virtually all industries becoming more competitive, with shorter product life cycles and more sophisticated customers, the ability to continuously develop and improve products and services is critical to an organization's long-term survival. Likewise, often the ability to offer new products and deliver new services is dependent on the development and enhancement of production processes. At other times, the key to improving the quality of products and services and driving their costs down is a function of an organization's ability to innovate its production processes. The way outputs are designed, the materials used, and the production processes employed substantially impact an organization's carbon footprint and thus provide significant opportunities in helping organizations achieve their sustainability goals and commitments. Finally, if an organization is using the wrong production process, perhaps because the organization has changed or the market has changed over time, it will not be competitive.

The chapter begins with some examples and an overview of the design of the product or service, including the role of innovation and product/service development. Then we describe the five major types of transformation processes and their respective advantages and disadvantages. Next, issues related to the selection of a competitive transformation process, such as considerations of volume, variety, and life cycles, are discussed. Last, explicit attention is given to some of the unique aspects of designing service operations.

3.1 Introduction

- No discussion of global competitiveness would be complete without the inclusion of Apple Inc.'s amazing comeback from its near-death experience in the late 1990s. Under the futuristic vision of the late Steve Jobs, the firm's ability to innovate and develop user-friendly devices has been unparalleled in the electronics industry. Leveraging its capabilities to design user-friendly products and experiences, it has expanded the breadth of its offerings from personal computers to portable digital music players, smartphones, digital content through its iTunes, App, and iBook online stores, watches, tablet computers, and retail stores.

Unfortunately for the existing players in an industry, Apple's entrance into a new industry tends to disrupt the entire industry. For example, Apple's entry into the smartphone industry impacted a number of other industries. For instance, the mobile communication capabilities and productivity tools provided by smartphones have reduced the need for some people to own a personal computer. The telecom industry has also been impacted. Prior to smartphones, the main product of telecom companies was providing voice services. With the introduction of smartphones, the focus of telecoms has shifted to data services. As a side note, when was the last time you saw someone using a pay phone? The TV and movie industry has also been impacted by smartphones. With smartphones, consumers are as likely, if not more likely, to watch a TV show or movie on their smartphone as opposed to watching them on TVs or going to a movie theatre. The gaming industry represents yet another industry impacted by smartphones. In the past, playing video games required a computer, video game console, or dedicated handheld gaming device. Now these same video games can be played on a smartphone.

The watch industry is another industry impacted by Apple. In April 2015, Apple introduced the first version of its watch. By the fourth quarter of 2017, Apple's watch became the best-selling watch brand. Indeed, in a little over two years, Apple's watch outsold the entire Swiss Watch Industry, which includes major brands such as Rolex, Swatch, and Omega.

Beyond disrupting existing industries, Apple has created entirely new industries. For example, in July 2008 Apple launched its App Store with 500 Apps. By mid-2022, the number of apps in its App Store increased to almost 3.8 million and a total of 375 billion apps had been downloaded in the five-year period from 2017 to 2021. The success of Apple's App Store has greatly expanded the functionality of the iPhone as well as has created employment opportunities for almost 3 million app developers.

Beyond developing highly innovative and user-friendly products, Apple has also distinguished itself on the sustainability front. More specifically, designing and producing its products to have a smaller carbon footprint is an important component of its commitment to achieving its sustainability goals. For example, the gold used in the plating of its main logic boards, the rare earth elements used to produce magnets used in its products, the tungsten used in the Taptic Engine, and the solder on main logic boards are all made from 100% recycled materials. Apple has also designed its products to be more energy efficient. The result has been a 70 percent reduction in the amount of energy used by its products over a 12-year period. As another design example, Apple removed power adapters for its iPhone and Apple Watches. This in turn resulted in reducing the amount of copper, tin, and zinc used by 861,000 metric tons. The smaller and lighter packaging further reduces Apple's carbon footprint. Finally, Apple makes use of robots to disassemble iPhones and recover rare earth and other materials that can be used in new products.

Apple nicely illustrates the important role that operations capabilities in areas such as innovation and product design play in organization's global competitiveness. Apple also illustrates that pursuing sustainability objectives does not have to come at the expense of reduced competitiveness. Indeed, Apple's overwhelming success is reflected in its market capitalization. At the end of 2014, Apple became the most valuable company of all time as its market capitalization crossed the $700 billion mark. In August of 2018 Apple became the first company to reach a market capitalization of $1 trillion and in August of 2020 it became the first company to reach a $2 trillion market capitalization (Cheng and Intindola 2012; Bajarin 2017; Statistica 2019).

- Louis Vuitton, one of the luxury goods brands of giant LVMH Moët Hennessy Louis Vuitton, has the unusual problem of making its products in volume for the world's rich, and aspiring rich, while maintaining an image that its products are limited edition and exclusive, which many of its products are. Vuitton has classically used a job shop to make their famous runway pieces, bags, travel cases, wallets, and other items. In the old days, some workers would cut fabric, others would sew together leather panels, some would glue in linings, still others would attach handles, and so on.

These days, technology has been used to replace manual labor for higher productivity and greater consistency, such as the robots that fetch shoe molds and the computer software that helps program how to cut leather to avoid flaws in the skins. Another approach – cellular manufacturing – has also been used for some items. In these cells, small teams of six or more workers performed a few different tasks around a U-shaped cluster of workstations and passed their work around the cluster to produce a finished product in one-eighth the time the job shop required. In addition, fewer workers were needed, and defects were caught sooner – returns of faulty handbags and wallets dropped by two-thirds after Vuitton implemented the cellular production process (Passariello 2006, 2011).

- Martin Marietta's aerospace electronics manufacturing facility in Denver, Colorado, was initially set up as a job shop with numerous functional departments. As is typical of most job shops, the Marietta plant had high levels of work-in-process (WIP) and long lead times, and parts had to travel long distances throughout the plant to have their processing completed. Also, as is typical of functional organizations, departmental divisions created barriers to communication and often resulted in conflicting goals. To address these problems, Martin Marietta organized its plant into three "focused factories." Each focused factory was completely responsible and accountable for building electronic assemblies for a particular application (e.g. flight, space, or ground use). The intent was to make each focused factory a separate business enterprise.

  A factory manager was assigned to each focused factory. The factory managers then engaged in a sort of "NFL draft" to select employees for their teams. Workers not drafted had to find other positions either inside or outside the company. Within the focused factories, product families were identified; these were based on the technology and processing requirements of the products. Next, standardized routings and sequences were identified for each product family. The plant realized a number of improvements as a result of these and other changes, including seven consecutive months of production with no scrap, a 50% reduction in WIP inventory, a 21% average reduction in lead times, and a 90% reduction in overtime (Ferras 1994).

These examples illustrate topics related to product and process design projects that are addressed in this chapter. Apple, well known for its ability to design electronic devices that are intuitive and easy to use, demonstrates the competitive advantage an organization can obtain through the design of superior products and services and the increasing importance of considering sustainability in the design of outputs. And because product and process design initiatives are typically completed via projects, the material in this chapter exemplifies the growth of the project economy described in Chapter 1 earlier.

Once outputs are designed, attention next shifts to properly designing the value-creating transformation process.[1] As we explore in the chapter, there are several generic types of transformation systems. The Louis Vuitton factory was originally organized as a *job shop* that had specialized departments for cutting, stitching, gluing, and so on. Although some of its products are still produced in this manner, others (typically those with higher volumes) are produced using a *cellular production process*. Martin Marietta was also originally organized as a job shop but converted into *focused factories*, which actually takes cellular production a step further. One question that naturally arises is: How important is it for an organization to select the appropriate transformation process?

As we noted in Chapter 1, the sand cone model of additive and complementary competitive strengths emphasizes operations that can deliver quality, delivery dependability, speed, and low cost.

---

[1] We use the term *value-creating process* here to be clear that the overarching objective of the transformation process or transformation system is to create value for the customer. However, in the spirit of being more concise, for the remainder of the chapter we will mainly use the terms transformation process or transformation system noting that these terms include the implied purpose of creating value for the customer.

An important ingredient in achieving these strengths is selecting the most appropriate transformation process design and layout for the organization's operations. There are various basic forms of transformation process designs, each with its own layout, as well as myriad combinations and hybrids of them. This chapter describes these transformation systems, how the operations are laid out for each of them, and how to select the most appropriate one for maximum competitiveness.

The general procedure for selecting a transformation system is to consider all alternative forms and combinations to devise the best strategy for obtaining the desired outputs. The major considerations in designing and selecting the transformation system – *efficiency, effectiveness, volume, capacity, lead time, flexibility*, and so on – are so interdependent that changing the system to alter one will change the others as well. And the layout of the operations is another aspect that must be considered in the selection of the transformation system. The main purpose of *layout analysis* is to maximize the efficiency (cost orientation) or effectiveness (e.g. quality, lead time, and flexibility) of operations. Other purposes also exist, such as reducing safety or health hazards, minimizing interference or noise between different operational areas (e.g. separating painting from sanding), facilitating crucial staff interactions, or maximizing customers' exposure to products or services.

In laying out service operations, the emphasis may instead be on accommodating the customer rather than on operations per se. Moreover, capacity and layout analyses are frequently conducted simultaneously by analyzing service operations and the wait that the customer must endure. Thus, *waiting line* (or *queuing*) *theory,* a topic discussed in Chapter 4, is often used in the design of a service delivery system. The layouts of parking lots, entry zones, reception rooms, waiting areas, service facilities, and other points of customer contact are of top priority in service-oriented organizations such as clinics, stores, nightclubs, restaurants, and banks.

In the frequently changing environment of the project economy, the transformation system and its layout will have to be constantly monitored and frequently redesigned to cope with new demands, new products and services, new government regulations, and new technology. The project economy, technology, increasing global competition, sustainability, the green movement, and shortages of materials and energy are only a few examples of changes in the recent past that have forced organizations to recognize the necessity of adapting their operations.

3.2 Output Design and Innovation

It is widely recognized that the environment confronting organizations today is increasingly competitive due to the globalization of markets, shorter product life cycles, and rapidly changing technology. As a result, organizations in all industries are searching for ways to improve their competitive position, reduce their carbon footprint, and attain world-class standards. From an operations management perspective, firms can enhance their competitiveness and help achieve their sustainability goals by developing new products and services (the topic of this section), selecting a more appropriate transformation process or system (discussed in the following two sections of this chapter), and/or improving their existing business processes (discussed in Chapters 8 and 9).

3.2.1 Output Development

In Chapter 1, it was noted that the field of research and development (R&D) is primarily responsible for developing innovative new product and service ideas. R&D activities focus on creating and developing (but not producing) the organization's outputs. More specifically, Figure 3.1 illustrates the stages of product and service development moving from pure research to applied research and finally to development as the output becomes more clearly defined. In the early years of a new output, development is oriented toward removing "bugs," increasing performance,

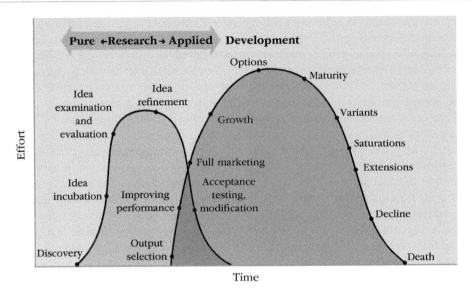

FIGURE 3.1   Stages of Product and Service Development

improving quality, and so on. In the middle years, options and variants of the output are developed. In the later years, development is oriented toward extensions of the output that will prolong its life.

Unfortunately, the returns from R&D are frequently meager, whereas the costs are great. Figure 3.2 illustrates the mortality curve (fallout rate) associated with the concurrent design, evaluation, and selection for a hypothetical group of 50 potential products, assuming that the 50 candidate products are the result of earlier research. Initial evaluation and screening reduce the 50 to about 22, and economic analysis further reduces the number to about 9. Development reduces this number even more, to about 5, and design and testing reduce it to perhaps 3. After two and a half more year's commercialization and production are completed, there is only one successful

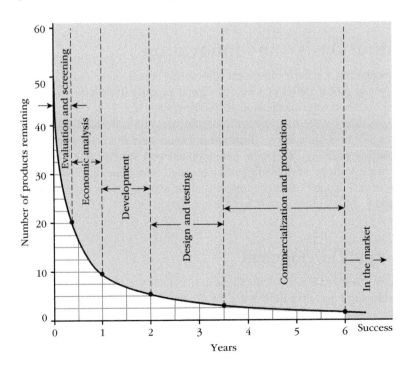

FIGURE 3.2   Product Mortality Curve

product left. (Sometimes there are none!) One study found that, beyond this, only 64% of the new products brought to market were successful or about two out of three. Although Figure 3.2 was developed from records of product developments, we believe the same type of curve applies to services.

3.2.2 Innovation

An *innovation* is the introduction to the *market* of a new, or improved, product, process, or service, as distinguished from an *invention* which is the creation of a product or process for the first time. The innovation may be a patented invention or a new combination of existing elements that has created a unique product, process, or service that was previously unavailable. Keeley et al. (2013) point out that there are at least ten different ways, and perhaps more, that an organization can innovate beyond just coming out with a new product or service – the process, the brand, the way of profiting, etc. Some of the following is based on the insights of Keeley et al.'s book and another excellent book *On Innovation* from *HBR's 10 Must Reads* series (2013).

Before attempting to innovate a new product or service, it is worth taking the time to examine your previous innovation attempts to learn from your successes and failures. What types of innovations worked and what types did not? What went right, and what went wrong? Could you have used a different type of innovation, or combined a few different types? Then identify where and how your competitors are innovating; again, could you employ a different type of innovation? Then address what seems important to customers and how that has evolved over time. In general, successful innovations arise from analyzing a range of different areas and finding a common consumer factor for either success or failure, such as greater convenience, lower costs, greater flexibility or features, and other such generic factors.

Perhaps what was innovative recently needs to change for the next evolution – what might that be, how can organizations profit from it, who is best positioned to benefit from that change, and why? Broadly speaking, the source of ideas for new products and services are often categorized as either market pull or technology push. With *market pull*, market research is conducted to identify unmet customer needs and/or opportunities for better meeting customer needs. In contrast, a *technology push* approach begins with a new technology and then seeks to identify ways the technology can be incorporated into new products and services. What is possible with the technologies today, and what will become possible in the near future? Who among your competitors is best positioned to take advantage of the new technologies? Can you take advantage of the coming changes instead, and if so, how might you profit from it?

A tool that is particularly useful in helping organizations identify opportunities for new products and services is the perceptual map. *Perceptual maps* help organizations understand how customers feel about the existing products and services that are currently being offered across two general dimensions. As an example, Figure 3.3 uses the scales of price and quality for an organization that is considering offering a service that allows customers to use an app to upload

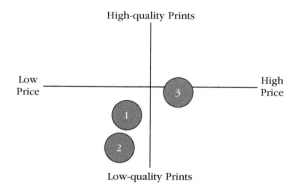

FIGURE 3.3
Example Perceptual Map for Photo Printing Smartphone App

photos they have taken with their smartphones and then receive printed photos through the mail. As shown in the figure, there are currently three competitors offering this service. In this case, the perceptual map suggests there may be an opportunity for the organization to offer a high-quality option at perhaps a somewhat higher price, which would position the offering in the upper right-hand corner of the perceptual map. But the scales can be anything, such as convenience, technological level, speed, and so on.

Next, we address some common mistakes during the innovation process. First, it is always a fortuitous outcome when an analysis shows there are some easy, profitable innovations that can be implemented, commonly called "low-hanging fruit." These should certainly be implemented asap but not by the innovation team – by separate, typically functional groups. The innovation team should instead focus on the big, high-potential breakthroughs which have more risk, will be more expensive, and probably involve innovations in two or more areas which may even change the strategic direction of the organization.

One useful tool to help analyze these innovations is the risk diagram, two typical versions of which are illustrated in Figure 3.4 (Meredith and Shafer, 2022, pp. 62, 266). Figure 3.4a illustrates the simple "risk matrix" where a box is divided into 4, 9, or even 25 smaller boxes based on two scales that could be anything, such as distance versus quality. Rectangles could be used also, such as one axis being acceptable or unacceptable, and the other axis having four categories, and the internal divisions could be curves instead of linear boxes. In our case, the matrix axes are Impact of a threat and its Probability of occurrence, where the most critical threats are shaded dark, and the least critical are unshaded. Then the different threats, five in this case, are placed in the appropriate boxes. If two factors like distance and quality had been used, then regions of risk or probability of failure could be sketched across the box with curves separating them. Then the various innovation projects would be plotted within the figure, possibly with circles indicating the size of their required investments or some other parameter.

In Figure 3.4b, we see a detailed aggregate project plan as described in Chapter 2, illustrating different types of innovation projects based on the degree of their product and process changes, with more change implying more risk. Here, the low-hanging fruit is in the lower right corner (least amount of change) and the highest risk projects still in R&D in the upper left corner, as well as the medium risk breakthrough and platform projects between the two extremes. Note the

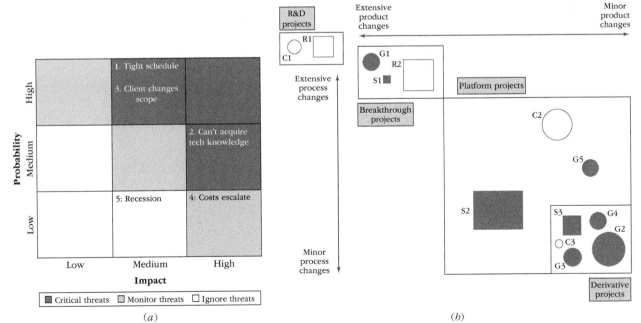

FIGURE 3.4   Two Versions of Risk Diagrams (*a*) Risk matrix (*b*) Risk portfolio

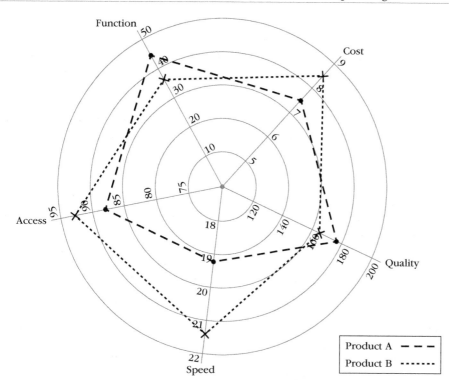

FIGURE 3.5 Spider/Star Chart

wide variety of identifications that can be put on the various projects: different shapes, different colors, different purposes (C, G, R, and S), and different generations within each purpose (1–4).

There are many other ways of illustrating the pros and cons of different innovation projects, such as a spider (sometimes called a "star") chart where each project is scored on multiple factors. Each slice of the pie can then represent different relevant considerations about the innovation. If values are listed along the spokes of a circle and the major common values connected with circles (which then looks like a spider's web), connecting the values for each innovation results in a unique shaped star for each project that allows comparisons across the portfolio of innovations, as shown in Figure 3.5.

Another common mistake is to use existing performance or justification criteria such as hurdle rates, discounted cash flows, and net present values to evaluate major innovations. These commonly used measures are based on the erroneous thinking that sticking with existing technologies and sunk costs will remain competitive in the future, but only guarantees that the organization will *not* be competitive in the future. Nor will it be easy to catch up because the competition is already one wave ahead of the organization and is working on implementing the next wave.

Similarly, new innovations should be insulated from the standard tools of quality and cost control such as large volumes, zero-defects, high utilization of processes, and such. Instead, their evaluations should be flexible in terms of budgets, plans, stage reviews, etc. until they have been solidified as feasible and desirable. Moreover, in Section 3.2.2.3 we suggest that their evaluations should not be in terms of money but rather on the reality of the assumptions that were made when they were approved, called "discovery-driven planning."

3.2.2.1 Design Thinking

Design Thinking is an approach that organizations are increasingly employing to facilitate their innovation initiatives related to the design of new products, services, and customer experiences. Indeed, the title of a recent Forbes article "These Days, Everyone Needs to Engage in Design Thinking" captures the sentiment of many leading organizations (McKendrick 2020).

Beyond providing some practical advice on how to adopt Design Thinking, the article also notes that approximately 90% of progressive companies have plans to significantly increase their investments in Design Thinking. Examples of well-known organizations that use Design Thinking include Nordstrom, Bank of America, Starbucks, Nike, Oral B, and GE Healthcare (Namdarian 2022).

Design Thinking is a human-centered design process developed by IDEO, a highly rated design firm. IDEO has developed or partnered with numerous organizations to develop new products, services, and experiences including the first notebook computer, the first ergonomic mouse, a portable defibrillator, a modular voting system for the largest voting district in the United States, and a new line of acoustic guitar amps for Fender.

Design Thinking is grounded in an understanding of people with the overarching goal of designing better product and service experiences. The application of Design Thinking principles in an actual design project is often referred to as a Deep Dive. As shown in Figure 3.6, IDEO's Deep Dive process consists of three major phases: Inspiration, Ideation, and Implementation.

The Inspiration Phase consists of two major activities, namely: observe and inquire, and telling stories. The focus of observation and inquiry is to gain insights into people's needs by watching what they do. As Yogi Berra so eloquently put it, "You can see a lot by just observing." Advocates of Design Thinking argue that the best way to reveal issues and opportunities is to go out into the field and see how people behave in their environment. Observing firsthand is important because quite often there is a gap between what people say they do and what they actually do. Also, importantly, there can be a gap between what people say they do and what they *think* they do.

One approach for observation and inquiry is to have people talk through their processes as they are engaging with a product or service. Another approach is to ask people to recount a specific event such as asking the subject to recount a recent experience with a product or service. Of course, it is critically important when soliciting stories in this fashion not to bias the respondents. Finally, it is helpful for the observer to put themselves in the shoes of the person being observed.

There are a number of other observation techniques that are commonly used. Shadowing involves observing people using products and services. Behavioral mapping involves photographing people within a space over a short period such as photographing customers shopping at a grocery store. Customers can also be asked to create camera journals which are visual diaries of their activities supplemented with written comments related to their impression of a product or service.

The second major activity in the Inspiration Phase is telling stories. Storytelling occurs during informal team meetings and is a powerful way for the design team members to share their experiences and the insights they gained from their direct observations. Telling stories also helps design team members make connections between their varied observations. In storytelling, team members can share what they actually saw and heard, and how they felt about what they observed. As a guideline, team members should be as descriptive as possible in sharing what they observed and

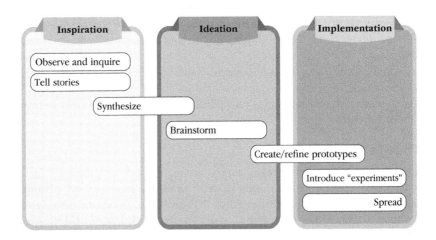

FIGURE 3.6   IDEO's Deep Dive Process

follow the general rules of reporting including addressing the who, what, when, where, why, and how. By the same token it is important that the members sharing the stories remain objective and not prescribe what *should* have happened or judge what was observed.

In transitioning from the Inspiration Phase to the Ideation Phase, the next step is to synthesize what was learned from the direct observations and begin to clarify what some of the key challenges are. Along these lines, one way to synthesize the observational data is to phrase it in terms of design challenges. More specifically, this involves taking the stories and insights that were shared among the team members and translating them into design challenges. One way to phrase these design challenges is:

A design challenge we see is _____ because we saw _____.

For example, in observing college students in a classroom, assume it was observed that some students finished in-class exercises much faster than others and that the students who finished early were bored waiting for the instructor to go over the exercise. In this case a design challenge could be phrased as:

A design challenge we see is that class time was not utilized efficiently because we saw several students texting while waiting for the instructor to go over the assigned exercise.

It is advisable for the design team to keep the information collected during the observation and inquiry phase (e.g. pictures, videos, and notes) close by so that it can be referred to when crafting the design challenges.

As you can likely imagine, successfully completing a Deep Dive requires a great deal of creativity. A widely used approach in business to foster creativity is brainstorming. Brainstorming was developed to capitalize on the synergistic effect of teams. No doubt you have heard the saying that "two heads are better than one." Brainstorming was also developed to limit the tendency to prematurely evaluate ideas as they are being generated (see Chapter 8 for additional details on brainstorming).

To incorporate brainstorming into a Deep Dive, the design challenges can be translated into brainstorm prompts. In Deep Dives such brainstorm prompts are often phrased beginning as "How might we" statements. It is recommended that brainstorm prompts be phrased optimistically such as "How might we increase student engagement" as opposed to "How might we minimize students' use of cell phones in class."

One way to conduct a brainstorming session using a brainstorm prompt is to write the prompt on a sheet of paper and attach the sheet to a wall. Then team members can write their ideas on sticky notes and place the ideas on the wall during a brainstorming session. Ideas that are similar or build on other ideas can be placed together.

There are several guidelines to consider in developing brainstorm prompts. First, they should not be overly broad or ambitious. Likewise, they should not be too abstract. How might we improve the communication in the hospital exemplifies a brainstorm prompt that is too abstract. In particular, it is not clear which functions need to communicate better, what type of communication needs to be improved (e.g. written, verbal), and who needs to communicate better (e.g. communication between doctors and nurses, communication between departments in the hospital). A better brainstorm prompt would be: How might we improve communication between nurses on different shifts? As you can see, this brainstorm prompt is much more specific and has a reasonable scope. By the same token, we also want to avoid brainstorm prompts that are too narrow and as such generate only a few solutions. "How might we reduce call response time from 15 minutes to 10 minutes" exemplifies a brainstorm prompt that is too narrow. A better brainstorm prompt would be "How might we provide customer service reps and customers with tools to reduce call times?" Unfortunately, determining whether a brainstorm prompt is too broad or too narrow is more art than science. Thus, the best advice is to be aware of the tendency to frame them too broadly or too narrowly and then to evaluate them considering these tendencies.

Once a number of brainstorm prompts have been developed, the next step is to decide which ones to actually brainstorm on. There are several guidelines that are helpful to the design team related to selecting the brainstorming prompts to focus on. First, the team members should consider what they are most passionate about. The energy and creativity the team brings to addressing a design challenge will be impacted by how passionate and excited they are about it. It is also advisable to consider the impact addressing a particular design challenge will have on the overall project. In other words, if the team came up with a great solution to the design challenge, how much of an impact would this have on the overall project? Finally, it is worth considering whether the team has a couple of initial ideas versus having no idea where to begin. In solving challenges, often the hardest part is getting started. The tendency to procrastinate can creep in when the team doesn't have some initial ideas on how to get started. On the other hand, the team can gain significant momentum and in turn increase its odds of success by starting with challenges that they have some initial thoughts on where to start.

In engaging in a brainstorming session there are a number of guidelines that should be followed. To begin, team members should not criticize ideas during the brainstorming session. Being critical of ideas will make people reluctant to share their ideas and will ultimately stifle the creativity of the team. Of course, the ideas will eventually be evaluated, just not during the brainstorming session. Second, team members should express all ideas no matter how radical, bizarre, unconventional, ridiculous, or impractical they may seem. Even if the idea is too radical, unconventional, and so on, and is ultimately not used, the idea may stimulate other ideas that are incorporated in the final solution. Third, the goal of a brainstorming session is to generate as many ideas as possible. Thus, it is the quantity of ideas generated that counts, not the quality. Finally, it is important for team members to combine, extend, and/or improve on one another's ideas. Thus, rather than criticizing ideas, the goal is to try to make ideas work.

Transitioning to the next major phase of the Deep Dive project, activities associated with creating and refining prototypes span the Ideation Phase and the Implementation Phase. A prototype is anything that helps communicate or test the solution being developed. Prototypes might take the form of mockups, models, or simulations of the process, service, experience, or environment that is being designed. There are numerous benefits associated with developing and using prototypes including helping the team obtain fast feedback at little cost, comparing alternative ideas to one another, and allowing concepts to be experienced rather than remaining abstract ideas.

A key principle associated with developing prototypes for Deep Dives is that they should be rough and rapid. Being rough means that the prototype should be just good enough to test the idea. No extra effort should be expended in the creation of prototypes beyond what is needed to evaluate the idea. It is also important that the team does not develop an emotional attachment to the prototype. If the ideas being tested don't pan out, it's time to move on to other ideas.

In addition to rough, prototyping should be rapid. This means prototypes should be developed quickly and at minimum expense. This enables the team to quickly experiment with a variety of ideas and get quick and regular feedback.

A couple of additional comments regarding prototypes are worth noting. First, prototypes should be shared with people outside the team such as with colleagues and customers to get additional feedback. Second, current organizational roles, processes, and budgets should not constrain the team's thinking. These constraints and limitations can be considered later because considering them too early in the process can significantly stifle the team's creativity.

In the Implementation Phase, prototypes are further refined, experiments or pilots of the design are tested, and eventually the ideas are spread more widely throughout the enterprise. Importantly, implementation doesn't mean that what the team has created is final. Rather, introducing new ideas as an experiment allows the team to test its viability while at the same time letting others see what is possible. Thus, with Deep Dives new ideas are always introduced as an experiment.

Introducing new ideas as experiments provides several benefits. First, it gives people a chance to co-develop the idea which increases their interest in the idea and buy-in. But beyond this, ideas can almost always be improved by people who are part of the experience. Finally, since the purpose of the experiment is to get more feedback on ideas, the team should measure the impact of the experiment. In a similar fashion to developing minimally acceptable prototypes, the team doesn't need months of baseline data. Rather, it requires utilizing some simple measures to demonstrate to others whether the idea is working or not.

3.2.2.2 Disruptive Innovations

Disruptive innovations are typically those that offer a set of performance characteristics that are not valued by current mainstream customers but rather by niche customers (Bower and Christensen 1995). These apparently small markets for the disruptive innovation compared with the size of the established market makes it unappealing to traditional organizations who would have to change their resources to meet the needs of this niche market. However, the organizations offering these disruptive innovations soon start improving the performance of the innovation along the dimensions valued by the mainstream customers at a fast rate. In addition, the mainstream customers may come to appreciate some of the performance characteristics of these new innovations. The result is that the innovative organizations start to invade the mainstream market. The traditional organizations then try to improve their outputs using their current resources to satisfy their original mainstream customers, but their rate of improvement is slower than that of the disruptive organizations, typically due to their older technology. This effect is because disruptive organizations are not weighed down by the older technology investments that traditional organizations have been using (Keeley et al. 2013, p. 104). Their fixed and sunk costs almost ensure that they will not be replacing their older technologies with the newer ones.

Taking an unbiased view of the market and seeing where new technologies may offer substantial advantages and performance improvements for the market is key to successful disruption. A classic example is that of Dell Computers and their multiple disruptive innovations in terms of up-front payment, 24/7 ordering and tech support, building to spec from their suppliers, and online sales (Keeley et al. 2013, p. 88).

Recent examples of disruptive innovations are cellphones and television streaming, which originally were inferior and appealed to a niche market, but then kept improving and dropping in price until they surpassed the mainstream technologies. For example, streaming eventually offered more selection of programming (movies, serials, weather, news, etc.) than cable television, and for a substantially lower cost. Of course, the big internet providers are trying to compete by setting up their own streaming systems but typically do not have the libraries of movies and so on that the streaming services have, or the contacts and resources to contract with other organizations to provide them. And cell phones have allowed people to drop their landline phones, which are now mostly used by advertisers hoping to sell their wares. And with the advent of digital cables, those old backup landline phones do not even use a landline anymore anyway, so if your cable goes out, so does your "landline"!

3.2.2.3 Discovery Driven Planning

McGrath et al. (1995) and Rice et al. (2008) propose reversing the innovation evaluation process. Instead of trying to determine whether an innovation meets the investment hurdle rate based on estimates of profitability, try to discover how valid the initial assumptions were, like whether the product will "sell itself" or there will be "no competition" (Harvard Business Review Press, pp. 127, 170). That is, instead of trying to determine whether the project is achieving the numbers it needs to at each stage of the project, determine how valid the initial assumptions about the innovation project now appear to be regarding the market, the competition, the funder's needs, the progress that has been made, expected future performance, costs to date and expected at completion, schedule to date and expected at completion, and so on.

An assumptions checklist for each project stage should be prepared with the most critical, make-or-break assumptions first and then when the project reaches that stage, the assumptions are checked for their validity. If a critical assumption is not met, the project must be replanned, or the assumptions revised as appropriate. As the innovation is being developed, then use each stage to check on those early or revised assumptions. If no plan can satisfy all the assumptions for that stage, the project should be terminated while the costs are still minimal.

The majority of innovation failures are rooted in the failure to *identify* a critical assumption, or assumptions, rather than having checked the assumption and come up with an incorrect answer (Harvard Business Review Press, p. 171). It is not technological difficulties that usually kill an innovation, but commonplace managerial behavior, such as optimism bias (Flyvbjerg 2021).

3.2.3 Post-Innovation

Given how competitive most industries are, once new ideas have been generated for new products, organizations are eager to test them and get them to market as quickly as possible. *Rapid prototyping* is a group of techniques that allow organizations to quickly produce physical models of new product ideas. In particular, rapid prototyping can be used for *concept* modeling to test and refine new product concepts by actually touching and feeling physical prototypes. With this functional modeling, organizations can actually see how the prototype performs.

The primary approach for rapid prototyping is three-dimensional (3D) printing. With 3D printing, solid items are created based on drawings created in computer-aided design (CAD) software. The 3D item is produced through what is referred to as an *additive process* whereby successive layers of the material are "printed." In effect, each layer is a cross section of the final item. This is in contrast to traditional *subtracting* production techniques where material is removed from an item such as drilling a hole or cutting an item to the desired length. Because material is added with 3D printing as opposed to being removed, typically less material is needed. Other advantages of 3D printing include the following:

- The speed with which prototypes can be created. Complex designs for an item can be "printed" in a few hours, which greatly facilitates getting timely feedback on products as they are being designed.

- The items are produced in a single step. Producing parts using traditional subtraction methods requires the development of detailed processing instructions such as what size drill bit to use, how much material should be cut off, and in what sequence all the subtraction operations should be performed in.

- There is little to no direct labor cost in producing the items.

- Custom designed products can be easily produced.

3D items can be made in a wide variety of materials including plastics, metals, nylon, resins, and wax. The cost of 3D printers ranges from a couple of hundred dollars to over $100,000.

In the world of product design, designers often follow a number of well-established principles to guide their design work. *Design for Excellence* is an umbrella term that includes collections of design principles for various design objectives. More specifically, Design for Excellence is abbreviated as DfX, which can be interpreted as Design for X, where the X is a placeholder to a specific design objective. For example, DfM stands for Design for Manufacturability and includes guidelines to ensure products can be produced defect free. Likewise, DfA stands for Design for Assembly and provides guidelines to ensure component parts can be easily assembled into the final end product. DfL refers to Design for Logistics (or Supply Chain) and includes guidelines that facilitate the distribution of products. As can be seen, Design for Excellence addresses a wide variety of design objectives as well as including Design for Cost, Design for Reliability, Design for Serviceability, and Design for Sustainability (discussed in more detail in the next section) to name a few others.

There are other options beyond generating and developing ideas in-house for new products and services. Two alternatives to research frequently used by organizations are *imitation* of a proven new idea (i.e. employing a second-to-market strategy) or outright *purchase* of someone else's invention. The outright purchase strategy is becoming extremely popular in those industries where bringing a new product to market can cost huge sums, such as pharmaceuticals and high technology. It is also employed in those industries where technology advances so rapidly that there isn't enough time to employ a second-to-market strategy. Although imitation does not put the organization first in the market with the new product or service, it does provide an opportunity to study any possible defects in the original product or service and rapidly develop a better design, frequently at a better price. The second approach – purchasing an invention or the inventing company itself – eliminates the risks inherent in research, but it still requires the company to develop and market the product or service before knowing whether it will be successful. Either route spares the organization the risk and tremendous cost of conducting the actual research leading up to a new invention or improvement.

In addition to output or "product research" (as it is generally known), there is also process research, which involves the generation of new knowledge concerning how to produce outputs. The production of many familiar products out of plastic (toys, pipe, furniture, automobile components, etc.) exemplifies successful process research. Motorola, to take another example, extensively uses project teams that conduct process development at the same time as product development. As product life cycles become increasingly shorter, developing outputs and the processes that will produce or deliver them concurrently is becoming increasingly important. Clearly, it is of little to no value to develop new outputs that the organization cannot produce or deliver. Developing the product and process simultaneously is referred to as *concurrent design*.

3.2.4 Design for Sustainability

The traditional focuses of output design are on reducing costs, improving functionality, and ease of use. However, as was noted earlier in the chapter, the design of an organization's outputs and the materials used in their production and delivery have a significant impact on the organization's carbon footprint. Indeed, it is widely acknowledged that 80 percent of the environmental impact of a product is determined by its design. Thus, before leaving the topic of output design, it is of value to highlight some of the ways output design can be leveraged to support an organization's sustainability goals and commitments.

More formally, Design for Sustainability (DfS) is an approach to output design that seeks to minimize the negative impact the output will have on people and the environment. A key aspect of DfS (also referred to as Green Design and Design for the Environment) is the efficient use of resources and the use of environmentally friendly and sustainable materials in the design of both the outputs themselves and processes used to create them.

A key element of DfS is choosing the materials that are used to produce the output and its packaging to reduce the negative impact on the environment. For example, polylactic acid (PLA) is fabricated from corn or tapioca plant starch and has the feel of a normal plastic cup but its use results in 75 percent less gas emissions compared to traditional plastics. Indeed, like many other products, plastics have a negative environmental impact both when they are produced (emitting CO_2 when made) and when they are discarded and placed in landfills. Apple has made the commitment that all of its products well be carbon neutral by 2030. To achieve this, all materials used in its products will come from recycled materials or renewable materials. Likewise, Microsoft introduced Xbox wireless controllers using post-consumer recycled (PCR) materials and is further investigating how recovered plastic waste from the oceans can be processed for use in consumer products.

Because the natural resources that serve as the raw materials for outputs are finite, they can eventually become depleted. Additionally, harvesting these natural resources often takes an additional toll on the environment. To counter this, recycling and reuse become critical. Importantly then, beyond incorporating environmentally friendly materials into the design of outputs, the outputs also need to be designed so that when they reach their end of life, they can be effectively recycled, reused, and disassembled.

In even more extreme cases, some raw materials are actually hazardous to people and the environment. Progressive companies like HP and Dell are intentionally identifying hazardous materials and developing plans to phase out their use. There are several public databases available to help organizations identify hazardous materials such as the Hazardous Substances Data Bank (HSDB) maintained by the U.S. National Library of Medicine (pubchem.ncbi.nlm.nih.gov).

Beyond the output itself, many products require some type of packaging. Environmental and competitive concerns are leading organizations to investigate ways to reduce product packaging. Unfortunately, in their pursuit of reduced packaging, organizations often don't adequately consider the ramifications that reduced packaging will have on the rate of damaged product (Terreri 2011). Indeed, product packaging that is not able to withstand the rigors of the supply chain can actually lead to more damage and waste and thereby negate all the anticipated environmental and cost benefits. Avoiding this pitfall requires that organizations holistically evaluate the impact packaging changes will have across their entire supply chain.

While many factors come into play when designing outputs including costs, functionality, ease of use, and impact on the organization's reputation, the environmental impact is becoming increasingly important at many organizations. Likewise, while selecting the materials used in the output and its packaging also require the consideration of multiple factors such as costs, availability, quality, and lead time, the impact on the environment is becoming an increasingly important consideration.

3.3 Forms of Transformation Systems

With our overview of output design complete, we now turn our attention to determining the best way to produce or deliver the output. We begin with an overview of five generic transformation systems originally developed for products, but most can also apply to services: continuous process, flow shop, job shop, cellular production, and project operations. Included in the overview are the advantages and disadvantages associated with each transformation system and approaches for developing the physical layout for each system. The chapter continues with a discussion of key considerations related to the selection of a transformation system including volume and variety of the output and what stage the output is in its life cycle. The rest of the chapter discusses some differences with the design of service processes.

3.3.1 Continuous Process

The *continuous transformation process* is commonly used to produce highly standardized outputs, usually fluidic products, in extremely large volumes. In some cases, these outputs have become so standardized that there are virtually no real differences between the outputs of different firms. Examples of such *commodities* include water, gases, chemicals, electricity, ores, rubber, flour, spirits, cements, petroleum, and milk. The term *continuous process* reflects the typical practice of running these operations 24 hours a day, 7 days a week. One reason for running these systems continuously is to spread their fixed costs over as large a volume as possible, thereby reducing unit costs. This is particularly important in commodity markets, where price can be the single most important factor in competing successfully. Another reason for operating these processes continuously is that stopping and starting them can be prohibitively expensive.

Continuous process industries constitute about half of the manufacturing industry in the United States. Although not all of this industry produces commodities, those are what is typically envisioned. The operations in these commodity industries are highly automated, with very specialized equipment and controls, often electronic and computerized. Such automation and the expense it entails are necessary because of strict processing requirements. Because of the highly specialized and automated nature of the equipment, changing the rate of output can be quite difficult. The facility is typically a maze of pipes, conveyors, tanks, valves, vats, and bins. The layout follows the processing stages of the product, and the output rate is controlled through equipment capacity and flow and mixture rates. Labor requirements are low and are devoted primarily to monitoring and maintaining the equipment.

Research (Dennis and Meredith 2000), however, has shown that there is a much wider range of continuous process industries than just commodity manufacturers. In fact, these industries range all the way from intermittent forms akin to *job shops* to rigidly continuous *flow shops* (both described next). In fact, there appear to be at least seven clearly differentiable forms of continuous processes. Some run for a short time making one product and then switch over to make another product, largely on demand and to the specification of individual customers, which is almost the opposite of commodity production. In addition to these two extremes, there are also blending types of continuous processes as well as unusual hybrids of both job and flow shops.

The major characteristic of processing industries, especially commodities, is that there is often one primary, "fluid"-type input material (gas, wood, wheat, milk, etc.). This input is then often converted into multiple outputs, although sometimes there may be only one output (e.g. clean, chlorinated water). In contrast, in discrete production, many types of materials are made or purchased and combined to form the output.

Although human variation in continuous processing firms does not usually create the problems it creates in discrete manufacturing, the demands of processing are usually more critical. For example, chemical reactions must be accurately timed. The result is that the initial setup of equipment and procedures is even more complex and critical than it is for flow shops. Fixed costs are extremely high; the major variable cost is materials. Variable labor (excluding distribution) is usually insignificant.

3.3.2 Flow Shops

The *flow shop* is a transformation system similar to the continuous process, the major difference being that in flow shops, there is a discrete product or service, whereas in continuous processes, the end product is not naturally divisible. Thus, in continuous processes, an additional step, such as bottling or canning, might be needed to get the product into discrete units. Like the continuous process, flow shops treat all the outputs as basically the same, and the flow of work is thus relatively continuous. Organizations that use this form are heavily automated, with large, special-purpose equipment. The characteristics of flow shops are a fixed set of inputs, constant throughput times, and a fixed set of outputs. Examples of the flow form for discrete products are manufacturing paper clips, steelmaking, and automobile assembly, whereas for services, some examples include the car wash, the processing of insurance claims, and the ubiquitous fast-food restaurant.

An organization that produces, or plans to produce, a high volume of a small variety of outputs will thus probably organize its operations as a flow shop. In doing so, the organization will take advantage of the simplicity and the savings in variable costs that such an approach offers. Because outputs and operations are standardized, specialized equipment can be used to perform the necessary operations at low per-unit costs, and the relatively large, fixed costs of the equipment are distributed over a large volume of outputs.

Continuous types of materials-handling equipment, such as conveyors – again operating at low per-unit costs – can be used because the operations are standardized, and typically, all outputs follow the same path from one operation to the next. This standardization of treatment provides for a known, fixed throughput time, giving managers easier control of the system and more reliable delivery dates. Flow shops are easier to manage for other reasons as well: routing, scheduling, and control are all facilitated because each output does not have to be individually monitored and controlled. Standardization of operations means that fewer skilled workers can be used and each manager's span of control can increase.

The general form of flow shops is illustrated in Figure 3.7, which shows a *production line.* (If only assembly operations were being performed, as in many automotive plants, the line would be called an *assembly line.*) This production line could represent new military inductees taking their physical exams, small appliances being assembled, or double-decker hamburgers being prepared.

Note that both services and products can be organized as flow shops and can capitalize on the many advantages of this form of processing.

3.3.2.1 Advantages of the Flow Shop

The primary advantage of a flow shop is the low per-unit cost that is attainable owing to specialized high-volume equipment, bulk purchasing, lower labor rates, efficient utilization of the facility, low in-process inventories, and simplified managerial control. In addition, with everyone working on all the required tasks simultaneously, referred to as overlapping, product or service outputs are produced very quickly.

Because of the high rate of output, materials can often be bought in large quantities at significant savings. Also, because operations are standardized, processing times tend to remain constant so that large in-process inventories are not required to queue up for processing. This minimizes investment in in-process inventory and queue (*buffer*) space. Furthermore, because a standardized product is produced, inventory control and purchasing decisions are routine.

Because the machines are specialized, less skilled operators are needed, and therefore, lower wages can be paid. In addition, fewer supervisors are needed, further reducing costs. Since flow shops are generally continuous, with materials handling often built into the system itself, the operations can be designed to perform compactly and efficiently with narrow aisles, thereby making maximum use of space.

The simplification in managerial control of a well-designed flow shop should not be overlooked. Constant operations problems requiring unending managerial attention penalize the organization by distracting managers from their normal duties of planning and decision-making.

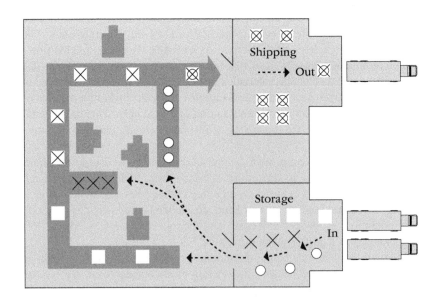

FIGURE 3.7
A Generalized Flow
Shop Operation

3.3.2.2 Disadvantages of Flow Shops

Despite the important cost advantage of flow shops, they can have some serious drawbacks. Not only is variety of output difficult to obtain, even changes in the rate of output are hard to make. Changing the *rate* of output may require using overtime, laying off workers, adding additional shifts, or temporarily closing the plant. Also, because the equipment is so specialized, minor changes in the design of the product often require substantial changes in the equipment. Thus, important changes in product design are infrequent, and this could weaken the organization's competitive position.

A well-known problem in flow shops is boredom and absenteeism among the labor force. Since the equipment performs the skilled tasks, there is no challenge for workers. And, of course, the constant, unending, repetitive nature of the manufacturing line can dehumanize workers. Because the rate of workflow is generally set (*paced*) by the line speed, incentive pay, and other output-based incentives are not possible.

The flow production line form has another important drawback. If the line should stop for any reason – a breakdown of a machine or conveyor, a shortage of supplies, and so forth – production may come to an immediate halt unless WIP is stored at key points in the line. Such occurrences are prohibitively expensive.

Other requirements of flow shops also add to their cost and their problems. For example, parts must be standardized so that they will fit together easily and quickly on the assembly line. And, since all machines and labor must work at the same repetitive pace in order to coordinate operations, the workloads along the entire line are generally *balanced* to the pace of the slowest element. To keep the line running smoothly, a large support staff is required, as well as large stocks of raw materials, all of which also add to the expense.

Last, in flow shops, simplicity in *ongoing operation* is achieved at the cost of complexity in the initial *setup*. The planning, design, and installation of the typically complicated, special-purpose, high-volume equipment are mammoth tasks. The equipment is costly not only to set up originally but also to maintain and service. Furthermore, such special-purpose equipment is very susceptible to obsolescence and is difficult to dispose of or to modify for other purposes.

3.3.2.3 Layout of the Flow Shop

The crux of the problem of realizing the advantages of a flow shop is whether the workflow can be subdivided sufficiently so that labor and equipment are utilized smoothly throughout the processing operations. If, for example, one operation takes longer than all the others, this single operation (perhaps a machine) will become a bottleneck, delaying all the operations following it and restricting the output rate of the entire process.

Obtaining smooth utilization of workers and equipment across all operations involves assigning to groups tasks that take about the same amount of time to complete. This balancing applies to production lines, where parts or outputs are produced, as well as to assembly lines, where parts are assembled into final products.

Final assembly operations usually have more labor input and fewer fixed-equipment cycles and can therefore be subdivided more easily for smooth flow. Either of two types of lines can then be used. A *paced line* uses some sort of conveyor and moves the output along at a continuous rate, and operators do their work as the output passes by them. For longer operations, the worker may walk or ride alongside the conveyor and then have to walk back to the starting workstation. The many disadvantages of this arrangement, such as boredom and monotony, are, of course, well-known. An automobile assembly line is a common example of a paced line. Workers install doors, engines, hoods, and the like as the conveyor moves past them.

In unpaced lines, workers build up queues between workstations and can then vary their pace to meet the needs of the job or their personal desires; however, average daily output must remain the same. The advantage of an unpaced line is that a worker can spend longer on the more difficult outputs and balance this with less time spent on the easier outputs. Similarly, workers can vary their pace to add variety to a boring task. For example, a worker may work fast to get ahead of the pace and then pause for a few seconds before returning to the task.

There are some disadvantages with unpaced lines, however. For one thing, they cannot be used with large, bulky products because too much in-process storage space is required. More important, minimum output rates are difficult to maintain because short durations in one operation usually do not dovetail with long durations in the next operation. When long durations coincide, operators downstream from these operations may run out of in-process inventory to work on and may thus be forced to sit idle.

For operations that can be smoothed to obtain the benefits of a production line, there are two main elements in designing the most efficient line. The first is formulating the situation by determining the necessary output rate, the available work time per day, the times for operational tasks, and the order of precedence of the operations. The second element is actually to solve the balancing problem by subdividing and grouping the operations into balanced jobs. To illustrate the concept of a balanced production line, we will give an example that addresses both of these main elements. In reality, of course, one of a variety of software packages would be employed.

3.3.2.4 Balancing the Production Line

We illustrate the formulation of the *line balancing* situation with an example. Longform Credit receives 1200 credit applications a day, on average. Longform competes on the basis of its ability to process applications within hours. Daily application processing tasks, average times, and required preceding tasks (tasks that must be completed before the next task) are listed in Table 3.1.

The *precedence graph* for these tasks is shown in Figure 3.8; it is constructed directly from Table 3.1. This graph is similar to the network diagram developed for projects (see Chapter 2) and is simply a picture of the operations (boxed) with arrows indicating which tasks must precede others. The number or letter of the operation is shown above the box, with its time inside.

Table 3.1   Tasks in Credit Application Processing

Task	Average time (minutes)	Immediately preceding tasks
a. Open and stack applications	0.20	None
b. Process enclosed letter; make note of and handle any special requirements	0.37	a
c. Check off form 1 for page 1 of application	0.21	a
d. Check off form 2 for page 2 of application; file original copy of application	0.18	a
e. Calculate credit limit from standardized tables according to forms 1 and 2	0.19	c, d
f. Supervisor checks quotation in light of special processing of letter and notes type of form letter, address, and credit limit to return to applicant	0.39	b, e
g. Administrative assistant types in details on form letter and mails	0.36	f
Total	1.90	

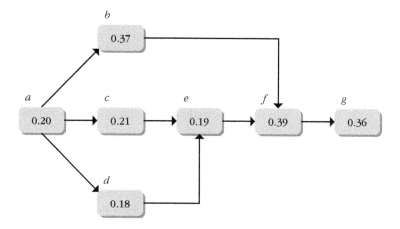

FIGURE 3.8 Precedence Graph for Credit Applications

In balancing a line, the intent is to find a *cycle time* in which each workstation can complete its tasks. A workstation is usually a single person, but it may include any number of people responsible for completing all the tasks associated with the job for that station. Conceptually, at the end of this time, every workstation passes its part on to the next station, and, of course, one item comes off the end of the line fully complete. (The Lean term *takt time* to be discussed in Chapter 9 is now commonly used in practice instead of *cycle time*. This switch in terminology has been made in part to help clear up the confusion created when the term *cycle time* was erroneously used to refer to the throughput time, or the time it takes to complete all the work to produce a finished item.)

Task elements are thus grouped for each workstation so as to utilize as much of this cycle time as possible but not to exceed it. Each workstation will have a slightly different *idle time* within the cycle time.

$$\text{Cycle time} = \text{Available work time/demand}$$

$$= \frac{8\,\text{h} \times 60\,\text{min/h}}{1200\,\text{applications}} = 0.4\,\text{min/application}$$

The cycle time is determined from the required output rate. In this case, the average daily output rate must equal the average daily input rate, 1200. If it is less than this amount, a backlog of applications will accumulate. If it is more than this, unnecessary idle time will result. Assuming an eight-hour day, 1200 applications per eight hours means completing 150 every hour or one every 0.4 minute – this, then, is the cycle time.

Adding up the task times in Table 3.1, we can see that the total is 1.9 minutes. Since every workstation will do no more than 0.4 minute's work during each cycle, it is clear that a minimum of 1.9/0.4 = 4.75 workstations are needed – or, always rounding *up*, five workstations.

$$\text{Number of theoretical workstations,}\ N_T = \Sigma\,\text{task times / cycle time}$$

$$= \frac{1.9}{0.4} = 4.75\,(\text{i.e. } 5)$$

It may be, however, that the work cannot be divided and balanced in five stations – in which case six, or even seven, may be needed. For example, precedence relationships may interfere with assigning two tasks to the same workstation. This is why we referred to N_T as the *theoretical* number of workstations needed. If more workstations are actually needed than the theoretical number, the production line will be less efficient. The *efficiency* of the line with N_A actual stations may be computed as

$$\text{Efficiency} = \frac{\text{Output}}{\text{Input}} = \frac{\text{Total task time}}{\left(N_A \text{ stations}\right) \times \text{cycle time}}$$

$$\frac{1.9}{5 \times 0.4} = 95\% \text{ if the line can be balanced with 5 stations}$$

$$\frac{1.9}{6 \times 0.4} = 79\% \text{ if 6 stations are required}$$

In the formula for efficiency, input is represented by the amount of work required to produce one unit, and output is represented by the amount of work that actually goes into producing one unit.

Now that the problem has been formulated, we can attempt to balance the line by assigning tasks to stations. We begin by assuming that all workers can do any of the tasks and check back on this later. There are many heuristic rules for deciding which task to assign to a station next, but these rules won't guarantee the best solution. Thus, it is wise to check for even better solutions. We will use the LOT rule; select the task with the *longest operation time* next. The general procedure for line balancing is as follows:

- Construct a list of the tasks whose predecessor tasks have already been completed.

- Consider each of these tasks, one at a time, in LOT order and place them within the station.

- As a task is tentatively placed in a station, add new follower tasks to the list whose precedence relationships are now met.

- Consider adding to the station any tasks in this list whose time fits within the remaining time for that station.

- Continue in this manner until as little idle time as possible remains for the station.

We will now demonstrate this procedure with reference to Longform, using the information in Table 3.1 and Figure 3.8. The first tasks to consider are those with no preceding tasks. Thus, task *a,* taking 0.2 of the 0.4 minute available, is assigned to station 1. This, then, makes tasks *b* (0.37 minute), *c* (0.21 minute), and *d* (0.18 minute) eligible for assignment. Trying the longest first, b, then c, and last d, we find that only *d* can be assigned to station 1 without exceeding the 0.4-minute cycle time; thus, station 1 will include tasks *a* and d. Since only 0.02 minute remains unassigned in station 1 and no task is that short, we then consider assignments to station 2.

Only *b* and *c* are eligible for assignment (since *e* requires that *c* be completed first), and *b* (0.37 minute) will clearly require a station by itself; *b* is, therefore, assigned to station 2. Only *c* is now eligible for assignment, since *f* requires that both *e* and *b* be completed, and *e* is not yet completed. But when we assign *c* (0.21 minute) to station 3, task *e* (0.19 minute) becomes available and can also be just accommodated in station 3. Task *f* (0.39 minute), the next eligible task, requires its own station; this leaves *g* (0.36 minute) to station 5. These assignments are illustrated in Figure 3.9 and Table 3.2.

We now check the feasibility of these assignments. In many cases, several aspects must be considered in this check (as discussed later), but here, our only concern is that the administrative assistant does not do task *f* and that the supervisor does not do task *g* (or, we hope, much of *a* through *e*). As it happens, task *f* is a station by itself, so there is no problem.

As we saw, short tasks are often combined to reach the cycle time. However, long tasks may have to be split up to meet the cycle time requirements. If a task cannot be split, we can "clone"

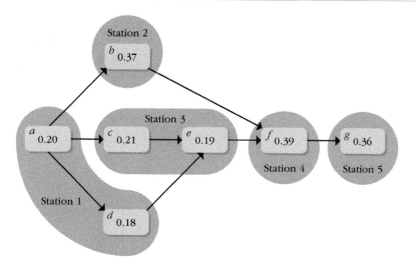

FIGURE 3.9   Station Assignments

Table 3.2   **Station Task Assignments**

Station	Time available	Eligible tasks	Task assigned	Idle time
1	0.40	a	a	
	0.20	b, c, d	d	
	0.02	b, c	None will fit	0.02
2	0.40	b, c	b	0.03
	0.03	c	c will not fit	
3	0.40	c	c	0.00
	0.19	e	e	
4	0.40	f	f	0.01
	0.01	g	g will not fit	
5	0.40	g	g	0.04

the station as many times as needed to effectively reduce its cycle time, with each station alternating in its output to match, in essence, the required cycle time.

3.3.3 Job Shops

Job shops use what is known as a *functional* layout because unique jobs must be produced through a variety of different machines or processes. In this form of transformation system, each output, or each small batch of outputs, is processed differently. Therefore, the flow of work through the facility tends to be intermittent.

The general characteristics of a job shop are a *grouping* of staff and equipment according to their function; using a large *variety* of inputs; requiring a considerable amount of *transport* of staff, materials, or recipients; and exhibiting large *variations* in system flow times (the time it takes for a complete "job"). In general, each output takes a different route through the various functions of the organization, requires different operations, uses different inputs, and takes a different amount of time.

This transformation system is common when the outputs differ significantly in form, structure, materials, or processing required. For example, an organization that has a wide variety of outputs

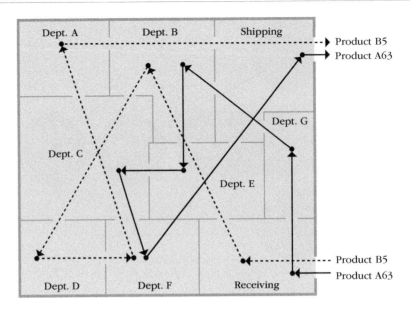

FIGURE 3.10
A Generalized Job
Shop Operation

or does custom work (e.g. custom guitars) would probably be a job shop. Specific examples of product and service organizations of this form are tailor shops, general offices, machine shops, fitness centers, hospitals, universities, automobile repair shops, local governmental services, and department stores. By and large, job shops are especially appropriate for service organizations because services are often customized, and hence, each service requires different operations.

Clearly, the efficient management of a job shop is a difficult task, since every output must be treated differently. In addition, the resources available for processing are limited. Furthermore, not only it is management's task to ensure the performance of the proper functions of each output, where considerations of quality and deadlines may vary, but management must also be sure that the available resources (staff, equipment, materials, supplies, and capital) are being efficiently utilized. Often, there is a difficult trade-off between efficiency and flexibility of operations. Job-based processes tend to emphasize flexibility over efficiency.

Figure 3.10 represents the flow through a job shop. This facility might be a hospital, an auto repair shop, or an office. Each particular "job" travels from one area or department to another, and so on, according to its unique routing, until it is fully processed. Temporary in-process storage may occur between various operations, while jobs are waiting for subsequent processing (standing in line for the coffee machine).

To illustrate this, refer to Figure 3.10. Product B5 begins its processing in Dept. B, followed by processing in Departments D, F, and A. Product A63 follows a completely different path through the job shop beginning in Dept. G and then being processed in Departments B, E, C, and F. As another example, consider a local gym with six departments: a room with cardio equipment, a room with free weights, a room with resistance machines, an area to consult with personal trainers, and an indoor pool area. A person training for a triathlon might begin by swimming, followed by a run on a treadmill in the cardio room, and ending with a leg workout in the room containing the resistance machines. Alternatively, a body builder might only visit the area containing the free weights. And someone interested in simply getting some exercise to stay healthy might begin by visiting the room containing the resistance machines followed by using an elliptical machine in the cardio room.

3.3.3.1 Advantages of Job Shops

The widespread use of the job shop form is due to its many advantages. A job shop is usually selected to provide the organization with the flexibility needed to respond to individual, small-volume demands (or even custom demands). The ability to produce a wide variety of outputs at reasonable cost is thus the primary advantage of this form. General-purpose equipment is used, and this is in greater demand and is usually available from more suppliers at a lower price than special-purpose equipment. In addition, used equipment is more likely to be available, further reducing the necessary investment. There is a larger base of experience with general-purpose equipment; therefore, problems with installation and maintenance are more predictable, and replacement parts are more widely available. Last, because general-purpose equipment is easier to modify or use elsewhere and disposal is much easier, the expense of obsolescence is minimized.

Because of the functional arrangement of the equipment, there are also other advantages. Resources for a function requiring special staff, materials, or facilities (e.g. painting or audiovisual equipment) may be centralized at the location of that function, and the organization can thus save expense through high utilization rates. Distracting or dangerous equipment, supplies, or activities may also be segregated from other operations in facilities that are soundproof, airtight, explosion proof, and so forth.

One advantage to the staff is that with more highly skilled work involving constantly varying jobs, responsibility and pride in one's work are increased, and boredom is reduced. Other advantages to the staff are that concentrations of experience and expertise are available and morale increases when people with similar skills work together in centralized locations (all market researchers together). Because all workers who perform similar activities are grouped together, each worker has the opportunity to learn from others, and the workers can easily collaborate to solve difficult problems. Furthermore, because the pace of the work is not dictated by a moving "line," incentive arrangements may be set up. Last, because no line exists that must forever keep moving, the entire set of organizational operations does not halt whenever any one part of the operation stops working; other functional areas can continue operating, at least until in-process inventory is depleted. Also, other general-purpose resources can usually substitute for the nonfunctioning resource: one machine for another, one staff member for another, and one material for another. For example, in the gym example mentioned earlier, if the leg curl machines break down in the resistance equipment room, squats using free weights can be used as a substitute.

3.3.3.2 Disadvantages of Job Shops

The general-purpose equipment of job shops is usually slower than special-purpose equipment, resulting in higher variable (per-unit) costs. In addition, the cost of direct labor for the experienced staff necessary to operate general-purpose equipment further increases unit costs of production above what semiskilled or unskilled workers would require. The result, in terms of costs of the outputs, is that the variable costs of production are higher for the general purpose than for the special-purpose equipment, facilities, and staff, but the initial cost of the equipment and facilities is significantly less. For small-output volumes, the job shop results in a lower total cost. As volume of output increases, however, the high variable costs begin to outweigh the savings in initial investment. The result is that, for high production volumes, the job shop is not the most economic approach (although its use may still be dictated by other considerations, as when particular equipment threatens workers' health or safety).

Inventories are also frequently a disadvantage in job shops, especially in product organizations. Not only do many types of raw materials, parts, and supplies have to be kept for the wide variety of outputs anticipated, but *in-process inventories,* that is, jobs waiting for processing, typically become very large and thereby represent a sizable capital investment for the organization. It is not unusual for batches of parts in these environments to spend 90–95% of the time they are in the shop either waiting to be moved or waiting to be processed. Furthermore, because there is so much in-process inventory that must travel between operating departments in order to be processed, the cost of handling materials is also typically high. Because job routings between operations are not identical, inexpensive fixed materials handling mechanisms like conveyor belts cannot be used. Instead, larger and more costly equipment is used; therefore, corridors and aisles must be large enough to accommodate it. This necessitates allocating even more space, beyond the extra space needed to store additional inventories.

Finally, managerial control of the job shop is extremely difficult, as mentioned earlier. Because the output varies in terms of its processing requirements, there is much uncertainly regarding what will arrive and when it will arrive to the various departments. This also complicates the managerial tasks of routing the orders, scheduling the orders, and allocating costs to the orders. Expediters must track down lost jobs and reorder priorities. In addition to watching the progress of individual jobs, management must continually strive to achieve the proper balance of materials, staff, and equipment; otherwise, highly expensive resources will sit idle, while bottlenecks occur elsewhere.

3.3.3.3 Layout of Job Shops

Because of its relative permanence, the layout of the operations is probably one of the most crucial elements affecting the efficiency of a job shop. In general, the problem of laying out operations in a job shop is quite complex. The difficulty stems from the variety of outputs and the constant changes in outputs that are characteristic of organizations with an intermittent transformation system. The optimal layout for the existing set of outputs may be relatively inefficient for the outputs to be produced six months from now. This is particularly true of job shops where there is no proprietary product and only for-contract work is performed. One week such a shop might produce 1000 wheels, and the next week, it might produce an 8000-gallon vat. Therefore, a job shop layout is based on the historically stable output pattern of the organization and expected changes in that pattern, rather than on current operations or outputs.

A variety of factors can be important in the interrelations among the operations of a job shop. If all the qualitative and quantitative factors can be analyzed and combined, the relative importance of locating each department close to or far from each of the other departments may be used to determine a layout. This approach is particularly useful for service operations where movements of materials are not particularly significant. To illustrate how this concept might be achieved in practice, we next present a simplified example. Following this, we illustrate how a purely cost-based layout could be achieved.

3.3.3.4 Directly Specified Closeness Preferences

As a simplified example, consider Table 3.3, where six departments have been analyzed for the desirability of closeness to each other. Assume we are given the organization's *closeness preferences,* indicated by the letters A, E, I, O, U, and X, with the meanings given in the table. In general, the desirability of closeness decreases along the alphabet until U, which is "unimportant,"

Table 3.3 Directly Specified Closeness Preferences

| Department | Department | | | | | | Note: |
	1	2	3	4	5	6	
1		E	A	U	U	U	
2			U	I	I	U	A = Absolutely necessary
3				U	U	A	E = Especially important
4					I	U	I = Important
5						I	O = Ordinary closeness is OK
6							U = Unimportant
							X = Undesirable

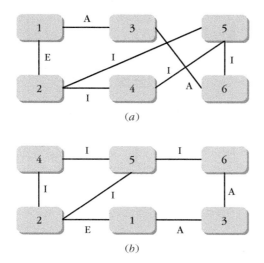

FIGURE 3.11 Closeness Preferences Layout: (*a*) Initial Layout; (*b*) Final Layout

and then jumps to "undesirable" with X; there is no range of undesirability in this case, although there could be, of course.

One way of starting the layout process is simply to draw boxes representing the departments in the order given in the table and show closeness preferences on the arcs (line segments) joining them. Figure 3.10*a* illustrates this for Table 3.3. The next step is to shift the departments with A on their arcs nearer each other and those with X away from each other. When these have been shifted as much as possible, the E arcs, then the I arcs, and finally the O arcs will be considered for relocation, resulting in an improved layout, such as in Figure 3.11*b*.

3.3.3.5 Cost–Volume–Distance Model

In the cost–volume–distance (CVD) approach, the desirability of closeness is based on the total cost of moving materials or people between departments. Clearly, a layout can never be completely reduced to just one such objective, but where the cost of movement is significant, this approach produces reasonable first approximations. The objective is to minimize the costs of interrelations among operations by locating those operations that interrelate extensively close to one another. If we label one of the departments i and another department j, then the cost of moving materials between departments i and j depends on the distance between i and j, D_{ij}. In addition, the cost will usually depend on the amount or volume moving from i to j, such as trips, cases, volume, weight, or some other such measure, which we will denote by V_{ij}. Then, if the cost of the flow from i to j per-unit amount per-unit distance is C_{ij}, the total cost of i relating with j is $C_{ij}V_{ij}D_{ij}$. Note that C, V, and D may have different values for different types of flows and that they need not have the same values from j to i as from i to j, since the flow in opposite directions may be of an entirely different nature. For example, information may be flowing from i to j, following a certain paperwork path, but sheet steel may flow from j to i, following a lift truck or conveyor belt path.

3.3.4 Cellular Production

Cellular production combines the advantages of job shops and flow shops to obtain the high variety possible with the job form and the reduced costs and short response times available with the flow form. Figure 3.12 contrasts a job shop with cellular production for a manufacturing firm. The job shop in Figure 3.12*a* has separate departments for welding, turning, heat treat, milling,

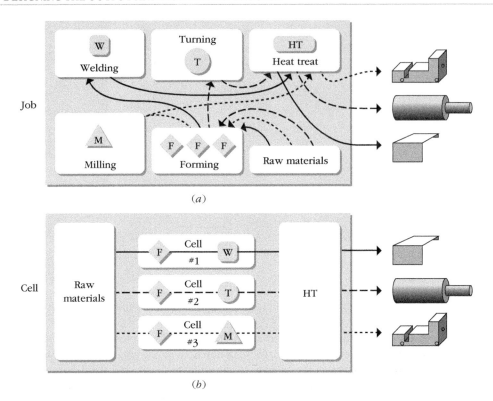

FIGURE 3.12
Conversion of (*a*) a
Job Shop Layout into
(*b*) a Cellular Layout for
Part Families

and forming. This type of layout provides sufficient flexibility to produce a wide range of products simply by varying the sequence in which the products visit the five processing departments. Also, flexibility is enhanced, as machines are easily substituted for one another should a specified machine be busy or nonoperational.

Figure 3.12*b* shows a reorganization of the plant for cellular production. The cellular form is based on *group technology,* which seeks to achieve efficiency by exploiting similarities inherent in parts. In production, this is accomplished by identifying groups of parts that have similar processing requirements. Parts with similar processing requirements are called *part families.* Figure 3.13 provides an example of how a population of parts can be organized into part families.

After the parts are divided into families, a *cell* is created that includes the human skills and all the equipment required to produce a family. Since the outputs are all similar, the equipment can be set up in one pattern to produce the entire family and does not need to be set up again for another type of output (as is necessary in a job shop). Some cells consist of just one machine producing a complete product or service. Other cells may have as many as 50 people working with dozens of machines.

A facility using cells is generally organized on the basis of *teams.* That is, a team is completely responsible for conducting the work within its cell. The team members usually schedule and inspect the work themselves, once they know when it is due. Occasionally, work must be taken outside a cell for a special treatment or process that is unavailable within the cell, but these outside transfers are minimized as much as possible.

The families are derived from one of a number of different approaches. Sometimes, the basis is the machines that are needed to produce the output, or the families may be based on the size of the equipment, the quality required, the skills needed, or any other overriding considerations. This is called the *classification* stage. Items are classified into families – sometimes by simple inspection and other times by complex analysis of their routing requirements, production

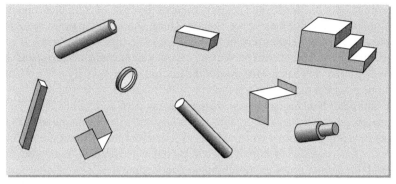

Unorganized parts

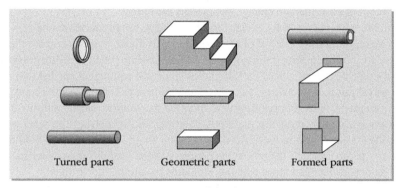

| Turned parts | Geometric parts | Formed parts |

Parts organized by families

FIGURE 3.13
Organization of
Miscellaneous Parts
into Families

requirements, part geometry, and the like. It is generally not feasible to classify all the outputs into one of a limited number of families, so at some point, all the miscellaneous outputs are placed in a "remainder" cell, which is operated as a minijob shop.

3.3.4.1 Advantages of Cellular Production

Organizations adopt the cellular form to achieve many of the efficiencies associated with products and services that are mass-produced using flow transformation systems in less repetitive job shop environments. However, not all the advantages of a full flow shop or a full job shop can be obtained because not enough high-volume equipment can be purchased to obtain the economies of scale that flow shops enjoy. And because the equipment is dedicated to part families, some of the variety afforded by job shops is lost.

One of the most important advantages of the cellular form is reduced machine setup times. In a job shop, when a worker completes the processing of one batch, the machine is set up for the next batch. Because a wide variety of parts typically flow through each department in a job shop, the next batch of parts processed by the worker will likely be different from the one just completed. This means that the worker may have to spend several hours or more simply setting up and preparing the machine for the next batch of parts. In cellular production, machine setup times are minimized because each cell processes only parts that have similar (or identical) setup and processing requirements. It is extremely desirable to minimize machine setup times because setup time takes away from the amount of time machines can be used to produce the outputs.

Decreasing machine setup times provides several benefits. First, as we have just noted, when setup times decrease, the amount of time equipment is available to process parts increases. Second, increased capacity means that the company can produce at a given level with fewer machines.

Reducing the number of machines used not only reduces the costs of equipment and maintenance but also reduces the amount of floor space needed. Third, shorter setup times make it more economical to produce smaller batches. For instance, if the setup time is four hours, it would not be efficient to produce a small number of parts using a particular machine only to spend another four hours to set it up for the next batch. However, if the machine required only a few minutes of setup time, it might be practical to produce a few parts on the machine.

There are numerous benefits associated with producing parts in small batches. To begin with, producing small batches enhances an organization's flexibility in responding to changes in product mix. Also, reducing the size of batches leads to reductions in WIP inventory. Less inventory means that less space is needed to store it and less capital is tied up in it. Also, product lead times are shorter, and throughput times are faster due to overlapping the tasks. Shorter lead times and faster throughput facilitate more accurate forecasting, faster response to market changes, faster revenue generation, and perhaps, the most important advantage of all, less time for engineers to change the output or customers to change (or cancel) the order!

Another major advantage of the cellular form is that parts are produced in one cell. Processing the parts in one cell simplifies control of the shop floor. To illustrate this, compare the amount of effort required to coordinate the production activities in job shops and the cellular layout. Producing parts in a single cell also reduces the amount of labor and equipment needed to move materials because travel distances between successive operations are shorter. Additionally, producing the parts in one cell provides an opportunity to increase the workers' accountability, responsibility, and autonomy. Finally, reducing materials handling and increasing the workers' accountability typically translate into reduced defects. In a job shop, it is difficult to hold the workers accountable for quality because the product is processed in several different departments, and the workers in one department can always blame problems on another department.

A unique advantage of the cell form is that it maximizes the inherent benefits of the team approach. In a flow shop, there is little teamwork because the equipment does most of the work; the labor primarily involves oversight and maintenance. Job shops are organized by department, and this allows for some teamwork – but not in terms of specific jobs because everyone is working on a different job. In a cell, all the workers are totally responsible for completing every job. Thus, the effect is to enrich the work, provide challenges, encourage communication and teamwork, meet due dates, and maintain quality.

An additional advantage for manufacturers is the minimal cost required to move to cellular production. Although some cells may be highly automated, with expensive special-purpose equipment, it is not necessary to invest any additional capital in order to adopt the cellular form. It requires only the movement of equipment and labor into cells. Or, with even less trouble, though with some loss of efficiency, the firm can simply designate certain pieces of equipment as dedicated to a single-part family but not relocate them. The term used in this case is *virtual cell* or *logical cell* (also known as *nominal*) because the equipment is not physically adjoining but is still reserved for production of only one part family.

Another form of cellular production is called a miniplant. Here, the cell not only does the manufacturing but also has its own industrial engineer, quality manager, accountant, marketing representative, and salesperson as well as almost all the other support services that a regular plant has. Only far-removed services, such as R&D and human resources, are not dedicated to the miniplant. The entire facility of the firm is thus broken down into a number of miniplants, each with its own general manager, production workers, and support services so that it can operate as an independent profit center.

3.3.4.2 Disadvantages of Cellular Production

Some disadvantages of the cellular form are those of flow shops and job shops, but they are not as serious. As in a flow shop, if a piece of equipment should break down, it can stop production in the cell; but in a cell form – unlike a flow shop, where that might be the only piece of equipment in the facility – work might, if permissible, temporarily be shifted to other cells to get a job out.

However, obtaining balance among the cells when demands for a product or service family keep changing is a lesser problem in both flow and job shops. Flow shops are relatively fixed in capacity and produce a standard output, so there is no question of balance. Job shops simply draw from a pool of skilled labor for whatever job comes in. With cells, by contrast, if demand for a family dries up, it may be necessary to break up that cell and redistribute the equipment or reform the families. In the short run, though, labor can generally be assigned to whatever cell needs it, including the remainder cell.

Of course, volumes are too small in cellular production to allow the purchase of high-volume, efficient equipment that flow shops use. The cellular form also does not allow for the extent of customization usually found in job shops, since the labor pool has largely been disbursed to independent cells (although the remainder cell may be able to do the work). Moreover, the fostering of specialized knowledge associated with various operational activities is reduced because the workers who perform these activities are spread out and therefore have limited opportunities to collaborate.

3.3.4.3 Cellular Layout

Cellular production creates teams of workers and equipment to produce families of outputs. The workers are cross-trained so that they can operate any of the equipment in their cell, and they take full responsibility for the proper performance or result of the outputs. Whenever feasible, these outputs are final products or services. At other times, particularly in manufacturing, the outputs are parts that go into a final product. If the latter is the case, it is common to group the cells closely around the main production or assembly line so that they feed their output directly into the line as it is needed.

In some cases, a *virtual cell* is formed by identifying certain equipment and dedicating it to the production of families of outputs but without moving the equipment into an actual, physical cell. In that case, no "layout" analysis is required at all; the organization simply keeps the layout it had. The essence of the problem, then, is the identification of the output families and the equipment to dedicate to each of them.

It is more common for an organization to actually form physical cells. When physical cells are created, the layout of the cell may resemble a sort of miniflow shop, a job shop, or a mix of these, depending on the situation. Thus, we will direct our attention here to the formation of the part or product families and their associated equipment, leaving the issues of physical layout to be addressed in the discussions of flow shops and job shops.

In practice, organizations often use the term *cell* to include a wide range of very different situations: a functional department consisting of identical machines, a single machine that automatically performs a variety of operations, or even a dedicated assembly line. Earlier, we also referred to the portion of a shop that is not associated with a specific part family as a cell: a *remainder cell.* Nevertheless, we do not consider all these groups to be part of what we are calling cellular production.

Organizations that formally plan their shop layouts typically choose to group their equipment on the basis of either the function it performs (i.e. job shops) or the processing requirements of a product or group of products (i.e. flow shops). As we discussed, the purpose of grouping equipment on the basis of its function is to maximize flexibility, whereas the purpose of grouping it on the basis of processing requirements is to maximize efficiency.

Companies that adopt cellular manufacturing typically create a *pilot cell* initially to experiment with the cellular approach, and therefore, most of the equipment in the shop remains in functional departments at this stage. As these firms gain experience with the cell and become convinced that it is beneficial, they begin a phase of implementing additional cells. This can be referred to as the *hybrid stage* because as the shop is incrementally converted to cells, a significant portion of the facilities are still arranged in functional departments. At some point, the formation of additional cells is terminated, and the firm may or may not have the majority of its equipment arranged in cells. Often, companies stop creating new cells when the volume of the remaining parts is insufficient to justify forming additional cells.

3.3.5 Project Operations

Project operations are typically of large scale and have a finite duration; also, they are nonrepetitive, consisting of multiple, and often simultaneous, tasks that are highly interdependent. However, the primary characteristics of the tasks are their limited duration and, if the output is a physical product, their immobility during processing. Generally, staff, materials, and equipment are brought to the output and located in a nearby *staging area* until needed. Projects have particularly limited lives. Resources are brought together for the duration of the project; some are consumed, and others, such as equipment and personnel, are deployed to other uses at the conclusion of the project. Typically, the output is unique (a dam, product development, a presidential campaign, and a trial).

In designing a processing system, a number of considerations may indicate that the project form is appropriate. One of these is the rate of change in the organization's outputs. If one department must keep current on a number of markets that are rapidly changing, the typical organization would quickly fall behind its competition. The project form offers extremely short reaction times to environmental or internal changes and would thus be called for. In addition, if the tasks are for a limited duration only, the project form is indicated. Finally, the project form is chosen when the output is of a very large scale with multiple, interdependent activities requiring close coordination. During the project, coordination is achieved through frequent meetings of the representatives of the various functional areas on the project team.

One of the advantages of the project form, as noted earlier, is its ability to perform under time and cost constraints. Therefore, if meeting a due date or staying within budget is crucial, the project form is most appropriate. Planning and managing projects was discussed in detail in Chapter 2.

3.3.6 Service Examples of these Transformation Forms

All of the previous five forms of transformation systems except for continuous processes can also be used for services. Using the example of personal fitness, a flow shop is commonly used for circuit training where five to ten specialized pieces of equipment are laid out in sequence with each piece of equipment (station) targeting a different muscle group. Completing a circuit entails visiting each station in sequence and completing a specified number of repetitions at the station or exercising for a specified amount of time. The stations are arranged in the order they are needed to facilitate completing the exercises in the correct order.

The local YMCA that one of the authors occasionally worked out at provides an example of a job shop, or functional, layout. At this particular YMCA, the workout equipment was arranged functionally with a room containing the equipment for cardio workouts (e.g. treadmills, exercise bikes, stair climbing machines), a room containing free weights, and another room with machines for performing resistance training. Other areas of the building had spaces for racket sports and swimming sports. In addition to the overall layout of the building being organized functionally, the layout within each functional area was often functionally laid out. For example, in the room containing the machines used for resistance training, the machines were arranged based on the muscle group the machine targeted. Thus, the machines for working out the legs were located together on one side of the room while the machines used to work out the chest were located together on another side of the room. The same YMCA also had a cellular transformation system. More specifically, behind the room containing the machines for resistance training was another room. This room was used by professional trainers who worked with high school athletes and other elite athletes. The room contained a variety of general-purpose equipment that was used to help the athletes develop their strength, endurance, and flexibility. Having all the equipment needed in one room meant that the athletes could complete their training in one location rather than having to travel to the rooms that contained the equipment based on its function.

Finally, training for a marathon exemplifies a project related to personal fitness. The dimensions of time (deadline) and performance would likely be the most important project goals.

3.4 Selection of a Transformation System

This section addresses the issue of selecting the appropriate transformation system, or mix of systems, to produce an output. From the preceding discussion, it should be clear that the five transformation systems are somewhat simplified extremes of what is likely to be observed in practice. Few organizations use one of the five forms in a pure sense; most combine two or more forms in what we call a *hybrid* shop. For example, in manufacturing computer keyboards, some parts and subassemblies are produced in job shops or cells but then fed into a flow shop at the final assembly line, where a batch of one model is produced. Then the line is modified to produce a batch of another model. Even in "custom" work, jobs are often handled in groups of generally common items throughout most of their processing, leaving minor finishing details such as the fabric on a couch or the facade of a house to give the impression of customizing.

Although services typically take the form of a job shop, the emphasis has recently been on trying to mass-produce them (using cells or flow shops) so as to increase volume and reduce unit costs. Some examples are fast-food restaurants, multiphasic medical screening, and group life insurance. Even with services, we often find combined forms of process design: McDonald's prepares batches of Big Macs but will accept individual custom orders. Burger King uses a conveyor assembly line for its Whoppers but advertises its ability to customize its burgers to suit any taste.

The problem for the operations manager is to decide what processing form(s) is most appropriate for the organization, considering long-run efficiency, effectiveness, lead time, capacity, quality, and flexibility. Selection may be even more difficult because, as mentioned previously, it is possible to combine processing forms to attain efficiency in some portions of the production process and flexibility in other portions. It is clear that the trade-offs must be well understood by the manager, and the expected benefits and costs must be well known.

Unfortunately, most plants do not have the luxury of time for completely reorganizing their processes. As a result, they often grow into a hodgepodge of machines and processes scattered somewhat randomly around the plant, barely resembling any of the aforementioned five forms, even if they started out with one of them. In that regard, services have an advantage since they are usually not loaded down with physical assets, yet their labor may be even harder to retrain or move than physical assets.

3.4.1 Considerations of Volume and Variety

One of the most important factors in the design of a transformation system is establishing the volume and variety of outputs the organization will produce. High volumes tend to indicate that highly automated mass production will be necessary. High variety, on the other hand, implies the use of skilled labor and general-purpose tools and facilities.

A related consideration here is whether the output will be make-to-stock or make-to-order. A *make-to-stock* product is produced in batches of some size that is economical (for the firm) and then stocked (in a warehouse, on shelves, etc.) but it is hard for many services to "stock" their service for their customers. As customers purchase them, the items are withdrawn from stock. A *make-to-order* item is usually produced in a batch of a size set by the customer (sometimes just one) and is delivered to the customer upon its completion. This is where services will usually operate. Generally, make-to-stock items are produced in large volumes with low variety, whereas make-to-order items are produced in low volumes with high variety. (Quite often, *every* item is different.) However, there are many variants of these two major categories, such as *engineer-to-order*, where a firm takes a customer's specifications for a product and actually designs the product and then makes it. (In the typical make-to-order process, the product is one that the firm already knows how to make and may even be listed in its sales catalog.) Another variant is called *assemble-to-order*, where the components of a set of products are stocked ahead of time (made-to-stock); when an order for one of the items in that set arrives, they are then quickly assembled to produce the final desired product.

Organizations in the same industry may deliver their outputs using alternative approaches. For example, a bakery that designs and bakes custom wedding cakes exemplifies engineer-to-order. A five-star restaurant that prepares your steak to your specific doneness specification exemplifies make-to-order. A pizza restaurant that adds the toppings you request to your pizza illustrates an assemble-to-order operation. Finally, a fast-food restaurant that prepares hamburgers ahead of time is employing a make-to-stock operation.

Clearly, *many* services will not normally be of a type that can be stocked, even if every service is identical (e.g., a physical examination). Also, exceptions to these generalizations are abundant. Automobiles, for example, are made to order but are produced in high volumes and with high varieties. (However, autos are really *assembled* to order, with the assembly components produced to stock *and already available*.) And general-purpose machine shops often produce high volumes of low-variety items for specific customers.

Figure 3.14*a*, based on the *product–process matrix* developed by Hayes and Wheelwright (1979), illustrates these points as they relate to the various transformation systems. The horizontal axis shows volume, as measured by the batch size, and the left vertical axis shows the variety of outputs. Organizations making a single unit of output that varies each time (such as dams, custom-built machines, and many services) use the project form or sometimes the job shop. Job

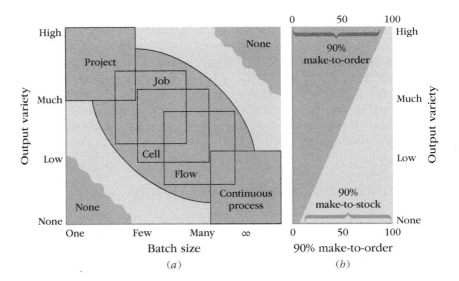

FIGURE 3.14 Effect of Output Characteristics on Transformation Systems – the Product-Process Matrix

shop and cellular systems, however, are mainly used when a considerable variety of outputs are required in relatively small batches. This is also characteristic of many services. When the size of a batch increases significantly, with a corresponding decrease in variety, then a flow shop is appropriate. Some services also fall into this category. Last, when all the output is the same and the batch is extremely large (or essentially infinite, as in the ore, petrochemical, and food and drink industries), the continuous process is appropriate. Very few services exist here.

Note that the standard, viable transformation forms lie on the diagonal of the product–process matrix. Operating at some point off this diagonal can be dangerous for the organization unless done carefully as a well-planned strategy. Essentially, no organizations operate in the upper right or lower left segments of this grid. The lower left does, however, represent manufacturing 200 years ago. If you wanted four identical dressers, say, for your four children, they were made one at a time by hand (whether identical or all different, for that matter). Today, however, it is simply too expensive to produce items this way; if the items are all identical, they are made in a large batch and then sold separately. In some cases, it is almost impossible to buy a single unit of some items, such as common tenpenny nails – you have to buy a blister pack of 10 or so. Similarly, the upper right may represent manufacturing in the future, when advanced technology can turn out great masses of completely customized products as cheaply as standard items. Currently, however, we have trouble doing this (in spite of popular concepts such as "mass customization" discussed in Chapter 1). Some products, however, lend themselves to approximations to this goal through specialized techniques such as assemble-to-order: fast food, computers purchased online, and so on. These firms have developed strategies, and the production techniques to accompany them, for successfully using "off-diagonal" transformation processes.

Note the overlap in the different forms. This means, for example, that on occasion, some organizations will use a flow shop for outputs with smaller batches or a larger variety, or both, than the outputs of organizations using a job shop. There are many possible reasons for this, including economic and historical factors. The organization may also simply be using an inappropriate transformation system. The point is that the categories are not rigid, and many variations do occur. Many organizations also use hybrids or combinations of systems, such as producing components to stock but assembling finished products to order, as in the auto industry.

Note in Figure 3.14b the general breakdown of make-to-order and make-to-stock with output variety and size of batch. Project forms (high variety, unit batch size) are almost always make-to-order, and continuous processing forms (no variety, infinite batch size) are almost always make-to-stock, though exceptions occasionally occur.

3.4.2 Output and Process Life Cycles

Earlier in this chapter we described the life cycle of an output: how long it takes to develop, bring to market, and catch on; how quickly it grows in popularity; how different versions are developed for different market segments; how the output reaches market saturation; and how price competition emerges. A similar life cycle occurs in the production system for an output. As a result, a project form of transformation system may be used for the development of a new output, may evolve into a job shop or cellular layout as a market develops, and finally may evolve into a flow shop as full standardization and high volumes develop. (We assume here that a continuous process is not appropriate for the output.) We briefly elaborate on this production life cycle.

In the R&D stage, many variations are investigated during the development of a product. As the output is being developed, prototypes are made in small volumes in a relatively inefficient, uncoordinated manner typically in a job shop. As demand grows and competitors enter the market, price competition begins and a cellular or flow system, with its high volume and low variable costs, becomes preferred. At the peak of the cycle, demand may increase to the point where such a system is justified. At the stage of project development and initiation (R&D and initial production), the cost of fixed equipment is nil, and labor is the predominant contributor to high variable costs. In the expansion stage, the job shop allows some trade-off of equipment for labor with a corresponding reduction in variable unit costs, thus leading, at these volumes, to a reduction in overall unit costs. Finally, at high volumes characterizing maturity, a nearly complete replacement of expensive labor with equipment is possible, using the cellular form and the flow shop.

Be advised, however, that not all outputs can or should follow this sequence. The point is that the transformation system should evolve as the market and output evolve. But many organizations see their strength in operating a particular transformation system, such as R&D or low-cost production of large volumes. If their outputs evolve into another stage of the life cycle in which a different transformation system form is preferable, they drop the output (or license it to someone else) and switch to another output more appropriate to their strengths.

Failing to maintain this focus in the organization's production system can quickly result in a "white elephant" – a facility built to be efficient at one task but being inefficiently used for something else. This can also happen if the organization, in an attempt to please every customer, mixes the production of outputs that require different transformation systems. Japanese plants are very carefully planned to maintain one strong focus in each plant. If an output requiring a different process is to be produced, a new plant is acquired or built.

From the previous discussion, it is clear that there is a close relationship between the design of a product or service (discussed earlier in this chapter) and the design of the production system. Actually, the link is even closer than it seems. Figure 3.15 illustrates the relationship between the innovations throughout the life cycle of a product or service and innovations throughout the life cycle of its production system. At the left, when the product or service is introduced, innovations and changes in its design are frequent. At this point, the production system is more of the project or job shop form since the design is still changing (the number of *product* innovations is high). Toward the middle, the product design has largely stabilized, and cost competition is forcing innovations in the production process, particularly the substitution of cellular or flow shop machinery for labor (the number of *process* innovations is high). At the right, this phenomenon has subsided and innovations in production methods are primarily the result of competitors' actions, government regulations, and other external factors.

Although not typically involved on the research side of such innovations in production methods (a laboratory engineering function), the operations manager is intimately involved with implementing them and improving them once implemented, as described in more detail in Chapters 8 and 9. It is also important that people representing the operations function be

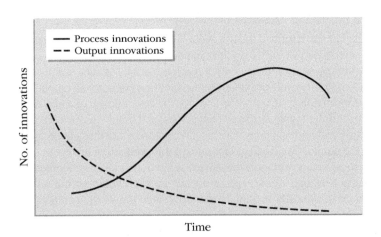

FIGURE 3.15
Output–Process Innovations over Time

involved in evaluating the possible trade-offs that exist in the development of new production processes. For example, the new production system might be more expensive but might produce a higher-quality output (and thus, the repeat volume may be higher, or perhaps the price can be increased). Or the new production system might be more expensive and might produce a lower-quality output but be simpler and easier to maintain, resulting in a lower total cost and, ultimately, higher profits. Clearly, many strategic and operational considerations – labor, maintenance, quality, materials, capital investment, and so on – are involved in the successful application of research to operations.

A final consideration related to product and process life cycles is how to implement the knowledge gained from product and process research. Frequently, organizations invest in a *pilot plant* to investigate a new product or process on just a small or limited scale prior to committing significantly more resources to full-scale production. As was noted earlier, the success rate of new production introductions can be quite low, and utilizing a pilot plant can greatly mitigate the risks associated with commercializing new products. Such pilot plants can be used to test and develop new production processes as well as use them for trial production in order to obtain intelligence about the market, including the size of the market and customer interest in the new product. For example, in the pharmaceutical industry, new drugs are typically first produced in small quantities in laboratories, followed by production in a pilot plant, and if all goes well, ultimately in full-scale production plants. It is also important to point out that it may not be possible to predict how a process will perform as it is scaled up. In the case of the pharmaceutical industry, it is not always possible to simply increase the scale of the lab process. An entirely different production process may be needed to produce a drug in large quantities.

Given the tradeoffs noted above, it is important for the operations manager to present a solid proposal to upper management to justify the acquisition of a new technology such as a robot or computer, or the implementation of a new method of producing a service or product such as cellular layouts. The *justification* process for such a proposal, or a full business case, is complex because there will typically be both soft and hard benefits, and the hard benefits may include both monetary and nonmonetary benefits such as higher volumes or quality. The soft benefits, such as improved morale in the organization or a better image with the public, are near impossible to monetize, and management usually will prefer them quantified if possible but left as subjective, such as a "30 percent" improvement. For many proposals, especially strategic proposals, the primary benefit of the change will be the soft benefits, such as positioning the organization for greater strength or competitiveness in the future, or increased social capital in the organization, or gaining an option to employ a revolutionary new technology later. Clearly, trying to accurately monetize these kinds of benefits would be virtually impossible.

3.4.3 Environmental Considerations

Another important consideration in selecting the transformation system that is gaining increasing importance at many organizations is the impact their operations will have on the environment. An organization's operations, and indeed other organizational activities as well, often require large amounts of energy and water and as a byproduct, may produce large quantities of emissions. To address this concern, organizations are turning to the use of clean technologies in the production of their outputs. The United Nations Environment Programme (UNEP) defines cleaner production as:

> *the continuous application of an integrated, preventive environmental strategy to processes, products, services to increase overall efficiency, and reduce risks to humans and the environment (UNEP 2006).*

Thus, in pursuing cleaner production, organizations seek to reduce the environmental impact of their production activities by using energy, water, and raw materials more efficiently and reducing the emissions generated. Not surprisingly, other important benefits beyond reducing the negative environmental impact of production activities typically accrue to organizations that pursue cleaner production such as increased revenue and improved cost efficiencies. The strategy of reducing the use of energy and natural resources while at the same time producing more goods and services is referred to as eco-efficiency. The definition of eco-efficiency may sound familiar to you. Referring back to our discussion of productivity in Chapter 1, we observe that eco-efficiency is a multifactor measure of productivity using energy and natural resources as the inputs.

Another element of cleaner production is minimizing waste, which can be accomplished by utilizing technology, enhancing operating practices and processes, and through reuse and recycling initiatives. The ultimate goal of waste minimization efforts is *zero* waste, meaning that no waste from production processes is sent to landfills. The principles of cleaner production related to increasing productivity by reducing the quantities of raw materials and energy used in the production process and reducing waste are also consistent with the principles of Lean Management discussed in Chapter 9.

3.4.4 Service Processes

In review of the differences between services and products in terms of selection and design consider the following:

- The amount of customer contact with a pure service (i.e. no accompanying physical good, as with a medical examination) is usually significantly higher than with a product, such as a chair. A measure of this factor is termed the contact intensity of the output, represented by the percentage of time the customer needs to be present compared to the total time required for the delivery of the output.

- Pure services are generally perceived to be much more labor intensive than products, which are more capital intensive, although this is not always the case.

- Similarly, pure services are generally thought to be more personalized and lower paying than mass-merchandised products, although this is not true for services that require high amounts of training or education.

- Because most services generally cannot be patented like products, service providers themselves are often certified or licensed by some accrediting agency such as in the medical, legal, and other such professional fields.

- Since pure services cannot be stored like products, there is difficulty matching the supply with the arrival of demand for the service. If capacity is made available for the highest possible demand peak, then the lower demand periods will experience poor utilization and efficiency.

- Services generally require less lead time to select, design, and offer, and can thus be changed easier and faster than with a product output. This is particularly true if the service is labor intensive (more flexible, trainable) rather than capital equipment intensive. However, this also means that competition can move in faster and easier.

As with the design of transformation systems for products, the design of transformation systems for services depends heavily on knowing exactly what characteristics of the service need to be emphasized: its explicit and implicit benefits, cost, time duration, location, and accessibility.

Knowing the importance of each of these allows the designer to make the necessary trade-offs in costs and benefits to offer an effective yet reasonably priced service.

Unfortunately, service transformation systems are frequently implemented with little development or pretesting, which is also a major reason why so many of them fail.

Consider the extensive development and testing of the McDonald's fast-food production system, airline reservations systems, and many life insurance policies. Each of these also illustrates the many hours of training required to use equipment and procedures properly and efficiently. Yet most new service firms frequently fail to train their personnel adequately, again inviting failure.

In most cases, the various forms and layouts of manufacturing transformation processes apply equally well to services. Flow shops are seen in fast-food restaurants, job shops are seen in banks and hospitals, and projects are seen in individual services such as wedding planning and house construction. Chapter 4 includes an example of a *service blueprint* that is commonly used for process flow and capacity analysis purposes but may also be helpful when designing the service up front.

However, one important service element that is usually missing from manufacturing transformation design is extensive customer contact during delivery of the service. This presents both problems and opportunities. For one thing, the customer will often add new inputs to the delivery system or make new demands on it that were not anticipated when it was designed. In addition, customers do not arrive at smooth, even increments of time but instead tend to bunch up, as during lunch periods, and then complain when they have to wait for service. Furthermore, the customers' biased perception of the server, and the server's skills, can often influence their satisfaction with the quality of the service. Obviously, this can either be beneficial or harmful, depending on the circumstances.

On the other hand, having the customer involved in the delivery of a service can also present opportunities to improve it. Since customers know their own needs best, it is wise to let them aid in the preparation or delivery of the service – as with automatic teller machines, salad bars, and pay-at-pump gas stations. In addition to improving the quality of the service, this can save the firm money by making it unnecessary to hire additional servers. However, the customer can also negligently – and quickly – ruin a machine or a tool and may even sue if injured by it, so the service firm must carefully consider how much self-service it is willing to let the customer perform.

Chase and Tansik (1983) devised a helpful way to view this customer contact when designing service delivery systems. Their suggestion is to evaluate whether the service is, in general, high contact or low contact, and what portions of the service, in particular, are each. The value of this analysis is that the service can be made both more efficient and more effective by separating these two portions and designing them differently. For example, the high-contact portions of the service should be handled by workers who are skilled at social interaction, whereas the low-contact portion should employ more technical workers and take advantage of labor-saving equipment. For example, a bank might have a back office, where checks are encoded, located apart from the front office, where customers deposit them. In this back office, equipment and efficiency are the critical job elements, whereas in the front office, interpersonal skills and friendliness are critical.

Whenever possible, the low-contact portion of a service should be decoupled from the high-contact portion so that it can be conducted with efficiency, whereas the high-contact portion is conducted with grace and friendliness. Close analysis of the service tasks may also reveal opportunities for decreasing contact with the customer – through, for example, automated teller machines, phone service, self-service, or the Web, if this is appropriate – with a concomitant opportunity for improving both the efficiency and level of service. In particular, enabling customers to use the Web to obtain service (e.g. obtain account information, place orders) offers them convenient access – 24 hours per day, 365 days per year – and immediate attention (i.e. no longer being placed on hold for the next available representative).

Similarly, there may be some opportunities for increasing the amount of customer contact, such as phone or e-mail follow-ups after service, which should be exploited to improve the overall service and its image. The service provider should thoroughly investigate these opportunities.

3.4.4.1 Service Process Design

Like the "product–process" matrix for manufacturing, Schmenner (1986) has developed a similar matrix for services that not only classifies four major and quite different types of services but gives some insights into how to design the best service system. The service matrix is shown in Figure 3.16. Service systems are divided into those with high- versus low-contact intensity (similar to Chase and Tansik) and according to whether they are capital-intensive or labor-intensive. Schmenner names each of the quadrants with an easily understood identifier that captures the essence of that quadrant: service factory, service shop, mass service, and professional service.

Each of the quadrants represents a unique service transformation process, with unique managerial challenges and unique characteristics. Those services at the high-contact side of the matrix have low volumes with high customization and must attain their profitability through high prices. Those on the other side with low contact and customization attain profitability through high volumes. The investment axis identifies whether the service provider puts its resources into expensive equipment or into labor. Thus, one axis is a combination of customer variety and volume (like the product–process matrix), and the other axis is based on the inputs needed to provide the service. Examples of typical services in each quadrant are given in the figure.

The matrix is also useful in identifying the managerial challenges for each of the quadrants. In the low-contact left side, the managerial challenge is making the service appear warm and friendly so as to attract high volumes. If the level of contact is high, the managerial challenge is to try to be optimally efficient in using capital and labor resources while keeping prices high. If the service is equipment-intensive, the challenge is to keep capital investment costs low. If instead the service is labor-intensive, the challenge is to minimize wages and time spent on each customer.

The matrix is also useful in redesigning a service. For example, a firm may decide to move from one quadrant to another to better use its resources or environment. For example, a tax preparation service may start as a high-priced professional service but then move either toward a more

	CUSTOMER CONTACT INTENSITY	
	Low	**High**
Capital-Intensive	**Service factory** Airlines Package/postal services Hotels Recreation	**Service shop** Hospitals Cruise line Repair services Expensive restaurants
Labor-Intensive	**Mass service** Sporting events School classes Retailing Fast food	**Professional service** Legal services Physicians Interior decorators Tax preparers

FIGURE 3.16 The Service Matrix

automated service shop through computer preparation of the forms or a less personalized mass service using less skilled tax preparers.

3.4.4.2 Servicescapes

Bitner (1992) uses the term *servicescape* to stress the importance of the physical environment of the service and its influence on both the customer and the server, as well as the efficiency and the customer's perception of the service. The servicescape for a self-service operation is much more important to the successful delivery of a service than when the service is assisted or full service because the customer has to take cues from the layout or signage about how to serve him- or herself, such as at an ATM or cafeteria. When there is assistance from a server, such as at an airport kiosk or sit-down restaurant, the servicescape layout can be adjusted to be more efficient from a processing point of view. And when there is full service, especially remote service (e.g. phoned orders, online tech support), the layout of the service facility can be even more structured so as to help the servers complete their tasks (since the layout does not affect the customers).

Bitner emphasizes three elements of servicescapes: their ambient conditions, their spatial layout and functionality, and the signs, symbols, and artifacts in the physical environment. The *ambient conditions* refer to the sights, sounds, scents, temperature, humidity, and other such conditions that affect the service. For example, a restaurant featuring live, soft piano music communicates a different (and probably more expensive) sensation to a customer than the one where loud pop music is competing with loud noise from the bar and table guests. Lighting, scents, and decor can play similar roles.

The *spatial layout and functionality,* as noted earlier, play important roles in minimizing the cost of providing the service (and sometimes maximizing the revenue) and maximizing the satisfaction of the customer. Again, whether the facility is a self-service or full-service one is an important consideration to the layout and functionality, such as with fast-food versus sit-down service restaurants. In terms of revenue maximizing, who hasn't tried to rush into a department store to buy a shirt only to be obstructed by a 30-foot-wide cosmetics counter and then having to navigate through an array of jewelry counters?

Last, *signs, symbols, and artifacts* help tell customers what to expect of the service and their role in the process. This includes wall decorations, floor coverings, furniture, colors, room sizes, ceiling heights, and so on. Consider the heavy furniture, wood paneling, thick carpeting, wall art, and handsome receptionist in an expensive law office versus the trash and recycle bins and logo-imprinted shirts and aprons in a fast-food outlet.

3.4.4.3 Service Gaps

When designing services, it can be useful to inspect the service design and delivery for potential "gaps" between what the customer/client needs and what the service provider is offering (Parasuraman et al. 1988). By identifying the possible gaps in the service process, a service provider can better control the quality, productivity, cost, and performance of its service offering, thereby resulting in greater profit and market share. A gap analysis can also help identify service industries where better service might offer a competitive advantage.

Figure 3.17 illustrates the concept. Essentially, there is commonly a gap between what the customer/client actually needs and what is delivered that involves gaps throughout the selection, design, and delivery process. We start with gap 1, the reasonable difference between the ideal service that the customer actually needs and what the customer expects. This gap is often influenced heavily by advertising and other communications from the service provider. Gap 2 is the imbalance between what the customer expected and his or her perception of what was actually

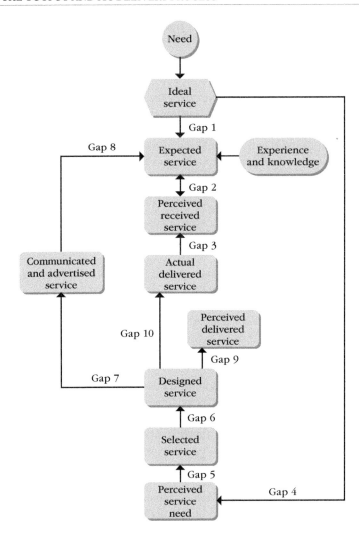

FIGURE 3.17 Potential Locations for Service Gaps

received. Gap 3 is the final gap on the customer's side; it represents the difference between what was actually delivered and the customer's perception of that reality.

The seven remaining gaps are all on the provider's side. Gap 4 is the misperception by the service provider of what the customer truly needs. Gap 5 is the difference between that misperception and what the provider chooses to offer (the selected service). Gap 6 is the discrepancy between the service that was selected and the service that was designed. Gap 7 concerns marketing and sales and is the disparity between the designed service and what these functions understand it to be. Continuing this path, gap 8 concerns the difference between what the provider is attempting to communicate to the customer and what the customer actually understands. Then, returning to the service delivery process, the last two gaps concern the contrast between what was designed and what was perceived as delivered (gap 9) or what was actually delivered (gap 10).

Clearly, with nine possible opportunities for the service provider to not meet the customer's expectations, not to mention the customer's needs (gap 1), there are a lot of ways to fail in the service provision process. It behooves all service (and product) providers to carefully examine each of these potential failure points in their own business to see if they can improve their service provision process, especially before someone else discovers the opportunity and moves to close the gaps.

3.4.4.4 Service Guarantees and Fail-Safing

Service guarantees are increasingly common among service providers who have confidence they can meet *the customer's service expectations* and who desire a competitive advantage in their industry. Package transportation companies were among the first to use them and since then have been adopted by hotels, restaurants, and others in those service businesses that have extensive contact with the public but a reputation for poor service.

There are four major elements of a service guarantee:

1. It must be meaningful to the customer in the sense that it in fact repays the customer for the failure of the service to meet his or her expectations. A guarantee with a trivial payoff that does not satisfy the customer will just increase the customer's dissatisfaction and negate the purpose of the guarantee program in the first place.

2. The guarantee must be unconditional. Again, if there are "exceptions" that exclude the common reasons why the service might fail, the customer will only be more dissatisfied.

3. The guarantee must be easy to communicate and for the customer (and employees) to understand. If the guarantee is complex or complicated to explain, it will not attract customers to the service provider. And employees who are charged with making good on the guarantee also need to fully understand it and be able to execute the guarantee provisions.

4. The guarantee must be easy to "use" in the sense of immediately invoking it when a service failure occurs. If the customer has to return home, mail in a coupon, and wait for satisfaction, the guarantee program will not achieve its purpose.

The information technology field is a leader in the development and use of formalized service guarantees, referring to them as service-level agreements (SLAs). Here, an SLA is a written contract between an information technology provider and the user of the technology specifying the level of service that will be provided, typically in measurable terms. In addition to using SLAs to specify the levels of service that will be provided by external organizations, it is also becoming increasingly common for internal information system departments to develop SLAs for the other departments they support within the enterprise. Representative SLA metrics for information technology providers include the percentage of uptime, help-desk response times, and the timely reporting of usage statistics.

One approach organizations use to help guarantee their service is a concept called *fail-safing* (Chase and Stewart 1994), which anticipates where a service failure might occur and installs preventive measures. The service blueprint in Chapter 4, mentioned earlier, includes potential failure points in the service process that should be considered for fail-safing. As an example of fail-safing, fast-food playgrounds are ubiquitous these days, but children who are too large can be a danger to smaller children (or to themselves) when they play on the equipment; hence, the "maximum height" signs at the playground entrance. And outpatient health clinics give vibrating beepers to patients who sign in so they aren't "lost" in the system.

But it is not only the customer who needs fail-safing, but also the service providers who need their systems to be designed to force them into performing the service correctly. A familiar example to both service providers and customers is computer screens that disallow entries in online forms that don't match the protocol or that reject the forms when required fields are inadvertently left empty. Another is McDonald's now-famous french fry scoop that picks up, straightens, and optimally sizes the amount of fries for the bag, all without human contact. Yet another is dangerous equipment that can't be activated unless the operator's hands and body are sensed to be out of danger.

In large part, the emergence of the concepts of service guarantees and fail-safing reflects the tremendous growth and availability of services in our economy and the increasingly poor record of satisfactory service being provided by so many of these new services. Examples abound: telephone answering systems with unending menus that keep customers from reaching a real person who can fix their problem, airline cancellations/delays/lost baggage, and so on. Although technology is often helpful in solving our problems, it can also multiply them.

EXPAND YOUR UNDERSTANDING

1. When a line cannot be perfectly balanced, some people will have more work time than others in each cycle. What might be a solution for this situation?

2. A current sociological trend is to move away from paced lines. Yet increasing automation is pushing workers to match their work pace to that of machines and computers. How can both of these trends be happening at the same time?

3. If a job shop was being laid out in a third-world country, how might the procedure be different? What other factors might enter in that would not exist in an industrialized country? Might the layout also differ among industrialized countries such as Europe and Japan? How about a flow shop?

4. In highly automated facilities, firms frequently increase the job responsibilities of the skilled workers who remain after automation has replaced the manual laborers, although there is less potential for applying their skills. Workers complain that they are under increased pressure to perform but have less control over the automated equipment. Is this ethical on the part of the companies involved? What approach would be better?

5. Cellular production is often conducted in a U-shaped (horseshoe-shaped) cell, rather than the rectangular cells shown in Figure 3.12b. What might be the advantages of this U shape?

6. What benefits would a virtual cell obtain, and not obtain, compared with a physical cell?

7. A number of firms are moving toward minifactories. What advantages might this offer over straight cellular production?

8. If efficiency, variety, and so on are the important measures of the low-contact or no-contact portion of a service, what are the important measures of the high-contact portion?

9. As the process life cycle changes with the product life cycle, should a firm change along with it or move into new products more appropriate to its existing process? What factors must be considered in this decision?

10. In Figure 3.14a, showing the five transformation systems, why don't firms operate in the regions marked "none"?

11. Identify the similarities in Figures 3.14a and 3.16. Identify the differences.

12. Describe how you would address the problem of framing a proposal's justification to reshore your current product made in China back to your home country.

13. In the discussion on Design Thinking, it is noted there can be gaps between what respondents tell market researchers when traditional techniques such as focus groups and interviews are used and what their actual behaviors are. What might be some reasons for these gaps? How does using direct observation help to mitigate these gaps?

14. Assume you are addressing the challenge of enhancing the educational experience of your Operations Management class. In your next class session observe the class and develop a design challenge and brainstorm prompt related to this challenge.

15. Does an organization have to accept higher product costs when designing an output or selecting a production process to reduce the negative environmental impact?

16. Name some other ways of innovating besides the product or service, the output process, the brand, and the way of profiting on the product or service.

17. In organizations you have worked for, has innovation come from market pull or technology push? Explain.

18. If you were to use a perceptual map of the market for the current or last organization you worked for, what scales would be most appropriate to use for the map? What would you do if there were 3 or 4 important factors to consider?

19. Describe why hurdle rates and ROI measures are inappropriate for innovations.

Apply Your Understanding

Paradise State University

Paradise State University (PSU) is a medium-sized private university offering both undergraduate and graduate degrees. Students typically choose Paradise State because of its emphasis on high levels of interaction and relatively small classes. University policy prohibits classes with more than 75 students (unless special permission is obtained from the provost), and the target class size is 25 students. All courses are taught by tenuretrack faculty members with appropriate terminal degrees. Faculty members teach two courses each semester.

The Business School at PSU offers only an MBA degree in one of six areas of concentration: accounting, finance, general management, management information systems (MIS), marketing, and operations management (OM). The MBA program is a one-year (two-semester) lockstep program. Since the Business School does not offer undergraduate business courses, students entering the program are required to have completed all the undergraduate business prerequisites from an accredited university. The faculty is organized into six functional departments. The table below lists the number of faculty members in each department and the average number of students each year who choose a particular concentration. Students are not permitted to have double concentrations, and PSU does not offer minors at the graduate level.

Department	Faculty	Number of students per year
Accounting	8	100
Finance	6	40
General management	7	70
MIS	10	150
Marketing	6	50
OM	10	30

The number of courses required by each concentration in each department is listed in the table below. For example, a student concentrating in accounting is required to take four accounting classes, one finance class, one management class, one MIS course, one marketing class, and two OM classes.

Concentration	Number of courses taken in respective departments					
	Accounting	Finance	Management	MIS	Marketing	OM
Accounting	4	1	1	1	1	2
Finance	1	4	1	1	1	2
General management	1	1	4	1	1	2
MIS	1	1	1	4	1	2
Marketing	1	1	1	1	4	2
OM	1	1	1	1	1	5

Questions

1. How many students must each department teach each semester? Given the target class size – 25 students – are there enough faculty members?

2. Conceptually, how could the cellular production approach be applied to the Business School?

3. What would be the advantages and disadvantages of adopting a cellular approach at the Business School? As a student, would you prefer a functional organization or a cellular organization? As a faculty member, what would you prefer?

4. On the basis of the information given, develop a rough plan detailing how the Business School faculty might be assigned to cells.

X-Opoly, Inc.

X-Opoly, Inc., was founded by two first-year college students to produce a knockoff real estate board game similar to the popular Parker Brothers' game Monopoly®. Initially, the partners started the company just to produce a board game based on popular local landmarks in their small college town, as a way to help pay for their college expenses. However, the game was a big success, and because they enjoyed running their own business, they decided to pursue the business full time after graduation.

X-Opoly has grown rapidly over the last couple of years, designing and producing custom real-estate trading games for universities, municipalities, chambers of commerce, and lately even some businesses. Orders range from a couple of hundred games to an occasional order for several thousand. This year, X-Opoly expects to sell 50,000 units and projects that its sales will grow 25% annually for the next five years.

X-Opoly's orders are either for a new game board that has not been produced before or repeat orders for a game that was previously produced. If the order is for a new game, the client first meets with a graphic designer from X-Opoly's art department, and then the actual game board is designed. The design of the board can take anywhere from a few hours to several weeks, depending on how much the client has thought about the game before the meeting. All design work is done on personal computers.

After the design is approved by the client, a copy of the computer file containing the design is transferred electronically to the printing department. Workers in the printing department load the file onto their own personal computers and print out the board design on special decals, 19.25 in. by 19 in., using high-quality color inkjet printers. The side of the decal that is printed on is usually light gray, and the other side contains an adhesive that is covered by a removable backing.

The printing department is also responsible for printing the property cards, game cards, and money. The money is printed on colored paper using standard laser printers. Ten copies of a particular denomination are printed on each 8.5-in. by 11-in. piece of paper. The money is then moved to the cutting department, where it is cut into individual bills. The property cards and game cards are produced similarly, the major difference being that they are printed on material resembling posterboard.

In addition to cutting the money, game cards, and property cards, the cutting department also cuts the cardboard that serves as the substrate for the actual game board. The game board consists of two boards created by cutting a single 19-in. by 19.25-in. piece of cardboard in half, yielding two boards each measuring 19.25 in. by 9.5 in. After being cut, game boards, money, and cards are stored in totes in a WIP area and delivered to the appropriate station on the assembly line as needed.

Because of its explosive growth, X-Opoly's assembly line was never formally planned. It simply evolved into the 19 stations shown in the following table.

Station number	Task(s) performed at station	Time to perform task
1	Get box bottom and place plastic money tray in box bottom. Take two dice from bin and place in box bottom in area not taken up by tray.	10 s
2	Count out 35 plastic houses and place in box bottom.	35 s
3	Count out 15 plastic hotels and place in box bottom.	15 s
4	Take one game piece from each of eight bins and place them in box bottom.	15 s
5	Take one property card from each of 28 bins. Place rubber band around property cards and place cards in box bottom.	40 s
6	Take one orange card from each of 15 bins. Place rubber band around cards and place cards in box bottom.	20 s
7	Take one yellow card from each of 15 bins. Take orange cards from box and remove rubber band. Place yellow cards on top of orange cards. Place rubber band around yellow and orange cards and place cards in box bottom.	35 s
8	Count out 25 $500 bills and attach to cardboard strip with rubber band. Place money in box bottom.	30 s

(continued)

Station number	Task(s) performed at station	Time to perform task
9	Count out 25 $100 bills. Take $500 bills from box bottom and remove rubber band. Place $100 bills on top of $500 bills. Attach rubber band around money and place in box bottom.	40 s
10	Count out 25 $50 bills. Take $500 and $100 bills from box bottom and remove rubber band. Place $50 bills on top. Attach rubber band around money and place in box bottom.	40 s
11	Count out 50 $20 bills. Take money in box and remove rubber band. Place $20 bills on top. Attach rubber band around money and place in box bottom.	55 s
12	Count out 40 $10 bills. Take money in box and remove rubber band. Place $10 bills on top. Attach rubber band around money and place in box bottom.	45 s
13	Count out 40 $5 bills. Take money in box and remove rubber band. Place $5 bills on top. Attach rubber band around money and place in box bottom.	45 s
14	Count out 40 $1 bills. Take money in box and remove rubber band. Place $1 bills on top. Attach rubber band around money and place in box bottom.	45 s
15	Take money and remove rubber band. Shrink-wrap money and place back in box bottom.	20 s
16	Take houses, hotels, dice, and game pieces and place in bag. Seal bag and place bag in box.	30 s

Station number	Task(s) performed at station	Time to perform task
17	Place two cardboard game board halves in fixture so that they are separated by ¼ in. Peel backing off of printed game board decal. Align decal over board halves and lower it down. Remove board from fixture and flip it over. Attach solid blue backing decal. Flip game board over again and fold blue backing over front of game board, creating a ¼ in. border. Fold game board in half and place in box covering money tray, game pieces, and cards.	90 s
18	Place game instructions in box. Place box top on box bottom. Shrink-wrap entire box.	30 s
19	Place completed box in carton.	10 s

Questions

1. What kind(s) of transformation system(s) does X-Opoly use?

2. What would be involved in switching the assembly line over from the production of one game to the production of another?

3. What is the cycle time of the 19-station line? What is its efficiency?

4. On the basis of the task descriptions, develop a precedence graph for the assembly tasks. (Assume that tasks performed in the 19 stations cannot be further divided.) Using these precedence relationships, develop a list of recommendations for rebalancing the line in order to improve its performance.

5. What would be the impact on the line's efficiency if your recommendations were implemented?

EXERCISES

3.1 Lay out the office shown below given the following desired closeness ratings:

1	2	3
4	5	6

Department	1	2	3	4	5	6
1		I	A	X	O	U
2			X	E	I	O
3				O	X	I
4					I	E
5						A
6						

3.2 Demand for a certain subassembly in a toy manufacturing facility is 96 items per eight-hour shift. The following six tasks are required to produce one subassembly:

Task	Time required (min)	Predecessor tasks
a	4	–
b	5	a
c	3	a
d	2	b
e	1	b,c
f	5	d,e

What is the required cycle time? Theoretically, how many stations will be required? Balance the line. What is the line's efficiency?

3.3 An assembly line has the following tasks (times shown in minutes).

  (a) Six assemblies are required per hour. Balance the line.

  (b) What is the efficiency of the line?

  (c) Rebalance the line if task e has a time of 1 minute.

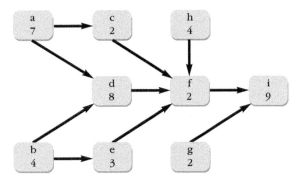

3.4 Use the CVD model to evaluate the following three locations in terms of access to five destinations: Site I is located 313, 245, 188, 36, and 89 ft, respectively, from the five destinations; site II, 221, 376, 92, 124, and 22 ft; and site III, 78, 102, 445, 123, and 208 ft.

3.5 Reevaluate Exercise 3.4 if the number of trips to each of the destinations is, respectively, 15, 6, 12, 33, and 21.

3.6 Kobenhavn Fine Products wishes to balance its line to meet a daily demand of 240 units. Kobenhavn works an eight-hour day on the following tasks:

Task	Time (min)	Preceding tasks
1	0.4	None
2	0.3	1
3	1.1	1
4	0.2	3
5	0.5	2
6	0.3	3
7	0.6	5
8	0.6	4, 6, 7

  (a) Find the cycle time, efficiency, and minimum number of stations. Balance the line.

  (b) Rebalance the line if task 8 requires 0.7 minute.

3.7 The head of the Campus Computing Center is faced with locating a new centralized computer center at one of three possible locations on the campus. The decision is to be based on the number of users in each department and the distance of the various departments from each possible location. Which location should be chosen?

Department	Number of users	Distance by location		
		1	2	3
1	25	0	3	5
2	30	5	4	3
3	10	2	0	1
4	5	3	2	0
5	14	6	2	3

BIBLIOGRAPHY

Apple, "The products you love also love the planet." apple.com/environment, February 11, 2022.

Bajarin, T. "How Apple's iPhone Changed These 5 Major Industries," time.com, June 26, 2017.

Bitner, M. J. "Servicescapes: The Impact of Physical Surroundings on Customers and Employees." *Journal of Marketing*, 52 (April 1992): 57–71.

Bower, J. L., and C. M. Christenson. "Disruptive Technologies: Catching the Wave." *Harvard Business Review* (January–February 1995): 43–53.

Chase, R. B., and S. Dasu. "Want to Perfect Your Company's Service? Use Behavioral Science." *Harvard Business Review* (June 2001): 78–84.

Chase, R. B., and D. M. Stewart. "Make Your Service Fail-Safe." *Sloan Management Review* (Spring 1994): 35–44.

Chase, R. B., and D. A. Tansik. "The Customer Contact Model for Organization Design." *Management Science*, 29 (September 1983): 1037–1050.

Cheng, J., and B. Intindola. "Apple's Size Clouds Market." *Wall Street Journal* (February 15, 2012).

Creative Mechanisms Staff. "Design for 'x' (DFX is for Excellence)," www.creativemechanisms.com/blog/design-for-x-dfx, August 3, 2016.

Dennis, D., and J. Meredith. "An Empirical Analysis of Process Industry Transformation Systems." *Management Science*, 46 (August 2000): 1085–1099.

Doerr, J., *Speed and Scale: An Action Plan for Solving our Climate Crisis Now*. Portfolio/Penguin, 2021.

Ferras, L. "Continuous Improvements in Electronics Manufacturing." *Production and Inventory Management Journal* (Second Quarter 1994): 1–5.

Flyvbjerg, B. "Top Ten Behavioral Biases in Project Management: An Overview." *Project Management Journal*, 52(6): 531–546.

Grant, D. B., Trautrims, A., and Wong, C. Y., *Sustainable Logistics and Supply Chain Management, 2nd Edition*. Kogan Page, 2017.

Harvard Business Review Press. *HBR's 10 Must Reads: On Innovation*. Boston, MA: Harvard Business School, 2013.

Hayes, R. H., and S. C. Wheelwright. "Link Manufacturing Process and Product Life Cycles." *Harvard Business Review* (January–February 1979): 133–140.

IDEO. "Products: A Selection of Case Studies," ideo.com/work/products, May 31, 2022.

Keeley, L., R. Pikkel, B. Quinn, and H. Walters. *Ten Types of Innovation: The Discipline of Building Breakthroughs*. Hoboken, NJ: Wiley, 2013.

McGrath, R. G., and I. Macmillan. "Discovery-Driven Planning." *Harvard Business Review*, July–August, 1995. Reprinted in Harvard Business Review Press (above): 125–142.

McKendrick, J. "These Days, Everyone Needs to Engage in Design Thinking." forbes.com, August 28, 2020.

Meredith, J. R., and S. M. Shafer. *Project Management: A Strategic Managerial Approach*, 11th ed. Hoboken, NJ: Wiley, 2022.

Namdarian, S. "6 Companies That Have Successfully Applied Design Thinking." collectivecampus.io.blog, May 31, 2022.

Parasuraman, A., V. A. Zeithaml, and L. L. Berry. "SERVQUAL: A Multiple-Item Scale for Measuring Consumer Perceptions of Service Quality." *Journal of Retailing*, 64 (1988): 12–40.

Passariello, C. "Brand-New Bag: Louis Vuitton Tries Modern Methods on Old Factory Lines." *Wall Street Journal* (October 9, 2006).

Passariello, C. "At Vuitton, Growth in Small Batches." *Wall Street Journal* (June 11, 2011).

Rice, M. P., G. C. O'Connor, and R. Pierantozzi. "Implementing a Learning Plan to Counter Project Uncertainty." *MIT Sloan Management Review* (Winter 2008).

Schmenner, R. W. "How Can Service Businesses Survive and Prosper?" *Sloan Management Review*, 28(3) (1986): 21–32.

Schmenner, R. W. "The Location Decisions of New Services." In J. A. Fitzsimmons and M. J. Fitzsimmons: *New Service Development*. Thousand Oaks, CA: Sage, 2000: 216–238.

Shafer, S.M., "Determining an Optimal Margin of Error for Supply Chain Audits." *Operations Management Research*, 11 (2018): 14–31.

Statistica. "Number of Apps Available in Leading App Stores as of 3rd Quarter 2018," www.statista.com/statistics/276623/number-of-apps-available-in-leading-app-stores/, January 14, 2019.

Terreri, A. "How green is Your Returnables Process?" *Food Logistics*, June 16–22, 2011.

UNEP, Environmental Agreements and Cleaner Production, unep.org, 2006

Capacity and Scheduling

4.1 Introduction

- The global business environment has become highly volatile, with up and down and up again gasoline prices, on and off regulation, supply chain disruptions, green challenges, terrorism, pandemics, and more. Airtel, India's largest telecom carrier, with 100 million subscribers, needed to gain agility between its costs, capacity, and customers so it could scale up and down rapidly in India's volatile business environment. Being agile means being able to break even at as low as 30% of capacity!

  As a telecom carrier, they decided to outsource their IT management to IBM and lease network capacity from Ericsson and Nokia, allowing them to pay for only the capacity they needed at any given time. They also knew that as customer demands change, the mix of skills needed would change, too, so they began cross-training their employees. And to minimize risk, they also don't allow any single customer to represent more than 5% of revenues; they also insist on drawing customers from across a variety of business sectors so that if one sector gets into trouble, other sectors could counterbalance it. As a result, they were probably the lowest-priced carrier in the world and one of the most profitable (Prahalad 2009).

- Ford Motor provides a recent example of the complications associated with determining the needed capacity for a new product in a developing market. More specifically, as a result of receiving 200,000 reservations for its F-150 Lightning all-electric truck, Ford decided to virtually quadruple its annual capacity from 40,000 trucks to 150,000 prior to launching the truck in April 2022. Further complicating Ford's capacity decision is the uncertainty surrounding how quickly the market for electric vehicles (EVs) will develop. Jim Farley, Ford's CEO, estimates that by the start of the next decade EVs may account for as much as half of Ford's global sales. Clearly, how rapidly the market transitions to EVs has major implications for both the amount of capacity Ford will need to produce its vehicles that use internal combustion engines and how much capacity will be needed to produce its EVs. Indeed, Farley characterized Ford's investment in the Lightning as a bet-the-company proposition (Naughton 2022).

- Waiting in line for service is one of the banes of many service industries, from airlines to retailing to entertainment to government services. Better service processes can often make a big difference in customers' satisfaction with their waiting. Alaska Airlines pioneered the self-service kiosk check-in and baggage-drop process in 2003 and then patented it in 2006. The new process cuts about 80% of the time off check-in and gives 50% more usable space. And although Alaska Air expected 20% to 30% increases in agent productivity, instead it got 100%, being able to serve passengers in half the time (Carey 2007).

  Recent research on waiting lines has found that up to three minutes of waiting, customers are fairly accurate about how long they've been waiting, but after that the wait estimates multiplied with every passing minute so that four minutes seemed like five or six and five minutes seemed like 10. In addition, if the line moved more slowly as a person approached the server, even if it had moved faster initially, the customer was highly dissatisfied, but if it speeded up toward the end, the customer felt much more positive. And even though the "cattle-stall" single line with multiple registers has been shown to be three times faster than separate lines for each register, many people would rather jockey for position between the separate lines.

  Both customers and organizations have come up with their own solutions to the problem. Customers may select a line that has customers with less full carts, no accompanying children, no old people, or a server who doesn't chat with the customers. Organizations use some of their own weapons, in addition to the ubiquitous impulse purchases along the waiting line, to distract the customers: adding line expediters to begin scanning upcoming customers' purchases, super helpers who can ring up purchases on handheld devices anywhere in the store, and baggers for the cashier. Some insist that cashiers stand out in front of their registers to show that their line is empty, others are installing self-checkout registers, and some put an employee or electronic screen at the line to direct shoppers to the next open register (Smith 2011).

- In industries, such as fashion, that are characterized by highly volatile demand, the combined costs of stockouts and markdowns can be greater than total manufacturing costs. One approach to forecasting in these highly volatile industries is to determine what can and cannot be predicted well. Products in the "predictable" category are made farthest in advance, saving manufacturing capacity for the "unpredictable" products so that they can be produced closer to their actual selling season. Using this approach, Sport Obermeyer, a producer of fashionable skiwear, increased its profits between 50% and 100% over a three-year period (Fisher et al. 1994).

- Bo Burlingham, editor-at-large of *Inc.* magazine, claims that "small giants" – firms that made a conscious choice to stay small and not expand, go public, or sell out to a larger corporation – are the "heart and soul" of the American economy. They are also "giants" because they are recognized in their industry for their achievements, and their employees express high levels of contentment and self-satisfaction with the way they do business. As one owner says, "I've made more money by choosing the right things to say no to than by choosing things to say yes to. I measure [success] by the money I haven't lost and the quality I haven't sacrificed."

  Fritz Maytag, brewmaster at Anchor Brewing, one of the "small giants," says, "Just because [your product] is the best around doesn't mean you have to franchise or even expand. You can stay as you are and have a business that's profitable and rewarding and a source of great pride."

  Burlingham says these small giants all have a strong commitment to great customer service and always "go the extra mile." Yet, in a seeming contradiction, he also points out that what really sets them apart is their belief that the customer comes second – their employees come first! It's a contradiction that makes fans wish they worked for one of these small giants instead (Burlingham 2006).

As we will discuss in more detail throughout this chapter, *capacity* represents the rate at which a transformation system can produce outputs. Because a project involving changing the amount of capacity is often a multiyear endeavor and requires significant financial resources, capacity planning and management are important components of an organization's strategy. In the case of Airtel, having the ability to quickly adjust capacity was critical to its ability to maintain its competitiveness on a cost basis. To effectively manage its capacity, Airtel leased capacity, cross-trained its workers, and diversified its customer base. The Ford Lightning example demonstrates how determining the amount of capacity needed can be especially challenging in new and rapidly developing markets. Likewise, Sport Obermeyer managed its capacity to mitigate the cost of stockouts and markdowns. In particular, Sport Obermeyer "saved" some of its limited capacity for products whose demand was less predictable. Anchor Brewing addresses another important strategic issue with implications related to required capacity, namely, the extent to which the organization desires to grow.

In manufacturing, semiconductor firms incur enormous costs associated with expanding capacity. To further complicate matters for manufacturing businesses, shorter product life cycles as we now see in our project economy mean that they have less time to recoup their investment, especially when the next generation of products makes their current products obsolete.

Planning and managing capacity is as important to service organizations as it is to manufacturing organizations. The Alaska Airlines example illustrates the important relationship between having adequate capacity and customer waiting, which in turn is strongly related to customer satisfaction, a critically important factor in a highly competitive project economy. As another example, the transformation process at Burger King is designed so that capacity can be quickly adjusted to match a highly variable demand rate throughout the day.

Thus, as our discussion to this point suggests, capacity is a very important element of a firm's competitive strategy. In fact, it plays a major role in the sand cone competitive dimensions described in Chapter 1: quality, delivery dependability, speed, and cost. For example, if capacity is insufficient for demand peaks, then confusion and errors may result when attempting to meet higher than expected demand, lowering the quality of the firm's outputs. And without capacity, customers cannot depend on the availability of the output and may turn to competitors. In terms of speed, sufficient capacity allows the organization to meet demand quickly, whenever and wherever it arises. And finally, if the firm has insufficient capacity, it will cost considerably more to engage the extra resources to meet unexpected demand, whether the resources are additional labor in the form of overtime or hiring, subcontracting out a portion of the demand, or storing inventory to meet demand peaks.

Capacity planning decisions are driven by projected demand estimates for the organization's outputs. (The topic of demand planning is discussed in Chapter 6.) Following a discussion of long-term capacity planning, we move into a description of efficiently utilizing the available capacity through schedule management and then into a description of short-term capacity alternatives.

4.2 Long-Term Capacity Planning

Capacity and location decisions are highly strategic because they are very expensive investments and, once made, are not easily changed or reversed. Hence, they must be carefully and thoroughly analyzed beforehand, using all available tools at management's disposal. *Capacity* is generally taken to mean the maximum *rate* at which a transformation system produces outputs or processes inputs, though the rate may be "all at once." Table 4.1 lists measures of capacity for a number

Table 4.1   **Examples of Measures of Capacity**

Production system	Measure of capacity in terms of outputs produced	Measure of capacity in terms of inputs processed
Airline	Available seat miles per year	Reservation calls handled per day
Hospital	Babies delivered per month	Patients admitted per week
Supermarket	Customers checked out per hour	Cartons unloaded per hour
Post office	Packages delivered per day	Letters sorted per hour
University	Graduates per year	Students admitted per year
Automobile assembly plant	Autos assembled per year	Part deliveries per day

of production systems. Notice that since capacity is defined as a rate, measures should be clear about the *time dimension*. For instance, how meaningful is it to know that a hospital can perform 25 surgeries? Without knowing whether this is simultaneously, per day, per week, or possibly per month, the number is relatively meaningless.

As illustrated in Table 4.1, airlines often measure their capacity in *available seat miles* (ASMs) per year. One ASM is one seat available for one passenger for 1 mile. Clearly, the number of planes an airline has, their size, how often they are flown, and the route structure of the airline all affect its ASMs, or capacity. However, we may also talk about the capacity of a single plane, such as a 550-seat jumbo, and here we clearly mean "all at once." Nevertheless, this capacity measure is not very useful without knowing to what use the plane may be put, such as constantly being in the air generating ASMs or used to carry cargo to generate additional revenue. Similarly, an elementary measure of a hospital's capacity is often simply the number of beds it has (for the full year is implied). Thus, a 50-bed hospital is "small," and a 1000-bed hospital is "large." And a restaurant may measure its capacity in tables (per hour), a hotel in rooms (per night), and a public service agency in family contacts (per weekday).

Notice that these measures of capacity do not recognize the multiple types of outputs with which an organization may, in reality, be concerned. ASMs say nothing about the mix of first class and economy passengers, but the customer mix clearly impacts profits. Similarly, number of beds says nothing about outpatient treatment, ambulance rescues, and other services provided by a hospital. Thus, capacity planning must often consider the capacity to produce multiple outputs. Complicating the analysis, some of the outputs may require the same organizational resources as well as some very specialized resources.

The provision of adequate capacity is clearly a generic problem, common to all types of organizations, but in pure service organizations, capacity is a special problem because the output cannot normally be stored for later use. A utility, for example, must have the capacity available to meet peak power demands, yet the *average* power demand may be much, much lower. Where the provision of the service is by human labor, low productivity is a danger when staffing is provided to meet the demand peaks.

Another characteristic of capacity is that, frequently, multiple resources can limit it. For example, the capacity of a fast-food restaurant may be limited not only by the number of order takers on duty but also by the number of cooks, the equipment available to prepare the food, the amount of food in stock, the space in the restaurant, and even the number of parking spaces outside. Any one of these resources can become a *bottleneck* (discussed in a later section of the chapter) that limits the restaurant's normal operating capacity to something less than its theoretical or design capacity.

In addition, during the production process, there are often natural losses, waste (avoidable), scrap (unavoidable), defects, errors, and so on that again limit the capacity of a system. These losses are considered in a measure known as the *yield* of the process: the amount of output of acceptable quality emerging from a production system compared with the amount that entered it. *Yield management,* also known as *revenue management,* is a somewhat different topic but of high interest these days, particularly in services. We return to the topic of yield management later in the chapter.

In the process of trying to forecast the long-run capacity needs for the organization, the issue of location of the facility, or facilities, cannot be ignored because the demand may well be a function of *where* the facility is located. And if there are multiple facilities, the capacity needs for any one will certainly depend on how many others are serving the same geographic needs. Moreover, transportation may also be a factor if there is a facilitating good, or product, involved, as well as inventories, warehouses, and other such matters that concern *supply chain management.* In these days of intense worldwide competition, supply chain management is taking on significantly more importance, as it accounts for a greater and greater proportion of the total cost of all outputs. Here, we simply point out the important interrelationships between capacity planning and supply chain management and return to the topic of supply chain planning and management in Chapters 5 and 6.

4.2.1 Capacity Planning Strategies

Issues of capacity planning over the long run relate primarily to the strategic issues of initiating, expanding, and contracting the major facilities used in producing the output. Note the interdependence of the capacity decision with the location decision. Every capacity decision requires a corresponding location decision. For example, expanding an existing facility defines the location of the new capacity to be an existing facility. This section covers capacity planning strategies in terms of facility size, economies of scale and scope, timing of capacity increments, and capacity for multiple outputs.

4.2.1.1 Facility Size Planning

Figure 4.1 illustrates the issue of facility size in terms of capacity and unit cost. Product cost curves are shown for five sizes of production facilities. When plants are operated at their lowest-cost production level (A, B, or C), the larger facilities will generally have the lowest costs, a phenomenon known as *economies of scale.* However, if production levels must be set at a value other than the lowest-cost level, the advantage of a larger facility may be lost. For example, point D is characterized by congestion and excessive overtime and point E by idle labor and low equipment utilization. Points F and G illustrate some of the diseconomies of scale, as described next.

4.2.1.2 Economies of Scale and Scope

Obtaining lower unit costs through the use of larger facilities is known as *economies of scale.* Primarily, the economy or efficiency comes from spreading the required fixed costs – land, administration, sales force, facilities, and such other factors – over a larger volume of products or services, although there are also economies obtained through stronger purchasing power and learning curve effects (discussed in a later section). However, as illustrated by points F and G in Figure 4.1, there is a limit to the benefits that can be obtained, called diseconomies of scale, because the inherent inefficiencies of large facilities begin to counter their economic benefits. This occurs through increased bureaucracy, poor communication, long lines of responsibility and authority, delays in production, reduced productivity, increased scrap and errors, and the like. Thus, there are a set of costs that drop with increasing size and another set that increase with size. Some manufacturers even have a corporate policy that no plant will be larger than some optimum size.

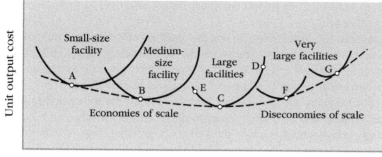

FIGURE 4.1
Envelope of Lowest
Unit Output Costs with
Facility Size

Managers frequently think in terms of economies of scale when making decisions about where to produce new products or services or whether or not to extend their line of products and services. However, the focus lost through adding these new production requirements can jeopardize the competitive strength of a firm. Managers would be well advised to examine more closely where the economies are expected to come from: sometimes it is from higher volumes, sometimes from the use of common technology, and sometimes from the availability of off-peak capacity. If the source of the economy results in offsetting diseconomies of scale, as a result of loss of focus or for other reasons, the firm should not proceed.

An allied concept related to the use of many advanced, flexible technologies, such as programmable robots, is called *economies of scope*. The phrase implies that economies can also be obtained with flexibility by offering variety instead of volume. However, upon closer examination, it is not clear why being flexible offers any particular economies. The real reason for economies of scope derives from the same economies as those of scale – spreading fixed costs among more products or services – but the scale is now obtained over many small batches of a wide variety of outputs, rather than large batches of only a few standard outputs.

4.2.1.3 Capacity Planning for Multiple Outputs

Realistically, organizations are not always expanding their capacity. For example, in November of 2018, General Motors announced that it was closing five of its production plants in the United States and Canada that produced passenger cars. In a similar fashion, in January 2018, Harley-Davidson announced it was closing its assembly plant in Kansas City and laying off 800 workers to cut costs in response to declining worldwide demand for its motorcycles. Even successful organizations occasionally need to reduce their capacity. Major ways of contracting capacity are to divest the firm of operations, lay off workers, outsource functions, and sell or lease equipment and facilities. Most organizations, however, try to contract only capacity that is inefficient or inappropriate for their circumstances, owing in part to a felt responsibility to the community. If it appears that organizational resources are going to be excessively idle in the future, organizations often attempt to add new outputs to their current output mix rather than contracting capacity (the latter frequently being done at a loss). This entails an analysis of the candidate output's life and seasonal demand cycles. In General Motors' case, the goal for closing the plants was to reduce costs and better align its capacity with a shifting market toward SUVs and pickup trucks.

It is also worth mentioning a caveat related to plant closings and layoffs. In the United States, the Worker Adjustment and Retraining Notification Act (WARN) requires that employers with 100 or more employees provide written notice at least 60 days prior to a plant closing or a layoff of 50 or more workers at a single location. Thus, a key managerial consideration associated with plant closures and layoffs is the impact employee morale will have as a plant closing and/or lay-offs are being phased in.

It is traditional in fire departments to use the slack months for performing building inspections, conducting fire prevention programs, giving talks on safety, and other such activities. The large investment in labor and equipment is thus more effectively utilized throughout the year by adoption of an *anticyclic* output (an output counter to the fire cycle) – fire prevention. For many of the same reasons, many fire departments have been given the responsibility for the city's or county's medical rescue service (although rescue alarms are not entirely anticyclic to fire alarms).

Clearly, many organizations, such as the makers of greeting cards, winter coats, swimming pool equipment, and fireworks, face this cyclic difficulty. A classic case of *seasonality* is that of furnace dealers. For the last 100 years, all their business typically was in the late autumn and winter, as illustrated in Figure 4.2. With the rapid acceptance of air conditioning in the 1950s and 1960s, many furnace dealers eagerly added this product to their output mix. Not only was it conceptually along the same lines (environmental comfort) and often physically interconnected with the home furnace, but, most importantly, it was almost completely anticyclic to the seasonal heating cycle. As shown in Figure 4.2, the addition of air conditioning considerably leveled dealers' sales throughout the year in comparison with furnace sales alone.

It is important to note that *seasonality* need not refer solely to the seasons of the year but can equally relate to daily, weekly, or monthly cycles, too. For example, fire departments are also well aware of the high demand for firefighting during the 3 P.M. to 9 P.M. period of the day between when children get out of school and when they go to bed.

In a similar manner, and for much the same reasons, organizations add to their mix outputs that are anticyclic to existing output *life cycles*. Figure 4.3 illustrates the expected life cycles of an organization's current and projected outputs. Total required capacity is found by adding together the needed capacities of each of the required outputs. Note the projected dip in required capacity five years in the future and, of course, beyond the eight-year R&D planning horizon.

The message of Figure 4.3 should be clear to the organization – an output with a three-year life cycle (appearing similar to the shaded area) is needed between years four and seven in order to maintain efficient utilization of the organization's available capacity. A priority output development program will have to be instituted immediately. At this point, it is probably too late to develop something through R&D; a more effective strategy, especially in light of the relatively low volume and short life cycle, might be an extension of an existing output.

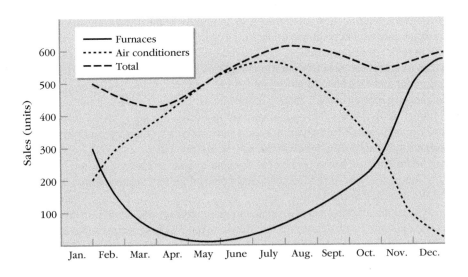

FIGURE 4.2
Anticyclic
Product Sales

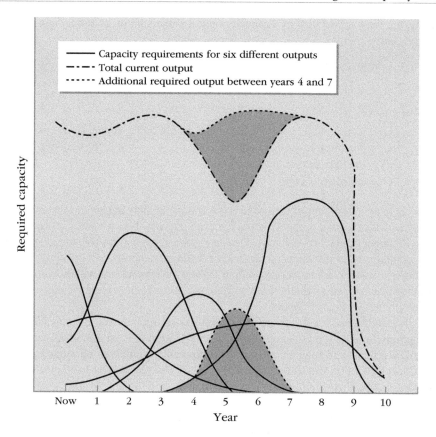

FIGURE 4.3
Forecast of Required
Organizational Capac-
ity from Multiple
Life Cycles

4.2.1.4 Breakeven Analysis of Capacity Options

Typically an organization has a number of options for adding capacity. For example, an organi-
zation may have choices between implementing highly automated production processes versus
more manual and labor-intensive production processes. ***Breakeven analysis*** can be used to per-
form an economic analysis among the options and thereby help management choose among the
capacity options identified. Breakeven analysis was originally developed as an accounting tech-
nique and as such is based on a simplified income statement:

$$P = R(Q) - \text{TC}$$

where

P = profit
R = revenue per unit
Q = annual demand
$R(Q)$ = total annual revenue
TC = total annual cost

For the purpose of comparing capacity options, we typically assume that the demand and unit
selling price remain constant across the capacity options. Therefore, when performing break-
even analysis of capacity options, we usually focus on the costs of the capacity options. More

specifically, the total annual cost of a capacity option is the sum of its annual variable cost and annual fixed cost:

$$TC = VC(Q) + FC$$

where

$$\begin{aligned}
TC &= \text{total annual cost} = \text{total annual variable cost} + \text{annual fixed cost} \\
VC &= \text{the variable cost per unit} \\
VC(Q) &= \text{total annual variable cost} \\
FC &= \text{annual fixed cost}
\end{aligned}$$

Clearly, there are many simplifications in this formula that may impact the accuracy of the calculation over a wide range of output volume. For example, variable cost per unit may decrease, or increase, with larger production volumes. Also, an organization may be able to reduce its material costs if its suppliers offer discounts on larger orders. And fixed costs will certainly jump if additional facilities are necessary to increase output capacity. Nevertheless, within a limited range of volumes, the basic total cost calculation is sufficiently accurate in helping management compare the costs of alternative capacity options.

To illustrate the use of breakeven analysis, consider an organization that has identified three capacity options for a new production line. Capacity Option A is an almost all-labor approach with VC of $160/unit and requires very little equipment resulting in an annual fixed cost of $20,000. Capacity Option B has a unit variable cost of $85 and annual fixed cost of $160,000. Capacity Option C utilizes highly automated equipment with an annual fixed cost of $400,000 and unit variable cost of $10.

As shown in Figure 4.4, the most cost-efficient capacity option depends on the expected level of demand. More specifically, the total costs of the three capacity options were plotted for alternative demand levels in Figure 4.4. For example, the total cost line for Capacity Option A can be found by plugging in alternative values of Q into the equation $160(Q) + 20,000$. From Figure 4.4, we observe that Capacity Option A is best at small volumes (has the lowest total annual cost), Option C is best for large volumes, and Option B is best for volumes in between.

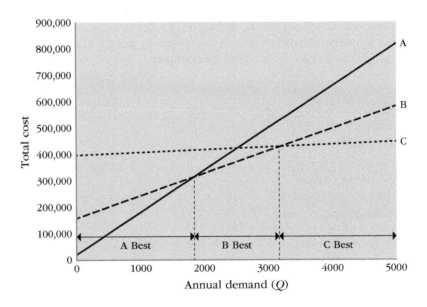

FIGURE 4.4
Comparison of Three
Capacity Options

To determine the precise demand volume Capacity Option A is best for, observe that the point where Capacity Option A's total annual cost line intersects Capacity Option B's total annual cost line, these two capacity options have the same total annual cost. At volumes below where these two lines intersect, Option A has a lower total annual cost and at volumes above where the two cost lines intersect Option B has lower total annual costs. At the point where the two lines intersect, the two capacity options have the same total annual cost. Thus, to find the demand level where the two options have the same total annual cost, we can set their total annual cost equations equal to each other and solve for Q. More specifically, the total annual cost for Option A is $160(Q) + 20,000$, and the total annual cost for Option B is $85(Q) + 160,000$. Setting them equal to each other yields $160(Q) + 20,000 = 85(Q) + 160,000$ and solving for Q results in a breakeven Q between these two options of 1866.7 units. In managerial terms this means that at demand levels of 1866 or less, Capacity Option A has the lowest total annual cost. In a similar fashion, the breakeven Q for Capacity Options B and C can be found to be $Q = 3200$. This indicates that Capacity Option B has the lowest total annual cost at demand levels between 1867 and 3199. At demand levels of 3201 Capacity Option C has the lowest total annual cost and at demand levels of exactly 3200 Capacity Options B and C have the same lowest total annual cost.

4.2.1.5 Timing of Capacity Increments

In addition to determining how much capacity is needed, we also need to determine how it will be added. Determining how capacity is added involves deciding on the timing of when the capacity will be added and the quantity of capacity to be added as illustrated in Figure 4.5.

Sometimes, there is an opportunity to add capacity in small increments such as one or more machines at a time (Figure 4.5a) rather than as one large chunk (Figure 4.5b), such as an entire production line or even an entire plant. Clearly, small increments are less risky, but they do not offer an opportunity to upgrade the entire production system at one time, as a single large chunk does. Other choices are to add capacity before (Figure 4.5c) or after (Figure 4.5d) the demand has arisen. Adding capacity before demand occurs upstages the competition and enhances customers' loyalty but risks the cost of the capacity if the expected demand never materializes. Adding capacity after demand arises encourages the competition to move into the market and increases the risk of losing market share. Clearly, the most appropriate strategy must be carefully evaluated for the situation at hand.

4.2.1.6 Environmental Considerations

In addition to considering the economics of different options for expanding capacity and the timing of when to expand capacity, organizations are increasingly considering the environmental impact related to their capacity decisions. For example, in addition to impacting customer service levels, responsiveness, and the organization's cost structure, there are also environmental implications associated with the choice of where to locate a new warehouse. In particular, pursuing a more centralized approach to managing inventory by expanding an existing warehouse as opposed to opening a new warehouse in closer proximity to customers has implications for the amount of energy needed to transport products. Of course, to appropriately consider the overall environmental impact in terms of the energy needed to transport an organization's products, the organization's sources of supply as well as the location of its customers should be considered.

Embedded in capacity expansion decisions are how the new capacity will be constructed as well has how it will be operated once constructed. There are significant environmental implications associated with both the construction of facilities and the operation of the facilities.

An important trend related to the construction of new facilities is obtaining LEED (Leadership in Energy and Environmental Design) certification. In 2019 there were over 70,000 LEED certified buildings in the United States up from under 3,200 in 2005. LEED is a broad framework

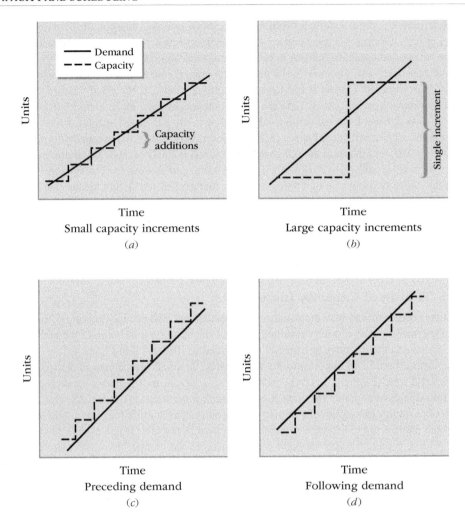

FIGURE 4.5 Methods of Adding Fixed Capacity

for improving the sustainability of buildings that addresses energy efficiency, carbon emissions, waste, and water usage. Through a third party verification and review process, points are awarded that determine if the building meets the requirements to achieve LEED certification. Becoming LEED certified requires earning 40 points. A building earning 50 points earns certification at the silver level, 60 points at the gold level, and 80 points or more at the platinum level. It is worth noting that LEED certification can also be obtained for the construction of new capacity such as for schools, retail, data centers, and warehouses as well as for existing buildings that are being improved.

There are a variety of strategies organizations can utilize to reduce the environmental impact associated with the construction of new facilities. One of the most important considerations is the choice of the construction materials to be used. For example, in constructing a warehouse, an organization might consider constructing walls with aluminum or perhaps using a timber frame with aluminum cladding. While both walls have a similar lifespan, a curtain wall made of aluminum requires about 2.5 times more energy to create than a similar wall constructed using a timber frame and aluminum cladding. As another alternative, a similarly constructed wall out of concrete would require approximately 20 percent less energy than the aluminum wall but has double the life expectancy.

Once constructed, the new facility will continue to have an impact on the environment based on how it was designed to be operated. For example, operating the new facility will require electricity for heating/cooling, lighting, and operating equipment. When evaluating the environmental impact of operating a facility, it is important to conduct a comprehensive analysis. To illustrate, on the surface a plant that employs heavy machinery and relatively fewer workers may appear to require more energy. However, when the energy used for the workers to commute to and from work is factored in, the picture may change.

It is also worth noting that there are often tradeoffs between the construction of a new facility and its operation regarding the facility's environmental impact. For example, adding additional insulation in the construction of the facility increases the energy embedded in the facility but provides energy efficiencies in operating the facility. Properly making these tradeoffs also requires considering the lifetime of the facility.

4.3 Effectively Utilizing Capacity Through Schedule Management

An important aspect of capacity worth emphasizing is its close tie to scheduling. That is, poor scheduling may result in what appears to be a capacity problem, and a shortage of capacity may lead to constant scheduling difficulties. Thus, capacity planning is closely related to the scheduling function. The difference is that capacity is oriented primarily toward the *acquisition* of productive resources, whereas scheduling concerns the *timing* of their use. However, it is often difficult to separate the two, especially where human resources are involved, such as in the use of overtime or the overlapping of shifts.

As a simple example, suppose that an organization has to complete the two jobs shown in Table 4.2 within two weeks. The table shows the sequential processing operations still to be completed and the times required. (The operations resources may be of any form – a facility, a piece of equipment, or an especially skilled worker.) In total, 60 hours of resource A is needed, 45 hours of B, and 25 hours of C. It would appear that two weeks (80 hours) of capacity on each of these three resources would be sufficient and additional capacity would, therefore, be unnecessary.

Figure 4.6 shows the resource requirements of the two jobs plotted along a timescale. Such a chart, called a *Gantt chart,* can be used to show time schedules and capacities of facilities, workers, jobs, activities, machines, and so forth. In Figure 4.6a, each job was scheduled on the

Table 4.2 Sequential Operations Required for Two Jobs

Job	Operations resource needed	Time required (hours)
1	A	10
	C	10
	A	30
	B	20
	C	5
2	B	15
	A	10
	C	10
	A	10
	B	10

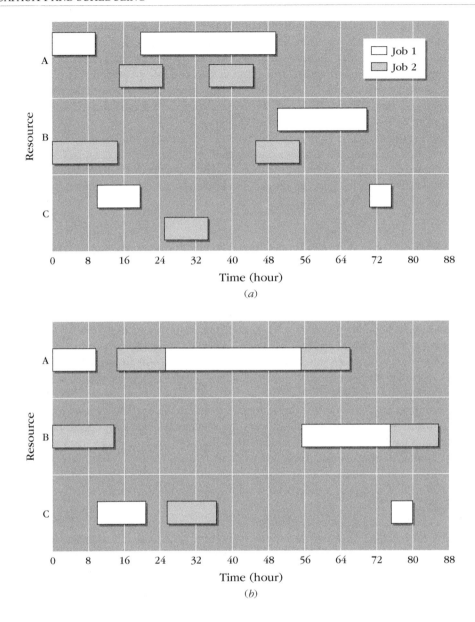

FIGURE 4.6 Gantt Charts for Capacity Planning and Scheduling

required resource as soon as it finished on the previous resource, whether or not the new resource was occupied with the other job. This infeasible schedule is called *infinite loading* because work is scheduled on the resource as if it had infinite capacity to handle any and all jobs. Note that in this way capacity conflicts and possible resolutions can be easily visualized. Shifting the jobs to avoid such conflicts – called *finite loading* – gives the longer but feasible schedule shown in Figure 4.6*b*.

The first resource conflict in Figure 4.6*a* occurs at 20 hours, when job 1 finishes on resource C and next requires resource A, which is still working on job 2. The second conflict, again at A, occurs at 35 hours, and the third, on B, at 50 hours. It is quickly found that deferring one job for the other has drastic consequences for conflicts of resources later (sometimes adding conflicts and sometimes avoiding them) as well as for job completion times. Another consideration, not specified here, is whether an operation can be stopped for a while and then restarted (called *operation splitting*) – for example, to let another job pass through (called *preemption*) – or, once started, must be worked on until completion. If splitting were allowed for job 2, we could have stopped work at resource A on job 2 at 20 hours to let job 1 begin and then finished the work starting at time 50 when job 1 was finished on resource A. Such operation splitting allows flexibility for rush work but hurts productivity because machines must be taken down and set up multiple times for the same job.

4.3.1 Scheduling Services

In this section, we consider the scheduling of pure services. Much of what was said previously applies to the scheduling of services as well as products, but here we consider some scheduling issues of particular relevance to services.

In the previous example, the focus was on scheduling jobs. There are, however, many operations for which scheduling of the jobs themselves is either inappropriate or impossible, and it is necessary to concentrate instead on scheduling one or more of the input resources. Therefore, the staff, the materials, or the facilities are scheduled to correspond, as closely as possible, with the expected arrival of the jobs. Such situations are common in service systems such as supermarkets, hospitals, urban alarm services, colleges, restaurants, and airlines.

In the scheduling of jobs, we are primarily interested in minimizing the number of late jobs, minimizing the rejects, maximizing the throughput, and maximizing the utilization of available resources. In the scheduling of resources, however, there may be considerably more criteria of interest, especially when one of the resources being scheduled is staff. The desires of the staff regarding shifts, holidays, and work schedules become critically important when work schedules are variable and not all employees are on the same schedule. In these situations, there usually exist schedules that will displease everyone and that will satisfy most of the staff's more important priorities – and it is crucial that one of the latter be chosen rather than one of the former.

4.3.1.1 Approaches to Resource Scheduling

The primary approach to the scheduling of resources is to match resource availability to demand (e.g. 7 P.M. to 12 A.M. is the high period for fire alarms). By so doing, we are not required to provide a continuing high level of resources that are poorly utilized the great majority of the time. However, this requires that a good forecast of demand be available for the proper scheduling of resources. If demand cannot be accurately predicted, the resulting service with variable resources might be worse than using a constant level of resources.

Methods of increasing resources for peak demand include using overtime and part-time help and leasing equipment and facilities. Also, if multiple areas within an organization tend to experience varying demand, it is often helpful to use *floating* workers or combine departments to minimize variability. On occasion, new technologies, such as 24-hour automated tellers, 24-hour order entry via the Web, and bill payment by telephone, can aid the organization.

The use of promotion and advertising to shift *demand* for resources is highly practical in many situations. Thus, we see *off-peak pricing* in the hotel and travel industries, matinée prices for movies, and cut rates for all-inclusive vacation destinations in off-peak seasons. Let us now consider how some specific service organizations approach their scheduling problems.

4.3.1.1.1 Hospitals. There are multiple needs for scheduling in hospitals. Although arrivals of patients (the jobs) are in part uncontrollable (e.g. emergencies), they are to some extent controllable through selective admissions for elective surgery, some maternity cases, inhospital observation, and so on. With selective admissions, the hospital administrator can smooth the demand faced by the hospital and thereby improve services and increase the utilization of the hospital's limited resources.

Very specialized, expensive equipment such as a dialysis machine is also carefully scheduled to allow other hospitals access to it, thus maximizing its utilization. By sharing such expensive equipment among a number of hospitals, more hospitals have access to modern technology for their patients at a reasonable level of investment.

Of all the scheduling in hospitals, the most crucial is probably the scheduling of nurses, as illustrated in the following example describing Harper Hospital (Filley 1983). This is because (1) it is mandatory, given the nature of hospitals, that nurses always be available; (2) nursing resources are a large expense for a hospital; and (3) there are a number of constraints on the scheduling of nurses, such as number of days per week, hours per day, weeks per year, and hours during the day.

Like many other hospitals, Harper Hospital of Detroit was under heavy pressure from Blue Cross, Medicare, and Medicaid to provide more health care at less cost. In addition, it needed to achieve more economies of scale from a merger that had taken place some years before. It also wanted to improve its patient care. One target to help achieve these goals was a better system for scheduling nurses.

Previously, nurses were scheduled on the basis of strict bed counts, problems with inadequate staffing during the prior day, and requests for extra help. What was developed was a *patient classification system* (PCS) that incorporated labor standards to determine what levels of nursing were needed. At the end of each shift, designated nurses evaluated each area's patients by their condition and assigned them to a "care level" ranging from minimal to intensive. An hour before the next shift began, the patients' needs for care were added up – accounting for new admissions, checkouts, and returns from surgery – to determine the total levels of care required. Given the levels in each area, nursing labor standards were used to determine how many nurses were needed on the next shift.

As a result of the new system, both the quality of patient care and the nurses' satisfaction went up. Annual labor savings from the new system were estimated as exceeding $600,000. Harper has further fine-tuned the PCS and now recalibrates its standards every two years.

4.3.1.1.2 Urban Alarm Services. In urban services that respond to alarms – such as police, fire, and rescue services – the jobs (alarms) appear randomly and must be quickly serviced with sufficient resources. Otherwise, extreme loss of life or property may result. In many ways, this problem is similar to that of a hospital, since the cost of staffing personnel is a major expense, but floating fire companies and police SWAT units may be utilized where needed, and some services (such as fire inspection) can be scheduled to help *smooth* demand.

Sometimes, a major difference vastly complicates some of these services (particularly fire): *duty tours* of extended duration, as opposed to regular shifts, run over multiple days. These tours vary from 24 to 48 hours in teams of two to four members. Common schedules for such services are "two (days) on and three off" and "one on and two off," with every fifth tour or so off as well (for a running time off, every three weeks, of perhaps $3 + 2 + 3 = 8$ days). Because living and sleeping-in are considered part of the job requirements, the standard workweek is in excess of 40 hours – common values are 50 and 54 hours. Clearly, the scheduling of such duty tours is a complex problem, not only because of the unusual duration of the tours but also because of the implications concerning overtime, temptations to "moonlight," and other such issues.

4.3.1.1.3 Educational Services. Colleges and universities have scheduling requirements for all types of transformations: intermittent (such as counseling), continuous (English 1), batch (field trips), and project (freshman orientation). In some of these situations, the jobs (students) are scheduled; in some, the staff (faculty, administrators) are scheduled; and in others, the facilities (classrooms, auditoriums) are scheduled.

The primary problem, however, involves the scheduling of classes, assignment of students, and allocation of facilities and faculty resources to these classes. To obtain a manageable schedule, three difficult elements must be coordinated in this process:

1. Accurate forecast of students' demand for classes

2. Limitations on available classroom space

3. Multiple needs and desires of the faculty, such as
   - Number of "preparations"
   - Number of classes
   - Timing of classes
   - Level of classes
   - Leave requirements (sabbatical, maternity, etc.)
   - Release requirements (research, projects, and administration)

Because of the number of objectives in such scheduling problems, a variety of multicriteria approaches have been used to aid in finding acceptable schedules, including simulation, goal programming, and interactive modeling.

In summary, the approach to scheduling services is usually to match resources and forecasted demand. Since demand cannot be controlled, it is impossible to build up inventory ahead of time, and backordering is usually not feasible. Careful scheduling of staff, facilities, and materials is done instead, with (limited) flexibility achieved through floating part-time and overtime labor and off-peak rates to encourage leveling of demand. The best schedule is often not the one that optimizes the use of resources or minimizes lateness for the expected demand, but rather the one that gives acceptable results under all likely operating conditions. As described later in this chapter, an important aspect of scheduling services is the queues that tend to build up if capacity is inadequate. Here, queuing theory and psychology concerning waiting can be profitably applied.

4.3.1.2 Yield/Revenue Management and Overbooking

Yield management, also called *revenue management,* is the attempt to allocate the fixed capacity of a service (although the process is now being used by retailers and manufacturers, too) to match the highest revenue demand in the marketplace. It appears that American Airlines was one of the first to develop this technique, but its use has spread to hotels, cruise lines, and other services. As described by Kimes (1989), yield management is most appropriate under the following circumstances:

1. **Fixed capacity:** There are only a limited, indivisible number of capacity openings available for the period. There is no flexibility in either dividing up the capacity or in finding additional capacity. For example, an airplane flight has a fixed number of seats.

2. **Perishable capacity:** Once the period passes, the capacity can no longer be used for that period. There is essentially no salvage value for the capacity. In the case of an airline, the revenue lost from unsold seats on a flight cannot be made up on future flights.

3. **Segmentable market:** The demand for the capacity must be segmentable into different revenue/profit classes, such as business versus pleasure, Saturday night stayover or not, first class versus economy, and so on.

4. **Capacity sold in advance:** The capacity is sold by reservation. Using yield management techniques, certain classes of capacity are held back for certain, more profitable classes of reservations or periods of the season. If the profitable classes fail to fill by a certain time point, some of the capacity is then released for the next-lowest profit class. This procedure cascades down through both reservation classes and time points as the period in question approaches.

5. **Uncertain demand:** Although demand for each reservation class may be forecast, the actual demand experienced in each class for each time period is uncertain.

6. **Low marginal sales cost and high marginal capacity addition cost:** The cost to add a unit of capacity is extremely high, but the cost to sell (rent) a unit of it for the period in question is low.

The technique used to determine how to allocate capacity among the different classes is similar to that used for *overbooking.* Overbooking is an attempt to reduce costs through better schedule management, as illustrated by Scandinavian Airlines (SAS) (Alstrup et al. 1989). SAS operated a fleet of DC-9 aircraft with 110 seats each. If SAS accepted reservations for only these 110 seats and "no-shows" (passengers who fail to show up for a flight) refused to pay for their reservations, SAS lost from 5% to 30% of the available seats. If there were 100 flights every day, these no-shows cost the airline as much as $50 million a year. To avoid this loss, most airlines overbook flights by accepting a fixed percentage of reservations in excess of what is available.

The management of SAS decided to develop an automated overbooking system to include such factors as class, destination, days before departure, current reservations, and existing cancellations. The objective of the system was to determine an optimal overbooking policy for the different classes on each flight, considering the costs of ill will, alternative flight arrangements, empty seats, and the upgrading or downgrading of a passenger's reserved class.

A number of interesting findings were made in the process of conducting the study. For example, an early finding was that the probability that a reservation would be canceled was independent of the time the reservation was made. When the system was completed, it was tested against the heuristics used by experienced employees who had a good "feel" for what the overbooking rate should be. It was found that the automated system would increase SAS's net revenue by about $2 million a year.

In contrast to the normal industry practice of overbooking flights, Southwest Airlines announced that by the end of June 2017, it would no longer overbook its flights. Southwest Airlines estimated that the move would have a small impact on its revenues as it typically only sold one extra ticket for a plane with 143 seats and the fact that the number of no-shows has been declining over the last two decades. Nevertheless, almost 15,000 of its passengers were required to give up their seats in the prior year.

4.4 Short-Term Capacity Planning

In the short term, capacity planning is primarily related to issues of scheduling, labor shifts, balancing of resource capacities, and other such issues. We will look into a variety of such approaches in this section.

4.4.1 Process-Flow Analysis

Earlier, we discussed some factors that might limit the output of a production system, such as bottlenecks in the system and yield considerations such as scrap and defects. Here, we will introduce some other terms relating to the use of a production system. One capacity measure that is commonly used is *utilization,* which is simply the actual output relative to some expected, designed, or normal output rate. For example, if a machine runs four hours a day in an American plant and the maintenance and setup time is usually two hours a day, the utilization for that day might be reported as 4/6 = 67%, which is considered to be fairly high utilization for a machine in a job shop. However, if the machine was in a Japanese plant, the utilization would probably be reported as 4/24 = 17%, since the machine could, in theory, have been used for all 24 hours in the day!

Clearly, utilization figures do not mean much unless one knows what the "normal" or expected output rate is based on. (When labor utilization measures are used for wage payment plans, this "normal" definition is often a heated subject of union negotiations. For example, should mandated "breaks" be included in the base or not? Should sick time be included? Lunch? Inactivity due to lack of materials to work on? And so on.) An advantage of basing the utilization on 24 hours is that this shows how much more could be done with the resource if it were needed. On the other hand, most managers would not like hearing that their expensive machinery was only being 17% utilized!

4.4.1.1 Bottlenecks in a Sequential Process

Another major concept in operations is that of *efficiency versus capacity (output rate)*. *Efficiency* was defined in Chapter 1 as output divided by input. Here, we measure output as the standard number of minutes needed to produce a unit and input as actual minutes of resource time spent overall in producing the item. It is important to understand what production situations are amenable to simple capacity improvements by adding capital resources and what production situations are not. Normally, we expect that the amount of productive capacity and the capital investment needed to gain this capacity will be about proportional. Suppose that blood samples are being analyzed in a spectroscope run by one nurse (and both spectroscope and nurse are constantly busy with this task) at the rate of 10 per hour and a capacity of 100 per hour is required. Then, the resource investment translates directly – 10 spectroscopes and 10 nurses will be needed.

However, if the production process is *sequential,* the resource investment may not translate so directly into the required output. Normally, many workers and machines are required to produce an output. In that case, the direct capacity-investment correspondence may not exist because of *bottlenecks* in the production process. Bottlenecks are places (there may be more than one) in the production process where production slows down because of a slow, or insufficient number of, machine(s), or perhaps because of a slow worker, or because the product needs to spend time drying. More formally, a bottleneck is the resource with the least amount of capacity and as such limits the capacity of the entire sequential production system. Fixing such bottlenecks usually only marginally improves the capacity of the system, however, because a new bottleneck arises somewhere else in the production process (this common problem is called "floating bottlenecks"). The following examples illustrate how this happens. For ease of understanding, we use a machine to illustrate the bottleneck, but any resource in a service operation could also be a bottleneck.

Assume that King Sports Products produces a variety of tennis rackets *sequentially* on four machines, and the times required on each machine for one typical racket are as shown in Figure 4.7. Note in this figure that the work embodied in each finished tennis racket is 4 + 3 + 10 + 2 = 19 minutes, which is also the *throughout time* for a racket if there are no other rackets being made – that is, the system is not busy. However, during a busy production day, this throughput time will increase, as we will see next.

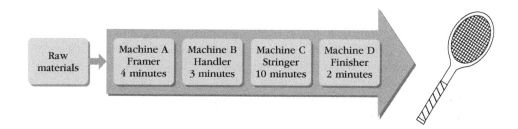

FIGURE 4.7 King Sports Production Process

To minimize the cost of equipment, King could use one of each machine. The resulting capacity or output rate will then be based on the bottleneck resource or in this case the *slowest* machine that has a processing time of 10 minutes, resulting in 6 units per hour. That is, since every item must go through *each* of the machines, in order, every racket must wait for machine C, the bottleneck, to finish before it can proceed. During this wait, the first, second, and fourth machines will be idle for six, seven, and eight minutes, respectively, out of every 10-minute cycle.

(Also, the throughput time during such a busy period now becomes $10 + 10 + 10 + 2 = 32$ minutes. The racket need not wait at the last machine to exit, but the machine must wait eight minutes for the next racket.) Since the output in this process embodies 19 minutes of work, whereas the input consists of four machines that spend 10 minutes each during every cycle that produces an item (not all of which is necessarily productive), this gives an overall efficiency of only 47.5%:

$$\text{Efficiency} = \frac{\text{output}}{\text{input}} = \frac{4+3+10+2}{4(10)} = \frac{19}{40} = 47.5\%$$

Note that it does not matter whether the bottleneck is at the end of the sequence, at the beginning, or in the middle. The process is still slowed, on average, to the output rate of the slowest machine. The capacity of this process is thus six units per hour, and the *cycle time of the process is 10 minutes*, or 1/6 of an hour – the output rate and the cycle time are always reciprocals. The process cycle time can be visualized as the time between items coming off the end of the production line, whereas the throughput time can be visualized as the time you would spend in the production process if you attached yourself to the item being produced and rode along through the production process – there is often no relationship between them! And the final output work time is the productive time the item spends in the process.

If King is willing to invest in another, fifth machine, it should purchase another machine of type C, since that is the bottleneck. Then, it could run machines C1 and C2 concurrently and put out two units every 10 minutes, obtaining an "effective" machine C processing time of five minutes for the machines by staggering their production. Note that machine C is still the bottleneck in the production process, so this effective five-minute machine processing time is once again the cycle time for the system. The effect of this single investment would be to *double* the capacity/output rate to 12 units per hour (five-minute cycle time) and increase the system efficiency to

$$\frac{4+3+10+2}{5(5)} = \frac{19}{25} = 76\%$$

Note in this efficiency calculation that the work output per racket is always 19 minutes, regardless of the number of machines; only the input changes. Now, the input is five machines running at a 5-minute cycle time. Continuing in this manner results in the data shown in Table 4.3 and sketched in Figure 4.8. In developing Table 4.3, the next machine added was always the machine that currently had the longest machine time. For example, when there were six machines, machine A had the longest machine time. Thus, the seventh machine added was a machine A.

Note from the table and figure that efficiency of production does not always increase when machines are added, although the general trend is upward. This is because some systems are fairly well "balanced" to begin with. (For example, the cycles across the machines are quite even with seven machines – 2, 3, 3.33, 2 – and even more so at 10 machines. Also note that the addition of only one extra machine at such points does not pay for itself.) If points of high efficiency are reached "early" (as machines are added), these points will tend to be natural operating solutions. For example, a tremendous gain in efficiency (and in output percentage) is reaped by adding a fifth machine to the system. Further additions do not gain much. The next largest gain occurs when the tenth machine is added to the system.

Table 4.3   Return to King for Using More Machines

Number of machines	Type of next machine	Machine times (min)				Cycle time (min)	Total hourly output	Efficiency (%)
		A	**B**	**C**	**D**			
4	–	4	3	10	2	10	6	47.5
5	C	4	3	5	2	5	12	76.0
6	C	4	3	3.33	2	4	15	79.2
7	A	2	3	3.33	2	3.33	18	81.4
8	C	2	3	2.5	2	3	20	79.2
9	B	2	1.5	2.5	2	2.5	24	84.4
10	C	2	1.5	2	2	2	30	95.0
11	D	2	1.5	2	1	2	30	86.0
12	A	1.33	1.5	2	1	2	30	79.2
13	C	1.33	1.5	1.67	1	1.67	36	87.5
14	C	1.33	1.5	1.43	1	1.5	40	90.5

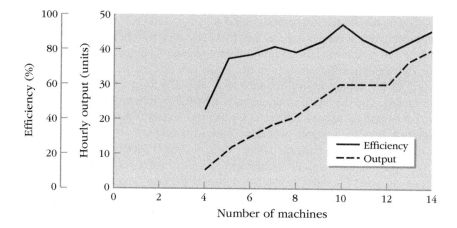

FIGURE 4.8
Efficiency and Output
Change as Machines
Are Added

Although this analysis describes the general trade-offs of the system, no mention has been made of demand. Suppose that demand is 14 units per hour. Then, to minimize risk but still keep an efficient system, King might use five machines and either work overtime, undersupply the market, or use a number of other strategies, as will be discussed later. Similarly, for a demand of 25 to 35 per hour, the use of 10 machines would be appropriate.

4.4.1.2 Mapping Product and Service Flows

With the role of a bottleneck in a production process in mind, let us now consider the more general procedure of conducting a process-flow analysis or process mapping, also known in service systems as "mapping" or "blueprinting." The purpose of conducting a process-flow analysis is normally to identify bottlenecks, inventory buildup points, and time delays in a production process, which are crucially important in determining the capacity of the process. Standard nomenclature is to use rectangles for tasks/activities, triangles for storage or waiting points, diamonds for decision points or branching (e.g. is the part good or defective?), and arrows for flows. An activity changes the characteristics of a product or service, whereas a flow simply indicates the next step in the process, which may involve a change in position.

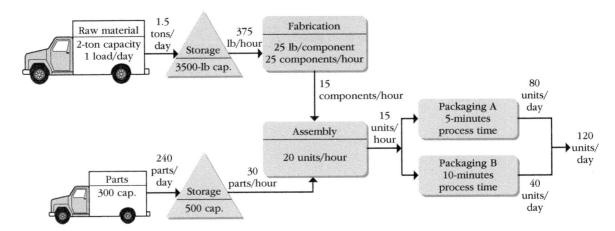

FIGURE 4.9   Process Flow for Manufactured Unit

A simplified process-flow diagram for a manufactured unit composed of two purchased parts and one fabricated 25-lb component is shown in Figure 4.9. Demand is currently 120 units per 8-hour day or 15 units per hour, for an effective process cycle time of one unit every 60/15 = 4 minutes. The inputs, on the left, consist of 1.5 tons (i.e. 3000 lbs) of raw materials delivered by a 2-ton-capacity truck once a day and 240 parts delivered by a 300-part-capacity truck once a day, both of which immediately go into different storage facilities (with different capacities, as shown). The capacities of each stage in the production process are as labeled. Fabrication of the 15 hourly 25-lb components will require 15 × 25 = 375 lbs per hour of raw material from the storage facility. The fabricated components will then flow into assembly, along with 30 parts withdrawn per hour from the parts of the storage facility. Assembly then produces the 15 units per hour, which flow into two separate packaging lines with different processing times due to their age. New line A packages 10 units each hour, while old line B packages 5 units an hour, for the required total demand. Although the output demand is currently 120 units a day, management anticipates an increase of perhaps as much as a third in the near future; their concern is whether the system can handle this increase in demand.

As we see from the diagram, there is currently excess capacity throughout the production system, but is there enough at each stage and process to handle the additional 0.333 × 120 = 40 units a day? Assembly, at 20 units per hour, could just handle the anticipated demand of 120 + 40 = 160 units a day: 20 × 8 = 160. However, the raw material storage facility, which can only hold 3500 lbs (enough to produce only 3500/25 = 140 units a day), is a bottleneck in the system, since we need 160 × 25 lbs/unit = 4000 lbs of storage (the limit of the delivery truck's capacity). Perhaps we could change our system to deliver a portion of the truckload directly to fabrication or run out 500 lbs to fabrication as the raw material is unloaded from the truck so there is enough space for the full required 2-ton delivery. Note that any activity, resources or storage, could have been the bottleneck in the process. What's more, even if we increase the capacity of the storage facility, the bottleneck will shift to the packaging machines, being able to produce only 12 units per hour from A and another six per hour from B, for a total of 18 per hour, or 144 units a day. And if their capacity is increased, the bottleneck will shift to the 300-part truck delivery because we will need 160 × 2 = 320 parts delivered each day. As you can see, the bottleneck shifts around the facility as we solve one problem after another. However, the process-flow diagram allows us to *anticipate* such shifts and head them off before they become real problems.

In a similar manner, Figure 4.10 presents a flow diagram for a simple photocopy service. When used for a service process, the process-flow diagram also typically illustrates potential failure points in the process and the *line of visibility* that divides those activities a customer perceives

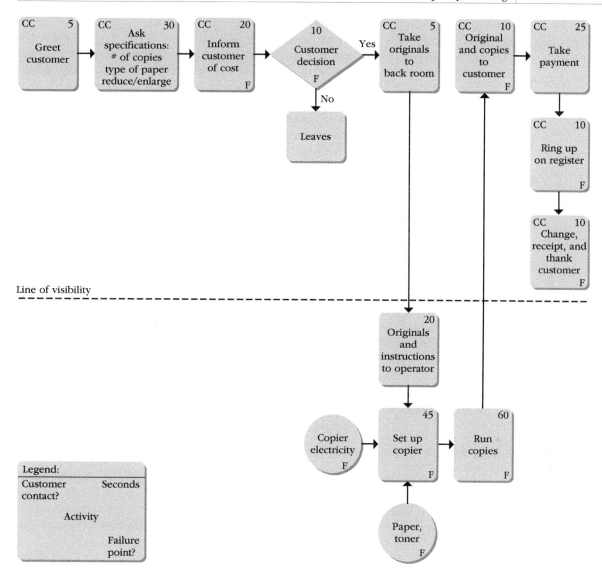

FIGURE 4.10   Process-Flow Map for a Service

from those that are conducted out of the customer's sight (the "backroom," as in an auto repair shop, where operations can be conducted with efficiency). The diagram is called a service "map" or "blueprint," as noted earlier, and shows the process times more prominently instead. Note the potential failure points in the photo-copy service diagram and the "line of visibility" that divides what the customer sees from the backroom operations. Although Figure 4.10 illustrates a simple service process for illustration purposes, service processes are frequently as complex as those in Figure 4.9, or even more so, and also involve bottlenecks and combined operations.

As these examples illustrate, process-flow analysis and the resulting process map are intuitive and powerful tools in helping managers understand the current process and identify opportunities for improvement. Indeed, process maps are a core tool in Six Sigma (discussed in Chapter 8). One recommended way to construct a process map is to use the technique of "being the part." With this approach, the analyst assumes the role of a part and follows its process flow, manually tracing each step of the part's journey (of course, the "part" could be other entities that are processed such as loan applications or patients). As the analyst arrives at each stage in the process, he/she interviews the employees that perform the work to understand the work that is performed at this stage. During the interview process, it is vitally important that the analyst remain objective and nonjudgmental about how the work is being done as the overarching goal is to understand how the process currently operates. If the workers feel they are being judged or even worse, at risk of losing their jobs, they may not be forthcoming with information and important opportunities to improve the process later on may remain hidden. It is also worth pointing out that developing a process map is typically an iterative process. As each new version is developed, it should be shared with the employees doing their work to make sure that it accurately reflects the way the work gets done. As workers see a version of the process map, it often triggers thoughts about other important details of the process that should be included in the process map.

Process maps are a powerful tool for helping managers understand work processes because they are easy to understand and very flexible. In the examples discussed earlier, the process map was used primarily to analyze capacity and identify the bottleneck. Process maps can be used for a variety of other purposes such as determining part throughput times, delays in the process, and nonvalue-added work activities. Furthermore, process maps can be modified in any way that helps the analyst gain important insights into the process. For example, additional symbols can be used or the symbols color-coded. Another way process maps are often embellished is by adding *swim lanes* to the process map to show which organizational units or departments perform which activities (see Exhibit 2 in the "BPO, Incorporated: Call Center Six Sigma Project" case in the Cases appendix for an example of a process map with swim lanes). Finally, it is worth mentioning that *Value Stream Maps* (VSM), a core lean tool, offer another approach for doing process-flow analysis. Typically, VSM document process flows beyond the organization's boundaries, while process maps focus on process flows *within* the organization's boundaries. VSM are discussed in more detail in Chapter 9.

4.4.2 Short-Term Capacity Alternatives

The problem of short-term capacity is to handle unexpected but imminent actual demand, either less than or more than expected, in an economical manner. It is known, of course, that the forecast will not be perfect; thus, managers of resources must plan what short-term capacity alternatives to use in either case. Such considerations are usually limited to, at most, the next six months, and usually much less, such as the next few days or hours.

Some alternatives for obtaining short-run capacity are categorized in Table 4.4. Each of the techniques in the table has advantages and disadvantages. The first set of alternatives concerns simply trying to increase the resource base. The use of overtime is expensive (time and a half), and productivity after eight hours of work often declines. It is a simple and easily used approach, however, that does not require additional investment, so overtime is one of the most common alternatives. The use of extra shifts requires hiring but no extra facilities. However, productivity of second and third shifts is often lower than that of the first shift. Part-time hiring can be expensive and is usually feasible for only low-skilled or unskilled work. Floating workers are flexible and very useful but, of course, also cost extra. Leasing facilities and workers is often a good approach, but the extra cost reduces the profit, and these external resources may not be available during the high-demand periods when they are most seriously needed. Subcontracting may require a long lead time, may be considerably difficult to implement, and may leave little, if any, profit.

The second set of techniques involves attempts to find ways to improve the utilization of existing resources. For daily demand peaks (seen especially in services, as discussed in the next section), shifts can be overlapped to provide extra capacity at peak times or staggered to adjust to changes in demand loads. Cross-training the workers to substitute for each other can effectively

Table 4.4 Techniques for Increasing Short-Run Capacity

I. Increase resources

  1. Use overtime

  2. Add shifts

  3. Employ part-time workers

  4. Use floating workers

  5. Lease workers and facilities

  6. Subcontract

II. Improve resource use

  7. Overlap or stagger shifts

  8. Cross-train the workers

  9. Create adjustable resources

  10. Share resources

  11. Schedule appointments/reservations

  12. Inventory output (if feasible) ahead of demand

  13. Backlog or queue demand

III. Modify the output

  14. Standardize the output

  15. Offer complementary services

  16. Have the recipient do part of the work

  17. Transform service operations into inventoriable product operations

  18. Cut back on quality

IV. Modify the demand

  19. Partition the demand

  20. Change the price

  21. Change the promotion

  22. Initiate a yield/revenue management system

V. Do not meet demand

  23. Do not supply all the demand

increase labor flexibility. And there may be other ways to make labor and other resources adjustable, too. A similar alternative is to simply share resources whenever possible. Especially for services, appointment and reservation systems, if feasible, can significantly smooth out daily demand peaks. If the output can be stocked ahead of time, as with a product, this is an excellent and very common approach to meeting capacity needs. If recipients are willing, the backlogging of demand to be met later during slack periods is an excellent strategy; a less accurate forecast is needed, and investment in finished goods is nil. However, this may be an open invitation to competition.

Modifying the output is a creative approach. Doing less customization, allowing fewer variants, offering complementary services, and encouraging recipients to do some assembly or finishing tasks themselves (as at self-service gasoline stations and checkout lines), perhaps with a small price incentive, are frequently employed and are excellent alternatives.

Attempting to alter the demand, partition it, or shift it to a different period is another creative approach. Running promotions or price differentials ("off-peak" pricing), or both, for slack periods is an excellent method for leveling demand, especially in utilities, hotels, and similar services. Prices are not easily increased above normal in high-demand periods, however. One formal method of partitioning both the demand and the resource supply is known as yield or revenue management, as discussed earlier. Last, the manager may simply decide not to meet the market demand – again, however, at the cost of inviting competition.

In actuality, many of these alternatives are not feasible except in certain types of organizations or in particular circumstances. For example, when demand is high, subcontractors are full, outside facilities and staff are already overbooked, second-shift workers are employed elsewhere, and marketing promotion is already low key. Thus, of the many possible alternatives, most firms tend to rely on only a few, such as overtime and, for product firms, stocking up ahead of demand.

So far, we have primarily discussed increasing capacity in the short run, but firms also have a need to *decrease* short-run capacity. This is more difficult, however, and most such capacity simply goes unused. If the output involves a product, some inventory buildup may be allowed in order to make use of the available capacity; otherwise, system maintenance may be done (cleaning, fixing, preprocessing, and so on).

4.4.3 Capacity Planning for Services

Capacity planning is often much more difficult for pure service operations than for products, and with a service, there is a clearer distinction between long- and short-run capacity planning. For services, the more difficult aspects of providing capacity occur in the short run, usually because the demand for a service is subject to daily peaks and valleys and the output cannot be stored ahead of time to buffer this fluctuation. For example, doctors' offices see demand peaks at 9 A.M. and 1 P.M., and college classes see a peak at 10 A.M. Or there may be weekly peaks, monthly peaks, or yearly peaks, such as Friday's demand on banks to deposit (or cash) paychecks and the first-of-the-month demand on restaurants when Social Security checks arrive in the mail. Some services, such as fire departments, experience multiple peaks, as illustrated in Figure 4.11a, which shows the regular *daily* cycle of fire alarms, with a peak from 3 P.M. to 7 P.M., and Figure 4.11b, which shows the *yearly* cycle of fire alarms, with a peak in April.

As noted earlier with regard to products, frequently, it is not clear whether a problem is a matter of scheduling or capacity; this is particularly true with services. The primary problem is matching availability of staff to demand in terms of timing and skills, both on a daily basis and over the longer term (such as weekly and monthly). As discussed earlier, service organizations have developed many novel approaches to this problem, as just briefly described: split shifts, overlapping shifts, duty tours (e.g. 48 or 72 hours for firefighters), part-time help, overbooking, appointment systems, and on-call staff. However, for services, a favorite alternative is to share capacity with neighboring units by pooling resources such as generators, police patrols, or hotel rooms. When one organization is temporarily overloaded, the neighbor absorbs the excess demand. Another favorite approach for some services that has even been too successful is that of shifting the demand to off-peak periods. When AT&T offered lower phone rates after 5 P.M., it found that it had to raise the Sunday night 5 P.M. to 11 P.M. rate owing to excessive shifted demand.

In many situations, it is almost impossible to measure an organization's capacity to produce a service because the service is so abstract. Thus, a more common approach is to measure *inputs,* rather than outputs, and assume (perhaps with regular checkups) that the production system is successful at transforming the inputs into acceptable services (outputs). For example,

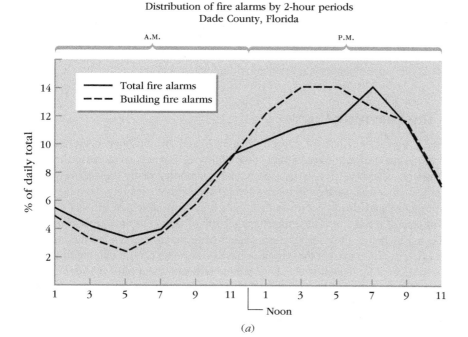

Distribution of fire alarms by 2-hour periods
Dade County, Florida

(a)

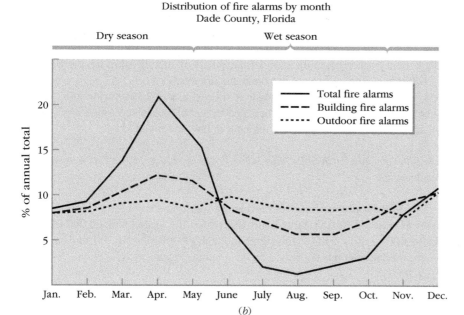

Distribution of fire alarms by month
Dade County, Florida

(b)

FIGURE 4.11 Fire Alarm Histories: (a) Hourly; (b) Monthly

organizations that offer plays, art exhibits, and other such intangible services do not measure their patrons' pleasure or relaxation; rather, they measure number of performances, number of actors and actresses, and number of paintings (or painting days, since many exhibits have a rotating travel schedule). Even fire departments do not attempt to measure their capacity by the number of fires they can extinguish; instead, they use the number of engines or companies they can offer in response to a call, the service or response time, or the number of firefighters responding.

Clearly, this manner of measuring service capacity can leave a lot to be desired. Do more paintings give greater satisfaction? Do higher-quality paintings give greater satisfaction? Might there be other factors that are equally or more important, such as the crowd, the parking facilities, or the lighting on the paintings? Is a hospital where more deaths occur providing worse service? Is a hospital with more physicians on staff providing better service?

4.4.4 The Learning Curve

An extremely important aspect of capacity planning, and an important operations concept in and of itself, is the *learning curve* effect – the ability of humans to increase their productive capacity through "learning." This issue is particularly important in the short-term start-up of new and unfamiliar processes, such as those involving new technologies (e.g. learning to use a new software program), and always occurs in the production ramp-up of new models of automobiles, planes, computers, and so on. Thus, the characteristic of slow, possibly error-prone output initially, followed by better, faster production, should be of major concern to marketing and sales, which are often trying to market the output or have promised a certain volume to a customer by a set date; to accounting, which is checking productivity and yield rates in order to determine a fair cost for the output; and to finance, which is concerned with the timing of cash flows related to purchases, labor, and revenues.

The improvement with experience is not necessarily due to learning alone, however. Better tools, improvements in work methods, upgraded output designs, and other such factors also help increase productivity. Hence, such curves are also known as *improvement curves, production progress functions, performance curves*, and *experience curves*. The learning curve effect, from this viewpoint, also affects long-term capacity and should be factored into longer term planning processes, another issue of interest to marketing and accounting as well as finance. The Japanese, in particular, count on increasing the long-term capacity of a facility through the workers' development of better work methods and improvements in tools.

The derivation of the learning curve began in the airframe manufacturing industry during the 1930s, when it was found that the labor hours needed to build each successive airplane decreased relatively smoothly. In particular, the learning curve law was found to be

> *Each time the output doubles, the labor hours decrease to a fixed percentage of their previous value.*

In the case of plane production, this percentage was found to be 80%. Thus, when the first plane of a series required 100,000 labor hours to produce, the second took 80,000 labor hours, the fourth took $80,000 \times 0.80 = 64,000$, the eighth took $64,000 \times 0.80 = 51,200$, and so on. This type of mathematical relationship is described by the *negative exponential function*

$$T_n = T_1 n^r$$

where

T_n = labor hours for the nth unit
T_1 = labor hours for first unit
n = number of units produced
r = exponent of curve = ln (learning rate)/0.69

Two forms of the learning curve relationship are used in the practice. In one form, T_n corresponds to the cumulative average labor hours of all n units, and in the other form, T_n corresponds to the actual labor hours to produce the nth unit. The second interpretation is often more useful for capacity planning. For example, then, a learning rate of 90% would mean that each time production doubled from, say, n_1 to n_2, unit n_2 would require 90% of the labor hours that n_1 required. The ln in the above formula is the "natural" logarithm (the base e), and 0.693 is the natural logarithm of 2.0 (because the learning curve is based on a doubling of output). But base 10, or any other base, may be used if divided by the log of 2.0 to the same base. That is, $r = \log(\text{learning rate})/\log(2.0)$

To illustrate the equation, calculating the time it will take to build the second airplane for our example can be done as follows:

$$T_2 = (100,000)2^{\ln(0.8)/0.693}$$

$$= (100,000)2^{-0.322}$$

$$= 80,000 \text{ labor hours}$$

Figure 4.12 shows the learning curve for airplanes again assuming 100,000 labor hours for the first plane and a learning rate of 80%.

A number of factors affect the learning curve rate, but the most important are the complexity of the task and the percentage of human, compared with mechanical, input. The greatest learning – sometimes at a rate as much as 60% (lower rates meaning greater learning) – occurs for highly complex tasks consisting primarily of human inputs. A task that is highly machine automated clearly leaves little opportunity for learning. (Thus, a rate close to 100% would apply, because typically only the human can learn although this is changing with advances in artificial intelligence.) In airframe manufacturing, the proportion of human effort is about 75%, and an 80% learning rate applies. For similar work of the same complexity and ratio of human-to-machine input, approximately the same rate will apply.

But learning curves are not limited to manufacturing or even to product-oriented organizations. These curves apply just as well to hairdressing, selling, finding a parking space, and preparing pizza. As indicated, they also apply to *groups* of individuals and *systems* that include people and machines, as well as to individuals.

A recent and noteworthy application of learning curves is to the cost of lithium-ion batteries used in electric vehicles. A significant barrier to the broad adoption of electric vehicles has been the high cost of the batteries needed to store the energy to power the vehicles. As it turns out, however, the ability to learn and improve has resulted in a dramatic reduction in the cost of

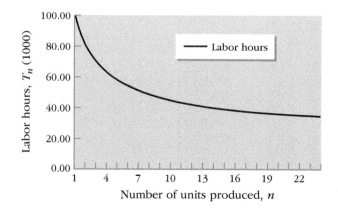

FIGURE 4.12 Eighty Percent Learning Curve for Airplane Production

lithium-ion batteries by 97% over the period from 1991 to 2018. More specifically, a lithium-ion battery with a one kilowatt-hour (kWh) capacity cost $181 in 2018 compared to $7500 for the same kWh capacity in 1991. In terms of learning curve theory, the cost of the lithium-ion batteries declined by an average of 19 percent each time capacity doubled. To help put this in perspective, in 2017 Tesla announced its Model 3 would have a 50-kWh battery. Producing a battery with this capacity in 1991 would have cost $375,000 (50 × 7500), well beyond what most people are willing to spend on a car and this is just for the battery. However, by 2018, producing the battery cost only $9,050 (50 × 181) which in turn enabled Tesla to offer the vehicle at a much more affordable price.

The primary question, of course, is what learning rate to apply. If previous experience is available, this may give some indication; if not, a close watch of the time it takes to produce the first few units should give a good indication. Let us illustrate the use of the learning curve, and some learning curve tables, with a simple example.

4.4.4.1 Creating Learning Curve Tables

Because working with the learning curve formula can be cumbersome, especially when you are interested in estimating the cumulative time required to produce multiple units, creating a table in a spreadsheet can greatly facilitate the analysis. To illustrate this, the unit times and cumulative times assuming an 80% learning rate (cell C1) and that the first item took 100,000 hours (cell C2) have been calculated and tabulated in the spreadsheet shown in Figure 4.13. The spreadsheet

	A	B	C
1	Improvement Rate:		80%
2	Hours for 1st Unit (m):		100,000
3			
4	Unit	Unit Time	Cumulative Time
5	1	100,000.0	100,000.0
6	2	80,000.0	180,000.0
7	3	70,210.4	250,210.4
8	4	64,000.0	314,210.4
9	5	59,563.7	373,774.1
10	6	56,168.3	429,942.4
11	7	53,449.0	483,391.4
12	8	51,200.0	534,591.4
13	9	49,295.0	583,886.3
14	10	47,651.0	631,537.3
15	11	46,211.1	677,748.4
16	12	44,934.6	722,683.1
17	13	43,791.6	766,474.6
18	14	42,759.2	809,233.8
19	15	41,819.9	851,053.7
20	16	40,960.0	892,013.7
21	17	40,168.3	932,182.0
22	18	39,436.0	971,618.0
23	19	38,755.5	1,010,373.5
24	20	38,120.8	1,048,494.3
25	21	37,526.7	1,086,021.0
26	22	36,968.9	1,122,989.9
27	23	36,443.6	1,159,433.5
28	24	35,947.7	1,195,381.2
29	25	35,478.4	1,230,859.6

Cell B5: =C2*A5^(LN(C1)/LN(2))
Copy to cells B6:B29

Cell C6: =C5+B6
Copy to cells C7:C29

FIGURE 4.13
Example Learning Curve Table

shows the time the nth unit will require (column B) and the cumulative amount of time that the first n units will take (column C).

From the spreadsheet in Figure 4.13, we observe that unit 2 will require 80,000 hours, that unit 4 will require 64,000 hours, that unit 8 will take 51,200 hours, and so forth. In addition, we also see that unit 3 will take 70,210.4 hours. The *total* labor hours to produce two, four, or eight planes are calculated in column C and are 180,000; 314,210.4; and 534,591.4 hours, respectively.

The spreadsheet shown in Figure 4.13 can be easily modified to accommodate other situations. For example, alternative improvement rates and first unit times can be entered in cells C1 and C2, respectively. Also, the number of rows can be easily expanded by copying the last row down to get unit and cumulative times over a wider range of units.

The learning curve is only a theoretical construct, of course, and therefore only approximates actual learning. A more realistic, and typical, learning pattern is illustrated in Figure 4.14. Initially, actual labor hours per unit vary around the theoretical curve until a "learning plateau" is reached at, perhaps, the tenth unit. At this plateau, no significant learning appears to occur, until there is a breakthrough. Learning typically involves a number of such plateaus and breakthroughs. At about 30 units, production is halted for a period of time and "forgetting" occurs, rapidly at first but then trailing off. When production is resumed, relearning occurs very quickly (as when someone relearns to ride a bicycle after 40 years) until the original efficiency is reached (at about 33 units). If the conditions are the same at this time as for the initial part of the curve, the original learning curve rate will then hold. After sufficient time passes, the improvement due to learning becomes trivial in comparison with natural variability in efficiency, and at that point, we say learning has ceased.

4.4.5 Capacity and Waiting

Another reason why capacity is important is because it impacts waiting times, whether it be parts waiting in front of a machine for processing, customers waiting in line to be checked out at a grocery store, or patients waiting to receive treatment from a doctor in the emergency department of a hospital. The technical term used for a single waiting line is queue. Thus, the words waiting

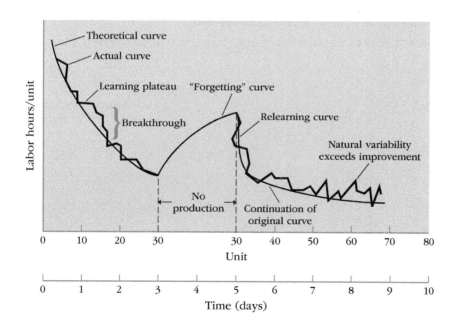

FIGURE 4.14
Typical Pattern of Learning and Forgetting

line or queue can be used interchangeably. ***Queuing theory*** is the branch of mathematics dedicated to modeling waiting lines so that their performance can be evaluated and ideas for improvement investigated. In particular, queuing theory provides a mechanism to determine several key performance measures of an operating system based on the rate of arrivals to the system and the system's capacity (specified as the system's service rate).

With an unpaced production line, for example, inventory between operations builds up at some times and disappears at other times, owing to natural variability in the mix of products produced and the processing times at various stages in the production process. In the delivery of services, this variability is often greater because of the unpredictability in serving humans who may play an important role in the service delivery process. What is more, when the "items" in queue are people, they tend to complain and create other challenges if kept waiting too long. Thus, it is incumbent for the operations manager to provide adequate capacity to keep long queues from forming. Of course, this costs more money for service facilities and staff. But long queues also cost money in the form of in-process inventory, unfinished orders, lost sales, and customer ill will. Figure 4.15 conceptually illustrates, as a function of the capacity of the service facility, the trade-offs in two costs:

1. *Cost of waiting.* In-process inventory, ill will, and lost sales. This cost decreases with increases in service capacity. However, there may be other ways to decrease these costs such as using lean processes (Chapter 9) or, particularly for services, those discussed later in this section.

2. *Cost of service facilities.* Equipment, supplies, and staff. This cost increases with increases in service capacity. Again, there are ways to also reduce the cost of service capacity, such as self-service, or automating the service.

At some point, the total of the two costs in Figure 4.15 is minimized, and it is at this point that managers typically wish to operate. But while the cost of adding capacity can be calculated fairly easily, the cost of waiting is more difficult to determine since it may depend on human aspects and thus can only be estimated by experimenting with different capacity levels. We will return to the human aspects associated with waiting, but first we address how to model queuing systems.

4.4.5.1 The Structure of a Queuing System

As illustrated in Figure 4.16, a queuing system is composed of the following parts:

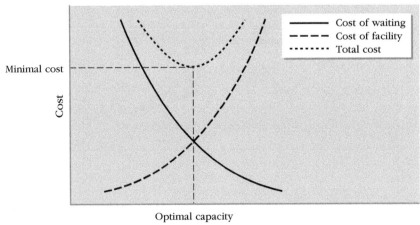

FIGURE 4.15 The Relevant Queuing Costs

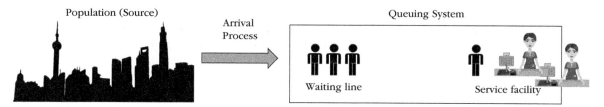

FIGURE 4.16 The Structure of a Queuing System

4.4.5.1.1 The Customers and Their Source. Customers are defined as those in need of service. Customers can be people waiting in line for an ATM, airplanes waiting to takeoff, machines waiting for repair, jobs waiting for processing, or raw materials waiting to be transported. The customers come from a *population* or a source, which can be considered either infinite (i.e. so large that our model is unaffected by the size) or finite. As an example of an infinite population, a hospital's "population" would be the people in the surrounding community, and the "customers" would be those people in the population requiring hospitalization for sickness or injury. While technically speaking, the population in a community is not infinite because of its large size, for all practical purposes it can be considered to be infinite. An example of a finite population might be a set of machines in a factory, or elevators in an office building, that are serviced by a repair crew.

4.4.5.1.2 The Arrival Process. An important element of waiting line analysis is the arrival of customers to the system. Customers don't necessarily have to arrive physically. For example, an arrival could be a phone call to a customer service rep. Arrivals to the queuing system are described or modeled by an arrival rate. The *arrival rate* represents the number of arrivals within a specified period of time. Examples of arrival rates include 100,000 visits per month to a website, 20 calls per hour to a help desk, and 15 walk-in customers per day to a hair salon. Notice that arrivals are expressed as a rate and therefore a period of time must be specified. Knowing that 10 customers arrive does not tell us much. Knowing that 10 customers per hour arrive tells us much more. A key assumption in waiting line analysis is that the arrivals are independent of one another and they vary randomly over time. Often the number of arrivals that occur in a given time period can be modeled using the Poisson distribution. The arrival rate is represented by the Greek symbol λ.

4.4.5.1.3 The Service Facility and the Service Process. The service is provided by a service facility(ies). This may be a person (bank teller, hair stylist, nurse), a machine (elevator, gasoline pump, printer), or a space (airport runway, parking lot), to mention just a few. A service facility may include one person or several people, operating either as a team or in parallel (multiple service channels).

4.4.5.1.4 The Queue or Waiting Line. Whenever an arriving customer finds that the service facility is busy, a queue, or waiting line, is formed. There may be single, multiple, or even priority lines and the order of service may be random, by appointment, first come-first served, or some other order. The queue can also be considered to be either infinite or finite. An example of the former is callers placed on hold for the next available service rep. An example of the latter is when there are only a limited number of waiting spaces available, such as parking spaces for cars.

4.4.6 Measuring the Performance of the Basic Queuing System

The classical and probably best known of all waiting line models is the common *Poisson-exponential single-server system*. In this model, the arrival rate λ is assumed to be random and follow the *Poisson* distribution. The service time is assumed to follow the *negative exponential distribution.* The average service rate is designated by the Greek letter μ, and the average service time by $1/\mu$. The *major assumptions* underlying the basic queueing system model are as follows:

- There is a single server.

- The source of population is infinite.

- Arrivals are processed on a first-come, first-served basis.

- The ratio λ/μ is less than 1. This ratio is designated by the Greek letter ρ and is a measure of the utilization of the system. If ρ is greater than or even equal to 1.0, the waiting line will increase without bound (explosive), a situation that is unacceptable to management (and even more so to customers). This is the case even when $\rho = 1$ because of the variability of the arrivals.

- Steady state (equilibrium) exists.

- Our interest is in the "long-run" behavior of the system, commonly known as steady state.

- There is unlimited space and no limit on the queue length.

A queuing system is usually evaluated by one or more of the following measures of performance (given with their respective formulas). These measures depend on only two parameters, λ and μ, which must be stated in the same time units.

The Average Waiting Time, W. The average time a customer spends in the system, waiting for the service and being served, is:

$$W = \frac{1}{\mu - \lambda}$$

The Average Waiting Time in the Queue, W_q. This is the average time a customer will wait, in the queue, before the service starts.

$$W_q = \frac{\lambda}{\mu(\mu - \lambda)}$$

The Average Number of Customers in the System, L. The average number of customers in both the queue and being served is:

$$L = \frac{\lambda}{\mu - \lambda}$$

The Average Number of Customers in the Queue, L_q. The length of the waiting line, not including the customer being served, is:

$$L_q = \frac{\lambda^2}{\mu(\mu - \lambda)}$$

The Probability of an Empty (Idle) Facility, P(0). The probability that there are no customers in the system, either waiting or being served, is:

$$P(0) = 1 - \frac{\lambda}{\mu}$$

The Probability of the System Being Busy, ρ. The probability the system is busy is the same as *not* finding an empty system:

$$\rho = 1 - P(0) = \frac{\lambda}{\mu}$$

The Probability of Finding Exactly N Customers in the system, P(N).

$$P(N) = \rho^N (1 - \rho)$$

The Probability that the Number of Customers in the System, N, Exceeds a Given Value, n.

$$P[N > n] = \rho^{n+1}$$

The following relationships, developed by the scholar J.D.C. Little, are extremely important because they hold for any queuing system and enable us to find L, L_q, W, and W_q as soon as any one is computed.

$$L = \lambda W$$

$$L_q = \lambda W_q$$

$$W = W_q + \frac{1}{\mu}$$

These measures of performance can be used in a cost analysis, or just to aid in determining service level policies. For example, a fast-food restaurant wants to design its service facility so that a customer will not wait, on the average, more than two minutes (i.e. $W_q \leq 2$ minutes) before being served. Or as another example, a helpdesk wants to ensure that its technicians are busy at least 75% of the day (i.e. $\rho \geq 0.75$).

4.4.7 Human Aspects and the Psychology of Waiting

As noted earlier, determining the cost of adding capacity is relatively straightforward, while determining the cost of waiting is more challenging as it depends on each person's unique perceptions. However, before investing resources by adding expensive service facilities, the manager may find it worthwhile trying to reduce the cost of waiting instead. Given that perceptions and expectations may have more to do with customer satisfaction than actual waiting time, Maister (1984) has formulated eight insightful "principles" of waiting, which, if addressed carefully, may be more effective in reducing the overall cost of waiting to the organization than adding service facilities:

1. *Unoccupied time feels longer than occupied time.* Give customers something to do while waiting, hopefully something that will facilitate the service that is to come. An example is having customers key in their Social Security or account number while waiting on the phone so the representatives will have their file on screen as they answer the call.

2. *Preservice waiting feels longer than in-service waiting.* Using staging areas to complete portions of the service, such as taking a patient's temperature and blood pressure, communicates that the service has begun.

3. *Anxiety makes waiting seem longer.* Offer information to relieve anxiety or distracters (even music and mirrors) to allay anxiety.

4. *Uncertain waiting is longer than known, finite waiting.* Provide cues, or direct announcements, to indicate how soon the service will be coming or finishing (especially in the case of an unpleasant or painful procedure).

5. *Unexplained waiting is longer than explained waiting.* Keep customers informed about why they are being delayed and how long it will be before they can be serviced.

6. *Unfair waiting is longer than fair waiting.* Make sure that priority or express customers are handled in a manner transparent to other customers and treated out of sight if possible.

7. *Solo waiting is longer than group waiting.* In part, this reflects principles 1 (someone else to talk to), 3 (seeing and talking to others can reduce anxiety), and 5 (other waiting customers may communicate reasons for the waiting), as well as the general principle that there is more security in groups.

8. *The more valuable the service, the longer it is worth waiting for.* The use of marketing and other means to increase the perception of the value of the service will reduce the impatience with waiting.

EXPAND YOUR UNDERSTANDING

1. Exactly what decreases in unit cost occur with larger facilities as a result of economies of scale? Might any costs increase with the size of a facility?

2. Why has the concept of economies of scope never arisen before? List where the economies come from.

3. How ethical is it for airlines, hotels, and other service providers to overbook their limited-capacity facilities intentionally, knowing that at some point they will have to turn away a customer with a "guaranteed" reservation?

4. Describe how the concept of bottlenecks would apply to services as well as products. Give some examples from your experience.

5. What elements would be measured if a product firm were to measure its capacity by its inputs, as do some service firms?

6. Does the learning curve continue downward forever?

7. Would the failure points, line of visibility, and processing times used in service maps be useful in process-flow diagrams for products?

8. Are the principles of waiting captured in the 23 capacity techniques of Table 4.4? Which ones?

9. Would a firm that simply expanded its current product line gain economies of scope? Might highly flexible and proficient labor also offer economies of scope?

10. Many services, such as airlines, conduct their scheduling in two stages. First, an overall macroschedule is constructed and optimized for costs and service to the customer. This schedule is then considered to be the baseline for detailed scheduling to attempt to achieve. The second, detailed stage is then a real-time schedule to adjust the macroschedule for any necessary changes, emergencies, and so on. Describe how this might work for airlines, hospitals, schools, and urban alarm services. What serious problems might arise with this approach?

11. Referring to the Yield/Revenue Management and Overbooking section, why might an early reservation be canceled? A late reservation?

12. Referring to Table 4.1, what actions could an airline do to increase its ASM? Are there any aspects beyond management's control that limit the ability of the airline to increase its ASM?

13. Why might unit variable cost increase with larger volumes? Why might it decrease?

14. Frequently, simple models such as breakeven analysis are much more appealing to management than more sophisticated models such as linear programming. Why might this be so?

15. In terms of the breakeven chart, such as Figure 4.4, how would manufacturing overseas compare with domestic production?

16. Under what conditions would it be best to precede an expected demand with additional capacity increments? When would it be best to follow expected demand?

17. How might you go about trying to determine the cost of customer ill will?

18. The queuing model in this chapter assumes that the system is in steady state. How valid is this assumption?

Apply Your Understanding

Bangalore Training Services

Bangalore Training Services (BTS) was an entrepreneurial start-up developed by Deepa Anand and Monisha Patel, two recent MBA graduates from the United States who had served internships in the summer with a U.S. call center that was considering setting up operations in India but was unsure how to find suitable employees. Their plan was to offer training to Indian men and women in call center activities such as sales, service, and troubleshooting for electronic goods of all sorts and then to match those employees to the needs of foreign firms looking to set up call centers. The training consisted of a dozen sessions covering culture, speaking fluency, electronic awareness, buying and service behaviors, and other such basic matters that all call centers required.

Questions

Discuss how the following topics from this chapter might be of relevance to Deepa and Monisha in setting up their new firm:

1. Capacity planning

2. Learning curve

3. Bottlenecks

4. Psychology of waiting

5. Scheduling

6. Service map/blueprint

Exit Manufacturing Company

The planning committee of Exit Manufacturing Company (made up of the vice presidents of marketing, finance, and production) was discussing the plans for a new factory to be located outside of Atlanta, Georgia. The factory would produce exterior doors consisting of prehung metal over styrofoam insulation. The doors would be made in a standard format, with 15 different insert panels that could be added by retailers after manufacture. The standardization of construction was expected to create numerous production efficiencies over competitors' factories that produced multidimensional doors. Atlanta was felt to be an ideal site because of its location – in the heart of the Sunbelt, with its growing construction industry. By locating close to these growing Sunbelt states, Exit would minimize distribution costs.

The capital cost for the factory was expected to be $14 million. Annual maintenance expenses were projected to total 5% of capital. Fuel and utility costs were expected to be $500,000 per year. An analysis of the area's labor market indicated that a wage rate of $10 per hour could be expected. It was estimated that producing a door in the new facility would require 1.5 labor hours. Fringe benefits paid to the operating labor were expected to equal 15% of direct labor costs. Supervisory, clerical, technical, and managerial salaries were forecast to total $350,000 per year. Taxes and insurance would cost $200,000 per year. Other miscellaneous expenses were expected to total $250,000 per year. Depreciation was based on a 30-year life with the use of the straight-line method and a $4 million salvage value.

Sheet metal, styrofoam, adhesive for the doors, and frames were projected to cost $12 per door. Paint, hinges, doorknobs, and accessories were estimated to total $7.80 per door. Crating and shipping supplies were expected to cost $2.50 per door.

Exit's marketing manager prepared the following price–demand chart for the distribution area of the new plant. Through analysis of these data, the committee members felt that they could verify their expectation of an increase from 15% to 25% in the current market share, owing to the cost advantage of standardization.

Average sales price ($/door)	Area sales (in units)
$90	40,000
$103	38,000
$115	31,000
$135	22,000

Questions

Develop a breakeven capacity analysis for Exit's new door and determine the following:

1. Best price, production rate, and profit.

2. Breakeven production rate with the price determined in Question 1.

3. Breakeven price with the production rate determined in Question 1.

4. Sensitivity of profits to variable cost, price, and production rate.

EXERCISES

4.1 Three professors are grading a combined final exam. Each is grading different questions on the test. One professor requires three minutes to finish her portion, a second takes six minutes, and the third takes two minutes. Assume that there is no learning curve effect.

a. What will be their hourly output?

b. If there are 45 tests to grade, how long will the grading take?

c. If each professor were to grade the exams separately in 18 minutes, how long would it take to grade the 45 tests? How long if another professor (who also required 18 minutes) joined them?

d. If another professor pitches in just to help the second professor in the original arrangement, how long will it take the four of them to grade the tests?

e. If a fifth professor offers to help, what might happen?

4.2 A toy firm produces drums sequentially on three machines – A, B, and C – with cycle times of three, four, and six minutes, respectively.

a. Determine the optimum efficiency and output rates for adding one, two, . . . , six more machines.

b. Assume now that two identical lines are operating, each with machines A, B, and C. If new machines can be shared between the lines, how should one, two, and then three new machines be added? What are the resulting efficiencies and outputs of the two lines? Is it always best to equally share extra machines between the two lines?

4.3 If unit 1 requires six labor hours and unit 5 requires 1.8324, what is the learning rate? What will unit 6 require? What have the first five units required in total?

4.4 A production lot of 25 units required 103.6 hours of effort. Accounting records show that the first unit took seven hours. What was the learning rate?

4.5 If unit 1 required 200 hours to produce and the labor records for an Air Force contract of 50 units indicate an average labor content of 63.1 hours per unit, what was the learning rate? What total additional number of labor hours would be required for another Air Force contract of 50 units? What would be the average labor content of this second contract? Of both contracts combined? If labor costs the vendor $10 per hour on this Air Force contract and the price to the Air Force is fixed at $550 each, what can you say about the profitability of the first and second contracts and hence the bidding process in general?

4.6 All the reports you wrote for one class had three sections: introduction, analysis, and conclusion. The times required to complete these sections (including analysis and creating the report) are shown below in hours.

Report	Introduction	Analysis	Conclusion
1	1.5	6	2
2	–	(Lost data)	–
3	1	3	0.8

The class requires five reports in all. You are now starting report 4, and, although you are working faster, you can afford to spend only 1 hour a day on these reports. Report 5 is due in one week (7 days). Will you be done in time?

4.7 A defense contractor is bidding on a military contract for 100 radar units. The contractor employs 30 machine operators who work 165 hours a month each. The first radar unit required 1145 operator hours, and the learning curve for this type of work is known to be 75%. It takes a month to order and receive raw material components, which cost $500 per radar unit. The material is then paid for in the month it is received. Fixed costs include a month to tool up, which costs $10,000 and then $5000 per month for every month of production. Direct labor and variable overhead are $8 per hour. The contractor can deliver only completed units and is paid the following month. Profit is set at 10% of the bid price. Find the bid price, derive the production schedule, and calculate the cash flow schedule.

4.8 Given the following four capacity alternatives, find the best production method for every production volume.

Method	Fixed Cost ($)	Variable Cost ($/unit)
A	200	5
B	100	10
C	150	4
D	250	2

4.9 Ace Machinery is forecasting demand of 70,000 units of demand next year a major increase from its demand this year of 50,000 units. By adding a third shift, it could produce 75,000 units, up from its current capacity of 50,000 units. The variable cost would increase from $1.10 to $1.50 on the third shift. Another option is to purchase additional equipment, which could reduce the variable cost to $1.

In addition to adding a third shift, Ace has identified two options for investing in additional equipment. One option is to invest $100,000 in new equipment, which would increase capacity by 20,000 units per year and result in variable costs of $1.20. The other equipment option is to invest $120,000 in additional equipment, which would also increase capacity by 20,000 units per year but would result in a variable cost of $1. In both cases, the equipment is expected to last for 10 years. What would you recommend Ace do?

4.10 Referring to Exercise 4.5, assume that the learning rate for each unit can vary by as much as ±5% from its average. In other words, if the learning rate averaged 70% it could vary by as much as ±3.5%. Thus, the second unit would take between 66.5% and 73.5% of the time it took to produce the first unit, the fourth unit would take between 66.5% and 73.5% of the time it took to produce the second unit, and so on. Furthermore, assume that all learning rates between the lower and upper bounds are equally likely. Reanalyze Exercise 4.5 incorporating this uncertainty into your analysis. How does it impact your results? Does it make sense to incorporate this uncertainty into the analysis?

4.11 A service system has an average interarrival time of two minutes and an average service rate of 60 per hour. *Find:*

a. The probability that a customer will have to wait.

b. The probability that four persons are in the system.

c. The probability of finding more than three in the system.

d. The probability that fewer than four are in the system.

4.12 The Pelican is a yogurt shop where people arrive at the average rate of 20 per hour. Joe, the proprietor, serves a customer, on the average, in two minutes. During the noontime rush, the arrival rate increases to one arriving customer every two minutes. *Find:*

a. How fast must Joe work to ensure that a noontime customer will not wait for service, on the average, more than 10 minutes?

b. What is the probability that six or more people are in the shop during the nonrush period?

c. What is the average waiting time during the nonrush hours?

4.13 Customers arrive at a one-person hair salon with an average interarrival time of 20 minutes. The average time for a haircut is 12 minutes.

a. The owner wishes to have enough seats in the waiting area so that no more than 5% of the arriving customers will have to stand. How many seats should be provided?

b. Suppose there is only sufficient space in the waiting area for five seats. What is the probability that an arriving customer will not find a seat?

BIBLIOGRAPHY

Alstrup, J., S. E. Andersson, S. Boas, O. B. G. Madsen, and R. V. V. Vidal. "Booking Control Increases Profit at Scandinavian Airlines." *Interfaces* (July–August 1989): 10–19.

Bomey, N., "GM Poised to Close Plants in Michigan, Ohio, Maryland, will Cut 15% of Salaried Workers." *USA Today*, November 26, 2018, www.usatoday.com/story/money/cars/2018/11/26/gm-general-motors-plantclosures-job-cuts/2113275002/

Burlingham, B. *Small Giants: Companies That Choose to Be Great Instead of Big*. New York: Portfolio, 2006.

Cameron, D. "Southwest to End Overbooking." *Wall Street Journal* (April 28, 2017): B6.

Carey, S. "Case of the Vanishing Airport Lines." *Wall Street Journal* (August 9, 2007).

Doerr, J., *Speed and Scale: An Action Plan for Solving our Climate Crisis Now*. Portfolio/Penguin, 2021.

Filley, R. D. "Putting the 'Fast' in Fast Foods: Burger King." *Industrial Engineering* (January 1983): 44–47.

Fisher, M. L., J. H. Hammond, W. R. Obermeyer, and A. Raman. "Making Supply Meet Demand in an Uncertain World." *Harvard Business Review*, 72 (May–June 1994): 83–93.

Grant, D.B., Trautrims, A., and Wong, C.Y., *Sustainable Logistics and Supply Chain Management, 2nd Edition*. Kogan Page, 2017.

Kimes, S. E. "Yield Management: A Tool for Capacity Constrained Service Firms." *Journal of Operations Management*, 8(4) (1989): 348–363.

Maister, D. H. "The Psychology of Waiting Lines." *Harvard Reprint* No. 9-684-064 (May 1984).

Naughton, K. (2022). America's Favorite Truck is About to Test Tesla's Dominance, Bloomberg.com, April 14, 2022.

O'Malley, A. "Green Buildings in the US: A Simple Guide." planradar. com, April 15, 2021.

Prahalad, C. K. "In Volatile Times, Agility Rules." *BusinessWeek* (September 21, 2009): 80.

Ritchie, H. "The Price of Batteries has Declined by 97% in the Last Three Decades." ourworldindata.org, June, 4, 2021.

Smith, R. A. "Find the Best Checkout Line." *Wall Street Journal* (December 8, 2011).

Tangel, A. "Harley to Close Plant in Missouri." *Wall Street Journal* (January 31, 2018), p. B10.

U.S. Department of Labor, "Plant Closings & Layoffs," www.dol.gov/general/topic/termination/plantclosings, January 9, 2019.

USGBC, "LEED Rating System." usgbc.org, June 6, 2022.

Strategic Management of Supply Chains

5.1 Introduction

- No other event in recent history has likely drawn greater attention to supply chain management than the COVID-19 pandemic that began in early 2020. During the pandemic we heard daily about shortages of a wide range of products, from staples like toilet paper and basic cleaning supplies to major purchases including vehicles and home appliances. To add some objectivity to this, consulting firm Procurement Tactics reported that in 2020 $1.14 trillion of goods were out of stock compared to $626 billion of items that were overstocked. Grocery stores were especially hard hit where it was estimated that the value of out-of-stock items was five times the value of overstocked items.

The industry that received perhaps the greatest amount of attention regarding shortages of products was the semiconductor industry. Shortages of semiconductors, or chips as they are more commonly referred to, resulted in shortages for many other products including home appliances, vehicles, and smartphones. While on the surface it is easy to imagine why a shortage of chips would impact smartphones, it may be less obvious why a shortage of chips would impact the sales of vehicles. As it turns out, chips are used to control virtually all aspects of vehicles from the motors used to open the windows to the onboard navigation systems. Deloitte estimated that cars manufactured in 2022 contained $600 worth of chips.

According to Vincent Roche, CEO of Analog Devices, the shortage of chips in the auto industry stems from the auto manufacturers significantly reducing their purchases of chips at the start of the pandemic and then relying on their inventories, given the much lower expected demand for vehicles. According to Roche, when demand for vehicles picked up, the chip manufacturers were not able to meet the demand for chips as a result of the vehicles needing more chips per vehicle, a delayed response from the chip manufacturers to ramp up production capacity, and the time required to ramp up capacity.

As a result of the chip shortage, some vehicle manufacturers were required to shut down their production facilities. For example, Ford was forced to shut down its Louisville, KY, plant for a full week in January 2021. Across the entire industry, vehicle sales in the United States fell by over 17% from 2019 to 2020 (from 17 million vehicles to 14.5 million).

To avoid the need to shut down production facilities and to meet as much demand as possible, vehicle manufacturers employed a variety of strategies. In some cases, chips in short supply were replaced by chips that have greater availability. But replacing chips required updating software. In other cases, vehicle features that depended on chips in short supply were being suspended. For example, General Motors (GM) temporarily stopped offering the heated seat option on some of its vehicles. GM did take steps to ensure that the suspended features could be added at a later date once the required chips were available. Vehicle manufacturers were also pressuring the chip producers to give them higher priority, which in turn required the chip producers to negotiate with their other customers.

At the same time, chip manufacturers were making commitments to expand their chip production capacity. For example, Taiwan Semiconductor Manufacturing Company (TSMC) committed to investing $100 billion over the next couple of years to increase its production capacity. Unfortunately, just as the semiconductor industry appeared to be making progress in terms of catching up with demand, the supply of neon gas used in the production of chips was being disrupted as a result of the war in Ukraine (Cherney 2021; Preston 2021; Procurement Tactics 2022; Statistic 2022; Yang and Yang 2021).

- While Apple's enormous success is most commonly attributed to its ability to design highly innovative products that are easy to use, the significant contribution its operations makes to its success gets much less publicity. Nevertheless, experts and analysts that closely follow Apple readily acknowledge that Apple's operations excellence is as much an asset to Apple as is its product innovation and marketing. Indeed, it is Apple's operational capabilities that allow it to pull off its massive, high-volume product launches by managing its inventory efficiently.

It is not widely known, but Apple's focus on improving its supply chain dates back to the return of Steve Jobs in 1997. For example, to ensure that there was an adequate supply of Apple's new translucent blue iMacs, Apple spent $50 million to acquire all the available holiday air transport capacity. Not only did this ensure that Apple could get its products to the customers but also the move crippled competitors, such as Compaq, that didn't recognize the need to ship products by air until it was too late. Based on this example and other similar examples, Apple has learned that making investments in its supply chain up front pays for itself in the long run in the form of greater volumes. Greater volumes also yield additional benefits. For example, when the sales volume of iPods increased in 2001, Apple discovered it could air-ship the iPods economically from the Chinese factories directly to its customers' homes. Not only does this help Apple reduce its investment in inventory but also provides an added level of service for the customer.

Beyond investing financial resources in its supply chain, Apple invests in its human capital as well. For example, to facilitate projects involving the process of translating product proto-types into successful new products, Apple's design engineers live in hotels for months to be close to their suppliers in order to help them perfect their production processes. For example, when Apple designed a new MacBook with a case that was made from a single piece of aluminum, Apple's design engineers worked with the suppliers to develop the equipment to fabricate the cases.

With a huge cash war chest, Apple planned to almost double its supply chain capital expen-ditures in 2011 to $7.1 billion. In part, this investment was used to purchase capacity from its suppliers to ensure the prices and availability of its products. For example, prior to the intro-duction of iPhone 4 in June 2010, supplier capacity for screens was being used for iPhones, forcing Apple's competitor HTC to scramble for sources of phone screens. Likewise, during Apple's project to launch iPad 2, it purchased so many of the high-end drills used to produce the tablet's internal casing that the lead time for other companies to get these drills extended to as long as six months.

Turning the tables, being selected by Apple to be one of its suppliers can be very profitable. However, this comes at a price. For example, when a potential supplier is asked to provide a price quote for a part or assembly that will go into an Apple product, the supplier is required to submit in great detail how it arrived at the quote, including the specific material costs, labor costs, and its estimated profit. Furthermore, to guard against supply disruptions, Apple requires its suppliers to maintain a two-week supply of inventory within a mile of the Asian assembly plants.

Carefully orchestrated events announcing new products are eagerly anticipated by industry analysts and loyal customers. Here, too, Apple's supply chain management (SCM) practices play an important role. For example, supplier factories work overtime weeks in advance of new product launches to build up inventory to meet the often-overwhelming demand for new Macs, iPhones, and iPads. Furthermore, the success of the new product debuts centers on the secrecy Apple is able to maintain about the features of its new products. To ensure that the secrecy of its new products was not breached and to discourage leaks, Apple placed electronic monitors in a subset of the boxes of parts that went into its products so that it was able to moni-tor the parts through the production process. Through this monitoring, Apple was able to track every part handoff from the loading docks through the distribution centers. And not to leave anything to chance, once the new products were finished, they were shipped in plain boxes or even disguised boxes, such as tomato boxes.

A final piece of Apple's supply chain that contributed to its operational excellence was its retail stores. Apple tracked the sales at its stores hour by hour and, based on these sales, adjusted its production forecast each day. When a risk of a product shortage was identified, Apple immediately deployed teams, and the added capacity was acquired (Satariano and Bur-rows 2011).

- Even with the lean inventories that have resulted from the prevalence of just-in-time (JIT) inventory systems, shifts in economic cycles can still wreak havoc for industry-wide supply chains. The electronics industry during the global recession of 2008–2009 illustrates this well.

  At one end of the electronics supply chain were the retailers that sell electronic products to end consumers. With the financial crisis rapidly escalating in the fall of 2008, Minnesota-based retailer Best Buy experienced a significant decline in sales. Best Buy ordered elec-tronic products such as DVD players six weeks prior to when they are needed. With the 2008

Thanksgiving shopping season approaching, Best Buy revised its prior forecast and dramatically reduced its orders to its suppliers, such as Japan's Toshiba and Korea's Samsung Electronics in early October 2008. As the financial crisis was uncharted territory, Best Buy's merchandising chief had to make his best guess in deciding how to modify the forecast.

Lacking a direct relationship with the final consumers, Best Buy's suppliers were caught off guard by its revised forecast and reduced orders. As expected, these suppliers in turn reduced orders from their suppliers. As an example, Zoran Corp, a designer of specialty chips used in electronic products, such as televisions (TVs), cameras, cell phones, DVD players, and digital picture frames, saw its revenue decline in the fourth quarter of 2008 by 42%. Zoran, which only designed chips, relied on companies like Taiwan Semiconductor Manufacturing Company (TSMC) to produce its chips. Faced with decreased orders for its chips, Zoran slashed its orders to TSMC. In January and February of 2009, TSMC saw its revenue decrease by 58% compared to the prior year and was only utilizing 35% of its plant capacity.

With decreased demand for its chips, TSMC in turn reduced its orders for chip-making equipment by 20%. Applied Materials is one company that made the equipment used in chip-making factories. With the downturn in demand for chip-making equipment, Applied Materials was forced to lay off 2000 workers and require another 12,000 workers to take an unpaid leave.

With the downturn in its business, Applied Materials reduced orders to its suppliers. For example, D&H Manufacturing Company, which made aluminum parts for chip-making equipment, reduced its employment from 600 to 150 workers in 18 months because of the drop-off in business. It also found itself sitting on a one-year supply of inventory versus its usual three months of inventory.

This example illustrates how the effects and decisions made at one end of the supply chain are often amplified as they cascade to the other end. And because the players at different stages in the supply chain are often caught off guard, it is not surprising that they frequently overreact to the situation. In this case, Best Buy was actually having trouble keeping its shelves stocked in the early part of 2009 despite the decline in demand. In fact, Best Buy estimated in March 2009 that it could have sold more in the preceding three months had its suppliers made less drastic reductions to their production plans (Dvorak 2009).

- Milwaukee, WI, is home to two of the biggest multibillion-dollar manufacturers of earth-moving equipment that sold for up to $180 million: Bucyrus International, Inc., and Joy Global, Inc. However, they disagreed completely on how to locate their production facilities. Bucyrus made all their machines in the United States and Europe, where they developed highly efficient, low-cost production processes, and then shipped them from there to customers all over the globe. Moreover, they expected the U.S. dollar and the euro to remain relatively weak currencies, making manufacturing there affordable. Although they were invited to build a plant in China in the 1970s, they declined to do so because the Chinese government decided to make the production of industrial mining machinery "strategically critical," meaning that they would be heavily subsidizing their own domestic manufacturers.

  In contrast, Joy preferred to design and engineer in the United States but build their plants close to emerging markets and in low-cost developing countries, such as China, where the mining market was growing, and customers and domestic suppliers were plentiful. Joy's Chinese factory operating costs were fully 20% less than in the United States or Europe, though they admitted to having had some early quality problems. As Bucyrus's CEO says, "It's going to be interesting to see how it plays out. One of us is more right than the other" (Matthews 2010).

The concept of SCM has taken on the nature of a crusade in U.S. industry. This is in part because of the tremendous benefits that can accrue to firms participating in a well-managed supply chain, the result of intensive, complicated, and continuing projects, especially when an unexpected disruption like the COVID-19 pandemic hits. The examples above illustrate this by highlighting the important role SCM plays in an organization's competitiveness. The COVID-19 pandemic illustrates how interrelated our supply chains are where a shortage of chips resulted in shortages of many other products. In Apple's case, it implemented supply chain practices to ensure a stable supply of its highly demanded products, which, in turn, leads to satisfied customers and minimizes potential lost sales. On the other hand, the Best Buy and COVID-19 examples illustrate the potential for lost sales and profits when the organizations along the supply chain overreact.

It is also worth noting that, although the benefits of superior SCM are clear for manufacturing and distribution firms, even service organizations benefit from good SCM. This is not only because services use supplies and facilitating goods in the delivery of their service (as noted in Chapter 1) but also because they, too, outsource many of their internal functions, such as information technology, accounting, and human resource management, just like manufacturers do. Thus, the provision of these services becomes part of another supply chain, a chain of services rather than goods, but nonetheless one requiring the same attention to strategy, purchasing, logistics, and management oversight, just like for goods.

We begin the chapter with some definitions of the supply chain and SCM. As with any new concept, not everyone envisions SCM in the same way. We then discuss some of the important strategic advantages that accrue from wise management of the supply chain. From this overview, we then consider the elements of the supply chain in depth, including purchasing/procurement, logistics, transportation, global sourcing, and supplier management. An important element of SCM is the critical role of information technology as a major catalyst in the supply chain movement. Next, we provide some guidelines for successful SCM. We conclude with a discussion of closed-loop supply chains. It is also worth noting that because no other area across an enterprise has the potential to influence an organization's overall environmental impact more than its supply chain management practices, the topic of sustainability is integrated throughout this chapter.

5.2 Defining SCM

The term *supply chain* generally refers to all the activities involved in supplying an end user with a product or service. The perception of each organization that is involved – the ore refiners, the transporters, the component producers, the manufacturer, the wholesaler, the retailer, and the customer – being a link in the process makes the analogy of a chain quite appropriate. Figure 5.1 shows the position of a typical company (A) in the chain, with its suppliers to the left of it, all the way "upstream" (as it is often called) to the raw materials, and its customers to the right, all the way "downstream" to the end consumer. However, company C in the chain (a downstream

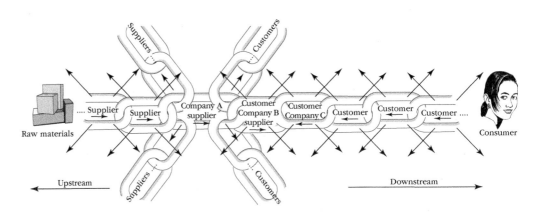

FIGURE 5.1 The Supply Chain

"customer" as far as company A is considered) sees the same thing as company A, with its suppliers (including upstream supplier company A) to its left and its customers to its right. And as is seen, company B in the middle is the customer of one firm and the supplier to another firm, as is the situation of almost all the companies in the chain.

Of course, all these companies typically need multiple materials and services to serve their immediate customer in the chain, so there are really a lot of upstream supplier company links connected on the left side of each link in the chain (only shown with links for company A, arrows for all others). And most firms typically sell to more than one customer, so there are also multiple downstream customer links connected on the right side of each link in the chain (again shown only for company A). Clearly, managing all these links – that is, suppliers and customers – even if only those directly connected to your company, is a major task!

Given such a lengthy process, it may behoove companies to store inventories of their outputs (if feasible) for immediate delivery. Moreover, it must be remembered that it is not just goods that are flowing along the chain but also information, funds, paper, people, and other such items, and they are flowing in *both* directions along the chain. In addition, the green revolution encourages recycling, recovery, and reuse of products, so even the used product may be flowing back up the chain. (We will return to the topic of closed-loop supply chains later in this chapter.) In addition, the supply chain also involves other functional areas and activities such as product/service design, finance, accounting, marketing, human resources, and engineering. Thus, instead of a chain, we should probably think of the supply process as more of a network, with everyone communicating with, and passing monies and items between, everyone else.

The Council of Supply Chain Management Professionals (CSCMP) defines supply chain management as encompassing

> *the planning and management of all activities involved in sourcing and procurement, conversion, and all logistics management activities. Importantly, it also includes coordination and collaboration with channel partners, which can be suppliers, intermediaries, third party service providers, and customers. In essence, supply chain management integrates supply and demand management within and across companies.*

SCM, then, concerns the process of trying to manage this entire chain from initial receipt of the ultimate consumer's order all the way back to the raw material providers and then ultimate delivery back to the consumer. Note that SCM is not restricted to managing only the links that connect with your company's position in the chain but *all* the links along the chain, so that savings (or increased value) in any part of the chain can be shared or leveraged by other companies along the chain. For example, Toyota is famous for teaching their suppliers how to install and operate their famed Toyota Production System (also known as *lean manufacturing* and discussed in Chapter 9). But the teaching doesn't stop there, since Toyota's first-tier suppliers can gain additional improvements by teaching their suppliers, the second tier, and so on up the supply chain. The interest in SCM has exploded primarily because of the development of new information technologies such as intranets, e-mail, electronic data interchange (EDI), and, of course, the Internet. These technologies, in conjunction with greater global competition, have fostered an interest and ability in improving processes along the entire supply chain, resulting in better performance at reduced cost.

SCM can also be considered to include a number of other managerial thrusts, such as quality management (Chapters 1 and 7), inventory management (discussed later), enterprise resource planning (ERP, also discussed later), and lean production (including JIT; Chapter 9). But it is even more comprehensive than that. For example, it includes marketing aspects in terms of communication with the customer, engineering issues involved in product/service design, financial aspects in terms of payments and float, purchasing elements such as sole sourcing, and, of course, technological initiatives such as the omnipresent Internet. To a large extent, this breakthrough in conceptualizing the potential for improvement in customer value by including all elements of the value chain is due to the development of advanced information technologies, such as the Internet.

Other definitions of SCM include the following points (Walker and Alber 1999):

- SCM coordinates and integrates all the supply chain activities into a seamless process and links all of the partners in the chain, including departments within an organization as well as the external suppliers, carriers, third-party companies, and information system providers.

- SCM enables manufacturers to actively plan and collaborate across a distributed supply chain to ensure that all parties are aware of commitments, schedules, and expedites. By actively collaborating as a virtual corporation, manufacturers and their suppliers can source, produce, and deliver products with minimal lead time and expense.

- The goal of SCM is to optimally deliver the right product to the right place at the right time while yielding the greatest possible profit.

The SCM objective of attempting to manage activities that lie outside a manager's normal realm of internal responsibility (i.e. managing second- or third-tier suppliers or downstream customers) is to reduce the costs of delivering a product or service to a user and improve its value. Sometimes, a distinction is made between a "value" chain, a "demand" chain, and a narrowly defined supply chain that simply manages suppliers to obtain the lowest cost. The conceptualization of the *value chain* is that it considers other important aspects of customer value besides cost, such as timeliness, quality, and functionality. That is, where the supply chain tends to focus on efficiency, the value chain focuses on effectiveness. These important issues will be discussed in more detail in the next section.

Also, as many have pointed out (e.g. Lummus and Vokurka 1999), the current conceptualization of the supply chain still has many elements of the old "push" system of production based on forecasts of demand. (See Section 6.3 on demand planning for more information on this topic.) The newer "pull" systems, consisting of JIT deliveries, lean manufacturing, and so on, dictate a different view of the value chain called a *demand chain*. In this conceptualization, a customer order *pulls* the product through the chain on demand, thereby further improving costs and benefits. Of course, acting after the fact rather than anticipating demand will put even further stress on the ability of the value chain to respond in a timely manner.

Another layer of complexity is often added when managing service supply chains, as the customers of the service can also serve as suppliers. For example, you supply the yard to your landscaping service. Likewise, your lifestyle and budget are important inputs to the architect you hire to design your dream house. Because the customers of a service may also be a supplier, it is likely that these customer–suppliers need to be handled differently than suppliers that are not customers. For example, suppliers that are not customers need to be selected, but customer–suppliers need to be attracted.

The dual nature of the customer–supplier role further compounds the complexity of the service supply chain. With a more manufacturing-oriented supply chain, the goods tend to flow in one direction downstream although this is changing as organizations seek to reduce their impact on the environment. In service supply chains and the dual customer–supplier role, services flow in both directions, with the customer both upstream and downstream from the service provider. Finally, service providers may require additional flexibility to deal with the added variation that is associated with customer-supplied inputs compared to other situations where the inputs are supplied by a more limited set of suppliers.

Attempts to reduce the costs of supply (previously considered as "purchasing" or "procurement") have been ongoing for decades, of course. However, management has also realized that there are costs other than strict materials and production costs in the supply chain that can be reduced with better information sharing and tighter management, and these costs are at the fore-front of attention in SCM. For example, costs of multiple shipments, costs of inappropriate functionality, costs of low quality, and costs of late delivery are all costs that can be eliminated with better information sharing and managerial oversight. And lowering all these costs provides additional benefits related to achieving sustainability objectives.

5.3 Supply Chain Strategy

The concept of the value chain was mentioned earlier, and it should be emphasized that an organization's supply chain strategy needs to be tailored to meet the needs of its customers, which isn't always the lowest cost. In fashion goods, for example, fast response to short fashion seasons is much more important than lowest cost. And in high technology, new functionality (or reliability or security) may be more important than cost. Thus, the strategy for building an organization's supply chain should focus on maximizing the value to its customers, where value can be considered to be benefits received for the price paid or benefits/cost (see Chapter 1).

In situations where the goods are basic commodities with standard benefits (food, home supplies, and gasoline), then cost reduction will be the focus. But in fashion goods, timeliness should be the focus of the supply chain, meaning quick deliveries, stockpiling of long lead time items, and so on. In new notebook computers, the focus might be on identifying firms that offer new functionality; in telecom, the focus might be on reliability; and in music, the focus might be on flexibility to meet quickly changing tastes or talent. Thus, the supply chain needs to be carefully matched to the firm's market and needs. Where the firm operates in multiple markets or appeals to multiple needs within the same market, it may find it necessary to operate different supply chains for each focus. Although most of the remaining discussion in this chapter is directed toward the traditional supply chain strategy of minimizing costs, which is always an important consideration and probably the major focus of most supply chains today, the other possible strategic purposes should be kept in mind also.

It is also important to point out that many organizations choose to outsource portions of the SCM function to the so-called third-party logistics (3PL) companies. These 3PL companies provide a range of services, including handling the distribution of the organization's products, receiving incoming materials, managing the organization's warehouses, managing the purchasing function, and handling product returns. The balance of activities kept in-house and those outsourced vary by company and should be driven by the organization's strategy and competencies.

There are a number of reasons why organizations choose to outsource portions of or the entire supply chain function to a 3PL. First, assuming that SCM is not the organization's core competency, shifting these activities to a 3PL allows the organization to focus more directly on its core competencies. Second, outsourcing these activities reduces the capital investments in the infrastructure needed to support these activities. In effect, the use of a 3PL converts a significant portion of what was a fixed cost into a variable cost. Finally, by utilizing a 3PL, the organization gains access to the best practices and technologies that it might not be able to afford or develop if the function was kept in-house. 3PLs are able to make the investment to develop these best practices and technologies because these development costs are spread across multiple organizations served by the 3PL.

However, there are also disadvantages in using 3PLs, such as the longer response time and greater risk of disruption in the supply chain when customers are wanting faster, more reliable response. An added danger of all outsourcing is the natural tendency for management to measure only the internal response time of the firm when the customer is measuring the total time from order to obtaining the good or service. In any outsourcing decision, the added time and risk of delay from outside suppliers need to be considered. This response time is also affected by the production process adopted, since make-to-stock (MTS) will have the fastest response because the order can simply be pulled off the shelf and sent to the customer, assemble-to-order (ATO) is a bit slower, make-to-order (MTO) is slower still, and engineer-to-order (ETO) is the slowest of all.

5.3.1 Strategic Need for SCM

To understand the potential for obtaining strategic advantage from better management of the supply chain, whether it is kept in-house or outsourced to a 3PL, it is useful to realize that total supply chain costs represent more than half, and in some cases three-quarters, of the total operating expenses for most organizations (Quinn 1997). To understand these values, bear in mind that the broader concept of the supply chain includes the supply, storage, and movement of materials, information, personnel, equipment, and finished goods within the organization and between it and its environment. The objective of SCM is to integrate the entire process of satisfying the customer's needs all along the supply chain. This includes procuring different groups of raw materials from multiple sources (often through purchasing or recycling or recovery), transporting them to various processing and assembly facilities, and distributing them through appropriate distributors or retailers to the final consumer. Within this process are a great variety of activities such as packaging, schedule coordination, credit establishment, inventory management, warehousing, maintenance, purchasing, order processing, and supplier selection and management.

As organizations have continued to adopt more efficient production techniques such as lean manufacturing, total quality management, and inventory reduction techniques to reduce costs and improve the quality, functionality, and speed of delivery of their products and services to customers, the costs and delays of *procuring* the requisite inputs and *distributing* the resulting goods and services are taking a greater and greater fraction of the total cost and time. For example, the cost of just physical distribution itself is now up to 30% of sales in the food industry. To achieve quick response with quality goods that accurately satisfy the need at the lowest possible cost requires taking a broad, long-range, integrated perspective of the entire customer fulfillment process instead of focusing on the narrow segments and pieces of the chain.

For instance, if each segment of the supply chain is acting in a way to optimize its own value, there will be discontinuities at the interfaces and unnecessary costs will result. If an integrated view is taken instead, there may be opportunities in the supply chain where additional expense or time in one segment can save tremendous expense or time in another segment. If a broad enough view is then taken, the savings in the one segment could be shared with the losing segment, so everyone would be further ahead. This broad, integrated view of the supply chain is more feasible these days due to the recent capabilities of advanced information technology and computer processing (e.g. bar codes, computerized manufacturing, the Internet, ERP systems, and electronic funds transfer).

Other factors are also driving the need to better manage the supply chain:

- *Increasing global competition.* In addition to increased pressure on cost from global competitors who have lower labor rates, they also frequently offer better quality, functionality, and customer responsiveness. This is pressuring firms to look globally for better or cheaper suppliers, resulting in increased outsourcing and offshoring.

- *Outsourcing.* Since more organizations are outsourcing and thereby increasing the need for transportation, this has pushed up transportation costs.

- *E-commerce.* The advent of e-commerce and other electronic technologies has made it easier and cheaper to outsource, either domestically or even globally.

- *Shorter life cycles.* Customers are demanding greater variety, faster response, higher quality, and cheaper prices. One result of these demands is shorter product life cycles, which means constantly changing supply chains and using more chains over the same period of time.

- *Greater supply chain complexity.* The increased complexity of supply chains requires much more attention and better management of these chains. For example, in early 2001, when the bottom fell out of the telecom market, Solectron Corp., the world's biggest electronics contract manufacturer, was holding $4.7 billion of inventory from its 4000 suppliers to fill firm orders from Cisco, Ericsson, Lucent, and other telecoms. But when the telecoms canceled their orders, no one knew who owned all that inventory (Engardio 2001)!

- *Increasing levels of concern for the environment.* Addressing environmental concerns impacts virtually all aspects of SCM from the sourcing of parts to the distribution of the product and even to the disposal of the product once it reaches the end of its useful life. Green sourcing seeks to identify suppliers in such a way that the organization's carbon footprint and overall impact on the environment are minimized. Reducing the waste associated with products is another way organizations minimize the negative impact they have on the environment. Along these lines, and as is discussed in greater detail further on, organizations can deploy a strategy referred to as the three Rs: reduce, reuse, and recycle.

Implementing SCM has brought significant documented benefits to many companies. Ferguson (2000) reports, for example, that compared to their competitors, such firms enjoy a 45% supply chain cost advantage, an order cycle time and inventory days of supply 50% lower, and finished product delivery 17% faster. Lummus and Vokurka (1998) note that these firms operate with 36% lower logistics costs, which, by itself, translates into a 4% increase in net profit margins. One firm reported a 25–50% reduction in finished product inventories, a 10% reduction in cost, and a 10–25% improvement in production process reliability.

Of course, these are primarily the cost aspects of the SCM process, which are more easily measured than the qualitative benefits, such as more loyal customers and a larger market share. There are also significant effects on other important aspects of an organization, such as its ability to learn new procedures and ways of operating, the morale of its employees, and the ability to change direction quickly.

5.3.1.1 Mitigating Supply Chain Risk

There are numerous benefits associated with extending the supply chain globally, including access to more markets and assess to cheaper materials and labor. However, increased globalization can also increase the risk of supply disruptions. More formally, supply chain disruptions are "unforeseen events that interfere with the normal flow of goods within a supply chain" (Ellis *et al.* 2010). While recently the COVID-19 pandemic has been cited as the major cause of supply disruptions, in more normal times the leading causes of supply disruptions are IT outages, weather, cyberattacks, and fires, according to the consulting firm Procurement Tactics. Overall, Procurement Tactics found that supply disruptions increased by 14% in 2020 from the previous year to 4,200. In addition to having a significant negative impact on an organization's reputation, supply disruptions can also have a significant impact on an organization's profitability. Along these lines, Procurement Tactics found that supply disruptions resulted in up to a 62% reduction in profitability.

There are numerous frameworks and approaches available for mitigating supply chain disruptions. In general, mitigating the risk of supply chain disruptions involves five steps:

1. *Risk identification.* The first step is to identify the potential threats that may disrupt supply chain activities. There are a wide variety of risks that can lead to supply chain disruptions including uncertainty related to demand, disruptions to supplier operations, disruptions to the organization's operations, security threats, and changes to the economy, to name a few.

2. *Assess and evaluate identified risks.* There are numerous approaches available to help organizations assess and evaluate risk including Failure Mode and Effect Analysis (see Chapter 7), the Likelihood-Impact Graph (see Chapter 7), the Delphi Method (see Chapter 6), and the use of a Risk Register (a common tool used in project management).

3. *Identify risk management strategies:* Broadly speaking, common risk management strategies include accepting the risk, acquiring insurance, identifying and investing in countermeasures to reduce the impact of the risk, developing backup plans, and investing in countermeasures that reduce the risk. A useful framework for managing risks is shown in Figure 5.2 (Knemeyer *et al.* 2009). According to the framework, threats are categorized on the dimensions of how likely they are to occur and their potential impact. In situations where both the potential loss and likelihood are low the recommended strategy is to accept the risk and the loss, particularly in cases where the cost of the countermeasures exceeds the potential loss. In cases where there is a high likelihood of the threat materializing but the potential loss is low, the recommended strategy is to develop measures to reduce the risk such as subscribing to a cloud-based security system to protect against cyberattacks. At the opposite end of the continuum where the likelihood of the threat is high, but the potential loss is low, the recommended strategy is to focus on reducing the loss. Purchasing insurance is a common approach organizations use to reduce their losses. Finally, for threats that have both a high likelihood of occurring and have high potential losses, the recommended strategy is to focus on simultaneously reducing the risk and the potential loss. For example, both purchasing insurance and developing backup contingency plans.

4. *Implement the strategy.* The goal in implementing the strategies identified in the previous step is to enhance the resilience of the supply chain to potential threats. The more resilient the supply chain, the faster it will be able to return to the desired state after a disruption materializes.

5. *Monitor the situation.* The earlier a disruption is detected, the better positioned the organization will be in addressing the threat. Monitoring the supply chain in real-time with the aid of advanced IT can greatly facilitate the early detection of potential threats.

To conclude our discussion of mitigating supply chain risk, it is worth noting that there is a number of well-established frameworks and certifications that focus on addressing risk more generally, as well as for areas specific to supply chain management. ISO 22301 is a standard for Business Continuity Management. More specifically, ISO 22301 provides a framework for preparing for, responding to, and recovering from threats and disruptions. Organizations can also become ISO 22301 certified which can be used as a criterion in selecting suppliers. More specific to supply chain management are PAS (Publicly Available Specification) 7000 Supply Chain Risk Management developed by the British Standards Institute and PAS 555 which provides a framework for cybersecurity.

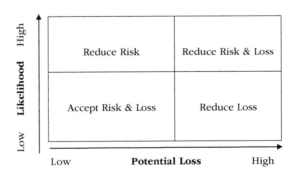

FIGURE 5.2 Strategies for Managing Risk

5.3.2 Measures of Supply Chain Performance

Better supply chain performance will show up in a number of standard financial measures of a company's health. Lower inventories, normally considered an asset, will be reflected in less need for *working capital* (WC) and a higher *return on assets* (ROA) ratio (since assets are reduced). And the lower cost to carry these inventories (as well as other reduced costs in the supply chain) will be seen in a reduced *cost of goods sold* (CGS) and thus a higher *contribution margin, return on sales* (ROS), and *operating income.* Moreover, if the supply chain is also better managed to provide other benefits to the consumer, as mentioned earlier, the effect should be seen in higher *total revenue,* since the consumer will be willing to pay more. Lower costs, if used to reduce prices, will also result in higher volumes, which will further increase revenues.

One performance measure that provides managers with a broad view of the supply chain is the cash conversion cycle (CCC). This financial performance metric helps a company assess how well it is managing its capital. In effect, the CCC is the amount of time the organization's cash is tied up in working capital before being returned by customers as they pay for delivered products or services. The CCC is made up of three components that track the organization's cash flows from its purchase of inventory to the sale of its products: (1) the amount of time needed to sell its inventory, (2) the amount of time needed to collect its receivables from its sales, and (3) the amount of time the organization has to pay its suppliers. Logically, low values indicate better performance for the first two components and higher values are preferable for the third component.

Days inventory outstanding (DIO) or supply is used to measure the amount of time an organization needs to sell inventory (the first component of CCC) and is calculated as follows:

$$DIO = \frac{\text{Average inventory}}{\text{COGS}/365}$$

The average inventory for a given year is typically calculated as the average of the beginning and ending inventory. Thus, for a particular year, the average inventory can be calculated by adding the inventory on the balance sheet for the current year to the inventory from the previous year and dividing by 2. Essentially, the inventory from the previous year represents the beginning inventory for the current year. The denominator in the DIO formula represents the *cost of goods sold (COGS)* per day and is calculated by dividing the COGS from the income statement by the number of days in the year. Also note that some organizations use the term cost of revenue (or sales) instead of COGS.

Days sales outstanding (DSO) is used to measure the amount of time an organization needs in order to collect cash from the sales of its inventory (the second component of CCC) and is calculated as follows:

$$DSO = \frac{\text{Average accounts receivable}}{\text{Revenue}/365}$$

The average accounts receivable for a given year is typically calculated as the average of the beginning and ending accounts receivable. Accounts receivable are reported on an organization's balance sheet. In a similar manner to average inventory, average accounts receivable is typically calculated as the average of the accounts receivable for the current year and previous year. The denominator in the DSO formula represents the revenue per day and is calculated by dividing total revenue from the income statement by the number of days in the year.

Finally, *days payables outstanding (DPO)* is used to measure the amount of time an organization has before paying its suppliers (the third component of CCC) and is calculated as follows:

$$DPO = \frac{\text{Average accounts payable}}{\text{COGS}/365}$$

The average accounts payable for a given year is typically calculated as the average of the beginning and ending accounts payable. Accounts payable is reported on an organization's balance sheet. In a similar fashion to average inventory and average accounts receivable, average accounts payable is typically calculated as the average of the accounts payable for the current year and previous year. The denominator in the DSO formula represents the daily COGS.

Bringing these three components together, the cash conversion cycle (CCC) is calculated as follows:

$$CCC = DIO + DSO - DPO$$

A positive CCC represents the number of days the organization's capital is tied up waiting for the customer to pay for the products or services. A negative CCC represents the number of days the organization is able to receive cash from its sales before it pays its suppliers. Thus, the smaller the CCC, including negative numbers, the better the organization is performing.

As was noted in Chapter 1, Amazon is an exemplar of efficiently managing its inventory. In 2017, Amazon achieved a negative 33.5 CCC compared to CCCs of positive 4.4 and 9.3 at Costco and Walmart, respectively. Amazon's negative 33.5 cash conversion cycle means that it gets paid from its customers 33.5 days before it pays its suppliers. Effectively then, Amazon is using its suppliers' cash to fund and expand its own operations!

Beyond these standard financial measures, however, we can also look at some more operations-oriented measures that we typically use to see how well operations is performing, such as defect rates, lead times, inventory turns, and productivity ratios. Since one of the major cost savings in SCM is the cost of inventories, it is worthwhile to examine some performance measures related to inventory reduction. One such measure is the inventory turnover (or "turns," as it is sometimes called):

$$\text{Inventory turnover} = \frac{\text{COGS}}{\text{Average inventory}}$$

Turnover essentially represents how often the average inventory is used up to obtain the total sales for the year. An inventory turnover of 1, for example, means it takes an organization an entire year to use up its inventory, while an inventory turnover of 5 means the organization uses up and therefore must replenish its inventory five times over the year. Like ROA, the more the inventory and assets can be reduced and still maintain the same sales, the better!

Note that if in the inventory turnover formula, daily COGS is used in the numerator instead of annual COGS, the formula becomes the reciprocal of DIO discussed earlier. Thus, we see there is a direct relationship between DIO and inventory turns. For example, an organization that turns over its inventory 5 times per year has an average of 73 (i.e. 365/5) days' supply of inventory. In some firms that have achieved supply chain excellence, they measure their supply of inventory in *hours* instead of days. Dell Computer is one of these firms (Dignan 2002; Magretta 1998) due to the outstanding job they have done on fine honing their supply chains.

5.3.3 Sustainable Supply Chain Management

The increasing commitments that many leading organizations are making to sustainability has been highlighted throughout this book. It is appropriate at this point to mention that perhaps no other area has the potential to influence an organization's overall environmental impact more than its supply chain management practices. Aligning the management of the supply chain with an organization's sustainability objectives is referred to as sustainable supply chain management. According to the Sustainable Supply Chain Foundation (SSCF), sustainable supply chain management

> *involves integrating environmentally and financially viable practices into the complete supply chain lifecycle, from product design and development to material selection (including raw material extraction or agricultural production), manufacturing, packaging, transportation, warehousing, distribution, consumption, return, and disposal. Environmentally sustainable supply chain management and practices can assist organizations in not only reducing their total carbon footprint, but also in optimizing their end-to-end operations to achieve greater cost savings and profitability. All supply chains can be optimized using sustainable practices.*

There are a variety reasons why products need to be transported to customers. Perhaps the most obvious reason is when key raw materials are not located near the producers or customers. For example, most of the timber harvested in the United States for the lumber industry comes from Maine, the Lake States, the Southeast, and the Pacific Northwest regions of the country. The supply chain question that naturally arises is how to get the lumber from where it is harvested to other parts of the country where it is to be processed and ultimately used?

Beyond the physical separation that often exists between the source of raw materials and the users, lower transportation costs have reduced the need for the various manufacturing stages to be in close proximity to one another, as well as for manufacturers to be in close physical proximity with their suppliers and their customers. Indeed, lower transportation costs have greatly facilitated the migration of production to developing countries with lower labor costs. Advances in information technology have also reduced the need for manufacturers to be in close physical proximity to their customers and suppliers.

While lower transportation costs can make it economically viable for organizations to be physically separated from their customers and suppliers, the increased distances materials must be transported can work against an organization's sustainability goals. Perhaps no organization exemplifies this better than Amazon which cofounded the Climate Pledge corporate movement requiring organizations that sign the pledge to achieve net-zero emissions by the year 2040. This is an especially difficult challenge for Amazon, as it requires an enormous amount of air transport and ground delivery vehicles to deliver 10 billion items annually. To help achieve its commitment to being net-zero by 2020, Amazon invested in electric vehicle manufacturer Rivian and purchased 100,000 electric delivery vans with the first 10,000 to be put in service by the end of 2022.

By the middle of 2022, over 300 organizations in 29 countries have signed the Climate Pledge. According to Jeff Bezos, Amazon's CEO, "You can't get to net zero on your own. It can only be done in collaboration with other large companies, because we're all part of each other's supply chains (Doerr 2021, p. 209). This is well illustrated by another major retailer, Walmart, which has also pledged to be carbon neutral by 2040. More specifically, analyses conducted at Walmart indicated that its own assets such as its trucks and retail stores accounted for only 8–10% of its carbon footprint while the remaining 90–92% was driven by its supply chain.

In an effort to reduce its carbon footprint across its entire supply chain, Walmart created what it called Sustainable Value Networks (SVN). Participation in the SVN was optional for Walmart's suppliers, and membership opportunities were also extended to universities and other nongovernmental organizations. The goal of SVN is to inform policy based on science and address issues such as reducing the carbon footprint associated with operating a distribution fleet and how to improve packaging.

5.4 Supply Chain Design

As shown in Figure 5.3, the supply chain consists of the network of organizations that supply inputs to the business unit, the business unit itself, and the customer network. Note that the supplier network can include both internal suppliers (i.e. other operating divisions of the same organization) and external suppliers (i.e. operating divisions of separate organizations). Also, note how design activities cut across the supplier network and the business unit and how distribution activities cut across the business unit and the customer network. This broader view of the entire process of serving customer needs provides numerous benefits. For example, it focuses management attention on the entire process that creates value for the customer, not the individual activities. When viewed in this way, information is more freely shared up and down the supply chain, keeping all parties informed of one another's needs. Furthermore, activities can be performed at the point in the supply chain where they make the most sense. To illustrate, instead of providing Johnson Controls with detailed specifications for car seats, car manufacturers provided broad specifications and relied on Johnson Controls' expertise to design and manufacture their car seats.

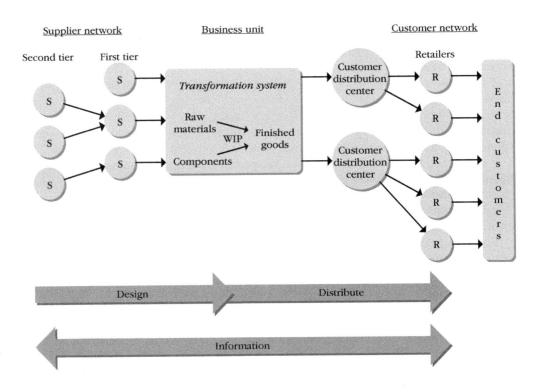

FIGURE 5.3 Simplified Supply Chain

In this section, we will look at each of the major logistical elements of the supply chain to better understand how they operate and interact to deliver value to the final customer: the "bullwhip" effect, transportation, and location. Outsourcing, purchasing, supplier management, and the role of information technology are discussed later in the chapter.

5.4.1 Logistics

Logistics can be defined as planning and controlling the efficient, effective flows of goods, services, and information from one point to another. As such, it consists of inventories, distribution networks, storage and warehousing, transportation, information processing, and even production – a rather all-enveloping term.

In these days of intense worldwide competition, international production in supply chains, and global distribution, logistics is taking on tremendous importance. Labor cost is dropping as a proportion of total output cost, as are manufacturing costs in general, but the costs of acquisition and distribution have remained about the same and now account for, as noted previously, approximately 20% of the United States' gross national product.

Generally speaking, when organizations design their supply chains, they tend to focus on one of two overarching goals: maximizing efficiency and minimizing the cost of the supply chain versus maximizing the flexibility and responsiveness of the supply chains. A logical question is: Are there guidelines that can help an organization determine whether its supply chain focus should be on efficiency or responsiveness? The good news is that there are indeed guidelines for this and, as you might suspect, the emphasis on efficiency versus responsiveness depends largely on the demand pattern of the outputs.

More specifically, Professor Marshall Fisher of the Wharton School distinguishes two fundamentally different types of outputs that he refers to as functional and innovative products. Functional products tend to be staples that we routinely purchase. As such, functional products tend to be more mature products with predictable demand patterns, long life cycles, and relatively low contribution margins. Examples of functional products include frozen vegetables, batteries, paper towels, soft drinks, and printer paper. At the other extreme, innovative products represent products that are continuously being improved and enhanced with new styles, features, capabilities, and so on. Because they are continuously updated, innovative products have unpredictable demand, short life cycles, and relatively high contribution margins as well as being offered in many varieties and options. Examples of innovative products include smartphones, tablet computers, tennis rackets, and designer blue jeans.

Using this classification, Professor Fisher suggests that focusing on supply chain efficiency is appropriate for functional outputs, while focusing on responsiveness is appropriate for innovative products. In fact, when seeking to identify the root cause of supply chain problems, quite often you will find that the problems are the result of the supply chain not being properly aligned with the demand pattern of the product. Most often, this occurs when an organization seeks to offer innovative products but is focusing on the efficiency of the supply chain. In these cases, the organizations would be well served to either consider marketing their products as functional products or placing greater emphasis on improving the responsiveness of their supply chain as opposed to optimizing its efficiency.

5.4.1.1 The Bullwhip Effect

While all products have an underlying demand pattern, the way the supply chain is managed can distort our perception of what the true underlying pattern of demand is. We now have a better understanding of one logistical effect that distorts the demand pattern known as the *bullwhip effect,* named after the action of a whip where each segment further down the whip goes faster than that above it. Unfortunately, this same effect occurs in a supply chain, but in reverse order, and has been well documented. More specifically, in supply chains, the bullwhip effect results when the variability of demand increases from the customer stage upstream to the factory stage. This is often the result of different parties in the supply chain being overly reactive in their ordering practices, as in the Best Buy example at the beginning of the chapter. For example, this happens when a small percentage increase in a retailer's orders results in the wholesaler increasing its orders by an amount greater than that of the retailer – a safety stock – just to be covered in case demand is increasing. Then, the distribution center sees this greater demand from its wholesalers and increases its orders by some safety percentage, also to be safe. The end result is that the factory sees a huge jump in demand. As it orders more equipment, labor, and materials to satisfy this big increase, too much is fed into the pipeline, and the retailer cuts back, with the wholesaler and distribution center likewise cutting back even more. The factory then sees a tremendous drop in demand and reverses the cycle, cutting excessively into production and initiating another round of excessive demand. This boom–bust cycle is particularly prevalent in some industries, such as commercial building. Obviously, both overproduction and underproduction are expensive and drive up supply chain costs. The Beer Game discussed in the appendix to this chapter is a staple of MBA programs and is used to provide students with firsthand experience with the bullwhip effect.

The bullwhip effect can occur whenever any one of the three conditions is extreme enough to cause the boom–bust cycle. The first condition is simply long lead times between the stages of the supply chain, so that changes in demand requirements are slowly moving up and down the chain, thereby allowing excessive changes to occur in the other stages of the chain. The second condition is large lot sizes with infrequent orders, resulting again in lags in information. And the third condition is the slow transmission of information occurring by handoffs from one link of the chain to the next.

The ways to eliminate the bullwhip effect are to reverse these three conditions. Reducing lead times through JIT programs, for example, will result in immediate deliveries of the ordered amounts, so safety stocks are unnecessary. Reducing lot sizes means smaller, more frequent deliveries, which again eliminates the need for large safety stocks. And, finally, the sharing of information from the retailer throughout the supply chain gives the factory, as well as the other supply chain partners, accurate information, so appropriate amounts of items are produced and delivered.

In addition to these three conditions, there are a number of business practices that also contribute to the bullwhip effect. One business practice is the tendency for customers to prefer placing all their orders either at the beginning or the end of the week (or month) rather than spacing orders out evenly. This leads to a situation where incoming orders will be bunched up around the beginning and end of the week (or month), thereby increasing the variability of the supplier's daily demand beyond the variability of the customers' daily demand. Furthermore, this problem tends to be amplified as the orders cascade upstream.

Another business practice that contributes to the bullwhip effect is the use of standard batch sizes. For example, if a particular product is packaged in cases of 24 units, then replenishment orders for this product will be done in multiples of 24. This practice further bunches up orders and again results in the supplier's daily demand being larger than that of the customers placing the orders.

Trade promotions are yet another practice that contributes to the bullwhip effect. Trade promotions are short-term discounts suppliers offer their customers. These discounts provide customers with an incentive to order more products than they need, called forward buying. Because customers will choose to place their orders when the trade promotion is offered and even delay orders in anticipation of a trade promotion, these trade promotions create another order-bunching problem.

A final practice that contributes to the bullwhip effect is shortage gaming. This practice occurs in situations where a product is in short supply. Anticipating that the supplier will allocate its inventory to its customers, some suppliers inflate their orders, fearing that they will be shipped less than they ordered. Attempting to game the system in this manner exacerbates the shortage problem, as some customers end up with less than they can sell because they did not inflate their orders, while others end up with more than they can sell. In some cases, the suppliers themselves further compound this problem by allowing their customers to return unsold inventory.

There are several actions suppliers can take to mitigate these practices. For example, suppliers can ask their customers to share information more frequently about actual demand. Likewise, suppliers can coordinate with their customers to eliminate the batching of orders. Alternatively, suppliers can encourage their customers to make greater use of technology such as the Web and EDI to place smaller but more frequent orders. Furthermore, suppliers can eliminate the practice of offering trade promotions. Finally, suppliers can enhance the value proposition they provide their customers and at the same time helping smooth out incoming orders by taking over the management of their customers' inventory, referred to as "vendor-managed" inventory.

5.4.1.2 Transportation

The four major *transportation modes* are, historically, water, rail, truck, and air. The main factors considered in choosing a transportation mode are the economics of the transportation mode and characteristics of the product including the product's weight, value, and perishability. Water is the least expensive mode and is good for long trips with bulky, low value-high volume, and non-perishable items. But it is very slow and of limited accessibility; thus it is often combined with truck. It handles the majority of ton-miles of traffic. However, railroads handle the most total tons of traffic and are used for shorter hauls than water. They have many advantages: ability to handle small as well as large items, specialized services (e.g., refrigeration, liquids, cattle), and still a relatively low cost. Rail also has a lower impact on the environment than trucking but limited accessibility often requires it to be used in combination with trucking.

Trucking holds more advantages for short hauls with small volumes to specialized locations. Truck transport has grown at the expense of rail for several reasons, such as growth of the national highway system, increase use of just-in-time, better equipment, high flexibility, good accessibility, and liberalized regulations.

Air transport is used for small, high-value, or perishable items such as electronic components, lobsters, optical instruments, and important paperwork. Its main advantage is speed of delivery over long distances. Thus, for the appropriate products, typically high value items, it can significantly reduce lead times, inventory, and warehousing costs, with a corresponding improvement in customer service. It also has the largest negative environmental impact.

Beyond the economics of the transportation mode and the characteristics of the product, organizations are increasingly considering the environmental impact of their supply chains. As shown in Figure 5.4, there are significant differences between the various modes of transportation in terms of their environmental impact. More specifically, Figure 5.4 shows the grams of CO_2e emissions to transport one ton of freight one kilometer. Referring to the figure, transporting freight by water is the most environmentally friendly mode of transporting freight while air transportation is the least environmentally friendly. Indeed, the CO_2e emissions from air transport are almost 150 times more than that of water.

There are a number of strategies available to reduce environmental impact of the transportation activities comprising an organization's supply chain. As Figure 5.4 demonstrates, one option may be to rely on more environmentally efficient modes of transportation. Of course, the accessibility of any mode may limit the extent this strategy can be pursued. Also, shifting to utilize alternative modes may require significant investments in infrastructure. In these cases, organizations

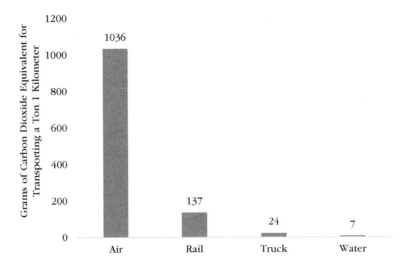

FIGURE 5.4 Environmental Impact of Alternate Modes of Transportation (Source: EEA 2022)

may be able to utilize a hybrid or multi-modal approach. The handoffs required with multi-modal approaches can be facilitated using standardized pallets and containers.

Perhaps an even better strategy is to simply reduce the need to transport outputs. While reverse globalization trends and nearshoring may result in higher labor costs, they may also help to reduce supply chain risks and, through reduced lead times, improve the responsiveness of the supply chain.

Of course, there are limits to how much transportation distances can be reduced. Recognizing this, another strategy is to perhaps reduce emissions using alternative fuels (e.g. biofuels, LNG, hydrogen fuel cells), and the use of electric vehicles (EVs). It is also important to point out that important tradeoffs exist that need to be considered across these options. For example, the use of biofuels requires crops which may reduce food grown for human consumption or lead to increases in deforestation. Hydrogen fuel cells can be substituted in most places where fossil fuels are used. The only emission in the process of converting hydrogen to electricity is water. However, producing hydrogen can have a significant impact on the environment, depending on whether the energy used to create it came from conventional or renewable sources. Another hurdle regarding the use of hydrogen cells is that the infrastructure for a hydrogen distribution network is needed. And like the use of hydrogen cells, the environmental impact of EVs depends on where the electricity comes from.

Finally, there are operational tactics that can be employed to reduce the environmental impact associated with transportation. For example, engines can be operated at optimal levels. In the shipping industry, running ships at slower speeds to save fuel is referred to as slow steaming. Another tactic is to improve the efficiency of transportation assets by ensuring they are fully loaded, that they are not traveling empty, increasing the aerodynamics of transportation vehicles, using software to optimize transportation routes (discussed below) and taking into account traffic congestion so that deliveries can be scheduled at off-peak times, and further developing autonomous vehicles that operate more fuel efficiently.

Taking all the pros and cons of each mode of transportation into consideration in planning is a complex task. Table 5.1 lists the major considerations that should be factored into the decision. Each particular situation may have additional factors to consider.

Independent of the specific mode of transport are additional transportation problems involving such considerations as the *number* of transporting vehicles, their capacities, and the *routes* that each vehicle will take. In general, these interrelated problems are frequently included as part of the *routing problem*. Solving the routing problem involves finding the best number of vehicles

TABLE 5.1   Factors to Consider in Transportation Decisions

Cost per unit shipped

Ability to fill the transporting vehicle

Total shipment cost

Protection of contents from theft, weather, and the like

Shipping time

Availability of insurance on contents, delivery, and so forth

Difficulty of arranging shipment (governmental regulations, transportation to shipment site, etc.)

Delivery accommodations (to customer's site, transfer to another transportation mode, extra charges)

Seasonal considerations: weather, holidays, and so on

Consolidation possibilities (among multiple products)

Risk (to contents, to delivery promises, to cost, etc.)

Size of product being shipped

Perishability of product during shipment

Environmental impact

and their routes to deliver the organization's output to a group of geographically dispersed recipients. When only one vehicle is serving all the recipients, the problem is known as the *traveling salesman problem*. In this problem, a number of possible routes exist between the organization and all the recipients, but only a few or perhaps just one of these routes will minimize the total cost of delivery. In the routing and traveling salesman problems, certain procedures are available to minimize either the distance traveled or the cost, but quite often there are other considerations, such as balancing workloads among vehicles or minimizing idle or delay time.

5.4.1.3 Warehousing

Despite the increased interest in just-in-time (JIT) as a method for reducing inventory with its increased frequency of deliveries in smaller quantities, most supply chains still rely heavily on warehouses. These warehouses not only store inventory, but provide other important functions, including receiving the goods and facilitating the distribution of them. More recently, warehouses have been used in the final processing of the output, customizing outputs, and preparing the output for sale such as putting price tags on merchandise and clothing on hangars.

Another approach for reducing inventory is to use larger centralized warehouses as opposed to using a larger number of smaller warehouses located closer to suppliers or customers. While using centralized warehouses can reduce the total amount of inventory needed, it may also result in greater transportation cost.

As was noted in Chapter 4, organizations are increasingly considering the environmental impact of their decision-making related to warehouses, in addition to the more traditional considerations of the impact on customer service levels, responsiveness, and the organization's cost structure. As was noted in Chapter 4, there are significant environmental implications related to the construction of warehouses and as well as how they are operated. For example, and as noted above, pursuing a more centralized approach to managing inventory by expanding existing warehouses as opposed to opening new warehouses in closer proximity to customers has implications for the amount of energy needed to transport products. Another environmental consideration is the specialized material handling equipment selected for use in the warehouse.

In our current Information Age, a new type of warehouse referred to as data centers is emerging for the purpose of storing information electronically. While there may be little physical traffic to data centers, as there is no need to transport or store physical materials, data centers often require 15 times more energy and some cases as much as 100 times more energy than a similarly sized office building. Perhaps no organization has more at stake in terms of optimizing the efficiency of its data centers than Meta (previously known as Facebook) which at the time of this writing has 21 data centers in operation or under construction. As a backdrop, Meta has already achieved being carbon neutral across its global operations and has further committed to being carbon neutral across its entire value chain by 2030. Additionally, its data centers are Leed certified at the Gold Level (see Chapter 4) and all energy is sourced from renewable sources. Compared to industry standards, Meta's data centers consume 32% less energy and are 80% more water efficient providing Meta both economic as well as environmental benefits.

As can be imagined, a variety of tactics were employed at Meta to achieve these results. For example, in 2016 Meta developed MyRocks that allowed it to double the compression used to store data which thereby allowed it to reduce the number of storage servers needed by 50%. Importantly, MyRocks is open-source software that other organizations can use. As another example, Meta minimizes energy usage at off-peak hours. Meta also developed servers that require less material to make and can operate at higher temperatures, thereby requiring less energy to cool them. As a final example, Meta uses a large network of sensors to monitor environmental conditions including air temperature, airflow, and humidity that is processed by a central computer that identifies trends and averts potential problems if they arise.

5.4.1.4 Location

Another key supply chain design decision is determining the location of the facilities relative to suppliers and potential customers. In general, the decision about location is divided into three stages: regional (including international), community, and site. Sources of information for these stages are chambers of commerce, realtors, utilities, banks, suppliers, transportation companies, savings and loan associations, government agencies, and management consultants who specialize in relocation. For some pure service organizations (e.g. physicians), only the site selection stage may be relevant because they are already focused on a specific region and community. Before discussing these stages in detail, however, we first highlight the relationship between the location decision and the development of core capabilities.

5.4.1.5 Developing Capabilities and the Location Decision

In examining the rationale offered by organizations regarding their decisions to relocate existing facilities or open new ones, it often appears that these decisions are being driven primarily by short-term considerations such as differentials in wage rates and fluctuations in exchange rates. In addition to having the appearance of being more band-aid solutions than addressing how to improve long-term competitiveness, these decisions are often dominated by operational factors such as wage rates and transportation costs. The problem with such static and one-dimensional analyses is that conditions change. For example, if one competitor chooses a location based on low wage rates, there is very little to prevent its competitors from locating in the same region. Furthermore, the benefit of low wages is likely to be short lived, as the demand for labor will increase when more organizations locate in the region, which in turn will result in higher wage rates.

An alternative approach for the location decision is to consider the impact these decisions have on the development of key organizational capabilities. In Chapter 1, we defined core capabilities as the organizational practices and business processes that distinguish an organization from its competition. Clearly, the way various organizational units are located relative to one another can have a significant impact on interactions between these units, which in turn impacts the development of core capabilities.

In order to leverage the location decision to enhance the development of long-term capabilities, Bartmess and Cerny (1993) suggest the following six-step process:

1. Identify the sources of value the company will deliver to its customers. In effect, this translates into identifying the order winners discussed in Chapter 1.

2. Once the order winners have been defined, identify the key organizational capabilities needed in order to have a competitive advantage.

3. Based on the capabilities identified, assess the implications for the location of organizational units. For example, if the company determines that a rapid product development capability is needed, then it follows that design needs to be in close contact with manufacturing and leading-edge customers. Alternatively, if operational flexibility is needed, then it follows that manufacturing needs to be in proximity to design, marketing, and management information systems.

4. Identify potential locations.

5. Evaluate the sites in terms of their impact on the development of capabilities, as well as on financial and operational criteria.

6. Develop a strategy for building an appropriate network of locations.

Having highlighted the relationship between the choice of a location and the development of capabilities, we next turn our attention to the actual stages that location decisions typically progress through.

5.4.1.5.1 Stage 1: Regional–International
In the regional–international stage, an organization focuses on the part of the world (e.g. North America, Europe, and Pacific Rim) or perhaps the region of a country (e.g. Southwest, Midwest, and Northeast) in which it wants to locate its new facility. For example, when Mercedes-Benz needed a new facility to produce its new multipurpose vehicle (MPV), it initially decided that its new facility should be located in North America and subsequently further narrowed the region to sites in the Southeastern United States. There are four major considerations in selecting a national or overseas region for a facility: *proximity, labor supply, availability of inputs,* and *environment.*

To minimize transportation costs and provide acceptable service to customers, the facility should be located in a region in *proximity* to customers and suppliers. Although methods of finding the location with the minimum transportation costs will be presented later in this chapter, a common rule of thumb in the United States is that the facility should be within 200 miles of major industrial and commercial customers and suppliers. Beyond this range, transportation costs begin to rise quickly.

The region should have the proper *supply of labor* available and in the correct proportions of required skills. One important reason for the past expansion of American firms abroad, particularly to Japan in the 1980s, was the availability of labor there at wage rates much lower than rates at home. Currently, this disparity has been eliminated because of Japan's increased wages. However, the real consideration should not be wage rates but rather the productivity of domestic labor relative to productivity abroad. This comparison would thus involve considering level of skills, use of equipment, wage rates, educational levels, and even work ethics (which differ even between regions within the United States) to determine the most favorable labor supply in terms of output per dollar of wages and capital investment. The organization of the labor pool should also be given consideration – that is, whether all the skills are unionized or whether there is an open shop. Some states have passed *right-to-work laws* that forbid any requirement that all employees join a union in order to work in an organization. Often, these laws result in significantly lower wage rates in these states and greater flexibility in worker assignments.

The region selected for location of the facility should have the necessary *inputs* available. For example, supplies that are difficult, expensive, or time consuming to ship and those that are necessary to the organization (i.e. no reasonable substitutes exist) should be readily available. The proper type (rail, water, highway, and air) and supply of transportation; sufficient quantities of basic resources such as water, electricity, gas, coal, and oil; and appropriate communication facilities should also be available. Obviously, many American industries are located abroad in order to use raw materials (oil, copper, etc.) available there.

The regional *environment* should be conducive to the work of the organization. Not only should the weather be appropriate, but the political, legal, and social climate should also be favorable. The following matters should be considered:

1. Regional taxes

2. Regional regulations on operations (pollution, hiring, etc.)

3. Barriers to imports or exports

4. Political stability (nationalization policies, kidnappings)

5. Cultural and economic peculiarities (e.g. restrictions on working women)

6. Incentives such as funding infrastructure development, funding for worker training, and tax breaks.

These factors are especially critical in locating in a foreign country, particularly an underdeveloped country. Firms locating in such regions should not be surprised to find large differences in the way things are done. For example, in some countries, governmental decisions tend to move slowly, with extreme centralization of authority. Very little planning seems to occur. Events appear to occur by "God's will" or by default. The pace of work is unhurried, and at times, discipline, especially among managers, seems totally absent. Corruption and payoffs often seem to be normal ways of doing business, and accounting systems are highly suspect. Living conditions for the workers, especially in urbanized areas, are depressing. Transportation and communication systems (roads, ports, phone service) can be incomplete and notoriously unreliable. Attempting to achieve something under such conditions can, understandably, be very discouraging. When locating in such countries, a firm should allow for such difficulties and unexpected problems. In such an environment, Murphy's law thrives.

With the escalating use of outsourcing, and especially offshoring, the roles of location and capacity in the competitive elements of a firm's strategy take on increased importance. By subcontracting production to another firm, an organization can often save substantially on labor costs (especially when offshoring) and at the same time reduce its own asset base tremendously, thereby increasing both its profit margins and ROA. Contract manufacturers such as Flextronics, Selectron, and Jabil Circuit are quick to point out these advantages and others, such as leaving the organization free to concentrate on its strengths, such as design, brand building, marketing, and strategy. There are, however, also disadvantages in both outsourcing and offshoring. One is the loss of control of the product. Another is a probable reduction in speed of response to customers. A third, which is especially sensitive in communities and is increasingly publicized by the media, is the loss of domestic jobs when the company outsources its work. And outsourcing production is always a dangerous action for two reasons: (1) Engineering and then design typically must follow production overseas, meaning the additional loss of these capabilities within the organization. (2) There is the increased potential that the firm is simply training a powerful competitor (especially if engineering and design have also been outsourced), thereby "hollowing itself out." In the 1980s, many firms in the TV and VCR industries outsourced all their production overseas, simply slapping on their own logo to sell their product domestically. Then, the foreign producers started introducing their own brands, and all the formerly domestic producers went out of business, losing the entire industry to foreign competition.

5.4.1.5.2 Stage 2: Community   After the region of a new facility has been selected, candidate communities within the region are identified for further analysis. Many of the considerations made at the regional–international stage should also be considered at this next stage. For example, the availability of acceptable sites, attitudes of the local government, regulations, zoning, taxes, labor supply, the size and characteristics of the market, and the weather would again be considered. In addition, the availability of local financing, monetary inducements (such as tax incentives) for establishing operations there, and the community's attitude toward the organization itself would be additional factors of interest to the organization.

Last, the preferences of the organization's staff should play a role in selecting a community. These would probably be influenced by the amenities available in the community, such as homes, religious congregations, shopping centers, schools and universities, medical care, fire and police protection, and entertainment, as well as local tax rates and other costs. Upper-level educational institutions may also be of interest to the organization in terms of opportunity for relevant research and development (R&D). For example, it was no coincidence that major IBM plants were located in Lexington, Kentucky; in Denver, Colorado; and in Austin, Texas, all of which are also sites of major state universities.

The standard "breakeven" or "cost–volume–profit" model (discussed in Chapter 4) can be helpful for this stage of the location decision, except that there is no revenue line and there are multiple costs lines, each representing a different community's costs. We assume that the problem is to choose from among a set of predetermined communities, on the basis of a range of fixed and variable costs. Although the relevant *factors* for comparison between the communities may be known (e.g. labor costs, taxes, and utility charges), their values may be uncertain, particularly if they are a function of the output rate of the facility being located. The various alternatives for location are then compared by graphing total operating costs for each alternative at different levels of demand, as in Figure 5.5.

This is accomplished by dividing the total operating cost into two components – fixed costs that do not vary with the demand for the output (e.g. land, buildings, equipment, property taxes,

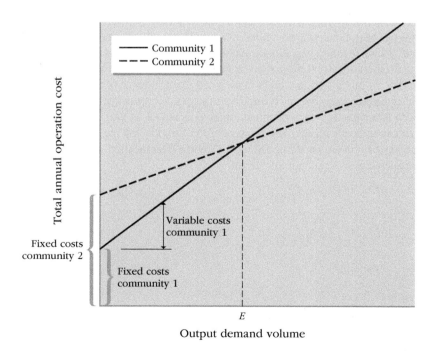

FIGURE 5.5 Break-even Location Model

and insurance) and variable costs such as labor, materials, and transportation – and plotting them on the axes of a graph. At the demand point E (the intersection of the two lines), the costs for the two alternatives are the same; for demand levels in excess of E, community 2 has the lowest annual cost, and for levels less than E, community 1 has the lowest annual cost. Thus, if the range of uncertainty concerning the output volume is entirely *above* point E, the manager need not be concerned about which community to choose – community 2 is preferred. Similar reasoning holds for any uncertainty existing entirely *below* point E – community 1 is preferred.

If the range of uncertainty is closely restricted to point E, then either community may be selected because the costs will be approximately the same in either case. However, if the range of uncertainty is broad and varies considerably from point E in both directions, then the breakeven chart will indicate to the manager the extra costs that will be incurred by choosing the wrong community. Before selecting either community, the manager should probably attempt to gather more information in order to reduce the range of uncertainty in demand.

5.4.1.5.3 Stage 3: Site After a list of candidate communities is developed, specific sites within them are identified. The *site* – the actual location of the facility – should be appropriate to the nature of the operation. Matters to consider include size; adjoining land; zoning; community attitudes; drainage; soil; the availability of water, sewers, and utilities; waste disposal; transportation; the size of the local market; and the costs of development. The development of industrial parks in some communities has alleviated many of the difficulties involved in choosing a site, since the developer automatically takes care of most of these matters. Before any final decision is made, a cash-flow analysis is conducted for each of the candidate sites; this includes the cost of labor, land, taxes, utilities, and transportation.

A model that can help with the site selection is the *weighted score model*. This approach can combine cost measures, profit measures, other quantitative measures, and qualitative measures to help analyze multiple locations (as well as any other multicriteria decision). Deciding on a location, whether for products or services, is complicated by the existence of multiple criteria such as executives' preferences, maximization of facility use, and customers' attitudes. These and other criteria may be very difficult to quantify or even to measure qualitatively; if they are important to the decision, however, they must be included in the location analysis.

Locations can be compared in a number of ways. The most common is probably just managerial intuition: Which location best satisfies the important criteria? The weighted score model is a simple formalization of this intuitive process that is useful as a rough screening tool for locating a single facility. In this model, a weight is assigned to each factor (*criterion*), depending on its importance to the manager. The most important factors receive proportionately higher weights. Then, a score is assigned to each of the alternative locations on each factor, again with higher scores representing better results. The product of the weights and the scores then gives a set of weighted scores, which are added up for each location. The location with the highest weighted score is considered best. In quantitative terms,

$$\text{Total weighted score} = \sum_i W_i S_i$$

Where

i = index for factors

W_i = weight of factor i

S_i = score of the location being evaluated on factor i

Quebec City, Canada, provides a good example of almost exactly this process (Price and Turcotte 1986). The Red Cross Blood Donor Clinic and Transfusion Center of Quebec City was located in a confined spot in the downtown area and wanted to expand in another location. The center's main activities affecting the choice of a new location were receiving donors, delivering blood and blood products throughout the community and the province of Quebec, and holding blood donor clinics across the same region.

Accordingly, the following criteria for a site were identified:

- Highway access for both clinics and blood deliveries

- Ability to attract more donors as a result of improved accessibility and visibility

- Convenience to both public and private transportation

- Ease of travel for employees

- Internal floor space

- Lot size

- Acceptability of the site to management and governmental authorities involved in the decision.

The analysis of the problem was very complicated, owing to conflicting requirements and the unavailability of data. Nevertheless, five sites were finally identified and evaluated on the basis of four final criteria. The five sites were then ranked on each of these criteria, and a scoring model was constructed to help management determine the best location. The weights were to be determined by management, and they could be modified to determine if changing them would have any effect on the best location. The final scores and rankings, with equal weights across the four criteria, are shown in Table 5.2.

5.4.1.6 Locating Pure Services

Although all the material presented so far applies equally to services and product firms, some aspects of locating service organizations are worth noting. First, service location decisions are usually based on how the location will help increase the organization's service revenues, with particular attention paid to avoiding poor locations, which can be fatal to some services. Since the majority of services are highly dependent on physical interaction with the customer, the most important factor in service location is being close to and easily accessible by customers. And if the service relocates, it does not want to move too far from its original location. The second major factor is usually access to qualified labor at a reasonable cost. Then come various other factors such as rent, infrastructure, business climate, competition, and so on. There are some exceptions, such as competitive clustering (auto dealers, motels) and saturation marketing (Walgreens, Starbucks).

There are various approaches to analyzing service locations, depending on some distinctions such as whether the issue is locating a single facility or multiple facilities. Another distinction involves the recipient coming to the facility, as in retailing, as opposed to the facility going to the recipient, as with a limousine service.

Table 5.2 Comparison of Quebec City's Site Factors

Site	Road access	Bus access	Proximity	Availability	Rank
1	0.4	0.0	0.4	0.7	1
2	0.2	0.2	0.3	0.7	2
3	0.3	0.3	0.2	0.0	4
4	0.0	0.4	0.1	0.0	5
5	0.1	0.1	0.0	0.7	3

5.5 Sourcing Strategies and Outsourcing

As was noted in Chapter 1, one trend in business is the emphasis organizations are placing on the sourcing of their products. In the past, sourcing decisions were frequently viewed as primarily tactical in nature with the overarching goal of obtaining the lowest possible unit cost. Often, the strategy used to obtain the lowest cost was to play one supplier against another. Now, we see organizations increasingly discussing *strategic sourcing* and thinking more holistically in terms of the total cost of ownership, not just the unit cost.

Outsourcing is the process of contracting with external suppliers for goods and services that were formerly provided internally and offers an important benefit for SCM. Global sourcing is an important aspect of supply chain outsourcing strategy, and we see it occurring more and more. In the news, we read and hear about the meetings of the World Trade Organization (WTO), the latest accords of the G7 major trading nations, the dangers of North American Free Trade Agreement (NAFTA), the job losses due to overseas outsourcing (furniture manufacturers closing U.S. plants and sourcing from Asia, call centers being relocated to India), and so on.

The classic example of global outsourcing has been Nike, where the shoes are designed in the United States, but all the production is done overseas. The strategic appeal of this lean model of business to other manufacturing and consumer firms is multiple. First, overseas production offers the promise of much cheaper labor costs, clearly a strategic benefit. But equally attractive to many firms that are outsourcing, whether globally or domestically, is the ability to dump a large portion of their capital-intensive production assets and staff, thus giving a big boost to their balance sheets, especially their ROAs. In addition, not being burdened with fixed, unchangeable capital production assets allows firms to be more flexible and responsive to their customers' changing needs.

There is a danger to outsourcing, however, particularly overseas outsourcing, and that is the possibility of being *hollowed out,* as noted in Chapter 1. To summarize, this is the situation where the supplier has been trained to produce, and even sometimes design, the customer's product so well that it can simply sell the product under its own brand and compete successfully against its former customer. In many cases, the customer has gone so long without designing or producing its own product – simply slapping its logo on the foreign-produced item – that it has lost the knowledge and skills to even compete in the market. This happened in the 1980s when American manufacturers trained foreign firms in how to produce TV sets and other electronic goods – and lost those entire industries. Clearly, decisions about outsourcing at this level are strategic ones for the organization, involving great potential benefits but also great risks, and should be deliberated thoroughly.

A more recent phenomenon is the trend toward outsourcing the entire production process to third-party *contract manufacturers.* In this case, the firms often conclude that their core competency is not in manufacturing per se but rather in system innovation or design. In the electronics industry, this is becoming a major element of SCM strategy for firms like Cisco, Apple, IBM, and many others. Cisco, for example, hardly makes any products itself. The big players in this growing industry are Jabil, Flex (formerly Flextronics), and SCI Systems. In fact, in the electronics sector, contract manufacturing was growing faster than the rate of growth of electronics itself in the late 1990s. In spite of the provision of products, these contract manufacturers consider themselves manufacturing *service* providers, and, indeed, this is a substantial service they offer their customers. However, in addition to the major impacts outsourcing involves for operations, it also has major impacts on other functional areas of the organization, such as marketing, finance, R&D, and human resource management. Outsourcing also has implications related to an organization's overall environmental impact. Moreover, to use this approach successfully requires that the firm maintain a strong, perhaps even core, competence in outsourcing. Many failures have resulted when firms jumped into outsourcing but didn't have the skills to manage it properly.

Outsourcing in general is a strategic element of SCM these days, not just for production materials but for a wide range of services as well. For example, organizations are coming to realize that many of the activities they perform internally, such as accounting, human resources, R&D, and even product design and information systems, are not part of their *core competencies* and can be performed more efficiently and effectively by third-party providers, often at a fraction of the cost of in-house workers. There is thus a growing movement toward increasing the span of SCM to include the acquisition of these services.

Recently, beginning in the early 2000s, there has been a trend toward reshoring or moving the production of products that had been offshored back to the United States. In making the decision to reshore the production of products, organizations consider a number of factors such as taxes, regulations, wages, oil prices, transportation, and fluctuations in the values of currencies. A survey conducted at MIT in 2012 found that of the 105 firms participating in the survey, 39% were considering reshoring some of their products produced overseas (Hagerty 2012, 2013). As one example, in 2012, Whirlpool made the decision to reshore the production of its hand mixers after offshoring them to China six years earlier. And in 2013, Whirlpool moved the production of some of its washing machines to a plant in Ohio from a plant in Mexico. As another example, Apple began producing some of its high-end desktop computers in Austin, Texas, in 2013. The nonprofit organization The Reshoring Initiative estimates that between 2010 and 2013, 80,000 manufacturing jobs had been created in the United States as a result of reshoring. It appears that heavy, bulky, and/or expensive products are the best candidates for reshoring.

While often the primary considerations for offshoring and reshoring focus on the supply side of the equation (e.g. taxes, regulations, wages, oil prices, and fluctuations in the values of currencies), the latest trend referred to as next-shoring considers the demand side of the equation. More specifically, next-shoring recognizes the significant benefits that accrue by being in proximity to where the demand for products and services actually occurs. Indeed, the McKinsey Global Institute estimates that the share of global demand coming from emerging markets will increase from 40% in 2008 to 66% by 2025. Proponents of next-shoring recognize that being in proximity to the sources of demand enhances the ability of organizations to adapt to changes such as shifts in customer requirements and emerging technologies. By the same token, next-shoring also creates new challenges related to the development of new supply chain partnerships.

5.5.1 Purchasing/Procurement

Organizations depend heavily on purchasing activities to help them achieve their supply chain strategy by obtaining quality materials and services at the right cost when they are needed. Indeed, the consulting firm Kearney estimated that 30% of a service firm's revenues go to procurement while 50% or more of a manufacturer's revenues go to procurement (Kearney 2019). On the surface it might appear that organizations compete directly with one another (e.g. Coke versus Pepsi, General Motors versus Toyota, and Amazon versus Walmart). A more accurate perspective is that it is one organization's supply chain that is competing with its competitor's supply chains.

Purchasing is expected to be able to quickly identify and qualify suppliers, negotiate contracts for the best price, arrange for transportation, and then continue to oversee and manage these suppliers. Lately, purchasing has been given the added responsibility in many organizations for also supplying major services to the organization, such as information technology, accounting, human resources, and other previously internal functions.

Another common term for the purchasing function is *procurement*. While "purchasing" implies a *monetary* transaction, "procurement" is the responsibility for acquiring the goods and services the organization needs, by any means. Thus, it may include scrap and recycled as well as purchased materials. Procurement thus allows the consideration of environmental aspects of

obtaining and distributing products. For example, there is often the possibility of recovering certain materials through recycling, reuse, or scrap purchases. And remanufacturing of goods is an inexpensive alternative to virgin production. On the distribution side, the concept of *reverse logistics* is being practiced in Germany, where packaging must reverse the logistics chain and flow back to the producer that originated it for disposal or reuse.

The purchasing area has a major potential for lowering costs and increasing profits – perhaps the most powerful within the organization. Consider the following data concerning a simple manufacturing organization:

Total sales	= $10,000,000
Purchased materials	= 7,000,000
Labor and salaries	= 2,000,000
Overhead	= 500,000
Profit	= 500,000

To double profits to $1 million, one or a combination of the following five actions could be taken:

1. Increase sales by 100%.

2. Increase selling price by 5% (same volume).

3. Decrease labor and salaries by 25%.

4. Decrease overhead by 100%.

5. Decrease purchase costs by 7.1%.

Although action 2 may appear easiest, it may well be impossible, since competitors and the market often set prices. Moreover, raising prices almost always reduces the sales volume. In fact, raising prices often decreases the total profit (through lower volume). Action 5 is thus particularly appealing. Decreasing the cost of purchased material provides significant profit leverage. In the previous example, every 1% decrease in the cost of purchases results in a 14% increase in profits. This potential is often neglected in both business and public organizations. Of course, other factors beyond cost such as the quality of the goods purchased and the delivery reliability of the supplier also need to be considered. It would not serve an organization's purposes well to see costs associated with poor quality rise more than the savings that result from lower purchasing costs.

This logic is also applicable to service organizations. For example, investment firms typically spend 15% of their revenues on purchases. However, manufacturing firms spend about 55% of their revenues for outside materials and services (Tully 1995)! And with factory automation and outsourcing increasing, the percentage of expenditures on purchases is increasing even more. In addition, with lean and JIT programs at so many firms (discussed in greater detail in Chapter 9), "JIT purchasing" is even further increasing the importance of purchasing and procurement, since delays in the receipt of materials, or receiving the wrong materials, will stop a JIT program dead in its tracks.

It is also important to recognize that not all suppliers (and purchased items) are equally important to an organization's competitiveness. The Kraljic matrix is a useful framework for helping organizations classify purchases from their supplier base. As shown in Figure 5.6, the Kraljic matrix classifies suppliers based on two dimensions: supply risk (or complexity of the item purchased) and the impact on profits. Factors that impact supply risk include availability of the item, the number of suppliers, whether the item could be produced in-house if needed, whether substitutes are available, price stability, and the likelihood of supply disruptions. Factors that are related to the profit impact include the quantity of the item needed, the percent of the total cost

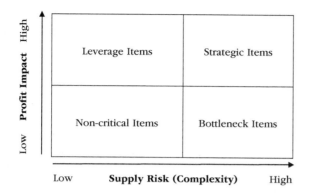

FIGURE 5.6 Kraljic Matrix for Classifying Suppliers

the item accounts for, and the impact the item will have on the final product or service's perceived quality. Using these two dimensions, purchased items can be placed into one of four categories.

Non-critical items in the lower-left quadrant in the Kraljic matrix correspond to purchased items with low supply risk that have little impact on profitability. Examples of non-critical items include copier paper, screws, and other standardized items. Because there tends to be an abundant supply (low supply risk) of these items and they have little impact on profitability, the focus in dealing with suppliers of these items is on using automation to maximize efficiency and lower costs.

Moving to the upper-left quadrant are leverage items. Like noncritical items, leverage items have low supply risk. However, in contrast to noncritical items, leverage items have a large impact on profitability. Because of the high impact leverage items have on profitability, organizations seek to capitalize on their bargaining power when negotiating with suppliers of leverage items. Standard commodities with abundant sources exemplify leverage items such as the plastic used in Legos building blocks.

Bottleneck items are the opposite of leverage items having high supply risk but low profit impact. Collaborating with suppliers to ensure adequate supplies is important. Alternatively, supply risk can be reduced by identifying new suppliers and/or substitute items. The rechargeable battery that is an integral part of a digital camera exemplifies a bottleneck item.

Finally, strategic items have both high supply risk and high profit impact. Establishing partnerships is the preferred strategy for dealing with suppliers of strategic items. Examples of strategic items are the chips that go into cars.

The category a supplier falls into in the Krajlic matrix also has implications with respect to achieving sustainability goals. For example, joint product development may be required when sustainability performance criteria are added in selecting suppliers for strategic items. Achieving sustainability objectives is perhaps most difficult for bottleneck items as the supplier tends to be in the more powerful position. In such cases, the purchasing company can leverage internal strategies such as making greater use of recycling. On the other hand, achieving sustainability objectives for leverage items is relatively straightforward and can be accomplished by sharing best practices. Finally, for noncritical items, sustainability objectives can be addressed as part of supplier selection.

SCM programs are putting ever greater emphasis on the purchasing function. Thus, we are seeing multiple new initiatives for cutting purchasing costs, including reverse auctions and joint venture websites by organizations that are normally competitors. Reverse auctions use a website to list the items a company wants to buy and bidders make proposals to supply them, the lowest qualified bidder typically winning the auction. Joint venture websites are typically for the same purpose, but combine the purchasing power of multiple large players in an industry – automobile manufacturing, aerospace, and health care, for example – in order to obtain even bigger cost savings. Such sites are virtual online bazaars, including all the goods and services the joint partners wish to outsource. But the range and volumes are massive, considering that the old Big Three U.S. auto companies each spent close to $80 billion a year on such purchases.

5.5.1.1 Value Analysis

A special responsibility of purchasing, or purchasing working jointly with engineering/design and operations (and sometimes even the supplier), is to regularly evaluate the *function* of purchased items or services, especially those that are expensive or used in high volumes. The goal is to either reduce the cost of the item or improve its performance. This is called "value analysis" because the task is to investigate the total value of the item to see if it can be eliminated, redesigned for reduced cost, or replaced with a less expensive or more beneficial item, or even if the specifications can be relaxed. Other aspects are investigated, too, such as the packaging, the lead time, the transportation mode, the materials the item is made from, whether the part can be combined with another part or parts, and so on.

Recent efforts in this area have extended the reach farther up the supply chain to involve second- and third-tier suppliers, even bringing them in before the product is designed in order to improve its value up front, called *early supplier involvement*. Value analysis should be a continuing effort to improve supply chain performance and increase its value to the ultimate consumer.

5.5.1.2 Key Elements of Effective Purchasing

Organizations that are highly effective in SCM purchasing seem to follow three practices:

1. *They leverage their buying power.* The advantages associated with decentralization are typically not achieved when it comes to purchasing. For example, HCA Healthcare combined the purchases of its 200-plus hospitals to increase its overall purchasing power. By combining all of its purchases for supplies ranging from cotton swabs to IV solutions, for instance, it was able to reduce purchasing costs by $200 million and boost profits by 15%.

2. *They commit to a small number of dependable suppliers.* Leading suppliers are invited to compete for an organization's business on the basis of set requirements, such as state-of-the-art products, financial condition, reliable delivery, and commitment to continuous improvement. The best one-to-three suppliers are selected from the field of bidders on the basis of the specified requirements. Typically, one- to five-year contracts are awarded to the selected suppliers. These contracts provide the supplier with the opportunity to demonstrate its commitment to the partnership. The customer shares information and technology with the supplier, and the supplier responds in turn. If a supplier is able to consistently improve its performance, the organization reciprocates by increasing the volume of business awarded to that supplier and extending the contract.

3. *They work with and help their suppliers reduce total cost.* Often, organizations will send their own production people to a supplier's plant to help the supplier improve its operating efficiency, improve its quality, and reduce waste. Additionally, an organization may benchmark key aspects of a supplier's operation such as prices, costs, and technologies. If it is discovered that a supplier has slipped relative to the competition, the organization can try to help the supplier regain its lead. If the supplier is unable or unwilling to take the steps necessary to regain its leadership position, the organization may need to find a new partner.

5.5.1.3 Sustainability and Procurement

Earlier in this chapter it was noted that Meta committed to being carbon neutral across its entire value chain by 2030. Like Meta, numerous other organizations have recognized that there is only so much that can be accomplished working individually and that achieving significant gains toward sustainability objectives requires the participation of their supply chain partners. Along these lines, sustainable procurement involves considering sustainability issues in sourcing decisions and supplier selection. Based on the extent to which sustainability is considered in an organization's practices, they can be classified into four categories (Walton *et al.* 1998):

- *Resistant adapters* employ sustainable practices only if they are required, perhaps through regulations.

- *Reactive adapters* seek to comply with environmental laws, often to avoid penalties.

- *Receptive adapters* consider how sustainable improvements can contribute to their competitive advantage.

- *Constructive adapters* recognize the value in embracing sustainability initiatives.

While organizations such as Meta demonstrate that reducing the organization's environmental impact and its competitiveness can be achieved simultaneously, there are challenges related to supplier selection that may need to be addressed including:

- Materials required from suppliers employing sustainable practices may cost more.

- Sustainability is a relatively new concept and, as such, organizations may not know how to evaluate suppliers in terms of their sustainability practices or have processes in place to evaluate them. Likewise, the supplier's sustainability practices and commitments to sustainability may lag their customers, requiring the suppliers to quickly define appropriate sustainability metrics and implement the associated measurement processes.

- Unfortunately, some organizations engage in the practice referred to as *greenwashing* where they give lip service to their sustainable practices typically to enhance their image. Employing greenwashing complicates the task of assessing a supplier's commitment to and achievement of sustainability goals.

- Incorporating sustainability criteria into supplier selection may result in reducing the number of suppliers. While there are benefits associated with reducing the number of suppliers, supply risk is also increased as the number of suppliers is reduced.

There are a number of third-party organizations that assess sustainability practices. Reviewing these assessments can help mitigate the challenges of assessing potential suppliers in terms of their sustainability practices. Examples of third-party organizations and certifications that can be consulted to assess the sustainability practices of potential suppliers include:

- International Fairtrade Organization certifies that farmers of crops such as cocoa, sugar, and coffee are paid a fair price. Certified organizations can use the Fairtrade label.

- Maritime Stewardship Council establishes standards based on fish stock levels and other criteria to ensure the sustainability of wild-caught fish. Some have criticized the council of not setting standards sufficiently high.

- Carbon Trust is an organization that advises businesses and assesses them on their carbon footprint.

- LEED (see Chapter 4) established standards related to the sustainability of buildings. The standard considers the purpose of the building (e.g. office, warehouse, and factory) and whether the building is new construction or already exists.

- The International Standards Organization (ISO) created ISO 14001 which are standards for creating and improving an environmental management system (EMS). ISO's focus is only on the creation of the standard and does not set environmental targets for the standards nor does it audit organizations seeking to become ISO certified. Rather, third party auditors are responsible for performing the audits which may complicate comparing potential suppliers that are ISO certified to one another.

Another important issue related to procurement is that depletion of key resources can create significant challenges related to acquiring needed inputs. Relevant countermeasures for materials at high risk include developing backup sources of supply, considering possible material substitutes, and implementing recycling programs. To facilitate identifying materials in short supply, the European Commission periodically publishes a report listing critical minerals and metals. This list of critical materials has increased over time consisting of 14 materials in 2011, 20 materials in 2014, 27 in 2017, and 30 in 2020. The new materials added to the 2020 list were bauxite, lithium, titanium, and strontium (helium was removed due to a decline in its importance to industry despite its supply still being of concern).

5.5.2 Supplier Management

Our discussion of the management of an organization's suppliers will focus on three areas: (1) selecting the suppliers, (2) contemporary relationships with suppliers, and (3) certification and auditing of ongoing suppliers.

5.5.2.1 Supplier Selection and Vendor Analysis

The general characteristics of a good supplier are as follows:

- Deliveries are made on time and are of the quality and in the quantity specified.

- Prices are fair, and efforts are made to hold or reduce the price.

- The supplier is able to react to unforeseen changes such as an increase or decrease in demand, quality, specifications, or delivery schedules – all frequent occurrences.

- The supplier continually improves products and services.

- The supplier is willing to share information and be an important link in the supply chain.

However, these are not the only factors to be considered in selecting a supplier. Additional considerations involve the supplier's reputation/reliability, having a nearby location (especially important for JIT delivery), its financial strength, the strength of its management, and even what other customers and suppliers are involved with it. For example, if we are a relatively small customer, we might be more at risk of not getting a delivery if a larger customer experiences a problem and needs our supplier's immediate help. Or if our supplier has weak or unreliable second- or third-tier suppliers, we might encounter a problem getting our supplies through no fault of our direct supplier.

Another important factor to consider in selecting a supplier is the total cost of ownership. In particular, one pitfall that organizations should avoid is the tendency to overly emphasize the unit cost being charged for a purchased item to the exclusion of other important aspects that also impact the organization's costs. In many cases, the actual costs of using, maintaining, transporting, inspecting, reworking, servicing, and handling a purchased item can be much greater than its unit cost. For example, after-sales service or the amount of maintenance required for a purchased item may have a larger impact on an organization's costs than simply the cost of acquiring the product or service. Thus, the objective for employing a total cost of ownership approach is to consider and analyze all costs related to a purchase, not just the obvious purchase price. It is also worth pointing out that when all costs of the purchase are considered (e.g. import costs, duties, and currency fluctuations), outsourcing overseas may not be as advantageous as when only the unit cost of the item is considered.

Finally, a supplier's commitment to sustainability is becoming an increasingly important consideration in the selection and evaluation of candidate suppliers at many organizations. Patagonia well exemplifies this. In particular, Patagonia's Supply Chain Environmental Responsibility Program focuses on measuring, reducing, and eliminating the impact the manufacturing of its products and the materials used in its products has on the environment. In addition to meeting minimum requirements, Patagonia suppliers are encouraged to demonstrate their commitment to environmental excellence. Supplier manufacturing facilities are evaluated and assessed in terms of whether they conform to Patagonia's minimum environmental performance requirements. These assessments are part of how they approve new suppliers and manage existing suppliers. A current focus at Patagonia is working with their raw material suppliers to help them decarbonize their operations. But beyond simply specifying environmental standards, Patagonia is a true supply chain partner. For example, they finance energy and carbon audits to help their supply chain partners improve their energy efficiency, implement renewable energy, and reduce the use of carbon-intensive fuels in the production of raw materials used in its products.

5.5.2.2 Supplier Relationships

In these days of intense global competition and SCM, the relationship between customers and suppliers has changed significantly. In the past, most customers purchased from the lowest bidders who could meet their quality and delivery needs, often maintaining at least two or three suppliers in case one was suddenly unable to meet their needs due to a wildcat strike or delivery problem. As pressure mounted to reduce costs, they often pressured their suppliers to cut costs by promising larger volumes to those that had the lowest costs and provided smaller amounts to other suppliers.

To implement SCM, customers are seeking a closer, more cooperative relationship with their suppliers. They are cutting back the total number of their suppliers by a factor of 10 or 20 and combining their purchases, with those remaining getting the overwhelming volume of all their business. They are also asking suppliers to do a greater portion of assembly, such as with automobile seats and other automotive components, which can then simply be installed as a package rather than assembled first and then installed. Not only does the reduced assembly labor save them cost, but in return for the higher volumes, they are expecting even further reductions in cost from their reduced number of suppliers.

5.5.2.3 Supplier Certification and Audits

As can be seen, these *sole-sourcing* arrangements are becoming virtual partnerships, with the customer asking the supplier to become more involved even at the design stage and asking for smaller, more frequent JIT deliveries of higher-quality items. This means longer-term relationships, help with each other's problems, joint planning, sharing of information, and so on. To do this, suppliers are being *certified* or *qualified* so that their shipments do not need to be inspected by the customer – the items go directly to the production line. This is often referred to as *stockless purchasing* because the items do not sit in the stockroom, costing capital for holding and securing them. To ensure that the contracted supplies will be available when needed, the customers periodically conduct *supplier audits* of their vendors, checking for potential production or delivery problems, quality assurance, design competence, process improvement procedures, and the management of corrective actions. Some customers rely on standard industry certifications such as ISO 9000 (see Chapter 7) rather than incurring the time and expense of conducting their own certification. Such certified suppliers are sometimes known as *world-class* suppliers.

Of course, most of the benefits of this partnership accrue to the customer rather than the supplier. The main immediate benefit to the supplier is that it stays in business and even grows. If managed properly, it should even become more profitable. However, with the help of its customers, its production processes should improve substantially, both in quality and efficiency, resulting in cost reductions that are shared between the partners. Toyota is known for helping their suppliers, and even their second- and third-tier suppliers, in this kind of fashion.

In the not too distant past, when JIT production was still novel, customers were using sole sourcing as a way to put pressure on their suppliers, forcing the supplier to stock inventories of items for immediate delivery rather than holding the stock themselves. Singing the praises of JIT – and insisting that the supplier implement JIT so that its deliveries could be made in smaller, more frequent batches – was often just a ploy to accommodate the customers' own sloppy schedules, because they never knew from week to week what they were going to need the following week. Today, firms are moving to lean/JIT (described in detail in Chapter 9) and bringing their suppliers along with them. In many cases, the customer, like Toyota, is teaching the supplier how to implement effective lean/JIT programs in their own organizations.

5.6 Role of Information Technology

Everyone knows that computers are everywhere these days and embedded in all kinds of products that one would not have expected. But why is this, and why now? Professor Richard Chase of the University of Southern California believes that the answer lies in two esoteric laws – one about physical goods and the other about abstract information. The first is the better known of the two: Moore's law, which states that computing power doubles every 18–24 months. The unstated surprise about Moore's law is that this doubling of power comes at the same or lower cost as before the doubling. Clearly, with enough money, our big computer companies could double computing power every 18 (or 12 or 6) months, but the size of the computers would grow enormously, as would their costs. Yet, this law implies that the cost and size do *not* increase. As a result, more and more computing power is becoming available for less and less money; hence, it is becoming omnipresent, appearing everywhere we go and in everything we buy.

The second law is less familiar to the public but derives from the fact that information assets, like knowledge, tend to grow with use rather than dwindle, as with physical assets. This second law is called Metcalfe's law, which says that the value of a network is proportional to the square of the number of elements (or users) connected to the network. This is why Facebook, Microsoft, and eBay have been so successful – with more people in a network, the value of the network to the user is enhanced, so more people join this network. And competing networks with fewer users are of less value and hence fade away.

As a result of these two laws, the growth of computers, which support networks, and networks, which support people's needs (business transactions, communication, blogging, etc.), has exploded. This phenomenon has been particularly prevalent in business, where it has contributed to both increased value (and thus revenues) and reduced costs, thereby having a double impact on increased profits. Next, we will look at some particular types of information technology that are commonly used in business, especially to support SCM.

Arguably, the most significant information technology development for SCM is the *Internet*, and its graphical component the *World Wide Web* (Web). Without a doubt, the Web offers enormous opportunities for members of a supply chain to share information.

One technology in particular supported by the Internet is mobile computing. As its name suggests, *mobile computing* allows users to access both data and software resources regardless of their location. In addition to the Internet, mobile computing is enabled by the ubiquity of wireless communication technologies (e.g. Wi-Fi and 5G cellular data services) and portable computing devices (e.g. smartphones, tablet computers, and notebook computers). Applications of mobile computing span the entire supply chain from helping employees working in warehouses pick the right inventory items for customer orders to helping logistics managers optimize the routes of delivery fleets. For example, using mobile computing, an organization can capture driver performance data as well as obtain real-time locational information on delivery vehicles.

Another technology having a significant impact on business in general and supply chain management in particular is the *cloud*. The cloud refers to software running and/or data stored on servers that users connect to via the Internet. This is in contrast to having data stored and/or software programs running locally on the user's computer. You most likely use a number of cloud-based services in your personal and educational/professional life including services such as Gmail, Apple iCloud, and Dropbox. The cloud offers users and organizations a number of important benefits including the ability to access information using different types of devices (e.g. smartphone, computer) via the Internet, not having to purchase computer memory, not having to incur the cost and effort to upgrade software, and greater opportunities for collaboration. Of course, there are potential drawbacks of using cloud services such as times when connecting to the Internet is interrupted or unavailable and the risk of the data being hacked. Software that is accessed and used via the cloud is also referred to as *Software as a Service (SaaS)* in contrast to the more traditional approach of installing and running software on individual user computers. As you can imagine, organizations can save much time and effort with SaaS since the need to install and update software on each end user's computer is eliminated.

The cloud facilitates managing the supply chain in numerous ways including the following:

• Enhancing an organization's agility to respond to changes due to the ease with which data can be accessed across the supply chain

• Enhancing integration due to the ease with which data can be shared both internally and externally

• Enhancing planning as real-time data on key aspects of the supply chain such as inventory levels or the location of delivery vehicles is available

• Better customer service and a stronger competitive position resulting from enhanced agility, integration, and planning.

5.6.1 ERP

ERP systems greatly facilitate communication throughout the supply chain and over the Internet. The ERP system embodies much more than just the supply chain, however; it also includes all the electronic information concerning the various parts of the firm. These massive systems can not only reduce costs and allow instant access to the entire firm's database but can also help increase revenues by up to 25% in some cases (Mabert et al. 2001, p. 50).

As the name suggests, the objective of these systems is to provide seamless, real-time information to all employees who need it, throughout the entire organization (or enterprise), and to those outside the organization. Figure 5.7 provides a broad overview of SAP's MySAP ERP system. MySAP, announced in 2003, represents the latest evolution of SAP's ERP system. SAP introduced its R/2 system in 1979, which was an ERP system that ran on mainframe computers, and its R/3 system for client–server computing environments in 1992. MySAP takes the evolution one step further and is based on SaaS whereby organizations will be able to access the SAP software via the Internet and thereby have access to the full functionality of the software without having to actually install and deploy the software throughout the enterprise. With the introduction of MySAP, SAP has announced that they will no longer continue to develop R/3.

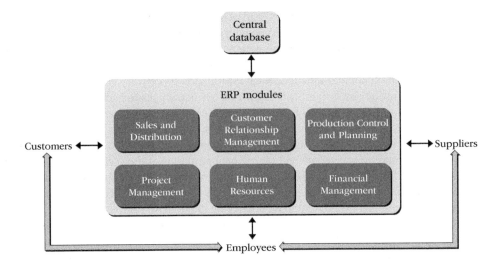

FIGURE 5.7
SAP's MySAP ERP

As shown in Figure 5.7, an ERP system consists of a number of modules that provide the functionality to support a variety of organizational processes. In particular, note how the three modules in the top row are directly aligned with managing the supply chain. These modules all access data from the central database, and changes made via these modules update the central database. Using ERP, each area interacts with a centralized database and servers, so suppliers can check on the latest demands and customers can determine the status of their order or available capacity for new orders. ERP can also handle international complications such as differences in taxes, currency, accounting rules, and language.

With the ERP approach, information is entered once at the source and made available to all stakeholders needing it. Clearly, this approach eliminates the incompatibility created when different functional departments use different systems, and it also eliminates the need for people in different parts of the organization to reenter the same information over and over again into separate computer systems. Although ERP ties all these areas together, the actual implementation of an ERP system in an organization may include only portions of these modules on an as-needed basis.

Davenport (1998) provides an example that illustrates the opportunity to automate tasks in a business process with an ERP system. In the example, a Paris-based sales rep of a U.S. manufacturer prepares a quote for a customer in Paris. After the rep enters the customer information into a notebook computer, the ERP system creates the sales contract in French. Included in the sales contract are important details of the order, such as the product's configuration, quantity ordered, price, delivery date, and payment terms. When the customer agrees to the terms of the quote, the sales rep submits the order electronically with a single keystroke. The system then automatically checks the customer's credit and accepts the order if it is within the customer's credit limit. Upon accepting the order, the ERP system then schedules the shipment of the completed order based on the agreed-upon delivery date and then, based on the delivery date and appropriate lead times, reserves the required raw materials. The system also determines if the required materials will be available and, if not, automatically generates the orders for the needed materials from suppliers. Next, the ERP system schedules the actual assembly of the order in one of the organization's Asian facilities. In addition, sales and production forecasts are updated, the commission due to the rep is calculated and credited to his or her account (in French francs), and the profitability of the order (in U.S. dollars) is computed. Finally, the business unit's and corporate financial statements such as balance sheets, accounts payable, accounts receivable, and cash flows are immediately updated.

As this example illustrates, the integration offered by ERP systems provides organizations with the potential to achieve dramatic improvements in the execution of their business processes. Owens Corning achieved this integration by replacing 211 legacy systems with one ERP system. Much of the benefit associated with this integration stems from having real-time access to operating and financial data. For example, after implementing an ERP system, Autodesk reduced the time it took to deliver an order from an average of two weeks to shipping 98% of its orders within 24 hours. Before implementing an ERP system, it took IBM's Storage Systems Division five days to reprice all of its products. After implementing an ERP system, it was able to accomplish the same task in five minutes. IBM also reduced the time required to ship replacement parts from 22 days to 3 days and reduced the time to perform credit checks from 20 minutes to 3 seconds! Fujitsu Microelectronics achieved similar benefits, reducing its order fulfillment time from 18 days to less than 2 days and reducing the time required to close its financial books from 8 days to 4 days.

Although ERP systems were originally developed for and adopted by manufacturing firms, employees working in service organizations have the same need for seamless, real-time information. To meet the needs of service organizations, numerous ERP systems specific to the needs of service organizations have been developed. For example, Carroll Hospital Center in Westminster, Maryland, adopted an ERP system to help streamline its operations and reduce costs (Monegain 2009). Carroll Hospital used the ERP to facilitate a variety of functions from payroll to budgeting and planning. According to the CIO of Carroll Hospital, the ERP system has impacted all aspects of the hospital from how patients receive their care to how employees are paid. Employees at Carroll Hospital appreciated the ERP system's ability to provide them with the information they need and eliminate paperwork. Overall, Carroll Hospital has found that the ERP system provides everyone with more timely and accurate information, which, in turn, facilitated the work of all employees.

In a similar fashion to the health-care industry, a number of specialized ERP systems have been developed for higher education. These ERP systems contain a number of specialized modules that universities can select from for maintaining and developing relationships with alumni, student services such as financial aid and course registration, finance and human capital management, and academic applications for tasks such as monitoring student progress and retention.

5.6.2 Customer Relationship Management Systems

Another important information technology is *customer relationship management (CRM) systems*. CRM systems are designed to collect and interpret customer-based data (Ragins and Greco 2003). This could be from internal sources such as marketing, sales, or customer support services or from external sources such as market research or the customer. The aim is to develop a process for improving the firm's response to its customers' needs, especially the most profitable customers. CRM systems thus provide comprehensive customer data so the firm can provide better customer service and design and offer the most appropriate products and services for its customers. CRM systems can be purchased as a standalone system or may be part of the organization's ERP system as shown in Figure 5.4.

5.6.3 Block Chain Technology

We conclude our discussion of the role of information technology with blockchain, the newest technology. At the time of this writing, blockchain was generating tremendous excitement given the significant impact it is expected to have on numerous industries, especially financial services and health care. As was noted in Chapter 1, while the blockchain technology was originally deployed in 2009 to track transactions for the cryptocurrency Bitcoin, the technology is applicable to a wide variety of situations that require the ability to securely record and share transactional information.

Essentially, a blockchain can be thought of as a computer file (or ledger) for storing data that possesses the following three properties:

1. The file (or ledger) is distributed or duplicated across multiple computers referred to as nodes. No one node has control over the content in the file. Rather, changes to the content in the file can only be made when there is a consensus among the nodes in the network that store the separate but identical information in the blockchain.

2. The data in the blockchain is encoded using cryptography. With cryptography, changes to the blockchain can only be made by someone possessing what is referred to as a private key. If the codes corresponding to the private key don't match, the changes are not accepted, and thus not distributed to the other nodes in the network.

3. Blockchains are public in the sense that anyone with the proper permission can view it. Of course, viewing the blockchain and being able to change the data in the blockchain require different levels of permission.

As its name suggests, blockchains store data in blocks. While each block in the chain can be a different size, each block contains a link to the previous block thereby forming a chain. Blocks also contain timestamps to keep track of when information in a given block was added or updated. And of course, each blockchain contains the data it was created to store such as data on the purchases and sales of goods and services.

While the first blockchain was created to track transactions related to the ownership of the cryptocurrency Bitcoin, blockchains can be used in any situation that requires the recording of transactions in a secure manner. In fact, blockchains can even be used to execute what are referred to as smart contracts where actions are automatically taken if certain conditions are met. For example, funds could automatically be transferred from an airline to the passengers of a cancelled flight.

In the case of supply chain management, blockchains can be used to track goods in a supply chain from the manufacturer through the distributor and ultimately to the end consumer. An example of this was mentioned in Chapter 1 where Walmart was able to track a mango from the time it was picked in Mexico through the packing house and other processing points along the supply chain to its store shelves in less than three seconds with the blockchain technology. Using its traditional technology and systems, it took Walmart over six days to track the same bag of mangoes.

5.7 Successful SCM

The basic requirements for successful SCM are trustworthy partners, good communication, appropriate performance measures, and competent managers with vision. Innovation to suit the particular situation of the individual organization is particularly desirable. Here are some examples of visionary SCM innovations that have been developed:

- Dell's "direct model" (Magretta 1998).

- Walmart's "*cross-docking*" technique of off-loading goods from incoming trucks at a warehouse directly into outbound distribution trucks instead of placing them into inventory.

- The relatively common approach used by Dell and many others of "*delayed differentiation,*" where final modules are either inventoried for last-minute assembly to customer order or differentiating features are added to the final product upon receipt of the customer's order.

- Sport Obermeyer's and Hewlett-Packard's "*postponement*" approach to delayed differentiation, where variety and customization are delayed until as late in the production process as possible, sometimes even arranging with the carrier to perform the final customization (called *channel assembly*). In Sport Obermeyer's (Fisher *et al.* 1994) version, those product lines where demand is better known are produced first, while customer demand volume information is being collected on less easily forecast lines whose production has thus been postponed. Similarly, Hewlett-Packard shipped generic printers to regional centers around the globe, where local workers added country-specific power supplies, power cords, and local language instructions.

One framework that is particularly useful in helping organizations assess the current performance of their supply chain and identify opportunities for improvement is the supply chain operations reference (SCOR) model, which was developed by the Supply Chain Council (which more recently merged with APICS). The emphasis of the SCOR model is on modeling the supply chain process, determining and using appropriate performance metrics, and identifying best practices through techniques such as benchmarking (discussed in detail in Chapter 8).

More specifically, the SCOR model helps managers understand their supply chain at four levels that become increasingly detailed as one progresses down the levels. At the highest level (level 1), the SCOR model identifies the five fundamental supply chain processes:

- *Plan.* Develop a strategy for aligning available supply with anticipated demand.

- *Source.* Procure the needed inputs to execute the plan.

- *Make.* Transform the inputs into outputs in order to meet the plan.

- *Deliver.* Move the finished outputs to the places where they are needed.

- *Return.* Process outputs that have reached the end of their useful life (discussed in more detail in the next section).

The second level in the SCOR model breaks the first level into greater detail and is referred to as the configuration level. For example, the level 1 general Make process can be further broken down into the more specific processes MTS, MTO, and ETO. Level 3 (Process Elements) focuses on the process activities needed to execute the level 2 processes, and level 4 addresses the topic of implementation.

5.7.1 Closed-Loop Supply Chains and Reverse Logistics

Guide and Van Wassenhove (2009, p. 10) define closed-loop SCM as "the design, control, and operation of a system to maximize value creation over the entire life cycle of a product with dynamic recovery of value from different types and volumes of returns over time." An important aspect of closed-loop SCM is recovering value from returned products. The potential for recovering value from returns is enormous, as the National Retail Federation (NRF) estimates that in 2021, 16.6% of the total merchandise purchased was returned, representing over $761 billion in merchandise (Repko 2022). It is estimated that the rate of returns is even higher at 20.8% in 2021, according to the NRF, for online purchases.

Closed-loop supply chains or reverse logistics are not new and have been practiced for decades. However, it is an area of increasing importance, partially due to the growth of e-commerce, as well as increasing interest in the "greening" of supply chain activities to reduce their environmental impact and waste (discussed in next section). The key players in reverse logistics include:

- Retailers who handle product returns, warranty exchanges, and on occasion perform repairs.

- Original equipment manufacturers (OEMs) that operate or outsource the operation of return centers.

- Reprocessors that disassemble, repair, remanufacture, refurbish, and recycle used goods.

- Customers that need to return or dispose of their used products.

Product returns are categorized as commercial returns, end-of-use returns, end-of-life returns, and repair and warranty returns. Commercial returns are typically returns to the reseller and occur within 90 days of purchase. For example, many cell phone companies allow customers to return their cell phones for any reason within 30 days of purchase. End-of-use returns occur when a product is returned so that its functionality can be upgraded. For example, in the United States, it is estimated that smartphone owners upgrade to a new smartphone every 24.7 months on average. End-of-life returns occur when the product still functions but is technologically obsolete. Finally, between commercial returns and end-of-life returns, customers return products to be repaired.

The type of product return has important implications for how the return is handled. For example, commercial returns have usually been only lightly used. Therefore, they typically require minor processing, such as cleaning and perhaps some minor repairs. End-of-use returns have been used more heavily, and there is likely to be more variability in the quality of these returns. Given this, these returns will typically require more extensive processing. The focus in end-of-life returns is on parts recovery and recycling, since these products are technologically obsolete. In summary, then, commercial returns are repaired, end-of-use returns are remanufactured, and end-of-life returns are recycled.

Some key differences between managing the forward supply chain for new products and the reverse supply chain include (Grant et al. 2017):

- There is often more uncertainty about the quantity and quality of returned products, making forecasting more complicated (forecasting is discussed in Chapter 6).

- There is additional uncertainly related to how customers will perceive refurbished products.

- The condition and quality of packaging is another source of uncertainty.

- Typically, detailed inspection is needed, which can be expensive and labor intensive.

From a strategic perspective, the key questions related to reverse logistics that need to be addressed include (Grant et al. 2017):

1. What materials can be returned, recovered, and/or recycled?

2. What are the responsibilities of various SC partners?

3. What is the economic value and benefit to the environment?

In summary, beyond providing significant environmental benefits, the goal of operating a closed-loop supply chain is to generate more value through the recovery activities than the cost of performing these activities. The steps involved in operating a closed-loop supply chain include acquiring the right quantities of the used product with the right quality and at the right time; using reverse logistics or moving the product back upstream from the customer to the repair/remanufacturing operations; sorting, testing, and grading the returned products to determine their disposition; repairing/remanufacturing the returned products; and, finally, remarketing the refurbished products. Some products, such as consumer electronics and computers, have short life cycles and therefore lose a significant portion of their value per week. In these cases, a slow reverse supply chain can erode much if not all of the potential value that can be recovered.

5.7.1.1 Reducing the Environmental Impact of Waste

Traditionally, supply chains were viewed linearly as materials flowed in one direction, where virgin raw materials were taken from the planet, made into products, and ultimately disposed of (i.e. take, make, and dispose). According to the EPA, 292.4 million tons of solid waste, or the equivalent of almost 5 pounds per person per day, were generated in the United States in 2018. Of the total solid waste generated, almost a quarter of it was recycled. In fact, in 2018 only 50% of the solid waste generated in the United States ended up in landfills compared to 94% in 1960. Food accounted for almost a quarter (24.1%) of the solid waste going to landfills in 2018 followed by plastics (18.5%) and paper/paperboard (11.8%) (EPA 2021).

In supply chain terminology, the linear flow of materials from raw materials to the end customers is referred to as forward flow. In contrast, in the circular view of supply chains (aka closed-loop supply chains or reverse logistics), tactics such as recycling and reuse seek to eliminate the need to dispose of waste. Thus, in addition to the forward flow, there is a backward (reverse) flow of materials, from the customer back up to the producer or other organizations that identify alternate avenues for used goods beyond disposal in a landfill. Beyond filling up landfills, there are finite quantities of natural resources that will eventually be depleted. Circular economy allows for reuse of natural resources. Germany, Scotland, and Sweden are currently at the forefront of achieving the zero-waste goal.

Figure 5.8 provides a hierarchy of alternative approaches for dealing with waste. The strategies are listed in order of most environmentally friendly to least environmentally friendly moving from the top of the inverted pyramid to the bottom of the pyramid. The approaches include:

- *Reduce:* Decreasing the quantities of natural resources and energy used. Tactics for reducing the use of natural resources and energy include designing products that use more energy-efficient materials and decreasing the amount of packaging used.

- *Product recovery:* If the product is still functional, it can be reused, as in the case of purchasing a used car. In other cases, the entire product or parts of the product can be refurbished, repaired, or remanufactured. This tactic is commonly used for electronic products such as cell phones and notebook computers, as noted earlier. The management of used and discarded products in order to maximize the economic value recovered and reduce the amount of waste is referred to as product recovery management. Approaches for product recovery management will be discussed in more detail shortly.

- *Recycle:* The goal of recycling is to recover materials from used products that can be reused. Sometimes, new versions of the existing product can be produced while in other cases the recovered materials are used to produce other products. Typically recycling requires some type of reprocessing, which necessitates the use of energy. On the other hand, recycling helps reduce the amount of virgin materials that are needed and there are also energy savings associated with using recycled materials. For example, all metals can be recycled. Recycling efforts are often driven by regulations at the state and local level in the United States. For example,

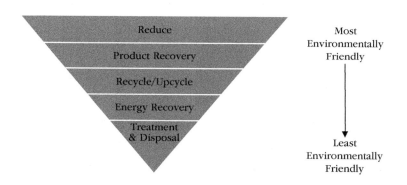

FIGURE 5.8 Waste Management Hierarchy. Adapted from Grant, Trautrims, and Wong (2017).

General Statutes in North Carolina require state agencies to collect and recycle aluminum cans, newspapers, office paper, recyclable glass, and plastic.

- *Upcycling:* This is a relatively new approach that is similar to recycling, but the goal is to creatively produce a new product from recovered materials that has more value than the used product. Often the new product is a one-of-a-kind product such as custom furniture or clothing. Converting old computer monitors to fish tanks is another example.

- *Energy recovery:* Also known as waste-to-energy, where waste is converted to energy, often through incineration.

- *Treatment and disposal:* As the least environmentally friendly approach for dealing with waste, the goal is to avoid it. Most commonly, disposal involves dumping waste into landfills or the oceans.

As noted above, product recovery seeks to maximum the economic value recovered and reduce the amount of waste. Approaches for product recovery include:

- *Repair:* Returning used products to good working order. Often repair requires the replacement of parts. Repair activities can be performed at various locations in the supply chain including retailers or specialized repair centers. Examples of products that are commonly repaired include washing machines and cars.

- *Refurbishing:* Returning used products to a specified quality level. While similar to repair, one key difference is that repair does not typically involve the disassembly of products while refurbishing typically involves the disassembly of components, inspection of components, and the repair/replacement of components. Examples include electronic products such as smartphones and computers.

- *Remanufacturing:* Similar to refurbishing but with the goal to return used products to the quality level of new products. Copiers and engines are examples of products that are commonly remanufactured.

- *Cannibalization:* In some instances, only a subset of parts can be reused and thus recovered from used products. Cannibalization often entails limited disassembly and inspection. Parts that cannot be reused are disposed of. As an example, parts of a car totaled in an accident may be recovered to be sold as used replacement parts.

Many organizations utilize an environmental management system (EMS) to facilitate their product recovery. In particular, the EMS can provide a database of all materials used to make a product, as well as the regulations that govern the disposal of these materials. ISO 14001, discussed previously, provides a standard for creating and improving an environmental management system.

Finally, there are a number of factors that organizations need to consider in developing their product recover strategy including:

- How can the product be designed so that materials can be recovered using the minimum amount of energy?

- Does the product lend itself to product recovery? Some products, especially perishable products such as food, cannot be recovered.

- Is there a reliable supply in terms of both quantity and quality of used products?

- Will there be sufficient demand for the repaired/refurbished/remanufactured products?

- What are the economic and environmental benefits?

As an example of a closed-loop supply chain, Tesla cofounder J.B. Straubel launched the startup Redwood Materials in 2017. The purpose of the startup was to recycle batteries in order to reduce and ultimately eliminate the mining needed for materials such as nickel, copper, and cobalt.

EXPAND YOUR UNDERSTANDING

1. Why is SCM such a topic of interest lately? Why wasn't it previously?

2. What appears to be the primary "secret" of successful SCM?

3. Given that the current conceptualization of the supply chain includes JIT and lean manufacturing, what other elements of SCM need to be changed to move toward the idea of a *demand* chain?

4. In what way can contract manufacturers consider themselves service providers? Hasn't Nike been doing this for years? What's the difference?

5. To date, it appears that purchasing has been one of the primary beneficiaries of SCM. Why do you think this is so? What do you expect will happen in the future?

6. The bullwhip effect is often blamed for the boom-and-bust cycles in our national economy. Which of the remedies for eliminating this effect in a supply chain might also benefit the national economy?

7. How does postponement differ from assemble-to-order?

8. Contrast CRM systems with ERP systems. Which do you suspect are larger and more costly?

9. In many of today's firms, the customer's computer is tied to the supplier's computer so that purchase orders go directly into the supplier's production planning system. What are the implications of this close relationship?

10. Discuss the pros and cons of relying on outside expertise in the selection and implementation of an ERP system.

11. When might an organization not use all three stages of the location selection process described here?

12. Might the breakeven model be used for the national or site stage of location? Might the weighted scoring model be used in the national or community stage of location? What factors would be used in these models at other stages?

13. In reflecting on the discussions of vehicle manufacturers and Best Buy described at the beginning of the chapter, do you see any similarities across these examples?

14. The chapter makes the argument that an organization's supply chain management practices have the largest impact on its environmental impact than any other area. In what ways do supply chain management practices affect an organization's environmental impact?

15. Referring to Figure 5.2, what risk management strategy would be appropriate for a global pandemic such as COVID-19?

Apply Your Understanding

Peak Nutrition, Inc.

Peak Nutrition, Inc. (PNI) offers a line of premium sports recovery drinks. Its drinks are made from all-natural fruit juices that are supplemented with protein, creatine, vitamins, and minerals. Each flavor is offered in both a 12- and 20-oz bottle. Eighty percent of PNI's sales are to two national health food chains, and the remaining 20% are to independent health food stores and online retailers.

PNI has a single production and bottling line, which has sufficient capacity to meet its current demand. Setting up the production line to produce a particular flavor requires an entire eight-hour shift. Most of the setup time is related to flushing out the equipment in order to not contaminate the new flavor to be produced with the flavor that was last produced. Given the long setup times, the production and bottling lines are dedicated to producing a single flavor for an entire week. The typical production schedule involves setting up the line on Monday, producing 12-oz bottles on Tuesday and Wednesday, and producing 20-oz bottles on Thursday and Friday. The plastic bottles and labels are purchased from outside suppliers. There is a one-week lead time for both the bottles and labels. PNI maintains a four-week

(continued)

inventory of plastic bottles and orders labels three weeks before they are needed. Changing over the bottling line from 12- to 20-oz bottles requires about an hour and a half, which also includes changing the labels.

Since each flavor is produced every six weeks, PNI historically produced an eight-week supply for each flavor to provide a safety net in the event demand exceeded its forecasts. Despite having an extra two weeks of inventory, PNI often experienced stockouts. Given the problem with stockouts, PNI recently acquired additional warehouse space and now plans to produce 10 weeks of demand during each production run. It is expected that producing a 10-week supply may result in the need for a small amount of overtime in some weeks.

PNI has limited communication with its customers, primarily consisting of the purchase orders it receives from its customers and the invoices and products it sends to them. PNI's goal is to meet all orders from its inventory. In this way, it is able to provide its customers with a one-week lead time. When the inventory level is insufficient to meet the quantity ordered, lead times increase to an average of two to three weeks, depending on how soon the product is next scheduled for production. Once last year, PNI was stocked out of a flavor for almost four weeks.

At the end of each quarter, PNI offers its customers discounts for orders above certain order quantity thresholds. The purpose of the discounts is to provide retailers with an incentive to put the sports drinks on sale and help boost quarterly sales. As a result of these incentives, PNI's sales tend to be 5 to 10 times higher in the last two weeks of the quarter compared to other times. In anticipation of the increase in sales, PNI builds up its inventory. However, while, on average, it has plenty of inventory across all flavors, it often experiences mismatches in its available supply and demand for specific flavors. In other words, it often finds that it has too much inventory of some flavors and too little of other flavors.

Questions

1. What concerns do you have about PNI's SCM practices?

2. What would you recommend PNI do to address your concerns?

3. Do you have any concerns about the way PNI determines its level of safety stock?

4. Should PNI focus on enhancing the efficiency or responsiveness of its supply chain? Why?

Stafford Chemical, Inc.

Stafford Chemical, Inc., is a privately held company that produces a range of specialty chemicals. Currently, its most important product line is paint pigments used by the automobile industry. Stafford Chemical was founded more than 60 years ago by Phillip Stafford in a small town north of Cincinnati, Ohio, and is currently run by Phillip's grandson, George Stafford. Stafford has more than 150 employees, and approximately three-quarters of them work on the shop floor. Stafford Chemical operates out of the same plant Phillip built when he founded the company; however, it has undergone several expansions over the years.

Recently, a Japanese competitor of Stafford Chemical, Ozawa Industries, announced plans to expand its operations to the United States. Ozawa, a subsidiary of a large Japanese industrial company, decided to locate a new facility in the United States to better serve some of its customers: Japanese automobile manufacturers who have built assembly plants in the United States.

The governor of Ohio has been particularly aggressive in trying to persuade Ozawa Industries to locate in a new industrial park located about 30 miles from Stafford's current plant.

She has expressed a willingness to negotiate special tax rates, to subsidize workers' training, and to expand the existing highway to meet Ozawa's needs. In a recent newspaper article, she was quoted as saying:

> *Making the concessions I have proposed to get Ozawa to locate within our state is a good business decision and a good investment in our state. The plant will provide high-paying jobs for 400 of our citizens. Furthermore, over the long run, the income taxes that these 400 individuals will pay will more than offset the concessions I have proposed. Since several other states have indicated a willingness to make similar concessions, it is unlikely that Ozawa would choose our state without them.*

George Stafford was outraged after being shown the governor's comments.

> *I can't believe this. Stafford Chemical has operated in this state for over 60 years. I am the third generation of*

Staffords to run this business. Many of our employees' parents and grandparents worked here. We have taken pride in being an exemplary corporate citizen. And now our governor wants to help one of our major competitors drive us out of business. How are we supposed to compete with such a large industrial giant? We should be the ones who are getting the tax break and help with workers' training. Doesn't 60 years of paying taxes and employing workers count for something? Where is the governor's loyalty? It seems to me that the state should be loyal to its long-term citizens, the ones who care about the state and community they operate in – not some large industrial giant looking to save a buck.

Questions

1. How valid is George Stafford's argument? How valid is the governor's argument? Is Stafford Chemical being punished because it was already located within the state?

2. How ethical is it for states and local governments to offer incentives to attract new businesses to their localities? Are federal laws needed to keep states from competing with one another?

3. Does the fact that Ozawa is a foreign company alter the ethical nature of the governor's actions? What about Ozawa's size?

4. What are George's options?

Dart's Parts, Inc.

Z. "Dart" Mitchell leaned forward in his chair to read the e-mail that had just arrived from one of his major customers, Avery Machine Corp. It read as follows:

To all our preferred suppliers:

Due to our commitments to our primary customer, Globus Enterprises, we will in the future be doing all of our supply chain business by way of the Internet, e-mail, and EDI. This includes order preparation, bidding, forecasting, production scheduling, delivery monitoring, cost control, accounts payable and receivable, credit and financing, market and advertising planning, human resource acquisition, engineering specifications, and so on. To maintain compatibility with our systems, you will have to invest in a specific set of EDI hardware and software, available from GoingBust.com on the Web. Although the hardware and software are expensive, we anticipate that the cost savings and increased business this will provide over the coming years can more than offset the additional cost. Please let us know if we can continue to count on you as one of our preferred suppliers as we move our supply chain into the information age.

J. R. Avery, Chairman Avery Machine Corp.

Dart's Parts had been founded in 1974 when the country was coming out of the 1973–1974 recession and the need for machine part fabricators was great. Over the years, Dart had built up the business to where it now had a solid base of major customers and a comfortable backlog of orders. Dart had increased the capacity of the plant substantially over the years, moving from a small, rented facility to its own 200,000-square-foot plant, with a separate 50,000-square-foot warehouse located adjacent to the main plant. Although not a "first adopter" when it came to new technology, Dart's embraced proven advanced technologies both on the plant floor, with innovations such as robots and numerically controlled machine tools, and in the office, with computers, digital copiers, and other such office equipment.

Dart Mitchell had been reading industry magazines about some of these new technologies and had to admit they sounded promising. However, he had read about some horror stories, too, when the much-advertised features turned into a nightmare. In one case, a customer had forced its suppliers to obtain production schedules off its website. Initially responding to high growth in a new product line, the firm had put its component needs on its website, but when a major order was canceled, it was late in changing the Web production schedule. As a result, the suppliers were stuck with hundreds of unneeded components, and the company wouldn't reimburse them. In another case, a manufacturer had made a bid for electronic parts on a Web auction and won. However, when it received the parts, they were too large to fit in the standard-sized enclosure it was using, and they all had to be scrapped.

Dart believed that this new technology was indeed the future of the industry, but he was concerned about getting in too early and being stuck with the wrong equipment. The new supply chain technology would undoubtedly open avenues to increased business, but it would also result in a number of costs. Of course, it would also save the company's reputation with Avery, a major customer. However, obtaining the EDI system would be a major financial investment for the firm, particularly if Avery later dropped this approach and went to an all-Internet ERP system like some customers had been talking about doing. At this point, Dart wasn't sure what to do.

Questions

1. Identify the trade-offs facing Dart's Parts.

2. What are the pros and cons of each alternative?

3. What additional information would be useful to have?

4. What recommendations would you make to Dart Mitchell?

EXERCISES

5.1 The location subcommittee's final report to the board has focused on three acceptable communities. Table 15b in the appendix to the report indicates that the cost of locating in communities 1, 2, and 3 is approximately €400,000, €500,000, and €600,000 per year (respectively), mortgaged over 30 years. Paragraph 2 on page 39 of the report indicates that the variable cost per unit of product will increase 15% in community 1 but decrease 15% in community 3, owing to differences in labor rates. As plant manager, you know that variable costs to date have averaged about €3.05 per unit, and sales for the next decade are expected to average 20% more than the last 10 years, during which annual sales varied between 40,000 and 80,000 units. Which location would you recommend?

5.2 Nina is trying to decide in which of four shopping centers to locate her new boutique. Some cater to a higher class of clientele than others, some are in an indoor mall, some have a much greater volume than others, and, of course, rent varies considerably. Because of the nature of her store, she has decided that the class of clientele is the most important consideration. Following this, however, she must pay attention to her expenses; and rent is a major item – probably 90% as important as clientele. An indoor, temperature-controlled mall is a big help, however, for stores such as hers, where 70% of sales are from passersby slowly strolling and window-shopping. Thus, she rates this as about 95% as important as rent. Last, a higher volume of shoppers means more potential sales; she thus rates this factor as 80% as important as rent. As an aid in visualizing her location alternatives, she has constructed the following table. "Good" is scored as 3, "fair" as 2, and "poor" as 1. Use a weighted score model to help Nina come to a decision.

	Location			
	1	2	3	4
Class of clientele	Fair	Good	Poor	Good
Rent	Good	Fair	Poor	Good
Indoor mall	Good	Poor	Good	Poor
Volume	Good	Fair	Good	Poor

5.3 A new product involves the following costs associated with three possible locations. If demand is forecast to be 3900 units a year, which location should be selected?

	Location		
	A	B	C
Annual cost ($)	10,000	40,000	25,000
Unit variable cost ($)	10.00	2.50	6.30

5.4 Select any publicly traded organization you are familiar with and calculate its CCC.

5.5 Use a weighted score model to choose between three locations (A, B, C) for setting up a factory. The weights for each criterion are shown in the following table. A score of 1 represents unfavorable, 2 satisfactory, and 3 favorable.

		Location		
Category	Weight	A	B	C
Labor costs	20	1	2	3
Labor productivity	20	2	3	1
Labor supply	10	2	1	3
Union relations	10	3	3	2
Material supply	10	2	1	1
Transport costs	20	1	2	3
Infrastructure	10	2	2	2

5.6 A manufacturer is considering three possible locations for its new factory. The choice depends not only on the operating costs at each location but also on the cost of shipping the product to the three regions it serves. Given the operating and distribution costs in the following tables, which location would you recommend for a production volume of 80,000 units per year?

	Location		
	A	B	C
Construction cost (amortized over 10 years)	$1,000,000	$1,800,000	$950,000
Material cost per unit	2.46	2.17	2.64
Labor cost per unit	0.65	0.62	0.67
Overhead: fixed	100,000	150,000	125,000
Overhead: variable per unit	0.15	0.18	0.12

Total Distribution Costs

	Location		
To region	A	B	C
1	$10,000	$20,000	$26,000
2	17,000	10,000	15,000
3	12,000	18,000	10,000

5.7 Referring to Exercise 5.6, management has collected additional information and determined that the annual production volume might be as low as 70,000 units, most likely will be 80,000 units, and might reach 85,000 units. Reanalyze the situation using this additional information assuming that the annual production volume follows a triangular distribution. What insights does your analysis provide you? Are there other costs in this situation that should also be modeled as variables as opposed to assuming their values are known with certainty?

BIBLIOGRAPHY

Bartmess, A., and K. Cerny. "Building Competitive Advantage Through a Global Network of Capabilities." Chapter 7 in R. A. Hayes, G. P. Pisano, and D. M. Upton. *Strategic Operations: Competing Through Capabilities*. New York: Free Press, 1996.

Cherney, M.A. "There is an Auto Chip Shortage That Will Slow Down Car Makers Says Analog Devices CEO, Barons (online), January 13, 2021.

CSCMP, "Supply Chain Management Definitions and Glossary," cscmp.org, June 8, 2022.

Davenport, T. "Putting the Enterprise into the Enterprise System." *Harvard Business Review* (July–August 1998): 121–131.

Dignan, L. "Is Dell Hitting the Efficiency Wall?" MSNBC News.com, July 29, 2002, pp. 1–5.

Doerr, J., *Speed and Scale: An Action Plan for Solving our Climate Crisis Now*. Portfolio/Penguin, 2021.

Dvorak, P. "Clarity Is Missing Link in Supply Chain." *Wall Street Journal* (May 18, 2009): A1, A14.

EEA, Rail and Waterborne Best for Low-carbon Motorized Transport, eea.europa.eu, February 25, 2022.

Ellis, S.C., R.M. Henry, and J. Shockley, "Buyer Perceptions of Supply Chain Disruption Risk: A Behavioral View and Empirical Assessment," *Journal of Operations Management*, 28 (2010): 34–46.

EPA, National Overview: Facts and Figures on Materials, Wastes, and Recycling, epa.gov, Jul7 14, 2021.

European Commission, "Critical Raw Materials Resilience: Changing a Path Towards Greater Security and Sustainability." eur-lex-europa.eu, March 9, 2020.

Engardio, P. "Why the Supply Chain Broke Down." *Business Week* (March 19, 2001): 41.

Ferguson, B. R. "Implementing Supply Chain Management." *Production and Inventory Management Journal*, 40 (Second Quarter 2000): 64–67.

Fisher, M. L., J. H. Hammond, W. R. Obermeyer, and A. Raman. "Making Supply Meet Demand in an Uncertain World." *Harvard Business Review*, 72 (May–June 1994): 83–93.

Grant, D.B., Trautrims, A., and Wong, C.Y., *Sustainable Logistics and Supply Chain Management, 2nd Edition*. Kogan Page, 2017.

Guide Jr., V. D. R., and L. N. Van Wassenhove. "The Evolution of Closed-Loop Supply Chain Research." *Operations Research*, 57(1) (January–February 2009): 10–18.

Hagerty, J. R. "Remade in the USA; Once Made in China: Jobs Trickle Back to U.S. Plants." *Wall Street Journal Online* (May 2, 2012).

Hagerty, J. R. "Whirlpool Jobs Return to U.S." *Wall Street Journal* (December 20, 2013): p. B4.

Kearney, *Realizing the Power of Procurement*, co.kearney.com, 2019.

Knemeyer, J., W. Zinn, and C. Eroglu, "Proactive Planning for Catastrophic Events in Supply Chains," *Journal of Operations Management*, 27 (2009): 141–153.

Lummus, R. R., and R. J. Vokurka. "Strategic Supply Chain Planning." *Production and Inventory Management Journal*, 39 (Third Quarter 1998): 49–58.

Lummus, R. R., and R. J. Vokurka. "Managing the Demand Chain Through Managing the Information Flow: Capturing 'Moments of Information.'" *Production and Inventory Management Journal*, 40 (First Quarter 1999): 16–20.

Mabert, V. A., A. Soni, and M. A. Venkataramanan. "Enterprise Resource Planning: Measuring Value." *Production and Inventory Management Journal*, 42 (Third/Fourth Quarter 2001): 46–51.

Magretta, J. "The Power of Virtual Integration: An Interview with Dell Computer's Michael Dell." *Harvard Business Review* (March–April 1998): 72–84.

Marr, B. "What Is Blockchain? A Super Simple Guide Anyone Can Understand." bernardmarr.com/default.asp?contentID=1389, November 16, 2018.

Matthews, R. G. "Mining-Gear Giants Diverge on How to Prosper." *Wall Street Journal* (March 2, 2010).

Meta, Sustainability at Meta, sustainability.fb.com, June 17, 2022.

Meta, A Green New Data Center in the New Mexico Desert, tech.fb.com, June 17, 2022.

Meta, Meta Data Centers, June 2022.

Monegain, B. "Maryland Hospital Implements ERP Technology." *Healthcare IT News*, www.healthcareitnews.com/news/maryland-hospital-implements-erp-technology, October 26, 2009.

Nash, K. S. "Firms Try Out Blockchain." *Wall Street Journal* (February 7, 2018): p. B5.

Patagonia, "Supply Chain Environmental Responsibility Program." patagonia.com, March 4, 2022.

Present, B. "Global Chip Shortage Makes it Tough to Buy Certain Cars" consumerreports.com, July 13, 2021.

Price, W. L., and M. Turcotte. "Locating a Blood Bank." *Interfaces* (September–October 1986): 17–26.

Procurement Tactics, Supply Chain Statistics – 18 Key Figures of 2022, procurementtactics.com, June 21, 2022.

Quinn, F. J. "What 's the Buzz? Supply Chain Management; Part 1." *Logistics Management*, 36 (February 1997): 43.

Ragins, E. J., and A. J. Greco. "Customer Relationship Management and e-Business: More Than a Software Solution." *Review of Business* (Winter 2003): 25–30.

Reference for Business, "Physical Distribution." www.referenceforbusiness.com/small/Op-Qu/Physical-Distribution.html, January 23, 2019.

Repko, M. "A More Than $761 Billion Dilemma: Retailer's Returns Jump as Online Sales Grow" cnbc.com, January 25, 2022.

Satariano, A., and P. Burrows. "Apple's Supply-Chain Secret? Hoard Lasers." *Bloomberg Business Week*, www.businessweek.com, November 3, 2011.

SSCF (Sustainable Supply Chain Foundation), "Welcome to the Sustainable Supply Chain Foundation (SSCF)" www.sustainable-scf.org, June 8, 2022.

Statista, "Light Vehicles Sales in the United States from 1976 to 2021", statista.com, June 22, 2022,

Stock, J., T. Speh, and H. Shear. "Many Happy (Product) Returns." *Harvard Business Review*, 80(7) (2002): 16–17.

Tully, S. "Purchasing's New Muscle." *Fortune* (February 20, 1995): 75–83.

USDA Forest Service, "Current U.S. Forest Data and Maps." www.fia.fed.us, June 9, 2022.

Verity, J. W. "Invoice? What's an Invoice?" *Business Week* (June 10, 1996): 110–112.

Walker, W. T., and K. L. Alber. "Understanding Supply Chain Management." *APICS—The Performance Advantage*, 9 (January 1999): 38–43.

Walton, S.V., R.B. Handfield, S.A. Melnyk, "The Green Supply Chain: Integrating Suppliers into Environmental Management Processes," *International Journal of Purchasing and Materials Management*, 34(2), (1998): 2–11

Yang, S., J. Yang, "TSMC Expects Auto-Chip Shortage to Abate this Quarter; A Dearth of Semiconductors has Stymied Manufacturing Activity in the Auto Industry", Wall Street Journal (online), July 15, 2021.

Appendix A

The Beer Game[1]

The *Beer Game* has become a staple of the operations management course in MBA programs across the country. In effect, the game simulates material and information flows in a simplified supply chain. As shown in Figure 5A.1, the supply chain consists of four stages. Moving from the factory downstream, the supply chain consists of a factory, wholesaler, distributor, and retailer. Accordingly, each stage in the supply chain is required to manage its inventory levels given the receipt of orders from its downstream customer through the placement of orders with its upstream supplier. The only exceptions to this are that the retailer's demand comes from the final consumer and the factory schedules production requests as opposed to placing an order from an upstream supplier.

There is a two-week delay between the retailer, wholesaler, and distributor. Thus, orders from the retailer to the wholesaler in a given week arrive two weeks after the wholesaler ships them. Likewise, orders from the wholesaler to the distributor in a particular week arrive two weeks after the distributor ships it. Production orders at the factory are available to ship three weeks after the production requests.

Your objective in playing the game is to minimize the sum of your total weekly costs. Weekly costs consist of two components: an inventory cost and a backlog cost. More specifically, weekly inventory cost is calculated at the rate of $0.50/keg of beer in inventory at the end of the week, while backlog costs are calculated at the rate of $1.00/keg on backlog at the end of the week. Obviously, only one of these costs can be positive in any given week (although it is possible that they both could be zero in a particular week).

Because a supply chain for the beer industry in reality would likely be characterized by multiple factories, dozens of distributors, hundreds of wholesalers, and tens of thousands of retailers, it is often the case that the only information shared between a supplier and its customer is order information. Therefore, in the game, the only communication you may have with your upstream supplier is the placement of your order.

In terms of the initial conditions, as it turns out, the demand at the retailer stage has been quite stable at four kegs per week for the last several weeks. Therefore, every order placed throughout the entire supply chain has been for four kegs over this period. Furthermore, each stage has maintained an inventory level of 12 kegs or the equivalent of three weeks of demand. However, as the weather turns warmer in the near future, demand is expected to increase. Also, it is expected that there will be one or more promotions over the coming months.

In playing the game, you will be assigned to one of the four stages in the supply chain. During each week of simulated time, you will be required to perform the following five tasks. It is important that these tasks be completed in the order listed below and that each stage in the supply chain complete the task simultaneously with the other stages. Note that only the final task requires you to make a decision.

---

[1] Adapted from Sterman, J. "Instructions for Running the Beer Distribution Game." Massachusetts Institute of Technology (October 1984); Hammond, J. H. "The Beer Game: Description of Exercise." *Harvard Business Schoolss* 9-964-104.

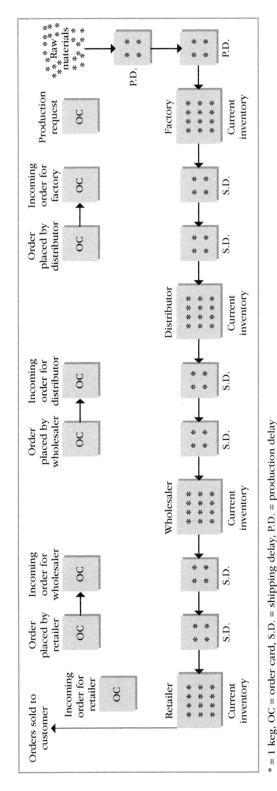

* = 1 keg, OC = order card, S.D. = shipping delay, P.D. = production delay

FIGURE 5A.1 The Beer Game Board and Initial Conditions

1. Deliver your beer and advance shipments. Move the beer in the Shipping Delay box (on the right, adjacent to your Current Inventory box) into the Current Inventory box. Next, move the beer in the other Shipping Delay box to the right to the now empty Shipping Delay box. (Factories move the inventory from the Production Delay box directly to the right of the Current Inventory box into the Current Inventory box. Then move inventory from the top Production Delay box to the bottom Production Delay box.)

2. Pick up the incoming order from your downstream customer in your Incoming Order box at your top left (retailers read incoming order from the consumer). Fill as much of the order as you can from your current inventory by placing the appropriate quantity of kegs in the Shipping Delay box directly to the left of your Current Inventory box. Quantities ordered above your current inventory level become part of your current backlog. More specifically, the amount to ship this week is calculated as follows:

$$\text{Quantity to ship} = \text{Incoming order this week} + \text{Previous week's backlog}$$

3. Calculate and record in Figure 5A.2 your ending inventory or backlog position (as a negative number). Count the number of kegs remaining in your current inventory after

Week	Inventory	Order placed	Week	Inventory	Order placed
1			26		
2			27		
3			28		
4			29		
5			30		
6			31		
7			32		
8			33		
9			34		
10			35		
11			36		
12			37		
13			38		
14			39		
15			40		
16			41		
17			42		
18			43		
19			44		
20			45		
21			46		
22			47		
23			48		
24			49		
25			50		

FIGURE 5A.2 Data Sheet

the shipment for the week has been made. If you get into a backlog situation, the backlog must be accumulated from week to week, since quantities ordered but not shipped must be made up. The week's ending backlog position is calculated as follows:

Current week's backlog = Previous week's backlog +
Incoming order − Shipments received this week

4. Advance your order cards. (Factories fill their production requests.) Advance the order from the Order Placed box to the Incoming Order box (or, for the factory, read the Production Request and fill the Production Delay box from the raw materials inventory). Make sure to keep the order cards facedown as you move them.

5. Decide how much to order, write it down on your order card (and in Figure 5A.2), and place the card facedown in the Orders Placed box. Factories decide how much to schedule for production, write it down on your order, and place the card facedown in the Production Request box.

6. Repeat steps 1–5.

Most likely, your instructor will have the class complete one or more practice runs or go through the first couple of weeks at a slow pace.

Supply Chain Planning and Analytics

6

CHAPTER IN PERSPECTIVE

The previous chapter addressed strategic topics related to the management of an organization's supply chain including supply chain strategy, supply chain design, sourcing strategies, and the role of information technology in supply chain management. We now turn our attention to topics related to more detailed planning including demand planning, sales and operations planning, and inventory and supply planning.

Supply chain planning has become much more sophisticated in the last decade and a large part of it is concerned with attempting to predict what the actual demand is going to be for the service or product. The good news is that we now have a much greater amount of data ("big data") to help us make this forecast, but the bad news is that we need substantially more powerful tools to analyze all this data. To help make these forecasts, organizations are turning to *analytics* to dissect and analyze the data to turn it into information for managerial use. The chapter starts with some elementary statistical forecasting techniques to illustrate how historical data can be analyzed to determine some limited range of future demand. Having these forecasts in hand, the next step is for management to decide how much of this forecast the organization wants to and can supply, called the *service level*, and then bring sales and operations together to create an aggregate plan for producing that amount. The chapter concludes with a discussion of the use of inventory as an important tool for supply planning and helping the organization achieve its service-level goals.

While the topics of demand planning, sales and operations planning, and inventory and supply planning may be more tactical in nature, poor execution in these areas can have significant negative effects on an organization's competitiveness. For example, a demand forecast that is too low often results in dissatisfied customers while over forecasting demand can result in excess inventory, which in turn translates into higher costs as a result of maintaining and disposing of the excess inventory. Likewise, having a service level below the industry norm may put an organization at a competitive disadvantage while providing a higher service level may translate into a competitive advantage. In any case, the topics addressed in this chapter all relate to helping an organization match the supply of their products and services with the demand. And beyond the strategic consequences just mentioned, poor execution in these areas is often highly visible to both customers and senior management.

6.1 Introduction

- Red Wing Shoes is a privately held manufacturer and distributor of footwear and personal protective equipment. It offered 26,000 footwear SKUs and 72,000 garment SKUs. To supply these products, Red Wing operated 14 manufacturing plants and had a complex global supply chain. Its in-house operations spanned much of the supply chain from company-owned tannery operations to company-owned Red Wing Shoe retail outlets.

  Given the breadth of its product offerings and the complexity of its supply chain, it was not surprising that Red Wing faced significant challenges in coordinating the activities of various departments spread out across the enterprise. Indeed, as recently as 2008, it took the company six weeks to complete its Sales and Operations Planning (S&OP). One problem with having such a long process was that by the time forecasts were sent to its suppliers, they were already out of date! Managers further criticized the process as being overly reactive, manual, having too much of an emphasis on what happened in the past, and not facilitating the needed collaboration with suppliers and the internal manufacturing team. Managers felt a clear need for a system that provided better visibility of the true demand for its products in order to be better positioned to coordinate the plans of the various functional areas across the organization. For example, if there was insufficient manufacturing capacity to meet the forecasted demand, what were the sales department's highest priority products and customers? Or could manufacturing increase capacity by using overtime or adding a shift? On the other hand, if there was excess capacity relative to the forecast demand, what actions (e.g. special promotions) could the sales department take to more fully utilize the available capacity?

  To address these challenges, Red Wing embarked on a several year journey to improve its S&OP process. One weak link in the process was the two-week delay it took simply to enter the data into the spreadsheet-based planning system. And because the data were manually entered, it was prone to error. For example, in one case, the employee entering the data forgot to add a subtotal to a spreadsheet, which resulted in underestimating the amount of capacity needed to meet actual demand. To address the data entry challenge, Red Wing developed a way to transfer the data from its ERP system directly into its planning spreadsheets, which eliminated the two weeks spent keying in the data and at the same time significantly reduced the number of data entry errors.

  Through its initiatives, Red Wing reduced the time required to complete the process by 50% from six to three weeks. Furthermore, the new process ensured that all functional teams were involved in the planning process and working toward the same goals. Another benefit of the new S&OP process was that questions from senior management that in the past took days to answer could be answered in minutes. In just two years, Red Wing was able to reduce inventory by 27% while at the same time improving fill rates by 8% to 10%. Finally, demurrage charges were reduced by 50%. As one senior manager at Red Wing put it, "This will be a game changer for us" (Grothe 2014).

- AmBev is Latin America's largest beverage company. It operates 49 production facilities and a fleet of 16,000 trucks to serve a distribution network consisting of 11,000 resellers and over one million final points of sale. Supporting this complex network were large quantities of raw materials and finished goods in its pipeline. Given this complexity, AmBev realized that effective production and distribution planning would need to go beyond simply using historical data. Rather it needed more sophisticated analyses to develop better predictions of demand which in turn would facilitate better decisions. AmBev turned to software made by SAS to combine data from multiple sources including demand and replenishment planning systems to develop weekly forecasts of demand. These weekly forecasts in turn drove sales targets, production goals, and distribution plans. Using this approach the company was able to increase its inventory turnover rate by 50%. For example, products that used to sit in inventory 14 to 15 days were held in inventory seven to eight days (IW/SAS 2010).

- As the UK's largest retailer, Tesco had a significant amount of capital tied up in inventory. Thus, a key challenge its supply chain management team faced was identifying ways to reduce inventory stock levels. To address this challenge, the company completed a number of supply chain analytics projects that generated savings of £100m annually across its retail stores. In one project, four years of sales data were collected and used to develop a simulation model of its distribution system. Inputting updated forecasts of demand into the model, the company was able to use the model to reduce inventory levels and save £50m annually. In another project, the company used regression analysis to study the relationship between weather patterns and sales. Interestingly, the company discovered that in addition to weather being an important factor in predicting demand, the location of the stores and other contextual factors are also important predictors of demand. For example, a warm day had a different impact on the demand in Scotland than the demand in more southern locations. Likewise, the impact of a hot spell starting on a weekend was different than a weekend in the middle of a heat wave. By incorporating information about the weather into its forecasts of demand, Tesco was able to reduce over- and under-stocking, generating annual savings of £6m. As a final example, Tesco developed an algorithm to help it better determine how to discount products as they reached the end of their shelf-life. Prior to the development of the algorithm, these decisions were based on management judgment. Tesco estimated that by removing the guesswork associated with determining when to discount a product, and by how much, it has reduced £30m of wasted stock annually (Computer Weekly 2013).

A by-product of the computerization of virtually every aspect of modern life is the explosion in the volumes of data available. Quite frankly, it is becoming increasingly common for businesses to become overwhelmed by the amounts of data available. At the same time, organizations are becoming increasingly aware of the central role their supply chains play to their competitiveness. In particular, in projects involving designing and managing their supply chains, organizations must carefully balance the often-competing objectives of efficiency and responsiveness. And at the same time, organizations need to consider other objectives such as managing risks and minimizing their carbon footprint, as discussed in the previous chapter. The good news is that by operating at the intersection of these trends, organizations can leverage advanced analytical tools to gain key insights into their supply chains and thereby enhance collaboration both within their organization and across their supply chain. And as the examples above illustrate, the benefits of doing so can be substantial.

We begin this chapter by further elaborating on the importance of supply chain planning and analytics. This is followed by a discussion on demand planning where the emphasis is on developing a forecast of future demand using techniques such as time series analysis and regression analysis. The chapter continues with a discussion of sales and operations planning where aggregate planning strategies and the determination of the appropriate service level are discussed. The chapter concludes with a discussion of the use of inventory as an important tool for supply planning and helping the organization achieve its service-level goals.

6.2 Importance of Supply Chain Planning and Analytics

Although supply chain management gained heightened interest during the COVID-19 pandemic, many organizations had already been focusing their attention on their supply chains as the next frontier for gaining competitive advantage. As Deloitte Consulting points out "Supply chains are a rich place for competitive advantage, partly because of their complexity, and partly because of the significant role they play in a company's cost structure" (Deloitte Consulting 2012). To address these challenges, many organizations are discovering ways to combine the volumes of data they accumulate with advanced analytical techniques to manage and improve their supply chains in ways that were unthinkable in the past.

Typically, organizations evolve through a number of stages as they gain experience with analytics and become more sophisticated in applying it toward the goal of developing a world-class supply chain. In the first stage, organizations simply summarize and report data to decision makers to inform them about what happened in the past – for example, sales by region last quarter. In the second stage, organizations develop the capability to analyze real-time data to understand what is currently happening (e.g. current inventory levels). As their sophistication increases, organizations may progress to the next stage where they seek to predict what will happen in the future (e.g. what will sales be next month?). In the most advanced stage, organizations use prescriptive analytical models to determine what should happen (e.g. how much should we produce of each product next quarter to maximize expected profits?). In summary, as organizations become increasingly sophisticated in their use of data and analytical methodologies, they can progress from using data to simply determine what happened in the past, to understanding what is currently happening, to predicting what will happen in the future, to prescribe what the organization should do about the future.

The evolution of using data and analytics as described above is representative of organizations that take a proactive approach to managing and improving their supply chains. Unfortunately, many organizations are not as proactive in their planning and execution and as a result use a more reactive approach. This leads to less effective supply chain planning and execution which in turn creates a number of problems that often get the kind of attention from senior management that junior managers would rather avoid. Examples of the types of problems that arise as a result of poor supply chain planning and execution include:

- Customer dissatisfaction because their orders are received late or the product was not available when they needed it.

- Increased costs when supplies need to be expedited.

- Strained relationships with suppliers that result from the organizations constantly changing and updating the outstanding orders they placed with their suppliers.

- Increased costs when orders need to be expedited to customers.

- Incurring the wrath of the finance department because of the excessive amount of cash that is tied up in inventory.

While the challenges and problems listed above are serious, they at least have the benefit of being visible. Another factor that compounds effective supply chain execution is that many problems such as inefficiencies and waste are not as visible or only become apparent after it is too late. These are exactly the types of challenges where more sophisticated data analytics can be beneficial.

At a more general level, another significant challenge confronting organizations today is the increasing amounts of uncertainty present in the current business environment. What will customer demand be this month? Will there be sufficient quantities available of key raw materials and at what price? Will suppliers be able to deliver my orders on time? What actions will competitors take, and even who will be my competitors in the future? The need to deal with the rising uncertainty in the business environment is another reason why effective supply chain planning and the use of data analytics are becoming increasingly important.

Broadly speaking then, effective supply chain planning and analytics consists of three major activities: demand planning, sales and operations planning, and supply planning. The focus of demand planning is developing a forecast or estimate of future demand. With a forecast in hand, sales and operations planning addresses the issue of how much of the expected demand the organization will attempt to meet, or in other words, determining its *service-level* objective. Supply planning in turn addresses the tactical issues of managing procurement, production, and distribution to ensure the targeted service level is met. In the remainder of this chapter, we address demand planning and sales and operations planning. The topic of supply planning was addressed in the previous chapter on the Strategic Management of Supply Chains.

6.3 Demand Planning

Fundamentally, demand planning is concerned with developing a point of view on what future demand will be over some forthcoming period of time (e.g. next week, month, quarter, and/ or year). This point of view of future demand or forecast of future demand drives a number of important organizational activities including:

- Determining how much of each product to produce.

- Determining how much inventory is needed to meet sales and production targets.

- Determining the capacity of resources (e.g. equipment and staff) needed to achieve the production and sales targets.

- Determining the amount of working capital that will be needed to meet production and sales targets.

Like all business activities, the process of demand planning in general and forecasting in particular can be improved. It falls to senior management to determine whether investing in such improvements is justified, for example, through an appropriate cost-benefit analysis. The remainder of this section provides a brief introduction to methods that can be used to develop a forecast of demand.

6.3.1 Forecasting Methods

Forecasting methods can be grouped in several ways. One classification, illustrated in Figure 6.1, distinguishes between formal forecasting techniques and informal approaches such as intuition, spur-of-the-moment guesses, and seat-of-the-pants predictions. Our attention here will obviously be directed to the formal methods.

Formal forecasting methods can be broadly classified as quantitative or qualitative techniques. In general, qualitative forecasting methods are often used for long-range forecasts, especially when external factors (e.g. a particularly cold winter) may play a significant role. They are also of use when historical data are very limited or nonexistent, as in the introduction of a new product or service, or estimating the impact of a global pandemic.

Some of the most significant decisions made by organizations, frequently strategic decisions, are made on the basis of *qualitative* forecasts. These often concern predicting the demand for a new product or service, a product that is reaching the end of its life, or a replacement product for an existing product. Also, qualitative techniques can be useful for predicting how the organization's outputs will evolve over time. In all of these cases, either historical data on demand are not available or the historical data that are available are no longer representative of the product's future demand.

Qualitative forecasts are made using information such as phone or mail surveys of consumers' attitudes and intentions, consumer panels, test marketing in limited areas, expert opinion and panels, and analyses of historical demand for similar products or services – a method known as *historical analogy*. One example of historical analogy would be the use of demand data for CD-ROMs to predict the demand curve for DVDs, or Broadway shows to predict the demand for movies.

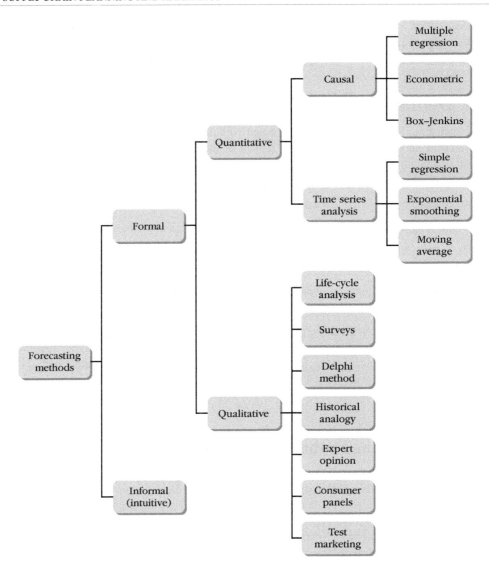

FIGURE 6.1
A Classification of
Forecasting Methods

A special type of expert panel uses what is called the *Delphi* method. The RAND Corporation developed the Delphi method as a group technique for forecasting the demand for new or contemplated products or services. The intent was to eliminate the undesirable effects of interaction between members of the group (such as loud and dominating individuals) while retaining the benefits of their broad experience and knowledge. The method begins by having each member provide individual written forecasts, along with any supporting arguments and assumptions. These forecasts are submitted to a Delphi researcher, who edits, clarifies, and summarizes the data. These data are then provided as feedback to the members, along with a second round of questions. This procedure continues, usually for about four rounds, when a consensus among panel members can often be reached on some of the issues.

Another qualitative device often used in forecasting is called *life-cycle analysis*. Experienced managers who have introduced several new products are often able to estimate how long a product will remain in each stage of its life cycle. This forecast, coupled with other market information, can produce reasonably accurate estimates of demand in the medium to long range.

Quantitative forecasting methods are generally divided between methods that simply project the past history or behavior of the variable into the future (*time series analysis*) and those that also include external data (*causal*). Time series analysis is the simpler of the two and ranges from just using an average of the past data to using regression analysis corrected for seasonality in the data. Simple projection techniques are obviously limited to, and primarily used for, very short-term forecasting. Such approaches often work well in a stable environment but cannot react to changing industry factors or changes in the national economy.

Causal methods, which are usually quite complex, include histories of external factors and employ sophisticated statistical techniques. In addition to using spreadsheets, many software packages are available for the quantitative techniques, both time series analysis and causal.

6.3.2 Factors Influencing the Choice of Forecasting Method

Which method is chosen to prepare a demand forecast depends on a number of factors. First, long-range (two- to five-year) forecasts typically require the least accuracy and are only for general (or aggregate) planning, whereas short-range forecasts require greater accuracy and are for detailed operations. Thus, the most accurate methods are usually used for short-term needs and, fortunately, the data in the near term are usually the most accurate.

Second, if the data are available, one of the quantitative forecasting methods can be used. Otherwise, nonquantitative techniques are required. Attempting to forecast without a demand history is almost as hard as using a crystal ball. The demand history need not be long or complete, but some historical data should be used if at all possible.

Third, the greater the limitation on time or money available for forecasting, the more likely it is that an unsophisticated method will have to be used. In general, management wants to use a forecasting method that minimizes not only the cost of making the forecast but also the cost of an *inaccurate* forecast; that is, management's goal is to minimize the total forecasting costs. Costs of inaccurate forecasting include the cost of over- or understocking an item, the costs of under or overstaffing, and the intangible and opportunity costs associated with loss of goodwill because a demanded item is not available.

Fourth, with the advent of computers, the cost of statistical forecasts based on historical data and the time required to make such forecasts have been reduced significantly. It has therefore become more cost-effective for organizations to develop more sophisticated forecasts.

In the remainder of this section, we briefly overview several of the quantitative forecasting methods including time series analysis and causal methods.

6.3.3 Time Series Analysis

A time series is simply a set of values of some variable measured either at regular points in time or over sequential intervals of time. We measure stock closing prices at specific points in time and quarterly sales over specific intervals of time. If, for example, we recorded the number of books sold each month of the previous year at Amazon and kept those data points in the order in which they were recorded, the 12 numbers would constitute a 12-period time series. Time series data can be collected over very short intervals (such as hourly sales at a fast-food restaurant) or very long intervals (such as the census data collected every 10 years).

6.3.3.1 Components of a Time Series

We analyze a time series because we believe that knowledge of past demand behavior might help us understand (and therefore help us predict) demand in the future, normally just the next period. Our goal is to find a forecasting model that is easy to compute and use, responsive to changes in the data, and accurate in its predictions. To begin our discussion of time series analysis, let us consider the component parts of any time series.

To analyze time series data, it is often helpful to think of it as being comprised of four components:

1. Trend, T

2. Seasonal variation, S

3. Cyclical variation, C

4. Random variation, R

The *trend* is the long-run direction of the time series, including any constant amount of demand in the data. Figure 6.2 illustrates three fairly common trend lines showing changes in demand; a horizontal trend line would indicate a constant, unchanging level of demand.

A straight line or linear trend (showing a constant amount of change, as in Panel A of Figure 6.2) could be an accurate fit to the historical data over some limited range of time, even though it might provide a rather poor fit over an entire time series. Panel B in the figure illustrates the situation of a constant percentage change. Here, changes in demand depend on the current size of the demand (rather than being constant each period, as in Panel A of Figure 6.2). The trend line shown in Panel C of Figure 6.2 resembles the life cycle or "stretched-S" growth curve that describes the demand many products and services experience over time.

Seasonal fluctuations are fairly regular fluctuations that repeat within one year's time, or whatever period encompasses the full set of seasons. Seasonal fluctuations result primarily from nature, but they are also brought about by human behavior. Sales of heart-shaped boxes of candy and pumpkins are brought about by events that are controlled by humans. Snow tires and gloves enjoy a brisk demand during the winter months, whereas sales of golf balls and bikinis peak in the spring and summer months. Of course, seasonal demand often leads or lags behind the actual season. For example, the production season for meeting retailers' demand for Christmas goods is August through September. Also, seasonal variation in events need not be related to the seasons of the year. For example, fire alarms in New York City reach a "seasonal" peak at 7 P.M. and a seasonal low at 7 A.M. every day. And restaurants reach three seasonal demand peaks every day at 7:00 A.M., 12:30 P.M., and 7 P.M.

The *cycle* or *cyclical component* is obvious only in time series that span several sets of seasons or more. A cycle can be defined as a long-term oscillation, or a swing of the data points about the trend line over a period of at least three complete sets of seasons. National economic cycles of booms as well as recessions and periods of war and peace are examples of such cycles.

Cycles, particularly business cycles, are often difficult to explain, and economists have devoted considerable research and speculation to their causes. Identification of a cyclic pattern in a time series requires the analysis of long periods of data. For most decision-making situations, forecasting the cyclic component is not considered, since long-term data are typically unavailable to determine the cycle. In addition, cycles are not likely to repeat in similar amplitude and duration; hence, the assumption of repeating history does not hold.

Random variations are, as the name implies, without a specific assignable cause and without a pattern. Random variations are the fluctuations left in the time series after the trend, seasonality, and cyclical behaviors have been accounted for. Random fluctuations can sometimes be explained after the fact, such as an increase in the consumption of energy owing to abnormally harsh weather, but cannot be systematically predicted and, hence, are not included in time series models.

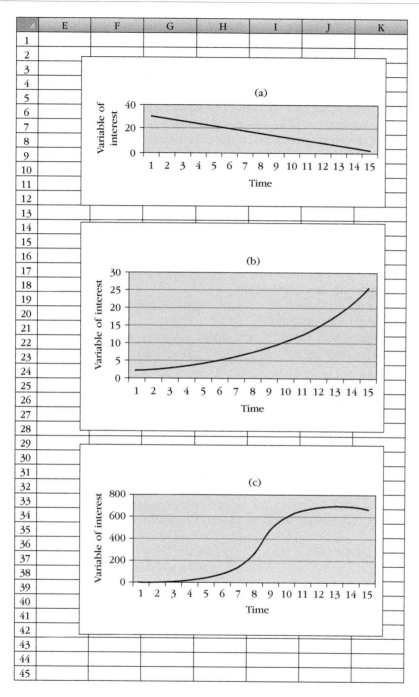

FIGURE 6.2 Three Common Trend Patterns. (a) Constant Change, (b) Constant Percent Change, and (c) Standard "S" Curve

The objective of time series analysis is to determine the magnitude of one or more of these components and to use that knowledge for the purpose of forecasting demand in the next period. We now turn our attention to three models of time series analysis:

1. Moving averages (trend component of the time series)

2. Exponential smoothing (trend component of the time series)

3. Linear trend, multiplicative model (trend and seasonal components)

6.3.3.2 Moving Averages

The *moving average* technique is one of the simplest ways to predict a trend. It generates the next period's forecast by averaging the actual demand for only the last n time periods (n is often in the range of 4 to 7). That is: Forecast = average of actual demand in past n periods.

Any data older than n are thus ignored. Note also that the moving average weights old data just the same as more recent data. The value of n is usually based on the expected seasonality in the data, such as 4 quarters or 12 months in a year; that is, n should encompass one full cycle of data. If n must be chosen arbitrarily, then it should be based on experimentation; that is, the value selected for n should be the one that works best for the available historical data.

Mathematically, a forecast using the moving average method is computed as

$$F_{t+1} = \frac{1}{n} \sum_{i=(t-n+1)}^{t} A_i$$

where

t = period number for the current period
F_{t+1} = forecast for the next period
A_i = actual observed value in period i
n = number of periods of demand to be included in the moving average (known as the "order" of the moving average)

To illustrate the use of the moving average, data were collected on quarterly iPad sales, as shown in Figure 6.3. The graph with the actual time series of iPad sales and moving average illustrates how a moving average smoothes out the fluctuations in the time series.

The plot also demonstrates one of the weaknesses associated with using moving averages. Specifically, whenever there is an upward or downward trend in the data, a forecast based on the moving average approach will always lag the time series. Referring to Figure 6.3, sales of the iPad peaked in the first quarter of 2014 and have been generally declining since. However, the four-period moving average line is typically above the actual demand in each period following the first quarter of 2014. Therefore, the moving average approach is most appropriate for situations where the decision maker would like to simply smooth out fluctuations around an assumed horizontal trend.

A refinement of the moving average approach is to vary the weights assigned to the values included in the average. Such an approach is called a *weighted moving average*, with the newer data typically weighted more heavily, rather than using equal weights. The reason for weighting the newer data more heavily is that since it is more current, it is often considered to be more representative of the future.

Referring to the iPad sales data, a weighted moving average could be constructed by weighting the fourth-oldest observation in the average by 0.1, the third-oldest by 0.2, the second-oldest by 0.3, and the most recent observation by 0.4. Of course, any combination of weights that summed to 1 could be used. Likewise, any number of periods could be included in the weighted moving average.

Time series analysis involves two inherent difficulties, and a compromise solution that addresses both must be sought. The first problem is producing as good a forecast as is possible with the available data. Usually, this can be interpreted as using the most current data because those data are more representative of the present behavior of the time series or iPad demand in our case. In this sense, we are looking for an approach that is responsive to recent changes in the data.

The second problem is to smooth the random behavior of the data. That is, we do not want a forecasting system that forecasts increases in demand simply because the last period's demand

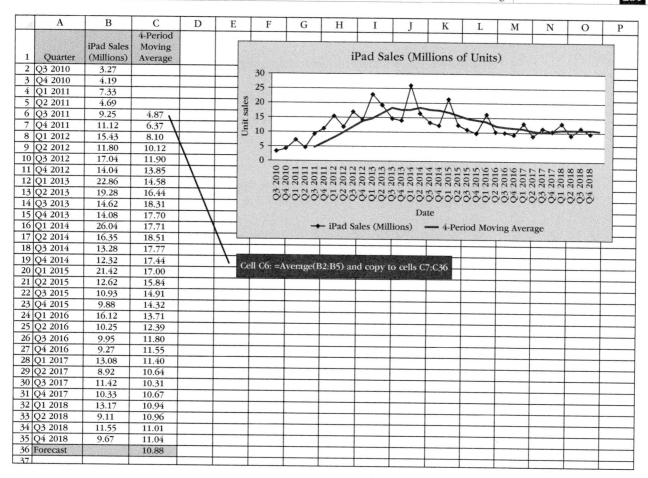

FIGURE 6.3 Four-Period Moving Average of iPad Sales. Statista, www.statista.com, January 11, 2019

suddenly increased, nor do we want a system that indicates a downturn just because demand in the last period decreased. All time series data contain a certain amount of this erratic or random movement. It is impossible for a manager to predict this random movement of a time series, and it is folly to attempt it. The only reasonable conclusion is to avoid overreaction to a fluctuation that is simply random. The general interpretation of this objective is that several periods of data should be included in the forecast so as to "smooth" the random fluctuations that typically exist. Thus, we are also looking for an approach that is stable, even with erratic data.

Clearly, methods used to attain both responsiveness and stability will be somewhat contradictory. If we use the most recent data so as to be responsive, only a few periods will be included in the forecast; but if we want stability, large numbers of periods will be included. The only way to decide how many periods to include is to experiment with several different approaches and evaluate each on the basis of its ability to produce good forecasts and still smooth out random fluctuations.

6.3.3.3 Exponential Smoothing

As noted above, we generally want to use the most current data and, at the same time, use enough observations of the time series to smooth out random fluctuations. One technique perfectly adapted to meeting these two objectives is exponential smoothing.

The computation of a demand forecast using exponential smoothing is carried out with the following equation:

New demand forecast $= (\alpha)$ current actual demand $+ (1 - \alpha)$ previous demand forecast or

$$F_{t+1} = \alpha A_t + (1 - \alpha) F_t$$

where α is a smoothing constant that must be between 0 and 1, F_t is the exponential forecast for period t, and A_t is the actual demand in period t.

The smoothing constant can be interpreted as the weight assigned to the last (i.e. the current) data point. The remainder of the weight $(1 - \alpha)$ is applied to the last forecast. However, the last forecast was a function of the previous weighted data point and the forecast before that. To see this, note that the forecast in period t is calculated as

$$F_t = \alpha A_{t-1} + (1 - \alpha) F_{t-1}$$

Substituting the right-hand side of this formula for F_t in the original formula yields

$$F_{t+1} = \alpha A_t + \left(1 - \alpha\right)\left[\alpha A_{t-1} + \left(1 - \alpha\right) F_{t-1}\right]$$

Thus, the data point A_{t-1} receives a weight of $(1 - \alpha)\alpha$, which, of course, is less than α. Since this process is iterative, we see that exponential smoothing automatically applies a set of diminishing weights to each of the previous data points and is therefore a form of weighted averages. Exponential smoothing derives its name from the fact that the weights decline exponentially as the data points get older and older. In general, the weight of the nth most recent data point can be computed as follows:

Weight of nth most recent data point in an exponential average $= \alpha \left(1 - \alpha\right)^{n-1}$

Using this formula, the most recent data point, A_t, has a weight of $\alpha (1 - \alpha)^{1-1}$, or simply α. Similarly, the second most recent data point, A_{t-1}, would have a weight of $\alpha (1 - \alpha)^{2-1}$, or simply $\alpha(1 - \alpha)$. As a final example, the third most recent data point, A_{t-2}, would have a weight of $\alpha (1 - \alpha)^{3-1}$, or $\alpha (1 - \alpha)^2$.

The higher the weight assigned to the current demand, the greater the influence this point has on the forecast. For example, if α is equal to 1, the demand forecast for the next period will be equal to the value of the current demand. The closer the value of α is to 0, the closer the forecast will be to the previous period's forecast for the current period. (Check these results by using the equation.)

Rearranging the terms of the original formula provides additional insights into exponential smoothing, as follows:

$$\begin{aligned} F_{t+1} &= \alpha A_t + (1 - \alpha) F_t \\ &= \alpha A_t + F_t - \alpha F_t \\ &= F_t + \alpha A_t - \alpha F_t \\ &= F_t + \alpha (A_t - F_t) \end{aligned}$$

In this formula, $A_t - F_t$ represents the forecast error made in period t. Thus, the formula shows that the new forecast developed for period $t + 1$ is equal to the old forecast plus some percentage of the error (since α is between 0 and 1). Notice that when the forecast in period t exceeds the actual demand in period t, we have a negative error term for period t and the new forecast will be reduced. On the other hand, when the forecast in period t is less than the actual demand in period t, the error term in period t is positive and the new forecast will be adjusted higher.

Our objective in forecasting with exponential smoothing is to choose the value of α that results in the best forecasts. Forecasts that tend always to be too high or too low are said to be biased – positively if too high and negatively if too low. The value of α is critical in producing good forecasts, and if a large value of α is selected, the forecast will be very sensitive to the current demand value. With a large α, exponential smoothing will produce forecasts that react quickly to fluctuations in demand. This, however, is irritating to those who have to constantly change plans and activities on the basis of the latest forecasts. Conversely, a small value of α weights historical data more heavily than current demand and therefore will produce forecasts that do not react as quickly to changes in the data; that is, the forecasting model will be somewhat insensitive to fluctuations in the current data.

Generally speaking, larger values of α of are used in situations in which the data exhibit low variability and can therefore be plotted as a rather smooth curve. On the other hand, a lower value of α should be used for data that exhibit a high degree of variability. Using a high value of α in a situation where the data exhibit a high degree of variability would result in a forecast that constantly overreacted to changes in the most current demand.

As with n, the appropriate value of α is usually determined by trial and error; values typically lie in the range of 0.01 to 0.30. One method of selecting the best value is to try several values of α with the existing historical data (or a portion of the data) and choose the value of α that minimizes the average forecast errors. As you can probably imagine, spreadsheets can greatly speed the evaluation of potential smoothing constants and the determination of the best value of α. For example, in the spreadsheet shown in Figure 6.4 that forecasts iPad sales using exponential smoothing, various values of α can be easily investigated by simply changing the value of α entered in cell B1. Also note that when exponential smoothing is used, a forecast value is needed for the very first period. Since a forecast value for the first period is typically not available, it is common to simply set $F_1 = A_1$.

Thus, the forecasts proceed as follows:

$$F_1 = A_1 = 3.27$$
$$F_2 = 0.2(3.27) + 0.8(3.27) = 3.27$$
$$F_3 = 0.2(4.19) + 0.8(3.27) = 3.45$$

and so on as shown in Figure 6.4.

6.3.3.4 Simple Regression: The Linear Trend Multiplicative Model

Figure 6.5 presents the quarterly number of visitors to a fictitious website providing medical information (Medfo.com). Demand is seen to be generally increasing, as is indicated by the linear trend line fit by Excel to the data. Given the apparent quality of the fit between quarter number and the number of visitors, the webmaster has decided to try a linear trend time series model. The model parameters for the regression model with quarter number as the independent variable and visitor volume as the dependent variable were calculated in cells A19 and B19 using Excel's LINEST function (discussed later). However, careful observation of the data reveals that the number of visitors is above average during the second and fourth quarters and below average during the first and third quarters, perhaps due to weather-related illnesses.

There are several versions of the linear trend time series model (for example, there are additive and multiplicative versions) and also many different approaches for determining the components of these forecasting models. We will present one method for determining the two demand components of a simple multiplicative model. Conceptually, the model is presented as

$$\text{Forecast} = \text{trend component (or } T) \times \text{seasonal component (or } S)$$

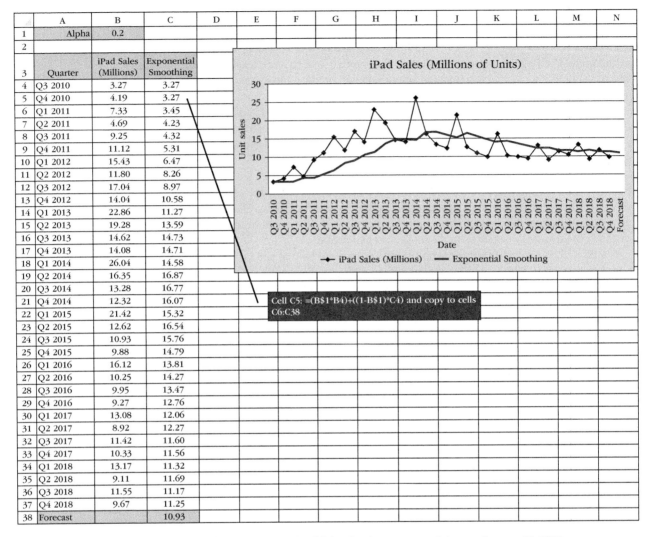

	A	B	C
1	Alpha	0.2	
2			
3	Quarter	iPad Sales (Millions)	Exponential Smoothing
4	Q3 2010	3.27	3.27
5	Q4 2010	4.19	3.27
6	Q1 2011	7.33	3.45
7	Q2 2011	4.69	4.23
8	Q3 2011	9.25	4.32
9	Q4 2011	11.12	5.31
10	Q1 2012	15.43	6.47
11	Q2 2012	11.80	8.26
12	Q3 2012	17.04	8.97
13	Q4 2012	14.04	10.58
14	Q1 2013	22.86	11.27
15	Q2 2013	19.28	13.59
16	Q3 2013	14.62	14.73
17	Q4 2013	14.08	14.71
18	Q1 2014	26.04	14.58
19	Q2 2014	16.35	16.87
20	Q3 2014	13.28	16.77
21	Q4 2014	12.32	16.07
22	Q1 2015	21.42	15.32
23	Q2 2015	12.62	16.54
24	Q3 2015	10.93	15.76
25	Q4 2015	9.88	14.79
26	Q1 2016	16.12	13.81
27	Q2 2016	10.25	14.27
28	Q3 2016	9.95	13.47
29	Q4 2016	9.27	12.76
30	Q1 2017	13.08	12.06
31	Q2 2017	8.92	12.27
32	Q3 2017	11.42	11.60
33	Q4 2017	10.33	11.56
34	Q1 2018	13.17	11.32
35	Q2 2018	9.11	11.69
36	Q3 2018	11.55	11.17
37	Q4 2018	9.67	11.25
38	Forecast		10.93

Cell C5: =(B$1*B4)+((1-B$1)*C4) and copy to cells C6:C38

FIGURE 6.4   Using Exponential Smoothing to Forecast iPad Sales. Statista, www.statista.com, January 11, 2019

In order to develop this model, we must first analyze the available historical data and attempt to break down the original data into trend and seasonal components.

As indicated earlier, a trend is a long-run direction of a series of data. In our example, the trend in the number of visitors to the website appears to follow a straight line – that is, to be a trend with respect to time. In order to project this linear trend into the future, we first estimate the parameters of the trend line using simple linear regression discussed in more detail shortly. Referring to Figure 6.5, we see that the trend line for the visitor volume is

$$\text{Number of visitors}_X = 27{,}253 + 15{,}462X$$

where X represents the quarter number.

As was noted earlier, and made even clearer in Figure 6.5, the data are above the trend line for all of the second and fourth quarters and below the trend line for all of the first and third quarters. Recognizing this distinct seasonal pattern in the data should allow us to estimate the amount of seasonal variation around the trend line (i.e. the seasonal component, S).

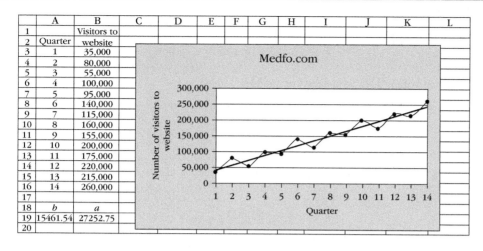

	A	B	C	D	E	F	G	H	I	J	K	L
1		Visitors to										
2	Quarter	website										
3	1	35,000										
4	2	80,000										
5	3	55,000										
6	4	100,000										
7	5	95,000										
8	6	140,000										
9	7	115,000										
10	8	160,000										
11	9	155,000										
12	10	200,000										
13	11	175,000										
14	12	220,000										
15	13	215,000										
16	14	260,000										
17												
18	b	a										
19	15461.54	27252.75										
20												

FIGURE 6.5
Number of Visitors
to Medfo.com

The trend line is the long-run direction of the data and does not include any seasonal variation. We can compute, for each available quarter of data, a measure of the "seasonality" in that quarter by dividing the actual number of visitors by the computed value of the trend for that quarter. This method is known as the ratio-to-trend method. Using the notation developed thus far, we can write the seasonal component for any quarter X as

$$\frac{Y_X}{T_X}$$

where Y_X is the number of visitors to the website in quarter X and T_X is the trend estimate for quarter X. Excel's TREND function (discussed later) can be used to calculate the trend estimate for each quarter, as shown in column C of Figure 6.6.

Consider the second and third quarters of the first year. The computed trend value for each of these two quarters is

$$T_2 = 27,253 + 15,462(2) = 58,176$$

	A	B	C	D
1				Seasonal
2		Visitors to		factor
3	Quarter	website	T_x	(Y/T)
4	1	35,000	42714.29	0.82
5	2	80,000	58175.82	1.38
6	3	55,000	73637.36	0.75
7	4	100,000	89098.90	1.12
8	5	95,000	104560.44	0.91
9	6	140,000	120021.98	1.17
10	7	115,000	135483.52	0.85
11	8	160,000	150945.05	1.06
12	9	155,000	166406.59	0.93
13	10	200,000	181868.13	1.10
14	11	175,000	197329.67	0.89
15	12	220,000	212791.21	1.03
16	13	215,000	228252.75	0.94
17	14	260,000	243714.29	1.07

FIGURE 6.6 Calculation of Quarterly Seasonal Factors

and

$$T_3 = 27,253 + 15,462(3) = 73,638$$

The actual volumes (in thousands) in quarters 2 and 3 were

$$Y_2 = 80,000$$
$$Y_3 = 55,000$$

Dividing Y_2 by T_2 and Y_3 by T_3 gives us an indication of the seasonal pattern in each of these quarters:

$$\frac{Y_2}{T_2} = \frac{80,000}{58,176} = 1.38$$

$$\frac{Y_3}{T_3} = \frac{55,000}{73,638} = 0.75$$

Similar indices were calculated for all quarters in the spreadsheet shown in Figure 6.6. In quarter 2, the actual number of visitors was 138% of the expected volume (i.e. the number of visitors predicted on the basis of a linear trend), but in quarter 3, the number of visitors was only 75% of that expected. Note that over the 14 periods of available data we have four observations of the number of visitors for the first and second quarters and three observations of the number of visitors for the third and fourth quarters. We can compute the average of each of these sets of quarterly data and use the averages as the seasonal components for our time series forecasting model, as shown in Figure 6.7.

Using both the trend component and the seasonal component, the webmaster now can forecast the number of visitors to the site for any quarter in the future. First, the trend value for the forecast quarter is computed and is, in turn, multiplied by the appropriate seasonal factor. For example, to forecast for the last quarter of the fourth year (quarter 16) and the first quarter of the fifth year (quarter 17), the webmaster would first compute the trend values:

$$T_{16} = 27,253 + 15,462(16) = 274,645$$
$$T_{17} = 27,253 + 15,462(17) = 290,107$$

Next, the forecast is computed by multiplying the trend value by the appropriate seasonal factor. For the fourth-quarter S_4 is 1.07, so the forecast for quarter 16 is

$$F_{16} = 274,645 \times 1.07 = 293,870$$

The seasonal factor for the first quarter is 0.90; therefore, the forecast for quarter 17 is

$$F_{17} = 290,107 \times 0.90 = 261,096$$

FIGURE 6.7
Calculating Seasonal
Component (S) for
Quarters 1 Through 4

	A	B	C	D	E
1	Year	Quarter 1	Quarter 2	Quarter 3	Quarter 4
2	1	0.82	1.38	0.75	1.12
3	2	0.91	1.17	0.85	1.06
4	3	0.93	1.1	0.89	1.03
5	4	0.94	1.07		
6	Average	0.90	1.18	0.83	1.07

These two forecasts correspond to the previous results for fourth and first quarters in that the fourth-quarter forecast is above the trend and the first-quarter forecast is below the trend. Seasonal indexes can be used in a similar way with exponential smoothing or moving averages. Again, simple ratios are calculated, averaged out, and then applied to the exponential smoothing or moving average forecasts.

6.3.4 Causal Forecasting with Regression

In this section, we discuss causal forecasting with regression analysis. We begin the section with an overview of the simple linear regression model.

6.3.4.1 The Simple Linear Regression Model

Simple linear regression analysis involves using the values of a single independent variable to predict or explain the values of the dependent variable. If we wish to include more than one independent variable in our model, we have a *multiple regression model*, which is beyond our scope here. Prior to using simple linear regression analysis, it is appropriate to plot the values of the independent and dependent variables to visually verify a key assumption that the variables are linearly related to one another. Figure 6.8 illustrates three common ways two variables can be related to each other. If it is discovered that the variables are not linearly related to each other, it may be possible to "transform" one or both of the variables so that they are approximately linearly related. Frequently used transformations include taking the square root, inverse, or logarithm of the data.

The mathematical form of the simple linear regression model is as follows:

$$Y = \alpha + \beta X + \varepsilon$$

where X corresponds to the independent variable, Y to the dependent variable, and α and β are the parameters of the model. According to this model, the value of the dependent variable Y is equal to the regression model constant plus the model parameter β times the value of the independent variable X. Also notice that a *residual,* or error term, is included in the model to account for the fact that it is typically not possible to determine the exact value of the dependent variable based on just the two model parameters α and β and therefore there is likely to be a difference between the predicted value of the dependent variable and the actual value.

Because our regression models are typically based on sample data, the true parameters of the regression model are unknown. In cases where the regression model is based on sample data, the model is written as

$$Y = a + bX$$

where a and b are estimates based on sample data of the unknown population parameters α and β, respectively.

Earlier in your academic career, perhaps in an algebra class, you may have seen the equation of a line expressed as

$$y = mx + b$$

where y represents the value on the vertical axis, x corresponds to the value on the horizontal axis, m represents the slope of the line (i.e. the amount the line rises for a unit change in x), and b corresponds to the y-intercept, or the point where the line intersects the y-axis (which is also the point on the line where $x = 0$). The regression model presented earlier is completely analogous to this, the only differences being that a is used to represent the y-intercept (b in the standard equation of a line) and b is used in place of m to represent the slope of the line.

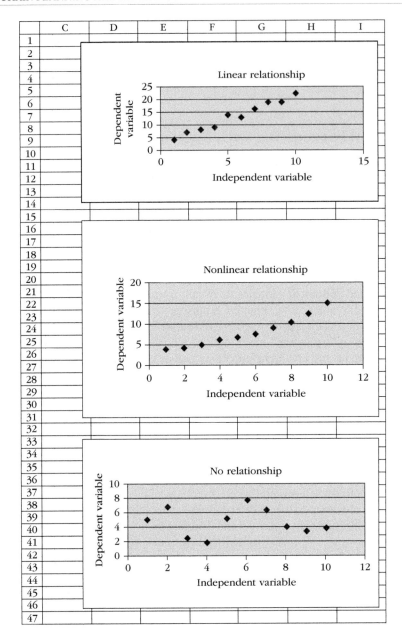

FIGURE 6.8
Example Relationships
Between Variables

There are a wide variety of ways that a line could be fit to a set of data. One way would be to simply use a ruler and visually determine which line provides the best fit to a set of points plotted on a graph by adjusting the angle of the ruler. The best line could then be drawn and its equation determined. While this approach often yields good results, statisticians and decision makers often favor the use of more formal, less subjective approaches. The approach typically used is based on minimizing the sum of the squared vertical distances between the data points and the regression line fit to the data points (that is, the *errors* from using the regression line to make a prediction). Because of this, it is often referred to as the *least squares regression* model.

To illustrate how the least squares approach works, consider the small data set consisting of four observations as shown in Figure 6.9. In the figure, the vertical distance from each point to the line fit to the data is shown. These vertical distances can be thought of as errors, e_i, since they represent the difference between what the line predicts the value of Y will be for a given value of X and what Y actually is for the given value of X. The least squares approach fits the line to the data such that the sum of the squared errors, $\sum e_i^2$, is minimized. In the example shown in Figure 6.9, this means fitting a line to the data so that the sum is minimized.

Fortunately, spreadsheets and other software programs have built-in functions that greatly facilitate the calculation of the regression model parameters. For example, Excel's LINEST function can be used to calculate the regression model parameters. The syntax of this function is

$$= \text{LINEST(range of } Y \text{ values, range of } X \text{ values)}$$

Note that the LINEST function is a special type of function called an *array function* because it is used to return multiple values (i.e. the parameters a and b) rather than a single value such as the average or standard deviation of a range of data. Because we are using the LINEST function as an array function, when the equation is entered into a cell, we must press and hold down the Ctrl key and the Shift key as we press the Enter key. When using an array function in Excel, you must first highlight the cells where you want the results of the function displayed and then enter the formula in the usual way beginning with an equal (=) sign.

Another useful Excel function is the TREND function. This function fits a straight line to a range of X and Y values and then returns the values that would appear on the trend line for each value of X. The syntax for the TREND function is as follows:

$$= \text{TREND(range of } Y \text{ values, range of } X \text{ values)}$$

Like the LINEST function, the TREND function returns multiple values; therefore, the Ctrl and Shift keys must be held down while pressing the Enter key.

To illustrate the use of the LINEST and TREND functions, sample data for the square footage and price of homes in a particular neighborhood are shown in Figure 6.10. The goal in developing the model is to be able to predict the price of a house based on its square footage. Note: to enter the TREND function in column D, cells D3:D12 were first highlighted. Then while these cells were highlighted, the formula shown in the callout in Figure 6.10 was entered. Once the formula was entered, the Ctrl and Shift keys were held down while the Enter key was pressed. Likewise, cells B15:C15 were highlighted prior to entering the LINEST function.

In developing regression models, the analyst must often make judgments about how to handle outliers, or extreme data points. In some cases, outliers may be the result of data entry errors and therefore should be corrected. At other times, outliers may be the result of unusual circumstances (e.g. a labor strike and a natural disaster); in these cases, they can perhaps be justifiably omitted

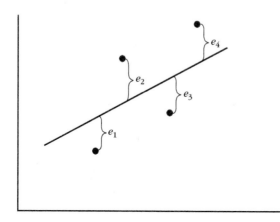

FIGURE 6.9 Least Squares Approach to Fitting Line to Set of Data

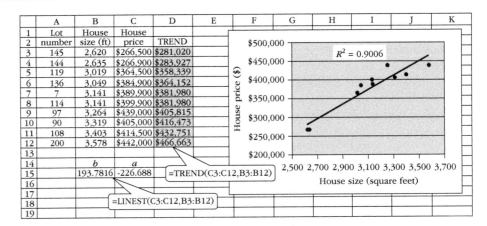

FIGURE 6.10 Using Excel's LINEST and TREND Functions

or adjusted. In the remaining cases where no error or unusual circumstance can be discovered, it is difficult to justify eliminating or adjusting an outlier.

The issue of outliers is important because of the impact these data points can have on the regression model. As is illustrated in Figure 6.11, an outlier is a data point that has an extreme value on the independent variable dimension, an extreme value on the dependent variable dimension, or on both dimensions. As shown in the top graph in Figure 6.11, an outlier on the independent variable

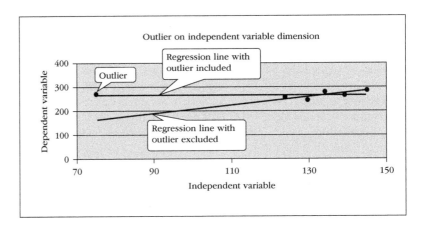

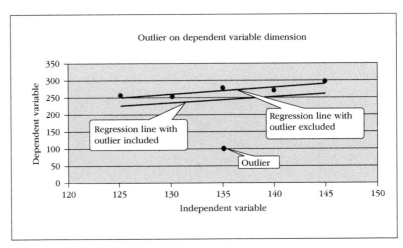

FIGURE 6.11 Impact of Outliers on Regression Line Fit to Set of Data

dimension can have a profound impact on the regression line fit to the data, altering both the slope of the line and its *y*-intercept. In contrast, an outlier on the dependent variable dimension primarily shifts the *y*-intercept of the regression line in the direction of the outlier but generally has little impact on the slope of the line. Thus, the predicted change in the dependent variable for a unit change in the independent variable remains much the same in the case where the outlier is the result of an extreme value of the dependent variable. This is not the case when the outlier is the result of an extreme value of the independent variable, since the slope of the regression line also changes.

Having gone through the process of fitting a linear trend line to a set of data, it is next logical to consider how well the model fits the data. One way to assess the quality of the model is to simply plot the trend line and data on the same graph and visually evaluate the quality of the fit. Another, more objective, approach is to determine the proportion of variation in the dependent variable that can be explained by the independent variable. This measure is called the *coefficient of determination* and is typically represented symbolically as R^2. Since R^2 corresponds to the proportion of variation in the dependent variable that is explained by the independent variable, it should not surprise you to learn that the R^2 will be between 0 and 1. An R^2 of 1 indicates that the independent variable completely accounts for the variation in the dependent variable, even though it may not *cause* it. (There could be a third factor causing both, or the direction of causation may be the reverse. For example, it has been observed that overweight people drink more diet soft drinks than others, but which causes which?) In this case, all data points will fall precisely on the trend line. Alternatively, an R^2 of 0 indicates that there is no relationship between the independent and dependent variables.

The *correlation coefficient, R,* is another measure for assessing the extent to which two variables are related to each other. More specifically, the correlation coefficient measures the degree to which there is a linear relationship between two variables and is calculated by taking the square root of R^2 and appending a plus or minus sign, according to whether the slope is positive or negative. The correlation coefficient can thus range between -1 and $+1$. It is positive if *Y* tends to increase as *X* increases and negative if *Y* tends to increase when *X* decreases. Like the coefficient of determination, a correlation of 0 suggests that there is no linear relationship between *X* and *Y*, but a large value does not necessarily imply causation.

Both R^2 and *R* are typically provided as standard output of statistical packages, including spreadsheets. Finally, we note that because R^2 provides precise information regarding the percent of *Y*'s variation that can be explained by *X*, its interpretation is more meaningful than the correlation coefficient, and it is therefore the preferred measure of the two.

6.3.4.2 Regression Analysis Assumptions

In addition to the assumption that there is a linear relationship between the dependent and independent variables, regression analysis also assumes the following:

- *The residuals are normally distributed.* That is, for a particular value of the independent variable, a plot of all the errors around the regression line at this point would be normally distributed.

- *The expected value of the residuals is zero, $E(e_i) = 0$.* The plot of the errors would be centered about 0 in terms of their mean value. This also implies that the expected value of the dependent variable falls directly on the regression line for each possible value of the independent variable.

- *The residuals are independent of one another.* The value of one error does not have any effect on the value of another error, either positive or negative.

- *The variance of the residuals is constant.* The spread of the errors about the regression line does not vary with the independent variable.

Perhaps the most common way to verify that these assumptions are met is to perform an analysis of the residuals (or errors). For a particular value of X, the residual is calculated by subtracting the trend line estimate of Y for that value of X from the actual Y value corresponding to that value of X. For example, referring to Figure 6.10, the residual for the 2620 ft^2 house is the actual price of the house minus what the trend line estimates a 2620 ft^2 house would cost, or

$$\$266,500 - \$281,020 = -\$14,520.$$

6.3.4.3 Using the Regression Model

In addition to ensuring that the regression model assumptions are not violated, it is equally important to understand how to properly use the results of a regression analysis. Generally speaking, new users of regression analysis should be aware of three common pitfalls. The first pitfall, or improper use of a regression model, is to use it to make predictions outside the range of data that were used to develop the model. As an example, it would be improper to attempt to use the regression model fit to the data in Figure 6.10 to predict the price of a 4500 ft^2 house. This would be improper since none of the observations in the data set are representative of a house of this size. Attempting to use a model to predict values that are not represented in the data set is called *extrapolation.*

A second pitfall to be aware of is attempting to overly *generalize* the results of a regression model. For example, the data shown in Figure 6.10 were collected for the new homes built in a particular subdivision in North Carolina. It is not at all clear whether the regression model fit to this data could be used to predict the price of a new house in other subdivisions in the same city. And it is even less likely that the regression model could be used to predict the price of a new house in other parts of the state or regions of the country.

The problem of generalization may at first glance appear to be similar to the problem of extrapolation. There is, however, an important difference. In the case of extrapolation, we are attempting to make a prediction beyond the values in our data set. Referring to our house price model, attempting to use the model to predict the price of a 4500 ft^2 home in the subdivision of interest is an extrapolation of the model.

Alternatively, generalization occurs when we attempt to use the model fit to data collected from one population to predict values in another population. Again, referring to the house price model, we can think of each subdivision or region as a population. Clearly, house construction costs could vary from subdivision to subdivision based on a variety of factors, including the cost of the land, quality of schools, distance to important destinations, available amenities, and so on. Thus, the problem of extrapolation occurs when we attempt to use a model to predict values for a population of interest that is not represented in our data set, while generalization occurs when we are attempting to use the model to make predictions for an entirely different population. Of course, it is possible to make both mistakes at the same time.

The final pitfall to be aware of is to improperly assume that the development of a regression model proves that there is a cause-and-effect relationship between the independent and dependent variables. Generally speaking, a regression model can be used to help validate that such a cause-and-effect relationship exists, but the actual existence of a cause-and-effect relationship must have its basis in some underlying theory. As a rather extreme example, suppose you collected monthly data for a number of years on ice cream sales and the number of drownings in the United States. If you were to develop a regression model with the number of drownings as the dependent variable and ice cream sales as the independent variable, you would likely get a pretty high R^2. Of course, concluding that the use of ice cream causes drownings (or worse, vice versa) on the basis of this regression model is a bit ludicrous. What is actually happening in this situation is that both variables are correlated with another variable – namely, weather. Thus, we reiterate that while regression analysis may be well suited to establishing the extent that two variables are correlated with each other, inferring causation between the variables is far more tenuous.

6.3.5 Assessing the Accuracy of Forecasting Models

Up to this point, we have discussed several statistical methods for developing forecasts including moving averages, exponential smoothing, the linear trend multiplicative model, and developing causal models using regression analysis. With so many alternative methods for developing a forecast, a logical question is how does one go about selecting a forecasting approach? The answer is that we assess and compare alternative forecasting models by measuring the forecast error. Forecast error can be quantified as the difference between the forecast and the actual demand in a given period. Three commonly used measures of forecast error are the mean absolute deviation (MAD), the mean absolute percent error (MAPE), and bias:

$$\text{MAD} = \frac{1}{n} \sum_{i=1}^{n} |F_i - A_i|$$

$$\text{MAPE} = \frac{1}{n} \sum_{i=1}^{n} \frac{|F_i - A_i|}{A_i}$$

$$\text{Bias} = \frac{1}{n} \sum_{i=1}^{n} (F_i - A_i)$$

where

F_i = the forecast of demand for period i
A_i = the actual demand in period i
n = the number of periods of data

Though similar in appearance, these measures assess forecasting performance from different perspectives. Since the MAD and MAPE sum only the absolute values of the forecast error, both positive and negative errors add to the sum of the *errors* and the average size of the error (MAD) and average percent error (MAPE) are determined. Both of these measures provide a sense of the *accuracy* of the forecasting model. A manager might use this knowledge by saying, "Our forecasts are typically accurate only within 10%; we had better maintain an extra stock of 10% or so to hedge against the potential error in our forecast."

Bias, on the other hand, indicates whether the forecast is typically too low or too high, and by how much. A manager knowing this might say, "On average, we are forecasting 10% too high; we can safely make 5–10% less to hedge against this potential error in our forecast." That is MAD and MAPE show the average size and percent of the error relative to demand, whereas bias shows the average total error and its direction.

Clearly, the preferred forecasting method is the one that produces the least amount of forecast error. However, because measures of accuracy (MAD and MAPE) and measures of bias provide a different perspective of forecast errors, it is important to use both types of measures in combination to get a complete picture of how well the forecasting models perform.

To illustrate this, suppose that two methods of forecasting are tested against demand data for a four-month period. Method A gives forecasts for January through April of 105, 107, 109, and 109, respectively; Method B yields forecasts of 108, 107, 105, 106; and the actual demands are

103, 106, 106, and 111. MAD for Method A would be $(|105 - 103| + |107 - 106| + |109 - 106| + |109 - 111|)/4 = 2$, and bias of $((105 - 103) + \cdots + (109 - 111))/4 = 1$. Thus, MAD indicates that the average forecast error using Method A is 2, and the bias of +1 indicates that the forecast tends to exceed demand. For Method B, MAD is 3 but bias is 0 (the reader should verify this). With Method B, positive and negative forecast errors cancel out, resulting in no bias. However, examining the MAD indicates that even though there is no bias, the actual forecasts developed using Method B are less accurate than those generated using Method A. Thus, with Method B the average forecast is off by 3; however, Method B is as likely to overestimate as to underestimate demand.

The ratio of bias to MAD is also sometimes used as a "tracking signal" in certain adaptive forecasting models. Briefly, adaptive forecasting models *self-adjust* by increasing or decreasing the smoothing constant α when the tracking signal becomes too large. Since this ratio can range only from −1 to +1, its absolute value is used as the smoothing constant, α. Ratios approaching −1 indicate that all or most of the forecast errors tend to be negative (i.e. the forecasts are too low). Ratios approaching +1 indicate that all or most of the forecast errors tend to be positive. Regardless, as the tracking signal gets closer to −1 or +1, α automatically increases, making the model more responsive and (it is hoped) leading to smaller forecast errors.

6.4 Sales and Operations Planning

Once the forecast of demand is developed, the next decision is to determine how much of the forecasted demand the organization should attempt to meet in order to achieve key organizational goals such as target levels of profitability. Determining the amount of demand to meet is operationalized by specifying target service levels or the percentage of demand to be met. These target service levels will likely differ by product and by customer. Therefore, while Demand Planning focuses on forecasting demand, Sales and Operations Planning addresses the question of how much of expected demand the organization should attempt to meet in order to be best positioned to achieve broader organizational goals.

In addition to determining appropriate service-level targets, another important purpose of Sales and Operations Planning is to develop an overall plan for the entire enterprise that is to be used to guide the efforts of all the different areas in the organization. This is in contrast to more traditional practices where each area of the organization develops its own plan independent of the plans of other departments. For example, consider the consequences of marketing developing a sales plan based on a newly developed promotional campaign without considering the production plan developed by the operations group.

To avoid the problems that can occur when each area of the organization develops its own plans independently, the Sales and Operations Planning process seeks to develop an *Aggregate Plan* that effectively matches supply and demand. It is referred to as an aggregate plan because the basic approach is to work with only "aggregate" units (that is, units grouped or bunched together such as product families). Aggregate resources are also used such as total number of workers and hours of available equipment time. In addition to helping coordinate planning across departments, the Aggregate Plan also helps minimize the consequences of short-sighted day-to-day decisions on longer-term performance. The Henry Ford Hospital provides an excellent example of how Aggregate Planning can be used to ensure that short-term decisions don't undermine the attainment of longer-term performance.

At the Henry Ford Hospital, aggregate planning was used to match available capital, workers, and suppliers to a highly variable pattern of demand. The hospital had 903 beds arranged into 30 nursing units, with each nursing unit containing 8 to 44 beds. For the purposes of planning, each of the nursing units is treated as an independent production facility.

A number of factors complicate the aggregate planning process at the hospital. First, as noted, demand exhibits a high degree of variability. For example, in one particular year, the average number of occupied beds was 770, but in one eight-week period during the year the average number of occupied beds was only 660. Further analysis uncovered that the number of occupied beds could change by as many as 146 beds in less than two weeks!

A second complicating factor was the large penalty incurred by the hospital for HMO patients who require care but could not be admitted because a bed was not available. In these cases, not only did the hospital lose revenue but it also had to pay another hospital for the patient's treatment. For a simple obstetrics case, the cost to the Henry Ford Hospital was approximately $5000 for each HMO patient that had to be turned away.

A third complication was the tight labor market for registered nurses, making it difficult and expensive to change the rate of production. On average, it took the hospital 12 to 16 weeks to recruit and train a nurse at a cost of approximately $7600.

A final complication is the high costs associated with idle facilities. The hospital estimated that the cost of one eight-bed patient module exceeds $35,000 per month.

At the Henry Ford Hospital, developing an Aggregate Plan is critical because without taking a sufficiently long-term view, decisions in the short-run may adversely impact performance over the longer term. For example, during one period at the hospital, a decision was made to reduce the staff. However, shortly after the staff was reduced, it was determined that the staff was needed and thus new staff members were recruited. The net result was that the hospital incurred both the costs associated with reducing the staff and the costs associated with recruiting and training new staff a short time later. A more effective approach would have been to compare the costs of reducing and hiring the staff with the costs of having excess staff during this period of time. Of course, the only way to accomplish this is to forecast far enough into the future to estimate if and when demand will pick up again.

6.4.1 Aggregate Planning Strategies

There are two Aggregate Planning strategies, known as *pure strategies,* which provide managers with a starting point to improve upon when developing an aggregate plan.

1. *Level production.* With a level production strategy, the same amount of output is produced each period. Inventories of finished goods (or backlogged demand) are used to meet variations in demand, at the cost of investment in inventory or the expense of a shortage (stock-out). The advantage is steady employment with no expenses associated with changing the size of the workforce. Since service outputs cannot be generally inventoried, this strategy, for a service firm, normally results in a constant but poorly utilized workforce (e.g. repair crews, cashiers, bank tellers, and food servers) of a size large enough to meet peak demand. If the service firm uses a smaller workforce, it risks losing some demand to a competitor.

2. *Chase demand.* In this strategy, production is identical to the expected demand for the period in question. This is typically obtained either through overtime or hiring and laying off. (Again, this assumes sufficient equipment and facilities.) The advantage of this policy is that there are no costs entailed by inventories of finished goods, except perhaps for buffer stock (also called safety stock) and no shortage costs, including loss of goodwill. Service firms use this strategy by making use of overtime, split shifts, overlapping shifts, call-in workers, part-time workers, and so on.

The vast majority of firms often achieve higher performance and lower costs by developing a hybrid (mixed) strategy that combines aspects of both pure strategies. Such strategies include a combination of using overtime, hiring and layoffs, subcontracting, and inventory. Product firms in particular have the option of trading off investment in inventories of finished goods for changes in capacity level or vice versa. For example, a product firm can build up inventory ahead of demand rather than acquiring all the capacity needed to meet peak demand.

6.4.2 Determining the Service Level: An Example Using the Newsvendor Problem

As was just noted, a key outcome associated with Sales and Operations Planning is determining the service level (or fill rate) for the organization's products and customers. In this section, we illustrate the process with the widely studied newsvendor problem.

The newsvendor problem applies to situations where there is a perishable product (e.g. newspapers, pumpkins, and mother's day cards) that must be ordered before the actual demand for the product will be known. The ordered product is either sold or scrapped depending on the actual level of demand. The following example will be used to illustrate the methodology.

For three years, Kacy has sold newspapers each morning on the corner of First and Banker Streets. She purchases the newspapers at 6:00 A.M. and stands on the corner from 6:30 to 8:30 A.M. each morning before walking two blocks to school. Kacy purchases the newspapers for $1.00 and sells them for $1.50.

It seems that Kacy is frequently either running out of newspapers before 8:30 A.M. and therefore missing potential sales or having several papers left over that cannot be sold or returned to the publisher. She wonders if there is some "best" order quantity to stock each day that will produce the largest average profit over the long run. Kacy knows that she cannot perfectly predict daily demand and that she is bound to run out on some days and to overstock on others. But she feels that a consistent policy will maximize her expected profits over the long run. How many newspapers should Kacy order each day to maximize her expected profit over the long run?

To answer this question, we must first consider the demand for newspapers on Kacy's corner. Suppose that Kacy has kept a record of the number of papers demanded each day for the last 100 days. That is, even when she ran out of papers, Kacy remained on the corner until 8:30 A.M. to count the number of people who asked for a paper, even though she had to tell them she had none left. Her summary of the 100 days' of demand is presented in Table 6.1.

Kacy's lowest demand was for 28 newspapers, and her highest demand was for 32. Therefore, she at least knows that she should never order more than 32 or less than 28.[1] But Kacy could order any of the five quantities in between on any given day. What order size will maximize profit?

One way to determine the optimal order quantity is through *incremental* (or *marginal*) analysis. The idea here is to start with a very small order for the items and compare the advantages and disadvantages of *ordering one more* unit. The advantage, of course, is the potential profit the unit might bring. The disadvantage is that the extra unit might not be sold (or needed), and then a loss might be sustained. Of course, for very low initial orders, the probability that one more unit will be sold is quite high, so it usually makes sense to order at least one more unit. For example, in Kacy's case, if she were to order 27 or less, it would certainly makes sense to order at least one more paper because the probability of selling it is 100%.

Table 6.1   Kacy's Newspaper Demand

Demand (newspapers)	Frequency (days)	Relative frequency
28	10	0.10
29	20	0.20
30	35	0.35
31	25	0.25
32	10	0.10
Total	100	1.00

[1] We are making the assumption here that 100 days' history is enough to predict the future. Obviously demand can change; Kacy must be aware of the possibility and monitor for it.

The next step is to consider adding still another unit to the order if the expected profit from ordering another unit is greater than (or equal to) the expected loss. This process is continued until ordering one additional unit cannot be justified on the basis of the expected return for that unit.

To frame this process mathematically, let

$$p = \text{the probability of selling } at \; least \text{ one more unit}$$
$$1 - p = \text{the probability of } not \text{ selling the unit}$$
$$\text{MCO} = \text{the marginal cost of ordering one more unit}$$
$$\text{MPU} = \text{the marginal profit of selling one more unit}$$

Then the expected gain from ordering one more unit is the probability of selling the unit times the profit to be gained. Mathematically,

$$\text{Expected gain} = p(\text{MPU})$$

Similarly, the expected loss from ordering the unit is the probability that it will not sell times the loss incurred (usually its price or price less salvage value):

$$\text{Expected loss} = (1 - p)\text{MCO}$$

Now, it is logical to keep increasing the order size as long as the expected gain from ordering one more unit exceeds the expected loss of ordering one more unit. Expressing this logic mathematically will allow us to identify that critical value of p *below which* it is not worthwhile to order another unit.

$$\text{Expected gain} \geq \text{Expected loss}$$
$$p(\text{MPU}) \geq (1 - p)\text{MCO}$$

or

$$p \geq \frac{\text{MCO}}{\text{MCO} + \text{MPU}}$$

In Kacy's problem, MCO = \$1.00 (the cost of the papers; there is no salvage value) and MPU = \$0.50 (the profit per paper sold). Thus

$$p \geq \frac{1.00}{1.00 + 0.50} = 0.67$$

Therefore, Kacy should increase the number of papers she stocks as long as the probability of selling the last paper stocked is at least 67%. Now we need a table showing the probability of selling N or more units as a function of order size, N. This is shown in Table 6.2.

Table 6.2 Probability Table for Kacy's Newspaper Ordering Problem

Order size, N	Probability of selling N units	Cumulative probability of selling more than N units
28	0.10	0.90
29	0.20	0.70
30	0.35	0.35
31	0.25	0.10
32	0.10	0

For example, if Kacy goes from stocking 28 to 29 papers, she has a 90% probability of selling the twenty-ninth paper. Notice that our value for $p = 0.67$ falls between $N = 29$ and $N = 30$. That is, if our current order size was 29, the probability is 0.70 of selling 30, 31, or 32 units, which is greater that the critical probability of 0.67, so stocking 30 is acceptable. But at $N = 30$, the value of 0.35 is less than 0.67, so 31 cannot be justified. Thus, our process is to go down the table of N values until we reach the first cumulative probability that is *less* than p.

This is a common problem. Retailers purchase seasonal clothing, perishable foods, and other items such as Valentine candy and cards, pumpkins, and fruit and vegetables in anticipation of demand. If too little demand is realized, then the remaining goods are scrapped if not salable or "reduced for clearance," either at a loss or at a reduced profit.

For Kacy's newspaper ordering problem, a fairly simple discrete probability distribution was used to model the demand for Newspapers. It is important to point out that the methodology presented here is equally applicable to situations where more complicated continuous distributions (e.g. the normal distribution) are used to model demand. In these cases, p is calculated as described above. Then the order quantity that provides this percent of area in the upper tail can be found. For example, if the demand is assumed to be normally distributed as shown in Figure 6.12, then the order quantity N can be determined such that there is the probability p that demand will exceed N. In other words, N is found such that the area in the upper tail equals p.

Taking these ideas one step further, we can more formally define the notion of service level. Conceptually, there are two possible outcomes when we order N units. One outcome is that the demand is less-than-or-equal to the N units that were ordered, in which case we have ordered enough to meet the demand. On the other hand, when demand exceeds the N units that were ordered, a stockout is incurred. In supply chain management terminology, the probability that we will have sufficient inventory to meet demand is referred to as the service level. The service level or the probability that demand will be less than or equal to the order quantity N is shown as the shaded region in Figure 6.13. Likewise, the stockout risk or the probability that demand will be greater than the order quantity of N is given by the area in the unshaded upper tail. Returning to the formula we used to calculate the critical value of p, we observe that the critical value of p provides a lower bound on the stockout risk.

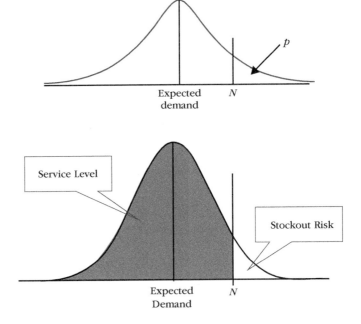

FIGURE 6.12 Determining the Order Size When the Distribution of Demand is Normally Distributed

FIGURE 6.13 Determining the Service Level and Stockout Risk.

Finally, before leaving the topic of Sales and Operations Planning, it is important to point out the importance of modeling demand properly. Too often managers rely too heavily on means at the expense of giving adequate attention to the variation and shape of the underlying distribution of demand. To illustrate this, assume that after collecting additional data, Kacy revised her probabilities of selling various quantities of newspapers as shown in Table 6.3 (we assume that the cost and revenue are unchanged). The expected daily demand for newspapers is 30.05 in both scenarios. However, using the same p of 0.67, the order quantity now changes from 29 papers to 28 papers despite the fact that the expected demand is identical in both scenarios. This example illustrates the impact the distribution of demand has on the determination of the optimal order quantity and the importance of modeling the distribution of demand as accurately as possible.

6.4.3 Collaborative Planning, Forecasting, and Replenishment

While using tools like aggregate planning to coordinate activities across all areas within an enterprise is important, this alone is not sufficient to meet world class standards of supply chain performance. Rather, organizations must be just as diligent in coordinating their planning efforts beyond their organizational walls and include their supply chain partners as well. Indeed, by recognizing their common business goals and interests, joint sales and operations plans can be developed that are mutually beneficial to all supply chain partners. Thus, in stark contrast to the more traditional "arms-length" approach of dealing with suppliers, more enlightened companies seek to build relationships with their supply chain partners based on collaboration. These organizations have learned that by viewing their suppliers and customers as partners, all parties in the supply chain benefit.

One approach that is gaining increasing acceptance to help coordinate the joint planning of supply chain partners is Collaborative Planning, Forecasting, and Replenishment (CPFR). Originally developed by Walmart in the mid-1990s, the goal of CPFR is to identify ways to improve supply chain performance (e.g. reducing inventory) by sharing planning and ordering information.

As its name suggests, CPFR involves three stages. In the first stage, planning, the supply chain partners define the parameters of their working relationship, identify key supply chain performance measures, and work toward developing a joint business plan. In the second stage, forecasting, the supply chain partners work together to develop a forecast and to continuously keep the forecast up to date as new information becomes available. Each partner in the supply chain has a different perspective and access to different information (e.g. upcoming sales promotions, store openings, products that will be discontinued) and the accuracy of the forecast can be improved by considering these multiple perspectives. The final stage, replenishment, focuses on execution. During this phase, actual orders are placed, orders are shipped, and payments are made. Across all three phases, performance is analyzed on key performance metrics and opportunities for improving the process are identified.

Table 6.3 Revised Probability Table for Kacy's Newspaper Ordering Problem

Order size, N	Probability of selling N units	Cumulative probability of selling more than N units
28	0.15	0.85
29	0.25	0.60
30	0.20	0.40
31	0.20	0.20
32	0.20	0

6.4.4 Back to Supplier Selection: Lifecycle Assessment

In addition to selecting suppliers that will be strong collaborative partners, sustainability is becoming an increasingly important consideration in selecting suppliers, as was noted in the previous chapter. The use of analytics can play an important role in assessing the environmental impact of potential suppliers. Conducting a lifecycle assessment (LCA) is the most comprehensive analytical approach for assessing the environmental impact of a product throughout its entire life. More specifically, as the name implies, LCA is an end-to-end approach beginning with obtaining raw materials from the planet and ending with the return of the materials to the planet. As such, LCA evaluates all aspects and stages in the supply chain including use of energy, raw materials, production, transportation, recycling, and disposal. The International Organization for Standardization (ISO) has developed the ISO 14040 standard for Life Cycle Assessment that defines the following four steps:

1. Define the scope of what will be included in the assessment. For example, will the assessment focus only on the environmental impact of the product to be acquired, the business unit of the supplier that produces the product, or the entire organization of the supplier?

2. Identify and inventory all the inputs within the defined scope used to produce the products across the entire supply chain.

3. Determine the environmental impact of inputs identified across the entire supply chain.

4. Assess the overall environmental impact.

Because of the enormous amount of data required to perform a lifecycle assessment, for practical reasons averages are typically used. For example, each truck in a fleet likely has different rates of emissions due to the age of the truck, the type of truck, how the truck is maintained, and even the driving habits of the truck driver and the routes used. Thus, rather than attempting to measure the actual emissions associated with each truck shipment, average values for the distance shipped and the amount of emissions per mile driven can be used to estimate the emissions associated with truck shipments. Additionally, for practical reasons, the number of tiers in the supply chain may be limited. For example, the lifecycle assessment could be limited to two tiers of suppliers up the supply chain and two tiers of customers down the supply chain.

Tetra Pak, headquartered in Switzerland, well illustrates how organizations use LCA. Tetra Pak is a producer of packaging equipment for liquid products such as milk, juices, and water. Its experience with performing LCAs dates back to the mid-1980s, with its most recent LCA being completed in 2020. The LCA performed was compliant with ISO 14040 and was reviewed by an independent research organization. The goal for the 2020 LCA was to provide Tetra Pak and its customers with a comprehensive view of its environmental impact. As such, the LCA investigated 11 different areas of environmental impact including climate change, acidification, air pollution, and energy use.

The results of the LCA identified areas where Tetra Pak had the lowest environmental impact, as well as areas where its products had a higher environmental impact than competing products. For example, Tetra Pak discovered that its beverage cartons had a higher environmental impact in the use of nature category compared to other options for packaging. Overall, Tetra Pak found that its beverage cartons had a lower impact on the climate than packaging made from glass, metal, and plastic. To illustrate the level of detail that went into the 2020 LCA, Tetra Pak determined that if producers in Europe switched from using bottles made of PET (a type of plastic) to a type of its beverage cartons, the amount that carbon emissions reduced equaled the emissions generated by 60,500 cars. Of course, this was based on the use of averages, including the assumption that, in Europe, an average car travels 12,000 km per year.

Sustainable supply chain performance measures traditionally focused on greenhouse gas emissions. However, as the Tetra Pak discussion highlights, performance measures across multiple dimensions need to be considered to appropriately assess supply chain performance in terms of sustainability.

ISO 14031 is a standard that provides specific guidance for evaluating environmental performance and performance indicators. Per ISO 14031, performance measures are classified as:

- *Environmental condition indicators.* Broadly assess an organization's environmental efforts and results to minimize its environment impact.

- *Management performance indicators.* Specific focus on measuring environmental efforts and performance of organization's management.

- *Operational performance indicators.* Specific focus on measuring environmental efforts and performance of organization's operations.

6.5 Inventory and Supply Planning

A key aspect of SCM is the use of inventory. In this section, we look at the use of inventory and the factors that help determine the best levels of inventories to hold. We describe the various functions of inventories, the forms of inventories, specific inventory-related costs, and the two fundamental inventory decisions all organizations must make. The appendix to this chapter provides additional details on using the economic order quantity model to determine how much inventory should be ordered.

Although inventory is inanimate, the topic of inventory and inventory control can arouse completely different sentiments in the minds of people in various departments within an organization. The salespeople generally prefer large quantities of inventory to be on hand. This allows them to meet customers' requests without having to wait. Customer service is their primary concern. The accounting and financial personnel see inventory in a different light. High inventories do not translate into high customer service in the accountant's language; rather, they translate into large amounts of tied-up capital that could otherwise be used to reduce debt or for other, more economically advantageous purposes. From the viewpoint of the operations manager, inventories are a tool that can be used to promote efficient operation of the production facilities. Neither high inventories nor low inventories per se are desirable; inventories are simply allowed to fluctuate so that production can be adjusted to its most efficient level. And top management's concern is with the "bottom line" – what advantages the inventories are providing versus their costs.

6.5.1 Functions of Inventories

There are many purposes for holding inventory, but, in general, inventories have five basic functions. Be aware that inventories will not generally be identified and segregated within the organization by these functions and that not all functions will be represented in all organizations:

1. *Transit inventories.* Transit inventories exist because materials must be moved from one location to another. (These are also known as *pipeline inventories*.) A truckload of merchandise from a retailer's regional warehouse to one of its retail stores is an example of transit inventory. This inventory results because of the transportation time required.

2. *Buffer inventories.* Another purpose of inventories is to protect against the uncertainties of supply and demand. Buffer inventories – or, as they are sometimes called, *safety stocks* – serve to cushion the effect of unpredictable events. The amount of inventory held over

and above the expected demand requirement is considered to be buffer stock held to meet any demand in excess of what is expected. The higher the level of inventory, the better the customer service – that is, the fewer the *stockouts* and *backorders*. A stockout exists when a customer's order for an item cannot be filled because the inventory of that item has run out. If there is a stockout, the firm will usually back-order the item immediately, rather than wait until the next regular ordering period.

3. Anticipation inventories. An anticipated future event such as a price increase, a strike, or a seasonal increase in demand is the reason for holding anticipation inventories. For example, rather than operating with excessive overtime in one period and then allowing the production system to be idle or shut down because of insufficient demand in another period, inventories can be allowed to build up before an event to be consumed during or after the event. Manufacturers, wholesalers, and retailers build anticipation inventories before occasions, such as Christmas and Halloween, when demand for specialized products will be high.

4. *Decoupling inventories.* It would be a rare production system in which all equipment and personnel operated at exactly the same rate. Yet, if you were to take an inspection tour through a production facility, you would notice that most of the equipment and people were producing. Products move smoothly even though one machine can process parts five times as fast as the one before or after it. An inventory of parts between machines, or fluid in a vat, known as decoupling inventory, acts to disengage the production system. That is, inventories act as shock absorbers, or cushions, increasing and decreasing in size as parts are added to and used up from the stock.

Even if a preceding machine were to break down, the following machines could still produce (at least for a while), since an in-process inventory of parts would be waiting for production. The more inventories management carries between stages in the manufacturing and distribution system, the less coordination is needed to keep the system running smoothly. Clearly, there is an optimum balance between inventory level and coordination in the operations system. Without decoupling inventories, each operation in the plant would have to produce at an identical rate (a paced line) to keep the production flowing smoothly, and when one operation broke down, the entire plant would come to a standstill.

5. *Cycle inventories.* Cycle inventories – or, as they are sometimes called, *lot-size* inventories – exist for a different reason from the others just discussed. Each of the previous types of inventories serves one of the major purposes for holding inventory. Cycle inventories, on the other hand, result from management's attempt to minimize the total cost of carrying and ordering inventory. If the annual demand for a particular part is 12,000 units, management could decide to place one order for 12,000 units and maintain a rather large inventory throughout the year or place 12 orders of 1000 each and maintain a lower level of inventory. But the costs associated with ordering and receiving would increase. Cycle inventories are the inventories that result from ordering in batches, or "lots," rather than as needed.

6.5.2 Forms of Inventories

Inventories are usually classified into four forms, some of which correspond directly with the previous inventory functions but some of which do not:

1. *Raw materials.* Raw materials are objects, commodities, elements, and items that are received (usually purchased) from outside the organization to be used directly in the

production of the final output. When we think of raw materials, we think of such things as sheet metal, flour, paint, structural steel, chemicals, and other basic materials. But nuts and bolts, hydraulic cylinders, pizza crusts, syringes, engines, frames, integrated circuits, and other assemblies purchased from outside the organization would also be considered part of the raw materials inventory.

2. *Maintenance, repair, and operating (MRO) supplies.* MRO supplies are items used to support and maintain the operation, including spares, supplies, and stores. Spares are sometimes produced by the organization itself rather than purchased. These are usually machine parts or supplies that are crucial to production. The term *supplies* is often used synonymously with *inventories*. The general convention, and the one that we will adopt in this book, is that supplies are stocks of items used (consumed) in the production of goods or services but are not directly a part of the finished product. Examples are copier paper, staples, pencils, and packing material. Stores commonly include both supplies and raw materials that are kept in stock or on shelves in a special location.

3. *Work in process (WIP).* WIP inventory consists of all the materials, parts, and assemblies that are being worked on or are waiting to be processed within the operations system. Decoupling inventories are an example of WIP. That is, they are all the items that have left the raw materials inventory but have not yet been converted or assembled into a final product.

4. *Finished goods.* The *finished goods* inventory is the stock of completed products. Goods, once completed, are transferred out of WIP inventory and into the finished goods inventory. From here, they can be sent to distribution centers, sold to wholesalers, or sold directly to retailers or final customers.

As you can see from this discussion, the inventory system and the operations system within an organization are strongly interrelated. Inventories affect customer service, utilization of facilities and equipment, capacity, and efficiency of labor. Therefore, the plans concerning the acquisition and storage of materials, or "inventories," are vital to the production system.

The ultimate objective of any inventory system is to make decisions regarding the level of inventory that will result in a good balance between the purposes for holding inventories and the costs associated with them. Typically, we hear inventory management practitioners and researchers speaking of *total cost minimization* as the objective of an inventory system. If we were able to place dollar costs on interruptions in the smooth flow of goods through the operations system, on not meeting customers' demands, or on failures to provide the other purposes for which inventories exist, then minimization of total costs would be a reasonable objective. But since we are unable to assign costs to many of these subjective factors, we must be satisfied with obtaining a good balance between the costs and the functions of inventories.

6.5.3 Inventory-Related Costs

There are essentially five broad categories of costs associated with inventory systems: ordering or setup costs, inventory carrying or holding costs, stockout costs, opportunity costs, and cost of goods. This section looks at these costs in turn.

6.5.3.1 Ordering or Setup Costs

Ordering costs are costs associated with outside procurement of material, and *setup costs* are costs associated with internal procurement (i.e. internal manufacture) of parts or material. Ordering costs include writing the order, processing the order through the purchasing system, postage, processing invoices, processing accounts payable, and the work of the receiving department, such as handling, testing, inspection, and transporting. Setup costs also include writing orders and processing for the internal production system, setup labor, machine downtime due to a new setup (e.g. cost of an idle, nonproducing machine), parts damaged during setup (e.g. actual parts are often used for tests during setup), and costs associated with employees' learning curve (e.g. the cost of early production spoilage and low productivity immediately after a new production run is started).

6.5.3.2 Inventory Carrying or Holding Costs

Inventory *carrying* or *holding* costs have the following major components:

- Capital costs

- Storage costs

- Risk costs

Capital costs include interest on money invested in inventory and in the land, buildings, and equipment necessary to hold and maintain the inventory, an item of special interest to both financial and top management. These rates often exceed 20% of the cost of the goods. If these investments were not required, the organization could invest the capital in an alternative that would earn some return on investment.

Storage costs include rent, taxes, and insurance on buildings; depreciation of buildings; maintenance and repairs; heat, power, and light; salaries of security personnel; taxes on the inventory; labor costs for handling inventory; clerical costs for keeping records; taxes and insurance on equipment; depreciation of equipment; fuel and energy for equipment; and repairs and maintenance. Some of these costs are variable, some fixed, and some "semifixed."

Risk costs include the costs of obsolete inventory, insurance on inventory, physical deterioration of the inventory, and losses from pilferage.

Even though some of these costs are relatively small, the total costs of carrying items in inventory can be quite large. Studies have found that for a typical manufacturing firm, the cost is frequently as large as 35% of the cost of the inventoried items. A large portion of this is the cost of the invested capital.

6.5.3.3 Stockout Costs

If inventory is unavailable when customers request it, a situation that marketing detests, or when it is needed for production, a stockout occurs. Several costs are associated with each type of stockout. A stockout of an item demanded by a customer or client can result in lost sales or demand, lost goodwill (which is very difficult to estimate), and costs associated with processing backorders (such as extra paperwork, expediting, special handling, and higher shipping costs). A stockout of an item needed for production results in costs for rescheduling production, costs of downtime and delays caused by the shortage, the cost of "rush" shipping of needed parts, and possibly the cost of substituting a more expensive part or material.

6.5.3.4 Opportunity Costs

Often, capacity and inventory costs can be traded off for one another. For example, capacity costs can be incurred because a change in productive capacity is necessary or because there is a temporary shortage of or excess in capacity. Why would capacity be too great or too small? If, for example, a company tried to meet seasonal demand (or any fluctuations in demand) by changing the level of production rather than by allowing the level of inventory to rise or fall, capacity would have to be increased during high-demand periods and lie idle during low-demand periods.

Also, capacity problems are often due to scheduling conflicts. These commonly arise when multiple products have to be produced on the same set of facilities.

Opportunity costs include the overtime required to increase capacity; the human resource management costs of hiring, training, and terminating employees; the cost of using less skilled workers during peak periods; and the cost of idle time if capacity is *not* reduced during periods when demand decreases.

6.5.3.5 Cost of Goods

Last, the goods themselves must be paid for. Although they must be acquired sooner or later anyway, *when* they are acquired can influence their cost considerably, as through quantity discounts.

6.5.4 Decisions in Inventory Management

The objective of an inventory management system is to make decisions regarding the appropriate level of inventory and changes in the level of inventory. To maintain the appropriate level of inventory, decision rules are needed to answer two basic questions:

1. When should an order be placed to replenish the inventory?

2. How much should be ordered?

The decision rules guide the inventory manager or computerized materials management system in evaluating the current state of the inventory and deciding if some action, such as replenishment, is required. Various types of inventory management systems incorporate different rules to decide "when" and "how much." Some depend on time and others on the level of inventory, but the essential decisions are the same. Even when complexities, such as uncertainty in demand and delivery times, are introduced, deciding "how many" and "when to order" still remains the basis of sound inventory management (refer to the appendix at the end of this chapter).

EXPAND YOUR UNDERSTANDING

1. In what situations would exponential smoothing as opposed to moving averages be most appropriate?

2. Why might a decision maker choose a qualitative forecasting method when extensive historical data are available?

3. To help pay their college expenses, two of your friends invested in a hot dog concession stand that they plan to operate during sporting events and during lunch on campus. They have asked for your help in forecasting the demand for hot dogs. How would you develop a forecast for demand, assuming that no historical data are available? What are the consequences of overestimating versus underestimating demand?

4. Provide an example of how data analytics can be used to uncover a hidden supply chain problem or inefficiency.

5. How can data analytics help managers cope with the increasing uncertainty inherent in the business environment?

6. How might you quantify the benefits of having a better forecasting model? What types of costs are incurred in developing a better forecasting model?

7. What circumstances might lead a forecaster to weight older data more heavily than recent data?

8. How might you evaluate a time series to see if there is any cyclic component in it? If you did identify a cyclic component, how could you use it to improve your forecast in the upcoming period?

9. What benefits accrue to a firm as it evolves from reporting data to using data to prescribe appropriate future actions?

10. Why is it important for all areas across the enterprise to be working off of the same forecast of demand?

11. What other inventory situations are similar to the "newsvendor problem" discussed in the chapter?

12. In making reservations for services, a common approach for dealing with the uncertain demand is to "overbook" to avoid the costs of no-shows. How ethical is this?

13. When determining the order size N when the distribution of demand is continuous, should the calculated value of N be rounded?

14. Do any of the five functions and four forms of inventories exist in service firms? If so, which ones, and why? If not, how are the functions served?

15. Contrast the functions and forms of inventories. Does every form exist for each function and vice versa, or are some more common?

Apply Your Understanding

Rush Airlines

Rush Airlines is a new low-cost airline that began operating three years ago. Its strategy is to identify pairs of cities that have a large number of travelers that need to commute between them and offer point-to-point flights between the cities. To keep its costs low, it has standardized its fleet of five planes on Boeing 737-800 aircraft. To further keep its costs down, it leases planes that are 10–15 years old at an average annual cost of $579,258. While the airline competes on the basis of offering low airfares, it is does not accept that low airfares must come at the expense of convenience. Thus, in addition to only offering point-to-point travel, the airline also offers its passengers the most leg room of any major airline. To accomplish this, it has configured its planes with 120 seats whereas other airlines squeeze in 160 seats in the same plane. Another way the company offers greater convenience to its customers is that it offers a full refund to passengers who cancel their reservation.

Perhaps as a result of its refund policy, one issue the company has been struggling with is no-shows. Every time a plane is in the air with an empty seat, the company has lost out on potential revenue. On the other hand, when a flight is overbooked and more passengers show up than the available seats, the company offers $250 gift cards to entice passengers to switch to a later flight. However, if it is the last flight of the day, the company also provides passengers with an extra $200 to cover a hotel stay and a meal.

To better understand the problem with no-shows, the company collected data on no-shows over the last 200 flights between New York City and Dallas. Currently, the airline has one plane dedicated to serving these cities and offers four flights a day between them (two a day in each direction). Total flight time including taxiing to and from the runway is 3.25 hours. The table below summarizes the no-show data collected:

Number of no-shows	Number of flights
0	50
1	60
2	40
3	30
4	20

The airfare for the flight between NYC and Dallas is $200. There are four major cost categories: fuel cost, the lease cost of the aircraft, flight staff cost, and maintenance costs. The fuel cost for the flight between NYC and Dallas is currently $4500 based on a fuel price of $1.85/gallon. The flight between NYC and Dallas is staffed with a pilot, copilot, and two flight attendants at an average cost of $629.20 per flight. In terms of maintenance cost, Rush creates a reserve fund for maintenance based on both the hourly length of the flight and the number of flights for each aircraft. The hourly charge for the maintenance reserve fund is $450 per hour (including taxiing time). In addition, there is a flat $320 maintenance charge per flight.

As noted earlier, the aircraft dedicated to the NYC/Dallas route makes four flights per day. The plane operates 300 days per year and the other 65 days are reserved for maintenance.

Questions

1. How many tickets would you recommend Rush sell for each NYC/Dallas flight (excluding the last flight of the day) to maximize its expected profit?

2. How many tickets would you recommend Rush sell for its last flight of the day between NYC and Dallas flight to maximize its expected profit?

3. In what ways is the challenge facing Rush Airlines both similar to but also different from the standard newsvendor problem?

Bardstown Box Company

Bardstown Box Company is a small, closely held corporation in Bardstown, Kentucky. Its stock is divided among three brothers, with the principal shareholder being the founding brother, Bob Wilson. Bob formed the company 20 years ago when he resigned as a salesman for a large manufacturer of corrugated boxes.

Bob attributes his success to the fact that he can serve the five-state area he considers "his territory" better than any of his large competitors. Bardstown Box supplies corrugated cartons to many regional distilleries and to several breweries. Also, it prints standard-size boxes for many small manufacturing firms in the region. Bob feels that the large box manufacturers cannot economically provide this personal service to his accounts.

Bob recognizes the danger of becoming too dependent upon any one client and has enforced the policy that no single customer can account for over 20% of sales. Two of the distilleries account for 20% of sales each, and hence are limited in their purchases. Bob has persuaded the purchasing agents of these two companies to add other suppliers, since this alternative supply protects them against problems Bardstown might have such as shipping delays, paper shortages, or labor problems.

Bardstown currently has over 600 customers with orders ranging from a low of 100 boxes to blanket orders for 50,000 boxes per year. Boxes are produced in 16 standard sizes with special printing to customers' specifications. Bardstown's printing equipment limits the print to two colors. The standardization and limited printing allow Bardstown to be price-competitive with the big producers while also providing service for small orders and "emergency" orders that large box manufacturers cannot provide.

Such personal service, however, requires tight inventory control and close production scheduling. So far, Bob has always forecast demand and prepared production schedules on the basis of experience, but because of the ever-growing number of accounts and changes in personnel in customer purchasing departments, the accuracy of his forecasts has been rapidly declining. The number of backorders is on the increase, late orders are more common, and inventory levels of finished boxes are also on the increase. A second warehouse has recently been leased because of the overcrowding in the main warehouse. Plans are to shift some of the slower-moving boxes to the leased space.

There has always been an increase in demand for boxes just before the holiday season, when customers begin stocking up. This seasonality in demand has always substantially increased the difficulty of making a reliable forecast.

Bob feels that it is now important to develop an improved forecasting method to help smooth production and warehousing volume. He has compiled the following demand data.

Sales (in number of boxes)

Month	20X1	20X2	20X3	20X4	20X5
January	12,000	8,000	12,000	15,000	15,000
February	8,000	14,000	8,000	12,000	22,000
March	10,000	18,000	18,000	14,000	18,000
April	18,000	15,000	13,000	18,000	18,000
May	14,000	16,000	14,000	15,000	16,000
June	10,000	18,000	18,000	18,000	20,000
July	16,000	14,000	17,000	20,000	28,000
August	18,000	28,000	20,000	22,000	28,000
September	20,000	22,000	25,000	26,000	20,000
October	27,000	27,000	28,000	28,000	30,000
November	24,000	26,000	18,000	20,000	22,000
December	18,000	10,000	18,000	22,000	28,000

Questions

1. Develop a forecasting method for Bardstown and forecast the total demand for 20X6.

2. Should Bob's experience with the market be factored into the forecast? If so, how?

EXERCISES

6.1 Plot the following data and then calculate and plot a three-period moving average. Then calculate and plot a five-period moving average. What do you observe in comparing the plots of the three- and five-period moving averages?

Period	1	2	3	4	5	6	7	8	9	10
Demand	60	52	55	42	57	33	26	42	35	31

6.2 Referring to Exercise 1, develop a forecast for period 11 using exponential smoothing and three values of α: 0.05, 0.30, and 0.90. Plot the actual data and the exponential averages for the three values of α. What do you observe?

6.3 Referring to Exercises 1 and 2, compare all five forecasting models. Which one would you recommend the firm use? Why?

6.4 Referring to the data in Exercise 1, use Excel's Solver or trial and error to find the value of α that minimizes the MAD. Restrict the value of α to be between 0.05 and 0.30.

6.5 Consider the following data for a children's toy:

Month	J	F	M	A	M	J	J	A	S	O
Demand (000)	0.2	0.5	1.0	2.0	4.0	8.0	25	45	59	66

(a) Forecast November demand using a three-month moving average.

(b) Forecast November demand using exponential smoothing and a smoothing constant of 0.3.

(c) Forecast November demand using linear regression.

(d) Plot the data and the linear trend line from c. What appears to be happening? Can you intuitively forecast the demand in November?

6.6 Given the following data, use a trend line and seasonals to predict demand for 20X8.

Year	Winter	Spring	Summer	Fall
20X4	123	133	172	281
20X5	155	189	205	286
20X6	151	186	288	303
20X7	178	225	272	296

6.7 Given the data below of visits to a walk-in medical clinic:

Month	20X4	20X5	20X6
January	12,000	15,000	15,000
February	8,000	12,000	22,000
March	18,000	14,000	18,000
April	13,000	18,000	18,000
May	14,000	15,000	16,000
June	18,000	18,000	20,000
July	17,000	20,000	28,000
August	20,000	22,000	28,000
September	25,000	26,000	20,000
October	28,000	28,000	30,000
November	18,000	20,000	22,000
December	18,000	22,000	28,000
Total	209,000	230,000	265,000

(a) Fit a linear trend line to the data and plot both the data and the trend line. What does the plot tell you?

(b) Develop a linear trend, multiplicative model for the data, including seasonality and forecast visits to the clinic for each month of 20X7.

(c) Use exponential smoothing with an α of 0.3 and forecast each month of 20X7, assuming after each forecast that the value calculated in (a) above is the actual demand. For F_1, use December 20X6 sales.

(d) Calculate MAD, MAPE, and bias resulting from the calculations in (b). What do they indicate?

6.8 Historical data suggests that demand for strawberries at Mary's Berry Patch is distributed as follows:

Demand (quarts)	Probability
13,000	0.1
15,000	0.5
18,000	0.3
20,000	0.1

Mary orders berries on Monday morning from a large wholesaler and pays $0.40 per quart. Any berries not sold at the retail price of $0.95 per quart are sold for $0.30 per quart to a local business that makes strawberry jelly. How many quarts of berries should Mary purchase to maximize profits?

6.9 Mario's Pizza serves pizza by the slice and does a substantial lunch business. The following table provides demand information based on an analysis of the last six months. Mario's direct cost for pizza is $2. He sells each pizza for a total of $5 in revenue. If Mario wants to maximize profits, how many pizzas should he make each day? Assume any pizzas left over at the end of the day must be disposed of and cannot be sold the following day.

Pizza demand	Probability
45	0.15
46	0.15
47	0.25
48	0.20
49	0.15
50	0.10

6.10 Referring to Exercise 6.9, develop a simulation model to estimate the annual daily profit for order quantities of 45–50. Are the results from the simulation model consistent with what you would expect given the optimal order quantity you calculated in Exercise 6.9?

BIBLIOGRAPHY

Bartmess, A., and K. Cerny. Building Competitive Advantage Through a Global Network of Capabilities. Chapter 7 In R. A. Hayes, Pisano, G. P., and D. M. Upton: *Strategic Operations: Competing Through Capabilities*. New York: Free Press, 1996.

Davenport, T. "Putting the Enterprise into the Enterprise System." *Harvard Business Review* (July–August 1998): 121–131.

Dignan, L. "Is Dell Hitting the Efficiency Wall?" MSNBC News.com, July 29, 2002, pp. 1–5.

Dvorak, P. "Clarity Is Missing Link in Supply Chain." *Wall Street Journal* (May 18, 2009): A1, A14.

Engardio, P. "Why the Supply Chain Broke Down." *Business Week* (March 19, 2001): 41.

Ferguson, B. R., "Implementing Supply Chain Management." *Production and Inventory Management Journal* 40 (Second Quarter 2000): 64–67.

Fisher, M. L., J. H. Hammond, W. R. Obermeyer, and A. Raman. "Making Supply Meet Demand in an Uncertain World." *Harvard Business Review* 72 (May–June 1994): 83–93.

Grant, D. B., A. Trautrims, and C.Y. Wong, *Sustainable Logistics and Supply Chain Management, 2nd Edition*. Kogan Page, 2017.

Guide Jr., V. D. R., and L. N. Van Wassenhove. "The Evolution of Closed-Loop Supply Chain Research." *Operations Research* 57(1) January–February (2009): 10–18.

Hagerty, J. R., "Remade in the USA; Once Made in China: Jobs Trickle Back to U.S. Plants," *Wall Street Journal Online* (May 2, 2012).

Hagerty, J. R., "Whirlpool Jobs Return to U.S." *Wall Street Journal* (December 20, 2013), p. B4.

Lummus, R. R., and R. J. Vokurka. "Strategic Supply Chain Planning." *Production and Inventory Management Journal*, 39 (Third Quarter 1998): 49–58.

Lummus, R. R., and R. J. Vokurka. "Managing the Demand Chain Through Managing the Information Flow: Capturing 'Moments of Information'." *Production and Inventory Management Journal* 40 (First Quarter 1999): 16–20.

Mabert, V. A., A. Soni, and M. A. Venkataramanan. "Enterprise Resource Planning: Measuring Value." *Production and Inventory Management Journal* 42 (Third/Fourth Quarter 2001): 46–51.

Magretta, J. "The Power of Virtual Integration: An Interview with Dell Computer's Michael Dell." *Harvard Business Review* (March–April 1998): 72–84.

Matthews, R. G., "Mining-Gear Giants Diverge on How to Prosper," *Wall Street Journal*, March 2, 2010.

Monegain, B. "Maryland Hospital Implements ERP Technology." *Healthcare IT News*, www.healthcareitnews.com/news/maryland-hospital-implements-erp-technology, October 26, 2009.

Price, W. L., and M. Turcotte. "Locating a Blood Bank." *Interfaces* (September–October 1986): 17–26.

Quinn, F. J. "What 's the Buzz? Supply Chain Management; Part 1." *Logistics Management* 36 (February 1997): 43.

Ragins, E. J., and A. J. Greco. "Customer Relationship Management and e-Business: More Than a Software Solution." *Review of Business* (Winter 2003): 25–30.

Satariano, A., and P. Burrows. "Apple's Supply-Chain Secret? Hoard Lasers." *Bloomberg Business Week*, www.businessweek.com, November 3, 2011.

Stock, J., T. Speh, and H. Shear. "Many Happy (Product) Returns." *Harvard Business Review* 80(7) (2002): 16–17.

Tetra Pak, "Comparative Life Cycle Assessment of Tetra Pak ® Carton Packages and Alternative Packaging Systems for Beverages and Liquid Food on the European Market," www.tetrapak.com, March 9, 2020.

Tully, S. "Purchasing's New Muscle." *Fortune* (February 20, 1995): 75–83.

Verity, J. W. "Invoice? What's an Invoice?" *Business Week* (June 10, 1996): 110–112.

Walker, W. T., and K. L. Alber. "Understanding Supply Chain Management." *APICS—The Performance Advantage* 9 (January 1999): 38–43.

Appendix A

The Economic Order Quantity Model

The concept of *economic order quantity* (EOQ) applies to inventory items that are replenished in *batches* or *orders*. This is in contrast to inventory items that are replenished continuously such as through an in-house assembly line. Although we have identified a number of costs associated with inventory decisions in the chapter, only two categories, carrying cost and ordering cost, are considered in the basic EOQ model. Shortage costs and opportunity costs are not relevant because shortages and changes in capacity should not occur if demand is constant, as we assume in this basic case. The cost of the goods is considered to be fixed and, hence, does not alter the decisions as to *when* inventory should be reordered or *how much* should be ordered.

More specifically, we assume the following in the basic EOQ model:

1. Rate of demand is constant (e.g. 50 units per day).

2. Shortages are not allowed.

3. Lead times are known with certainty, so stock replenishment can be scheduled to arrive exactly when the inventory drops to zero.

4. Purchase price, ordering cost, and per-unit holding cost are independent of the quantity ordered.

5. Items are ordered independently of each other.

Let us consider a water distributor that sells 1000 5-gallon bottles per month (30 days) and purchases in quantities of 2000 bottles per order. Lead time for the receipt of an order is six days. The cost accounting department has analyzed inventory costs and has determined that the cost of placing an order is $60 and the annual cost of holding one 5-gallon bottle in inventory is $10.[1]

Under its current policy of ordering 2000 bottles per order, what is the water distributor's total annual inventory cost? Its inventory pattern is represented by the "sawtooth" curve of Figure 6A.1. For simplicity, let

$$Q = \text{order quantity}$$
$$U = \text{annual usage or demand}$$
$$C_O = \text{cost to place one order}$$
$$C_H = \text{annual holding cost per unit}$$

To determine the total annual incremental cost of the distributor's current inventory policy, we must determine two separate annual costs: total annual holding cost and total annual ordering cost.

---

[1] Sometimes holding cost is given as a fixed value per year and other times as a percentage of the value of the inventory, especially when interest charges represent the major holding costs.

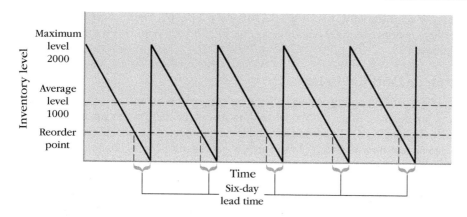

FIGURE 6A.1
Water Distributor's
Inventory Pattern

The *ordering* cost is determined by C_O, the cost to place one order ($60), and the number of orders placed per year. Since the distributor sells 12,000 5-gallon bottles per year and orders 2000 per order, it must place six (that is, 12,000/2000) orders per year, for a total ordering cost of $360 (6 orders per year × $60 per order). Using our notation, we write the annual ordering cost as

$$\text{Annual ordering cost} = \frac{U}{Q} \times C_O$$

The annual holding cost is determined by C_H, the cost of holding one 5-gallon bottle for one year ($10), and the number of bottles held as "cycle stock." Notice that the inventory level is constantly changing and that no single bottle ever remains in inventory for an entire year. On average, however, there are 1000 bottles in inventory. Consider one cycle of the distributor's inventory graph, as shown in Figure 6A.2. The inventory level begins at 2000 units and falls to 0 units before the next cycle begins. Since the rate of decline in inventory is constant (i.e. 1000 per month), the average level is 1000 units, or simply the arithmetic average of the two levels: (2000 + 0)/2 = 1000.

If, on the average, there are 1000 bottles in inventory over the entire year, then the annual inventory holding cost is $10,000 (i.e. $10 per unit × 1000 units). Or, in our general notation,

$$\text{Annual holding cost} = \frac{Q}{2} \times C_H$$

Adding annual ordering cost and annual holding cost gives the following equation for total annual cost (TAC):

$$\text{TAC} = \frac{U}{Q}C_O + \frac{Q}{2} \times C_H$$

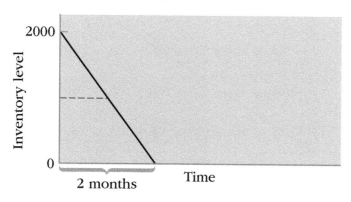

FIGURE 6A.2
Water Distributor's
Inventory Graph

For the water distributor, TAC is $360 + $10,000 = $10,360. Thus, its current inventory policy of ordering quantities of 2000 bottles is costing $10,360 per year. Is this the best policy, or can it be improved?

Finding an Optimal Policy

We can graph annual holding cost and annual ordering cost as a function of the order quantity, as shown in Figure 6A.3. Since the annual holding cost is $(Q/2)C_H$, which can be written $(C_H/2)Q$, we see that holding cost is linear and increasing with respect to Q. Annual order cost is $(U/Q)C_O$, which can be rewritten as $(UC_O)/Q$. We can see that ordering cost is nonlinear with respect to Q and decreases as Q increases.

Now, if we add the two graphed quantities for all values of Q, we have the TAC curve shown in Figure 6A.3. Note that TAC first decreases as ordering cost decreases but then starts to increase quickly. The point at which TAC is minimized is the optimal order quantity; that is, it gives the quantity Q that provides the least total annual inventory cost. This point is called the EOQ, and for this inventory problem it happens to occur where the order cost curve intersects the holding cost curve. (The minimum point is not *always* where two curves intersect; it just happens to be so in the case of EOQ.) From Figure 6A.3, we can see that EOQ is approximately 400 bottles per order.

We can compute an accurate value algebraically by noting that the value of Q at the point of intersection of the two cost lines is the EOQ. We can find an equation for EOQ by setting the two costs equal to one another and solving for the value of Q:

$$EOQ = \sqrt{\frac{2UC_O}{C_H}}$$

For the water distributor, we can compute EOQ as

$$EOQ = \sqrt{\frac{2(12,000)60}{10}} = \sqrt{144,000} = 379.5$$

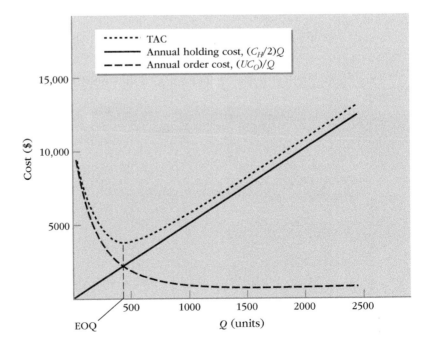

FIGURE 6A.3
Graph of Annual
Inventory Costs

Obviously, since we cannot order a fraction of a bottle, the order quantity would be rounded to 380 units.

The TAC of this policy would be

$$TAC = \left(\frac{12,000}{380}\right)60 + \left(\frac{380}{2}\right)10 = 1894.74 + 1900 = \$3794.74$$

Note that this is an improvement in TAC of $6565.26 over the present policy of ordering 2000. Actual inventory situations often exhibit relative "insensitivity" to changes in quantity in the vicinity of EOQ. To the inventory manager, what this means is added flexibility in order quantities. If, for example, shipping and handling was more convenient or economical in quantities of 500 (perhaps the items are shipped on pallets in quantities of 250), the additional 120 units per order would cost the organization only an extra $145.26 per year.

Cautions Regarding EOQ

The EOQ is a computed minimum-cost order quantity. As with any model or formula, the GIGO rule (garbage in, garbage out) applies. If the values used in computing EOQ are inaccurate, then EOQ will be inaccurate – though, as mentioned previously, a slight error will not increase costs significantly. EOQ relies heavily on two variables that are subject to considerable misinterpretation. These are the two cost elements: holding cost (C_H) and order cost (C_O). In the derivation of EOQ, we assumed that by ordering fewer units per order, the cost of holding inventory would be reduced.

Similarly, it was assumed that by reducing the number of orders placed each year, the cost of ordering could be proportionately reduced. Both assumptions must be thoroughly questioned in looking at each cost element that is included in both C_H and C_O.

For example, if a single purchasing agent is employed by the firm, and orders are reduced from 3000 to 2000 per year, does it stand to reason that the purchasing expense will be reduced by one-third? Unless the person is paid on a piecework basis, the answer is clearly no. Similarly, suppose that we rent a warehouse that will hold 100,000 items and that we currently keep it full. If the order sizes are reduced so that the warehouse is only 65% occupied, can we persuade the owners to charge us only 65% of the rental price? Again, the answer is no. Clearly, then, when costs are determined for computations, only real, out-of-pocket costs should be used. Costs that are committed, or "sunk," no matter what the inventory level or number of orders is, should be excluded.

Note also that C_H and C_O are *controllable* costs. That is, they can be reduced, if this is advantageous. This is exactly what the Japanese recognized. They saw the following problems with holding inventory:

- Product defects become hidden in the inventory, thereby increasing scrap and rework later in the production system, when defects are harder to repair. Just as important, the problem in the system that led to the defective part cannot be tracked down so easily later.

- Storage space takes up precious room and separates all the company's functions and equipment, thereby increasing problems with communication. Space itself is extremely expensive in Japan (directly increasing the variable C_H).

- More inventory in the plant means that more control is needed, more planning is required, larger systems are required to move all that stock, and in general more "hassle" is created, which leads to errors, defects, missed deliveries, long lead times, and more difficulty in product changeovers.

Rarely do U.S. firms consider these real costs in the EOQ formula. More typically, these costs are considered part of the indirect, overhead, or "burden" costs that are assumed to be uncontrollable. Again, the message is be very careful about the values used in the EOQ formula.

Also, it should be noted that very small EOQ values (e.g. 2) will not usually be valid, because the cost functions are questionable for such small orders. Last, EOQ order sizes should not be followed blindly. There may not be enough cash just now to pay for an EOQ, or storage space may be insufficient.

Apply Your Understanding

Delta Products Inc.

Delta Products, of Omaha, Nebraska, makes a line of door hardware, including doorknob sets and deadbolts. Its product line is particularly well known for excellent quality, a high level of security, and ease of installation.

Delta hired Gina Scott, a first-year MBA concentrating in operations management, for one of its summer internships. Her task was to spend the summer analyzing the operation and usage of the large transfer press, the plant's current bottleneck machine. The transfer press stamps out the doorknobs used in Delta's door hardware and is available 2000 hours per year for this task. At the end of the summer, in a report to the plant manager, Gina was to submit her recommendations for improving the operation of the transfer press.

Gina spent the first week familiarizing herself with the operation of the transfer press by observing and questioning the machine operator. By the end of the first week, she determined that Delta uses six unique doorknobs in its door hardware.

She decided that her next task was to get an estimate of the annual demand for the knobs. She studied Delta's product catalogs and determined which products each knob was used in. Next, she got from the sales manager a copy of a spreadsheet that contained the complete sales figures for each product over the last three years. After casually looking over the data, she observed that the sales were remarkably stable over the three-year period. Gina added formulas to the spreadsheet to average the sales data over the three-year period and to calculate the number of knobs of each type that were used.

With her analysis of the demand for knobs completed, Gina turned her attention to the actual production of the knobs. She spent the next couple of weeks collecting data on the individual processing times of the knobs on the transfer press, the time required to set up the press to produce a new batch of knobs, and the production batch sizes currently being used. She also worked closely with the cost accountant to determine the cost of holding knobs in inventory, and she found that machine operators are paid $15 per hour, including fringe benefits. Gina summarized the information for her report in the following spreadsheet.

Item	Annual Demand	Unit Processing Time (hrs.)	Setup Time (hrs.)	Annual Holding Cost ($/unit)	Current Batch Size
Knob A	6000	0.0500	6.2	3.25	1500
Knob B	3000	0.0420	4.6	3.85	1500
Knob C	7000	0.0400	7.2	2.75	1500
Knob D	10,000	0.0380	5.4	3.70	2000
Knob E	8400	0.0375	3.8	4.20	1500
Knob F	9400	0.0480	6.8	2.25	2000

Her next task was to analyze the information she had compiled and look for ways to improve the operation. Given the information she had available, she began by developing a spreadsheet to calculate the EOQ. She then developed another spreadsheet to compare the TAC of using the current batch sizes with the economic order quantities she had calculated. Gina was extremely pleased when she realized she could save Delta almost $7000 per year in just one department if it adopted her recommended economic order quantities. After rechecking her calculations, she was convinced of the validity of her analysis and couldn't wait to see the plant manager's reaction to her report. She was actually hoping that the plant manager would be impressed enough with her work to offer her a full-time position upon graduation. The final spreadsheet she developed to summarize the potential savings to Delta is shown next.

Item	Current Batch Size	Economic Order Quantity	TAC Current Batch Size	TAC EOQ
Knob A	1500	586	2810	1904
Knob B	1500	328	3026	1262
Knob C	1500	741	2567	2039
Knob D	2000	662	4105	2448
Knob E	1500	477	3469	2005
Knob F	2000	923	2729	2077
Total			$18,705	$11,737
Annual Savings			$6968	

(continued)

On the Monday of her last week, Nikki met with the plant manager, Joe Thomas, and the press department manager, Mike Willis. After complimenting Gina on a very thorough and well-written report, Joe asked Mike what his reaction was. Mike commented:

> *I also was very impressed with the thoroughness of Gina's analysis. The data that she collected on setup times, production times, and holding costs are the best data we have ever had about our operations. Unfortunately, while I have not had a chance to thoroughly run the numbers, I think there is a problem with Gina's analysis. Her analysis requires significant reductions in our batch sizes. While I agree that we could save money by cutting the batch sizes, the fact of the matter is that the transfer press she analyzed is one of our major bottlenecks. We are currently using every second of the 2000 hours we have available on the machine. Cutting the lot sizes as Gina has suggested will require more setups, and we simply don't have the time for additional setups.*

> *Gina was quite distraught by the outcome of the meeting. She still had a week left in her internship, and she desperately wanted to salvage the work she had spent an entire summer on. She was determined to spend her final week finding a way to save Delta money while at the same time not exceeding its available capacity.*

Questions

1. Verify Gina's calculations of the EOQ and total annual cost.

2. Is Mike's intuition correct – that using Gina's economic order quantities will exceed the 2000 hours of capacity available on the transfer press?

3. Are there any opportunities for Delta to save money without exceeding its available capacity?

EXERCISES

6A.1 Frame-Up, a self-service picture framing shop for tourists in Sevilla, Spain, orders 3000 meters of a certain molding every month. The order cost is €40, and the holding cost is €0.05 per meter per year. What is the current annual inventory cost? What is the maximum inventory level? What is the EOQ?

6A.2 The Corner Convenient Store (CCS) in northern Chicago receives orders from its distributor in three days from the time an order is placed. Light Cola sells at the rate of 860 cans per day. (It can sell 250 days of the year.) A six-pack of Light Cola costs CCS $1.20. Annual holding cost is 10% of the cost of the cola. Order cost is $25.00. What is CCS's EOQ?

6A.3 A Liverpool, England, camera supplies wholesaler purchases £1 million worth of camera equipment each year. It costs £100 to place and receive an order, and the annual holding cost per item is 20% of the item's value.

  a. What is the £ value of the EOQ?

  b. How many months' supply is the EOQ?

  c. How often should orders be placed?

  d. How much will the annual holding cost change if the company orders monthly? How much will the annual ordering cost change?

  e. What should the £ value of the EOQ be if the wholesaler doubles its annual purchases? What should it be if (instead) the ordering cost doubles? What should it be if the holding cost drops to 10%?

6A.4 Wing Computer Corporation of Xiamen, China, uses 15,000 keyboards each year in the production of computer terminals for major computer manufacturers headquartered in Taiwan. Order cost for the keyboards is 50 renminbi, and the holding cost for one keyboard is 1.5 renminbi per unit per year. What is the EOQ? If Wing orders 1250 per month, what will be the total annual cost? What is the average inventory level?

6A.5 Management at Wing Computer referred to in the previous exercise collected additional information. In particular is determined that the annual demand for keyboards is normally distributed with a mean of 15,000 keyboards and standard deviation of 1000. Likewise, order cost for the keyboards ranges between 40 and 60 renminbi with all costs within this range equally likely. Finally, holding cost for one keyboard ranges between 1.0 and 2.0 renminbi per unit per year, again with all outcomes in the range equally likely. What are the implications of having this additional information related to the calculation of the EOQ?

BIBLIOGRAPHY

Axsater, S. *Inventory Control*, 3rd ed. Springer International Publications AG, Switzerland, 2015.

Silver, E. A., D. F. Pyke, and D. J. Thomas. *Inventory and Production Management in Supply Chains*, 4th ed. CRC Press/Taylor and Francis Group LLC, Boca Raton, FL, 2017.

Taleizadeh, A. A. *Inventory Control Models with Motivational Policies*. Springer International Publications AG, Switzerland, 2018.

Vollmann, T. E., W. L. Berry, D. C. Whybark, and F. R. Jacobs. *Manufacturing Planning and Control Systems for Supply Chain Management*, 5th ed. New York: McGraw-Hill, 2004.

Waters, D. *Inventory Control and Management*. Hoboken, NJ: Wiley, 2003.

Zipkin, P. H. *Foundations of Inventory Management*. New York: Irwin/McGraw-Hill, 2000.

PART 3

MANAGING AND IMPROVING THE PROCESS

In this final part of the book, we begin in Chapter 7 with the crucial role of monitoring and controlling the processes that we have so carefully planned and designed based on the methods discussed in the earlier chapters. Once again, just planning and designing the supply chain and other processes is no guarantee of success or especially continued success. They must be monitored to ensure they are achieving their goals and being properly executed on a constant basis, and then management must intercede to correct, as well as improve, them. One of the major ways of improving these processes is through Six Sigma projects, described in Chapter 8, which utilize a well-defined and structured approach. Another major way of improving processes is through the technique of lean production, described in Chapter 9, which reduces waste in all forms within any type of process.

The book then concludes with a variety of cases that focus on many of the concepts and techniques presented in the previous chapters.

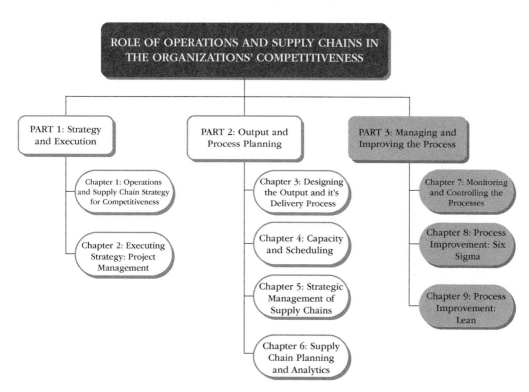

Monitoring and Controlling the Processes

Having selected an appropriate value-creating transformation process and designed a supply chain to deliver the value to customers (Part 2 of this book), we now turn to the need to manage, control, and improve these processes. With the organization's processes designed, they must now be implemented. The effective and efficient execution of processes is complicated by changes that occur both inside and outside the organization. Hence, every process must be monitored and controlled to be sure it continues to achieve its objectives in support of the organization's overall competitiveness.

This chapter discusses the task of monitoring and control. It includes some discussion of the measures that will be monitored and ways to then exercise control to correct the process. We illustrate the control process with the example of controlling quality through the use of quality control charts. Other topics include well-popularized subjects such as ISO 9000 and ISO 14000, benchmarking, process capability, and service defections. After we complete our discussion of how to plan for process monitoring and control, the next two chapters will then delve into ways to improve these processes.

While more tactical in nature, the topic of monitoring and controlling processes has important strategic implications. For example, effective monitoring of its value-creating processes positions an organization to proactively take corrective action to correct defects and other quality-related issues and thereby minimize the impact they have on customer satisfaction. This is important as customer satisfaction is a critical driver of competitive success.

7.1 Introduction

- The Columbus air mail processing center (AMC) was one of 77 AMCs operated by the United States Postal Service (USPS). Each AMC was responsible for processing letters and packages that are to be distributed via air mail. A top priority of the USPS was outstanding customer service, which is assessed in part on the basis of the percent of letters and packages delivered on time. The USPS contracted with IBM Consulting Services to monitor its on-time delivery performance.

  Each year, the Columbus AMC processed in excess of 50 million first-class letters that originate in central Ohio. Unfortunately, 8.7% of the letters processed there did not meet the established on-time delivery commitments. To address this problem, a Six Sigma project was initiated at the Columbus AMC with the objective of improving its on-time delivery performance. A key improvement made as a result of the Six Sigma project was the creation and documentation of a standardized process. In addition, improvements were incorporated into the new standardized process to "mistake-proof" it in order to further prevent late deliveries. As a result of the process improvements implemented, late deliveries were reduced by 14.3%. Furthermore, the improved process generated $15,000 in annual savings.

While making these types of process improvements is certainly important, it is equally important to carefully monitor and control the process to ensure that the improved level of performance is maintained. At the Columbus AMC, on-time delivery performance was continuously monitored using a type of control chart called a p-chart. The use of the p-chart enabled the Columbus AMC to track the proportion of late deliveries and discover when corrective measures were needed in a timely manner (Franchetti 2008).

- Movistar is a mobile phone operator owned by the Telefónica Group, based in Argentina. In early 2008, Movistar raised concerns about the reliability of Telefónica's network service, citing over 400 service interruptions that resulted in lost revenue of $500,000. To address the concerns raised by Movistar, Telefónica initiated a Six Sigma project to better understand the root causes of the service interruptions. Over the course of the project, many process improvement tools were used to help better understand the problem, including process mapping, control charts, and box plots. In the end, the project resulted in dramatic reductions in service interruptions and in monthly savings of $300,000, allowing the project to recoup all its costs in six months. In reflecting on the success of the project, managers cited the use of control charts incorporated into a scorecard that enabled the team to monitor the progress of the project and enhance communication among all stakeholders (Krzykowski 2011).

- North Shore-Long Island Jewish (LIJ) Health System, located in Great Neck, New York, found that its "accessioning" registration process was out of control. Accessioning occurs when the information in the paper requisition for obtaining specimen samples is entered into the lab's information system and a label is generated and placed on a sample tube. LIJ performed more than 3.5 million tests annually for all 18 of the system's hospitals as well as all the microbiology, molecular diagnostics, complex reference tests, long-term care facilities, clinical trials, and physician offices in the network. Accessioning errors had been measured for years and had been a chronic problem. However, when the rate of incomplete or inaccurate specimens reached 5% (i.e. 175,000!), LIJ decided to step in and exercise control. A multidisciplinary project team was formed to investigate and correct the problem. Before the study began, the team assumed that the handwriting of the physicians would be the culprit, but it was found that half the errors were due to incorrect entering of the patients' Social Security numbers. This was due to the difficulty in reading an addressograph label, which was then replaced with a barcode reader. In addition, it was found that a small percentage of the staff made the majority of errors, indicating additional training was desirable. Further investigation showed that a lack of established best practices in the laboratory was another major source of errors, and discussion with the staff led to the creation of a "lead accessioner" position to set standard practices for the laboratory. As a result of these changes, the laboratory increased its accuracy rate to 99% and its handling capacity by 43%, resulting in a positive financial impact of about $339,000 a year (Riebling et al. 2004).

As these examples illustrate, monitoring and control are central to achieving the purposes for which processes and projects were initially designed. It doesn't matter if the process or project issue needing control is related to cost, quality, time, progress, or something else; to properly obtain the objectives we desire, we need to identify measures to track and, when needed, exercise control to bring results into agreement with our plans.

We begin the chapter with a general overview of the topics of monitoring and control. We then focus on process monitoring. Here we discuss the tasks of identifying possible risks to the processes, the most appropriate measures to monitor, and the collecting and reporting of the data. Next, we consider the task of process control, analyzing the data and taking action. We illustrate one of the most fully developed control systems, statistical process control, using the control of quality as an example. Finally, we discuss a special case of control, that of service quality.

7.2 Monitoring and Control

As we noted in Figure 1.1 back in Chapter 1 when we described the production system, we will want to monitor not only our processes but also our output – and even the environment – to make sure that our strategy, inputs, and value-creating transformation processes are appropriate to achieve our goals. To do this, we first need to identify the key factors to be monitored and controlled, which in turn depend on our goals for the production system. Once we know this, we can design a monitoring system to track and report on the activities which are needed to achieve our goals. But if these activities fail to perform correctly, or the environment changes, we may need to take action to alter the activities and regain control of the process. The actions needed to control activities depend on the situation, but the *process* and *tools* of control are well known and will be described following our discussion of monitoring.

The monitoring system is a direct connection between planning and control. But if it does not collect and report information on some significant element of the production system, control can be faulty. Unfortunately, it is common to focus monitoring activities on data that are easily gathered – rather than important – or to concentrate on "objective" measures that are easily defended at the expense of softer, more subjective data that may be more valuable for control. When monitoring output performance, we should concentrate primarily on measuring various facets of output rather than intensity of activity. It is crucial to remember that effective managers are not primarily interested in how hard their employees work – they are interested in the results achieved. Also, it is imperative that the information be timely enough to exert control.

7.3 Process Monitoring: Goals, Risks, Data Collection, and Reporting

Although we will be monitoring the environment and our processes as well as our outputs, the measurement of output performance usually poses the most difficult data-gathering problem. There is a strong tendency, particularly in service operations, to let inputs serve as surrogate measures for output. If we have spent 50% of the budget (or of the scheduled time), we assume we have also completed 50% of the work or reached 50% of our goal.

Given all this, performance criteria, standards, and data collection procedures must be established for each of the factors to be measured. However, more often than not, standards and criteria change because of factors that are not under the control of management. For example, the market, our competitors, or government regulations may change. Standards may also be changed by the community as a response to some shift in public policy – witness the changes in the performance standards imposed on nuclear power installations or automotive exhaust systems. Shifts in the prime rate of interest or in unemployment levels often alter the standards that management must use in making decisions. The monitoring process is based on the criteria and standards because they dictate, or at least constrain, the set of relevant measures.

Next, the information to be collected must be identified. This may consist of accounting data, operating data, engineering test data, customer satisfaction data, regulations, competitors' prices, specification changes, and the like. The fundamental problem is to determine precisely which of all the available data should be collected. It is worth repeating that the typical determinant for collecting data too often seems to be simply the ease with which they can be gathered. Again, the nature of the required data is dictated by the organization's objectives or goals. The overarching consideration in determining the data to be collected should be the potential insights the data can provide into how the process is performing, not the ease with which it can be collected. Such measures are often referred to as key (or critical) *performance indicators* or *KPIs*.

Perhaps the most common error made when monitoring data is to gather information that is clearly related to performance but has little or no probability of changing significantly from one collection period to the next. Prior to its breakup, the American Telephone and Telegraph Company used to collect monthly statistics on a very large number of indicators of operating efficiency. The extent of the collection was such that it filled a telephone book-sized volume known as "Ma Bell's Green Book." For a great many of the indicators, the likelihood of a significant change from one month to the next was extremely small. When asked about the matter, one official remarked that the mere collection of the data kept the operating companies "on their toes." We feel that there are more positive and less expensive ways of motivating personnel. Certainly, "collect everything" is inappropriate as a monitoring policy. There are a wide variety of elements of the production system and environment that we may wish to monitor, but too much data can be worse than too little data since it can obscure the information that may be most important in the various measures we are watching.

Therefore, the first task is to identify the objectives desired from the production system. Data must be identified that measure achievement against these goals and how effective the production system is. Then mechanisms can be designed that will gather and store such data. Next, we must examine the purposes of the various processes and find measures that provide us with insight into how these processes are performing and what the risks are to that performance. As an aside, if at least some of the data do not relate to the individual work level, no useful action is apt to be taken. In the end, it is the detailed work of the processes that must be altered if any aspect of performance is to be changed. The fascinating book *The Soul of a New Machine* (Kidder 1981) reveals the crucial roles that organizational factors, interpersonal relationships, and managerial style play in determining process success. And finally, we need to monitor the environment continually – the market, the economy, technology, competition, etc. – to make sure that our goals are still appropriate. We need to be especially sensitive to risks and any changes in the environment, internal or external, that may pose new or increased risks.

7.3.1 Goals and Standards

Let us begin with the objective of identifying what our goals are for the production system. We can certainly list a large set of criteria for our operations to meet, but what is actually realistic? We need a standard, such as what our competitors do, or perhaps a global expectation, otherwise known as "world class" or "best-in-class." Fortunately, there are some well-formulated concepts for monitoring how our competitors are doing. One such approach is called "benchmarking," essentially documenting the level of competence of either competitors or even noncompetitor "best-in-class" organizations (Thamhain 1996; Toney 1997). This can show how our competitors are doing on those measures of importance to our customers or clients as well as on other measures of interest to us. Gupta and Graham (1997) offer a case study showing the importance of customer benchmarking. But benchmarking can also be used simply to find out how well some key aspects of the organization's operations can be done. Ibbs and Kwak (1998) present a benchmarking study of industry processes, tools, and techniques. Industry leaders, often in a different industry from our own, can help us to improve our own operations even if our competitors are not at that level, giving us a potential competitive advantage. Benchmarking is one of the major improvement tools of the "Six Sigma" system, so it will be described in detail in the next chapter. However, there is also a global standard that organizations can use known as ISO.

7.3.1.1 ISO 9000 and 14000

ISO 9000 was developed as a guideline for designing, manufacturing, selling, and servicing products; in a sense, it is a sort of checklist of good business practices. Thus, the intent of the ISO 9000 standard is that if an organization selects a supplier that is ISO 9000 certified, it has some assurance that the supplier follows accepted business practices in the areas specified in the standard. However, one criticism of ISO 9000 is that because it does not require any specific actions, each organization determines how it can best meet the requirements of the standard.

ISO 9000 was developed by the International Organization for Standardization and first issued in March 1987. A major revision to ISO 9000 was completed in December 2008; the new standard is commonly referred to as ISO 9000:2008. Since its introduction, ISO 9000 has become the most widely recognized standard in the world. To illustrate its importance, in 1993, the European Community required that companies in several industries become certified as a condition of conducting business in Europe. In December of 2017, 1,058,504 organizations were ISO 9000 certified globally and 16,463 were ISO 14000 certified.

As mentioned in Chapter 5, ISO 14000 is a series of standards covering environmental management systems, environmental auditing, evaluation of environmental performance, environmental labeling, and life-cycle assessment. Like ISO 9000, ISO 14001 (a subset of the ISO 14000 series) is a standard in which organizations can become certified. The focus of ISO 14001 is on an organization's environmental management system. However, like ISO 9000, ISO 14001 does not prescribe specific standards for performance or levels of improvement. Rather, its intent is to help organizations improve their environmental performance through documentation control, operational control, control of records, training, statistical techniques, and corrective and preventive actions.

Clearly, this set of international standards for both production and environmental maintenance certification will lead to a range of measures that should be considered for monitoring the proper functioning of the production system. But there are other measurement systems available also which are sometimes more intuitive and simpler, as discussed next.

7.3.1.2 Stages of Operational Effectiveness

Wheelwright and Hayes (1985) suggest that organizations can progress through four stages of effectiveness in terms of the role their operations play in supporting and achieving the overall strategic objectives of the organization. As a diagnostic tool, this framework helps determine the extent to which an organization is utilizing its operations to support and possibly attain a sustainable competitive advantage. As a prescriptive tool, the framework helps focus an organization on appropriate future courses of action because it is argued that stages cannot be skipped. Important managerial challenges are also identified for each stage of effectiveness.

Organizations in stage 1 of the model are labeled *internally neutral*. These organizations tend to view operations as having little impact on the organization's competitive success. In fact, these organizations often consider the operations area as primarily a source of problems (e.g. quality problems, late shipments, and too much capital tied up in inventory). Thus, believing that operations have little strategic importance, these organizations place an emphasis on minimizing the negative impact of operations.

Stage 2 is labeled *externally neutral*. As the name suggests, organizations at this stage attempt to match the operational practices of the industry. Thus, organizations in this stage still tend to view operations as having little strategic importance, but they at least attempt to follow standard industry practices and achieve operational parity with their competitors. Because these organizations follow industry practice, they tend to be more reactive than proactive in the operations area. Furthermore, operational investments and improvements tend to be tied to reducing costs.

Stage 3 is called *internally supportive*. In this stage of development, the organization expects its operations to support the overall business strategy and competitive position. In many cases, this is stated as a formal operations strategy. Thus, operational decisions are evaluated based on their consistency with and the extent to which they support the organization's overall mission. Internally supportive organizations tend to be more proactive in terms of identifying opportunities to support the organization's overall competitiveness. It is important to point out, however, that while stage 3 organizations expect operations to support the overall business strategy, operations is typically not involved in actually formulating it.

Stage 4 organizations depend on their operations to achieve a competitive advantage and are referred to as *externally supportive*. In effect, these organizations use core capabilities residing in the operations area to obtain a sustainable competitive advantage.

Because different parts of an organization may evolve at different rates, determining an organization's stage of effectiveness may require making a judgment about where the balance of the organization is positioned. Thus, it is possible that some departments or areas of a stage 2 organization exhibit characteristics of a stage 3 organization. However, if the majority of the organization is most appropriately characterized as being in stage 2, then the organization should be categorized as being in stage 2. Thus, evaluating an organization's evolution is based not on its most evolved area but rather on the balance of its organizational practices.

Using the definitions of the four operational effectiveness stages above, Dangayach and Deshmukh (2006) developed perceptual measures for each of these stages based on company practices, some of which are given in Table 7.1. By asking managers how closely their organization followed each of these practices (on a 1–5 scale), they were able to classify them into one of the four stages and relate them to the organization's overall performance. Thus, these measures would be excellent items for monitoring the evolving competitive strength of organizations and taking control actions when they show competitive slippage.

7.3.2 Identifying and Evaluating the Risks

Once we have the measures we are interested in monitoring, we can anticipate what might go wrong, or right, for each of these practices, such as firefighting or supporting the business strategy in Table 7.1. Flow charts of the process, SWOT analysis, brainstorming, and other approaches can help in identifying the risk factors affecting the measures, but a simple method for identifying them is a cause–effect diagram, also known as a fishbone chart, as shown in Figure 7.1.

Table 7.1 Perceptual Measures for Operational Effectiveness

Stage	Assessment of Organizational Practices
Internally neutral	The organization's objective is to minimize operations' negative impact.
	Firefighting is common.
	Outside experts are called in for strategic decisions.
	Operations is primarily reactive.
Externally neutral	Standard industry practices are followed.
	The aim is to achieve competitive parity in the operations area.
Internally supportive	Operations investments support the business strategy.
	An operations strategy is formulated and pursued.
Externally supportive	Operations is involved upfront in major strategic decisions.
	The aim is to achieve a competitive advantage through operations.
	The goal is to achieve competitive superiority.

Fishbone chart

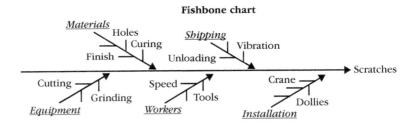

FIGURE 7.1
The Cause–Effect or
"Fishbone" Chart

In the figure, we see that scratches on a piece of furniture may come from several causes, such as shipping, or the equipment used to produce the item. After we identify all the likely causes, we then try to identify what processes or equipment in that cause may have been responsible for the scratches. The next step would be to find reasons for each of those processes scratching the furniture and then what factors we could measure and monitor that might lead us to the problem. We could also use the same kind of chart for a good outcome, such as support for the business strategy, as a way to improve the organization's operations. This technique is more fully described in the next chapter on the Six-Sigma system.

Another, more structured, approach to evaluate the risk factors for a process is Failure Mode and Effect Analysis (FMEA). FMEA was developed by the space program in the 1960s (Stamatis 2003) as a structured approach to help identify and prioritize for close monitoring and control those elements of a system that might give rise to failure. It employs a scoring model approach setup in a series of six straightforward steps, as follows:

1. List the possible ways a production system or service delivery system might fail.

2. Evaluate the severity (S) of the consequences of each type of failure on a 10-point scale, where 1 is "no effect" and 10 is "very severe."

3. For each cause of failure, estimate the likelihood (L) of its occurrence on a 10-point scale where 1 is "remote" and 10 is "almost certain."

4. Estimate the ability to detect (D) a failure associated with each cause. Using a 10-point scale, 1 means detectability is almost certain using normal monitoring/control systems and 10 means it is practically certain that failure will not be detected in time to avoid or mitigate it.

5. Find the *Risk Priority Number* (RPN), where RPN = S×L×D.

6. Consider ways to reduce the S, L, and D for each cause of failure with a significantly high RPN.

Table 7.2 illustrates the application of FMEA to a new concept for a fast-food restaurant. Here, we are primarily illustrating how to apply the approach, but in other situations our items of failure could be more specific and narrower: a particular machine, a particularly difficult process, a unique government regulation, and other such items that clearly could result in missing our goals for the new concept. In the table, we have identified training and marketing as the elements with the highest RPNs and thus those we particularly want to monitor and control very carefully. We might invest additional time and effort in training our employees to offset the first threat, but since L is low already, it might be more productive to find ways to detect this inadequacy faster, such as surveying our customers to monitor their perceptions of our service. This might then reduce D to 3 instead of 5 and thereby mitigate the threat. In addition, we could include a question on the survey to help determine which marketing approaches are having the greatest results, reducing D from 8 to perhaps 5.

Table 7.2   **FMEA for a New Fast-Food Concept**

Potential ways to fail	S	L	D	RPN
Inadequate training	8	4	5	160
Weak marketing	6	3	8	144
Poor location	7	5	3	105
Defective concept	9	3	3	81
Local restaurant regulation change	3	5	8	120
Competitors' reactions (e.g. price, ads)	4	6	4	96

It was noted above that more specific items might be included in the FMEA list, such as a particular machine or difficult process. One way to identify such items for inclusion in the FMEA list, or for monitoring in general, is by evaluating their "process capability," a topic we explain in detail in Chapter 8 when we talk about process improvement. In essence, however, if the specifications for a machine (or process) are relatively tight compared to the natural variation in the machine, we have to carefully monitor the machine's process capability to satisfy the requirements of the production system. For example, in our fast-food example, if the process required a difficult and time-consuming step in the preparation of a particular menu item, we might fail because our customers got tired of waiting for their food. Hence, we would want to monitor the time this process required very carefully and take controlling steps if it started to exceed the required specifications of our production system.

7.3.3   Data Collection and Reporting

After we have decided upon the data measures we need to collect for monitoring, when we should collect it, and how, we then need to turn it into information that can be used for controlling the process. This usually involves some analysis or processing of the data, such as averaging the values, or perhaps something as complex as fitting statistical distributions to the data to determine trends or relationships. For example, a common figure used in quality control, described later in the chapter, shows the range of daily values – the largest minus the smallest. If this range is increasing over time, it may mean that this process is wearing out or nearing failure for some reason, and control must be taken to return the process to its normal range.

It will be necessary to create a method for determining when the monitored values are out of control and thus need to be reported to the appropriate authority for action. It is better to correct a process before it goes out of control, of course, so timely collection and reporting are also necessary. There are three kinds of reports that organizations typically use: routine reports, exception reports, and special analysis reports. Routine reports are usually not read carefully except for those that are needed by upper management for other purposes. These reports should be timed to allow the recipient to exercise control of a process before any problem occurs, as noted earlier. Exception reports are usually intended to help with special decisions or unexpected situations where employees or managers need to be made aware of a change, and to document that change. Special analysis reports are used to disseminate the results of a study or test concerning something new, such as a new opportunity or problem, a new government regulation, a new material that has become available, or some new software package.

Frequently, the reports are presented orally in a meeting, especially if upper management is interested in the report. These meetings can range from regular, formal meetings to informal get-togethers, sometimes even on a golf course for one-to-one (or three) meetings. Given that most employees are as enthused about going to a meeting as catching COVID-19 or getting a cavity filled, there are some meeting guidelines that can help, as follows:

1. Only use meetings for dealing with a crisis or generating ideas for dealing with an important problem or opportunity and face-to-face interaction or input is needed, and no other alternative such as email is adequate.

2. Make sure a written agenda for the meeting is distributed far enough in advance of the meeting that attendees will have the time to prepare their comments about the item(s).

3. Set clear, feasible start and stop times and stick to them. By all means, never penalize those who show up on time by delaying the meeting for those who are late.

4. If the meeting is for a crisis, restrict the agenda to just that issue, and the stop time can be "when the crisis is resolved."

5. The chair should also take the minutes, and indicate what is to be done, by whom, and when.

6. Leave Robert's Rules of Order outside.

7.4 Process Control: Analyzing the Data and Taking Action

Process control is the act of reducing differences between plan and reality for each process; that is, taking action by altering activities in order to improve the results. Monitoring and comparing activities with the plan and then reporting these findings is of no avail if actions are not taken when reality deviates significantly from what was planned. In fact, the simple act of noting and reporting discrepancies may motivate the actions required to correct the deviations. When it does not, however, active control is needed to bring performance back in line with the plan. Control has the primary purpose of ensuring that the process is in compliance with its objectives. In large production systems particularly, early control is crucial since the longer we wait, the more difficult it is to correct the deviation.

Control is one of the manager's most difficult tasks, invariably involving both mechanical and human elements. In addition, control can be difficult because problems are rarely clear-cut and hence the need for change and redirection may be fuzzy. Determining what to control raises further difficulties – did someone take an incorrect action or is the system to blame, or perhaps simply Mother Nature?

A good control system should also possess some specific characteristics:

- The system should be flexible. Where possible, it should be able to react to unforeseen changes in system performance.

- The system should be cost-effective, and the cost of control should never exceed the value of control. For example, bear in mind that control is not always less expensive than scrap.

- The system should be as simple as possible to operate.

- The system must operate in a timely manner. Problems must be reported while there is still time to do something about them.

- Sensors and monitors should be sufficiently precise to control the process within limits that are truly functional for the organization.

- The control system should be easy to maintain.

- The system should signal the manager if it goes out of order.

- The system should be capable of being extended or otherwise altered.

- Control systems should be fully documented when installed, and the documentation should include a complete training program in system operation.

- The system must operate in an ethical manner.

Next, we turn to a common tool for controlling processes, the control chart, and illustrate it with the case of controlling quality. However, it can also be used for controlling many other measures, such as scrap, turnover, revenues, progress (see Meredith and Shafer 2022, pp. 450–455), costs, and so on. We might note that control charts are based on the concept of *cybernetic* control, where deviations away from the desired level are noted and correction applied to bring the process back to its nominal or desired level. This is the same principle that a house thermostat uses, increasing the level of heat or air conditioning when the temperature deviates from the setpoint, and when you correct your car's steering after taking your eyes off the road for even a few seconds.

7.4.1 Statistical Process Control

One of management's most difficult decisions in quality control centers on whether an activity or process needs adjustment or corrective action. The use of control charts can greatly facilitate this task. More specifically, *control charts*, developed in the 1920s, provide a simple tool for determining when a process has only random or chance variation present versus times when there is an assignable source of variation. Let's examine the distinction between chance variation and assignable variation in more detail and discuss why it is important.

To begin, it is important to point out that a repetitive operation or process will not produce exactly the same outputs over and over again. For example, it is not possible for a worker at a fast-food restaurant to put *exactly* the same amount of ketchup on each hamburger made in a batch of hamburgers. Thus, there will be some variability in the amount of ketchup put on each hamburger. Because there is variation in the amount of ketchup put on the hamburgers, the amount of ketchup put on a hamburger can be described by a distribution with some mean and standard deviation. For the purpose of control charts, we typically assume the pattern of variability can be described by the normal distribution.

Some of the variation in the outcomes of a process are due to the equipment and machinery that is used, the operators, and a variety of other factors. This type of variation is a natural and inherent aspect of the process and is therefore to be expected.

At other times, there is an *assignable* cause for some of the variation present in the process. Because the source of this variation can be assigned to a specific cause, assignable variation is said to be the result of *special causes*. And because there is an assignable source of this variation, it is desirable to identify the source of this variation so that it can be eliminated. Logically, eliminating a source of variation in a process results in the process producing more consistent outcomes or in the case of our fast-food restaurant, doing a better job of putting the same amount of ketchup on each hamburger.

In the case of putting ketchup on hamburgers, there are numerous potential special or assignable causes that would result in creating inconsistencies in the amount of ketchup put on the hamburgers. For example, perhaps the workers were not trained properly so they don't know how much ketchup should be put on the hamburgers. If this were the case, workers would have to rely on their own judgment about how much ketchup to put on the hamburgers. Here, the lack of training is an assignable cause for some of the variation in the amount of ketchup put on hamburgers. Another example of an assignable source of variation would be a fatigued worker that is not paying close enough attention to the amount of ketchup being put on the hamburgers. Or perhaps the ketchup was watered down too much so that when the ketchup bottle is squeezed, too much ketchup runs out. As a final example, perhaps the nozzles were clogged so that when the bottle is squeezed, not enough ketchup comes out. In all of these cases, there is a clear assignable reason or cause for the wrong amount of ketchup being put on the hamburgers. Based on these examples, it stands to reason that management would want to know when assignable sources of variation were present so that the situation could be corrected and the source of the assignable variation eliminated. We note that a process is said to be *in-control* when there is only chance variation present and said to be *out-of-control* when there is an assignable source of variation present.

Control charts can be constructed using two types of data. *Attribute* data refers to assessing a discrete characteristic of the output. For the purpose of control charts, the characteristic most often assessed is whether the output is good or bad, or alternatively, *defective* or *not defective*. Also, if the output can have more than one defect, such as more than one typo on a page, then the number of defects can be counted.

In contrast to attribute data, *variable* data refers to a characteristic that is continuous and can be measured. Examples of characteristics that can be measured include the weight and length of an output. Other characteristics that can be measured include temperature, profit, and elapsed time.

The process of constructing control charts begins by taking a number of samples of the output being produced and assessing the units in the sample in terms of the quality. For attribute control charts, this often entails determining whether each unit in the sample is defective or not defective. For variable control charts, each unit would be measured on a quality dimension of interest such as the length, weight, or diameter of the part. Using the data from a number of samples, the average of the process, or the *process mean*, is calculated, and this is plotted as the centerline of the control chart as shown in Figure 7.2.

The data in the samples are also used to calculate the *upper and lower control limits* for the control chart. In practice, the upper control limit is typically set at three standard deviations above the process mean and the lower control limit is set at three standard deviations below the mean. We know from statistics that the chance that a normally distributed point will be outside plus or minus three standard deviations due to random chance is less than 0.3% (0.003) or less than three samples out of 1000 samples. Thus, the chance that data points from samples collected in the future will fall outside of the control limits is so small that this occurrence provides strong evidence of assignable variation. Using higher limit control charts (more than three standard deviations) would increase the risk of not detecting a process that is out of control.

The calculated control limits are also plotted on the control chart as shown in Figure 7.2. Finally, summary statistics from future sample data are plotted on the control chart and the

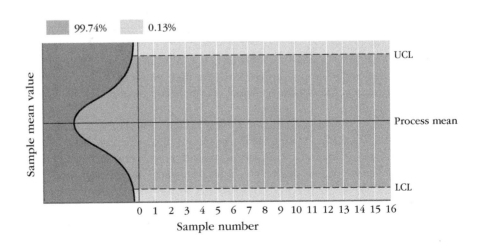

FIGURE 7.2 Control Chart with the Limits Set at Three Standard Deviations

patterns of the points plotted on the control chart assessed. If there is only chance variation in the process, no systematic pattern should be evident in the points plotted. When there is an assignable source of variation present in the process, a systematic pattern will appear in the points plotted.

The best use of control charts is to use them proactively to predict when an out-of-control situation is likely to occur rather than waiting for a process to actually go out of control. If only chance variation is present in the process, the points plotted on a control chart will not typically exhibit any pattern. On the other hand, if the points exhibit some systematic pattern, this is an indication that assignable variation may be present and corrective action should be taken.

The control chart, though originally developed for quality control in manufacturing, is applicable to all sorts of repetitive activities in any kind of organization. Thus, it can be used for services as well as products, for people or machines, for cost or quality, and so on. For example, the beginning of the chapter mentioned the USPS's use of control charts to monitor on-time delivery performance.

For the control of *variables* – that is, *measured characteristics* – two control charts are required:

1. Chart of the *sample means* $(\overline{X})$

2. Chart of the *range* (R) of values in each sample (largest value in sample minus smallest value in sample).

It is important to use two control charts for variables because of the way in which control of process quality can be lost. To illustrate this phenomenon, we will use the data supplied in Table 7.3, which correspond to the minutes needed to process a form at an insurance company. Three samples are taken each day: one in the morning, one near noon, and one just before closing. Each sample consists of three forms randomly selected from the staff working on these forms in the processing department.

Referring to scenario 1, we can easily determine that the average of sample 1 is five minutes and the range is two minutes ($\overline{X}_1 = 5$, $R_1 = 2$). Similarly, $\overline{X}_2 = 7$, $R_2 = 2$, $\overline{X}_3 = 8$, and $R_3 = 2$. If we consider only the ranges of the samples, no problem is indicated because all three samples have a range of two (assuming that a range of two minutes is acceptable to management). On the other hand, the behavior of the process means shows evidence of a problem. Specifically, the process means (minutes) have increased throughout the day from an average of five minutes to an average of eight minutes. Thus, for the data listed in scenario 1, the sample ranges indicate acceptable process performance, while the sample means indicate unacceptable process performance.

The sample statistics can be calculated in the same way for scenario 2: $\overline{X}_1 = 5$, $R_1 = 2$, $\overline{X}_2 = 5$, $R_2 = 4$, $\overline{X}_3 = 5$, and $R_3 = 6$. In contrast to scenario 1, the sample means show acceptable performance, while the sample ranges show possibly unacceptable performance. Thus, we see the necessity of monitoring both the mean and the variability of a process.

Figure 7.3 illustrates these two patterns of change in the distribution of process values more formally. These changes might be due to boredom, tool wear, improper training, the weather, fatigue, or any other such influence. In Figure 7.3a, the variability in the process remains the same, but the mean changes (scenario 1); this effect would be seen in the means ($\overline{X}$) chart but not in the range (R) chart. In Figure 7.3b, the mean remains the same, but the variability tends to increase (as in scenario 2); this would be seen in the range (R) chart but not the means ($\overline{X}$) chart.

Table 7.3   **Sample Data of Process Times (minutes)**

Sample	Scenario 1	Scenario 2
1	4, 5, 6	5, 4, 6
2	6, 7, 8	3, 5, 7
3	7, 9, 8	8, 2, 5

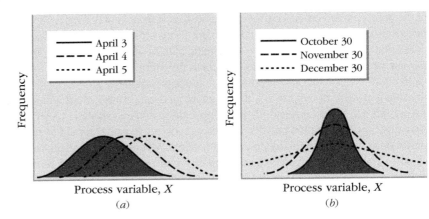

FIGURE 7.3
Patterns of Change in
Process Distributions

In terms of quality of the output, either type of change could result in lower quality, depending on the situation. Regarding control limits, the LCL for the means chart may be negative, depending on the variable being measured. For example, variables such as profit and temperature can be negative, but variables such as time, length, diameter, and weight cannot. Since (by definition) the range can *never* be negative, if calculations indicate a negative LCL for the range chart, it should simply be truncated to zero.

As indicated earlier, control limits for the means chart are usually set at plus and minus 3 standard deviations. But if a range chart is also being used, these limits for the means chart can be found by using the average range, which is directly related to the standard deviation, in the following equations (where $\bar{\bar{X}}$ is the grand mean or the average of the sample means):

$$\text{UCL}_{\bar{X}} = \bar{\bar{X}} + A_2\bar{R}$$
$$\text{LCL}_{\bar{X}} = \bar{\bar{X}} - A_2\bar{R}$$

Similarly, control limits for the range chart are found from

$$\text{UCL}_R = D_4\bar{R}$$
$$\text{LCL}_R = D_3\bar{R}$$

The control chart factors A_2, D_3, and D_4 vary with the sample size and are tabulated in Table 7.4.

7.4.2 Constructing Control Charts

The best way to illustrate the construction of control charts is by example. Assume that a bank with 10 branches is interested in monitoring the age of the applications for home mortgages being processed at its branches. To maintain a continuing check on this measure of customer responsiveness, one could select branches at random each day and note the ages of the applications. To set up the control charts, initial samples need to be taken. These data will, if considered representative by management, be used to set standards (i.e. control limits) for future applications. For our example, we assume that a sample of $n = 4$ of the 10 branches each day will give the best control for the effort involved. More specifically, each day four branches are chosen at random, and then, from each of these branches, an in-process application is selected at random. The age of the randomly selected application is then recorded. The mean age and range in ages for the initial samples were entered into the spreadsheet shown in Table 7.5. Note that each sample mean and sample range shown in Table 7.5 is based on data collected by randomly visiting four branches.

Table 7.4 Control Chart Factors to Determine Control Limits

Sample size, n	A_2	D_3	D_4
2	1.880	0	3.267
3	1.023	0	2.575
4	0.729	0	2.282
5	0.577	0	2.115
6	0.483	0	2.004
7	0.419	0.076	1.924
8	0.373	0.136	1.864
9	0.337	0.184	1.816
10	0.308	0.223	1.777
12	0.266	0.284	1.716
14	0.235	0.329	1.671
16	0.212	0.364	1.636
18	0.194	0.392	1.608
20	0.180	0.414	1.586
22	0.167	0.434	1.566
24	0.157	0.452	1.548

The grand mean $\bar{\bar{X}}$ and the average range were also calculated (cells B23 and C23, respectively). The grand mean is then simply the average of all the daily means:

$$\bar{\bar{X}} = \frac{\sum \bar{X}}{N}$$

where N is 20 days of samples and the average range is

$$\bar{R} = \frac{\sum R}{N}$$

The data in Table 7.5 can now be used to construct control charts that will indicate to management any sudden change, for better or worse, in the ages of the mortgage applications. Both a chart of means, to check the age of the applications, and a chart of ranges, to check consistency among branches, should be used.

The grand mean and average range will give the centerline on these charts, respectively. The values of A_2, D_3, and D_4 are obtained from Table 7.4 for $n = 4$, resulting in the following control limits:

$$\text{UCL}_{\bar{X}} = 11 + 0.729(14) = 21.206$$
$$\text{LCL}_{\bar{X}} = 11 - 0.729(14) = 0.794$$
$$\text{UCL}_R = 2.282(14) = 31.948$$
$$\text{LCL}_R = 0(14) = 0$$

The control charts for this example were developed using a spreadsheet and are shown in Figures 7.4 and 7.5. In addition, the data in Table 7.5 are graphed on the charts. As seen in Figure 7.4, no pattern is apparent from the data; the points appear to fall randomly around the grand mean (centerline) and thus are considered by management to be representative.

Table 7.5   Mean and Range of Ages of Mortgage Applications

	A	B	C
		Sample	Sample
1		Sample	Sample
2	Date	mean	range
3	June 1	10	18
4	June 2	13	13
5	June 3	11	15
6	June 4	14	14
7	June 5	9	14
8	June 6	11	10
9	June 7	8	15
10	June 8	12	17
11	June 9	13	9
12	June 10	10	16
13	June 11	13	12
14	June 12	12	14
15	June 13	8	13
16	June 14	11	15
17	June 15	11	11
18	June 16	9	14
19	June 17	10	13
20	June 18	9	19
21	June 19	12	14
22	June 20	14	14
23	Average	11	14

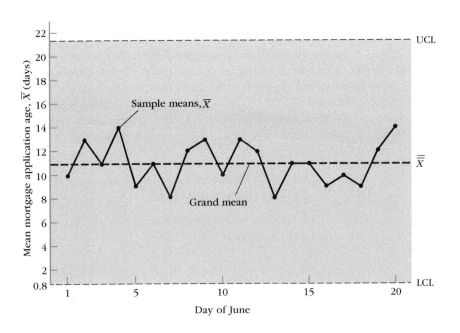

FIGURE 7.4 Mean Mortgage Application Age

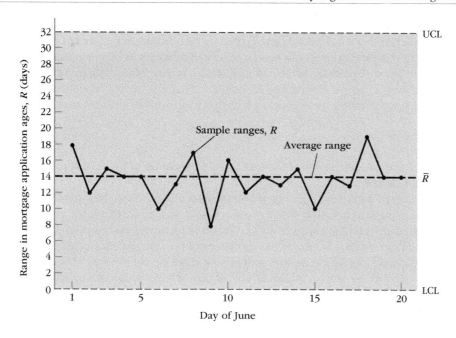

FIGURE 7.5
Range in Mortgage
Application Age

The range chart, Figure 7.5, again shows no apparent pattern and is also acceptable to management. Each day, as a new sample is taken, $\bar{X}$ and R will be calculated and plotted on the two charts. If either $\bar{X}$ or R is outside the LCL or UCL, management must then investigate to identify the assignable cause for the variation.

Control charts can also be used for controlling attributes of the output, the second type of inspection we described earlier. The most common of these charts are the *fraction-defective p-chart* and the *number-of-defects c-chart*. As with the range chart, the LCL for attribute charts can never be negative.

The fraction-defective p-chart can be used for any two-state (*dichotomous*) process such as heavy versus light, acceptable versus unacceptable, on time versus late, defective versus not defective, or placed properly versus misplaced. The control chart for p is constructed in much the same way as the control chart for $\bar{X}$. First, samples of historical data are gathered (a common rule of thumb is 25 samples), and the fraction (percent) having the characteristic in question (e.g. too light, defective, or misplaced) in each sample, p is computed. Then the average p, $\bar{p}$, is calculated across the samples which is used as the centerline for the p-chart.

Large samples are usually taken because the fraction of interest is typically small, and the number of items in the samples should be large enough to include some of the defectives. For example, a fraction defective may be 3% or less. Therefore, a sample size of 33 would have to be taken (i.e. 1/0.03 = 33) to expect to include *even one* defective item. Since the control limits depend in part on the sample size used, it is best to use the same sample sizes for constructing the control charts and then collect additional data to monitor the process.

Since the fraction defective follows a *binomial* distribution (*bi* means "two": either an item is or it is not) rather than a normal distribution, the standard deviation may be calculated directly from $\bar{p}$ as

$$\sigma_p = \sqrt{\frac{\bar{p}(1-\bar{p})}{n}}$$

where n is the uniform sample size to be used for controlling quality. Although the fraction defective follows the binomial distribution, if $n\bar{p}$ and $n(1-\bar{p})$ are both greater than 5, the normal distribution is a good approximation and the control limits of $3\sigma_p$ will again represent 99.7% of the sample observations. Again, the LCL cannot be negative.

The number-of-defects c-chart is used for a single situation in which any number of incidents may occur, each with a small probability. Typical of such incidents are scratches on tables, fire alarms in a city, typesetting errors in a newspaper, and the number of improper autoinsertions per printed circuit board. An average number of incidents, $\bar{c}$, is determined from past data by dividing the total number of incidents observed by the number of items inspected. The distribution of such incidents is known to follow the *Poisson distribution* with a standard deviation of

$$\sigma_c = \sqrt{\bar{c}}$$

Again, the normal distribution is used as an approximation to derive control limits with a minimum LCL of zero.

As noted earlier, we typically use control limits set at plus or minus three standard deviations, so that we don't have to intercede with a process unless we are sure that it has gone out of control. However, there is nothing magical about three standard deviations. Sometimes we may want to be absolutely sure that it has not gone out of control because someone could be harmed if it has, so waiting for 3 chances of the process harming someone out of every 1000 cycles may be waiting too long and we want to intercede, sooner, say at two standard deviations, or even one. Of course, this will be more costly, but we may be willing to pay this cost to avoid the chance of harm. Additionally, the risk of concluding that the process is out of control when it is in control increases as the control limits are tightened.

Similarly, control charts can be used for other purposes, where the limits on one side of the chart, say, above the mean, may be different from those below the mean. That is, something different is happening on one side of the mean than the other, like one side is favorable for us and the other side is highly undesirable. Figure 7.6 shows an example of this situation, where something good is happening for values above 1.0 but bad for values less than 1.0. The figure

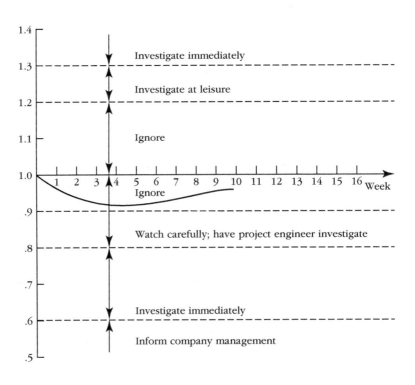

FIGURE 7.6 Nonsymmetrical Control Chart

reflects a situation above 1.3, if the process is looking so good, we should investigate to see what is going on. Perhaps the monitoring equipment has become defective, or someone has done something innovative to significantly improve the process and we would like to add this improvement throughout our facility.

7.5 Controlling Service Quality

For process control, control charts can also be used for controlling the quality of services, assuming that the right measures are being monitored. However, measuring the quality of the service portion of an output is often more difficult than measuring the quality of the facilitating good for a variety of reasons – including the service portion being abstract rather than concrete, transient rather than permanent, and psychological rather than physical. One way to cope with these difficulties is to use customer satisfaction surveys. For example, J.D. Power and Associates (www.jdpower.com) makes extensive use of customer satisfaction surveys to rate airlines, hotel chains, and rental car companies. For example, its ratings of airlines in 2022 were based on 7004 flight evaluations supplied by a national survey of travelers from March 2021 to March 2022. In the surveys, overall customer satisfaction was assessed on the basis of the airlines' performance in eight areas: cost and fees, in-flight service, flight crew, aircraft, boarding, baggage, check-in, and reservations. In 2022, JetBlue had the highest customer satisfaction score, followed by Alaska Air and Delta in the first/business class segment. These same three airlines also had the highest customer satisfaction in the premium category segment with Delta moving into second and Alaska Air moving to third. In the basic economy segment, Southwest had the highest customer satisfaction followed by JetBlue and Delta.

J.D. Power ranks hotel chains, wireless carriers, and rental car companies in a similar manner. For example, in 2021, J.D. Power ranked the overall satisfaction for eight categories of hotels (luxury, upscale, economy, etc.) on the basis of 32,963 individual evaluations. The rankings were based on respondents completing a survey with 150 questions over the period of May 2020 to June 2021. In 2021, Ritz-Carlton was the highest ranked luxury hotel and for the 16th year in a row, Drury Hotels was the highest ranked upper-midscale hotel.

A common approach to improving the quality of services is to methodically train employees in standard procedures and to use equipment that reinforces this training. Perhaps the ultimate example is McDonald's Hamburger University, where managers are intensively trained in the McDonald's system of food preparation and delivery. Not only is training intensive, but follow-up checkups are continuous, and incentives and rewards are given for continuing to pay attention to quality. Furthermore, the equipment is designed to reinforce the quality process taught to employees and to discourage sloppy habits that lead to lesser quality.

Financial services can also benefit from better quality. Some years ago, a major bank noticed that its requests for letters of credit were handled by nine different employees who conducted dozens of steps, a process that consumed four days. By retraining its employees so that each would be able to process a customer's request through all the steps, the bank was able to let each customer deal with only one employee who could complete the process within a day. Now each time a letter of credit is ordered, the customer is placed back with the same employee. As a result, the department involved has been able to double its output of letters of credit using the services of 49% fewer employees.

By paying attention to the quality delivered to customers, American Express was able to cut the processing time for new credit applications from 22 days to 11 days, thereby more than doubling the revenue per employee in its credit card division. It had previously tracked errors and processing time internally but had ignored the impacts on the customer. When it began focusing on the customer, it suddenly found that speed in the credit department was often immaterial in shortening the customer's waiting time for credit approval because four more departments still had to process every new application.

7.5.1 Service Defections

When a tangible product is produced, quality is often measured in terms of defects. In many services, the analogy to a product defect is a defecting customer – that is, a customer who takes his or her business elsewhere. Thus, service defections can be measured in a variety of ways, such as the percent of customers that do not renew their membership (health clubs), the percent of sales from new versus repeat customers (office supply retailer), and the number of customers that cancel their service (video streaming). Of course, the concept of a defecting customer is equally applicable to organizations that produce tangible outputs.

Organizations should monitor their defecting customers for a number of reasons. First, research suggests that long-time customers offer organizations a number of benefits. For example, the longer a customer has a relationship with an organization, the more likely that customer is to purchase additional products and services and the less price-sensitive he or she is. In addition, no advertising is necessary to get the business of long-term customers. In fact, long-term customers may actually be a source of free advertising for the company. One study published in the *Harvard Business Review* concluded that cutting defections in half more than doubles the average company's rate of growth. Likewise, improving customer retention rates by 5% can double profits.

Defections by customers can provide a variety of useful information. First, feedback obtained from defecting customers can be used to identify areas that need improvement. Also, the feedback can be used to determine what can be done to win these customers back. Finally, monitoring for increases in the defection rate can be used as an early warning signal that control actions are immediately needed.

EXPAND YOUR UNDERSTANDING

1. We often divide "control" into two categories: preventive and corrective. Would you classify FMEA as a tool for monitoring, preventive control, or corrective control? Explain.

2. Since service defections are analogous to defects in products, could they be controlled with control charts in the same way? Would they use charts based on inspection of variables or attributes? Give an example(s).

3. Under what kinds of circumstances might an organization wish to use control limits of two standard deviations or even one standard deviation? What should it bear in mind when using these lower limits?

4. Why are two control charts not necessary in controlling for attributes? Might not the variability of the fraction defective or the number of defects also be going out of control?

5. It is generally not appropriate to apply control charts to the same data that were used to derive the mean and limits. Why? What are the two possible outcomes if this is done, how likely is each, and what are the appropriate interpretations?

6. In deriving the p-chart, why can the sample size vary? What must be remembered if the p-chart is applied to a different sample size each time?

7. Firms regularly employ a taster for drinkable food products. What is the purpose of this taster?

8. How is quality handled differently in service firms and product firms? Does quality mean something different in a service firm?

9. Referring to the Stages of Operational Effectiveness framework, name an organization you believe exemplifies an organization in stage 4.

10. Should management be just as concerned with sample points below the lower control limit on a *p*-chart as points above the upper control chart?

11. Name an organization that would be a good example for benchmarking "best-in-class" regarding product development. Name one that would be a good benchmark of high reliability.

12. Set up a cause–effect diagram for getting an A in one of your classes.

13. Create a FMEA chart for creating a business for yourself, identifying all the ways you might fail.

14. What is the purpose of the ISO Standards? Why does this system work so well?

Apply Your Understanding

Investor's Friend

Four years ago, Ava Chase graduated from a prestigious business school with a major in finance and decided to start her own online financial weekly newspaper, *Investor's Friend*, with an emphasis on service to her subscribers. Her main competitive weapon was to reduce the cost of the subscription each year to renewing subscribers so that they remained loyal to her newspaper service. They also could go back to any previous issue and read any article from earlier editions. In addition, she provided an index of previously published articles so subscribers could easily and quickly find investing articles of interest to them. Finally, there was an extensive glossary of financial terminology so they could quickly grasp the details of various financial products.

At this point in the life of the newspaper, as shown in Table A, she was getting more subscribers to her paper, as well as more ads to increase her revenues, but production costs were escalating, her own advertising costs to solicit new subscribers and advertisers were increasing, and of course her revenues from renewals were going down. And like any newspaper, she also lost some of her previous subscribers, as well as advertisers. Ava initially didn't make money on the newspaper but improved every year, although the improvement started slowing down. As a result, her finances were getting tight, and she wondered what she should do: increase the new subscription price, alter the discount either up or down for renewals, change her newspaper's advertising rates, change the amount of her own advertising, some combination of these, or something else entirely?

Year	Number of new subscribers	Number of renewals	Total subscriber revenues	Advertiser revenues	Production cost	Advertising cost
20X1	531	0	10,620	0	12,444	3109
20X2	163	482	13,595	2124	12,802	2817
20X3	210	571	17,783	3509	14,311	3055
20X4	228	706	21,227	4788	17,975	2478

Questions

1. What is *Investors Friend's* average defection rate?

2. What is the current growth rate? What would it be if the defection rate were halved?

3. Estimate the percent of sales from new versus repeat subscribers.

4. What have been Ava's profits each year?

5. What would the profit be next year if the retention rate were increased by 5%? Where do the new profits come from?

6. What should Ava do to improve the newspaper's financial situation?

(continued)

Sammy's Jumbo Franks

Late last month, Jim Runnels, a sales representative for Sammy's Jumbo Franks (SJF), was called to the office of the Greenville Coliseum and Sport Complex, his largest account. The manager for food and beverages for the Greenville Coliseum was complaining that the jumbo hot dogs it had received over the last couple of weeks were not within the specified range of 4.9–5.1 oz.

The off-weight hot dogs had not been detected by the coliseum's receiving staff. The problem arose when the coliseum began serving the hot dogs to people attending sporting and other events. In particular, the off-size hot dogs created two problems for the coliseum: the hot dogs were either too big or too small for the hot dog buns, and the variation in the weights meant that standard cooking times resulted in either over- or undercooking the hot dogs.

In consequence, the coliseum had to issue special cooking instructions to all of its food servers that required them to weigh each hot dog and sort them by weight so that batches of similar weight hot dogs could be cooked together. The manager of food services at the coliseum made it clear that a new supplier for jumbo hot dogs would be sought if this problem continued.

SJF's quality control department was immediately summoned to assist in determining the cause of the problem.

SJF's quality manager, Ronald Wilson, speculated that the cause of the problem was with the second shift. To analyze the problem, he entered into a spreadsheet the data from all the previous samples taken over the last two months. As it turned out, 15 random samples had been taken over the two-month period for both the first and the second shifts. Samples always consisted of 10 randomly selected hot dogs. Also, separate sampling schedules were used for the first and second shifts so that the second shift would not automatically assume that it would be subject to a random sample just because the first shift had been earlier in the day.

After entering the sample weight data of the hot dogs into the following spreadsheet and calculating the sample means, Ronald was quite puzzled. There did not seem to be any noticeable difference in the average weights across the two shifts. Furthermore, although the lines were running at less than full capacity during the first six samples, there still did not seem to be any change in either line after reaching full production with the start of the basketball season.

	A	B	C	D	E	F	G	H	I	J	K	L	M	N	O	P
1	First shift															
2							Sample number									
3	Observation	1	2	3	4	5	6	7	8	9	10	11	12	13	14	15
4	1	4.90	5.05	4.96	4.92	4.96	5.03	4.99	5.00	5.02	5.03	5.01	4.95	5.02	4.96	5.06
5	2	5.03	5.04	4.96	5.00	5.00	4.99	5.03	5.01	5.05	4.90	4.94	4.95	4.95	4.97	4.97
6	3	5.00	5.00	4.92	5.05	5.03	4.98	5.01	4.95	5.00	4.95	5.00	5.06	5.00	4.93	5.00
7	4	5.03	5.11	5.01	5.03	4.98	4.99	5.02	5.01	5.01	5.01	5.00	5.02	4.98	5.01	5.00
8	5	5.02	4.94	4.98	5.01	5.00	4.98	5.01	4.99	5.03	5.01	4.96	4.94	5.04	5.00	5.03
9	6	4.92	5.02	5.00	5.02	5.02	5.01	4.99	4.98	5.00	4.94	4.98	4.99	5.02	5.04	5.08
10	7	5.04	5.03	4.98	5.02	5.00	4.99	5.06	4.96	5.01	4.98	5.01	4.97	4.99	4.98	4.97
11	8	4.92	5.00	5.00	4.96	5.01	5.01	5.05	5.00	4.97	4.98	4.97	4.97	5.05	5.08	4.98
12	9	4.95	4.95	4.94	5.02	4.95	4.98	4.97	4.94	5.07	5.00	5.00	4.96	5.02	4.94	5.00
13	10	5.02	4.99	5.08	4.94	5.00	4.95	5.04	4.98	5.02	5.01	4.98	5.02	5.06	5.02	4.97
14	Average	4.98	5.01	4.98	5.00	5.00	4.99	5.02	4.98	5.02	4.98	4.99	4.98	5.01	4.99	5.01
15																

	A	B	C	D	E	F	G	H	I	J	K	L	M	N	O	P
16																
17	Second shift															
18							Sample number									
19	Observation	1	2	3	4	5	6	7	8	9	10	11	12	13	14	15
20	1	5.03	5.02	4.99	4.96	5.03	5.02	5.08	5.10	5.16	5.00	4.97	5.11	5.11	4.90	5.02
21	2	4.90	4.95	4.97	4.97	4.98	5.03	4.97	4.93	4.92	4.97	4.91	5.05	4.98	4.92	4.98
22	3	5.02	4.94	5.04	4.98	5.00	4.98	4.93	4.92	4.99	5.08	5.15	4.93	5.13	4.97	4.86
23	4	4.98	5.05	5.02	5.00	4.97	5.06	4.84	4.93	5.00	5.07	4.96	5.15	5.15	4.92	4.94
24	5	5.01	4.95	5.02	5.02	4.98	5.04	5.07	5.03	4.98	4.94	4.91	4.98	5.10	5.04	4.93
25	6	4.99	4.99	4.99	5.03	5.00	5.04	4.95	4.96	4.99	4.96	5.07	4.88	5.12	5.03	4.97
26	7	4.99	4.97	5.00	4.98	4.99	4.99	4.93	4.86	5.01	5.13	5.15	4.74	5.01	4.91	5.05
27	8	5.02	5.00	5.00	4.96	4.98	4.98	4.99	5.08	5.07	4.93	4.95	4.90	4.93	4.95	4.97
28	9	5.01	5.00	5.05	5.02	5.03	4.97	4.82	4.96	4.93	4.96	4.91	5.03	5.04	4.98	5.03
29	10	4.97	4.99	4.95	5.03	5.00	4.99	5.05	5.14	5.03	4.91	5.11	5.04	5.03	5.08	4.92
30	Average	4.99	4.99	5.00	5.00	5.00	5.01	4.96	4.99	5.01	5.00	5.01	4.98	5.06	4.97	4.97

Questions

1. Can you identify any difference between the first and second shifts that explains the weight problem? If so, when is this difference first detectable?

Koala Tech, LTD.

Koala Tech, Ltd., of Sydney, Australia, produces office equipment for small businesses and home offices. Several months ago, it launched its PFS 1000, a single unit that functions as a color printer, color scanner, color copier, and fax machine. The PFS 1000 won rave reviews for its functionality, affordable price, and innovative design. This, coupled with Koala Tech's reputation for producing highly reliable products, quickly led to a severe backlog. Koala Tech's plant simply could not keep up with demand.

Initially, Koala Tech's president, Nancy Samuelson, was extremely concerned about the backlog and put a great deal of pressure on the plant manager, George Johnson, to increase production. However, Nancy abruptly shifted gears when a new report indicated that returns and complaints for the PFS 1000 were running four times higher than the usual industry rate. Because Koala Tech's reputation was on the line, Nancy decided that the problem required immediate attention. She also decided that the quickest way to diagnose the problem and to avoid the usual mentality of "blaming it on the other department" would be to bring in an outside consultant with expertise in these matters.

Nancy hired Ken Cathey to investigate the problem. Nancy and Ken agreed that Ken should spend his first week interviewing key personnel in an effort to learn as much about the problem as possible. Because of the urgency of the problem, Nancy promised Ken that he would have complete access to – and the cooperation of – all employees. Nancy would send out a memo immediately informing all employees that they were expected to cooperate and assist Ken in any way they could.

The next morning, Ken decided to begin his investigation by discussing the quality problem with several of the production supervisors. He began with the supervisor of the final assembly area, Todd Allision. Todd comment

> *I received Nancy's memo yesterday and, frankly, the problem with the PFS 1000 does not surprise me. One of the problems we've had in final assembly is with the casing. Basically, the case is composed of a top and a bottom. The problem we are having is that these pieces rarely fit together, so we typically have to force them together. I'm sure this is adding a lot of extra stress on the cases. I haven't seen a breakdown on what the problems with quality are, but it wouldn't surprise me if one of the problems was cracked cases or cases that are coming apart. I should also mention that we never had this problem with our old supplier. However, when purchasing determined that we could save over $A1 per unit, we switched to a new supplier for the cases.*

(continued)

The meeting with Todd lasted for about an hour and a half, and Ken decided that rather than meet with someone else, he would be better off reviewing the notes he had taken and filling in any gaps while the conversation was still fresh in his mind. Then he would break for lunch and meet with one or two additional people in the afternoon.

After returning from lunch, Ken stopped by to talk with Steve Morgan, the production supervisor for the printed circuit boards. Ken found Steve and an equipment operator staring at one of the autoinsertion machines used to place components such as integrated circuits, capacitors, and resistors on the printed circuit board before wave soldering. Upon arriving, Ken introduced himself to Steve and asked, "What's up?" Steve responded:

We are having an extremely difficult time making the printed circuit boards for the PFS 1000. The designers placed the components closer together than this generation of equipment was designed to handle. As a result, the leads of the components are constantly being bent. I doubt that more than 25% of the boards have all their components installed properly. As a result, we are spending a great deal of time inspecting all the boards and reworking the ones with problems. Also, because of the huge backlog for these boards and the large number that must be reworked, we have been trying to operate the equipment 20% faster than its normal operating rate. This has caused the machine to break down much more frequently. I estimate that on a given eight-hour shift, the machine is down one to two hours.

In terms of your job – to determine the cause of the problems with quality – faulty circuit boards are very likely a key contributor. We are doing our best to find and correct all the defects, but inspecting and reworking the boards is a very tedious process, and the employees are putting in a lot of extra hours. In addition, we are under enormous pressure to get the boards to final assembly. My biggest regret is that I didn't have more input when they were building the prototypes of the PFS 1000. The prototypes are all built by highly trained technicians using primarily a manual process. Unfortunately, the prototypes are built only to give the engineers feedback on their designs. Had they shown some people in production the prototypes, we could have made suggestions on changes that would have made the design easier to produce.

Ken decided to end the day by talking to the plant manager, Harvey Michaels. Harvey was in complete agreement with Todd and Steve and discussed at length the enormous pressure he was under to get product out the door: "The bottom line is that no one cooperates. Purchasing changes suppliers to save a few bucks, and we end up with components that can't be used. Then our own engineers design products that we can't produce. We need to work together."

On his second day, Ken decided to follow up on the information he had gathered the day before. He first visited the director of purchasing, Marilyn Reagan. When asked about the problem of the cases that did not fit together, Marilyn responded:

The fact of the matter is that switching suppliers for the cases saved $A1.04 per unit. That may not sound like a lot, but multiply that by the 125,000 units we are expecting to sell this year, and it turns out to be pretty significant. Those guys in production think the world revolves around them. I am, however, sympathetic to their problems, and I plan on discussing the problem with the supplier the next time we meet. That should be sometime next month.

After wrapping up the meeting with Marilyn, Ken decided he would next talk to the director of engineering. On the way, he recognized a person at a vending machine as the worker who had been standing next to Steve at the auto-insertion machine. Ken introduced himself and decided to talk with the worker for a few minutes. The worker introduced himself as Jim and mentioned that he had been working in the shipping department until just two weeks ago. The operator before Jim had quit because of the pressure. Jim hadn't received any formal training in operating the new equipment, but he said that Steve tried to check on him a couple of times a day to see how things were going. Jim appreciated Steve's efforts, but the quality inspectors made him nervous, and he felt that they were always looking over his shoulder.

Ken thanked Jim for his input and then headed off to meet with the director of engineering, Jack Carel. After introducing himself, Ken took a seat in front of Jack's desk. Jack began:

So, you are here to investigate our little quality snafu. The pressure that we are under here in engineering is the need to shrink things down. It used to be that fax machines, printers, scanners, and copiers were all separate pieces of equipment. Now, with the introduction of the PFS 1000, all this functionality is included in one piece of equipment not much larger than the original printer. That means design tolerances are going to be a lot tighter and the product is going to be more difficult to manufacture. But the fact of the matter is that manufacturing is going to have to get its act together if we are going to survive. The engineering department did its job. We designed a state-of-the-art piece of office equipment, and the prototypes we built proved that the design works. It's now up to the manufacturing guys to figure out how to produce it. We have done all that we can and should be expected to do.

To end his second day, Ken decided to meet with the director of quality assurance, Debbie Lynn. Debbie commented:

My biggest challenge as director of quality assurance is trying to convince the rest of the organization of the importance quality plays. Sure, everyone gives lip service to the importance of quality, but as the end of the month approaches, getting the product out the door is always the highest priority. Also, while I am officially held accountable for quality, I have no formal authority over the production

workers. The quality inspectors that report to me do little more than inspect product and tag it if it doesn't meet the specifications so that it is sent to the rework area. In all honesty, I am quite optimistic about Nancy's current concern for quality and very much welcome the opportunity to work closely with you to improve Koala Tech's quality initiatives.

Questions

1. **Which departments at Koala Tech have the most impact on** quality? What role should each department play in helping Koala Tech improve overall quality?

2. What recommendations would you make to Nancy concerning Koala Tech's problem with quality? What role should the quality assurance department play?

EXERCISES

7.1 The city government is planning a career fair weekend in two months and wishes to use an FMEA table to identify risk elements to monitor and determine possible actions to take in controlling the risks. They believe that there are four major risks to the fair:

1. Insufficient employer turnout – the severity if this happens they rate as an 8, the likelihood as a 4, and the detectability as a 5.

2. Insufficient job seeker turnout – for this, they rate the severity as a 6, likelihood as a 7, and detectability as a 5.

3. Inclement weather – severity 4, likelihood 5, detectability 4.

4. Economy – severity 7, likelihood 5, detectability 6.

Determine the most important risk elements and suggest ways to control them.

7.2 Pick two different processes on which to run an FMEA analysis, such as running an end-of-semester party and passing an upcoming advanced finance course. Identify the major risks for success with each one and give each a severity, likelihood, and detectability rating to calculate the RPN for each risk. How would you monitor each of these risk elements for impending failure and what steps might you take to control them?

7.3 Top management of the Royal Scottish Bank monitors the volume of activity at 38 branch banks with control charts.

If deposit volume (or any of perhaps a dozen other volume indicators) at a branch falls below the LCL, there is apparently some problem with the branch's market share. If, on the other hand, the volume exceeds the UCL, it means that the branch should be considered for expansion or that a new branch might be opened in an adjacent neighborhood.

Given the 10-day samples for each of the six months below, prepare an $\bar{X}$ chart for the deposit volume (in hundreds of thousands of pounds) for the Kilmarnock branch. Use control limits of $\pm 3\sigma$. The average range of the six samples was found to be £85,260.

Month	Average of 10 days of deposits (£100,000)
June	0.93
July	1.05
August	1.21
September	0.91
October	0.89
November	1.13

7.4 Using the following weekly demand data for a new soft drink, determine the upper and lower control limits that can be used in recognizing a change in demand patterns. Use $\pm 3\sigma$ control limits.

Week	Demand (six packs)
1	3500
2	4100
3	3750
4	4300
5	4000
6	3650

7.5 A control chart has a mean of 50 and 2 control limits of 40 and 60. The following data are plotted on the chart: 38, 55, 58, 42, 64, 49, 51, 58, 61, 46, 44, 50. Should action be taken?

7.6 Given the following data, construct a three-sigma range control chart.

Day of sample	Sample values
Saturday	22, 19, 20
Sunday	21, 20, 17
Monday	16, 17, 18
Tuesday	20, 16, 21
Wednesday	23, 20, 20
Thursday	19, 16, 21

a. If Friday's results are 15, 14, and 21, is the process in control?

b. Construct a three-sigma means control chart and determine if the process is still in control on Friday.

7.7 a. Using the following data, prepare a p-chart for the control of picking accuracy in a wholesale food warehouse. Sample size is expected to be 100 cases.

Day	Number of cases picked	Number of incorrect picks
1	4700	38
2	5100	49
3	3800	27
4	4100	31
5	4500	42
6	5200	48

b. Determine if days 7, 8, and 9 are under control.

Day	Number of cases picked	Number of incorrect picks
7	100	1
8	100	2
9	100	4

7.8 A new machine for making nails produced 25 defective nails on Monday, 36 on Tuesday, 17 on Wednesday, and 47 on Thursday. Construct an $\bar{X}$ chart, p-chart, and c-chart based on the results for Monday through Wednesday and determine if Thursday's production was in control. The machine produces 1 million or so nails a day. Which is the proper chart to use?

7.9 Construct a p-chart using two-sigma limits based on the results of 20 samples of size 400 in the following table.

Sample number	Number of defects
1	2
2	0
3	8
4	5
5	8
6	4
7	4
8	2
9	9
10	2
11	3
12	0
13	5
14	6
15	7
16	1
17	5
18	8
19	2
20	1

7.10 Twenty samples of 100 were taken with the following number of defectives: 8, 5, 3, 9, 4, 5, 8, 5, 3, 6, 4, 3, 5, 6, 2, 5, 0, 3, 4, 2. Construct a 3-sigma p-chart.

7.11 Sheets of styrofoam are being inspected for flaws. The first day's results from a new machine that produced five sheets are 17, 28, 9, 21, 14. Design a control chart for future production.

BIBLIOGRAPHY

Dangayach, G. S., and S. G. Deshmukh. "An Exploratory Study of Manufacturing Strategy Practices of Machinery Manufacturing Companies in India." *OMEGA: The International Journal of Management Science*, 34 (2006): 254–273.

Franchetti, M. "Six Sigma Receives USPS Stamp of Approval." *Six Sigma Forum Magazine* (February 2008): 15–17.

Gupta, V. K., and D. J. Graham. "A Customer-Driven Quality Improvement and Management Project at Diamond Offshore Drilling." *Project Management Journal* (September 1997).

Ibbs, C. W., and Y.-H. Kwak. "Benchmarking Project Management Organizations." *PM Network*, February 1998.

J.D. Power, North American Hotel Guests want Breakfast Back, jdpower.com, July 14, 2021.

J.D. Power, North American Airline Passenger Satisfaction Declines, jdpower.com, May 11, 2022.

Kidder, T. *The Soul of a New Machine*. Boston, MA: Little Brown, 1981.

Krzykowski, B. "Walking the Talk." *Quality Progress* (June 2011): 41–44.

Thamhain, H. J. "Best Practices for Controlling Technology-Based Projects." *Project Management Journal*, (December 1996).

Meredith, J. R., and S. M. Shafer. *Project Management: A Strategic Managerial Approach*, 11th ed. New York: Wiley, 2022.

Riebling, N. B., S. Condon, and D. Gopen. "Toward Error Free Lab Work." *Six Sigma Forum Magazine* (November 2004): 23–29.

Stamatis, D. H. Failure *Mode and Effect Analysis: FMEA from Theory to Execution*, 2nd ed. Milwaukee, WI: ASQ Quality Press, 2003.

Toney, F. "What the Fortune 500 Know About PM Best Practices." *PM Network*, February 1997.

Wheelwright, S. C., and R. H. Hayes. "Competing Through Manufacturing." *Harvard Business Review* (January–February 1985): 99–109.

8 Process Improvement: Six Sigma

CHAPTER IN PERSPECTIVE
While controlling the processes as described in Chapter 7, it is often determined that there are opportunities to improve the process. Thus, the focus of this chapter is on the redesign and continuous improvement of business processes in support of the overall business strategy.

To put our discussion in perspective, we begin with an overview of three alternative approaches for process improvement. We then turn our attention to the first process improvement strategy, Business Process Design. This is then followed by a detailed discussion of the second process improvement strategy, Six Sigma. Next, each phase in Six Sigma's DMAIC approach is discussed in more detail, including illustrating the use of representative Six Sigma tools in each phase. The chapter concludes with a discussion of Six Sigma in practice. Here, we discuss the various roles associated with Six Sigma, becoming certified, and the need for organizations to customize their approach to Six Sigma training and implementation. In the next chapter, we then continue our discussion of process improvement strategies and address the third process improvement strategy, namely, Lean. The trend toward integrating Six Sigma and Lean will also be discussed in the next chapter.

While often considered more tactical in nature, the topic of process improvement has important strategic implications. For example, as is discussed in greater detail in the chapter, organizations that have adopted Six Sigma have obtained substantial financial benefits. But beyond these financial benefits, process improvement is fundamentally concerned with identifying ways to better meet customer requirements, which in turn is perhaps the most important driver of competitive success. Indeed, meeting customer requirements is becoming progressively more important in fiercely competitive markets that result from shorter product life cycles, customers becoming more sophisticated given the ubiquity of information, and the globalization of markets.

8.1 Introduction

- Hewitt Associates provides human resource (HR) outsourcing services for client organizations. HR outsourcing involves having a service provider take over an organization's traditional HR functions, such as payroll processing, benefits administration, and employee recruiting. Customer service (CS) representatives are the Hewitt employees on the frontline delivering the HR outsourcing service to its clients. A key challenge Hewitt faced was that the annual turnover of its CS reps was close to 100%. Each time a CS rep left, Hewitt incurred significant costs associated with the separation process, hiring costs for the replacement, training costs, and costs related to lost productivity.

To address the turnover challenge, a team initiated a Six Sigma project using the traditional define, measure, analyze, improve, and control (DMAIC) methodology and multiple Six Sigma tools, including project charters, cause-and-effect diagrams, and prioritization matrices. At the outset of the project, the team determined that it first needed to quantify the costs of CS rep turnover using hard data in order to get senior management buy-in for investing in initiatives to reduce the turnover rate. Based on the team's analysis, it was estimated that CS rep turnover was costing Hewitt $14.5 million annually in lost productivity and another $1.5 million for training and recruiting costs.

To analyze the situation further, Hewitt used regression analysis to identify the key factors that impacted employee turnover. The regression analysis identified a number of potential factors, including providing employees with opportunities for growth, pay, recognition, work activities, and management positions. After studying the results, the team decided to experiment with one potential factor, base pay. To investigate the impact base pay had on retention, the team selected a group of CS reps to pilot test providing them with market adjustments to their base pay. Making these adjustments cost Hewitt $600,000. The result was that the retention rate of the CS reps who received the market adjustment to their base pay increased to 96%, which translated into not losing 80 proficient CS reps. The team further estimated that the lower turnover rate translated into a savings of $1.9 million, providing a 217% return on investment (Leatherbury 2008).

- Bank of America (B of A) was paying a steep price in terms of both money and customer dissatisfaction from errors and inefficiencies. As one example, on a 10-point scale, only 40% of B of A's customers rated their experience with the company at the top, that is, a 9 or 10. Internally, hundreds of thousands of defects were being created per million opportunities. Ken Lewis, the company's CEO, decided in 2001 that a change in strategy was needed. This entailed a shift from fueling growth by mergers and acquisitions toward more organic growth based on retaining and deepening the relationship with existing customers. Thus, in 2001, the company embarked on its quality journey. Based on his belief that the company needed a more disciplined and comprehensive approach to process improvement, Lewis turned to Six Sigma. A new senior manager reporting directly to Lewis was hired to oversee quality and productivity.

  Being a financial services organization, it was to be expected that many in the organization would be skeptical of the applicability of an approach that was developed for factories. One way CEO Lewis addressed this concern was by being among the first to personally complete a Green Belt project and further requiring all of his direct reports to complete projects as well. Each of these projects was a success, providing benefits such as improved customer satisfaction with problem resolution, significantly reduced travel expenses, and increased employee retention. If you asked executives at B of A, they would have told you Six Sigma was not a fad but the way we conducted business. To get its Six Sigma initiative off the ground, B of A recruited Black Belts and Master Black Belts from leading Six Sigma organizations such as General Electric, Motorola, and Honeywell. By 2004, B of A estimated that there were over 100 open senior leadership positions requiring a background in Six Sigma. One senior executive at B of A had gone so far as to speculate that Black Belt certification would become a mandatory qualification for leadership roles at B of A. By early 2004, B of A had trained more than 10,000 employees in the use of Six Sigma tools to support the DMAIC methodology. But perhaps the most compelling statistics relate to the overall benefits B of A has received as a result of its Six Sigma initiatives. In particular, B of A estimates that it obtained benefits in excess of $2 billion in less than three years while at the same time increasing its customer top ratings by 25% (Jones 2004).

- In 2002, the nuclear medicine department of Southside Hospital, a not-for-profit community hospital located in Bay Shore, New York, was receiving numerous complaints regarding the turnaround times for stress tests. Delays in receiving the results from stress tests impacted the timeliness of treating the patients, which in turn could affect the length of time a patient was required to stay in the hospital. To address the problem associated with excessive turnaround times, hospital administrators decided to test Six Sigma's approach with a team consisting of one Black Belt and three Green Belts. In the course of completing the project, the team utilized many traditional Six Sigma tools, including voice of the customer (VOC), "critical to quality" trees, process mapping, stakeholder analysis, defects per million opportunities (DPMO), cause-and-effect diagrams, regression analysis, and Pareto analysis. In the end, the team was able to reduce the turnaround times for stress tests by over 50%, from 68 to 32 hours (the standard deviation was also reduced from 32 to 9 hours). In addition, the project resulted in an overall increase in capacity with no additional cost. In fact, costs actually decreased by $34,000 due to savings in salaries. Hospital administrators were pleased by the extent to which such a data-driven approach enhanced the ultimate success of the project (Godin et al. 2004).
- 3M's journey with Six Sigma dates back to 2001. Fast forward to 2021 and 3M has continued to employ Six Sigma in a variety of areas: helping it optimize and improve its supply chain risk management processes, improve its internal production processes, and to achieve its sustainability goals. For example, 3M utilized Lean Six Sigma projects to help it meet the demand for respirators in Brazil during the COVID-19 pandemic. Likewise, 3M utilized a number of methodologies including Lean Six Sigma to reduce waste, which helped it improve both its internal processes while at the same time make progress toward its sustainability objectives.

  3M is a true pioneer in sustainability, having launched its Pollution Prevention Pays (3P)[1] program in the mid-1970s. To achieve important sustainability objectives, 3P projects have focused on reformulating products, modifying production processes, redesigning equipment, and recycling/reusing waste. More specifically, 3M's Environmental, Health, and Safety Operations (EHS) team has leveraged Lean Six Sigma tools to help achieve its sustainability goals. For example, in 2006, 3M discovered that 70% of its 3P projects utilized Six Sigma. In 2007, the EHS team included two Blackbelts and one Master Blackbelt. Additionally, all other members of the EHS team were required to take two weeks of training to become Greenbelts and lead a Six Sigma project. While the primary goal of its Six Sigma projects typically focused on improving operational efficiencies and product yields, a natural by-product associated with these goals was reductions in energy consumption, reduced emissions, and less waste.

  To evaluate its progress toward its sustainability objectives, 3M utilized a variety of metrics including water released, energy usage, waste generated, and greenhouse gasses emitted. As an example of its success, in 2000 3M established the goals of improving energy efficiency by 20% and reducing waste by 25% by 2005. It exceeded these goals, improving its energy efficiency by 27% and reducing waste by 30% (EPA 2021, 3M 2022).
- One of the tasks performed by TRW's corporate law department is the registration of trademarks. The company estimated that it costs an average of $1200 (not including processing costs) to renew a trademark worldwide. To evaluate the trademark renewal process, a team utilized many traditional Six Sigma tools, including VOC, determining the critical to quality characteristics, logistic regression analysis, and value-added process mapping to evaluate the process. One finding from the project was that in numerous cases, trademarks were being

---

[1] Is it a coincidence that a company that goes by 3M named an important enterprise-wide initiative 3P?

renewed more out of a sense of history and nostalgia as opposed to providing value to the business. In the end, the project produced hard savings of $1.8 million by eliminating the renewal of entire classes of trademarks. Numerous process improvements in the trademark renewal process were also identified, producing additional soft savings. Finally, by clearly defining defects in the trademark renewal process, the project team was able to establish a baseline process sigma level of 2.18, which can be used to assess the impact of future process improvements (Das et al. 2004).

These examples illustrate that the Six Sigma process improvement methodology is applicable to a wide variety of organizations and disciplines. The examples are also representative of significant gains organizations achieve in improving their processes through the use of Six Sigma. These improvements translate directly into helping organizations become more competitive. As a result of the success organizations have had with their Six Sigma initiatives, it has become a particularly timely topic in business. This has further resulted in people with a background in Six Sigma being in high demand. In fact, at 3M, 25% of the 1000 employees who completed Six Sigma training were promoted two levels or more! As further support, a search in June 2022 at Indeed.com using the keyword "Six Sigma" yielded over 23,000 job postings across virtually all industries, including manufacturing, consulting, technology, financial services, insurance, health care, and retail.

As further evidence of the value industry is placing on individuals with Six Sigma experience, consider the following quote taken from the letter to shareholders in GE's 2000 annual report, whose coauthors included chairman and CEO Jack Welch and president and chairman-elect Jeffrey Immelt (p. 6):

> It is reasonable to guess that the next CEO of this Company, decades down the road, is probably a Six Sigma Black Belt or Master Black Belt somewhere in GE right now, or on the verge of being offered – as all our early-career (3–5 years) top 20% performers will be – a two- to three-year Black Belt assignment. The generic nature of a Black Belt assignment, in addition to its rigorous process discipline and relentless customer focus, makes Six Sigma the perfect training for growing 21st century GE leadership.

A question that naturally arises is: What is driving industry's interest in Six Sigma? Perhaps the primary reason for the current popularity of Six Sigma is that it works, as exemplified by the significant benefits several high-profile organizations have reported from their Six Sigma initiatives.

To illustrate this, Table 8.1 summarizes the financial benefits obtained by organizations across a variety of industries. The table also provides summary information related to the number of employees who were trained at various Six Sigma levels.

Table 8.1 Examples of Six Sigma Training and Benefits

Company	Time period	Number of master black belts trained	Number of black belts trained	Number of green belts trained	Monetary benefits from Six Sigma ($M)
Air Canada	2002–2005	11	51	1200	$450
American Express	2002				$200
American Standard	2000–2004	44	673	4302	$170
Cummins	2000–2005	65	500		$1000
Merrill Lynch	2001–2005	20	406	874	
Sun Microsystems	2000–2005	6	122	207	$1170
Tyco International	2002–2005		263	870	$800

Six Sigma is equally applicable to organizations that produce a tangible output (e.g. Cummins and Sun Microsystems) or deliver an intangible service (e.g. Air Canada and American Express) as well as to organizations that exist to make a profit (e.g. B of A, American Standard, and Tyco International) or are nonprofit organizations such as Southside Hospital.

To put our discussion into perspective, we begin with a brief overview of alternative approaches to process improvement. Based on this overview, we then turn our attention to the first process improvement strategy, Business Process Design (BPD). This is then followed by a detailed discussion of the second process improvement approach – Six Sigma's DMAIC improvement methodology. Following this overview of the DMAIC approach, each of its phases is discussed in more detail, and representative Six Sigma tools are overviewed. The chapter concludes with a discussion of Six Sigma in practice. In the next chapter, we continue our discussion of process improvement and address a third process improvement approach, namely, the Lean approach to process improvement. The trend toward integrating Six Sigma and Lean will also be discussed in the next chapter.

8.2 Approaches for Process Improvement

The appropriate process improvement strategy to employ depends on the nature of the challenge to be addressed. Figure 8.1 provides a road map for selecting the appropriate process improvement strategy. As is shown in Figure 8.1, BPD and Design for Six Sigma (a set of six-sigma tools) are appropriate process improvement strategies for situations where it is determined that the process is fundamentally flawed or when a brand-new process must be created. In cases where the process is fundamentally flawed, it is best to start with a clean slate and redesign the process from scratch. In cases where the process is not fundamentally flawed but there are opportunities to improve it, we must consider the nature of the problem to determine the appropriate process improvement strategy. In cases where it is determined that there is too much variation in the process, the Six Sigma methodology is appropriate (variation in process outcomes was discussed in the previous chapter). In cases where it is determined that the efficiency of the process needs to be improved, Lean is the appropriate process improvement strategy. Of course, it is also common for a process to suffer from both too much variation and waste, in which case a combination of Six Sigma and Lean tools can be applied to the process improvement initiative. This is often referred to as Lean Sigma. We now turn our attention to discussing BPD and Six Sigma in more detail. Lean is the topic of the next chapter.

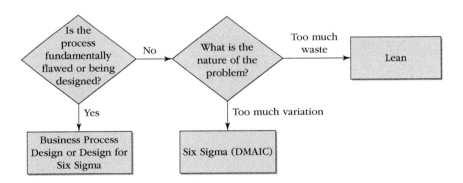

FIGURE 8.1 Alternative Process Design and Improvement Strategies

8.3 Business Process Design (Reengineering)

BPD is the appropriate strategy for processes that require improvements beyond what can be done via incremental enhancements or in situations where a new process that does not currently exist must be developed. BPD is often needed when there is a major advance in technology, a major shift in customer requirements, or where a process has not been improved over a long period of time. BPD is perhaps most commonly referred to as *reengineering*, but a wide variety of other names are also frequently used.

Although there have been dramatic advances in technology and significant shifts in customer requirements in the last few decades, it is only recently that organizations have begun to look for better ways to organize and integrate work. Despite the technological advances adopted by organizations, the dramatic improvements in performance that were expected did not materialize. One explanation for this is that organizations were not taking advantage of the capabilities the new technologies offered. Rather, companies were simply using technology to speed up and automate existing (and often ineffective) practices. Clearly, if an activity or a set of activities is not effective to begin with, performing it faster and with less human intervention does not automatically make it effective.

For instance, one major financial institution reported that more than 90 steps were required for an office worker to get office supplies. Given the capabilities of information technology, it is certainly true that these steps could be automated and speeded up. However, is automating all these steps the best solution? Might it not make more sense to eliminate most of them? Consider that even if the forms are generated and dispatched faster, valuable managerial time is still being used to examine and approve these requests every time an employee needs a pad of paper or ballpoint pen. Indeed, when the cost of the controls is weighed against the benefits, it might be much more effective to give employees access to the supply cabinet to retrieve their own supplies as needed. Dr. Michael Hammer used the term *paving cow paths* to describe organizations that simply implement a new technology without considering the capabilities it offers to perform work in entirely new and better ways.

There are several themes that generally underlie BPD. *First,* BPD's primary objective is designing business processes that best meet the needs of the customer. With BPD, the goal is not to improve the efficiency or effectiveness of a process simply for the sake of doing so. Rather, all improvements must ultimately translate into benefits the customer cares about. This brings us to a *second* theme associated with BPD, a concern with making *quantum* improvements in performance rather than small, *incremental* improvements. Reducing errors by 10% would generally be considered an incremental improvement. Reducing errors by 75% or more is a quantum improvement. A *third* important theme of BPD is the central role of technology. When new information technologies are adopted by companies, they should take advantage of the capabilities offered by the technology to perform activities in perhaps entirely different and better ways.

Hammer and Stanton (1995), in *The Reengineering Revolution,* define reengineering as "the fundamental rethinking and **radical redesign** of business **processes** to bring about **dramatic** improvements in performance" (p. 3). The keywords *radical, redesign, process,* and *dramatic* are particularly important to understanding the concept of reengineering or BPD. The word *radical* is used to signify that the purpose of BPD is to *profoundly* change the way work is performed, not to make *superficial* changes. It has to do with understanding the foundation upon which work is based and eliminating old ways that no longer make sense. In other words, it refers to *reinventing* the way work is performed and organized, not simply improving it. Radically changing work is often best accomplished by starting with a clean slate and making no assumptions about how work activities are performed.

The second keyword, *redesign*, denotes the fact that BPD is concerned with the design of work. Typically, people think of design as being primarily applicable to products. However, the way work is accomplished can also be designed. In fact, Hammer and Stanton point out that having intelligent, capable, well-trained, motivated employees is of little value if work is badly designed to begin with. The third keyword is *process*. Although all organizations perform processes, it was not until recently that they began organizing work on the basis of these processes. As they did this, they soon realized that customers are not particularly interested in the individual activities that are performed to create a product or service. Rather, they are more concerned about the final result of these activities. We use the term *process centered* to refer to organizations that have organized their work activities on the basis of specific customer value-creating processes.

The last keyword is *dramatic*. BPD is concerned with making quantum improvements in performance, not small or incremental improvements. Thus, BPD focuses on achieving breakthroughs in performance. A company that lowers its lead time by 10% from the previous year does not exemplify a dramatic improvement. On the other hand, a company that reduces its lead time from three weeks to three days does.

To illustrate these concepts, consider the experiences of IBM Credit Corporation. IBM Credit was in the business of financing purchases of IBM office equipment. Numerous companies – including General Motors, Ford, Chrysler, and General Electric – are in the lending business. These companies have found that operating financial units can be extremely profitable in addition to offering customers a higher level of service.

Originally, IBM Credit was organized into functional departments. The steps involved in processing a credit request are shown in Figure 8.2. The process began when an IBM sales rep closed a deal and the customer wanted to finance the purchase through IBM Credit. In this case, the sales rep would relay the pertinent information to one of 14 order loggers at IBM Credit. The order loggers sat in a conference room and manually wrote down on pieces of paper the information supplied by the sales reps. Periodically during the day, the pieces of paper were carted upstairs to the credit department. Employees in the credit department entered the pertinent information into a computer to check the borrower's creditworthiness. The results of this check were then recorded on another piece of paper.

Next, the documents would be transferred to the business practices department. This department would modify the standard loan covenant in response to specific requests by customers. The business practices department used its own computer system. After being processed in the business practices department, the documents were transported to the pricing department, where pricers entered the data into a software program to determine the appropriate interest rate. Finally, the entire dossier was transported to an administrator, who converted all the information into a "quote letter." The quote letter was then sent by Federal Express to the field sales rep.

The sales reps were extremely dissatisfied with this process. First of all, the entire process took an average of six days and sometimes as long as two weeks. What salesperson wants to give his or her customers two weeks to think over a purchase? On top of this, when a sales rep called to check on the status of a customer's credit request, often the request could not even be located.

As a result of complaints from the sales reps, a manager at IBM Credit decided to investigate the problem. The first thing this manager wanted to determine was how much work time actually went into processing a credit request. To determine this, the manager employed the strategy of "becoming the part" – or in this case, "becoming the loan request" – by walking an actual request through the entire process. First, he recorded the time it took to log an actual order. Then he took

FIGURE 8.2 Processing Credit Requests at IBM Credit

the order that was just called in and personally carried it to the credit department. Arriving at the credit department, he selected a worker at random and told the worker to stop what he or she was currently working on and perform the credit check. After repeating this in the other departments, the manager determined that the actual processing time of a credit request was about 90 minutes. Thus, out of an average of six days, each application was being processed for only about 90 minutes, indicating a significant opportunity for improvement.

IBM Credit's approach to improving this process was to combine all these activities into one job called a *deal structurer*. Thus, one worker handled all the activities required to process a credit request, from logging the information to writing the quote letter. As a result of using deal structurers, turnaround times were reduced to an average of 4 hours. Furthermore, with a small reduction in head count, the number of deals processed by IBM Credit increased 100 times (not 100%). Do these results qualify as dramatic?

Given these results, you may wonder why IBM Credit had ever adopted a functional organizational structure in the first place. To answer this, let's put ourselves in the shoes of a manager at IBM Credit. Suppose we were asked to develop an organization to process credit requests. One requirement that might occur to us is that the process should be able to handle any possible type of credit request. Given this requirement, if you look again at Figure 8.2, you will see that IBM Credit's original functional arrangement accomplishes this objective. For example, no matter how difficult checking a particular borrower's creditworthiness might be, the process could handle it because everyone in the credit department was a highly trained specialist. The same is true of all the other departments. However, another important question is: How often will this specialized knowledge be needed? In other words, what percent of the credit requests are relatively routine and what percent require deep, specialized knowledge? As IBM found out, the vast majority of credit requests could be handled relatively routinely.

Another explanation for why IBM Credit originally created a functional organization relates to the technology that was available at the time. A key ingredient that allowed IBM Credit to move to the deal-structurer model was advances in technology. For example, spreadsheets, databases, and other decision support tools were adopted so that the deal structurers could quickly check interest rates, access standard clauses, and check the creditworthiness of the borrowers. In effect, the new technology allowed the deal structurers, who had only general knowledge, to function as though they had the specialized knowledge of an expert in a particular discipline.

8.4 Six Sigma and the DMAIC Improvement Process

The Six Sigma concept was developed by Bill Smith, a senior engineer at Motorola, in 1986, as a way to standardize the way defects were tallied. As you probably already know, sigma is the Greek symbol used in statistics to refer to standard deviation, which is a measure of variation. Adding "six" to "sigma" combines a measure of process performance (*sigma*) with the goal of nearly perfect quality (*six*). More specifically, to some, the term *Six Sigma* literally translates into making no more than 3.4 mistakes (defects) per 1 million opportunities to make a mistake (defect).

While Six Sigma's original definition of 3.4 defects per million opportunities (DPMO) is a rather narrow measure of quality, Six Sigma itself has evolved and now encompasses a broad methodology for designing and improving business processes. In fact, many organizations (e.g. B of A and GE) viewed Six Sigma as an integral part of their overall business strategy. In the popular book *The Six Sigma Way* (Pande et al. 2000), Six Sigma is defined as

> *a comprehensive and flexible system for achieving, sustaining, and maximizing business success. Six Sigma is uniquely driven by close understanding of customer needs, disciplined use of facts, data, and statistical analysis, and diligent attention to managing, improving, and reinventing business processes. (p. xi)*

At Motorola, Six Sigma was defined as "a business improvement process that focuses an organization on customer requirements, process alignment, analytical rigor, and timely execution."[2] While numerous additional definitions of Six Sigma could be cited, common themes tend to emerge across the range of suggested definitions, including rigorous (often statistical) analysis, customer focus, data-driven analysis, and improvement of overall business performance. Likewise, a number of benefits are commonly associated with Six Sigma initiatives, including increased profitability, improved quality, improved employee morale, lower costs, higher productivity, market share growth, improved levels of customer retention and satisfaction, and shorter lead times. Interestingly, Motorola[3] became the first company to win the Malcolm Baldrige National Quality Award in 1988. Furthermore, Motorola estimated that as of 2006 it had saved in excess of $17 billion as a result of its Six Sigma initiatives.

Arguably, one reason for the success of Six Sigma programs where others have failed is that Six Sigma provides a structured, logical, and disciplined approach to problem solving. More specifically, as shown in Figure 8.3, Six Sigma projects generally follow a well-defined process

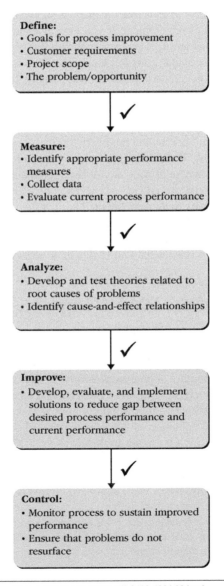

FIGURE 8.3 The Six Sigma DMAIC Approach for Process Improvement

---

[2] Retrieved September 20, 2004, from www.motorola.com/content/0,2409-4904,00.html.

[3] In January of 2011 Motorola was split into two independent companies: Motorola Mobility and Motorola Solutions.

consisting of five phases. The phases are *define, measure, analyze, improve, and control,* which are collectively referred to as *DMAIC* (pronounced dey-MAY-ihk). As the names of the phases suggest, the DMAIC improvement process can be thought of as an adaptation of the scientific method to process improvement.

Before discussing the DMAIC phases in more detail, a couple of comments are in order. First, as shown in Figure 8.3, the phases in a DMAIC project often serve as project milestones and can thus be used as tollgates to the next phase in the project. In particular, the progress and outcomes associated with the project are evaluated at the end of each phase to assess the merits of permitting the project to move on to the next phase. The extent to which organizational resources will continue to be allocated to the project is typically assessed at these milestones as well.

Second, there are large numbers of standard Six Sigma tools and methodologies that are used at various phases in a DMAIC project. Table 8.2 summarizes some frequently used Six Sigma tools and methodologies and lists the DMAIC phases where these tools/methodologies are most commonly used. Before turning our attention to discussing each DMAIC phase in more detail, we first provide a detailed example of an actual Six Sigma project.

8.4.1 Example Six Sigma Project

With increasing patient volumes, the North Shore University Hospital in Manhasset, New York, initiated a Six Sigma project in 2004 to reduce the bed assignment turnaround time. The bed turnaround time is the elapsed time from when the discharge instructions are given to a patient to the time the admission nurse is notified that a clean bed is ready. Within six months, the Six Sigma team was able to reduce the average bed turnaround time by over 2 hours.

The Six Sigma team began the define phase by developing a process map that identified all the steps in the process from the time the patient received the discharge instructions to the time the admission nurse was notified that a clean bed was ready. The team also defined the admission nurses as the customer of the process and surveyed these nurses to collect VOC data. Based on the VOC data collected, the team established a target bed turnaround time of 2 hours and an upper specification limit (USL) of 2.5 hours.

In the measure phase, the team developed the operational definition of a defect as any case where more than 2.5 hours were required to turn around a bed. The team also conducted a measurement systems analysis to verify the effectiveness of its measurement system and hence the data collected to study the process. In addition, the team calculated the DPMO of the current process. The team discovered that the average bed turnaround time was over 3.75 hours and that the DPMO was 672,725. Finally, the team created a cause-and-effect diagram to identify the variables that influenced the bed turnaround times.

In the analyze phase, the team performed hypothesis tests and used analysis of variance to identify variables that were statistically significant. As the team analyzed the data, they discovered communication and technical problems in two key steps. To address these problems, the team developed four recommendations in the improve phase. For example, one recommendation related to revising the discharge assessment sticker to include additional information. Another recommendation was to better utilize the admission RN beepers so they would be immediately notified of when a clean bed was ready.

In the control phase, control charts (discussed in the previous chapter) were created to monitor bed turnaround times. The control charts helped ensure that the improvements made to the process continued and also served as an early detection system should performance begin to deteriorate.

This example illustrates another characteristic of Six Sigma projects. Namely, with Six Sigma, we let the story naturally unfold as we objectively analyze the data. This means that, as difficult as it is to do at times, we resist the tendency to try to solve the problem as soon as it is defined. Rather, we engage in a process of progressively gaining additional insight into the root causes of

Table 8.2   Common Tools and Methodologies in the Six Sigma Toolkit

Six Sigma tool/methodology	DMAIC phase(s) most commonly used in
Affinity diagram	D, A
Benchmarking	D, M
Brainstorming	A, I
Business case	D
Cause-and-effect diagrams	M, A
Control charts	M, A, I, C
Critical to quality tree	D
Data collection forms	M, A, I, C
Data mining	M
Design for Six Sigma (DFSS)	An entire collection of tools/methodologies that can be used across all phases
Design of experiments (DOE)	A, I
Defects per million opportunities (DPMO)	M
Failure modes and effects analysis (FMEA)	M, I, C
Gantt chart	Tool used to manage entire DMAIC project
Kano model	D, M
Lean tools	An entire collection of tools/methodologies that can be used across all phases
Measurement systems analysis (gage R&R)	M
Nominal group technique	D, M
Pareto analysis	D, M, A, I
Process capability	M, A, I
Process maps	D, M, A, I, C
Process sigma	M, I
Project charter	D
Quality function deployment (QFD)	D, M
Regression	A
Rolled throughput yield (RTY)	D, M, A
Simulation	A, I
SIPOC	D
Stakeholder analysis	D, I
Theory of constraints (TOC)	One of the Lean tools
Voice of the customer (VOC)	D

the problem by sequentially answering new questions as they arise. Thus, as the insights we gain from investigating a particular issue often naturally lead to new questions, we utilize the tools in the Six Sigma toolkit to help find answers to these new questions. Through this process of applying the Six Sigma methodology and tools, we ultimately gain a clear understanding of the root causes of the problem, which in turn well positions us to address it. It also ensures that we are focusing on the real problem and not symptoms of the problem.

It is also worth pointing out that often the hardest part of solving a problem is simply figuring out where to start. The DMAIC approach not only provides a disciplined approach for solving problems but also adds structure to what otherwise might appear to be an unstructured problem. Of course, it is possible that what we learn in one phase of a Six Sigma project requires that we revisit an earlier phase. We now turn our attention to discussing each of the phases of a Six Sigma project in more detail.

8.5 The Define Phase

The define phase of a DMAIC project focuses on clearly specifying the problem or opportunity, determining the goals for the process improvement project, and identifying the scope of the project. Identifying the customers and their requirements is also critical, given that the overarching goal for all Six Sigma projects is improving the organization's ability to meet the needs of its customers. In this section, we overview three tools commonly used in the define phase of a DMAIC project: process mapping, benchmarking, and quality function deployment (QFD).

8.5.1 Process Mapping

Process mapping is closely aligned to the concept of process flow analysis discussed in Chapter 4. A key use of process maps is helping analysts and decision makers gain a better understanding of a process. As such, process maps are a core tool in the Six Sigma toolkit. They are especially useful in helping define the challenges and opportunities associated with the execution of a process.

More specifically, a process map is a graphic representation of a process and shows the sequences of tasks that comprise a business process. Typically, an *as-is* process map of the current process is developed. Then after the *as-is* process map has been analyzed and improvement opportunities identified, a *to-be* process map depicting the way the process should be executed is crafted.

A number of symbols are commonly used to create process maps. A rectangle is typically used to represent a process step such as a discrete work activity. Some examples of work activities include drafting a proposal, scheduling a meeting, entering quarterly results, measuring a patient's blood pressure, and reviewing customer satisfaction data. A diamond is used to represent a decision point or conditional branching. Some examples of decisions include deciding whether to make an offer or not, deciding on whether the shipment is of acceptable quality or not, deciding whether to hire a job candidate or not, moving the location of an event based on the weather, and choosing what to invest in based on interest rates. The rectangle for process steps and the diamond for decision points are used in virtually all process maps. Figure 8.1 discussed earlier in this chapter shows a very simple process map. Exhibit 2 in the BPO Incorporated case at the end of this book provides a more detailed example of a process map for an actual service delivery process. This process map was further enhanced with *swim lanes* to clarify which stakeholders performed the activities comprising the process.

To conclude this discussion of process maps, we offer several guidelines to follow in developing them. First, to identify the steps in the process, we recommend using the approach of *being the part* (also discussed in Chapter 4). In other words, if a manufacturing process is being analyzed, assume the role of a part and follow the part from the start of the manufacturing process to the end. At each stage in the process, interview the workers to find out what they do. This principle can be applied to all business processes. For example, if a health-care process is being analyzed, become the patient. If a warehouse operation is being analyzed, become the customer order.

A second guideline to follow is that when you are interviewing employees at the various stages in the process, it is critical that you be nonjudgmental regarding what they share with you.

If they get the sense that you are judging the way they do their jobs, they will not be forthcoming with the work they do, which in turn will result in a process map that is not an accurate reflection of the way work is actually being done. Not having an accurate picture of the process means that important process improvement opportunities may not be identified.

Finally, it is important to recognize that developing a process map is typically an iterative process. After you talk to employees and develop a draft of the process map, it is important for you to share the process map with the employees to verify that it captures what they shared with you accurately. Quite often when they see the process map, they will say things like, "yes that is what I told you, but now that I see it, it is actually a little more complicated than that." Iterating back and forth with the employees that do the work after each draft of the process map is completed is critical to having a process map that provides an accurate representation of the process as it is currently performed.

8.5.2 Benchmarking

In conjunction with their efforts to improve their products and processes, many organizations are engaging in an activity called *benchmarking*. Essentially, benchmarking involves comparing an organization's processes with the best practices to be found. Benchmarking is used for a variety of purposes, including the following:

- Comparing an organization's processes with the best organization's processes. When used in this way, benchmarking activities should not be restricted to other organizations in the same industry. Rather, the companies that are best in the world at performing a particular activity, *regardless of industry*, should be studied. For example, Xerox used L.L. Bean to benchmark the order fulfillment process.

- Comparing an organization's products and services with those of other organizations.

- Identifying the best practices to emulate.

- Projecting trends in order to be able to respond proactively to future challenges and opportunities.

Benchmarking generally involves three steps. The first step is concerned with preparing for the benchmarking study. In this phase, it is important to get the support of senior management and its input on what should be benchmarked. Problem areas, activities related to serving the customer better, and activities related to the mission of the organization are all appropriate candidates for inclusion in the benchmarking study.

The second phase of benchmarking consists of collecting data. There are two general sources of benchmarking data. One source is *published data*. These are often available from universities, financial filings (e.g. 10k reports), consultants, periodicals, trade journals, and books. The other source of data is *original research* conducted by the organization itself. If this approach is employed, a list of organizations to benchmark might include companies that have recently received quality awards or other business awards, are top rated by industry analysts, have been the subject of recent business articles, or have a track record of superior financial performance. Once the companies have been identified, data can be collected in a variety of ways, including interviews, site visits, and surveys.

The third and final phase of benchmarking involves using what has been learned to improve organizational performance. Once the second phase has been completed, identified gaps in performance can be used to set challenging but realistic goals (often called *stretch goals*). Also, the results of the benchmarking study can be used to overcome and eliminate complacency within the organization.

8.5.3 Quality Function Deployment (QDF)

Arguably, two key drivers of an organization's long-term competitive success are the extent to which its new products or services meet customers' needs and having the organizational capabilities to develop and deliver such new products and services. Clearly, no amount of clever advertising and no degree of production efficiency will entice customers to continue to purchase products or services that do not meet their needs. Likewise, it serves no purpose for an organization to design new products or services that it does not have the capability to produce or deliver. Of course, the desire to offer new products and services can serve as the impetus for acquiring additional process capabilities; however, organizations typically seek to develop new products and services that capitalize on their existing capabilities.

QFD is a powerful tool for helping translate customer requirements into needed process capabilities. In effect, the use of QFD ensures that newly designed or improved products and services satisfy customer requirements and are ultimately producible by the firm. As Figure 8.4 illustrates, the QFD methodology utilizes a series of tables to maintain links among customer requirements, technical requirements, component requirements, process requirements, and ultimately specific process activities. Because of their shape, these tables are often referred to as the *houses of quality*. Before discussing the contents of a house of quality in detail, we first broadly overview the QFD process and discuss the links between the four houses of quality.

8.5.3.1 Broad Overview of QFD

QFD begins by using *voice of the customer (VOC)* data to specify the customer requirements in the rows of the first house, the output planning matrix, shown in Figure 8.4. The name VOC stems from the fact that the customer's own language is used to capture these requirements. As examples, a sample of mountain bike riders might offer responses regarding their preferences for a new bike such as "the bike should shift effortlessly," "there should be no bob on climbs," "the bike should climb, descend, and handle great," "the bike should suck up the bumps," and "I like a bike that is well balanced with a low center of gravity."

Then, based on the customer requirements listed in the rows, the technical requirements for the product or service are generated and listed in the columns of this house. While the customer requirements are expressed in the customer's own language, the technical requirements are often expressed in a more specialized language such as that used by engineers. Thus, technical requirements for a product might be expressed in terms of dimensions, weights, performance, tensile strength, and compression.

Once the rows and columns are generated for the output planning matrix, the relationship matrix in the middle of the house is completed. The cells in the relationship matrix correspond to the intersection of a particular customer requirement and technical requirement. In each cell, the strength of the relationship between the corresponding customer requirement and technical

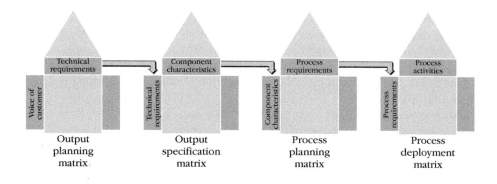

FIGURE 8.4 Quality Function Deployment Process

requirement is evaluated. An important use of the relationship matrix is to ensure that each customer requirement is addressed by one or more technical requirements. Likewise, the relationship matrix can be used to ensure that designers do not add technical requirements to the product or service that do not address and are therefore not linked to specific customer requirements.

In the next house of quality, the technical requirements that were the columns in the previous house of quality now become the rows, and the task now becomes generating a list of the elemental or component characteristics for the product or service that will become the columns in this house of quality. This process continues from house to house until all the process activities to satisfy the customers' requirements have been determined. Thus, we see that QFD provides a logical and straightforward approach for ensuring that designs for new or improved products and services meet customers' requirements and are ultimately producible.

8.5.3.2 House of Quality Details

With this general overview of QFD and its four houses of quality, we now turn our attention to the specific information listed in each house of quality. Besides the relationship matrix, which links the row requirements (or whats) to the column "hows," the roof of the house corresponds to a triangular correlation table where the correlations between the technical requirements are assessed. This assessment helps identify those technical requirements that are synergistic with each other and that conflict with each other and therefore where a trade-off may exist. At the far right of the house, customer importance ratings and the results of a competitive evaluation are summarized. Finally, at the bottom of the house, target values, a competitive evaluation, and importance weights are summarized for each how.

To illustrate the QFD process, consider a fast-food restaurant chain that is interested in improving its offerings. Figure 8.5 provides the completed output planning matrix for the chain. At the far left of the house, the VOC data are listed, including customer statements such as "food that tastes good" and "get what I ordered." Based on these customer requirements, a list of technical requirements was generated and listed in the columns. In the relationship matrix, the relationship between each customer requirement and technical requirement was assessed. Thus, we see that there is a strong relationship between the taste of the food and the use of fresh ingredients, while there is only a moderate relationship between the taste of the food and the time it takes to make and deliver it to the customer. In the roof of the house, the correlations between each of the technical requirements are evaluated and listed. In our example, we note that the requirements of "fresh ingredients" and "quality ingredients" are consistent with each other, while a trade-off exists between "limiting the fat and carbohydrate content of the food" and "keeping meal price down." At the far right, customer importance ratings and a competitive evaluation are summarized. Thus, we see that good taste, nutrition, and accuracy of the order are the most important aspects of the service to the customers surveyed. On these three dimensions, we see that the organization in question has the best-tasting food, has the second most nutritional offerings, and has the highest-order accuracy. At the bottom of the house, target values and a competitive evaluation are listed for each how. For example, in terms of using fresh ingredients, the chain in question has set a goal of achieving a score of 90 on this dimension and estimates that competitors A and B score 70 and 75, respectively, on this dimension. Finally, the importance weight or priority for each how is listed at the very bottom of the house. This can help in making trade-offs when conflicts are discovered in the roof of the house. In the present case, the most important technical requirement is the use of quality ingredients.

The other houses of quality are completed in a similar fashion. One key advantage of QFD is that it is a visual tool. Through the use of QFD, a firm can analyze its outputs in terms of customers' desires, compare its outputs with competitors' outputs, determine what it takes to better meet each customer's requirements, and figure out how to do it. In addition, it provides a means of

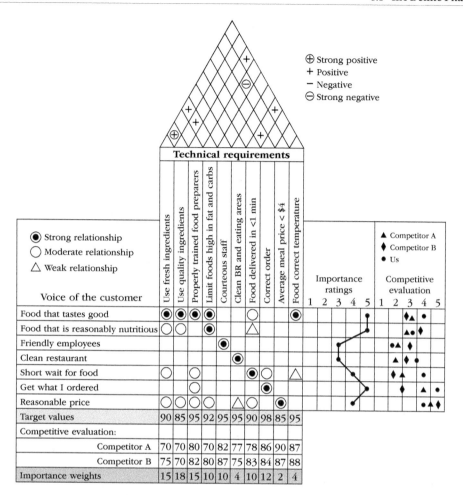

FIGURE 8.5 Example Output Planning Matrix for Fast-Food Restaurant Chain

linking these customer requirements through the entire planning process, ending with the specification of detailed process activities. A number of firms such as Toyota and Hewlett-Packard have adopted QFD and found that it cut their product development time by one-third to one-half and their costs by up to 60% (while improving quality).

8.5.4 The Kano Model

As has been noted previously in this chapter, the driving force of process improvement initiatives is that they provide benefits that ultimately translate into better meeting the needs of the customer. Of course, being positioned to better meet customer desires requires that the customer requirements be understood and well-defined in the first place. Thus, an important aspect of the define phase of a Six Sigma project is defining the customer and their requirements.

The Kano model, named after the Japanese engineer and consultant Noriaki Kano, provides a useful framework for classifying customer requirements. As shown in Figure 8.6, customer requirements can be placed into one of three categories:

- *Dissatisfiers.* Dissatisfiers concern aspects or features that customers expect to be included in a product or service. However, as shown in Figure 8.6, offering more of the feature only leads to less dissatisfaction and the feature in and of itself does not lead to satisfaction with

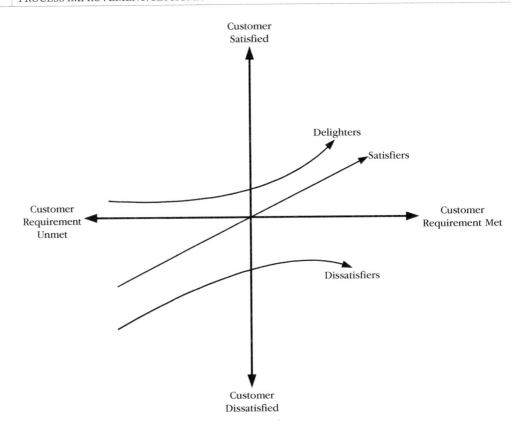

FIGURE 8.6 The Kano Model for Classifying Customer Requirements

the product or service. An example of this would be the spare tire that comes with a new car purchase. Some manufacturers offer what is referred to as a "50-mile" spare tire in that it is meant to be used only temporarily until the standard tire can be repaired or replaced. Some car models, however, come with an actual standard tire as the spare tire, thereby offering the customer more of this feature. It is unlikely, however, that many customers who purchase a car become satisfied with their purchase because it comes with a standard tire for the spare. Rather, most people purchasing cars likely expect there to be a spare tire with the car and don't consider it much in their purchase decision.

- *Satisfiers.* Satisfiers are features such that the more of this feature the product or service provides the more satisfied customers become. It is also important to point out that if the requisite amount of this feature is not provided, customers will be dissatisfied with the product or service. The price paid for a car exemplifies a satisfier. Above some price point, the customer will be dissatisfied with the purchase of a car. As the price moves higher and higher above this point the customer becomes more dissatisfied. On the other hand, as the price drops below this point, the customer becomes more and more satisfied as the discount increases.

- *Delighters.* Delighters are features of products and services that offer unexpected benefits and in doing so delight the customer. As an example, some years ago one of the authors purchased a new car and was delighted by the theater lighting in the car that gradually dimmed at night when the car doors were closed.

Beyond helping organizations better understand their customers' requirements, use of the framework has important implications for professionals involved with process design/

improvement and product design (discussed in Chapter 3). To begin, the framework can help ensure that aspects of a product or service that will delight the customer and thereby help to provide the organization with a competitive advantage are formally considered. Furthermore, as the intensity of competition continues to increase, it is important for management to recognize that the features of a product or service evolve over time. Thus, what was once a delighter will likely become a satisfier and what was a satisfier will likely eventually become a dissatisfier. For example, cars that come with a feature that automatically parallel parks the car likely delights current consumers. However, it seems inevitable that most car companies will eventually embed this technology into their cars, at which point the feature will likely become a satisfier.

8.6 The Measure Phase

Typically, the measure phase begins with the identification of the key process performance metrics. Correctly choosing process performance metrics is critical in order to have an accurate picture of how the process is actually performing in terms of meeting customer requirements. Unfortunately, it is not uncommon for managers to select performance metrics based on their ease of measurement and/or the availability of data, rather than on their ability to provide insights into how the process is meeting customer requirements. For example, some organizations use machine utilization to assess the performance of their manufacturing processes. In reality, machine utilization has at best an indirect relationship to what really matters to customers – shorter lead times, higher quality, the percent of orders shipped on time, and so on. As a service example, consider a call center. In this case, performance measures such as the percent of calls answered by the third ring, the percent of calls processed without having to be escalated, and the average hold time are all better indicators of how well the process is performing than, for example, labor utilization.

Once the key process performance metrics have been specified, related process and customer data are collected. One early use of these data is to evaluate the process's current performance, which can then be used as a baseline to evaluate the benefits of potential process improvements that are identified later in the project.

As shown in Table 8.2 earlier, there are a variety of tools in the Six Sigma toolkit that are useful during the measure phase. We begin our discussion of the measure phase with a commonly used process performance measure, namely, *defects per million opportunities (DPMO)*. We then conclude our discussion of the measure phase with a brief overview of measurement systems analysis.

8.6.1 Defects per Million Opportunities (DPMO)

An important advantage of using DPMO is that it provides a standard measure of process performance. As such, it provides a mechanism for comparing the performance across a range of processes that otherwise would be difficult to compare. In fact, as we now illustrate, DPMO makes such comparisons possible across varying processes by incorporating an adjustment for the complexity of each process.

To illustrate the calculation of the DPMO and how it adjusts for process complexity, consider a bank that processes two types of loans. Process A is used to process relatively simple loans, such as for a car, and consists of five steps; process B is used to process more complex loans, such as mortgages, and requires the completion of 25 steps. Let's further assume that of the last 10,000 loans processed by each process, a total of 100 errors were made in each process. In this case, the number of *defects per unit* (*DPU*) is the same for both methods and is calculated as follows (note that here a loan represents a unit):

$$DPU = \frac{\text{number of defects}}{\text{number of units}} = \frac{100}{10,000} = 0.01$$

This result suggests that each process is averaging 0.01 error (or defect) per loan, or 1 error per 100 loans. Is it then reasonable to conclude that both processes are performing at the same level? Because this comparison has not accounted for the differences between the methods in terms of their complexity, the answer is no. Thinking about this situation intuitively, we would generally expect the number of errors or defects to increase as the complexity of the process increases. Unfortunately, the DPU measure does not reflect this logic.

To account for the differences in the complexity of the processes, an adjustment is needed. Up to this point, we have counted each loan (unit) processed as representing one opportunity for a defect. In reality, there are typically multiple opportunities to create a defect (error). To illustrate, Figure 8.7 displays 33 specific defects organized into seven categories associated with staying at a hotel. As this figure illustrates, for virtually all products and services, there are numerous opportunities for introducing defects or making errors. Thus, rather than treating each unit or customer as a single opportunity for a defect, an alternative approach is to develop a list of all the opportunities for creating a defect for a given product or service. Then the *number of defects per opportunity* (*DPO*) can be calculated as follows:

$$DPO = \frac{\text{number of defects}}{\text{number of units(customers)} \times \text{number of opportunities}}$$

An important issue that must be addressed in using the DPO measure relates to developing the list of opportunities. In particular, it is possible to make it appear that performance is better than it actually is by padding the list with additional opportunities. To illustrate, in Figure 8.7, there are 33 specific opportunities for defects listed in seven categories. Let's assume that a survey of 100 customers revealed 200 occurrences of the 33 items listed in the figure. Based on this, if we consider each of these 33 items as a valid opportunity for a defect, then the DPO works out to be

$$\frac{200}{100 \times 33} = 0.06$$

Alternatively, if we consider each stage in the service delivery process (i.e. the seven categories listed in Figure 8.7) as an opportunity for a defect, then the DPO increases to

$$\frac{200}{100 \times 7} = 0.29$$

Thus, we see that increasing the number of opportunities considered can make the performance look better. Along these lines, then, a less than honest manager or supplier could inflate the list of opportunities for defects by including some opportunities that in reality never occur. Besides being unethical, pursuing this strategy greatly undermines the value of using DPO as a standardized measure of process performance. In the end, there are no firm rules for what to include and what not to include. As a general rule of thumb, however, it is suggested that only those defects that are meaningful to the customer be included. One strategy for determining the list of opportunities is to simply treat each stage as representing one opportunity for a defect. Based on this approach, there would be seven opportunities for a defect per hotel customer (of course, some of these defects could be repeated over a multiple-day stay). Thus, a hotel customer

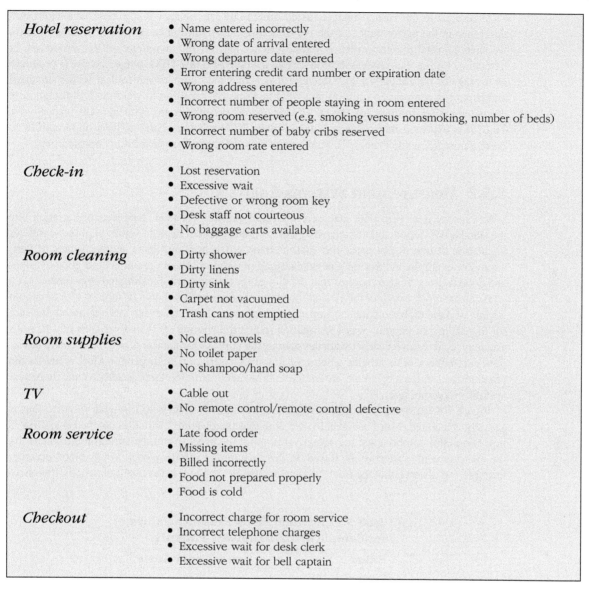

Hotel reservation	• Name entered incorrectly
	• Wrong date of arrival entered
	• Wrong departure date entered
	• Error entering credit card number or expiration date
	• Wrong address entered
	• Incorrect number of people staying in room entered
	• Wrong room reserved (e.g. smoking versus nonsmoking, number of beds)
	• Incorrect number of baby cribs reserved
	• Wrong room rate entered
Check-in	• Lost reservation
	• Excessive wait
	• Defective or wrong room key
	• Desk staff not courteous
	• No baggage carts available
Room cleaning	• Dirty shower
	• Dirty linens
	• Dirty sink
	• Carpet not vacuumed
	• Trash cans not emptied
Room supplies	• No clean towels
	• No toilet paper
	• No shampoo/hand soap
TV	• Cable out
	• No remote control/remote control defective
Room service	• Late food order
	• Missing items
	• Billed incorrectly
	• Food not prepared properly
	• Food is cold
Checkout	• Incorrect charge for room service
	• Incorrect telephone charges
	• Excessive wait for desk clerk
	• Excessive wait for bell captain

FIGURE 8.7   Defect Opportunities Associated with a Stay at a Hotel

whose reservation was lost and who experienced an excessive wait for check-in would count as one check in defect as opposed to two defects.

Based on this logic and returning to our original objective of comparing loan processes A and B, we determine that process A has five opportunities to create a defect, while process B has 25. Then, based on the data collected indicating that 100 errors were made in both processes out of the last 10,000 loans processed, we can calculate the DPO for both processes as follows:

$$\mathrm{DPO}_A = \frac{100}{10{,}000 \times 5} = 0.002$$

$$\mathrm{DPO}_B = \frac{100}{10{,}000 \times 25} = 0.0004$$

In contrast to our earlier analysis based on the DPU measure, we now observe a significant difference in the performance of the two processes. This difference is now observable because we have adjusted the performance measure to account for the complexity of the processes. In particular, we see that process A produces an average of 0.002 DPO, while process B produces an average of only 0.0004 DPO. Because it is somewhat cumbersome to deal with such small numbers, it is common to multiply the DPO measure by 1 million to yield the DPMO measure discussed earlier. In this case, the DPMO for processes A and B are 2000 and 400, respectively. Thus, it is expected that process A would make 2000 mistakes per 1 million opportunities to make a mistake, while Process B would make only 400 mistakes per million opportunities.

8.6.2 Measurement Systems Analysis

Whenever we deal with data that were collected via measurement, measures of variation like the standard deviation and variance may not accurately reflect the true variation in the sample or population of interest. In particular, measurement errors may introduce another source of variation. For example, measuring a person's blood pressure manually requires both good eyesight and good hearing. It also requires that the dial gauges be properly recalibrated over time.

As an example, consider the 10 systolic blood pressure values shown in Table 8.3 for a random sample of male diabetic patients. In particular, we note that the average systolic blood pressure for this sample of patients was 130.5 with a standard deviation of 21 and variance of 442.9. As you may recall from an earlier statistics course, the purpose for measures like the standard deviation and variance is to provide a sense of how much variation or dispersion there is across the population of interest or, in the present case, how much variation there is across male diabetics' systolic blood pressure.

Figure 8.8 illustrates that the measurement system contributes to the total variance that is actually calculated. More specifically, we note that the observed variation can be broken down into two major components: the actual variation in the process and the variation introduced by the measurement system itself. Based on this insight and referring back to our blood pressure example, we observe that the total calculated variance of 442.9 is the result of actual differences

Table 8.3 Systolic Blood Pressure Values for Sample of Male Diabetic Patients

Patient	Systolic blood pressure
S. Jones	123
K. Smith	106
T. Carter	136
F. Lance	145
J. Porter	153
L. Davis	157
H. Johnson	101
R. Jones	124
G. Scott	152
B. Regan	108
Average	130.5
Std. dev.	21.0
Variance	442.9

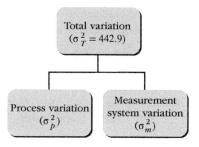

FIGURE 8.8 Components of Total Process Variation

in the patients' blood pressures (process variation) and perhaps errors made in measuring the patients' blood pressures (measurement system variation). Mathematically, this can be expressed as follows:

$$\sigma_T^2 = \sigma_p^2 + \sigma_m^2$$

where

σ_T^2 = the total observed or calculated variation

σ_p^2 = the actual variation inherent in the process and commonly referred to as the part-to-part variation (or, in our example, patient-to-patient variation)

σ_m^2 = variation introduced by the measurement system

Recall from basic statistics that calculating the total variation arising from multiple sources requires summing the variances from each source, not their standard deviations. Therefore, the total observed standard deviation, σ_T, is calculated as

$$\sigma_T = \sqrt{\sigma_p^2 + \sigma_m^2}$$

To assess the variation introduced by the measurement system, a *measurement systems analysis* study is conducted. The purpose of a measurement systems analysis study is to assess what percent of the observed variation is being introduced by the measurement system itself and what percent represents the actual underlying variation in the process. The smaller the percentage of variation introduced by the measurement system, the better.

In addition to considering the impact the measurement system has on the variation of observed values, it is also important to consider the impact the measurement system has on the mean (or location) of the observed values. To access the impact the measurement system has on the mean of observed values, three additional measurement system metrics are employed:

1. *Bias* represents the difference between the average of a number of observations and the true value. For example, assume that a nurse takes the systolic blood pressure of a patient three times and observes the following blood pressures: 126, 128, and 127. Further, assume that it was known at the time the patient's blood pressure was taken that the patient had an actual blood pressure of 125. In this case, we can average the three nurse readings and calculate an average blood pressure value of 127. Based on this, the bias would be 2 (i.e. 127–125), suggesting that the nurse tends to overestimate a patient's blood pressure by 2. Thus, bias is a measure of the tendency of the measurement system to underestimate or overestimate the measurement value of interest, perhaps due to a defective instrument, such as the sphygmomanometer. While errors may be made in taking individual

measurements, ideally these errors should cancel out over time, and the average should be close to the true value, which would in turn yield a bias of approximately zero.

2. *Linearity* of a measurement system corresponds to the accuracy of the measurement system across the entire range of possible entities to be measured. Ideally, a measurement system's accuracy should not be impacted by an entity's position in the range of possible values. Thus, a blood pressure measuring system that is more accurate for people with a blood pressure of 115 than for people with a blood pressure of 155 does not possess the characteristic of linearity.

3. *Stability* of a measurement system corresponds to the ability of the measurement system to get consistent results over time. For example, assuming that a patient's blood pressure remains constant over time, the results of taking the patient's blood pressure at his or her annual physical should yield similar results.

8.7 The Analyze Phase

Having first defined the problem/opportunity, the customer, and the goals for the Six Sigma project and then subsequently considered appropriate performance measures, collected the relevant data, and evaluated the process's current performance, we are now ready to begin the analyze phase. In this phase of the project, our objective is to utilize the data that have been collected to develop and test theories related to the root causes of existing gaps between the process's current and desired performance. Ultimately, our goal is to identify key cause-and-effect relationships that can be leveraged to improve the overall performance of the process.

Referring to Table 8.2 again, there are a number of tools in the Six Sigma toolkit that are useful in the analyze phase. In this section, we will overview three of these tools: (1) brainstorming, (2) cause-and-effect diagrams, and (3) process capability analysis. Because the design of experiments (DOE) is equally applicable to the improve phase, we defer our discussion of it until the next section.

8.7.1 Brainstorming

Brainstorming is among the most, if not the most, widely used techniques in business to stimulate and foster creativity. It is widely used to facilitate the identification of ways to improve business processes. Brainstorming was originally developed by Alex Osborn, an advertising executive, in the 1950s. The basis for brainstorming was Osborn's belief that while on the one hand there can be a synergistic effect associated with having people work in teams (i.e. two heads are better than one), the team's overall creativity and effectiveness is often limited by a tendency to prematurely evaluate ideas as they are being generated. In an effort to capitalize on the strengths of working in teams while at the same time eliminating the drawbacks, Osborn developed the brainstorming approach, which includes the following four guidelines:

1. Do not criticize ideas during the brainstorming session.

2. Express all ideas no matter how radical, bizarre, unconventional, ridiculous, or impractical they may seem.

3. Generate as many ideas as possible.

4. Combine, extend, and/or improve on one another's ideas.

As you can see, brainstorming focuses more on the quantity of ideas generated rather than the quality. This is intentional, the point being that there will be ample opportunity to critically evaluate the ideas after the brainstorming session has ended. Therefore, the temptation to criticize or judge ideas early in the process should be avoided so as to not stifle the creativity of the participants during the brainstorming session.

It is interesting to note that despite the wide acceptance and use of brainstorming in industry, much of the research in the area questions its effectiveness. As one example, Diehl and Stroebe (1987) compared both the quantity and quality of ideas generated by people working in teams and individually. In this study, they found that the teams generated an average number of 28 ideas, while the same number of people working individually generated an average of 74.5 ideas. Furthermore, when the ideas were evaluated by experts, only 8.9% of the ideas generated by the teams on average were considered "good ideas" compared with 12.7% of the ideas generated by the people working independently. Based on these results and the results of other studies, Professor Thompson (2003) identified four threats to team creativity:

1. *Social loafing.* When working in teams, people may feel they will not get credit for their ideas and therefore may not work as hard in groups compared with the amount of effort they would invest if working individually.

2. *Conformity.* When working in teams, people may be overly conservative with what they are willing to share with the team because of concerns they may have about the reaction of others.

3. *Production blocking.* There are physical limitations that can restrict the productivity of a team. For example, only one person can speak at a time. Likewise, people cannot listen and concentrate on what others are saying and simultaneously generate their own new ideas. When working alone, there are likely to be fewer distractions interrupting a person's train of thought.

4. *Downward norm setting.* Research on teams suggests that individuals working in a team environment tend to match the productivity of the least productive team member.

Fortunately, in addition to identifying these threats to team creativity, Professor Thompson also identified a number of specific actions that can be used to mitigate the threats and actually enhance team creativity. These actions include the following:

- *Create diversified teams.* Teams consisting of members with a variety of different skills, experiences, training, and so on will position the team to view a problem from multiple perspectives.

- *Use analogical reasoning.* With analogical reasoning, concepts from one discipline or area are applied to other areas. For example, Dr. Eliyahu Goldratt originally developed the theory of constraints (discussed in the next chapter) as a way to improve the efficiency of a factory. More recently, his theory has been extended and applied to the field of project management.

- *Use brainwriting.* Brainwriting involves having the participants in a brainstorming session take periodic breaks to write down their own ideas silently. A key benefit of brainwriting is that it can greatly eliminate production blocking.

- *Use the nominal group technique (NGT).* The NGT is often included as part of the Six Sigma toolkit, as shown in Table 8.2. With the NGT, team members first work independently for perhaps 5–10 minutes generating a list of ideas. The team members then share their ideas with the team, often in a round-robin fashion, and the ideas are listed. After all the ideas are listed, the team moves on to discussing, clarifying, and extending them. At the end of the discussion, team members individually rank-order the ideas. Depending on the number of ideas, the team may rank-order each idea or, alternatively, select their 5 or 10 favorite ideas and then rank-order this subset. The team then evaluates the results, perhaps considering the scores of the ideas or the frequency with which an idea was selected.

- *Record team ideas.* Recording ideas can help a team utilize its time together more effectively by eliminating repetitive discussions and ensuring that ideas are not forgotten.

- *Use trained facilitators to run the brainstorming session.* As experts in brainstorming, trained facilitators can ensure that the rules are followed and that the discussion stays on task.

- *Set high standards.* In some cases, a team's lack of performance may be the result of misunderstandings of what is expected or even possible. For example, feedback regarding how many ideas the team has generated in comparison to the number of ideas other teams have generated after similar durations may help increase the quantity of ideas generated.

- *Change the composition of the team.* Research supports the fact that periodically replacing team members helps increase both the quantity of ideas generated by the team and the number of different types of ideas generated.

- *Use electronic brainstorming.* With electronic brainstorming, team members are seated in a room with individual computer workstations for each team member. The team members work individually and enter their ideas into the computer. A computer screen located at the front of the room anonymously displays all ideas generated. Thus, the participants are able to build off of one another's ideas without the constraint that only one person can speak at a time and without having to listen to someone else while trying to think independently.

- *Make the workplace a playground.* Creativity can be fostered by making simple changes to the work environment. While the possibilities are endless, the common denominator is to make the environment fun. Some ideas include placing toys that foster creativity at each seat (e.g. Play-Doh, Legos, building blocks), painting a conference room in nontraditional colors, and changing the name of the room from "the conference room" to "the innovation zone."

8.7.2 Cause-and-Effect Diagrams

Cause-and-effect diagrams, a technique for identifying risks as noted in Chapter 7, are another widely used Six Sigma tool. In fact, developing a cause-and-effect diagram often goes hand in hand with brainstorming. For example, a cause-and-effect diagram provides an effective way to organize the ideas that are generated in a brainstorming session addressing the causes of a particular problem. Alternatively, a brainstorming session may be held to develop the cause-and-effect diagram.

As an example, Figure 8.9 provides a cause-and-effect diagram developed by a college professor to analyze the challenge of not having sufficient time to prepare for MBA classes.

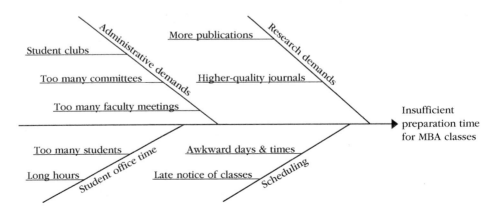

FIGURE 8.9 Cause-and-Effect Diagram to Analyze the Problem of Insufficient Preparation Time

Creating cause-and-effect diagrams is a fairly straightforward process. First, a box summarizing the problem is drawn at the far right of the workspace, and a horizontal line with an arrow terminating at the box is added. In Figure 8.9, the problem was defined at the far right of the diagram as insufficient preparation time for MBA classes. Next, the major causes of the problem are identified and connected to the original horizontal line. Referring to Figure 8.9, four major causes were identified regarding the problem of having insufficient preparation time: (1) scheduling, (2) research demands, (3) student office-hours time, and (4) administrative demands. The process of creating a cause-and-effect diagram continues by attempting to break down each major cause into more detailed causes and then possibly breaking down these detailed causes even further. For example, in examining Figure 8.9, we observe that issues related to late notices and inconvenient days and times contribute to the scheduling problem.

Not only can cause-and-effect diagrams be developed quickly, they provide an intuitive approach for better understanding problems. Furthermore, important insights are often obtained through the process of creating the diagram, as well as from the diagram itself. However, it should also be noted that, while the cause-and-effect diagram is well structured, the process of creating one is usually not. It is typical to bounce around from the detailed analysis of a particular cause to adding one or more additional major causes. Furthermore, as additional ideas are generated, it may be decided to eliminate, move, combine, and/or rename the major causes or the more detailed causes. Because of its appearance, this is why cause-and-effect diagrams are often referred to as "fishbone" diagrams.

8.7.3 Process Capability Analysis

With the advent of total quality management programs and their emphasis on "making it right the first time," organizations are becoming increasingly concerned with the ability of their production processes and service delivery processes to meet customer requirements. Process capability analysis allows an organization to measure the extent to which its processes can meet its customer requirements or the design specifications for the product or service. As shown in Figure 8.10, process capability depends on the following:

1. Location of the process mean

2. Natural variability inherent in the process

3. Stability of the process

4. Product's design requirements

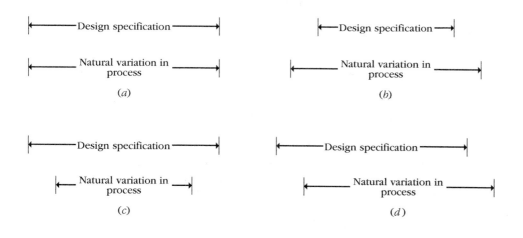

FIGURE 8.10
Natural Variation in a Production System versus Product Design Specifications

In Figure 8.10a, the natural variation inherent in the process and the product's design specifications are well matched, resulting in a production system that is consistently capable of meeting the design requirements. However, in Figure 8.10b, the natural variation in the production process is greater than the product's design requirements. This will lead to the production of a large amount of product that does not meet the requirements: the production process simply does not have the necessary ability. Options in this situation include improving the production process, relaxing the design requirements, or producing a large quantity of product that is unfit for use.

In Figure 8.10c, the situation is reversed: the product has wider design specifications than the natural variation inherent in the production system. In this case, the production process is easily able to meet the design specifications, and the organization may choose to investigate a more economical production process in order to lower costs. Finally, although the widths of design specifications and process variation are equal in Figure 8.10d, their means are out of sync. Thus, this process will produce a fair amount of output above the Upper Specification Limit (USL). In this situation, the solution would be to shift the process mean to the left so that it is better aligned with the design specifications.

More formally, the relationship between the natural variation in the production system and the product's design specifications can be quantified using a *process capability index*. The process capability index (C_p) is typically defined as the ratio of the width of the product's design specification to 6 standard deviations of the production system. Six standard deviations for the production process is used because 3 standard deviations above and below the production process's mean will include 99.7% of the possible production outcomes, assuming that the output of the production system can be approximated with a normal distribution. Mathematically, the process capability index is calculated as

$$C_p = \frac{\text{Product's design specification range}}{\text{Six standard deviations of the production system}} = \frac{\text{USL} - \text{LSL}}{6\sigma}$$

where LSL and USL are a product's lower and upper design specification limits, respectively, and σ is the standard deviation of the production system.

According to this index, a C_p of less than 1 indicates that a particular process is not capable of consistently meeting design specifications; a C_p greater than 1 indicates that the production process is capable of consistently meeting the requirements. As a rule of thumb, many organizations desire a C_p index of at least 1.3. Achieving *Six Sigma quality* with no more than 3.4 defective parts per million provides a C_p index of 2.0 (based on Motorola's original assumption that the process mean can shift by as much as 1.5 standard deviations).

Figure 8.11 illustrates the effect that changes in the natural variation of the production system have on the C_p index for fixed product design specifications. In Figure 8.11a, the natural variation in the process is much less than the product's design specification range, yielding a C_p index greater than 1. In contrast, in Figure 8.11b, the natural variation in the process is larger than product's design specifications, yielding a C_p index less than 1. Finally, in Figure 8.11c, the natural process variation and the design specifications are equal, yielding a C_p index equal to 1.

One limitation of the process capability index is that it only compares the magnitudes of the product's design specification range and the process's natural variation. It does not consider the degree to which these ranges are actually aligned. For example, the situations shown in Figures 8.10a and 8.10d both yield a C_p index of 1. However, as was pointed out earlier, a considerable amount of defective product would be produced in the situation shown in Figure 8.10d, owing to the lack of alignment between the design specifications and the process mean. While beyond our scope, we note that this limitation is easily addressed by using a one-sided capability index. Typically, the data collected to construct the control charts (see Chapter 7) for the process is used to calculate the process standard deviation used in the capability index formulas.

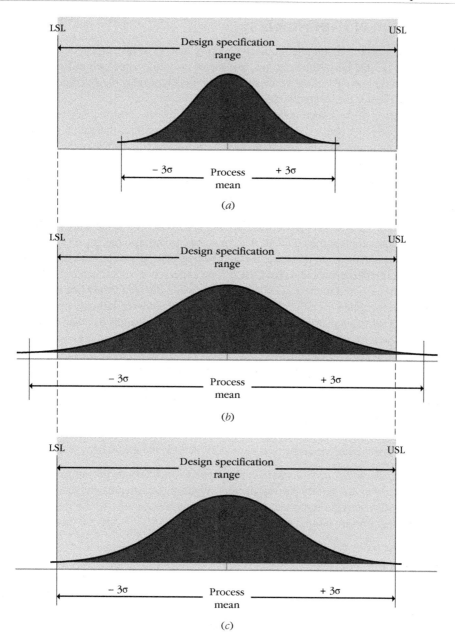

FIGURE 8.11 Effect of Production System Variability on Process Capability Index: (a) $C_p = 1.6$, (b) $C_p = 0.8$, (c) $C_p = 1.0$

8.8 The Improve Phase

Having defined the problem, measured the process's current performance, and analyzed the process, we are now in a position to identify and test options for improving the process. Bear in mind that changing a process is often a project in itself and as noted in Chapter 2, involves risk and change, both of which need to be identified and managed, possibly using tools such as FMEA as described in Chapter 7. Thus, each option for improvement needs to be put through screens to ascertain the risks and changes involved with that option. In the remainder of this section, our focus will be on the use of DOE as a process improvement tool.

8.8.1 Design of Experiments

Perhaps the most common approach to analyzing problems is to investigate one factor at a time (aka OFAT or 1FAT). Unfortunately, the one-factor-at-a-time approach suffers from several important shortcomings. To illustrate these shortcomings, consider the operation of a financial institution's call center for its credit cards.

A representative performance measure would be the time it takes the call center's customer service reps (CSRs) to process an incoming call. Factors or variables that might initially be identified as having an impact on the time to process a call include the nature of the call, the time of day, and the CSR who handles the call.

The first shortcoming with OFAT is that it is not typically possible to test one factor at a time and hold all the other factors constant. For example, assume that processing time data were collected for two CSRs over some period of time and it was determined that CSR A averaged 5 minutes per call, while CSR B averaged 7 minutes per call. Based on these data, can we conclude that CSR A is more efficient than CSR B? The answer is no because the impact of other variables has not been accounted for. In this case, it could be that CSR B's calls were of a more difficult nature to handle. Or perhaps the data for CSR A were collected around lunchtime when there was a high volume of calls and numerous callers on hold, while the data from CSR B were collected early in the morning when the call volume was lower and there were virtually no callers on hold. The point is that when one variable is studied at a time and the values of other variables are not controlled or otherwise accounted for, it is difficult, if not impossible, to draw valid conclusions about the impact of a single variable.

One approach to overcoming the shortcomings associated with the OFAT approach is to use DOE techniques. DOE techniques utilize the principles of statistics to design experiments to investigate multiple process variables simultaneously. With DOE techniques, multiple factors are varied and therefore studied simultaneously, and repeated measurements are typically taken for each combination of factor-level settings.

Some major considerations associated with DOE include the following:

- *Determining which factors to include in the experiment.* Interviewing subject-matter experts (SMEs) is one way to identify relevant factors. Work in the previous phases of the Six Sigma project may also provide important insights into relevant factors. Along these lines, cause-and-effect diagrams are often particularly helpful for identifying relevant factors.

- *Specifying the levels for each factor.* Once the factors are identified, the levels of each factor must be specified. For example, referring to the Southside Hospital example from the beginning of the chapter, Table 8.4 summarizes an experiment that investigates four factors that are hypothesized to have an impact on the lead time for stress tests. For the first factor, method used to order the stress test, two levels have been specified – using either a phone call or email to order the test. Thus, the study will investigate the impact these two alternative methods for ordering stress tests has on the overall stress test lead time. Notice that the factor related to the method used to educate the patients about the stress test has three levels, while each of the other factors has two levels.

- *Determining how much data to collect.* In the experimental design listed in Table 8.4, there are a total of 24 treatment combinations (2 levels of the method used to order the stress test × 2 levels of the patient scheduling method × 3 levels of the patient education method × 2 levels of the dictation technology). Therefore, 24 patients are needed in order to obtain one observation for each possible *treatment combination*. Of course, to have confidence in the results of a study, it is necessary to collect more than one observation. In DOE terminology, we refer to multiple observations for a treatment combination as *replication*. If historical data are

Table 8.4   Representative Factors and Their Levels for a Stress Test Study

Factor	Levels
Method used to order stress test	Phone; e-mail
Method used to schedule patient appointments	Fixed time appointments; patients given a time window
Method used to educate patients about stress test	Information sheet; phone call from nurse; in-person meeting with nurse
Dictation technology	Tape recorder and transcriber; speech recognition

available, preliminary calculations may be performed to determine how many replications are needed in order to obtain a specified level of statistical confidence. In other cases, limitations such as the time available to complete the study, personnel, or money may dictate the number of replications possible.

- *Determining the type of experimental design.* Fundamentally, there are two types of experimental designs. A *full factorial* experiment corresponds to a study where data are collected for all possible treatment combinations. A *fractional factorial* experiment corresponds to a study where data are collected for only a subset of all possible treatment combinations. Fractional factorial experiments are used when the number of treatment combinations is so large that it is not practical to collect data for each treatment combination. For example, a study with seven factors, each with three levels, would have 2187 treatment combinations (3^7). In many cases, investigating 2187 treatment combinations is not practical. Fortunately, in these cases, fractional factorial designs can be developed that reduce the number of treatment combinations while at the same time still providing the most relevant information. In effect, DOE techniques utilize statistical principles to maximize the amount of information that can be obtained from a given number of treatment combinations. Because the calculations are quite complex, the design of fractional factorial experiments is typically done with the aid of specialized statistics packages or published experimental design catalogs.

8.8.1.1 Taguchi Methods

Among the more popular approaches used to design experiments are Taguchi methods, named after Genichi Taguchi. According to Taguchi, most of the quality of products and services is determined at the design stage, and therefore, the production system can affect quality only slightly. Taguchi focused on this fact to develop an approach to designing quality into outputs. Rather than trying to constantly control equipment and workers to stay within specifications – sizes, finishes, times – he has devised a procedure for statistical testing to determine the best combination of product and process design to make the output relatively independent of normal fluctuations in the production system. To do this, statistical experimentation is conducted to determine what product and process designs produce outputs with the highest uniformity at lowest cost.

8.9 The Control Phase

As the Six Sigma project nears completion, the focus in the final phase shifts to the development of procedures to again monitor the process. Here, our purpose is to ensure that the process's new (hopefully) higher level of performance is maintained and that previous problems do not resurface. We discussed the use of control charts – the most commonly used control tool – in Chapter 7 and the use of "earned value" to control projects in Chapter 2.

8.10 Six Sigma in Practice

To conclude our introduction to Six Sigma, we now turn our attention to issues related to employing Six Sigma to improve business processes and performance. Here, our focus will be on the various roles played in Six Sigma initiatives, becoming certified in Six Sigma, and the need for each organization to customize its Six Sigma program to its unique needs.

8.10.1 Six Sigma Roles

One aspect that differentiates Six Sigma from earlier process improvement programs, including total quality management and reengineering, is that with Six Sigma, specific roles and titles for these roles have been defined and generally accepted. The central roles to Six Sigma include the following:

- *Master Black Belts.* Master Black Belts combine an advanced knowledge of the Six Sigma toolkit with a deep understanding of the business. The primary roles of Master Black Belts are to develop and execute Six Sigma training programs and to work with senior management to ensure that Six Sigma initiatives are being best leveraged to help the organization achieve its strategic goals.

- *Black Belts.* The two primary roles of Black Belts, who have a solid background in the Six Sigma toolkit, are conducting Six Sigma training and leading Six Sigma improvement projects. Both Black Belt and Master Black Belt roles tend to be full-time positions.

- *Green Belts.* Green belts have broad knowledge of the Six Sigma toolkit but not nearly as much depth in the tools as Black Belts and Master Black Belts. The majority of the work of Six Sigma projects is typically completed by Green Belts under the guidance and direction of Black Belts and, on occasion, Master Black Belts. Green Belts are not usually employed as full-time process improvement professionals, but rather are expected to use the Six Sigma methodology to improve their work processes.

- *Yellow Belts.* Although Yellow Belts are not as common as Master Black Belts, Black Belts, and Green Belts, some organizations have added this rank as a designation for those employees who have completed Six Sigma awareness training.

In addition to these central roles, there are also a number of important supporting roles, including the following:

- *Champions/Sponsors.* Champions are senior managers who support and promote Six Sigma projects. The employees working on a Six Sigma project rely on the champion's senior position within the organization to help them obtain the resources needed to successfully complete the project as well as to remove hurdles that might otherwise derail the successful completion of the project.

- *Process owners.* Although process owners are the managers with end-to-end responsibility for a particular business process, typically they do not direct Six Sigma projects. Rather, they are best viewed as being the customers of Six Sigma projects.

8.10.2 Becoming Certified

In addition to having well-defined roles, another aspect that differentiates Six Sigma from earlier programs is that accompanying each of the central Six Sigma roles is a certification process. Along these lines, it is a common practice for organizations to make a distinction between employees who are Six Sigma trained at a certain level and those who are certified at the level. In these organizations, becoming certified at a given level entails meeting additional requirements beyond receiving the training, such as passing an examination and/or successfully completing one or more Six Sigma projects.

Generally speaking, there are four alternative ways of obtaining Black Belt certification. Perhaps the most common approach is for employees to be trained and certified internally by their current employer. In fact, based on their success with Six Sigma, some organizations actually open their training programs to people outside their organizations. One notable example was Motorola University.

A second approach for obtaining certification is through numerous consulting organizations that offer both training and certification programs. These organizations can be easily found by doing a Web search using a search string such as "Six Sigma certification." Third, a number of universities have begun offering training and in some cases certification programs. Several universities even offer this training and certification through online programs. Finally, individuals can obtain certification through professional societies, perhaps most commonly through ASQ (www.asq.org).

Given the wide range of options for becoming certified, it is somewhat surprising to observe the extent to which these varied certification programs are standardized in terms of both duration and content. For example, the standard for Black Belt training is a four-month program during which students receive one week of formal in-class training each month and use the time between training sessions to work on a Black Belt project.

8.10.3 The Need to Customize Six Sigma Programs

Although there is a fair amount of consensus related to the roles, body of knowledge, and training practices surrounding Six Sigma programs, organizations that have succeeded with their Six Sigma programs also recognize the need to tailor their Six Sigma approach to their unique needs. ScottishPower, an electric and gas provider to more than 5 million customers in the United States and United Kingdom, serves as an excellent example of this. In May 2001, ScottishPower brought in an external consultant to begin training its first wave of 20 full-time Black Belts. Because of the limited data that were available and the relatively generic nature of the external consultant's training program, ScottishPower emphasized the use of the simpler tools in its early Six Sigma projects, including process mapping, Pareto analysis, cause-and-effect diagrams, and stakeholder analysis. Six months after the first wave of Black Belt training, a second group of 20 employees was selected for full-time Black Belt training. Based on their experience from the first round, ScottishPower identified the need to better use statistical analysis to identify the root causes of problems. Thus, the second wave of training, which was performed by ScottishPower's own Black Belts who had been trained in the first wave, emphasized statistical techniques such as the use of t-tests, ANOVA, correlation, regression, and DOE. Based on a desire to gain additional value from the data that were being collected, ScottishPower began emphasizing additional techniques in subsequent waves, including chi-square tests, nonparametric tests such as Mann–Whitney and Kruskal–Wallis and Box–Cox transformations. ScottishPower's experience and success with Six Sigma highlights the importance of customizing a Six Sigma program to the organization's unique needs and adopting the training as the organization becomes more sophisticated in its ability to both collect and analyze data.

8.10.4 Six Sigma and Sustainability

The primary focus of Six Sigma to reduce variability and thereby increase consistency, naturally overlaps with the goals of improving sustainability. For example, reducing the number of defects and rework translates directly into requiring less energy and materials, which align with

sustainability objectives. This direct connection between Six Sigma and sustainability was well illustrated by the 3M example at the beginning of the chapter. In particular, it was noted that while the primary goal of 3M's Six Sigma projects focused on improving operational efficiencies and product yields, a natural byproduct of these projects was reductions in energy consumption, reduced emissions, and less waste.

Broadly speaking, there are three ways Six Sigma can support an organization's sustainability goals: (1) using Sigma's DMAIC approach to complete projects specifically focused on improving sustainability, (2) ensuring that sustainability objectives are embedded in all Six Sigma projects, and (3) realizing sustainability benefits as a natural byproduct of traditional Six Sigma projects.

Regarding the use of DMAIC for sustainability projects, Six Sigma provides a disciplined and well-structured approach, as well as a robust set of tools to help ensure projects focused on sustainability are successful and achieve their goals. The specific Six Sigma tools that are used most frequently in sustainability projects include statistical process control (discussed in the previous chapter), FMEA (also discussed in the previous chapter), Pareto analysis, and ANOVA (Erdil *et al.* 2018).

Regarding the second way Six Sigma can support sustainability, embedding sustainability goals into all Six Sigma projects helps reinforce the importance senior management is placing on sustainability. Embedding sustainability goals into a traditional Six Sigma project requires identifying sustainability opportunities in the Define phase and identifying corresponding metrics in the Measure phase. In the Improve phase it may be necessary to undertake a cost-benefit analysis if pursuing sustainability goals will impact the achievement of other project goals. Of course, as was noted earlier, it is also likely that the traditional Six Sigma goals for the project are aligned with sustainability goals. Last, in the Control phase it may be appropriate to monitor one or more of the sustainability metrics defined in the Measure phase.

Finally, it also important to point out that organizations may encounter challenges associated with their sustainability improvement initiatives. Some of the more common challenges include lack of broad organizational support, limited resources available to support sustainability initiatives, and the difficulty in quantifying the benefits. The strategy discussed above of embedding sustainability objectives into traditional Six Sigma projects is often an effective strategy for addressing these challenges.

EXPAND YOUR UNDERSTANDING

1. Contrast Six Sigma and BPD.

2. Is there any relationship between DPMO and process capability?

3. Measurement systems analysis focuses primarily on the variation introduced into the measurement system by human operators. Can you think of other sources of variation introduced by the measurement system beyond the human operators?

4. Is the DMAIC approach more applicable to projects focusing on incremental change or radical change? Why?

5. Are there any limitations you see associated with QFD? Benchmarking?

6. What phase of DMAIC do you imagine is the most important phase? What phase do you imagine takes the longest?

7. Suppose that a restaurant's requirements for the "4-ounce" hamburger patties that it purchased from its supplier should be between 3.4 and 4.6 ounces. Why would the restaurant be concerned about hamburgers weighing too much?

8. In what ways might a traditional Six Sigma project align with helping an organization achieve its sustainability objectives? In what ways might tradeoffs exist between the goals associated with a Six Sigma project and sustainability?

Apply Your Understanding

Three Dot Four Capital Management

John Sale was recently promoted to Senior Vice President of Consumer Lending at Three Dot Four Capital Management. Three Dot Four is a large financial services organization ranked among the top 20 financial institutions in terms of total assets. A key consideration in John's promotion was his past success leading the bank's quality and productivity group. In particular, there appears to be a significant amount of dissatisfaction among both the bank's customers and the bank's loan officers with its online mortgage application process.

The online mortgage application process is initiated when a customer clicks on the Apply for a Home Mortgage Now link on Three Dot Four's homepage. This link takes the user to an Instruction page that overviews the application process and provides a checklist of the information the applicant will be asked to supply on subsequent Web pages. Clicking on the Continue button at the bottom of the Instruction page takes the user to the first of four Web pages, each containing a Web-based form to collect the required data.

The first Web page, Personal Information, solicits information regarding the applicant and requires entering information in 33 fields. Information collected on this page includes the applicant's and coapplicant's names, full addresses, previous addresses, dates of birth, Social Security numbers, phone numbers, e-mail addresses, and so on. To continue on to the next page, the user selects the Continue button located at the bottom of the Personal Information page. When the Continue button is selected on a given page, a check is made to ensure that none of the required fields has been left blank. If the validation check is passed, the next Web page in the application process is displayed. In cases where the validation check fails, the blank fields are highlighted and the user is asked to enter the information in these fields.

Once information has been entered for all required fields on the Personal Information page, the second page – Property, Loan, and Expenses – is displayed. This page is used to collect information about the property the loan will be used to purchase, the type of loan the applicant desires, and information about the applicant's monthly expenses. In total, the Property, Loan, and Expenses page contains 10 data fields.

Once the information has been entered for all required fields on the Property, Loan, and Expenses page, the Employment page is displayed. This page captures information about the applicant's and coapplicant's employment history, including salary and other income information. The Employment page contains 16 user fields. Finally, the last Web page in the application process captures information about the applicant's Assets and Liabilities. In particular, the user is asked to supply information about checking accounts, savings accounts, credit card accounts, investment accounts, car loans, and so on. In total, this page contains 22 data fields.

When the applicant clicks on the Submit Application button at the bottom of the Assets and Liabilities page, a final validation check is performed and the information is transferred to one of the bank's loan officers. The loan officers subsequently print out the information and then add the application to their backlog of other in-process applications. To even out the work across the loan officers, all loan officers process loan applications submitted via the Web, as well as applications received via the mail and applications completed at one of the bank's branch offices.

Initially, John identified two areas in need of improvement: the fairness of loan approval decisions and the accuracy of the information in loan applications submitted online. In terms of the fairness of loan approval decisions, over the last couple of years, the company has received numerous complaints from applicants questioning the organization's fairness in making loan approval decisions. To begin understanding this problem, John initiated a study in which 25 loan applications were randomly selected. These loan applications were then evaluated by a panel of three experts to determine whether the loan should be approved or rejected. Next, three loan officers were selected and asked to evaluate each of the 25 loans two times. The data collected from this study is summarized in Table 1.

To investigate the issue related to the accuracy of information in online mortgage applications, John formed a process improvement team. The team began by collecting data on the total number of hits each page in the Web application process received as well as the number of times the page was actually completed during the month of January. In addition, the team performed a detailed audit of all the information that was submitted during January and tallied the number of fields that contained errors across all submitted information. A summary of the team's preliminary results is given in Table 2.

(continued)

Table 1 Summary of Loan Approval Fairness Study

Loan	Expert panel	Loan officer 1		Loan officer 2		Loan officer 3	
		Jan 1	Feb 1	Jan 1	Feb 1	Jan 1	Feb 1
1	A	A	A	A	A	A	A
2	R	R	R	R	R	R	A
3	A	A	A	A	A	A	A
4	A	R	R	R	R	R	R
5	R	R	R	R	R	R	R
6	R	R	R	A	A	R	R
7	A	A	A	A	R	A	A
8	R	R	R	R	R	R	R
9	A	A	R	R	R	A	R
10	R	R	R	R	R	R	R
11	R	R	R	R	R	R	R
12	A	A	A	A	A	A	A
13	A	A	A	A	R	A	A
14	R	R	R	R	R	R	R
15	R	R	R	A	R	R	R
16	A	A	A	A	A	A	A
17	A	A	A	R	A	A	A
18	A	A	A	A	A	A	A
19	R	R	R	R	R	R	R
20	R	R	R	R	A	R	R
21	R	R	A	R	A	R	A
22	A	A	A	A	A	A	A
23	A	R	R	R	R	R	R
24	A	A	R	A	R	R	R
25	A	A	A	A	A	R	A

A = Loan approved.
R = Loan not approved.

Table 2 Online Mortgage Application Submissions, January

Web page	Number of hits	Number submitted	Number of errors
Personal information	108,571	68,400	45,144
Property, loan, and expense information	68,400	62,928	22,025
Employment information	62,928	59,781	28,695
Asset and liability information	59,781	52,009	51,489

Questions

1. What is the DPMO for the loan applications submitted via the Web?

2. What could be done to improve the DPMO?

3. Regarding the fairness of the loan approval process, what recommendations would you make?

Valley County Medical Clinic

Valley County Medical Clinic (VCMC) operates a walk-in medical clinic to meet the nonacute medical needs of its approximately 15,000 citizens. Patients arriving at the clinic are served on a first-come, first-served basis.

As part of a new total quality management program, VCMC conducted an in-depth, four-month study of its current operations. A key component of the study was a survey, distributed to all county citizens. The purpose of the survey was to identify and prioritize areas most in need of improvement. An impressive 44% of the surveys were returned and deemed usable. Follow-up analysis indicated that the people who responded were representative of the population served by the clinic. After the results were tabulated, it was determined that the walk-in medical clinic was located near the bottom of the rankings, indicating a great deal of dissatisfaction with the clinic. Preliminary analysis of the respondents' comments indicated that people were reasonably satisfied with the treatment they received at the clinic but were very dissatisfied with the amount of time they had to wait to see a caregiver.

Upon arriving at the clinic, patients receive a form from the receptionist requesting basic biographical information and the nature of the medical condition for which treatment is being sought. Completing the form typically requires 2 to 3 minutes. After the form is returned to the receptionist, it is time-stamped and placed in a tray. Clerks collect the forms and retrieve the corresponding patients' files from the basement. The forms typically remain in the tray for about 5 minutes before being picked up, and it takes the clerk approximately 12 minutes to retrieve the files. After a patient's file is retrieved, the form describing the medical problem is attached to it with a paper clip, and it is placed in a stack with other files. The stack of files is ordered according to the time stamps on the forms.

When the nurse practitioners finish with their current patient, they select the next file from the stack and escort that patient to one of the treatment rooms. On average, files remain in the stack for 10 minutes, but this varies considerably depending on the time of day and the day of the week. On Monday mornings, for example, it is common for files to remain in the stack for 30 minutes or more.

Once in the treatment room, the nurse practitioner reads over the form describing the patient's ailment. Next, the nurse discusses the problem with the patient while taking some standard measurements such as blood pressure and temperature. The nurse practitioner then makes a rough diagnosis, based on the measurements and symptoms, to determine if the ailment is one of the 20 that state law permits nurse practitioners to treat. If the condition is treatable by the nurse practitioner, a more thorough diagnosis is undertaken and treatment is prescribed. It typically takes about 5 minutes for the nurse practitioners to make the rough diagnosis and another 20 minutes to complete the detailed diagnosis and discuss the treatment with the patient. If the condition (as roughly diagnosed) is not treatable by the nurse practitioner, the patient's file is placed in the stack for the on-duty MD. Because of the higher cost of MDs versus nurse practitioners, there is typically only one MD on duty at any time. Thus, patients wait an average of 25 minutes for the MD. On the other hand, because of their greater training and skill, the MDs are able to diagnose and treat the patients in 15 minutes, despite the fact that they deal with the more difficult and less routine cases. Incidentally, an expert system for nurse practitioners is being tested at another clinic that – if shown to be effective – would initially double the number of ailments treatable by nurse practitioners and over time would probably increase the list even more as the tool continued to be improved.

Questions

1. Develop a process map for the medical clinic that shows the times of the various activities. Is the patients' dissatisfaction with the clinic justified?

2. What do you imagine are the patients' key requirements for the clinic?

3. What assumptions are being made about the way work is performed and treatment administered at the clinic?

4. Redesign the process of treating patients at the clinic, using technologies you are familiar with, to better meet the patients' needs as listed in Question 2.

EXERCISES

8.1 A call center has determined five types of defects can occur in processing customer calls: the customer spends too long on hold, the customer is given the wrong information, the customer rep handles the call in an unprofessional way, the customer is transferred to the wrong destination, and the customer is disconnected. A total of 468 calls were subject to a quality audit last month, and the results obtained from the audit are summarized in the list below. What is the DPMO for the call center?

Number of defects/call	Frequency
1	73
2	13
3	3
4	1
5	0

8.2 Over the last quarter, 742 shots were administered at a walk-in clinic. To be treated properly, patients must be given the correct dosage of the correct medication. During the quarter in question, it was determined that one patient received the incorrect dosage of the correct medication, another patient received the wrong medication, and a third patient received both the wrong medication and the wrong dosage given her age and weight. What is the DPMO for the clinic?

8.3 A silk screening company prints 6000 decals per month. A random sample of 150 decals is taken every week and inspected based on four characteristics. The data for the last four weeks are summarized in the table below. Assuming that the data in the table are representative of the process, what is the DPMO for the silk-screening process?

Decal characteristic	Number of defects observed
Color accuracy	10
Image alignment	7
Color consistency	8
Image sharpness	3

8.4 A hospital made 225 medication errors last year. Of these errors, 30% were errors with the prescription, while 70% were errors made while dispensing the medication. The hospital admitted 8465 patients last year, and the patients received an average of 4.8 prescriptions per hospital stay. Medications are dispensed at the time they are needed, and each medication is dispensed four times per day on average. The average patient stay at the hospital is 3.5 days. Compute the DPMO for the patient medicine process. What assumptions, if any, were needed to calculate the DPMO?

8.5 Customers of Dough Boy Ltd. have specified that pizza crusts they order should be 28–32 centimeters in diameter. Sample data recently collected indicate that Dough Boy's crusts average 30 centimeters in diameter, with a standard deviation of 1.1 centimeters. Is Dough Boy's pizza crust production system capable of meeting its customers' requirements? If not, what options does Dough Boy have to rectify this situation?

8.6 Design specifications for a bottled product are that it should contain 350–363 milliliters. Sample data indicate that the bottles contain an average of 355 milliliters, with a standard deviation of 2 milliliters. Is the filling operation capable of meeting the design specifications? Why or why not?

BIBLIOGRAPHY

3M, "2022 Global Impact Report, 3M.com, June 28, 2022.

Das, R., S. Colello, and H. Davidson. "Six Sigma in Corporate Law." *Six Sigma Forum Magazine* (November 2004): 30–36.

Diehl, M., and W. Stroebe. "Productivity Loss in Brain-Storming Groups: Towards a Solution of a Riddle." *Journal of Personality and Social Psychology*, 53 (1987): 497–509.

EPA, "3M – Lean Six Sigma and Sustainability," epa.gov, October 19, 2021.

Erdil, N. O., C. B. Aktas, and M. A. Omid, "Embedding Sustainability in Lean Six Sigma Efforts," *Journal of Cleaner Production*, 198 (2018): 520–529

Godin, E., D. Raven, C. Sweetapple, and F. R. Del Giudice. "Faster Test Results." *Quality Progress* (January 2004): 33–39.

Hammer, M., and S. A. Stanton. *The Reengineering Revolution.* New York: Harper Business, 1995.

Jones, M. H., Jr. "Six Sigma at a Bank?" *Six Sigma Forum Magazine* (February 2004): 13–17.

Leatherbury, J. "Talent Show: A Process Improvement Approach to Employee Retention Yields Impressive Business Results." *Quality Progress* (November 2008): 48–55.

Pande, P. S., R. P. Neuman, and R. R. Cavanagh. *The Six Sigma Way.* New York: McGraw-Hill, 2000.

Thompson, L. "Improving the Creativity of Organizational Work Groups." *Academy of Management Executive*, 17 (2003): 96–111.

Process Improvement: Lean

9

CHAPTER IN PERSPECTIVE

As an organization monitors its processes, opportunities may be identified to improve these processes either by completely redesigning the process through Business Process Design or reducing the variation inherent in the process through Six Sigma, as described in Chapter 8. In this chapter, we discuss another approach for process improvement that seeks to minimize waste and maximize value.

More specifically, "Lean management" has taken on the aura of a global competitive philosophy because so many firms that embrace it have been so successful: Toyota, Deere, and numerous others. We first address the history and philosophy of Lean and then make a comparison between traditional production systems and Lean enterprises. Following this, we continue with a discussion of five Lean principles: (1) specify value from the customer's point of view, (2) identify the value stream, (3) make value flow, (4) have the customer pull value, and (5) pursue perfection. The chapter concludes with a discussion of the benefits associated with Lean and Lean Six Sigma.

While often considered more tactical in nature, the topic of Lean has important strategic implications in the same way Six Sigma (discussed in the previous chapter) does. For example, organizations that have adopted Lean have obtained substantial cost savings, achieved significant improvements in shortening lead times and improving their on-time delivery performance, and have enhanced service delivery processes to provide higher service levels to customers. As these benefits illustrate, Lean makes important, if not critical, contributions toward enhancing an organization's competitive position. In fact, because of the value Lean provides, some organizations have adopted the Lean principles discussed in this chapter as the way they do all their business, making Lean an important element of the overall business strategy.

9.1 Introduction

- The city of Springdale, AR, was receiving complaints from its citizens that its commercial building permit process was too cumbersome. The problem in part stemmed from the fact that the staff had been downsized; yet, the process hadn't been modified to adapt to having fewer staff. Key complaints related to not being able to predict the time required to get approval and not being able to get updates on the status of a pending application. The city was concerned that people would choose to locate their businesses in adjacent cities as a result of their dissatisfaction with the process.

To address these concerns, the city undertook a three-day kaizen event. The goal of kaizen events is to rapidly identify and implement process improvement ideas. On the first day of the kaizen event, the process improvement team received some training about the kaizen approach including an introduction to process mapping. After the training, the team moved on and developed a clear problem statement and set goals for the kaizen event. The team defined reducing the time to process the applications and reducing the number of errors as the primary goals. Since there was no baseline data on application processing time and number of errors, the team decided to use a surrogate measure of performance, the complexity of the process – defined as the number of steps in the process. The team reasoned that as the number of steps in the process increased, the total processing time and opportunities for errors would also increase.

The team's next step was to better understand the current process. To accomplish this, the team "walked the process" by following a single commercial building permit packet through the entire process. The team was surprised to learn that the process consisted of 43 steps and 16 decisions. Armed with this insight, the team set a project goal of reducing the number of steps to 30 and the number of decisions to 12.

The experience of walking the process provided the team with numerous improvement ideas. The team captured these ideas by completing a future-state process map by early in the afternoon of the second day. The team then piloted the future-state process map, adjusted it, and finalized the new process by 3:00 p.m. of the second day. The new process developed by the team reduced the number of steps to 25 (which exceeded the goal of 30) and the number of decisions to 11. With the project complete and an entire day left, the team completed kaizen events for four other processes by lunchtime on the third day! (Smith 2012).

- It was not uncommon for chemotherapy patients at Virginia Mason Medical Center, a 350-bed hospital located in downtown Seattle, to spend an entire day receiving their weekly chemotherapy treatment. To illustrate the process, after arriving at 8:00 a.m. and checking in on the first floor, the patient would be asked to go to the laboratory for blood testing located on the sixth floor. After having the blood drawn, the patient would then wait for the results to be sent to the oncologist and then eventually meet with the oncologist on the second floor. If things progressed smoothly, the patient would begin receiving the intravenous chemotherapy treatment by noon in an open and noisy room that was shared with six other patients.

  To improve this process, Virginia Mason turned to the concepts of Lean pioneered by Toyota shortly after World War II. Virginia Mason's overarching goal was to improve the patient experience while at the same time increasing the overall efficiency of the process. Using Lean concepts, Virginia Mason completely redesigned the process for chemotherapy patients so that everything flows to the patient as opposed to the patient flowing through the process. For example, instead of being located on separate floors, the labs and doctors' offices are now adjacent to private patient treatment rooms. Furthermore, each private treatment room has a flat-screen TV, a computer, nursing supplies, and toilet facilities. A dedicated pharmacy was also added to the cancer treatment center, thereby eliminating delays for patients of up to 2 hours. Other improvements have reduced the preparation time for chemotherapy treatments from 3 hours to less than 1 hour. Across the entire medical center, hospital administrators estimate that its Lean initiatives have resulted in savings of $6 million in capital spending, freed up 13,000 square feet, reduced inventory costs by $360,000, and reduced the distance hospital staff walk each day by 34 miles. In addition to these tangible results, the hospital achieved a number of other benefits, including improved patient satisfaction, shorter bill collection times, and lower infection rates. To achieve these benefits, the hospital spent approximately $1.5 million, primarily for consultants, travel, and training (Connolly 2005).

- Xerox has a long track record in the area of quality management. Xerox's journey began in the early 1980s when it established its Leadership Through Quality Initiative, which focused on improving business processes in order to improve customer satisfaction, quality, and productivity. Fast-forward to the late 1990s and we see Six Sigma and Lean being adopted by Xerox's manufacturing and supply chain functions which improved its operating efficiency and effectiveness. In mid-2002, Xerox's leadership decided to integrate its Lean and Six Sigma programs across the entire enterprise, naming the initiative Xerox Lean Six Sigma. To support this initiative, Xerox kicked off an intense Black Belt (BB) training program in January 2003 that included employees from all functional areas. By August 2004, 400 BBs had been trained, 2500 employees had completed or were in the process of completing Green Belt training, 2000 leaders had completed a two-day workshop, and 10,000 employees had completed Yellow Belt awareness training. Furthermore, a total of 700 Lean Six Sigma projects have been completed across all areas of Xerox, including product design, supply chain, marketing and sales, customer service, and strategy deployment. Xerox estimated that it achieved an initial $6 million return in 2003 based on a $14 million investment in Lean Six Sigma and expected even bigger gains in the years ahead (Fornari and Maszle 2004).

- Honeywell International was another multibillion dollar, diversified technology company that successfully integrated Six Sigma's traditional emphasis on variation reduction with Lean's emphasis on waste reduction to create its Six Sigma Plus program. Honeywell competed in four major industry segments: (1) aerospace, (2) automation and control solutions, (3) specialty materials, and (4) transportation systems. The business unit for each of these industry segments was headed by a group president. Reporting to each group president was a Six Sigma Plus Leader (SSPL) who was responsible for developing the strategic plans and deploying these plans for Six Sigma Plus initiatives within the group. Reporting to the SSPL is a team composed of Master Black Belts (MBBs), Lean Masters (LMs), BBs, and Lean Experts (LEs). MBBs and LMs, also referred to as Honeywell Masters (HMs), worked on projects that had more than a $1 million financial impact and were also responsible for training, mentoring, and certifying BBs and LEs.

  In addition to the SSPLs in each business unit, Honeywell had a Vice President of Six Sigma who reported directly to the CEO. This VP chaired the Six Sigma Plus Executive Council, which in turn oversaw all training and ensured that a common curriculum was used company-wide. In 2002, Honeywell reported productivity improvement gains of $1.2 billion. Honeywell's 2004 Annual Report announced the introduction of the Honeywell Operating System (HOS). The HOS was based on the Toyota Production System and was used to provide a roadmap to further integrate Six Sigma and Lean tools (Hill and Kearney 2003).

- The hospital patient discharge process is often associated with substantial patient dissatisfaction. However, in addition to frustrating patients, delays in the discharge process create problems in other areas of the hospital such as admitting and the emergency department, as these areas must wait for the rooms vacated by discharged patients. To address the inefficiencies often associated with the patient discharge process, Valley Baptist Hospital in Harlingen, Texas, utilized Lean Six Sigma and changed management techniques. One specific goal of this project was to substantially reduce the time from when a patient discharge order was entered into the computer until the time the patient was transported from the room.

  The process improvement team began by mapping the current patient discharge process. In mapping the process, the team discovered that there was little consistency across the nurses in terms of their approaches to discharging patients. Further analysis of the process map was undertaken to identify the activities in the discharge process that were not "adding value," that is, helping discharge patients faster. All activities were classified as either value added, nonvalue added, or value enabler. The team further enhanced the process map to show rework loops, communication flows among the staff, and physical movements. Key performance metrics were also added to the process map, which highlighted a substantial amount of nonvalue-added time.

As the team further embellished and analyzed the process map, it was able to identify several primary drivers of waste in the patient discharge process. For example, the team discovered that in 21% of cases, nurses required clarification from a doctor before the discharge order could be entered into the computer. The need to clarify an order added an average of 33 minutes to the discharge process. As another example, the team discovered that in some cases the primary nurse took the patient's vital signs, while in other cases, a second nurse took the vital signs, which were then reported to the primary nurse. Having the primary nurse take the vital signs himself or herself reduced the elapsed time by an average of 64 minutes.

Based on these insights and others, the process improvement team developed a new standard operating procedure consisting of six steps for the patient discharge process. After adopting the new process, the mean time to discharge a patient was reduced by 74%, from 185 minutes to 48 minutes. Furthermore, the standard deviation of discharge times also decreased by 71%, from 128.7 minutes to 37.2 minutes. Finally, the percentage of discharged patients who vacated their rooms in 45 minutes or less increased from 6.9% to 61.7% (DeBusk and Rangel 2005).

As these examples illustrate, *Lean* is a philosophy that seeks to eliminate all types of waste, whether it be excessive delays in treating patients, excessive lead times, carrying excessive levels of inventory, workers or parts traveling excessive distances, spending too much time setting up equipment, unneeded space, reworking defective products, clarifying patient orders, idle facilities, and scrap. The examples also illustrate several other important themes associated with Lean. First, since waste can be thought of as those activities and outcomes that do not add value for the customer, a strong customer orientation is central to Lean. This was illustrated in the Virginia Mason example, where the chemotherapy process was redesigned so that the treatment process flowed to the patient as opposed to the patient flowing through the process. In fact, Virginia Mason made additional changes not mentioned in the example to improve the customer experience, including allocating the best rooms with windows to patients, adding a waterfall and meditation room to help ease patient stress, and adding an Internet café. A second theme relates to the large payoff that can be achieved through Lean initiatives. This is exemplified by Honeywell's $1.2 billion in productivity gains; Virginia Mason's cost, space, and travel savings; and Valley Baptist's 74% reduction in patient discharge time. Finally, a third theme that emerges from the examples is the trend for organizations to merge their Six Sigma (discussed in Chapter 8) programs with their Lean programs. This trend reflects the complementary nature of these two programs: Six Sigma's focus on variation reduction and Lean's focus on eliminating waste. Clearly, a process with little variation but lots of waste would not be desirable and vice versa.

In essence, the goal of Lean is to accomplish more with fewer resources: fewer workers and less inventory, space, equipment, time, scrap, and so on. To accomplish this goal, Womack and Jones, in their book *Lean Thinking* (2003), identify five Lean principles:

1. Specify value from the customer's point of view.

2. Identify the value stream, the complete set of activities required to create the output valued by the customer.

3. Make value flow through the value stream by eliminating nonvalue-added activities and streamlining the remaining value-added steps.

4. Have the customer pull value through the value stream.

5. Pursue perfection.

Lean cannot be reduced to a "formula," and therefore, every firm must apply the philosophy differently. In the remainder of this chapter, we discuss these five Lean principles in more detail. However, before doing so, we begin our discussion with an overview of the Lean philosophy to put it in proper context.

9.2 History and Philosophy of Lean

Lean production (also known as *synchronous manufacturing* or simply *Lean*) is the name given to the Toyota Production System. Toyota began developing its approach to manufacturing shortly after World War II. The Toyota system is known for its minimal use of resources and elimination of all forms of waste, including time.

Thus, for example, just-in-time (JIT) is an important element of the Toyota system. Similarly, Lean production is an integral element of its supply chain management. As such, it requires identifying and eliminating all forms of nonvalue-added activities throughout the entire supply chain. Teams of multiskilled workers are employed at all levels of the organization to root out inefficiency and waste. To understand why Lean was developed, it is important to understand a little about the history and culture of Japan.

Japan is a small country with minimal resources and a large population. Thus, the Japanese have always been careful not to waste resources, including space (especially land), as well as time, and labor. Waste is abhorrent because the country has so little space and so few natural resources to begin with. Therefore, the Japanese have been motivated to maximize the gain or yield from the few resources available. It has also been necessary for them to maintain their respect for each other in order to work and live together smoothly and effectively in such a densely populated space.

As a result, their work systems tend to be based on three primary tenets:

1. Minimizing waste in all forms

2. Continually improving processes and systems

3. Maintaining respect for all workers

During production, the Japanese studiously avoid waste of materials, space, time, and labor. They therefore pay significant attention to identifying and correcting problems that could potentially lead to such waste. Moreover, operations and procedures are constantly being improved and fine-tuned to increase productivity and yield, further eliminating waste. Equal respect is paid to all workers, and the trappings of status are minimized so that respect among all can be maintained.

Although low cost and consistent quality are important goals when a firm adopts Lean, many other benefits also have accrued in those firms where it has been implemented. Examples include reduced inventories of all types (and thus less need for the space they require), greater productivity among both labor and staff, shorter lead times, improved processes, increased equipment productivity and utilization, better quality, fewer errors, and higher morale among the workforce and managers. Additionally, many of these benefits also translate into improved sustainability as is discussed later in the chapter. Because of its broad nature and wide range of benefits, Lean has become for many companies a major element in their competitive strategy, as the Xerox example at the beginning of the chapter illustrated.

The second tenet of Japanese work systems is continuous improvement, which corresponds to the Lean principle of pursuing perfection. Accordingly, Lean is not simply considered a one-time event to streamline the transformation system from a sloppy, wasteful form to an efficient, competitive form. Rather, it is an ongoing journey that seeks to make continuing improvements throughout the system to keep the firm competitive and profitable in the future.

Perhaps, the most important of the three tenets is the third, maintaining respect for all workers. Unfortunately, U.S. industry seems to be moving more slowly in this direction, and U.S. firms seem far behind the Japanese in obtaining respect and loyalty from their workers. This is probably because these firms and industries do not show respect for and loyalty to their employees in the first place.

Initially, in the early 1980s, the Japanese approach to production was greeted with a great deal of ambivalence in the United States. Typical of the sentiment at this time was, "It will never work here." However, this view abruptly changed when a number of domestic companies, such as Hewlett-Packard and Harley-Davidson, began demonstrating the significant benefits of JIT, an important component of Lean.

Next, we describe the most common characteristics of Lean systems and compare them with the more traditional systems.

9.2.1 Traditional Systems Compared with Lean

Table 9.1 presents a dozen characteristics of Lean systems that tend to distinguish them from the more traditional systems historically used in U.S. industry. These characteristics range from philosophy and culture to standard operating procedures. Several of the contrasts summarized in Table 9.1 are elaborated on in the remainder of this section.

9.2.1.1 Priorities

Traditionally, most firms want to accept all customer orders or at least provide a large number of options from which customers may order. However, this confuses the production task, increases

Table 9.1   Comparison of Traditional Systems and Lean

Characteristic	Traditional	Lean
Priorities	Accept all orders Many product options	Limited market Few product options Low cost, high quality
Product/service design	Customized outputs Design from scratch	Standardized outputs Incremental design Simplify, design for manufacturing
Capacity	Highly utilized Inflexible	Moderately utilized Flexible
Transformation system	Job shop	Flow shops, cellular manufacturing
Layout	Large space Material-handling equipment	Small space Close, manual transfer of materials
Workforce	Narrow skills Specialized Individualized Competitive attitude Change by edict Status: symbols, pay, privileges	Broad skills Flexible Work teams Cooperative attitude Change by consensus No status differentials
Scheduling	Long setups Long runs	Quick changeovers Mixed model runs
Inventories	Large WIP buffers Stores, cribs, stockrooms	Small WIP buffers Floor stock
Suppliers	Many competitive Deliveries to central receiving area Independent forecasts	Few or single sourced Cooperative, network Deliveries directly to assembly line Shared forecasts
Planning and control	Planning-oriented Complex Computerized	Control-oriented Simple Visual
Quality	Via inspection Critical points Acceptance sampling	At the source Continuous Statistical process control
Maintenance	Corrective By experts Run equipment fast Run one shift	Preventive By operator Run equipment slowly Run 24 hours

the chance of errors, and increases costs. With Lean, the target market is usually limited and the options are also limited. A wise Lean firm knows which customers it does *not* want.

Thus, we see that right from the start the overall priorities of Lean firms are different from those of the traditional firm. This perspective is reflected in the approach Lean firms take to each of the other characteristics as well. In one sense, their "strategy" for competing is different from that of the traditional firm, and this strategy permeates their production system.

9.2.1.2 Product/Service Design

In line with the priorities, engineering in the Lean firm designs standard outputs and incrementally improves each design. The parts and subassemblies that make up each output are also standardized; over time, they are further simplified and improved. More traditionally, engineers attempt to design custom outputs to satisfy unique customers, starting from scratch each time and designing new parts and subassemblies. The reason for the new design is often that they cannot find the previous design or that the engineers change and do not know what their predecessors have already designed.

Furthermore, designers in Lean organizations usually include considerations about the manufacturability of the part or product. As was discussed in Chapter 3, this is called *design for manufacturability* (DFM) or *design for assembly* (DFA). Too often, the traditional firm whips up a new engineering design as quickly as it can and then passes the design on to manufacturing without giving a thought to how it can be made (sometimes it cannot). With this approach, poor quality and high costs often result and cannot be improved on the shop floor, since they were designed in from the start.

9.2.1.3 Layout

The traditional method of layout follows the job shop approach of using widely spread-out equipment with space for stockrooms, tool cribs, and work-in-process inventories between the equipment. To handle and move all this inventory, automated or semiautomated equipment such as conveyors, carousels, and forklifts is also required, which takes even more space.

With Lean, production equipment is moved as close together as possible so that parts can be actually handed from one worker or machine to the next. The use of cells and flow lines permits the production of parts in small lots with minimal work-in-process and material-moving equipment. The cells are often U-shaped so that one worker can easily access all the machines without moving very far and finished products will exit at the same point where raw materials enter the cell.

It is not unusual for the workflows in a traditional job shop to look like a plate of spaghetti when traced on a diagram of the shop layout. In fact, creating such a diagram in which the physical flows of the parts are mapped onto the shop floor is referred to as a *spaghetti chart* and is a commonly used Lean tool. In particular, spaghetti charts can be used to identify excessive travel distances, backtracking, and other sources of waste.

9.2.1.4 Workforce

A key element of Lean is the role of the workforce as a means of uncovering and solving problems. Rather than considering the workers as the traditional cogs in the great plant machine, each with its own tasks, skills, and narrow responsibilities, Lean strives for a broadly skilled, flexible worker who will look for and solve production problems wherever they appear.

In the traditional shop, much of the employees' time is nonworking time: looking for parts, moving materials, setting up machines, getting instructions, and so on. Thus, when actually working, the employees tend to work fast, producing parts at a rapid pace whether or not the parts are needed. (This, of course, results in errors, scrap, and machine breakdowns, which again provide a reason to stop working.) The outcome is a stop-and-go situation that, overall, results in a relatively inefficient, ineffective pace for most workers.

Conversely, with Lean, the workers produce only when the next worker is ready. The pace is steady and fast, although never frantic. In spite of the built-in rule that workers should be idle if work is not needed, the focus on smooth flows, short setups, and other such simplifications means that workers are rarely idle. (Of course, if they *are* idle, that is an immediate signal to the system designers that work is not progressing smoothly through the plant and adjustments need to be made.)

9.2.1.5 Inventories

In Japan, inventory is seen as an evil in itself. It is a resource sitting idle, wasting money. But, more important, inventory tends to hide problems. In the traditional plant, inventories are used to buffer operations so that problems at one stage don't affect the next stage. However, inventories also hide problems, such as defective parts, until the inventory is needed and then is found to be defective. For example, in a plant with lots of work-in-process inventory, a worker who discovers a batch of defective parts can simply put them aside and work on something else. By the time the worker returns to the defective batch, if ever, so much time has elapsed since the batch was processed upstream that the cause of the problem is unlikely to be discovered and corrected so as to prevent a recurrence. In contrast, in an environment where there is little or no buffer inventory, a worker who discovers a defective batch has no choice but to work on the batch. Furthermore, the worker can then notify upstream operations of the problem so they can correct it and ensure that it does not occur in the future.

The Japanese liken inventory, and the money it represents, to the water in a lake. They see problems as boulders and obstacles under the water, as shown in Figure 9.1. To expose the problems, they reduce the inventories (water level), also shown in Figure 9.1, and then solve the problems. Then, they lower the inventory more, exposing more problems, and solve those, too. They continue this until all the problems are solved and the inventory investment is practically gone. The result is a greatly improved and smoother production system.

Also, with minimal or no inventory, control of materials is much easier and less expensive. Parts don't get lost, don't have to be moved, don't have to be labeled, and don't have to be held in computer memory or inventory records. Basically, discipline and quality are much improved and cost is reduced, simultaneously.

9.2.1.6 Suppliers

As was discussed in Chapter 5, traditional practice has been to treat suppliers as adversaries and play them off against each other. Multiple sourcing purportedly keeps prices down and ensures a wide supply of parts. However, multiple sourcing also means that no supplier is getting an important fraction of the total orders; thus, there is no incentive to work with the firm to meet specifications for quality and delivery.

With Lean, the desire is for frequent, smooth deliveries of small lots, with the supplier considered part of the team. As part of the team, the supplier is even expected to help plan and design the purchased parts to be supplied. Schedules must be closely coordinated, and many

FIGURE 9.1
Lowering Inventory Investment to Expose Problems

small deliveries are expected every day. Thus, it is in the supplier's interest to locate a plant or warehouse close to the customer. From a sustainability point of view, having suppliers located in closer proximity also helps offset the more frequent deliveries. Clearly, then, the supplier must have a large enough order to make this trouble worthwhile; thus, *single sourcing* for 100% of the requirements is common. But with such large orders, the customer can expect the supplier to become more efficient in producing the larger quantities of items, so quantity discounts become available. Moreover, having just one source is also more convenient for a firm that must interact and coordinate closely with the supplier.

Perhaps equally significant, there is no incoming inspection of the materials to check their quality – all parts must be of specified quality and guaranteed by the supplier. Again, this requires a cooperative rather than an adversarial approach, with the supplier working with the team. Many Lean firms are now establishing a list of "certified" suppliers that they can count on to deliver perfect quality and thus become members of their production teams. In fact, many organizations implementing such programs will purchase products only from suppliers that pass their certification criteria.

Single sourcing also has some disadvantages, however. The largest, of course, is the risk of being totally dependent on one supplier. If the supplier, perhaps through no fault on its part, cannot deliver as needed, the firm is stuck. With the minimal buffers typical of a Lean organization, this could mean expensive idled production and large shortages. There is also some question about the supplier's incentive to become more creative in terms of producing higher quality or less expensive parts because it already has the single-source contract. Yet the Japanese constantly pressure their suppliers to continue reducing prices, expecting that, at the least, the effect of increased learning with higher volumes will result in lower prices.

9.2.1.7 Planning and Control

In the traditional firm, planning is the focus, and it is typically complex and computerized. Material Requirements Planning is a good example of the level of planning and analysis that goes into the traditional production system. Unfortunately, plans often go astray, but since the firm is focused on planning rather than control, the result is to try to improve planning the next time, and this, in turn, results in ever more complex plans. Thus, these firms spend most of their time replanning and very little time actually executing the plans.

In the Lean approach, the focus is on control. Thus, procedures are kept simple and visual and made as routine as possible. Rather than planning and forecasting for an uncertain future, the firm attempts to respond to what actually happens in real time with flexible, quick operations. Some planning is certainly conducted, but to be even more effective and efficient in responding to actual events, the planning is directed to simple expectations and improvements in the control system. Focusing on standardized products that are produced repetitively also helps simplify planning.

But is there any way to combine the advantages of the Lean JIT approach and MRP? Yes, there is a way. It consists of using MRP to pull the long-lead-time items and purchases *into* the shop, and it then employs JIT once the parts and raw materials have entered the shop. Dover's OPW Division used this approach, for example. It employed MRP's explosion and lead-time offsetting to identify and order the external parts and raw materials and used JIT's procedures to run a smooth, efficient plant once the parts and materials arrived. In other cases, MRP is used as a planning tool for order releases and final assembly schedules, while JIT is used to execute and implement the plan.

9.2.1.8 Quality

The traditional approach to quality is to inspect the goods at critical points in the production system to weed out bad items and correct the system. At the least, final inspection on a sample should be conducted before a lot is sent to a customer. If too many defectives are found, the entire lot is inspected and the bad items are replaced with good ones. Scrap rates are tracked so that the firm knows how many to initiate through the production system in order to yield the number of good items desired by the customer.

With Lean, the goal is zero defects and perfect quality. A number of approaches are used for this purpose, as described in Chapters 1 and 7. But the most important elements are the workers themselves – who check the parts as they hand them to the next worker – and the small lot sizes produced, as described earlier. If a part is bad, it is caught at the time of production, and the error in the production system is corrected immediately.

With our comparison of traditional and Lean organizations complete, we now turn our attention to the five principles of Lean and discuss each in more detail. This discussion will include an overview of representative tools and methodologies commonly used to support each principle.

9.3 Specify Value and Identify the Value Stream

At the heart of Lean is the concept of value. While producers and service providers seek to create value for their customers, it is important to recognize that value is ultimately defined by the customer. Thus, one way to define value is to consider what and how much a customer is willing to pay for a particular product or service. Of course, related to how much a customer is willing to pay for a product or service is the strength of the customer's desires and needs and the variety of options available to satisfy these needs.

Alternatively, another common definition of value is that it is the opposite of waste, or *muda*. Waste can be defined as those activities that consume resources but from the customer's perspective create no value. From this perspective, waste is often classified into one of the following seven categories:

1. *Overproduction.* Overproduction means creating more of an output than is needed at a particular point in time. Producing more than is needed creates the need for additional space to store the surplus, requires purchasing more raw materials than were needed, and often has a detrimental effect on profit margins as the surplus may need to be disposed of at distressed prices.

2. *Inventory.* Inventory takes a variety of forms, including raw materials, work-in-process, and finished goods (see Chapter 6). It requires space for its storage, leading to lease and utility expenses. Furthermore, the inventory must be insured, handled, financed, and tracked, further increasing the cost of holding it.

   However, despite all these efforts, some portion of inventory will tend to get damaged, some may become obsolete, and some may even be stolen. Unfortunately, most, if not all, of the work related to maintaining inventory is not value added in the eyes of the customer.

3. *Waiting.* Waiting relates to delays or events that prevent a worker from performing his or her work. A worker with nothing to work on because of a delay in an upstream activity, a worker who is idle because a piece of equipment broke down, or a worker who is idle while waiting for a piece of equipment to be set up all exemplify the waste of waiting.

4. *Unnecessary transport.* Any time a worker or a part must be moved, it is considered waste. One goal of Lean is to seek ways to reduce the distance that people or work must travel, as was illustrated by the Virginia Mason Medical Center example at the beginning of the chapter.

5. *Unnecessary processing.* Unnecessary processing relates to extra steps in a process. Examples of unnecessary processing include removing burrs from machined parts, reworking defective parts, and entering the same information into multiple databases. Also, from the Lean perspective, inspections are generally considered unnecessary processing.

6. *Unnecessary human motions.* Using the human body efficiently and effectively is vital not only to the health of the workers but also to the productivity of the organization. Time and motion studies as well as ergonomic studies are used to help design work environments that increase the efficiency, safety, and effectiveness of workers.

7. *Defects.* Parts that must be reworked, or in more extreme cases scrapped, represent the final category of waste. Having to perform rework requires repeating steps that were already performed, while scrapping parts results in extra material and processing charges with no corresponding output to offset these charges.

The key to providing outputs that are valued by the customer is developing a solid understanding of customer needs. Establishing the voice of the customer, perhaps through a quality function deployment initiative (discussed in the previous chapter), is one approach commonly used to help identify and better understand customer needs. Based on a better understanding of how the customer defines value, the next logical task is to define a target cost. Generally speaking, the low-cost producer in an industry has more options available to it than other organizations in the industry. For example, the low-cost producer has the option of matching its competitors' prices and thereby maintaining a higher profit margin. Alternatively, the low-cost provider can offer its products and services at a lower price than the competition in an effort to increase its market share.

9.3.1 Identify the Value Stream

Once value has been defined from the customer's perspective and a target cost established, the next step is to identify the set of activities or value stream required to create the customer-valued output. Broadly speaking, the value stream includes all activities (value added and nonvalue added) from the creation of the raw materials to the final delivery of the output to the end consumer. Within the organization, the value stream includes the design of the output; continues through the operations function, where raw materials are transformed into finished goods; and ends with the delivery of its output to the customer.

A useful tool for helping organizations identify the set of activities in their value stream is called a *value stream map*. A value stream map is similar to a process map as discussed in the previous chapter. However, it differs in one important way. Namely, the scope of a process map tends to be within the boundaries of an organization while a value stream map transcends organizational boundaries. Thus, a complete value stream map includes the organization's suppliers, the suppliers to its suppliers, and any distributors, retailers, and so on that are between the organization and the end customer.

The activities within a value stream map are often broadly categorized as follows:

- Value added (e.g. patient diagnosis)

- Nonvalue added but necessary (e.g. requiring patients to sign a HIPAA form)

- Nonvalue added and not necessary (e.g. waiting for the doctor)

The challenge associated with value-added activities is to identify ways to perform these activities in such a way that more value is created and/or fewer resources are consumed. Likewise, the challenge for both types of nonvalue-added activities is to identify opportunities to eliminate them or perhaps transform the activity into something that is valued by the customer.

An example value stream map for a service firm, in this case a contract manufacturer of metal cases for servers, is shown in Figure 9.2. In this example, the contract manufacturer provides the service of fabricating the metal cases for the servers that their customer, Allied Computer, Inc. (shown in the upper right-hand corner of the figure), assembles for *its* customers. The most frequently used value stream symbols are summarized in Table 9.2.

A value stream map displays the flow of materials and information with suppliers, shown on the left of the diagram, and customers on the right. In studying the value stream map shown in Figure 9.2, we see that our contract manufacturer gets a shipment of steel coils from its supplier, National Steel, Inc., every Monday. Also shown in the value stream map are the quantities of inventory held at each stage of the value stream and the details of the operational activities at each

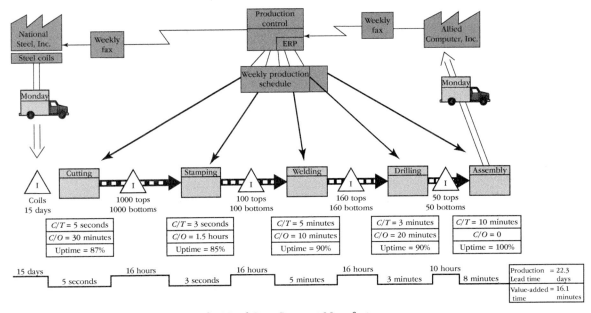

FIGURE 9.2   As-Is Value Stream Map for Metal Case Contract Manufacturer

Source: Adapted from www.mamtc.com.

Table 9.2   Commonly Used Value Stream Symbols

Value Stream Map Symbol	Description	Use
Customer/Supplier	Customer/Supplier	When in upper left represents a supplier. When in upper right represents a customer. Supplier or customer name entered inside symbol.
Frequency	External Shipment	Used to represent shipments from a supplier or to a customer. The frequency of the shipment is often entered inside the symbol.
(block arrow)	Shipments	Block arrows used to show the movement of raw materials and finished goods.
(triangle)	Inventory	Used to show inventory between stages in the process. The amount of inventory and a description of what is being stored is often entered below the symbol.
Process	Process	This symbol represents a process, operation, machine, or department that material flows through.
C/T = C/O = Avail =	Data Box	Data Boxes are used with other symbols to provide additional information. They most frequently are used with Process symbols. Information frequently captured about a process includes its cycle time (C/T), changeover time (C/O), uptime, available capacity, batch size, and scrap rate.

Table 9.2   Commonly Used Value Stream Symbols (*continued*)

Value Stream Map Symbol	Description	Use
NVA NVA VA VA VA	Timeline	A timeline is often placed at the bottom of the value stream map to show value added (VA) and nonvalue-added (NVA) time.
Production Control	Production Control	The Production Control symbol is used to capture how production is scheduled and controlled.
→	Manual Information	A straight thin arrow is used to show the flow of information that is conveyed manually such as memos, reports, and meetings. The frequency with which the information is conveyed can also be added.
(wiggle arrow)	Electronic Information	A wiggle arrow represents information that is conveyed electronically such as via the Web or e-mail. The frequency with which the information is conveyed can also be added.
(kaizen burst)	Kaizen Blitz	This symbol is used to document specific process improvement projects that are expected to be executed.
(workcell symbol)	Workcell	This symbol represents the production of part families in cells (see Chapter 3).
(push arrow)	Push Arrow	This symbol is used when the output of one process stage is pushed to the next stage in the process.
P W	Production and Withdrawal Kanbans	Production kanbans are used to trigger production. Withdrawal kanbans are used to authorize the material movement to downstream processes.
(supermarket symbol)	Supermarket	A supermarket is a small amount of inventory that is stored at the point of usage.

stage in the process. Inventory is represented by triangles and processing activities by rectangles in the value stream map. In the case of our contract manufacturer, a 15-day supply of coils is maintained in front of the cutting operation. Also, additional details about the processing steps are included in Data Boxes near each operational activity. Information often captured in Data Boxes includes the cycle time[1] of the activity, how long it takes to change over the equipment, the capacity of the processing stage, and other relevant details about the activity or operation.

---

[1] Note that usage of the term *cycle time* has a slightly different meaning compared to its usage in the context of assembly line balancing. Here, our usage of cycle time refers to the amount of time it takes the particular stage to complete its operation, which may vary across the different processing stages. In assembly line balancing, cycle time refers to the amount of time each station has to complete its activities where the cycle time is constant across all processing stations.

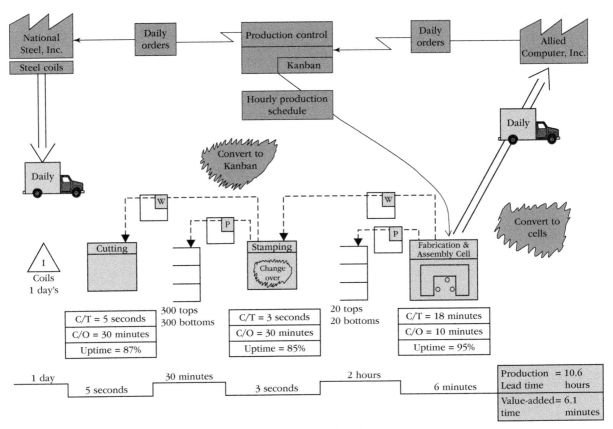

FIGURE 9.3 To-Be Value Stream Map for Metal Case Contract Manufacturer

Source: Adapted from www.mamtc.com.

We also see that a weekly production schedule is generated by an enterprise resource planning (ERP) system (discussed in Chapter 5) and that each stage in the process works at its own pace and pushes its product on to the next operation. We contrast push and pull systems later in this chapter. Along the bottom of the value stream map is a timeline that tracks value-added and nonvalue-added time. In our example, we see that out of the total lead time of just over 22.3 days, only 16.1 minutes are considered to be adding value. Finally, at the far right, we observe that the contract manufacturer makes weekly shipments on Monday to its customer, Allied Computer, Inc. Also note that information from the contract manufacturer's ERP system is used to generate orders for raw materials, which are faxed to its supplier, National Steel, weekly. Likewise, the contract manufacturer receives a weekly fax from its customer, Allied Computer, which is input into its ERP system.

The value stream map shown in Figure 9.2 is called an *As-Is* value stream map since it describes the current value stream. After the As-Is map is created, it is carefully studied to identify opportunities for improving the process, and a *To-Be* value stream map is crafted. Following this, a transition plan from the As-Is process to the To-Be process is developed.

Figure 9.3 provides the To-Be value stream map for the contract manufacturer. The To-Be map calls for the following process improvements:

- Reducing the quantity of steel coils held in inventory from 15 day's worth to 1 day's worth, made possible in part by getting daily shipments from National Steel as opposed to weekly shipments

- Reductions in work-in-process inventory levels made possible by eliminating the old push system and adopting a kanban pull system (discussed later in the chapter)

- Kaizen events (discussed later in the chapter) to reduce the changeover time of the stamping machine, convert to the kanban system, and convert from the functional layout to a cellular layout (as discussed in Chapter 3)

- Communicating electronically and daily with its suppliers and customers

- Reducing the production lead time from 22.3 days to 10.6 hours

9.4 Make Value Flow

Erratic flows in one part of the value stream often become magnified in other parts of the system, not only farther down the stream but, because of scheduling, farther *up* the line as well. This is due to the formation of queues in the production system, the batching of parts for processing on machines, the lot-sizing rules we use to initiate production, and many other similar policies. These disruptions to the smooth flow of goods are costly to the production system and waste time, materials, and human energy. Thus, having identified the value stream, the next step is to transform it from the traditional batch and wait approach to one where the flow is continuous. This is accomplished by eliminating nonvalue-added activities and streamlining the remaining value-added steps. In fact, many Lean organizations make the analogy that goods should "flow like water." A key aspect to achieving such a smooth flow is to master-schedule small lots of final products.

Another obstacle to smooth flows is the traditional functional organization structure. In the functional organization, work is organized based on the similarity of the work performed. Thus, you have accounting departments, marketing departments, radiology units, quality assurance departments, and so on. The problem with organizing work on the basis of the type of work performed is that work must then be handed off from department to department. Such hand-offs inevitably create delays in the process and introduce opportunities for making errors. Therefore, Lean organizations have a bias toward organizing work based on the value-creating process the work supports, as opposed to organizing work functionally.

It should also be pointed out that early production or delivery is just as inappropriate as late delivery. The goal is *perfect* adherence to schedule – without this, erratic flows are introduced throughout the value stream. With continuous, smooth flows of parts come continuous, level flows of work, so there are no peak demands on workers, machines, or other resources. Then, once adequate capacity has been attained, it will always be sufficient.

9.4.1 Continuous Flow Manufacturing

An important tenet to making value flow in Lean enterprises is continuous flow manufacturing (CFM). According to this tenet, work should flow through the process without interruption, one unit at a time, based on the customer's demand rate. Thus, once the processing of a unit has begun, the work should continue uninterrupted until the unit is completed. This is reflected by the phrase, "Don't let the parts touch the floor." To accomplish this, delays associated with setting up equipment, moving work between departments, storing work because a needed resource is unavailable, equipment breakdowns, and so on must be eliminated.

To synchronize the flow of work with the customer's demand rate, the *takt time* is calculated (the same as the cycle time, as noted in Chapter 3). The term *takt time*, German for the baton used by orchestra conductors, was coined by Toyota and translates the customer demand rate into time. In effect, the takt time defines the rhythm or pace at which work must be completed at in order to meet the customer demand rate. More specifically, takt time is calculated as

$$\text{Takt time} = \frac{\text{available work time}}{\text{customer required volume}}$$

To illustrate the concept of takt time, consider an insurance company that operates 9 hours per day processing claims. Assume that the employees get two 15-minute breaks and 1 hour for lunch. Further, assume that the company receives 6000 claims per month and that there are 20 working days per month. In this case, the takt time would be calculated as

$$\text{Takt time} = \frac{540 \text{ min} - 30 \text{ min} - 60 \text{ min}}{\dfrac{6000}{20}} = \frac{450}{300} = 1.5 \text{ minutes/claim}$$

In this case, the insurance company must process a claim every 1.5 minutes. But suppose the processing of an application requires 15 minutes of work. Then, in this case, 10 employees working in parallel would be needed. In other words, processing 10 applications every 15 minutes is equivalent to processing one application every 1.5 minutes.

9.4.2 The Theory of Constraints

The *theory of constraints* (TOC) (Goldratt 1990) offers a systematic way to view and analyze process flows. Key aspects of the TOC include identifying the bottlenecks (defined in Chapter 4) in the process and balancing the workflows in the system. Other names for the same concept are drum–buffer–rope (DBR), goal system, constraint management, and synchronous manufacturing. TOC is often compared to kanban (discussed later in this chapter) and MRP as another way to plan production and schedule operations. Studies comparing these systems seem to show that each has different strengths – MRP to generate time-phased requirements, TOC to plan medium-time-horizon bottleneck facilities, and JIT to maximize throughput – and manufacturers should employ a combination of the three.

The TOC was originally implemented through a proprietary package primarily used in the make-to-order and automotive industries, which is based on an alternative approach to capacity planning. The basic procedure is first to identify bottleneck workstations in the shop, schedule them to keep them fully utilized, and then schedule the nonbottleneck workstations to keep the bottlenecks busy so that they are never waiting for work. The following ten guidelines capture the essence of the theory:

1. *Flows rather than capacities should be balanced throughout the shop.* The objective is to move material quickly and smoothly through the production system, not to balance capacities or utilization of equipment or human resources.

2. *Fluctuations in a tightly connected, sequence-dependent system add to each other rather than averaging out.*

3. *Utilization of a nonbottleneck is determined by other constraints in the system, such as bottlenecks.* Nonbottleneck resources do not restrict the amount of output that a production system can create. Thus, these resources should be managed to support the operations of those resources (i.e. the bottlenecks) that do constrain the amount of output. Clearly, operating a nonbottleneck resource at a higher rate of output than the bottleneck resource does nothing to increase the output produced by the entire production system.

4. *Utilizing a workstation (producing when material is not yet needed) is not the same as activation.* Traditionally, managers have not made a distinction between "using" a resource and "activating" it. However, according to the TOC, a resource is considered *utilized* only if it is helping the entire system create more output. If a machine is independently producing more output than the rest of the system, the time the machine is operated to produce outputs over and above what the overall system is producing is considered activation, not utilization.

5. *An hour lost at a bottleneck is an hour lost for the whole shop.* Since the bottleneck resource limits the amount of output the entire system can create, time when this resource is not producing output is a loss to the entire system that cannot be made up. Lost time at a bottleneck resource can result because of downtime for maintenance or because the resource was starved for work. For example, if a hair stylist is idle for an hour because no customers arrive, this hour of lost haircuts cannot be made up, even if twice as many customers as usual arrive in the next hour.

6. *An hour saved at a nonbottleneck is a mirage.* Since nonbottlenecks have plenty of capacity and do not limit the output of the production system, saving time at these resources does not increase total output. The implication for managers is that time-saving process improvements to the system should be directed at bottleneck resources.

7. *Bottlenecks govern shop throughput and work-in-process inventories.*

8. *The transfer batch need not be the same size as the process batch.* The size of the *process batch* is the size of the batch produced each time a job is run. Often, this size is determined by trading off various costs, as is done with the economic order quantity (EOQ) model discussed in Appendix A to Chapter 6. On the other hand, the size of the *transfer batch* is the size of the batch of parts moved from one work center to another work center. Clearly, parts can be moved in smaller batches than the process batch. Indeed, considerable reductions in batch flow times can often be obtained by using a transfer batch that is smaller than the process batch. For example, assume that a manufacturer produces a part in batches of ten. This part requires three operations, each performed on a different machine. The operation time is 5 minutes per part per operation. Figure 9.4 demonstrates the effect on flow time when a process batch of ten units is reduced to a transfer batch of one unit. Specifically, in Figure 9.4a, the transfer batch is the same size as the process batch, and a flow time of 150 minutes results. In Figure 9.4b, the one-unit transfer batch reduces flow time to 60 minutes. The reason for long flow time with a large transfer batch is that in any batch, the first part must always wait for all the other parts to complete their processing before it is started on the next machine. In Figure 9.4a, the first part in the batch has to wait 45 minutes for the other nine parts. When the transfer batch is reduced to one unit, the parts in the batch do not have to wait for the other parts in the process batch.

9. *The size of the process batch should be variable, not fixed.* Because the economics of different resources can vary, the process batch does not need to be the same size at all stages of production. For example, consider an item that is produced on an injection molding machine and then visits a trimming department. Because the time and cost to set up injection molding equipment are likely to be very different from the time and cost to set up the trimming equipment, there is no reason why the batch size should be the same at each of these stages. Thus, batch size at each stage should be determined by the specific economics of that stage.

Time	5	10	15	20	25	30	35	40	45	50	55	60	65	70	75	80	85	90	95	100	105	110	115	120	125	130	135	140	145	150
Opn 1	P1	P2	P3	P4	P5	P6	P7	P8	P9	P10																				
Opn 2											P1	P2	P3	P4	P5	P6	P7	P8	P9	P10										
Opn 3																					P1	P2	P3	P4	P5	P6	P7	P8	P9	P10

(a)

Time	5	10	15	20	25	30	35	40	45	50	55	60
Opn 1	P1	P2	P3	P4	P5	P6	P7	P8	P9	P10		
Opn 2		P1	P2	P3	P4	P5	P6	P7	P8	P9	P10	
Opn 3			P1	P2	P3	P4	P5	P6	P7	P8	P9	P10

(b)

FIGURE 9.4 Transfer Batch Size and its Effects on Flow Time. (*a*) Transfer Batch Size Equals Process Batch Size. (*b*) Transfer Batch Size Equals One Part

10. *A shop schedule should be set by examining all the shop constraints simultaneously.* Traditionally, schedules are determined sequentially. First, the batch size is determined. Next, lead times are calculated and priorities set. Finally, schedules are adjusted on the basis of capacity constraints. The TOC advocates considering all constraints simultaneously in developing schedules (this is why it is also referred to as constraint management). The theory also argues that lead times are the result of the schedules and therefore cannot be determined beforehand.

The critical aspect of these guidelines is the focus on bottleneck workstations, not overloading the workstations, and splitting batches in order to move items along to the next workstation when desirable.

Based on these guidelines, the theory of constraints suggests three key performance measures to focus on when it comes to managing and improving processes. The first performance measure is *throughput*, which is defined as the rate at which the production system generates money through sales. To generate money from sales, the organization must complete units of production and get them "out the door" to the customer.

The second performance measure is *inventory*, which corresponds to all the money the system has invested in purchasing and transforming materials and items it ultimately intends to sell. The third performance measure is *operating expenses*, which corresponds to all the money the system spends to turn inventory into throughput. Based on these performance measures, the goal for management is straightforward. In particular, it should take actions and prioritize process improvement projects that result in increasing throughput while simultaneously reducing inventory and reducing operating expenses.

9.5 Pull Value Through the Value Stream

In the traditional firm, long lead times are often thought to allow more time to make decisions and get work performed. But in the Lean enterprise, short lead times mean easier, more accurate forecasting and planning. Moreover, a way to capitalize on the increasing strategic importance of fast response to the customer is to minimize all the lead times. If lead times are reduced, there is less time for things to go awry, to get lost, or to be changed. For example, it is quite common for an order placed two months ago to be changed every three weeks until it is delivered: change an option, change the quantity ordered, and so on. However, if the delivery time is one week or less, customers can place the order when they know exactly what they need and can therefore delay ordering until the week before they need it.

As opposed to the MRP approach of "pushing" materials through a plant, Lean enterprises rely on *pull systems* whereby actual customer demand drives the production process. Push systems are planning-based systems that determine when workstations will probably need parts if everything goes according to plan. However, operations rarely go according to plan; as a result, materials may be either too late or too early. To safeguard against being too late and to make sure that people always have enough work to keep busy, safety stocks are used, even with MRP; these may not even be needed, but they further increase the stocks of materials in the plant. Thus, in a push system, we see workers always busy making items and lots of material in the plant.

In comparison, a pull system is a control-based system that signals the requirement for parts as they are needed in reality. The result is that workers may occasionally (and sometimes frequently) be idle because more materials are not needed. This keeps material from being produced when it is not needed (waste). The appearance of a plant using a pull system is quiet and slow, with minimal material around.

To further contrast the differences between push and pull systems, consider the production system shown in Figure 9.5. The system consists of one machine of type A and one machine of type B. Machine A has the capacity to produce 75 units per day, and machine B has the capacity to produce 50 units per day. All products are first produced on machine A and then processed on machine B. Daily demand for the organization is 50 units.

In a push system, each work center would work as fast as it could and *push* the product on to work centers downstream, regardless of whether they needed additional materials. In Figure 9.5, after the first day of operation, machine A would produce 75 units, machine B would process 50 of the 75 units it received from machine A, and 25 units would be added to work-in-process inventory. Each day the system operates in this fashion, 25 more units will be added to the work-in-process inventory in front of machine B. This might seem irrational to you, but the only way for inventory not to be built up is for machine A to produce less than it is capable of producing. In this example, we could idle machine A 33% of the day and produce and transport only 50 units to machine B. However, if you were the plant manager and you noticed that the worker assigned to machine A was working only 67% of the time, what would you think? You might think that the worker was goofing off and order him or her to run the machine. Of course, doing this only increases the amount of money tied up in inventory and does nothing to increase the amount of product completed and shipped to the customer.

In a pull system, the worker at machine A would produce only in response to requests for more materials made by the worker at machine B. Furthermore, the worker at machine B is authorized

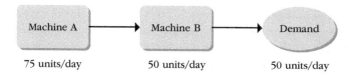

FIGURE 9.5 Sequential Production System with Two Machines

to make additional product only to replenish product that is used to meet actual customer demand. If there is no customer demand, machine B will sit idle. And if machine B sits idle, machine A will be idle. In this way, the production of the entire operation is matched to actual demand.

The signals used in a pull system to authorize production may be of various kinds. Dover Corporation's OPW Division made gasoline nozzles for gas pumps and used wire bins as signals. Each bin held 500 nozzles, and two were used at any time. Raw material was taken out of one bin until it was empty, and then material was drawn from the second bin. A bin collector constantly scouted the plant, looking for empty bins, and returned them to the stockroom, where they were refilled and returned to the workstations. In this manner, no more than two bins' worth of material (1000 units) was ever in process.

Hewlett-Packard used yellow tape to make squares about 1 foot on a side as the signals for its assembly lines. One square lied between every two workers. When workers finished an item, they drew the next unit to work on from the square between them and the previous worker. When the square was empty, this was the signal that another item was needed from the previous worker. Thus, there are never more than two items in process per worker.

These two examples are actually modifications of Toyota's original JIT system. Toyota's materials management system is known as *kanban*, which means "card" in Japanese. The idea behind this system is to authorize materials for production only if there is a need for them. Through the use of kanban authorization cards, production is "pulled" through the system, instead of pushed out before it is needed, and then stored. Thus, the Master Production Schedule (MPS) authorizes final assembly, which in turn authorizes subassembly production, which in its turn authorizes parts assembly, and so on. If production stops at some point in the system, immediately all downstream production also stops, and soon thereafter all upstream production as well.

9.5.1 Kanban/JIT in Services

Of course, many services, especially pure services, have no choice but to provide their service exactly when it is demanded. For example, a hair stylist cannot build up inventories of cuts and styles before the actual customers arrive. Now, JIT is being adopted in other services that use materials rather extensively. For example, professors can choose materials from a wide variety of sources and let a "JIT" publisher compile the material into a custom-made book as quickly and cheaply as a standard book. Supermarkets replenish their shelves on a JIT basis as customers withdraw purchases. And everyone is familiar with fast-turnaround operations such as dry cleaners, automobile oil changes, ride sharing services, and eyeglass lenses, not to mention fast food.

Many, if not most, of the techniques used in manufacturing to become Lean are equally applicable to services such as close supplier ties (food spoils), maintaining a flexible workforce (customization), and using reservation systems and off-peak pricing to keep level loads on the system. In addition, the general advantages that manufacturers accrue through defect-free operations, flexible layouts, minimal inventories, preventive maintenance, advanced technologies, standardized work methods, and other such approaches provide equal advantages to service organizations – and in some cases greater advantages.

9.6 Pursue Perfection

At the risk of stating the obvious, competition is a moving target. By the same token, opportunities to improve processes never end. Therefore, it is common for Lean enterprises to focus less on meeting the immediate challenges posed by the competition and to focus more on the long-term goal of achieving perfection. In the remainder of this section, we overview five commonly used tools that Lean organizations turn to in their pursuit of perfection: 5S, the visual factory, kaizen, poka yoke, and total productive maintenance.

9.6.1 5S

A widely used approach for increasing the efficiency of individual work activities is 5S. The approach consists of the following five steps:

1. *Sort.* Distinguish what work must be performed to complete a task from what does not need to be done. Eliminate the unnecessary steps.

2. *Straighten (Set in order).* A common phrase in industrial engineering is "a place for everything and everything in its place."

3. *Scrub (Shine).* Maintain a workplace that is clean and free of clutter.

4. *Systemize.* Develop and implement standardized procedures for maintaining an orderly work environment.

5. *Standardize (Sustain).* Make the previous four steps a habit.

9.6.2 The Visual Factory

With little or no slack to absorb disruptions, successful execution in a Lean environment requires that workers and decision makers be constantly up to date with the conditions in the work environment. One way Lean organizations accomplish this is through an approach called the visual factory. The objectives of the visual factory are to help make problems visible, help employees stay up to date on current operating conditions, and communicate process improvement goals. With the visual factory, problems can be made visible through the use of charts displayed throughout the workplace that plot trends related to quality, on-time delivery performance, safety, machine downtime, productivity, and so on. Likewise, visual factories make use of production and schedule boards to help employees stay up to date on current conditions. It should be noted that the concept of a visual factory is equally applicable to services. For example, a call center one of the authors visited had a board that displayed updated information on the percent of calls that were answered within the desired time frame.

9.6.3 Kaizen

The Japanese word kaizen literally translates as "continuous improvement." The Lean journey in the pursuit of perfection requires a continuous series of incremental improvements. In some cases, a continuous improvement initiative may take a year or longer to implement. However, recently a short-term approach to continuous improvement, called the *kaizen blitz* (aka kaizen workshops, kaizen events), is becoming increasingly popular. In a kaizen blitz, a cross-functional team completes a continuous improvement project in under a week. Often, the kaizen blitz begins with a day or two of formal training in Lean concepts. The training is then followed by the team completing a continuous improvement project. The project requires the team to collect any needed data, analyze the data, and then immediately implement the proposed improvements. Typical goals for a kaizen blitz include one or more of the following: reducing the amount of floor space needed, increasing process flexibility, improving workflows, improving quality, enhancing the safety of the working environment, and reducing or eliminating nonvalue-added activities.

9.6.4 Poka Yoke

The goal of poka yoke is to mistake-proof work activities in a way that prevents errors from being committed in the first place. Examples of poka yoke include supplementing electronic forms with computer code or scripts that check the validity of information entered into fields as it is being entered, designing a machine that requires the operator to press two buttons simultaneously to cycle the machine so that neither hand can be caught in the machine when it is operating, and placing parts in kits based on their assembly sequence.

9.6.5 Total Productive Maintenance

A key driver of waste and therefore an important component of Lean is the effective use of equipment. In particular, equipment impacts waste in a number of ways, including the following:

- *Breakdowns.* When a piece of equipment fails, it is no longer creating valued outputs, which can lead to customer dissatisfaction as well as economic repercussions for the firm. Furthermore, workers may be made idle during the breakdown, further adding to the firm's cost without corresponding increases in sales.

- *Setups.* As with breakdowns, a piece of equipment undergoing a setup or changeover is not creating valued outputs. Moreover, during the setup, workers are being paid to make the changeover; if a specialized group performs the setup, the machine operators may be idled during the setup period.

- *Stoppages.* At times, production on a piece of equipment may need to be halted because its output is unacceptable.

- *Reduced speed.* Another potential loss occurs when a piece of equipment is operated at a lower production rate than the rate at which it was designed to operate at.

- *Yields.* Yield relates to the percent of the total output produced that is acceptable. Lower yields correspond to greater amounts of waste in the form of scrap and rework.

Total productive maintenance (TPM) focuses broadly on the cost of equipment over its entire life cycle and encompasses a variety of tools and techniques to improve equipment maintenance practices as well as to help prevent and predict equipment failures. Key components of a TPM program include the following:

- Identifying ways to maximize equipment effectiveness

- Developing a productive maintenance system for maintaining equipment over its entire life cycle

- Coordinating the work of engineering, operations, and maintenance employees

- Giving employees the responsibility to maintain the equipment they operate

9.7 Benefits and Risks of Lean and Lean Six Sigma

In summary, the evidence to date suggests that Lean is not one of the annual fads of American management but rather a philosophy for efficiently and effectively using the resources an organization already has at its disposal. As such, it will not disappear from the scene, though its tenets are increasingly being merged with other programs such as Six Sigma, supply chain management, and sustainability. And in spite of concerns about the timely physical transportation of goods, a major challenge for the future will be the effective utilization of the many information technologies available to managers. In too many cases, organizations are relying too much on internal forecasts rather than using the Internet and other information and communications technologies to access their customers' real-time production schedules. In the future, Lean organizations will increasingly make use of satellite tracking systems, wireless communication, scanning technology, global positioning systems, two-dimensional bar codes and RFID tags, and paperless documentation across the entire value chain.

As we have seen, Lean offers a variety of possible benefits: reduced inventories and space, faster response to customers due to shorter lead times, less scrap, higher quality, increased communication and teamwork, and greater emphasis on identifying and solving problems. In general, the benefits associated with Lean can be placed into the following five categories: (1) cost savings, (2) revenue increases, (3) investment savings, (4) workforce improvements, and (5) uncovering problems.

1. *Cost savings.* Costs are saved in a number of ways: inventory reductions, reduced scrap, fewer defects, fewer changes due to both customers and engineering, less space, decreased labor hours, less rework, reduced overhead, and other such effects.

2. *Reduced impact on the environment.* Reductions in the space needed, defects, scrap, and rework all translate into needing less energy, natural resources, materials, and transportation, which in turn also results in reductions in emissions and waste that needs to be disposed of.

3. *Revenue increases.* Revenues are increased primarily through better service and quality to the customer. Short lead times and faster response to customers' needs result in better margins and higher sales. In addition, revenues will be coming in faster on newer products and services.

4. *Investment savings.* Investment is saved through three primary effects. First, less space (about a third) is needed for the same capacity. Second, inventory is reduced to the point that turns (discussed in Chapter 5) run about 50 to 100 a year (compared with 3 or 4, historically). Third, the volume of work produced in the same facility is significantly increased frequently by as much as 100%.

5. *Workforce improvements.* The employees of Lean firms are much more satisfied with their work. They prefer the teamwork it demands, and they like the fact that fewer problems arise. They are also better trained for the flexibility and skills needed with Lean (e.g. problem solving, maintenance), and they enjoy the growth they experience in their jobs. All this translates into better, more productive work.

6. *Uncovering problems.* One of the unexpected benefits is the greater visibility of problems that Lean allows if management is willing to capitalize on the opportunity to fix these problems. In trying to speed up a process, all types of difficulties are uncovered and most of them are various forms of waste, so not only is response time improved but cost is also.

However, there are also some risks with Lean, as more experience with Lean has shown. In some cases of Lean where a client used subcontracting, the subcontractor has stolen the technology and come out with a competing, possibly improved, product or service with a much cheaper price, then dropping their Lean client. In one case, for example, the overseas subcontractor was working two shifts to produce items for a client, and then, unknown to the client, running a third shift to produce more items which it sold on the black market. And this need not be the entire item, but instead a major sub-part of the item, like a computer chip or high-tech innovative element, which could then be sold to the client's competitors, or even used by the subcontractor itself to produce a competing product.

Another risk is designing or continuing to "optimize" the supply chain to be cheaper, but in the process making it less reliable, or longer, or having more subcontractors (points of failure). This lesson came to haunt many American producers who off-shored their production and then could not get their products during the COVID-19 pandemic due to shipping tangles, part shortages like chips, delays at ports, or subcontractor failures. The longer and more parts in the supply chain, the more unreliable the chain becomes. It also impacted many domestically outsourced products when one of the many suppliers couldn't deliver parts that the clients needed, like computer chips for automobiles.

Although it is tempting to take advantage of a subcontractor's offer to lower their price if you sole-source from them, you are laying 100 percent responsibility on their ability to provide those items in any circumstances that might arise. The same consideration is needed for a transportation subcontractor who offers to transport 100 percent of your products, or a distributor, or a retailer, and so on.

9.7.1 Lean Six Sigma

Earlier in the chapter, it was mentioned that a current trend is for organizations to merge their Lean and Six Sigma initiatives. Xerox called its merged program Lean Six Sigma, while Honeywell referred to its program as Six Sigma Plus. A company in India is reported to be the first company to introduce Lean Six Sigma in 1997 and currently, most organizations refer to their merged Lean and Six Sigma initiatives as Lean Six Sigma (Atmaca and Girenes 2013). Merging Six Sigma and Lean makes sense because being competitive in today's environment requires processes that are both efficient and consistent. An organization that focuses only on the elimination of waste through Lean and does not also address the consistency of its processes will be missing significant opportunities to enhance the effectiveness of its processes. Likewise, focusing only on reducing the variation inherent in an inconsistent process and not simultaneously addressing ways to make it more efficient also limits the overall effectiveness of the process.

However, beyond simply addressing different aspects of process effectiveness, Six Sigma and Lean have proven to be excellent complements to each other. For example, most of the tools associated with Lean are more applicable to the improve and control phases of the Six Sigma Define, Measure, Analyze, Improve, and Control (DMAIC) approach (discussed in the previous chapter). Thus, merging Lean with Six Sigma provides Lean practitioners with the disciplined and structured DMAIC approach and a richer set of tools, particularly those associated with the Define, Measure, and Analyze phases. Likewise, the Lean tools nicely complement the traditional Six Sigma tools and methodologies.

A project completed at one of Honeywell's European chemical plants provides an excellent illustration of the complementary nature of Lean and Six Sigma. The impetus for the project was the fact that the operation was losing almost $1 million per year. To turn around the operation, it was determined that capacity needed to be doubled, while prices needed to be reduced by 50%.

The project team began by analyzing a detailed process map and categorizing the steps in the process as value-adding or nonvalue-adding activities. Through this analysis, the team also discovered that each stage in the process was a bottleneck. Using the detailed process map, the team determined whether a quality requirement or an issue related to process flow was the cause of the bottleneck. As it turned out, one bottleneck was the result of a quality issue, and the bottlenecks at the other four stages were caused by issues related to process flow.

To resolve the bottleneck caused by quality issues, the team relied on traditional Six Sigma tools, including Measurement Systems Analysis, process mapping, FMEA, cause-and-effect matrices, and design of experiments (see Chapter 8 for a discussion of these tools). To address the bottlenecks that resulted from process flow issues, Lean tools were used to eliminate the nonvalue-adding steps such as unnecessary product movements and material handling. By utilizing both Lean and Six Sigma tools, the team was able to meet the goal of doubling capacity and reducing costs by 50%. And the profit of the operation increased from losing almost $1 million annually to generating a profit of $3.4 million annually. Of course, the similarity between the

$3.4 million in annual profit is just a coincidence with Six Sigma's goal of achieving no more than 3.4 defects per million opportunities. Or is it?

9.7.2 Lean Green

The term green manufacturing is used to describe initiatives that seek to reduce the negative environmental impacts of production activities, especially minimizing energy used, natural resources consumed, materials used, waste, emissions, and pollution. With the rising interest in sustainability and the significant overlap between the goals of Lean Six Sigma and sustainability, organizations are increasingly relying on Six Sigma, Lean, and Lean Six Sigma to achieve their sustainability objectives. Indeed, there is a growing body of research that supports a direct relationship between Lean, Six Sigma, and Lean Six Sigma and improved performance on sustainability objectives (see Chugani *et al.* (2017) and Erdil *et al.* (2018) for reviews of this research). For example, in a review of 16 operations management journals, a total of 70 research papers published between 2000 and 2015 that combined the process improvement methodologies of Lean, Six Sigma, or Lean Six Sigma with sustainability were identified (Chugani *et al.* 2017). The research also indicates increasing research in this area, as there were 12 papers published over the 5-year period from 2001 to 2005 and 41 papers published in these journals over the 5-year time period from 2011 to 2015. Additionally, major governmental organizations including the U.S. Environmental Protection Agency and the European Commission have advocated the use of Lean as an approach for improving sustainability performance.

Given the significant overlap between the objectives of sustainability and Lean, it is logical that many organizations would have combined their sustainability initiatives with Lean, creating yet another incarnation of Lean referred to as Lean Green or Green Lean Six Sigma (GLSS). If you are keeping count, this is the third time Lean has been discussed in combination with another methodology. Chapter 2 discussed the application of Lean principles to create Agile project management and in this chapter, we previously described the combination of Lean and Six Sigma.

EXPAND YOUR UNDERSTANDING

1. In your opinion, does it make more sense for an organization to merge its Lean and Six Sigma programs or keep them separate?

2. Describe how trying to please every customer turns into a "trap" for traditional production. Aren't customization and multiple options the way of the future, particularly for differing national tastes and preferences?

3. The Japanese say that "a defect is a treasure." What way do they mean, and how does this relate to Lean?

4. How smooth is a production flow where every item requires a setup? Wouldn't flows be smoother with long runs where no setups were required for days?

5. Does the TOC apply to services as well as to products?

6. One JIT consultant suggests that managers implement JIT by just removing inventories from the floor. What is likely to happen if they do this? What would the Japanese do?

7. With single sourcing, how does the firm protect itself from price gouging? From strikes or interruptions to supply?

8. How might Lean apply to a service like an airline? A retailer? A university?

9. American managers hate to see high-paid workers sitting idle, even maintenance employees. What is the alternative?

10. The TOC distinguishes between process batches and transfer batches. It also recommends that process batches vary according to the economics of efficiency at each stage of production. Considering the effects of order size and size of the preceding process batch, how should transfer batches be determined?

11. Consider a service you are familiar with. List examples for each of the seven categories of waste for the service.

12. In identifying the value stream, why is it important to go beyond the boundaries of the organization of interest?

13. List examples for each of the seven categories of waste in an office environment or for an office worker. Are the principles of Lean as applicable to an office environment as they are to a manufacturing environment?

14. It was noted at the end of the chapter that it is common to combine Lean principles with other approaches. Can you think of some reasons why this might be the case?

Apply Your Understanding

AIRCO, Inc.

AIRCO, Inc. offers a range of aviation services to airlines. Its primary services are repairing and overhauling planes and their interiors for its client airlines, which range in size from small regional carriers to large international carriers. As an extension to its seat repairing services, AIRCO recently expanded into the design and assembly of airplane seats.

Since it is new to the business, a typical seat order for AIRCO is for one plane, consisting of anywhere between 100 and 350 seats. Its more established competitors often receive seat orders for multiple planes. The process of filling each seat order is complicated by the fact that many variations of seats go into a single plane, based on how the seats are grouped together in the rows; whether the seat is an aisle seat, window seat, or middle seat; whether the seat will be placed in an exit row; and what class the seat will be placed in. There is additional variation across orders because different airlines require the use of different fabrics and cushion materials, require different types of electronics installed in the seats, and even have different dimensions of their seats.

AIRCO's seat design and assembly business completed the upfit of its South Carolina factory a couple of months ago. The facility houses both a group of design engineers and three assembly lines. In addition to designing the seats to the airlines' specifications, the design engineers also develop detailed instructions for the assembly workers, explaining the steps to follow in assembling the seats.

Currently, each of the three assembly lines consists of 12 stations. The takt time of the assembly lines is 30 minutes. Unfortunately, as is often the case for the startup of production operations, the assembly line is experiencing some significant challenges. For example, virtually no seats pass final inspection at the end of the line and are therefore routed to a "penalty box," where they wait to be reworked. Regarding the quality problems, Christine Chadwick, the supervisor of the penalty box, commented:

> While I haven't done a detailed analysis of why so many seats fail final inspection, my experience tells me that by far the number-one reason for the seats ending up here is because they are missing parts. Sometimes we also see seats where the parts were installed incorrectly or where a part was damaged when it was assembled.

Parts are delivered to the assembly line stations in carts. Each cart contains the parts for one seat, taken from the "supermarket." Supermarkets are locations on the shop floor where a small amount of inventory is stored to support production activities. While the assembly worker is assembling a seat, a second cart is being filled with the parts for the next seat. Two parts pickers support each assembly line. These parts pickers travel up and down the assembly line; when they find an empty cart, they take it to the supermarket, where they pick the parts that are needed at the station.

To replenish a cart, the parts pickers refer to the laminated list of parts needed by the workstation. The parts pickers then walk around the supermarket to find the needed parts. The supermarket was designed in a U-shape to facilitate replenishing the cart with the needed parts; however, the laminated list is rarely in the order in which the parts are stored, thus requiring the parts pickers to backtrack through the supermarket. As needed parts are found, they are tossed into the cart except for smaller items like bolts and washers, which are placed in a box attached inside the cart. Immediately after taking parts from the supermarket shelves, the parts pickers scan the bar code label on the shelf with a bar code reader and enter the quantities taken in order to update the inventory level.

Each assembly line has its own dedicated supermarket. Frequently, however, parts pickers find the inventory level depleted for some parts on their list; in these cases, they go to one of the other supermarkets to find the needed parts. Each assembly line is dedicated to the seats for a specific plane order. All the parts needed for the entire seat order are delivered to the supermarket at once. Typically, it takes one to two weeks to assemble all the seats for a plane order. Occasionally, there are some bulky items that do not fit in the supermarkets; in these cases, the parts pickers must travel a couple of hundred yards to retrieve these parts from bulk storage. Bulk storage also holds the parts that arrive before they are moved to the supermarkets.

The assembly workers refer to instructions displayed on monitors at their workstation to assemble the seats. After reading the instructions and looking at the diagrams, the assembly operator roots through the cart of parts to find the next pieces to install. With the parts in hand, the operator next searches for the needed tools and then installs the parts. This process is repeated until the seat is completed, with the operation cycling between reading instructions, finding parts, and finding tools. If the work is completed in less than the 30-minute takt time, the worker can take a short break. More typical, however, are cases where the assembly workers are waiting for their carts of parts so they can begin working on the next seat.

Questions

1. What types of waste are present at AIRCO's new South Carolina facility?

2. What Lean tools do you see as being particularly applicable to AIRCO? Explain the potential benefits these tools could provide to AIRCO.

Galt Lock Ltd.

Galt Lock Ltd., located in Sydney, Australia, produces a line of door locksets and hardware for the residential, light commercial, and retail markets. The company's single plant is just over 200,000 square feet and is organized into the following functional departments: screw machines, presses, machining, maintenance, tool and dies, latches, plating, buffing, subassembly, and final assembly. The company employs approximately 375 people, 290 of whom are hourly workers. The largest category of employees – assemblers – accounts for two-thirds of the workforce.

The company uses a proprietary planning and scheduling system that uses both an AS/400 minicomputer and spreadsheet analysis performed on a PC to determine production and purchasing requirements. At any given time, there are 1500 to 3000 open work orders on the shop floor. The average lot size is 50,000 parts, but for some products the size is as high as 250,000 parts.

The planning system creates work orders for each part number in the bills of materials, which are delivered to the various departments. Department supervisors determine the order in which to process the jobs, since the system does not prioritize the work orders. A variety of scheduling methods are used throughout the plant, including kanbans, work orders, and expeditters; however, the use of these different methods often creates problems. For example, one production manager commented that although a "kanban pull scheduling system is being used between subassembly and final assembly, frequently the right card is not used at the right time, the correct quantity is not always produced, and there are no predetermined schedules and paths for the pickup and delivery of parts." In fact, it was discovered that work orders were often being superseded by expediters and supervisors, large lag times existed between the decision to produce a batch and the start of actual production, and suppliers were not being included in the "information pipeline." One production supervisor commented:

> We routinely abort the plans generated by our formal planning system because we figure out other ways of pushing product. Although we use kanban systems in two areas of the plant, in reality everything here is a push system. Everything is based on inventory levels and/or incoming customer orders. We push not just the customer order but all the raw materials and everything that is associated with the product being assembled.

In an effort to improve its operations, Galt Lock hired a consulting company. The consultant determined that 36% of the floor space was being used to hold inventory, 25% was for work centers, 14% for aisles, 7% for offices, and 18% for nonvalue-adding activities. The production manager commented:

> We have an entire department that is dedicated to inventory storage consisting of 10 to 11 aisles of parts. What is bad is that we have all these parts, and none of them are the right ones. Lots of parts, and we still can't build.

The consultant also determined that the upstream "supplying" work centers were often far from the downstream "using" work centers, material flows were discontinuous because the parts were picked up and set down numerous times, and workers and supervisors often spent a considerable amount of time hunting for parts. The production manager commented:

> Work-in-process is everywhere. You can find work-in-process at every one of the stations on the shop floor. It is extremely difficult to find materials on the shop floor because of the tremendous amount of inventory on the shop floor. It is also very difficult to tell what state a customer order is in or the material necessary to make that customer order, because we have such long runs of components and subassemblies.

The plant manager commented:

> My biggest concern is consistent delivery to customers. We just started monitoring on-time delivery performance, and it was the first time that measurement had ever been used at this operation. We found out how poorly we are actually doing. It is a matter of routinely trying to chase things down in the factory that will complete customer orders. The challenge of more consistent delivery is compounded by the fact that we have to respond much faster. Our customers used to give us three to six weeks of lead time, but now the big retailers we are starting to deal with give us only two or three days. And if we don't get it out in that short period of time, we lose the customer.

Questions

1. Evaluate and critique the existing operation and the management of Galt Lock.

2. How applicable is JIT to a situation like this? Would converting from a functional layout to a cellular layout facilitate the implementation of JIT?

3. Where could the principles of Lean production be of value to Galt Lock?

EXERCISES

9.1 The time between patient arrivals to the blood-drawing unit of a medical lab averages two minutes. The lab is staffed with two nurses who actually draw the patients' blood. The nurses work from 9:00 A.M. to 5:30 P.M. and get two 10-minute breaks and a half hour for lunch. What is the takt time for drawing patient blood?

9.2 Referring to Exercise 1, assume that additional analysis was performed and it was determined that an average of 255 patients (with a standard deviation of 30) requiring blood work come to the lab each day. It was further determined that the duration of the nurses' breaks ranged from 9 to 13.5 minutes, with all times in the range equally likely, and that the time taken for lunch ranged from 28 minutes to 34 minutes, again with all times in the range equally likely. Using Crystal Ball or another simulation package, develop a distribution for the takt time, assuming that the number of patients that arrive on a given day is normally distributed. What are the managerial implications of your analysis?

BIBLIOGRAPHY

Atmaca, E., and S. S. Gireness, "Lean Six Sigma Methodology and Application," *Quality and Quantity*, 47(4) (2013): 193–212.

Chungani, B., V. Kumar, J. A. Garza-Reyes, L. Rocha-Lona, and A. Upadhyay, "Investigating the Green Impact of Lean, Six Sigma, and Lean Six Sigma: A Systematic Literature Review," *International Journal of Lean Six Sigma*, 8(1) (2017): 7–32.

Connolly, C. "Hospital Takes Page from Toyota." *Washington Post* (January 3, 2005): www.msnbc.msn.com/id/8079313/

DeBusk, C., and A. Rangel, Jr. "Creating a Lean Six Sigma Hospital Process," healthcare.isixsigma.com, May 30, 2005.

Erdil, N. O., C. B. Aktas, and M. A. Omid, "Embedding Sustainability in Lean Six Sigma Efforts," *Journal of Cleaner Production*, 198 (2018): 520–529

Fornari, A., and S. Maszle. "Lean Six Sigma Leads Xerox." *Six Sigma Forum Magazine* (August 2004): 11–16.

Goldratt, E. M. *Theory of Constraints*, 2nd rev. ed. Crotonon-Hudson, NY: North River Press, 1990.

Hill, W. J., and W. Kearney. "The Honeywell Experience." *Six Sigma Forum Magazine* (February 2003): 34–37.

Smith, C. "Seeing is Believing." *Six Sigma Forum Magazine* (November 2012): 22–26.

Womack, J. P., and D. T. Jones. *Lean Thinking: Banish Waste and Create Wealth in Your Corporation*, rev. ed. New York: Free Press, 2003.

CASES

BPO, Incorporated: Call Center Six Sigma Project

Scott M. Shafer

Allen J. (AJ) Lauren, executive vice president of BPO, Inc., shifted his gaze from the e-mail message he had just finished reading to the view of the neighboring manufacturing plant outside his spacious fourth-floor corner office. AJ was responsible for the operations of BPO's Employee Benefit Outsourcing (EBO) business. He often pondered the symbolism of the old manufacturing plant's reflection on his office building. If nothing else, the building's neighbor made an interesting contrast – the mature manufacturer versus BPO, an information age consultancy.

AJ's attention shifted back to the e-mail message he had just received from Sam Regan, the CEO of HA, one of BPO's major clients.

After considering different options for responding to the e-mail message, he decided to wait. Instead, he called his executive assistant and instructed her to contact Ethan Ekans, AJ's newly hired senior vice president of operations, and Jerry Small, assistant director of quality and a Six Sigma Black Belt candidate.[1] He asked her to set up a meeting for that afternoon. AJ wanted an immediate update on the ongoing Six Sigma project Jerry was completing to investigate ways to improve the efficiency and effectiveness of the Health and Welfare Service Delivery Process.

From:	Sam Regan
Sent:	May 10, 2005
To:	Allen Lauren
Cc:	Kacy Scott, Jim Regit, Larry Watts
Subject:	Process audit needed

AJ –

Pursuant to my divorce becoming final last month, I called to have my former wife removed from my benefits. I am sorry to report that the service BPO provided was far below my expectations. As a result of this experience, I have asked my human resources chief, Kacy Scott, to oversee a full audit of all HA transactions processed by BPO. We have identified an outside auditor to perform the audit. It is my expectation that BPO will provide the audit team with its full cooperation and that the audit will be performed at BPO's expense.

I consider this to be a very serious matter and emphasize that our business relationship is at risk. Pending the outcome of the audit, it may become necessary to renegotiate our contract.

If any of the above terms are unacceptable to you, please let me know at your earliest convenience.

Sam Regan, CEO
HA, Inc.

AJ was interested in learning if Sam Regan's experience was simply an isolated event or if this was a common occurrence. Perhaps there was a way to use Jerry's project to head off the process audit HA's CEO was demanding.

Returning to his desk with the e-mail message still displayed on his computer screen, AJ felt his stomach sink. When he first read the message, he had not noticed that Sam Regan had copied Jim Regit, BPO's chairman, and Larry Watts, BPO's president. He had already anticipated that the senior management team would review EBO's business operations at its mid-July quarterly performance review meeting. He was now concerned that this would be a top agenda item.

Although EBO's revenues had been growing 30% annually, the division had been losing about $5 to $10 million a year. AJ was glad he had asked Jerry to take on the project. He knew Jerry had been using simulation modeling to examine the Health and Welfare Service Delivery Process and hoped he would have some answers about how they could improve the process and profitability. He certainly would need some answers for the July meeting.

Business Process Outsourcing

Increased competition was forcing organizations across virtually all industries to reduce their costs while at the same time improving their service levels. Many had turned to business process outsourcing, the farming out of business activities to specialized service providers. For example, as early as 2001, Forrester found that two-thirds of the companies it surveyed outsourced at least one of their business processes.[2] Furthermore, Forrester found that of the firms that already outsourced one or more of their business processes, approximately 80% expected to outsource additional processes within the next two years. Business processes commonly outsourced included manufacturing, human resources, finance and accounting, claims processing, information technology, and marketing.

IDC, a leading provider of market intelligence for the information technology and communications industries, projected that by 2006 business process outsourcing sales would reach $1.2 trillion industry-wide[3] and human resource outsourcing (HRO) would experience a 29.8% compound annual growth rate (CAGR) with sales topping $15 billion.[4] Because of specializing in a particular business process, business process outsourcing providers sought to offer their clients faster innovation, improved quality, economies of scale, and extensive process expertise.

BPO, Inc.

BPO, a Fortune 500 professional services organization, offered its clients a range of services from risk management/insurance brokerage to management consulting. It had operations in over 100 countries, over 50,000 employees, and over 500 offices.

As Exhibit 1 shows, BPO had three divisions: (1) risk management/insurance brokerage, (2) human resource consulting, and (3) compensation consulting. The risk management/insurance brokerage division helped organizations understand and assess their risk profiles and then develop appropriate risk management/insurance programs to minimize their vulnerability to potential long-term setbacks. Its human resource consulting division offered organizations services in the areas of HRO, business process design (BPD), and management consulting. BPO established the HRO group to capitalize on the increasingly popular trend of outsourcing human resource activities. The compensation consulting division assisted organizations in the development of effective compensation and reward programs.

The HRO group consisted of EBO and employee processing outsourcing practices. Because of the increasing popularity of business process outsourcing, the EBO group was one of BPO's fastest-growing businesses and offered three primary services:

- **Defined benefit.** Administration of pension and retirement plans where a formula determined the amount of the employee benefit based on the employee's years of service and earnings.

- **Defined contribution.** Administration of retirement plans where employee benefits were a function of employee and/or employer contributions.

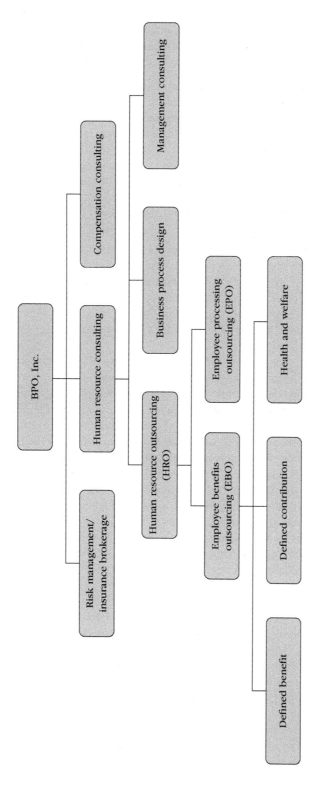

EXHIBIT 1   BPO, Inc. Lines of Business

- **Health and welfare.** Administration of medical, dental, vision, and survivor benefit plans. Administering these plans included enrolling employees in the programs, reporting benefit elections to insurance carriers, reporting deductions to payroll, answering questions about the plans, and processing changes to the plan (e.g. adding a new dependent). Also, the EBO group offered administrative services for flexible spending accounts (FSA) and COBRA.

The defined benefit service and health and welfare service each accounted for approximately $40 million in revenues. Revenues from the defined contribution service were negligible. Clients of the HRO group were interested in the potential cost savings associated with outsourcing their processes. Furthermore, they tended to view business process outsourcing services as a commodity and, based on this view, typically solicited bids from competing business process outsourcing providers, pitting one service provider against the others. This, coupled with high service-level expectations, made it difficult for outsourcing companies to earn a profit.

The Health and Welfare Service Delivery Process

The EBO group's Health and Welfare Service Delivery Process administered medical, dental, vision, and survivor benefit plans for its 18 client firms. In effect, the EBO group performed administrative tasks such as providing assistance to employees enrolling in company-sponsored benefit plans, changing benefit options, updating dependent information, and answering questions about coverage that were formerly performed in-house by its clients' human resource departments. Interestingly, the employees of its client firms were often unaware of the fact that they were actually talking to a third party, not a person employed in their organization's human resource department.

The EBO group interfaced with its client organizations on two levels. At the organizational level, client organizations provided the EBO group with a weekly update of the Employment Database. This database listed all employees, their position, employment status (e.g. full time, part time, terminated, and medical leave), salary, and so on. The EBO group used information in the database to determine employee eligibility and level of coverage.

At the participant level, individual employees contacted the EBO group directly either via the phone or the Web to resolve benefit program-related issues. Frequently, these requests came from newly hired employees who needed to enroll in company-sponsored benefit programs. In other cases, the participants needed to make a change to their benefit selections, such as adding a new dependent or adding/dropping a spouse. Participants also called when they had questions about their coverage. The typical contractual service level between BPO and its clients was that the BPO staff would answer 80% of the calls in 20 seconds or less. In addition, BPO established a handling-time goal of 6 minutes per call, although this was purely an internal metric, not part of the service-level agreement it negotiated with clients.

The Health and Welfare Service Delivery Process consisted of two primary subprocesses. The first subprocess, Database Update, was a weekly batch process that updated the Employee Benefits database based on the weekly Employment Database updates that client firms provided. The other subprocess, Participant Care, focused on responding directly to client employees' inquiries and requests. Although these two subprocesses were physically located on separate floors, they were highly inter-related and neither one alone offered clients a complete business solution. For example, the ability to answer customer inquiries accurately via the Participant Care subprocess depended largely on the weekly Database Update subprocess. Likewise, Benefit Administrators used information obtained from the Participant Care subprocess to update the Employee Benefits database during the weekly Database Update subprocess.

Exhibit 2 shows the process map Jerry developed in conjunction with his Six Sigma project.

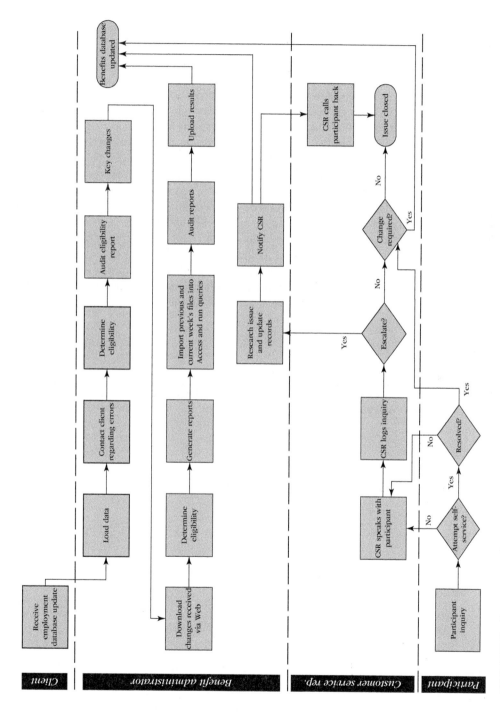

EXHIBIT 2   Process Map for Health and Welfare Service Delivery Process

The Database Update Subprocess

The Database Update subprocess began when a benefits administrator (BA) in the EBO group received the weekly Employment Database update from the client firm. The BAs worked for specific clients. In other words, the same BA processed a given client's data week in and week out. As shown in Exhibit 3, 15 of the 18 clients had one dedicated BA assigned, while the other three clients (CI, HA, and LO) had two dedicated BAs. The BAs worked from 8:00 A.M. to 5:00 P.M.[5] and had two 15-minute breaks and a 1-hour lunch break. All BAs had a four-year college degree and earned $30,000 to $60,000 per year.

Once the BA received the data from the client, he/she loaded it on a mainframe computer. The data Jerry collected suggested that loading the data most frequently took 80 minutes but had been done in as little as 20 minutes and on other occasions had taken as long as 5 hours.

Once the BA loaded the data, the next step was to contact the client regarding any errors discovered in the data. Jerry found that in 95% of the cases, this took between 10 and 60 minutes, with all times in this range equally likely. In the other 5% of cases, the time to contact the client required 150–210 minutes, again with all times in this range equally likely.

Once the BA corrected the errors, the BA determined the eligibility of the participants who had a change in their records since the last weekly update or for new employees. Most often, it took the BAs approximately 90 minutes to determine the eligibility of the participants, but in some cases, it had taken as little as 5 minutes and in other cases as long as 5 hours.

After the BAs determined the participant eligibility, they printed an audit report. The audit report was subject to 100% inspection and most often required approximately 2 hours to complete. On occasion, however, the BAs were able to audit the report in as little as 15 minutes, and on other occasions, it had taken as long as 6 hours.

Exhibit 3   Client Information

Clients	Number of BAs assigned to account	Calls before 6:00 P.M. (percent)	Calls after 6:00 P.M. (percent)	Calls accepted from 8 A.M. until
BM	1	2.9	0	6 P.M.
CS	1	6	0	6 P.M.
CI	2	3.2	0	6 P.M.
CO	1	1.3	0	6 P.M.
ED	1	6.6	0	6 P.M.
EQ	1	4.6	0	6 P.M.
HA	2	22.3	84.5	8 P.M.
IE	1	5.2	0	6 P.M.
LO	2	6.3	12.2	8 P.M.
ME	1	5	0	6 P.M.
MI	1	3	0	6 P.M.
NG	1	2.1	0	6 P.M.
OB	1	14.3	0	6 P.M.
PS	1	1.3	0	6 P.M.
RS	1	2.7	0	6 P.M.
TM	1	1.5	0	6 P.M.
US	1	9.7	0	6 P.M.
VA	1	2	3.3	8 P.M.

Based on the audit and the client's response to the errors detected after loading the data, the BAs next manually keyed in any needed changes to the database. Jerry's data suggested that the BAs could key in the changes in as little as 10 minutes, had occasionally taken as long as 5 hours, and most often required approximately 85 minutes.

These steps corresponded to processing the updates received directly from the client. In addition, participants could have updated their records directly via the Web or a customer service rep (CSR) could have updated them via the Web while speaking to the participant on the phone. Therefore, in the next step, the BA downloaded the changes received via the Web. Typically, this took the BA approximately 50 minutes but ranged between 15 minutes and 2 hours.

Based on this new information, the BAs next determined the participant eligibility exactly as they did for the updated data they received from the client. Most often, the BAs required 90 minutes to determine the eligibility of the participants. However, Jerry's data indicated that on one occasion, a BA was able to determine participant eligibility in as little as 5 minutes; however, on another occasion, a BA required 5 hours to complete this task.

Once the BAs determined participant eligibility, they then generated reports and files for the actual insurance carriers and payroll departments. Jerry's data indicated that it took the BAs approximately 40 minutes to generate the reports and files, but some had accomplished this in as little as 5 minutes and at other times had taken as long as 2 hours. After generating these reports, the BAs imported them and the reports from the previous week into an Access™ database program and then ran a number of queries. Jerry's data indicated that a BA had been able to import the files and execute the queries in as little as 5 minutes but in some cases had taken as long as 1 hour. Most often, it took the BAs 25 minutes to import the files and run the queries. Auditing these reports typically took the BAs an additional 45 minutes, but this had been done in as little as 15 minutes or as long as 3 hours.

In the last step, the BAs uploaded the results from all the previous steps to the Employee Benefits database. Uploading the data typically took the BAs 3 hours, but this had been done in as little as 30 minutes and on other occasions had taken as long as 495 minutes. The result of all these steps was an updated Employee Benefits database.

The Participant Care Subprocess

The Participant Care subprocess consisted primarily of a call center staffed with 31 CSRs organized into five teams (see Exhibit 4). Approximately half of the CSRs had four-year college degrees, and they earned $25,000 to $35,000 per year. Unlike the BAs, many of the CSRs supported more than one client. As shown in Exhibit 4, the schedules of the CSRs were staggered throughout the day based on the anticipated call volume and the need to schedule lunch and 15-minute breaks. For 15 of the 18 client organizations, the call center accepted calls between 8 A.M. and 6 P.M. The call center was staffed until 8 P.M. for the other three client organizations, which operated primarily on the West Coast. Exhibit 3 provides additional information on the volume of calls by client.

The Participant Care subprocess began when a participant had an inquiry or needed assistance with a company-sponsored benefit program. In such cases, the participant had two choices in attempting self-service: via the Web or through a voice response system via a telephone. The first point of contact for customers who did not attempt self-service or who were unable to resolve their issues on their own was the CSRs. As shown in Exhibit 5, there was considerable fluctuation in the volume of calls throughout the day.

Most frequently, the CSRs were on the phone with participants for 6.2 minutes. The CSRs handled simple requests such as providing a fax number in as short as 0.7 minute. In other more complicated cases, such as helping a participant select from a number of different insurance package options, the CSRs spent as much as 19.1 minutes. Following the completion of each call, the CSR logged the call in the computer system. Jerry's data indicated that CSRs spent from 0.75 to 1.5 minutes logging the calls, with all times in this range equally likely.

Exhibit 4   Customer Service Rep (CSR) Information

	CSR	Clients supported	Shift begins	Morning break	Lunch break	Afternoon break	Shift ends
Team 1	MC	CS, HA, OB, VA	8:00	10:45	1:00	3:15	5:00
	VH	CO, ME, TM, US	8:00	9:00	2:00	4:15	5:00
	YS	CS, OB, VA	8:30	11:00	2:00	3:30	5:30
	LL	CS, CO, ME, TM	8:30	10:30	12:00	4:30	5:30
	JA	OB, US	8:30	10:15	12:00	3:00	5:30
	KH	CS, US	9:00	11:00	2:00	4:45	6:00
	WB	LO, OB, VA	9:00	10:30	12:00	2:30	6:00
	NM	CS, CO, ME, TM	9:00	11:00	1:00	5:15	6:00
	RL	CS, LO, OB, VA	8:00	10:00	12:30	3:00	5:00
Team 2	MS	EQ	9:00	11:15	12:30	4:15	6:00
	LL	EQ, ME	8:00	10:00	2:00	3:45	5:00
	RS	EQ	8:00	9:30	11:30	3:00	5:00
	TP	ME	8:30	10:45	1:30	3:15	5:30
Team 3	TP	ED, NG, PS	8:00	10:00	12:00	3:30	5:00
	MB	BM, CI, LO, MI	8:00	9:30	11:30	3:00	5:00
	SW	ED, RS	8:00	9:30	11:30	2:30	5:00
	CS	BM, CI, RS, IE, LO	9:00	10:45	12:30	4:00	6:00
	TF	BM, ED, MI, NG, PS	9:00	11:15	1:30	4:15	6:00
	ID	LO, MI, NG, PS	9:00	10:30	1:00	4:00	6:00
	DW	ED, RS	9:00	10:15	12:30	3:00	6:00
	CC	ED, RS	9:00	10:30	2:00	4:00	6:00
	KP	CI, ED, RS, IE, LO	9:00	10:15	1:30	3:15	6:00
Team 4	AS	HA	11:00	1:15	3:00	4:45	8:00
	SL	HA	8:00	9:45	11:30	2:45	5:00
	BK	HA	11:00	12:45	2:00	3:45	8:00
	OW	HA	9:00	10:15	12:30	3:15	6:00
	GJ	HA	8:00	10:00	12:00	3:00	5:00
	CR	HA	9:00	9:00	1:30	3:30	6:00
	LK	HA, LO, VA	11:00	11:00	2:30	4:15	8:00
Team 5	KM	EQ	8:00	8:00	11:30	3:00	5:00
	VR	EQ, ME	8:30	8:30	12:30	3:30	5:30

In approximately 20% of the cases, the participant had an issue that the CSR could not handle. In these cases, the CSR acquired all the necessary information from the participant and explained to the participant that the company would contact him/her within two days. The CSR forwarded the collected information to the BA who served that client company. The BA then researched the issue, updated the client's records if necessary, and notified the CSR of the escalated issue's outcome. In approximately 60% of the cases, the BAs were able to research and update a case that had been escalated by a CSR in 5–10 minutes, with all times in this range equally likely. In the

Exhibit 5   Arrival of Calls to Customer Service Reps

Hour	Average number of calls per hour in April 2005
8:00 to 9:00	30.4
9:00 to 10:00	49.8
10:00 to 11:00	59.0
11:00 to 12:00	60.0
12:00 to 1:00	49.4
1:00 to 2:00	57.1
2:00 to 3:00	57.5
3:00 to 4:00	53.9
4:00 to 5:00	51.6
5:00 to 6:00	37.5
6:00 to 7:00	11.0
7:00 to 8:00	10.2

remaining 40% of the cases, it took the BA 45–60 minutes to research and update the case, again with all times in the range equally likely.

Once the BA notified the CSR of the outcome of the escalated issue, the CSR called the participant back to explain the outcome. In approximately 75% of the cases, the CSRs left voice messages, requiring approximately 30 seconds per message. In the other cases, the CSRs spent between 5 and 10 minutes explaining the outcome to the participant, with all times in this range equally likely.

There were four other important points about these subprocesses. First, there was no difference in the time the CSRs spent on the phone for calls that they handled versus calls that they sent to the BAs. In some cases, the CSRs were able to determine very early in the call that they needed to hand off to a BA, while in other cases, this did not become apparent until much later in the call. Second, the CSRs gave priority to new incoming calls over callbacks. Third, the BAs gave priority to the Database Update subprocess over researching calls escalated by the CSRs. Fourth, the tasks associated with the Database Update subprocess were in general more complex than researching escalated calls.

Meeting with Ethan and Jerry

When Ethan and Jerry arrived at AJ's office, AJ was in the middle of a phone conversation apparently related to a problem with a software upgrade. Ethan and Jerry seated themselves at the small round table at the far end of AJ's office. After completing his phone conversation, AJ removed his phone headset and walked across the office to close his glass office door. Joining Ethan and Jerry at the table, he started the meeting by noting:

> Today, I received a disturbing e-mail message from the CEO of HA. Apparently, he tried to update his benefits and the service we provided did not meet his expectations. He has requested a full audit of all transactions with HA and has made it clear to me that his business is at risk. I need to know if this was an isolated incident or if it is typical of the service we provide.
>
> As you know, Jim and Larry are expecting an update on our plans for addressing our operational problems in the performance review meeting scheduled for mid-July. This was exactly why I assigned Jerry to the Six Sigma project. What I need now is a full update on the status of the project, which will hopefully give me some ideas on how to reply to HA's CEO.

Jerry responded:

I began my Black Belt training the first week in March. The first week of training addressed the define phase and the measure phase of the project. During the week that followed this training, I worked with you and Ethan to develop a project charter and have a copy here for you if you need it (see Exhibit 6).

Having completed the project charter, I moved into the measure phase and turned my attention to developing a process map of the Health and Welfare Service Delivery Process. At first, I thought this was going to be a breeze as I was able to obtain a flowchart the IT group had developed for the process. However, as I began talking with BAs about the process, I realized the flowchart was missing important components of the process. I therefore spent a good week interviewing people who were familiar with various parts of the process to develop an accurate and detailed process map. Here is a copy of the most current version of the process map (see Exhibit 2).

A key challenge I faced in developing the process map was integrating the Database Update subprocess, which is done in batch mode, with the Participant Care subprocess, which is done in real time.

Continuing in the measure phase, I next used the process map to identify the data requirements for the simulation model you asked me to develop. In reviewing the process map, I determined I would need data on the arrival rate of calls by client, the processing times for all steps in the process, the

Exhibit 6   Project Charter for Jerry's Six Sigma Project

SIX SIGMA PROJECT CHARTER
Background

Project Name:	Health and Welfare Service Delivery Process
Project Sponsor:	AJ Lauren, Executive VP
Process Owner:	Ethan Ekans, Senior VP
Black Belt:	Jerry Small, Assistant Director

Project Objectives

Project Start Date:	March 7, 2005
Target Completion Date:	July 8, 2005
Project Mission Statement:	Develop a simulation model of the Health and Welfare Service Delivery Process to help better understand key operational problems, assess the impact of varying resource levels on key performance metrics, assist in the identification and test of solutions to improve profitability and customer service levels.

Problem Statement

Operational problems are negatively impacting the profitability and service levels of the Health and Welfare Service Delivery Process.

Project Scope

Health and Welfare Service Delivery Process, excluding FSA and COBRA.

Project Milestones

Milestones	Target Completion Date
Complete Define Phase	March 11, 2005
Complete Measure Phase	April 1, 2005
Complete Analyze Phase	April 29, 2005
Complete Improve Phase	June 3, 2005
Complete Control Phase	July 1, 2005

assignment of BAs and CSRs to clients, the percentage of calls that were escalated from the CSRs to the BAs, and the work schedules for the BAs and CSRs. I was able to obtain the arrival rate of calls by client, the assignment of CSRs and BAs to clients, the percent of allocated calls, and the work schedules without much difficulty.

On the other hand, obtaining the processing time data for both the BAs and CSRs was more of a challenge. For the BAs, I created a form listing all their tasks and asked them to record their processing times over a two-week period. In terms of the CSRs, while it is true that our system automatically tracks the duration of calls, I learned that the system does not include in the call duration times the time a CSR puts a customer on hold while he/she researches an issue. I observed a number of CSRs putting clients on hold despite the fact that they are trained not to do this. Therefore, in order to estimate the processing times, I obtained tapes for an entire week of calls for six CSRs and manually timed the duration of each call. I obtained tapes from two CSRs who have been here less than one year, two CSRs who have been here between two and three years, and two CSRs who have been with us more than three years. I fit individual distributions to the process time data that I collected for each task and used these distributions to model the work activities in the simulation model. Finally, I concluded the measure phase by collecting some baseline data on key performance metrics. Here is a copy for you to review (see Exhibit 7).

Regarding these performance metrics, I performed a small work sampling study over a two-week period to get an estimate of the CSR and BA utilization levels. I calculated the other performance metrics starting with system data and made appropriate adjustments based on the other data I obtained.

After completing the training on the analyze phase last month, I developed a simulation model of the "As-Is" process. After tweaking the model here and there, I am obtaining results from the model that are consistent with the baseline performance metrics. This provides me with confidence that the benefits observed in the simulation model corresponding to tested process improvements will accurately reflect the actual benefits obtained from implementing these improvements in the actual process.

Last week, I completed the third week of training corresponding to the improve phase. Ethan has an idea for improving the process that he would like to test with the simulation model.

Ethan explained:

I know I have only been here a couple of months, but I believe the Health and Welfare Service Delivery Process is fundamentally broken. Tweaking it here and there will not resolve the operational problems.

My suggestion is to create a new case manager position between the CSRs and BAs. The case managers would handle issues that the CSRs were handing off to the BAs. I envision the case managers, like the CSRs, being able to support multiple client organizations. I also would like to provide the CSRs with additional training in order to position them to handle more issues to reduce the number of escalated calls. The pay scale for the case managers would be midway between the CSRs and BAs, or about $35,000 per year, and we would need to include an additional 30 percent to account for benefits and taxes.

Exhibit 7   Baseline Performance Metric for the Health and Welfare Service Delivery Process

Performance metric	Value
CSR utilization	37%
BA utilization	74%
Average time on-hold waiting for CSR	1.77 minutes
Average processing time for calls not escalated (includes on-hold time and time speaking with CSR)	11.54 minutes
Average elapsed time from when CSR escalates call to when CSR calls customer back	6.7 hours (does not include nonwork hours)

I have discussed this idea with the BAs and they concur that the CSRs could research the less complex issues with a little training. I developed this plan to create a service delivery solution to improve customer service, optimize operational expenses, and facilitate career development. I call it my "high-touch, low-cost model" because the customer will have more direct contact with the service provider since fewer calls will be escalated. At the same time, we will be positioned to respond to the participant with lower-cost labor.

Signaling the end of the meeting, AJ stated:

This meeting has been helpful. I think I should be able to use the baseline performance information in my reply to HA's CEO. I will also note that we are currently investigating some fundamental changes to our service delivery process such as the high-touch, low-cost approach.

I will try to convey to him that we are aware of our operational problems and that the changes we will implement in the near future will fundamentally change our process, thereby making an audit of our current process of little value.

I would like the two of you to continue this project and evaluate options for improving the Health and Welfare Service Delivery Process. As I see it, we have two fundamental options. On the one hand, we can make incremental improvements to the current process. Jerry's baseline performance metrics confirmed my suspicion that there are underutilized resources. Perhaps you can identify ways to reallocate the staff to our bottlenecks or perhaps even eliminate some staff.

Eliminating staff could also help improve our profitability. There are probably additional opportunities to improve the resource allocation through better scheduling. It would be great if you could identify some process improvements that we could implement quickly and inexpensively to generate some immediate cost savings and service-level improvements.

On the other hand, I would also like you to consider more radical changes to the process such as Ethan's high-touch, low-cost approach. We need solutions that improve our profitability but not at the expense of our service levels. Let's schedule a meeting for early next week to discuss your process improvement recommendations.

More Analysis

As Jerry walked back to his office, he considered numerous questions. How much inefficiency existed in the current process and was it really beyond repair? How could the simulation model be modified to test Ethan's high-touch, low-cost model? In particular, how could the company determine the number of BAs, CSRs, and case managers it needed and how should they be allocated to clients? Where would the company get the new case managers? Would it be better to train CSRs for the case manager role or simply reallocate some of the BAs to the case manager role? Or perhaps some combination would be best? Using CSRs would require bumping their pay as well as providing them with additional training, while shifting BAs to the case manager role would entail paying the case managers more because AJ had made it clear that cutting the BAs' pay was not an option. Could the organization really save money by utilizing case managers?

Certainly, the simulation model could help in developing a plan for allocating the work across the different job functions. Then, based on this, he could assess the potential cost savings and also evaluate Ethan's idea for making a radical change in the process.

Notes

1. Consistent with industry practices, employees selected to serve in the Black Belt role at BPO completed a four-month training program during which the Black Belt candidates received one week of formal in-class training each month and used the time between classes to complete a Black Belt project. Also consistent with the practices of other organizations,

BPO made a distinction between employees who were Six Sigma Black Belt *trained* and those that were *certified* Six Sigma Black Belts. At BPO, certified Black Belts were required to pass a comprehensive 4-hour exam and to have successfully completed a Six Sigma project in addition to the four weeks of Black Belt training.

2. Ross, C. F. "Business Process Outsourcing Gains Momentum." *Techstrategy* (November 30, 2001).

3. Ante, S. E. "Savings Tip: Don't Do It Yourself." *Business Week* (June 23, 2003): 78–79.

4. Pramuk, M. "The Evolution of HR Outsourcing Services: The Impact of New Entrants and Changing Alliances on Building a Successful Competitive Strategy." *IDC* (December 2002).

5. All times in the case are Eastern Standard Time.

Peerless Laser Processors

Jack R. Meredith, Marianne M. Hill, and James M. Comer

Owner and president Ted Montague was sitting at his desk on the second floor of the small Groveport, Ohio, plant that housed Peerless Saw Company and its new subsidiary, Peerless Laser Processors, Inc. As he scanned over the eight-page contract to purchase their third laser system, a 1200-watt computerized carbon dioxide (CO_2) laser cutter, he couldn't help but reflect back to a similar situation he had faced three years ago in this same office. Conditions were significantly different then. It was amazing, Ted reflected, how fast things had changed in the saw blade market, especially for Peerless, which had jumped from an underdog to the technology leader. Market data and financial statements describing the firm and its market environment are given in Exhibits 1 and 2.

History of Peerless Saw Company

Peerless Saw Company was formed in 1931, during the Great Depression, in Columbus, Ohio, to provide bandsaw blades to Ford Motor Company. It survived the Depression and by 1971, with its nonunionized labor force, it was known for its quality bandsaws and circular saw blades.

But conditions inside the firm warranted less optimism. The original machines and processes were now very old and breaking down frequently, extending order backlogs to 20 weeks. However, the owners were nearing retirement and didn't want to invest in new machinery, much less add capacity for the growing order backlog that had been building for years.

By 1974, the situation had reached the crisis point. At that point, Ted Montague had appeared and, with the help of external funding, bought the firm from the original owners. Ted's previous business experience was in food processing, and he had some concern about taking charge of a metal products company. But Ted found the 40 employees, 13 in the offices and 27 (divided among two shifts) on the shop floor, to be very helpful, particularly since they now had an owner who was interested in building the business back up.

Within two years, Ted felt comfortable with his knowledge of the business. At that point, he had a feel for what he believed were the more serious problems of the business and hired both a

Exhibit 1 Peerless Financial Data, 1993

Sales		$5,028,067
Costs:		
Materials	1,860,385	
Labor	905,052	
Variable overhead	1,106,175	
G&A	553,087	
Contribution to profit		603,368

Exhibit 2 Sales and Market Data, 1993

Year	Sales (M)	Market share (%)
1993	$5.028	29
1992	3.081	27
1991	2.545	25
1990	2.773	25

manufacturing manager and a manufacturing engineer, Con Wittkopp, to help him solve the problems. The most shopworn machines at Peerless were the over-30-year-old grinding machines and vertical milling machines. Committed to staying in business, Ted arranged for capital financing to design and build a new facility and replace some of the aging equipment. In 1987, the firm moved into new quarters in Groveport, not far from Columbus, with 7000 additional square feet of floor space. He also ordered seven new grinders from Germany and five new vertical mills. In order to determine what bottlenecks and inefficiencies existed on the shop floor, Ted also devised and installed a cost-tracking system.

Laser Cutting Technology

By 1988, the competition had grown quite strong. In addition to the growing number of direct domestic competitors, foreign firms were mounting a devastating attack on the more common saw blade models, offering equivalent quality off the shelf for lower prices. Furthermore, many users were now tipping their own blades, or even cutting them themselves, further reducing the salable market. Sales were down, while costs continued to increase and the remaining equipment continued to age and fail. Ted and Con looked into new technologies for saw blade cutting. They felt that computer numerical control (CNC) machining couldn't be adapted to their needs, and laser cutting had high setup times, was underpowered, and exhibited a poor cut texture. (Ted remarked that "it looked as though an alligator had chewed on it.")

By early 1991, advances in laser cutting technology had received a considerable amount of publicity, so Ted and Con signed up to attend a seminar on the subject sponsored by Coherent, one of the leaders in industrial laser technology. Unfortunately, at the last minute, they were unable to attend the seminar and had to cancel their reservations.

Ted was under pressure from all sides to replace their worn-out punch presses. No longer able to delay, he had contracts made up to purchase three state-of-the-art, quick-change Minster punch presses. As he sat at his desk on the second floor of the Groveport building, scanning the Minster, Inc. contracts one last time before signing, Con came in with a small piece of sheet steel that had thin, smooth cuts through it.

It seems that a salesperson had been given Ted and Con's names from the seminar registration list and decided to pay them a call. He brought a small piece of metal with him that had been cut with a laser and showed it to Con. This was what Con brought into Ted's office. Impressed with the sample, Ted put the contracts aside and talked to the salesperson. Following their talk, Ted made arrangements to fly out to Coherent's headquarters in Palo Alto, California, for a demonstration.

In July 1991, Ted and Con made the trip to Palo Alto and were impressed with the significant improvements made in laser cutting technology in just a few years. Setups were faster, the power was higher, and the cuts were much cleaner. Following this trip, they arranged to attend the Hanover Fair in Germany in September to see the latest European technology. There they were guaranteed that the newer higher-powered lasers could even cut one-quarter-inch steel sheets.

In November, Ted and Con returned to Palo Alto, making their own tests with the equipment. Satisfied, Ted signed a contract for a 700-watt laser cutter,[1] one of the largest then available, at a price close to $400,000, although the cutter couldn't be delivered until September 1992.

In addition to the risk of the laser technology, another serious problem now faced Ted and Con – obtaining adequate software for the laser cutter. Ted and Con wanted a package that would allow off-line programming of the machine. Furthermore, they wanted it to be menu driven, to be operable by their current high school-educated workers (rather than by engineers, as most lasers required), and to have pattern search capability.

---

[1]The contract included extensive ancillary equipment and hardware.

Coherent, Inc. was simply not in the off-line software business. Since Ted and Con did not want to learn to write their own software for the cutter, Coherent suggested a seminar for them to attend where they might find the contact they needed.

Con attended the session but was shocked at the "horror stories" the other attendees were telling. Nevertheless, someone suggested that he contact Battelle Laboratories in Columbus for help. Fearing their high-class price tag but with no other alternative, Ted and Con made arrangements to talk with the Battelle people.

The meeting, in March 1992, gave Ted and Con tremendous hope. Ted laid out the specifications for the software and, surprisingly, it appeared that what they wanted could possibly be done. The price would be expensive, however – around $100,000 – and would require seven months to complete. The timing was perfect. Ted arranged for a September completion, to coincide with the delivery of the laser cutter. During the next seven months, Con worked closely with Battelle, constantly redesigning and respecifying the software to improve its capabilities and avoid unsolvable problems and snags.

Finally, in September 1992, a 2-inch-high printout of code, programmed into a computer, was delivered and matched via an interface with the recently delivered laser cutter. But when the system was turned on, nothing happened. As Ted remarked, "Disaster City!" The software problem was solved within a day, but the laser cutter had to be completely rebuilt on site. For almost 100 days, the bugs had to be worked out of the system. "It was just awful."

The months of debugging finally resulted in a working system by December 1992. Meanwhile, Ted and the machine operator, Steve, spent 4 hours every Friday morning in training at Battelle to learn how to use the system. Con and another operator did the same on Friday afternoons. Con and Ted later remarked that the "hardest" part of the training was learning to find the keys on the keyboard. Initially, Ted and Con thought that they might have enough business to keep the laser busy during one shift per day. As it turned out, running the system was considerably more operator dependent than they had expected for a computerized system. Though anyone in the shop could learn to use the system, the operator had to learn how to work with the system, finessing and overriding it (skipping routines, "tricking" it into doing certain routines) when necessary to get a job done. Ted described this as "a painful learning curve." Thus, only an experienced operator could get the volume of work through the system that was "theoretically" possible. Nevertheless, once thoroughly familiar with the system, one operator could easily handle two cutters at the same time, and probably even three.

Within the next 17 months, Peerless put 4000 saw patterns on the system and started running the cutter for two full shifts. Due to increased demand, they added another laser cutter, using the same computer system, and by November 1993 were running both cutters throughout two full shifts.

Marketplace and Competitive Effects

As of 1994, Peerless saw a number of improvements in their operations and some significant changes in their market as well. In 1989, they had a 14-week delivery lead time. Part of the reason for this was that 25% of their orders had to be renegotiated with the customer because the old tooling couldn't handle the job. This slowed down the work tremendously. With the laser cutter, this has been reduced to just three weeks, heat treating being the bottleneck (two full weeks).

Though they weren't making any blades that could not be made in 1989, their product mix changed considerably. In 1989, they made primarily 8-, 10-, 12-, and 14-inch saw blades. With the new capabilities of the laser cutter, they were now making a much wider variety of blades as well as more complex blades. As a matter of fact, they were producing the more difficult blades now, and at less cost. For example, with the laser cutter, it took one-seventh the amount of time to cut a blade as it did previously and one-eighth the number of machine operators. The resulting average cost saving was 5–10% per blade, reaching a maximum of 45% savings (on labor, material, and variable overhead) on some individual blades. Although cost savings allowed

Peerless to cut prices on their blades, more significantly, they had an improved product, faster lead times, and more production capability.

Production capability was of particular importance. Peerless found that the ability to do things for customers that simply couldn't be done before changed the way customers ordered their blades. Because of their new capability, they were now seeing fewer repeat orders (although the batch size remained about the same) and considerably more "creativity" on the part of their customers. Orders now came to them as "The same pattern as last time except . . ." Customers were using Peerless' new capability to incrementally improve their saw blades, trying to increase capacity, or productivity, or quality by even 1 or 2%, based on their previous experimentation. Peerless had discovered, almost by accident, a significant competitive advantage.

Ted was intrigued with the way the laser cutter had revived Peerless. He stated that, based on payback or return on investment (ROI) criteria, he could not have justified the investment in the laser cutter beforehand. But more significantly, if he were to go through the figures now, after the tremendous success of the laser cutter, he still would not be able to justify the cutter on payback or ROI grounds. The point was that the new technology had changed the market Peerless was selling to, although the customers remained largely the same. The laser cutter in fact "created" its own market, one that simply could not exist prior to this technology. It filled a need that even the customers did not know existed.

Despite the increased speed of the laser cutter, it was not necessary to lay anyone off, though some employees' jobs changed significantly. The laser system was purposely packaged so that the existing employees could work with it and contribute to its success, even though they may have had only high school educations.

Ted continued to push the concept of a small, high-quality, technologically advanced business staying ahead of the same foreign competition that was wreaking havoc on the major corporations in America.

Ted summarized the benefits the new technology brought as follows:

- Decreased product cost

- Increased product quality

- Ability to use a sophisticated technology

- Ability to do what couldn't be done before; more responsive to the market

- An inspiration to visiting customers

- A positive image for the firm

- Adds "pizzazz" and "mystique" to the firm

- Allows entry into new fields

Peerless in 1994

In September 1994, Ted created a new division, Peerless Laser Processors, Inc., to handle general laser cutting of other types of parts besides saw blades. By then, Peerless had logged 10,000 hours on the laser cutters and had placed 6000 patterns on the system, adding new ones at the rate of 300 a month. Due to continuing customer requests that had never originally been considered, or even dreamed of, the software has been under constant revision and improvement by Battelle. Ted noted that, even though the need for revisions is expected to continue, it would not pay to hire a software programmer, nor would the job be interesting enough to keep one for long.

Ted and Con felt that generic computer-assisted design/computer-aided manufacturing (CAD/CAM) systems available today would not help their situation. The unneeded capabilities tend to slow down the system, and in their new business, the main competitive factor, given other constants such as quality, is: "How fast can you do the job?"

Peerless also hired two additional sales representatives, with one now in the field and two in the office at all times. They also hired an engineer to develop new applications on a full-time basis for Peerless Laser Processing. As Con noted, "The problem is recognizing new applications while still doing your own work." They discovered, for example, that they could now make their own shuttles for their double-disk grinders instead of purchasing them.

Peerless now has five U.S. competitors in the laser cutting business. Of course, Germany and Japan, among others, are still major competitors using the older technology. For the future, Ted sees the lasers becoming more powerful and having better control. He sees applications growing exponentially, and lasers doing welding and general fabrication of parts as well. He sees other technologies becoming competitive also, such as water jet and electrodischarge machining (EDM).

For Peerless, Ted's immediate goal is to attain a two-week lead time for saw blades and even better customer service, possibly including an inventory function in their service offerings. For the long run, Ted's goal is to become a "showcase" operation, offering the best in technology and quality in the world. As Ted put it:

> A company is like a tree. It only succeeds if it continues to grow, and you've got to grow wherever there's an opportunity. There are a maximum number of saw blades needed in the world, but no cap on what else the technology can do. We're only limited by our own imagination and creativeness and desire to make technology do things. That's our only restriction. What it fundamentally comes down to is this: Is a railroad a railroad or a transportation company? Are we a saw blade company or are we a company that fabricates metals into what anyone wants?

General Micro Electronics, Inc.: Semiconductor Assembly Process[2]

Scott M. Shafer

Having just left a tense meeting with Tom Kacy (her boss) and Charles Samuelson (Kacy's boss), Brianna Regan, process engineer at General Micro Electronics (GME), was sitting in her office. She shifted her gaze from the data she was studying in the Excel spreadsheet to the sample semiconductor chips scattered on her desk. She tapped nervously with her pencil and stared at the chips. She was reflecting on what the data were saying and thinking about what her recommendations were going to be to turn around the performance of the new automated wire-bonder machine used in GME's assembly operation.

The company had purchased the new machine and had it all set up by the beginning of January. It was now May, and Regan was becoming increasingly frustrated with her inability to get control over the machine. She knew that if the new machine's performance continued to deteriorate, she would soon be getting the type of attention from senior management she would prefer to avoid.

GME purchased the new wire-bonder machine in part to support the company's contract assembly business which was growing three times faster than the company's proprietary semiconductor business. From its initial installation in January through February, the new machine performed well in terms of the wire-bond strength. However, beginning in March, its performance became more erratic, although still acceptable. By April, the machine's performance had grown more and more erratic to the point that it was finally deemed unacceptable to the operations managers at GME. Regan herself was becoming increasingly frustrated with the machine's inability to meet GME's internal standards. In fact, the continuous adjustments she had made on the machine in an effort to rectify the situation during the intervening months seemed to be making the situation worse.

The need to improve the performance of the new wire-bonding machine was becoming critical as overtime costs were mounting and the operation would soon constrain the growth of GME's contract assembly business. Tom Kacy, manufacturing manager and Regan's boss, reflected this at the meeting earlier that day when he told her:

> Brianna, we've got to correct the problems with the new machine ASAP! We're scheduling overtime on our existing outdated wire-bonding machines but they're very close to full utilization. We really need the capacity of the new machine.

The wire-bond strength was an important quality dimension for semiconductor chips. In particular, when chips were subjected during use to such external stresses as vibration and heat, the wire bonds could loosen causing the chips to fail. Given that the chips GME supplied to its customers represented a small percentage of the total unit cost of the products they were used in, GME's customers became very disgruntled when their products failed as a result of an inexpensive defective chip. In one instance, a $500 two-way radio used in a taxicab failed because a $2.00 chip was defective. At that same meeting, Charles Samuelson, VP of Operations, expressed his concern:

> Without additional capacity we won't be able to meet our promised delivery dates. We also can't afford to compromise on the quality our customers expect. Historically, fewer than 10 chips out of every million we ship have been returned because of quality problems.

[2]The authors are grateful to Dr. Deborah Ettington, the editor of the *Case Research Journal*, and three anonymous reviewers who gave invaluable advice and suggestions for improving this case and to John Waltman for his copy-editing expertise. This case was developed for the sole purpose of providing material for course analysis and class discussion. It is not intended to illustrate either effective or ineffective handling of a managerial situation. All characters, data, and events are real, but names of people, organizations, and dates have been disguised.

The Semiconductor Industry

Semiconductors (aka integrated circuits (ICs) and chips) had become a ubiquitous part of life and had transformed the way people worked and lived. They were the heart of most electronic products and greatly enhanced the functionality of numerous other products. Imagine how different life would have been over the last decade without cell phones, personal computers, GPS devices, and video games. Likewise, consider how semiconductors enhanced the functionality of numerous products including automobiles, medical equipment, TVs, cameras, dishwashers, and hearing aids, just to name a few.

Beyond transforming our lives, the semiconductor industry played a critical role in the U.S. economy. Semiconductors were a major category of U.S. exports, and U.S. sales accounted for almost half of worldwide sales. The industry was a significant source of employment in the United States, both directly and indirectly as the enabling technology for other products.

General Micro Electronics, Inc.

Founded in 1968, GME designed and supplied a range of low-power analog, digital, and mixed-signal semiconductors used to support communication applications. Its headquarters were in the United Kingdom, and it had operations in the United States, Germany, and Singapore.

GME operated in four major segments: wireless, memory management, wire line telecommunications, and networking. The wireless portion of its business accounted for 45% of sales and provided chips for voice, data, signaling, and radio-frequency applications. Memory management applications accounted for an additional 36% of sales.

GME's sales were approximately $30 million. GME was what industry experts called a fabless (literally "without fabrication") semiconductor company, meaning that it performed the assembly and test operations of its semiconductors in-house but outsourced the production of the silicon wafers (a process discussed in more detail in the Appendix).

More specifically, GME's primary business activity was contract assembly. As a contract assembler, it received semiconductor wafers, or chips, from its customers, assembled them into packages, and electrically tested the finished packages.

GME's Semiconductor Assembly Process

As a fabless semiconductor firm, GME outsourced wafer fabrication (the appendix provides additional details of the wafer fabrication process). When a completed wafer arrived, GME's technicians first tested each semiconductor or die within the wafer and recorded the locations of defective dies within the wafer. Next, the wafers went through "singulation," a process that used a diamond saw that separated the wafer into individual dies. After singulation, the defective dies were removed, and each good die was placed into a plastic container. Each wafer contained 50–200 dies, and consistent with industry standards, 90–99% of the dies on a given wafer were of good quality. The dies ranged in size from 0.1-inch sides to 0.25-inch sides.

To work with other electronic components in a particular product, chips were often mounted on printed circuit boards which were then used to support and connect electronic components to obtain the desired functionality. The first step to connect with the printed circuit board was to mount the dies on a lead frame with glue. Exhibit 1 shows a lead frame with six positions (i.e. the six squares at the center of the lead frame) prior to the semiconductor dies being mounted on them. The dies were mounted by gluing one in each position. While the six chips were processed together initially, eventually the lead frame shown in Exhibit 1 would be trimmed to create six individual chips.

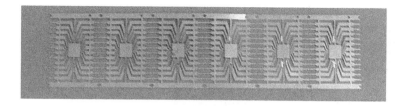

EXHIBIT 1
Example Lead Frame

After the die was mounted on the lead frame, a wire-bonding process was used to electrically connect the die to the lead frame. Exhibit 2 illustrates the lead frame's appearance after a die was mounted on it. As Exhibit 2 shows, each die contained a number of small square bond pads on its top surface around its perimeter. The die was connected to the lead frame by adding gold wires that connected the pads on the die to the pads on the lead frame. For example, in Exhibit 2, a gold wire was added to connect the pad labeled "PAD 1" on the die to the lead frame pad labeled "1." Additional wires were used to connect the other die pads to the lead frame pads.

To connect the die pads to the lead frame pads, the die was first heated. Next, a gold wire was fed through a capillary on the wire-bonding machine. A spark fired at the end of the gold wire created a small gold ball at the wire's end. The capillary then moved down to contact the appropriate pad on the die. By the use of temperature, pressure, and ultrasonic vibration, the machine created a bond between the gold ball and the pad on the die. Next, the capillary moved over to the pad on the lead frame and used ultrasonic energy to stitch the wire to the lead frame pad creating a wedge bond. Finally, a clamp on the capillary closed, cutting the wire, and the capillary moved to the next die pad to bond. Exhibit 3 shows a wire bond completed between the die and lead frame.

Following the wire-bonding process, the die and lead frame went through a molding process, which encapsulated them in plastic. Next, the lead frames were trimmed to create individual chips. Finally, the leads were bent at 90° to facilitate mounting on the printed circuit board.

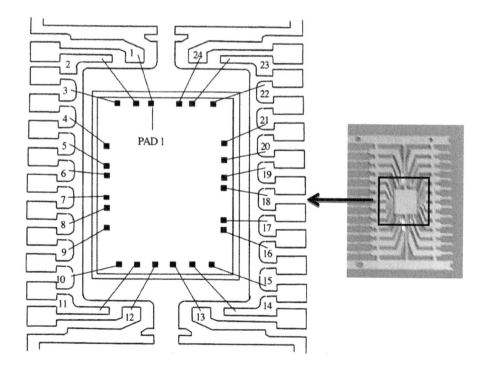

EXHIBIT 2 Schematic of Lead Frame with Mounted Die

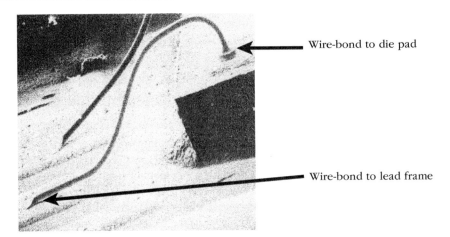

EXHIBIT 3
Completed Wire Bonds

Challenges with the New Wire-Bonding Machine

The pressure coming down on Brianna Regan and her boss Tom Kacy was escalating as GME's contract assembly business continued to grow. A key performance variable used to assess the quality of chips was the strength of the wire bond. As mentioned earlier, weak bonds could result in the chip failing since the connections between the semiconductor and the lead frame would loosen under the stresses the chip encountered in its normal operation. In the taxi example mentioned earlier, a chip used in a two-way radio in a taxicab was subjected to vibration stresses when the cab encountered bumps in the road. These stresses led to microcracks at the wire-bond interface that in turn created intermittent or permanent failures.

GME quantified the strength of the wire bond by a measure called pull strength. To measure the pull strength of a wire bond, a technician manually positioned a die/lead frame assembly on a piece of test equipment and then placed a small hook under the center of the wire spanning the die and lead frame (see Exhibit 4). The diameter of the wire was approximately 0.001 inch with a length of just a few hundredths of an inch. Given these small dimensions, the technician used a small, mounted magnifying glass to position the hook. The technician then used the apparatus to pull the hook upward with gradually increasing force until the wire bond broke. During this process, the dial gauge of the apparatus recorded the bond pull strength, the maximum force needed to break the wire bond. GME's internal requirement for the pull strength of wire bonds was at least 7 grams, which exceeded the military standard of 4 grams. Although military contracts accounted for a very small percentage of GME's business, the industry commonly used and cited military standards.

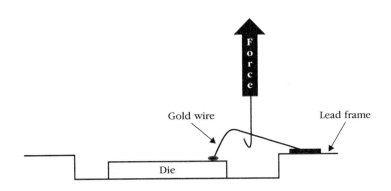

EXHIBIT 4 Measuring the Wire-Bond Pull Strength

The wire-bond strength measurement process was very operator dependent. For example, it was critical for the operator to place the hook in the center of the wire span because an off-center hook would apply more force on either the ball bond on the die or the wedge bond on the lead frame. In fact, improper placement of the hook was the primary source of error in the measurement process. To help ensure that the measurements taken were accurate, GME provided the operators performing this test with extensive training. Furthermore, the technician period-ically recalibrated the measurement apparatus by the attachment of a weight to the hook on the apparatus. The technician then ensured the reading on the dial matched the known value of the attached weight. Although automatic bond strength testers were available, GME's apparatus was a manual unit. While automatic testers greatly mitigated the chances of operator error in the measurement process, they were significantly more expensive than manual ones. In March, Charles Samuelson commented:

> *Industry still uses manual testers like ours, and with proper calibration and operator training these testers should be sufficient for our purposes. In my view, all we're compromising is test speed, but that's justified for us when we consider the cost of more automated testing equipment and our relatively low assembly volumes. Even with our current growth in volume, it will be quite some time before purchasing an automatic tester would be justified.*

Prior to the introduction of the new wire-bonder machine, GME had not encountered any problems meeting its internal pull-strength standard of 7 grams. In fact, the operations personnel were surprised that the new wire-bonder machine was not meeting the pull-strength standard, given that its process controls were so much more advanced compared to the existing equipment used on the production floor. Furthermore, GME was reluctant to consider lowering its pull-strength standard. Charles Samuelson commented in March:

> *Even though the military standard requirement of greater than four grams pull-strength provides some safety margin, I see no reason why we should dilute our long-term capability of greater than seven grams pull-strength. The new machine with its advanced features should perform as well or better than our existing equipment. I'm not willing to dilute our long-term performance specifications since this would make it easier to dilute other specifications. Let's not go down that slippery slope!*

Over the four months following the installation of the new machine, Regan had collected sample data on the wire-bond pull strength for the new machine. Typically, the technician took one sample each day, a frequency Kacy and Samuelson considered sufficient for a one machine, one shift per day operation. The sampling plan involved the technician first ran-domly selecting one of the six dies on the first lead frame produced in a production lot. For the selected die, the technician then measured the pull strength of two randomly selected wires on each of the die's sides. The semiconductors produced by GME generally required six wire bonds per side. Thus, to conduct the sample, the operator randomly chose only two of those six wires on each side of the die to test. This provided a total of eight observations (four sides × two wires per side). This was a destructive test and the tested die could not be reworked and sold after the test; however, the production quantities in the production plan factored in the need to perform these tests.

Exhibit 5 lists the data collected over the four-month period, and Exhibit 6 plots the sample means and ranges. In discussion with the test operators, Regan learned that virtually all the wire-bond breaks occurred at the bond to the lead frame.

In examining the patterns of the sample means and ranges shown in Exhibit 6, Regan was extremely concerned about the deterioration in the performance of the new machine. She won-dered whether the new machine was even capable of meeting GME's pull-strength requirement of greater than 7 grams.

Exhibit 5 Sample Data for New Wire-Bonding Machine

Sample	Obs1	Obs2	Obs3	Obs4	Obs5	Obs6	Obs7	Obs8
1	17.0	15.0	13.0	15.0	15.0	15.0	14.5	15.0
2	14.0	11.0	13.0	10.5	8.0	5.6	SO	10.0
3	7.0	17.5	17.5	17.2	16.5	16.5	16.5	18.5
4	13.0	20.0	16.0	13.5	14.1	17.5	10.5	17.0
5	14.5	15.5	14.5	14.0	11.5	13.5	13.5	14.2
6	15.0	12.3	16.5	14.5	15.5	19.0	14.0	8.0
7	17.0	14.0	18.0	17.0	16.4	17.0	17.5	12.5
8	11.5	11.7	12.0	11.5	16.5	12.0	12.5	11.5
9	14.5	14.0	14.5	15.5	10.5	16.0	16.0	15.5
10	15.0	15.0	14.5	14.8	14.0	12.0	15.0	16.5
11	13.0	13.0	13.0	13.0	12.6	11.0	13.5	12.5
12	15.5	15.0	12.0	14.6	12.0	15.0	12.0	17.0
13	11.5	16.0	16.0	15.0	16.5	15.5	15.0	15.0
14	18.5	15.5	13.0	15.0	15.0	14.5	12.0	16.5
15	14.5	12.0	13.0	15.0	12.0	11.5	16.5	14.9
18	11.5	16.0	12.0	16.0	11.5	11.5	11.7	11.5
17	12.6	11.5	12.5	14.5	11.0	10.5	15.5	14.0
18	13.5	14.0	5.0	11.0	9.0	9.0	10.5	14.5
19	11.0	10.5	12.0	16.5	13.5	11.5	13.5	15.5
20	15.0	16.0	16.5	14.5	14.5	13.5	13.5	12.0
21	12.0	14.0	12.0	12.5	12.0	14.5	13.0	17.5
22	12.5	10.0	12.5	13.5	13.3	13.5	12.5	12.5
23	11.5	12.0	10.5	11.5	17.5	12.0	13.0	12.0
24	12.8	8.5	11.5	15.0	11.5	12.5	13.5	14.0
25	9.0	13.5	12.0	13.5	13.5	12.2	12.5	12.5
26	14.3	14.5	14.0	12.0	12.5	14.0	9.5	11.5
27	10.0	13.0	11.2	16.5	12.5	13.0	12.5	13.0
28	15.5	13.3	16.5	11.5	13.0	14.0	11.5	11.5
29	18.0	13.0	9.0	14.0	11.0	13.5	13.0	11.0
30	11.7	13.5	7.0	15.0	14.5	14.5	17.0	12.0
31	12.0	13.0	11.5	12.7	10.5	15.0	13.5	14.0
32	13.5	13.5	14.5	13.5	12.5	MO	12.7	9.5
33	12.0	12.0	18.5	13.0	12.0	13.5	12.0	12 0
34	14.0	13.0	10.0	12.0	13.5	12.0	14.0	14.5
35	12.2	8.5	11.5	14.0	13.5	13.0	16.5	12.0
36	13.3	9.5	14.0	12.5	12.5	13.0	14.5	13.0
37	9.5	12.0	13.5	12.5	13.0	13.5	13.3	9.5
38	12.0	13.8	16.0	12.5	12.0	12.0	11.5	12.5
39	14.0	11.5	17.5	12.0	13.2	11.5	15.0	13.0
40	10.5	13.0	13.6	16.0	13.0	13.0	14.0	13.0
41	10.0	14.0	13.5	12.2	12.5	14.5	13.0	15.5
42	11.0	16.0	14.0	14.3	16.0	14.5	11.0	11.5

Sample	Obs1	Obs2	Obs3	Obs4	Obs5	Obs6	Obs7	Obs8
43	10.5	14.4	15.0	14.0	14.0	13.0	14.5	14.5
44	15.0	15.5	10.5	14.0	16.0	15.0	12.0	13.0
45	15.0	16.0	13.5	13.0	14.0	13.4	11.0	13.5
46	13.0	12.0	13.0	12.5	14.1	13.5	17.0	13.0
47	14.5	14.5	11.0	12.5	9.5	12.0	14.5	8.0
48	13.8	12.5	13.5	12.5	10.0	11.0	7.0	14.5
49	10.0	15.0	10.0	13.0	13.7	13.5	14.0	12.5
50	14.0	9.0	10.0	9.0	11.5	13.0	14.5	14.5
51	11.6	11.5	13.5	14.5	14.0	14.0	15.5	17.5
52	18.0	11.0	15.5	12.0	13.5	13.1	11.5	12.0
53	12.2	11.0	9.5	17.0	11.5	14.5	12.0	11.5
54	16.5	12.0	12.4	10.0	11.5	11.5	11.0	11.0
55	14.7	15.0	14.0	14.5	17.5	15.5	14.5	15.5
56	9.5	16.0	14.8	16.0	15.5	15.5	15.5	13.0
57	17.5	20.0	14.0	14.0	18.0	16.5	16.2	17.5
58	10.5	11.0	13.2	16.5	12.0	13.0	14.0	5.5
59	14.5	8.5	15.5	16.5	15.5	18.0	13.0	11.0
60	13.9	6.0	10.0	13.0	13.5	15.0	14.0	10.0
61	15.0	13.1	9.0	16.0	19.0	12.5	14.0	15.5
62	15.0	10.5	16.0	9.5	16.0	12.0	13.5	5.5
63	7.5	10.5	10.5	14.0	10.5	10.3	9.5	13.0
64	17.5	14.0	14.0	17.5	13.5	13.5	8.5	11.0
65	10.5	12.0	12.5	12.3	10.5	11.5	11.5	19.5
66	14.0	10.5	15.2	8.5	10.5	17.0	10.5	13.0
67	17.0	17.4	20.0	16.5	16.5	16.0	15.5	12.5
68	16.0	16.5	18.0	15.5	15.0	14.0	14.5	14.5
69	14.5	15.0	15.0	22.5	17.0	14.6	15.0	15.0
70	11.0	13.5	11.5	4.5	9.0	14.5	10.9	8.5
71	13.5	12.0	11.5	4.0	13.0	15.5	11.0	7.0
72	10.0	9.0	8.5	12.6	4.5	11.5	12.0	14.5
73	12.5	9.5	11.5	9.0	14.5	9.5	7.0	12.6
74	7.0	8.0	13.5	12.0	13.5	17.0	11.5	9.5
75	8.0	10.0	14.5	19.0	11.0	11.4	9.5	10.5
76	14.5	9.0	19.0	11.0	13.0	13.0	15.2	13.0
77	13.9	13.5	17.0	17.5	14.5	11.5	14.0	16.0
78	15.5	10.5	11.5	10.5	12.0	10.5	17.5	11.5
79	9.0	13.5	3.5	9.5	10.5	12.5	4.5	5.3
80	14.0	14.0	14.0	16.2	20.5	14.5	11.5	11.5
81	8.5	5.5	9.7	11.5	13.5	11.5	11.5	12.0
82	11.5	12.0	16.5	14.1	12.0	7.5	11.0	14.0
83	16.5	9.5	10.5	10.5	6.5	11.2	13.0	15.5
84	16.0	14.0	12.5	14.5	8.5	20.5	17.0	8.0

(continued)

Sample	Obs1	Obs2	Obs3	Obs4	Obs5	Obs6	Obs7	Obs8
85	12.0	11.2	11.5	13.5	14.0	10.0	19.0	11.5
86	10.5	7.5	10.5	10.5	7.5	10.5	8.5	12.5
87	13.5	13.5	13.5	13.0	13.0	13.5	12.7	3.5
88	21.5	15.5	17.0	10.5	14.5	16.0	15.0	17.9
89	11.5	12.2	12.5	20.0	12.5	10.0	9.0	13.5
90	12.5	12.5	10.3	7.5	12.0	18.5	10.0	9.0
91	13.0	20.5	15.3	12.0	15.0	9.0	11.0	17.0
92	9.0	11.0	16.3	13.0	11.5	12.0	8.5	19.5
93	12.3	12.0	17.0	12.5	5.5	12.0	12.5	14.5
94	18.0	9.0	12.0	11.0	19.5	14.0	16.0	13.1
95	13.5	18.5	17.0	12.2	9.0	17.0	13.5	11.5
96	17.5	11.5	4.5	9.0	7.5	12.5	9.5	7.0
97	11.0	12.0	12.5	11.0	18.0	8.5	13.5	11.5
98	10.0	6.0	15.0	12.5	12.0	11.5	12.0	12.0
99	8.5	17.0	11.5	10.0	14.0	9.5	10.5	12.0
100	12.0	14.5	16.0	14.0	14.0	14.5	15.0	18.5
101	16.5	4.5	11.7	6.5	5.0	12.5	8.5	8.5
102	3.5	10.5	10.0	5.0	9.5	6.0	8.5	15.5
103	11.5	17.0	12.0	12.0	12.0	12.0	11.0	12.5
104	5.0	5.0	5.0	5.0	15.5	5.5	4.5	5.5
105	13.0	11.5	4.5	10.0	7.2	15.0	13.5	16.5
106	12.5	9.0	4.5	6.5	9.0	10.5	9.0	11.0
107	10.5	13.0	13.0	8.0	12.5	13.0	11.5	9.5
108	4.0	2.5	3.0	3.8	5.5	2.5	10.5	5.5
109	6.0	6.0	9.0	6.5	3.0	5.0	6.0	3.8
110	9.5	12.0	9.5	3.0	11.8	7.5	10.5	10.5
111	12.0	12.5	13.2	12.0	8.0	11.5	14.0	12.0
112	13.0	10.5	12.5	14.5	13.5	12.0	13.5	13.5
113	11.9	12.5	10.5	13.0	10.5	11.5	13.0	15.5
114	13.5	8.0	5.5	9.5	8.0	9.5	7.5	8.5
115	7.0	7.0	7.5	10.0	7.5	5.0	5.5	8.0
116	13.0	15.0	12.5	13.0	10.0	11.0	13.5	14.0
117	10.5	5.5	9.3	12.5	11.5	11.5	7.5	10.0
118	6.0	9.0	9.0	9.5	10.5	10.0	12.0	8.0
119	6.5	9.0	8.5	9.5	10.0	13.5	7.5	9.0
120	16.0	7.5	4.0	4.5	8.0	4.0	4.0	9.7
121	9.0	9.5	9.0	16.5	4.5	5.2	8.5	9.5
122	5.5	8.4	5.5	7.5	18.5	6.0	6.0	6.0
123	5.5	6.0	5.5	5.5	5.0	5.5	10.0	4.0
124	5.0	5.5	5.5	6.1	7.0	13.0	7.5	5.0
125	16.5	12.0	7.0	8.0	11.0	15.3	12.5	5.5
126	5.5	9.5	10.0	10.5	9.0	9.5	9.5	10.5

Tom Kacy and Charles Samuelson met in early March to discuss their shared concerns regarding the ability of the new machine to meet the pull-strength requirement, at which time they decided to hire an employee of the bonding machine manufacturer as a consultant to assess the situation and offer recommendations to resolve the issues. Unfortunately, despite paying significant consulting fees to the manufacturer, they found that the problems with low bond strengths and excess variability continued throughout the rest of March and then April. In his exit meeting with Samuelson and Kacy, the consultant expressed his frustration with not being able to resolve the issue:

> *Our machine's not responsible for the problems you're experiencing. I recommend you look more closely at the input materials such as the wire, lead frames, and capillaries used. When you resolve the material issues, I'll be happy to come back and help you optimize the machine settings.*

Prior to the company's engaging the manufacturer as a consultant, Regan had enrolled in a training program to become a certified Six Sigma Black Belt. Six Sigma was a comprehensive approach for improving business performance. The key elements of the Six Sigma approach included a clear focus on the customers' needs, the use of performance metrics, a focus on improving business processes often through the reduction of inherent variation in the processes, clearly defined process-improvement specialist roles, the use of data-driven and highly structured problem-solving methodologies, and ultimately the generation of tangible business results. As part of her training, Regan learned to use the design of experiments (DOE) methodology. DOE used statistical principles to systematically and simultaneously investigate multiple process variables that potentially impact the outcome of the process, which in this case was the pull strength of the wire-bonding process. As she learned more about the DOE methodology, she became convinced that this approach could be extremely beneficial in helping understand and ultimately resolving the issues with the new wire-bonding machine.

In a formal meeting in April with Tom Kacy and Charles Samuelson, Regan pitched her idea for performing a DOE to investigate the problems with the new wire-bonding machine. At the meeting's conclusion, Kacy and Samuelson agreed with her recommendation to undertake a formal DOE study. They also decided that while Regan had no direct experience with DOE, her Six Sigma training best positioned her to lead the study. During the meeting, Regan stated:

> *We're at an impasse. The process the manufacturer set up in January worked great at first. Something happened, and we lost the handle on the process. To be perfectly honest, we're not sure how the variables interact. I've tried to improve the process by adjusting the machine, but my changes have only made the situation worse. With the hindsight of my Six Sigma training, I now see how I made our problems worse by not systematically studying the relevant variables. I believe that a DOE's the best way to learn how the variables interact and get this process back under control.*

In the meeting, Tom Kacy noted:

> *I completely agree with Brianna. We seem to have lost the handle on the process and everything we've tried so far is not working. We need to take a fresh, more systematic, approach.*

Charles Samuelson also concurred:

> *I agree with the DOE approach. What really irritates me is that the manufacturer did not employ this approach when we brought in its consultant. You know, I don't think that the consultant was even aware of DOE as he kept trying new settings without any apparent discipline or plan. I've heard of the success of DOE in process-improvement activities and think it can work here too. Brianna, I appreciate your honesty in admitting your mistakes; it took a lot of courage to do that!*

We will come out of this with a stronger process and a stronger organization! Brianna, right now you're our best choice for this project given your experience with wire bonding – both good and bad – and because you're the only one of us with any understanding of DOE.

For her part, Regan had mixed feelings concerning the outcome of the meeting. On the one hand, she felt good that management expressed confidence in her. On the other hand, she was a little apprehensive about getting what she had asked for. The pressure she had already imposed on herself to perform increased exponentially now that her credibility was at stake.

The Design of Experiments (DOE) Study

Regan began the DOE study by identifying the process parameters to include in it. Based on her personal knowledge of the process, Regan identified the following machine settings that were normally used to control wire-bond quality:

- **Power:** The ultrasonic energy applied to the wire-bond process to heat and recrystallize the wire to form the wire bond.

- **Force:** The downward force or pressure applied to the bond.

- **Work holder temperature:** The temperature of the work holder on which the die sat during the bond formation process. Work holder temperature was a secondary way of supplying energy to the bond process.

- **Time:** The duration of the capillary's contact with the die surface and lead frame and thus the amount of time the power and force were applied.

In the past, the work holder temperature had been held more or less constant, and the other three machine settings had been varied from run to run based on Regan's and the machine operators' best guesses, as they sought the best combination of settings to improve the machine's performance. Unfortunately, as Exhibit 6 shows, they made little progress toward understanding the key factors affecting bond quality and how the factors interacted.

In follow-up discussions with other subject matter experts (SMEs) including her counterparts at sister plants, the manufacturer of the machine, and people she had met at conferences, Regan identified other parameters that might also potentially impact bond quality:

- **Work holder cleanliness:** A dirty work holder impeded heat transfer between the work holder and the lead frame die pad.

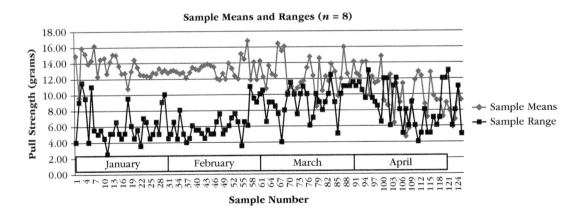

EXHIBIT 6   Sample Means and Ranges for the Data Provided in Exhibit 5

- **Work holder planarization:** An out-of-plane or uneven work holder would mean the same downward force would not be applied equally around the lead frame bond pads.

- **Capillary size and finish:** The bond wire was fed through the center of the capillary, and the size of the capillary and the capillary finish, such as smooth or matte, were believed to affect bond properties. These had varied throughout the use of the new machine.

- **Lead frame material:** Lead frames were made of a range of different materials, each one of which could affect the bond properties. Only one type of lead frame material had been used on the new machine.

- **Wire span shape and length:** The bonder was capable of producing different shapes in the wire-bond span. The shape of the wire bond was defined by the length of the wire connecting the die to the lead frame and the height of the wire above the die (see Exhibit 3). Different shapes were available to optimize wire-bond properties. The measurement equipment found that longer wire spans tended to have lower bond strengths.

- **Bond shape and/or imprint:** Visual inspection of the bonds could be used to roughly gauge whether the bond had been performed properly. For a "good" bond, the ball diameter on the die should have been about three to five times the wire diameter, and the wedge-bond imprint on the lead frame should have approximated a half circle. A wedge bond of less than a half circle indicated insufficient bonding, whereas more than a half circle indicated over bonding and excessive pinching of the wire at the neck.

- **The wire material:** Numerous properties of the wire used could affect the bond strength including the wire's diameter, its composition (e.g. gold vs. copper), its coefficient of expansion, its hardness, and so on.

Analysis and Recommendations

After carefully considering the list of potential factors, Regan decided to include four factors in the DOE study: power, force, work holder temperature, and time. Based on what she learned in her Six Sigma training, she decided that studying each factor at two levels was appropriate. Given this, she selected levels within the range of currently used operating values for each factor. Exhibit 7 summarizes the list of factors and the levels Regan chose for each factor. In total, the DOE study included 16 treatment combinations (two levels of power × two levels of force × two levels of work holder temperature × two levels of time). The wire-bonding machine was used to create the wire bonds on two dies for each treatment combination. The wire-bond pull strength was then measured on six randomly chosen wires for each die, yielding a total of 12 observations (or replications) for each treatment combination. Regan believed that obtaining 12 observations for each treatment combination was a sufficient number of observations to estimate the process average.

Regan completed her DOE study during May. Exhibit 8 summarizes the study's results. These results were the focus of the meeting Regan was just returning from with Kacy and Samuelson.

Exhibit 7 Factors and Levels for Wire-Bond DOE Study

Factor	Current levels used	Low level for DOE study	High level for DOE study
Force	50 to 250	130	190
Power	120 to 250	150	210
Temperature	200°	185°	225°
Time	25 to 80	40	80

Exhibit 8   Pull-Strength Results from DOE Study

Treatment Combinations	Power	Time	Force	Temp	Rep 1	Rep 2	Rep 3	Rep 4	Rep 5	Rep 6	Rep 7	Rep 8	Rep 9	Rep 10	Rep 11	Rep 12
1	150	40	130	185	7.0	12.0	10.0	9.0	9.0	6.0	8.0	8.0	10.0	9.5	9.0	10.0
2	150	40	130	225	13.0	12 5	13.0	14.0	13.0	15.0	11.0	11.0	12.0	13.0	13.0	13.0
3	150	40	190	185	6.0	10.5	11.5	11.0	9.5	9.0	8.0	9.0	7.0	9.5	8.0	10.5
4	150	40	190	225	11.5	11.5	11.0	12.0	12.0	15.5	13.0	12.0	13.0	13.5	13.0	13.0
5	150	80	130	185	7.0	10.0	7.5	8.0	8.0	15.0	10.0	9.0	10.0	10.0	6.5	3.0
6	150	80	130	225	13.0	12.5	13.0	13.0	13 5	15.0	13.0	13.0	12.0	13.0	14.0	14.0
7	150	80	190	185	13.0	13.0	12.0	12.0	12.0	16.0	11.0	12.0	12.0	12.0	10.5	13.0
8	150	80	190	225	13.0	12.0	13.0	13.0	12.0	17.0	14.0	12 5	12.0	13.0	16.0	14.5
9	210	40	130	185	9.0	8.5	10.0	8.0	9.0	6.0	9.0	10.0	10.0	9.0	6.5	12.0
10	210	40	130	225	11.5	11.5	11.0	9.5	12.0	13.0	9.0	4.0	8.0	8.0	6.0	6.0
11	210	40	190	185	15.0	13.0	9.0	11.5	10.0	16.0	10.0	13.0	13.0	13.0	6.0	13.0
12	210	40	190	225	13.0	12.0	11.5	11.0	11.0	10.0	12 5	12.0	8.0	10.0	12.0	14.5
13	210	80	130	185	9.0	9.5	10.5	8.5	9.5	6.0	7.0	13.0	12.0	13.0	11.0	6.0
14	210	80	130	225	15.0	15.0	12.0	12.0	12.0	12.0	10.5	10.0	10.5	10.0	10.0	13.5
15	210	80	190	185	13.0	11.0	11.0	11.5	11.5	10.0	9.0	10.0	11.0	10.0	10.5	13.0
16	210	80	190	225	12 5	9.5	11.5	12.0	12.0	12.5	15.5	15.0	14.0	14.0	13.0	12.0

. . .As Regan returned her attention to the spreadsheet in front of her containing the results of the DOE study, she began to reflect on how she was going to analyze the data from the study. Would she be able to use the data to develop a set of recommendations for improving the performance of the new wire-bonding machine? Regan mused to herself:

I am under a lot of pressure to get this machine back under control! And I've made the situation much worse with my adjustments to the machine. On top of this, we're incurring a lot of overtime costs trying to keep up with the increase in business using our old equipment. I really hope I can find something in the data that will help us better understand the variables that influence the strength of the wire bonds . . .

Appendix

Wafer Fabrication Process

While the functionality chips enabled in everyday products often amazed people, semiconductors were electronic devices that performed relatively basic functions such as switching between conducting electric currents to blocking them. Despite the fact that semiconductors performed fairly basic functions, the process of making them was quite complex and consisted of hundreds of steps.

Most semiconductors were made from silicon, which was created from abundantly available sand. The silicon first was heated to create a molten liquid after which a solid piece of silicon called a seed was dipped into the molten liquid, similar to the way a wick was dipped into liquid wax to create a candle. As the silicon seed was slowly withdrawn from the liquid silicon, it was cooled to form a cylindrical silicon ingot. The silicon ingot was then ground to a uniform diameter, and then a diamond saw blade was used to cut the ingot into thin individual silicon wafers. Following a series of smoothing and polishing operations on each wafer, they were ready for wafer fabrication.

The process of creating the actual semiconductor on the silicon wafer was referred to as wafer fabrication. The process was extremely complex, often taking a month or more to complete. Because a single dust particle could ruin an entire chip, wafer fabrication was done in an environmentally controlled clean room, a production space where airborne particles that could contaminate the wafers being made were continuously removed from the air. Each silicon wafer contained up to several hundred chips depending on the size of the wafer and the size of the chips.

The wafers were first cleaned to maximize the yield of the wafer fabrication process. Next, a uniform insulator film was created on the surface of the wafer by heating the wafer to 1000°C and exposing it to ultrapure oxygen.

Patterning, the next major step in wafer fabrication, involved coating the wafer surface with a light-sensitive film. Ultraviolet light was then projected through a mask to transfer an image on to the surface of the wafer.

After the patterning was completed on the wafer, it was ready for etching. In the etching phase, the image transferred to the wafer's surface was developed similar to the way a film photograph was developed with chemicals to create a negative. The developed image on the wafer's surface was then chemically removed or etched away.

After etching, the wafers went through a doping process that altered the electrical conducting characteristics. A finished wafer required numerous repetitions of the cleaning, patterning, etching, and doping steps.

Heublein: Project Management and Control System[3]

Herbert F. Spirer and A. G. Hulvey

Heublein, Inc., develops, manufactures, and markets consumer food and beverage products domestically and internationally. The business of Heublein, Inc., their sales revenue, and some of their better known products are shown in Figure 1. Highlights of Figure 1 include the following: The four major businesses ("Groups") use different manufacturing plants, equipment, and processes to produce their products. In the Spirits Group, large, continuous-process bottling plants are the rule; in the Food Service and Franchising Group, small fast food restaurants are the "manufacturing plants."

The amount of spending for capital projects and support varies greatly among the Groups, as would be expected from the differences in the magnitude of sales revenues.

The engineering departments of the Groups have responsibility for operational planning and control of capital projects, a common feature of the Groups. However, the differences among the Groups are reflected in differences in the sizes of the engineering departments and their support services. Similarly, financial tracking support varies from full external support to self-maintained records.

Prior to the implementation of the Project Management and Control System (PM&C) described in this paper, the capital project process was chiefly concerned with the financial justification of the projects, as shown in Figure 2. Highlights include:

- A focus on cost–benefit analysis.

- Minimal emphasis on execution of the projects; no mechanism to assure that nonfinancial results were achieved.

The following factors focused attention on the execution weaknesses of the process:

- Some major projects went over budget.

- The need for optimal utilization of capital funds intensified since depreciation legislation was not keeping pace with the inflationary rise in costs.

Responding to these factors, Heublein's corporate management called for a program to improve execution of capital projects by implementing PM&C. Responsibility for this program was placed with the Corporate Facilities and Manufacturing Department, which, in addition to reviewing all Capital Appropriation Requests, provided technical consulting services to the corporation.

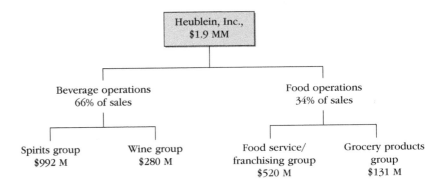

FIGURE 1   Heublein, Inc.

---

[3]Reprinted with permission from Herbert F. Spirer.

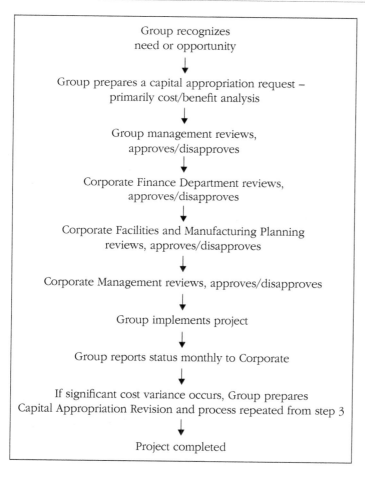

FIGURE 2 Capital Project Progress Prior to PM&C

Feasibility Study

Lacking specialized expertise in project management, the Director of Facilities and Manufacturing Planning (F&MP) decided to use a consultant in the field. Interviewing of three consultants was undertaken to select one who had the requisite knowledge, compatibility with the style and goals of the firm, and the ability to communicate to all levels and types of managers. The latter requirement was important because of the diversity of the engineering department structures and personnel involved. The first author was selected as the consultant.

With the consultant selected, an internal program manager for PM&C was selected. The deferral of this choice until after selection of the consultant was deliberate, to allow for development of interest and enthusiasm among candidates for this position and so that both the selected individual and the selection committee would have a clear picture of the nature of the program. A program manager was chosen from the corporate staff (the second author).

Having the key staff in place, ground rules were established as follows:

- The PM&C program would be developed internally to tailor it to the specific needs of the Groups. A "canned" or packaged system would limit this flexibility, which was deemed essential in this application of project management principles.

- The directors of the engineering departments of each of the Groups were to be directly involved in both the design and implementation of the PM&C system in total and for their particular Group. This would assure the commitment to its success that derives from ownership and guarantees that those who know the needs best determine the nature of the system.

To meet the above two ground rules, a thorough fundamental education in the basic principles of project management would be given to all involved in the system design.

The emphasis was to be project planning as opposed to project control. The purpose of PM&C was to achieve better performance on projects, not catch mistakes after they have occurred. Success was the goal, rather than accountability or identification of responsibility for failure.

Program Design

The option of defining a uniform PM&C system, to be imposed on all engineering departments by corporate mandate, was rejected. The diversity of projects put the weight in favor of individual systems, provided planning and control was such that success of the projects was facilitated. The advantage to corporate staff of uniform planning and reporting was given second place to accommodation of the unique needs of each Group and the whole-hearted commitment of each engineering manager to the effective use of the adopted system. Thus, a phased implementation of PM&C within Heublein was planned in advance. These phases were:

Phase I. Educational overview for engineering department managers. A three-day seminar with two top-level educational objectives: (1) comprehension by participants of a maximal set of project management principles and (2) explanation of the corporate objectives and recommended approach for any PM&C system.

Phase II. PM&C system design. A "gestation period" of three weeks was deliberately introduced between Phases I and II to allow for absorption, discussion, and review of the project management principles and objectives by the engineering department managers. At the end of this period, a session was called for the explicit purpose of defining the system. The session was chaired by the consultant, a deliberate choice to achieve the "lightning rod" effect whereby any negative concern was directed to an outsider. Also, the consultant – as an outsider – could criticize and comment in ways that should not be done by the engineering department managers who will have long-term working relationships among each other. It was agreed in advance that a consensus would be sought to the greatest possible extent, avoiding any votes on how to handle particular issues which leaves the "nay" votes feeling that their interests have been overridden by the majority. If consensus could not be achieved, then the issue would be sidestepped to be deferred for later consideration; if sufficiently important, then a joint solution could be developed outside the session without the pressure of a fixed closing time.

Phase III. Project plan development. The output of Phase II (the set of consensus conclusions) represented both guidelines and specific conclusions concerning the nature of a PM&C system. Recognizing that the PM&C program will be viewed as a model project and that it should be used as such, serving as an example of what is desired, the program manager prepared a project plan for the PM&C program. The remainder of this paper is primarily concerned with the discussion of this plan, both as an example of how to introduce a PM&C system and how to make a project plan. The plan discussed in this paper and illustrated in Figures 3 to 11 is the type of plan that is now required before any capital project may be submitted to the approval process at Heublein.

Phase IV. Implementation. With the plan developed in Phase III approved, it was possible to move ahead with implementation. Implementation was in accordance with the plan discussed in the balance of this paper. Evaluation of the results was considered a part of this implementation.

Project Plan

A feature of the guidelines developed by the engineering managers in Phase II was that a "menu" of component parts of a project plan was to be established in the corporate PM&C system and that elements of this menu were to be chosen to fit the situational or corporate tracking requirements. The menu is:

1. Introduction
2. Project Objectives
3. Project/Program Structure
4. Project/Program Costs
5. Network
6. Schedule
7. Resource Allocation
8. Organization and Accountability
9. Control System
10. Milestones or Project Subdivisions

In major or critical projects, the minimal set of choices from the menu is specified by corporate staff (the definition of a "major" or "critical" project is a part of the PM&C procedure). For "routine" projects, the choice from the menu is left to the project manager.

In the PM&C plan, items 6 and 7, Schedule and Resource Allocation, were combined into one section for reasons which will be described as part of the detailed discussions of the individual sections which follow.

Introduction

In this PM&C system, the Introduction is an executive summary, with emphasis on the justification of the project. This can be seen from the PM&C Program Introduction shown in Figure 3.

It is to the advantage of everyone concerned with a project to be fully aware of the reasons for its existence. It is as important to the technicians as it is to the engineers or the corporate financial department. When the project staff clearly comprehends the reason for the project's existence, it is much easier to enlist and maintain their support and wholehearted efforts. In the Heublein PM&C system, it is expected that the introduction section of a project plan will include answers to these questions: What type of project is involved? What is the cost–benefit relationship? What are the contingency plans? Why is it being done this way (i.e. why were alternatives rejected)? Figure 3 not only illustrates this approach but also is the executive summary for the Heublein PM&C system.

External and internal factors make it urgent to ensure most efficient use of capital funds. Implementation of a project management and control ("PM&C") system has been chosen as one way to improve the use of capital funds. The Corporate Management Committee defined this need.

Subsequently, Corporate Facilities and Manufacturing Planning performed a feasibility study on this subject. A major conclusion of the study was to develop the system internally rather than use a "canned" system. An internally developed system can be tailored to the individual Groups, giving flexibility which is felt to be essential to success. Another conclusion of the study was to involve Group engineering managers in the design and implementation of the system for better understanding and acceptance. This is the detailed plan for the design and implementation of a corporate-wide PM&C system. The short-term target of the system is major capital projects; the long-term target is other types of projects, such as new product development and R&D projects. The schedule and cost are:

Completion Date: 1 year from approval.
Cost: $200,000, of which $60,000 is out of pocket.

FIGURE 3 Introduction to PM&C Program Project Plan

Objectives

Goals for a project at Heublein must be stated in terms of deliverable items. To so state a project objective forces the definition of a clear, comprehensible, measurable, and tangible objective. Often, deliverable items resulting from a project are documents. In constructing a residence, is the deliverable item "the house" or is it "the certificate of occupancy"? In the planning stages of a project (which can occur during the project as well as at the beginning), asking this question is as important as getting the answer. Also, defining the project in terms of the deliverables tends to reduce the number of items, which are forgotten. Thus, the Heublein PM&C concept of objectives can be seen to be similar to a "statement of work" and is not meant to encompass specifications (detailed descriptions of the attributes of a deliverable item), which can be included as appendices to the objectives of the project.

Figure 4 shows the objectives stated for the Heublein PM&C program. It illustrates one of the principles for objective statements: that they be hierarchically structured, starting with general statements and moving to increasingly more detailed particular statements. When both particular and general objectives are defined, it is imperative that there be a logical connection; the particular must be in support of the general.

Project Structure

Having a definition of deliverables, the project manager needs explicit structuring of the project to:

- Relate the specific objectives to the general.

- Define the elements which comprise the deliverables.

- Define the activities which yield the elements and deliverables as their output.

- Show the hierarchical relationship among objectives, elements, and activities.

The work breakdown structure (WBS) is the tool used to meet these needs. While the WBS may be represented in either indented (textual) or tree (graphical) formats, the graphic tree format has the advantage of easy comprehension at all levels. The tree version of the WBS also has

General objectives
1. Enable better communication between Group and Corporate management with regard to the progress of major projects.
2. Enable Group management to more closely monitor the progress of major projects.
3. Provide the capability for Group personnel to better manage and control major projects.

Specific objectives[a]
1. Reporting and control system
    - For communication of project activity with Group and between Group and Corporate.
    - Initially for high-cost capital projects, then for "critical," then all others.
2. Procedures manual
    - Document procedures and policies.
    - Preliminary manual available by October 20, 1979, for use in general educational seminars.
3. Computer support systems
    - Survey with recommendations to establish need for and value of computer support.
4. General educational package
    - Provide basic project planning and control skills to personnel directly involved in project management, to be conducted by academic authority in field.
    - Technical seminars in construction, engineering, contract administration, and financial aspects of project management.

FIGURE 4 Objectives of PM&C Program

[a]Defined at the PM&C Workshop, attended by representatives of Operating Groups.

the considerable advantage that entries may be made in the nodes ("boxes") to indicate charge account numbers, accountable staff, and so on.

Figure 5 is a portion of the indented WBS for the PM&C program, showing the nature of the WBS in general and the structure of the PM&C program project in particular. At this point, we can identify the component elements and the activities necessary to achieve them. A hierarchical numbering system was applied to the elements of the WBS, which is always a convenience. The 22 Design-Phase Reports (2100 series in Figure 5) speak for themselves, but it is important to note that this WBS is the original WBS: All of these reports, analyses, and determinations were defined prior to starting the program, and there were no requirements for additional items.

Project Costs

The WBS provides a listing of the tasks to be performed to achieve the project objectives; with only the WBS in hand, it is possible to assemble a preliminary project estimate. The estimates based only on the WBS are preliminary because they reflect not only uncertainty (which varies considerably among types of projects) but because the allocation of resources to meet schedule difficulties cannot be determined until both the network and the schedule and resource evaluations have been completed. However, at this time, the project planner can begin to hierarchically assemble costs for use at any level. First, the lowest-level activities of work (sometimes called "work packages") can be assigned values. These estimates can be aggregated in accordance with the WBS tree structure to give higher-level totals. At the root of the tree, there is only one element – the project – and the total preliminary estimated cost is available.

Figure 6 shows the costs as summarized for the PM&C program plan. This example is supplied to give the reader an idea of the nature of the costs to be expected in carrying out such a

---

Work breakdown structure

HEUBLEIN PM&C PROGRAM
1000 Program plan
2000 PM&C system
  2100 Design-Phase reports
    2101 Analyze project scope
    2102 Define performance reports
    2103 Define project planning
    2104 Define revision procedure
    2105 Define approval/signoff procedure
    .
    .
    .
    2121 Define record retention policy
    2122 Define computer support systems requirements
  2200 Procedures manual
    2201 Procedures manual
    2202 Final manual
  2300 Reporting and control system
  2400 Computer support survey
    2401 PERT/CPM
    2402 Scheduling
    2403 Accounting
3000 General training
  3100 Project planning and control seminar
    3101 Objective setting
    3102 WBS
    .
    .

FIGURE 5 Project Structure

Labor costs	
Development and design	$40,000
Attendees' time in sessions	60,000
Startup time of PM&C in group	40,000
Basic educational package	
Consultants' fees	20,000
Attendees' travel and expenses	30,000
Miscellaneous	10,000
Total program cost	$200,000
Out-of-pocket costs: $60,000	

FIGURE 6   Program Costs

PM&C program in this type of situation. Since a project-oriented cost accounting system does not exist, out-of-pocket costs are the only incremental charges. Any organization wishing to cost a similar PM&C program will have to do so within the framework of the organizational approach to costing indirect labor. As a guide to such costs, it should be noted that in the Heublein PM&C program, over 80% of the costs – both out of pocket and indirect – were in connection with the General Training (WBS code 3000).

Seminars were limited to two and two-and-a-half days to assure that the attendees perceived the educational process as efficient, tight, and not unduly interfering with their work; it was felt that it was much better to have them leaving with a feeling that they would have liked more rather than the opposite. Knowing the number of attendees, it is possible to determine the labor-days devoted to travel and seminar attendance; consultant/lecturer's fees can be obtained (expect preparation costs) and the incidentals (travel expenses, subsistence, printing, etc.) are easily estimated.

Network

The PM&C system at Heublein requires networks only for major projects but encourages their use for all projects. Figure 7 shows a segment of the precedence table (used to create the network) for the PM&C plan. All the usual principles of network creation and analysis (e.g. for critical path) may be applied by the project manager to the extent that it facilitates planning, implementation, and control. Considerable emphasis was placed on network creation and analysis techniques in the educational phases of the PM&C program because the network is the basis of the scheduling methods presented, is potentially of great value, and is one of the hardest concepts to communicate.

In the Heublein PM&C system, managerial networks are desired – networks which the individual project managers will use in their own management process and which the staff of the project can use to self-direct where appropriate. For this reason, the view toward the network is that no one network should exceed 50 nodes. The top-level network represents the highest level of aggregation. Each activity on that network may well represent someone else's next lower-level network consisting of not more than 50 nodes. This is not to say that there are not thousands of activities possible in a Heublein project, but that at the working managerial level, each manager or project staff person responsible for a networked activity is expected to work from a single network of a scope that can be easily comprehended. It is not an easy task to aggregate skillfully to reduce network size, but the exercise of this discipline has value in planning and execution in its own right.

The precedence table shown reflects the interdependencies of activities for Heublein's PM&C program; they are dependent on the design of the program and the needs of the organization. Each organization must determine them for themselves. But what is important is that institution

Act'y short descr.	Time (weeks)	Immediate predecessors
4000 prepare final rpt	2	2000,2122,3200
2000 monitor system	6	2000: hold group workshops
2000 hold group workshops	2	2000: obtain approval
2000 prepare final proc	2	2000: monitor system
2000 prepare final proc manual, revise syst	2	2116–2121: approvals
2000 monitor system	8	2000: hold group workshops
2000 prepares for implementation	2	3100: hold PM&C seminar
2122 get approval	2	2122: define com and supp needs
2122 def comp supp needs	4	3100: hold PM&C sem
3200 hold tech seminars	4	3200: prepare seminars
3200 prepare seminars	8	3200 : obtain approvals
3200 obtain approvals	2	3200: def tech sem needs
3200 def tech sem needs	2	3100: hold PM&C sem
3100 hold PM&C seminar	3	3100: integrate proc man in sem 2201: revise prel proc man
3100 int. proc man in sem	1	2201: prel. proc manual
2201 revise prel proc man	6	2201–2300 : get approval

Note: Because of space limitations, the network is given in the form of a precedence table. An activity-on-node diagram may be directly constructed from this table. Numerical designations refer to the WBS in Figure 5.

FIGURE 7   Network of PM&C Program

of a PM&C program be planned this way. There is a great temptation in such programs to put all activities on one path and not to take advantage of parallel activities and/or not to see just what is the critical path and to focus efforts along it.

Schedule and Resource Allocation

The network defines the mandatory interdependency relationships among the tasks on a project; the schedule is the realization of the intent of the project manager, as it shows when the manager has determined that tasks are to be done. The schedule is constrained in a way that the network is not, for the schedule must reflect calendar limitations (vacations, holidays, plant and vendor shutdowns, etc.) and also the limitations on resources. It is with the schedule that the project manager can develop the resource loadings and it is the schedule which ultimately is determined by both calendar and resource constraints.

Organization and Accountability

Who is responsible for what? Without clear, unambiguous responses to this question there can be no assurance that the task will be done. In general, committees do not finish projects and there should be one organizational unit responsible for each element in the WBS and one person in that organizational unit who holds final responsibility. Thus, responsibility implies a single name to be mapped to the task or element of the WBS, and it is good practice to place the name of the responsible entity or person in the appropriate node on the WBS.

However, accountability may have multiple levels below the top level of complete responsibility. Some individuals or functions may have approval power, veto power without approval

Activity	PM&C Mgr	Consultant	Mgrs. of Eng.				Dir F&MP
			FS/F	GPG	Wines	Spirits	
Program plan	I	P					A
Design-phase reports	I	P	P	P	P	P	
Procedures manual	I						A
Reporting and control system	I	P	P	P	P	P	
Computer support survey	I	P					P
Project planning and control seminar	A	I					P
Technical seminars	I		P	P	P		A

Legend:

  I: Initiate/ responsibility

  A: Approve

  P: Provide input

FIGURE 8 Accountability Matrix for PM&C Program

power, others may be needed for information or advice, and so on. Often, such multilevel accountability crosses functional and/or geographical boundaries, and hence, communication becomes of great importance.

A tool which has proved of considerable value to Heublein where multilevel accountability and geographical dispersion of project staff is common is the "accountability matrix," which is shown in Figure 8.

The accountability matrix reflects considerable thought about the strategy of the program. In fact, one of its great advantages is that it forces the originator (usually the project manager) to think through the process of implementation. Some individuals must be involved because their input is essential. For example, all engineering managers were essential inputs to establish the exact nature of their needs. On the other hand, some individuals or departments are formally involved to enlist their support, even though a satisfactory program could be defined without them.

Control System

The basic loop of feedback for control is shown in Figure 9. This rationale underlies all approaches to controlling projects. Given that a plan (or budget) exists, we then must know what is performance (or actual); a comparison of the two may give a variance. If a variance exists, then the cause of the variance must be sought. Note that any variance is a call for review; as

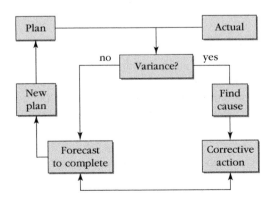

FIGURE 9 The Basic Feedback Loop of Control

experienced project managers are well aware, underspending or early completions may be as unsatisfactory as overspending and late completions.

The PM&C program did not involve large purchasing, or for that matter, many purchases. Nor were large numbers of people working on different tasks to be kept track of and coordinated. Thus, it was possible to control the PM&C program through the use of Gantt conventions using schedule bars to show plan and filling them in to show performance. Progress was tracked on a periodic basis, once a week.

Figure 10 shows the timing of the periodic reviews for control purpose and defines the nature of the reports used.

Milestones and Schedule Subdivisions

Milestones and Schedule Subdivisions are a part of the control system. Of the set of events which can be, milestones form a limited subset of events, in practice rarely exceeding 20 at any given level. The milestones are predetermined times (or performance states) at which the feedback loop of control described above (Figure 9) should be exercised. Other subdivisions of the project are possible, milestones simply being a subdivision by events. Periodic time subdivisions may be made, or division into phases, one of the most common. Figure 11 shows the milestones for the PM&C program.

SUMMARY

The Heublein PM&C program met the conditions for a successful project in the sense that it was completed on time and within the budgeted funds. As is so often the case, the existence of a formal plan and continuing

---

1. Periodic status checking will be performed monthly.

2. Labor costs will be collected manually and estimated where necessary from discussion with Group engineering management.

3. Out-of-pocket costs will be collected through commitments and/or invoice payment records.

4. Monthly status reports will be issued by the PM&C program project manager including:

   a. Cost to date summaries

   b. Cost variances

   c. Schedule performance relative to schedule in Gantt format

   d. Changes in scope or other modifications to plan

5. Informal control will be exercised through milestone anticipation by the PM&C program project manager.

FIGURE 10
Control System

Date	Description
5 Feb	Program plan approved by both Corporate and Groups
26 Feb	Reporting and control system approved by Corporate and Groups
5 Mar	Organizational impact analysis report issued
7 Apr	Basic project planning and control seminars completed
24 Aug	Final procedures manual approved Technical seminars completed Computer support systems survey completed
30 Nov	Final impact assessment report issued

FIGURE 11
Milestones

reference to it made it possible to deal with changes of scope. Initial reaction to the educational package was so favorable that the population of attendees was increased by Group executives and engineering managers.

To deliver on time and within budget but to deliver a product which does not serve the client's needs is also unsatisfactory. Did this PM&C program achieve the "General Objectives" of Figure 5? As is so often the case in managerial systems and educational programs, we are forced to rely on the perceptions of the clients. In this PM&C program, the clients are Corporate Management, Group Management, and, most importantly, the Managers of Engineering and their staffs. In the short run, the latter two operational clients are primary. In addition to informal feedback from them, formal feedback was obtained in the form of Impact Statements (item number 4000 in the WBS of Figure 5). The Impact Statements concerned the impact of the PM&C program on the concerned organization ("How many labor hours are expected to be devoted to the PM&C system?") and response to the PM&C program ("Has this been of value to you in doing your job better?").

Clearly, the response of perceived value from the operating personnel was positive. Can we measure the improvement which we believe to be taking place in the implementation of capital and other projects? It may be years before the impact (positive or negative) can be evaluated, and even then there may be such confounding with internal and external variables that no unequivocal, quantified response can be defined.

At this point, we base our belief in the value of the PM&C program on the continuing flow – starting with Impact Statements – of positive perceptions. The following is an example of such a response, occurring one year after the exposure of the respondent:

> . . . *find attached an R&D Project Tracking Diagram developed as a direct result of the [PM&C] seminar . . . last year. [In the seminar we called it] a Network Analysis Diagram. The Product Development Group has been using this exclusively to track projects. Its value has been immeasurable. Since its inception, fifteen new products have gone through the sequence . . . .*

D. U. Singer Hospital Products Corp.[4]

Herbert F. Spirer

D. U. Singer Hospital Products Corp. has done sufficient new product development at the research and development level to estimate a high likelihood of technical success for a product of assured commercial success: a long-term antiseptic. Management has instructed Singer's Antiseptic Division to make a market entry at the earliest possible time; they have requested a complete plan up to the startup of production. Marketing and other plans following startup of production are to be prepared separately after this plan has been completed.

Project responsibility is assigned to the division's Research and Development Group; Mike Richards, the project scientist who developed the product, is assigned responsibility for project management. Assistance will be required from other parts of the company: Packaging Task Force, R & D Group; Corporate Engineering; Corporate Purchasing; Hospital Products Manufacturing Group; and Packaged Products Manufacturing Group.

Mike was concerned about the scope of the project. He knew from his own experience that a final formula had yet to be developed, although such development was really a "routine" function. The remaining questions had to do with color, odor, and consistency additives rather than any performance-related modification. Fortunately, the major regulatory issues had been resolved, and he believed that submission of regulatory documentation would be followed by rapid approval as they already had a letter of approval contingent on final documentation.

But there were also issues in packaging that had to be resolved; development of the packaging design was one of his primary concerns at this time. Ultimately, there will have to be manufacturing procedures in accordance with corporate policies and standards: capital equipment selection and procurement, installation of this equipment, and startup.

Mike was concerned about defining the project unambiguously. To that end, he obtained an interview with S. L. Mander, the group vice president.

When he asked Mander where his responsibility should end, the executive turned the question back to him. Mike had been prepared for this and said that he would like to regard his part of the project as done when the production process could be turned over to manufacturing. They agreed that according to Singer practice, this would be when the manufacturing operation could produce a 95% yield of product (fully packaged) at a level of 80% of the full production goal of 10 million liters per year.

"But I want you to remember," said Mander, "that you must meet all current FDA, EPA, and OSHA regulations and you must be in compliance with our internal specification – the one I've got is dated September and is RD78/965. And you know that manufacturing now – quite rightly, I feel – insists on full written manufacturing procedures."

After this discussion, Mike felt that he had enough information about this aspect to start to pin down what had to be done to achieve these results. His first step in this effort was to meet with P. H. Docent, the director of research.

"You are naive if you think that you can just start right in finalizing the formula," said Docent. "You must first develop a product rationale (a).[5] This is a formally defined process according to company policy. Marketing expects inputs at this stage, manufacturing expects their voice to be heard, and you will have to have approvals from every unit of the company that is involved; all of this is reviewed by the Executive Committee. You should have no trouble if you do your homework, but expect to spend a good eight weeks to get this done."

"That certainly stretches things out," said Mike. "I expected to take 12 weeks to develop the ingredient formula (b) and you know that I can't start to establish product specifications (c) until the formula is complete. That's another three weeks."

[4]Reprinted with permission from Herbert F. Spirer.

[5]Tasks which must be accounted for in a network plan are identified by lowercase alphabetic symbols in parentheses. Refer to Exhibit 1.

"Yes, but while you are working on the product specifications you can get going on the regulatory documentation (d). Full internal specifications are not required for that work, but you can't start those documents until the formula is complete."

"Yes, and I find it hard to believe that we can push through both preparation of documents and getting approval in three weeks, but Environmental swears it can be done."

"Oh, it can be done in this case because of the preparatory work. Of course, I won't say that this estimate of three weeks is as certain as our other time estimates. All we need is a change of staff at the Agency and we are in trouble. But once you have both the specifications and the approval, you can immediately start on developing the production processing system (g)."

"Yes, and how I wish we could get a lead on that, but the designers say that there is too much uncertainty and they won't move until they have both specifications and regulatory documentation and approval. They are offering pretty fast response; six weeks from start to finish for the processing system."

"They are a good crew, Mike. And of course, you know that you don't have to delay on starting the packaging segment of this project. You can start developing the packaging concept (e) just as soon as the product rationale has been developed. If my experience is any judge, it will take a full eight weeks; you'll have to work to keep the process from running forever."

"But as soon as that is finished we can start on the design of the package and its materials (f), which usually takes about six weeks. Once that is done, we can start developing the packaging system (h), which shouldn't take longer than eight weeks," concluded Mike. At this point, he realized that although Docent would have general knowledge, he needed to talk directly to the Director of Manufacturing.

"The first step, which follows the completion of the development of processing and packaging systems," said the Director of Manufacturing, "is to do a complete study of the facilities and equipment requirements (i). You won't be able to get that done in less than four weeks. And that must precede the preparation of the capital equipment list (j) which should take about three-quarters as long. Of course, as soon as the development of both the process system and packaging system are completed, you could start on preparing the written manufacturing facilities procedures (q)."

"But," said Mike, "Can I really finish the procedures before I have installed the manufacturing facilities (p)?"

"No, quite right. What you can do is get the first phase done, but the last three of the ten weeks it will take to do that will have to wait for the installation of the manufacturing facilities."

"Then this means that I really have two phases for the writing, that which can be completed without the manufacturing facilities installation (q), and that which has to wait for them (q')."

"True. Now you realize that the last thing you have to do after completing the procedures and installing the equipment and facilities is to run a pilot test (r) which will show that you have reached a satisfactory level?"

"Yes. Since that must include debugging, I've estimated a six-week period as adequate." The director of manufacturing assented. Mike continued, "What I'm not sure of is whether we can run all the installation tasks in parallel."

"You can let the purchase orders and carry out the procurement of process equipment (k), packaging equipment (I), and facilities (m) as soon as the capital equipment list is complete. The installation of each of these types of equipment and facilities can start as soon as the goods are on hand (n, o, p)."

"What do you estimate for the times to do these tasks?" asked Mike. The director of manufacturing estimated 18, 8, and 4 weeks for the purchasing phases for each of the subsystems in that order and four weeks for each of the installations. "Then I can regard my job as done with the delivery of the procedures and when I show my 95% yield," said Mike, and the director of manufacturing agreed, but reminded Mike that none of the purchasing cycles could start until the capital equipment list had been prepared and approved (j), which he saw as a three-week task.

The executive committee of D. U. Singer Hospital Products Corporation set a starting date for the project of March 10 and asked Mike to project a completion date with his submission of the plan. The committee's request implied that whatever date Mike came up with was acceptable, but Mike knew that he would be expected to show how to shorten the time to complete the project. However, his task in making the schedule was clear; he had to establish the resource requirements and deal with calendar constraints as best as he could.

To this end, Mike had to get an estimate of resources, which he decided to do by making a list of the activities and asking each group involved what was their level of employee input. The results of this survey are shown in Exhibit 1. For example, activity a takes 8 weeks and requires 12 worker-weeks from R&D, or an average of 1.5 workers for the entire 8-week duration of activity.

For the purposes of overall planning, the accounting department told Mike that he could estimate a cost of $600 per week per employee. This would enable him to provide a cash flow forecast along with his plan, which the chief accountant said would be expected, something that Mike had not realized.

Mike knew that it was customary at D. U. Singer to provide the following inputs as parts of a plan to be submitted to the executive committee:

A. WBS.

B. An activity-on-node (PERT) network.

C. A determination of the critical path(s) and the duration along the path.

D. An activity list, early-start schedule, slack list, and master schedule. Assume that every activity begins at its early start, regardless of resource constraints.

E. A period labor requirements table for each group and the project as a whole.

F. A cash flow requirements graph for the project, assuming that charges are uniformly distributed throughout the activity.

Exhibit 1 Labor Requirements (Worker-Weeks)

Activity	Packaging task force	R&D group	Corp. eng.	H-P manuf.	Pack. prod. manuf	Maint.	Purchasing	Material and other direct charges
a – prod. rationale	1	12	1	1	2	0	0	$0
b – dev. formula	0	16	4	2	0	0	0	500
c – prod. spec.	1	6	3	1	1	0	1	0
d – reg. document	0	12	4	2	0	0	0	0
e – dev. pkg. concept	12	8	4	2	8	0	2	4000
f – design pkg.	12	2	3	0	3	0	3	2000
g – dev. proces. sys.	0	18	12	12	0	0	0	0
h – dev. pkg. sys.	24	8	8	0	8	0	2	0
i – study facil./eqpt. req.	0	4	16	2	2	0	0	0
j – capital equip. list	0	1	3	0	0	0	1	0
k – procure proces. eqpt.	0	1	1	1	0	0	7	40,000
1 – procure pkg. eqpt.	1	0	1	0	1	0	9	160,000
m – procure facil.	0	0	1	1	1	1	6	30,000
n – install proces. eqpt.	0	2	4	8	0	4	1	4000
o – install pkg. eqpt.	2	0	4	0	8	4	1	8000
p – install mfg. facil.	0	0	5	5	5	10	1	6000
q,q' – written procedures	5	5	5	10	15	10	0	5000
r – pilot test	3	6	6	6	6	6	0	0

Automotive Builders, Inc.: The Stanhope Project

Jack Meredith

It was a cold, gray October day as Jim Wickes pulled his car into ABI's corporate offices parking lot in suburban Detroit. The leaves, in yellows and browns, swirled around his feet as he walked into the wind toward the lobby. "Good morning, Mr. Wickes," said his administrative assistant as he came into the office. "That proposal on the Stanhope project just arrived a minute ago. It's on your desk." "Good morning, Debbie. Thanks. I've been anxious to see it."

This was the day Jim had scheduled to review the 2009 supplemental capital request, and he didn't want any interruptions as he scrutinized the details of the flexible manufacturing project planned for Stanhope, Iowa. The Stanhope proposal, compiled by Ann Williamson, project manager and managerial "champion" of this effort, looked like just the type of project to fit ABI's new strategic plan, but there was a large element of risk in the project. Before recommending the project to Steve White, executive vice president of ABI, Jim wanted to review all the details one more time.

History of ABI

ABI started operations as the Farm Equipment Company just after the First World War. Employing new technology to produce diesel engine parts for tractors, the firm flourished with the growth of farming and became a multimillion-dollar company by 1940.

During the World War II, the firm switched to producing tank and truck parts in volume for the military. At the war's end, the firm converted its equipment IN to the production of automotive parts for the expanding automobile industry. To reflect this major change in their product line, the company was renamed Automotive Builders, Inc. (ABI), though they remained a major supplier to the farm equipment market.

A Major Capital Project

The farm equipment industry had been doing well, but there were some disturbing trends. Japanese manufacturers had entered the industry and were beginning to take a significant share of the domestic market. More significantly, domestic labor costs were significantly higher than costs overseas and resulted in price disadvantages that couldn't be ignored any longer. Perhaps most important of all, quality differences between American and Japanese farm equipment, including tractors, were becoming quite noticeable.

To improve the quality and costs of their incoming materials, many of the domestic tractor manufacturers were beginning to single source a number of their tractor components. This allowed them better control over both quality and cost and made it easier to coordinate delivery schedules at the same time.

In this vein, one of the major tractor engine manufacturers, code-named "Big Red" within ABI, let its suppliers know that it was interested in negotiating a contract for a possible 100% sourcing of 17 versions of special piston heads destined for a new line of high-efficiency tractor engines expected to replace the current conventional engines in both new and existing tractors. These were all six-cylinder diesel engines and thus would require six pistons each.

This put ABI in an interesting situation. If they failed to bid on this contract, they would be inviting competition into their very successful and profitable diesel engine parts business. Thus, to protect their existing successful business and to pursue more such business, ABI seemed required to bid on this contract. Should ABI be successful in their bid, this would result in 100% sourcing in both the original equipment market (OEM) as well as the replacement market with its high margins. Furthermore, the high investment required to produce these special pistons at ABI's costs would virtually rule out future competition.

ABI had two plants producing diesel engine components for other manufacturers and believed that they had a competitive edge in engineering of this type. These plants, however, could not accommodate the volume Big Red expected for the new engine. Big Red insisted at their negotiations that a 100% supplier be able to meet peak capacity at their assembly plant for this new line.

As Jim reviewed the proposal, he decided to refer back to the memos that restated their business strategy and started them thinking about a new Iowa plant located in the heart of the farm equipment industry for this project. In addition, Steve White had asked the following basic yet rather difficult questions about the proposal at their last meeting, and Jim wanted to be sure he had them clearly in mind as he reviewed the files:

- ABI is already achieving an excellent ROI. Won't this investment simply tend to dilute it?

- Will the cost in new equipment be returned by an equivalent reduction in labor? Where's the payoff?

- What asset protection is there? This proposal requires an investment in new facilities before knowing whether a long-term contract will be procured to reimburse us for our investment.

- Does this proposal maximize ROI, sales potential, or total profit?

To address these questions adequately, Jim decided to recheck the expected after-tax profits and average rate of return (based on sales of 70,000 engines per year) when he reached the financial portion of the proposals. These figures should give a clear indication of the "quality" of the investment. There were, however, other aspects of capital resource allocation to consider besides the financial elements. One of these was the new business strategy of the firm, as recently articulated by ABI's executive committee.

The Business Strategy

A number of elements of ABI's business strategy were directly relevant to this proposal. Jim took out a notepad to jot down each of them and assign them a priority as follows:

1. Bid only on good margin products that have the potential for maintaining their margins over a long term.

2. Pursue only new products whose design or production process is of a proprietary nature and that exist in areas where our technical abilities enable us to maintain a long-term position.

3. Employ, if at all possible, the most advanced technology in new projects that is either within our experience or requires the next step up in experience.

4. Foster the "project champion" approach to innovation and creativity. The idea is to encourage entrepreneurship by approving projects to which individual managers are committed and that they have adopted as personal "causes" based on their belief that the idea, product, or process is in our best interest.

5. Maintain small plants of no more than 480 employees. These have been found to be the most efficient, and they enjoy the best labor relations.

With these in mind, Jim reopened the proposal and started reading critical sections.

Demand Forecasts and Scenarios

For this proposal, three scenarios were analyzed in terms of future demand and financial impacts. The baseline Scenario I assumed that the new line would be successful. Scenario II assumed that the Japanese would soon follow and compete successfully with Big Red in this line. Scenario III

Table 1   Demand Forecasts (000s Engines)*

Year	Baseline I	Scenario II	Scenario III
2010	69	69	69
2011	73	72	72
2012	90	81	77
2013	113	95	68
2014	125	87	62
2015	145	74	47

*Each engine requires six pistons.

assumed that the new line was a failure. The sales volume forecasts under these three scenarios are shown in Table 1.

There was, however, little confidence in any of these forecasts. In the preceding few years, Japan had become a formidable competitor, not only in price but also in more difficult areas of competition, such as quality and reliability. Furthermore, the economic situation in 2009 was taking a severe toll on American farmers and economic forecasts indicated there was no relief in sight. Thus, as stated in the proposal:

> The U.S. farm market will be a difficult battleground for world farm equipment manufacturers, and any forecast of a particular engine's potential in this market must be considered as particularly risky. How much risk do we want to accept? Every effort should be made to minimize our exposure on this investment and maximize our flexibility.

Manufacturing Plan

The proposal stressed two primary aspects of the manufacturing process. First, a learning curve was employed in calculating production during the 1000-unit ramp-up implementation period in order to not be overly optimistic. A learning rate of 80% was assumed. Second, an advanced technology process using a flexible manufacturing system (FMS), based largely on turning centers, was recommended since it came in at $1 million less than conventional equipment and met the strategy guidelines of using sophisticated technology when appropriate.

Since ABI had closely monitored Big Red's progress in the engine market, the request for bids had been foreseen. In preparation for this, Jim had authorized a special manufacturing process study to determine more efficient and effective ways of producing piston heads. The study considered product design, process selection, quality considerations, productivity, and manufacturing system planning. Three piston manufacturing methods were considered in the study: (1) batch manufacture via computer numerically controlled (CNC) equipment, (2) an FMS, and (3) a high-volume, low-unit-cost transfer machine.

The resulting recommendation was to install a carefully designed FMS if it appeared that additional flexibility might be required in the future for other versions or even other manufacturers. Though such a system would be expensive, the volume of production over the FMS's longer lifetime would offset that expense. Four preferred machine builders were contacted for equipment specifications and bids. It was ABI's plan to work closely with the selected vendor in designing and installing the equipment, thus building quality and reliability into both the product and the process and learning about the equipment at the same time.

To add further flexibility for the expensive machinery, all design features that would facilitate retool or changeover to other products were incorporated. For example, the machining centers would also be capable of machining other metals, such as aluminum or nodular iron, and would be fitted with variable feed and speed motors, feed-force monitors, pressure-controlled clamping of workpieces, and air-leveling pallets. Also, fully interchangeable chucks, spindles, pallets, tooling, and risers would be purchased to minimize the spare parts inventories.

Plant Operation and Organization

As stated in the proposal, many innovative practices were to be employed at the new plant:

- Machine operators will be trained to do almost all of their own machine maintenance.

- All employees will conduct their own statistical process control, and piston heads will be subject to 100% inspection.

- There will only be four skill classes in the plant. Every employee in each of those classes will be trained to do any work within that class.

- There will not be any time clocks in the plant.

The organizational structure for the 11 salaried workers in the new plant is shown in Figure 1, and the complete labor summary is illustrated in Figure 2, including the shift breakdown. As can be seen, the plant will be relatively small, with 65 employees in the ratio of 1:5 salaried to hourly. The eight-month acquisition of the employees during the ramp-up is illustrated in Figure 3, with full employment occurring by March 2010.

Financial Considerations

Financial aspects of new proposals at ABI were considered from a number of perspectives, in part because of the interdependent nature of many proposals. The results of not investing in a proposal are normally compared with the results of investing and the differences noted. Variations on the investment assumptions are also tested, including errors in the forecast sales volumes, learning rates, productivities, selling prices, and cancellations of both current and future orders for existing and potential business.

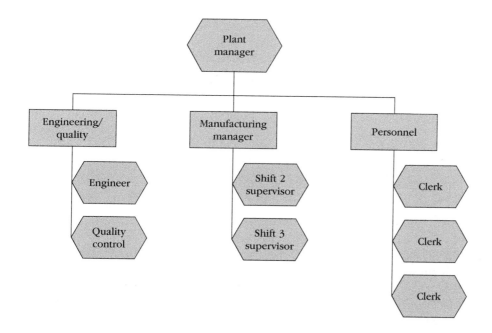

FIGURE 1 Stanhope Organization

Salaried labor	Number of staff
Plant manager	1
Manufacturing managers (three shifts)	3
Quality control manager	1
Engineering	2
Personnel manager	1
Clerical	3
	11

Hourly labor	Days	Afternoons	Night
Direct	14	14	10
Inspection	1	1	1
Maintenance	2	1	1
Tooling	2	2	1
Rec./shp./mtl.	2	1	1
Total	21	19	14

Summary

Salary	11
Hourly	54
Total	65

FIGURE 2 Stanhope Labor Summary

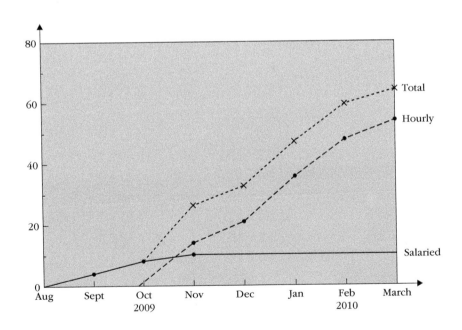

FIGURE 3 Stanhope Labor Buildup

For the Stanhope proposal, the site investment required is $3,012,000. The details of this investment are shown in Table 2. The total investment required amounts to $7,108,000 (plus required working capital of $1,380,000). The equipment is depreciated over an eight-year life. ABI, under the revised tax laws, is in the 34% tax bracket. The price of the piston heads has been tentatively set at $25.45 apiece. ABI's expected costs are shown in Table 3.

Table 2   Stanhope Site Capital Costs

Land and site preparation	
Land	$246,000
Access roads/parking lot	124,000
Landscaping	22,000
Building costs	
Building (67,000 sq ft)	1,560,000
Air conditioning	226,000
Power	205,000
Employee services	177,000
Legal fees and permits	26,000
Auxiliary equipment	
ABI company sign	25,000
Containers, racks, and so on	33,000
Flume	148,000
Coolant disposal	97,000
Furnishings	51,000
Forklift trucks	72,000
Total	3,012,000

Table 3   Piston Head Cost Summary

Material	$8.47
Labor	1.06
Variable overhead	2.23
Fixed overhead	2.44
Freight	0.31
Total factory cost	14.51
General and administrative	1.43
Scrap	0.82
Testing	0.39
Total cost	17.15

Some Concerns

Jim had spoken with some of his colleagues about the FMS concept after the preliminary financial results had been tabulated. Their concerns were what now interested him. For example, he remembered one manager asking: "Suppose Big Red's sales only reach 70% of our projections in the 2012–2013 time period, or say, perhaps as much as 150%; how would this affect the project? Does the FMS still apply or would you consider some other form of manufacturing equipment, possibly conventional or CNC with potential aftermarket application in the former case or a transfer machine in the latter case?"

Another manager wrote down his thoughts as a memo to forward to Jim. He had two major concerns:

- Scenario II analysis assumes the loss of substantial volume to competition. This seems rather unlikely.

- After-tax margins seem unreasonably high. Can we get such margins on a sole-source contract?

Jim wondered what these changes in their assumptions would do to the ROI of the proposal and its overall profitability.

Conclusion

Jim had concerns about the project also. He wondered how realistic the demand forecasts were, given the weak economy and what the Japanese might do. If the demand didn't materialize, ABI might be sorry they had invested in such an expensive piece of equipment as an FMS.

Strategically, it seemed like ABI had to make this investment to protect its profitable position in the diesel engine business. But how far should this argument be carried? Were they letting their past investments color their judgment on new ones? He was also concerned about the memo questioning the high profit margins. They did seem high in the midst of a sluggish economy.

AREA UNDER THE NORMAL DISTRIBUTION

Example: the area to the left of $Z = 1.34$ is found by following the left Z column down to 1.3 and moving right to the 0.04 column. At the intersection read 0.9099. The area to the right of $Z = 1.34$ is $1 - 0.9099 = 0.0901$. The area between the mean (dashed line) and $Z = 1.34$ is $0.9099 - 0.5 = 0.4099$.

Z	0	0.01	0.02	0.03	0.04	0.05	0.06	0.07	0.08	0.09
0.0	0.5000	0.5040	0.5080	0.5120	0.5160	0.5199	0.5239	0.5279	0.5319	0.5359
0.1	0.5398	0.5438	0.5478	0.5517	0.5557	0.5596	0.5639	0.5675	0.5714	0.5753
0.2	0.5793	0.5832	0.5871	0.5910	0.5948	0.5987	0.6026	0.6064	0.6103	0.6141
0.3	0.6179	0.6217	0.6255	0.6293	0.6331	0.6368	0.6406	0.6443	0.6480	0.6517
0.4	0.6554	0.6591	0.6628	0.6664	0.6700	0.6736	0.6772	0.6808	0.6844	0.6879
0.5	0.6915	0.6950	0.6985	0.7019	0.7054	0.7088	0.7123	0.7157	0.7190	0.7224
0.6	0.7257	0.7291	0.7324	0.7357	0.7389	0.7422	0.7454	0.7486	0.7517	0.7549
0.7	0.7580	0.7611	0.7642	0.7673	0.7704	0.7734	0.7764	0.7794	0.7823	0.7852
0.8	0.7881	0.7910	0.7939	0.7967	0.7995	0.8023	0.8051	0.8078	0.8106	0.8133
0.9	0.8159	0.8186	0.8212	0.8238	0.8264	0.8289	0.8315	0.8340	0.8365	0.8389
1.0	0.8413	0.8438	0.8461	0.8485	0.8508	0.8531	0.8554	0.8577	0.8599	0.8621
1.1	0.8643	0.8665	0.8686	0.8708	0.8729	0.8749	0.8770	0.8790	0.8810	0.8830
1.2	0.8849	0.8869	0.8888	0.8907	0.8925	0.8944	0.8962	0.8980	0.8997	0.9015
1.3	0.9032	0.9049	0.9066	0.9082	0.9099	0.9115	0.9131	0.9147	0.9162	0.9177
1.4	0.9192	0.9207	0.9222	0.9236	0.9251	0.9265	0.9279	0.9292	0.9306	0.9319
1.5	0.9332	0.9345	0.9357	0.9370	0.9382	0.9394	0.9406	0.9418	0.9329	0.9441
1.6	0.9452	0.9463	0.9474	0.9484	0.9495	0.9505	0.9515	0.9525	0.9535	0.9549
1.7	0.9554	0.9564	0.9573	0.9582	0.9591	0.9599	0.9608	0.9616	0.9625	0.9633
1.8	0.9641	0.9649	0.9656	0.9664	0.9671	0.9678	0.9686	0.9693	0.9696	0.9706
1.9	0.9713	0.9719	0.9726	0.9732	0.9738	0.9744	0.9750	0.9756	0.9761	0.9767
2.0	0.9772	0.9778	0.9783	0.9788	0.9793	0.9798	0.9803	0.9808	0.9812	0.9817
2.1	0.9821	0.9826	0.9830	0.9834	0.9838	0.9842	0.9846	0.9850	0.9854	0.9857
2.2	0.9861	0.9864	0.9868	0.9871	0.9875	0.9878	0.9881	0.9884	0.9887	0.9890
2.3	0.9893	0.9896	0.9898	0.9901	0.9904	0.9906	0.9909	0.9911	0.9913	0.9916
2.4	0.9918	0.9920	0.9922	0.9925	0.9927	0.9929	0.9931	0.9932	0.9934	0.9936
2.5	0.9938	0.9940	0.9941	0.9943	0.9945	0.9946	0.9948	0.9949	0.9951	0.9952
2.6	0.9953	0.9955	0.9956	0.9957	0.9959	0.9960	0.9961	0.9962	0.9963	0.9964

AREA UNDER THE NORMAL DISTRIBUTION

z	0	0.01	0.02	0.03	0.04	0.05	0.06	0.07	0.08	0.09
2.7	0.9965	0.9966	0.9967	0.9968	0.9969	0.9970	0.9971	0.9972	0.9973	0.9974
2.8	0.9974	0.9975	0.9976	0.9977	0.9977	0.9978	0.9979	0.9979	0.9980	0.9981
2.9	0.9981	0.9982	0.9982	0.9983	0.9984	0.9984	0.9985	0.9985	0.9986	0.9986
3.0	0.9987	0.9987	0.9987	0.9988	0.9988	0.9989	0.9989	0.9989	0.9990	0.9990
3.1	0.9990	0.9991	0.9991	0.9991	0.9992	0.9992	0.9992	0.9992	0.9993	0.9993
3.2	0.9993	0.9993	0.9994	0.9994	0.9994	0.9994	0.9994	0.9995	0.9995	0.9995
3.3	0.9995	0.9995	0.9995	0.9996	0.9996	0.9996	0.9996	0.9996	0.9996	0.9997
3.4	0.9997	0.9997	0.9997	0.9997	0.9997	0.9997	0.9997	0.9997	0.9997	0.9998

GLOSSARY

This glossary lists the major key terms in the book followed by the chapter section where it is mainly discussed. For other locations of the terms, please consult the Index.

3PL–a third-party logistics contractor that handles portions of or the entire supply chain function.

Aggregate planning–a preliminary, approximate schedule of an organization's overall operations that will satisfy the forecast of demand at minimum cost.

Agile project management–an approach to project management based on lean management principles that seeks to lower costs, improve project outcomes, and reduce project completion times by using quick turnaround stages. With Agile, the project is completed in short stages called sprints that last between 1 and 4 weeks with client feedback after each sprint to direct the next sprint.

Attribute data–a discrete characteristic of the output. For the purpose of control charts, the characteristic most often assessed is whether the output is defective or not defective.

Balanced scorecard–a method for monitoring the performance of an organization's strategy on multiple metrics.

Benchmarking–comparing an organization's processes to the best practices to be found.

Bias–a measure of forecast accuracy that assesses the tendency of the forecast to under or over-estimate demand.

Blockchain–an approach for storing information for a growing list of records (transactions). The records are stored as blocks of data with each block linked to the previous block, thereby providing a chain of records. In addition to being linked to the previous record, each block contains a timestamp and data related to a specific transaction. The data stored in the blockchain are distributed across a peer-to-peer network and can generally be read by the public.

Blueprinting–see process-flow analysis.

Brainstorming–a technique for generating solutions among a group.

Break-even analysis–methodology based on a simplified income statement that is used to perform an economic analysis among the options and thereby help management choose among the options, such as alternative capacity or location options.

Bullwhip effect–a causal chain of contractors where small perturbations anywhere in the chain are amplified along the chain to distort supplies.

Business case–the financial and strategic justification for a project.

Business process design–see Reengineering.

Capacity–the rate at which a transformation system can produce outputs.

Carbon dioxide equivalents (CO_2e) (Chapter 1 Appendix)–a measure for assessing the combined impact of alternative greenhouse gases.

Cash conversion cycle (CCC)–the amount of time the organization's cash is tied up in Working Capital before being returned by customers as they pay for delivered products or services. The CCC is made up of three components that track the organization's cash flows from its purchase of inventory to the sale of its products: (1) the amount of time needed to sell its inventory, (2) the amount of time needed to collect its receivables from its sales, and (3) the amount of time the organization has to pay its suppliers.

Causal methods–using related external data and factors to make a forecast.

Cause-effect diagram–a method for determining factors that may impact the performance of some processes.

CCC–cash conversion cycle.

Cellular production–a production system that combines the advantages of the job shop and flow shop to obtain the high variety possible with the job form and the reduced costs and short response times associated with the flow form.

Change manager–person with responsibility to help people and teams successfully transition to new roles or responsibilities.

Chase demand–a production strategy that uses hiring, layoffs, and overtime to exactly meet demand in each period.

Climate pledge–co-founded by Amazon, signatory organizations agree to have net-zero emissions by 2040.

Closed-loop supply chain–see Reverse logistics.

Cloud–software running and/or data stored on servers that users connect to via the Internet.

Cloud computing–storing and using information on a shared, external computer system.

Collaborative planning–coordinating with supply chain partners to continuously update forecasts.

Continuous-flow manufacturing, CFM–setting up a production system so that products flow continuously at the same rate as that of customer demand.

Continuous process–a transformation process used to produce standardized, fluidic products.

Contract manufacturer–a third party who produces all of a firm's outputs.

Control chart–a tool for determining if a process has an assignable cause of variation.

Core capabilities–the areas of knowledge and strength that distinguish an organization.

CPM–critical path method (see Project network).

Crashing–reducing the project completion time by using additional or better resources.

Crash time–refers to the shortest amount of time an activity can be completed. The crash cost refers to the cost of reducing the activity to the crash time.

Critical chain–an approach to project scheduling that considers three primary impediments to project completion.

Critical path–the longest path through a project network showing the earliest a project can be completed.

Customer relationship management, CRM–a system that collects customer data from internal and external sources to help the firm provide better service for its customers.

Cycle time–the amount of time to produce one unit.

Delphi method–a procedure for developing a forecast from a group of experts.

Design for excellence (DfX)–an umbrella term that includes collections of design principles for various design objectives. Design for Excellence is abbreviated as DfX, which can be interpreted as Design for X where the X is a placeholder to a specific design objective. For example, DfM stands for Design for Manufacturability, DfA stands for Design for Assembly, and DfL refers to Design for Logistics (or Supply chain).

Design for sustainability (DfS)–an approach to designing outputs that seeks to minimize the negative impact the outputs will have on people and the environment. Also referred to as design for the environment and green design.

Design thinking–a human-centered design process developed by IDEO.

DMAIC–design, measure, analyze, improve, and control; the basic process for conducting Six Sigma projects.

Earned value–a technique for monitoring and controlling both cost and time in a project by giving monetary credit for each activity in the project.

Economic order quantity (EOQ) model–a model for determining the optimal order quantity for inventory items that are replenished in batches or orders.

Economies of scale–obtaining lower unit costs by using larger facilities to spread the fixed costs over a greater volume.

Economies of scope–obtaining economies of scale but through flexible equipment that can produce greater variety to increase production volumes.

Efficiency–the amount of output divided by amount of input, in the same units, expressed as a percentage.

Enterprise resource planning, ERP–a comprehensive computer system that provides seamless, real-time information to all stakeholders that need it.

Exponential smoothing–a forecasting method that uses a weighted average of the current demand and the previous period's demand.

Facilitating good–the product portion of a service.

Fail-safing–installing preventive measures at likely service failure points.

Failure mode and effects analysis, FMEA–a technique to identify and prioritize risks.

Fishbone chart–see Cause-effect diagram.

Flow shop–a transformation process used to produce discrete products or services, typically on a single, continuous production line.

Focus–the one or two greatest areas of strength in an organization.

Green design–see design for sustainability.

Green manufacturing–Initiatives that seek to reduce the negative environmental impacts of production activities.

Greenhouse gases (Chapter 1 Appendix)–gases in Earth's atmosphere that absorb thermal energy and reflect a portion of it back to the Earth's surface.

Historical analogy–predicting demand for a new item through analysis of past demand for a similar item.

Hollowed out–when a supplier takes over a customer's production or design process and then goes into business competing with that customer.

House of quality–see QFD.

Innovation–the introduction to the market of a new or improved produce, process, or service.

Inventory turnover–represents how often the average inventory is used up to obtain the total sales for the year.

ISO 9000–checklist of good business practices.

ISO 14000–standards for creating an environmental management system.

ISO 22301–provides a framework for preparing for, responding to, and recovering from threats and disruptions.

Job shop–a transformation process used to produce unique products (or services) or batches of such in separate functional areas.

Kaizen–continuous improvement of a production system.

Kanban–a card that authorizes materials for production, thereby "pulling" production through the system.

Kano model–provides a useful framework for classifying customer requirements into one of three categories: dissatisfiers, satisfiers, and delighters.

Lean green–combination of Lean principles with sustainability objectives (aka Green Lean Six Sigma).

Lean production–see Toyota Production System.

Learning curve–a mathematical model that captures the human learning showing the decreasing amount of time required for each unit of additional production.

LEED (Leadership in Energy and Environmental Design)–a broad framework for improving the sustainability of buildings that addresses energy efficiency, car emissions, waste, and water usage.

Level production–a production strategy that uses inventory and stockouts to balance out the demand. Not easily used for services.

Life-cycle analysis–forecasting demand based on the expected life cycle of the product or service.

Lifecycle assessment (LCA)–the most comprehensive analytical approach for assessing the environmental impact of a product throughout its entire life.

Mass customization–making near-custom products or services as inexpensively as mass-produced ones.

Mean absolute deviation, MAD–a measure of forecast accuracy that gives the average amount of error regardless of whether the error was high or low.

Mean absolute percentage error, MAPE–similar to MAD but stated in terms of percentages.

Metcalfe's law–the value of a network is proportional to the square of the number of elements connected to it.

Mobile computing–allows users to access both data and software resources regardless of their location.

Moore's law–computing power doubles every 1824 months.

Moving average forecast–a method that averages the values of the last n periods.

Multifactor productivity–a measure of productivity that includes several inputs in the denominator, such as both labor and capital.

Next-shoring–moving production close to, or next to, the end customer.

Optimistic time–the soonest an activity may reasonably be completed, sometimes stated as one chance in a hundred.

Outsourcing–contracting with external suppliers for items that were formerly produced internally.

Overbooking–intentionally taking more orders than your service capacity to offset no-show customers.

Perceptual maps–a diagram that illustrates how customers feel about the existing products and services that are currently being offered across two general dimensions, such as scales of price versus quality

Performance frontier–the envelope showing the range of production possibilities given the technology employed.

PERT–program evaluation and review technique (see Project network).

Pessimistic time–the longest estimated time an activity may reasonably be completed, sometimes stated as one chance in a hundred.

Pilot plant–used to test and develop new production processes as well as use them for trial production in order to obtain intelligence about the market, including the size of the market and customer interest in the new product. Thus, they enable an organization to investigate a new product or process on just a small or limited scale prior to committing significantly more resources to full-scale production.

Process capability analysis–the extent to which a process can meet a customer's requirements.

Process-flow analysis/mapping–mapping the flows, waits, activities, and storages in a product or service production process.

Process map–a graphic representation of a process that shows the sequences of tasks that comprise a business process.

Product-process matrix–a diagram showing the ranges of variety and batch size combinations for alternate transformation processes.

Productivity–the ratio of outputs to inputs. In managerial terms, productivity is the output that is generated for a given level of input. Productivity is one measure of efficiency.

Project charter–an abbreviated description of a project used for information or funding purposes and the basis for a final project plan.

Project economy–The observation that the continually increasing use of projects to accomplish goals in our society will soon replace our *mass production economy with a project economy.*

Project life cycle–the start, growth, and ending stages of a project, usually shaped like a stretched S or a stretched J (exponential form).

Project network–a diagram of nodes connected by arrows showing the tasks and their precedences, usually of the PERT or CPM type.

Project owner–person with responsibility for obtaining the benefits described in the portfolio's business case for the project.

Project portfolio–all the projects an organization is involved in.

Quality function deployment, QFD–a method to translate customer requirements into process capabilities.

Queuing theory–branch of mathematics dedicated to modeling waiting lines so that their performance can be evaluated and ideas for improvement investigated.

RACI matrix–a table of the tasks versus human resources showing who is responsible, who is accountable, who to consult, and who to inform.

Rapid prototyping–a group of techniques that allow organizations to quickly produce physical models of new product ideas.

Reengineering–a process for making major rather than incremental improvements in a process.

Reshoring–moving production of an offshore product back home.

Revenue management–see Yield management.

Reverse logistics–flow back to the originating producer for reuse or disposal.

Risk diagram–a matrix divided into smaller boxes or curves based on two scales where each box or curve represents a different degree of risk

RFID–radio-frequency identification tags for attaching to inventory.

Sand cone–when firms build on previous areas of strength rather than trading them off. The usual order of strengths starts with quality and then adds delivery dependability, then speed, and last cost. The order or strengths may vary.

Service level–the percentage of demand served.

Servicescape–the environment of a service.

Simple regression–a statistical procedure used to forecast demand by fitting a linear trend line to the previous n periods.

Single measure of productivity–a measure of productivity that only considers one factor of production (or one input) such as labor hours in the denominator.

Six Sigma–a comprehensive methodology for improving business performance. Also a measure of process performance.

Slack time–the amount of time an activity can be delayed before delaying the project's completion.

Software as a Service (SaaS)–software that is accessed and used via the cloud.

Sole sourcing–working with only one supplier.

Spider/star chart–used where there are multiple factors represented by different spokes in a circle. When the factor values for each alternative are connected between the spokes, the spider/star shape shows the differences between the alternatives.

Stakeholders–anyone with an interest in a project.

Stockless purchasing–items that are delivered directly to where they will be used rather than to a storage facility.

Strategic sourcing–selecting a source by considering the total cost of ownership.

Strategy map–a map of the flows among four strategic perspectives to visualize the implementation of a strategy.

Suboptimization–when one part of a system is improved to the detriment of other parts or the whole system.

Supply chain–all the activities involved in supplying an end user with a product or service.

Supply chain operations reference, SCOR–a model to help identify best supply chain practices.

Sustainability–the ability of an entity such as a person, organization, society, or even the entire planet to maintain itself and thereby endure over time. In business often taken to mean the reduction of waste to minimize the negative impact on the environment.

Sustainable project management–the combination of traditional project management concepts with sustainability concepts including both social and environmental concerns.

Sustainable supply chain management–aligning the management of the supply chain with an organization's sustainability objectives.

Takt time–see Cycle time.

Taguchi methods–a technique that focuses on the design phase to improve quality.

Theory of constraints–an approach to help balance the work flows in a production system by identifying and removing the bottlenecks.

Time series analysis–making a forecast based on the past history of the relevant product or service demand.

Total factor productivity–a measure of productivity where all the inputs used (labor, capital, materials, and energy) are included in the denominator.

Toyota Production System, TPS–a comprehensive approach for eliminating waste ("muda") in all forms.

Transformation process–the portion of a production system where value is added to inputs to create outputs by either alter, transport, store, or inspect.

Triple bottom line–an approach for assessing organizational performance that considers profits, social responsibility (people), and environmental responsibility (planet).

Utilization–the percentage of time a resource is used.

Value analysis–evaluating the function of an item or service to reduce its cost.

Value Stream Map–a diagram showing the process flows of a production system.

Variable data–a characteristic of the output that is continuous and can be measured.

Voice of the customer, VOC–a method to determine customer requirements.

Work breakdown structure, WBS–the set of the tasks required to complete the project, organized in some fashion.

Yield management–a method of allocating fixed service capacity to the highest-paying customers first.

3D printing–method used to create solid items from drawings created in computer-aided design (CAD) software. With 3D printing, the item is produced through what is referred to as an additive process whereby successive layers of the material are "printed." In effect, each layer is a cross section of the final item so cavities and other difficult shapes and angles are easily made.

INDEX